广东知识产权年鉴

Guangdong Intellectual Property Yearbook 2016

二〇一六年版

广东省知识产权局 编

SPM 廣東省出版集團
广东人民出版社
广州·

图书在版编目（CIP）数据

广东知识产权年鉴. 2016／广东省知识产权局编. —广州：广东人民出版社，2016.10

ISBN 978-7-218-11351-7

Ⅰ. ①广… Ⅱ. ①广… Ⅲ. ①知识产权—工作—广东—2016—年鉴 Ⅳ. ①D927.650.34-54

中国版本图书馆CIP数据核字（2016）第266546号

广东知识产权年鉴（2016）

广东省知识产权局　编

出 版 人：肖风华

责任编辑：余小华　陈东英
责任技编：周　杰

出版发行：广东人民出版社
地　　址：广州市大沙头四马路10号（邮政编码：510102）
电　　话：（020）83798714（总编室）
传　　真：（020）83780199
网　　址：http://www. gdpph. com
印　　刷：广州市官侨彩印有限公司
开　　本：889毫米×1194毫米　1/16
印　　张：24　　**插　　页**：8　　**字　　数**：900千
印　　数：1—2000册
版　　次：2016年10月第1版　2016年10月第1次印刷
定　　价：280.00元

如发现印装质量问题，影响阅读，请与出版社（020-83795749）联系调换。
售书热线：（020）83790604　83791487　　**邮购**：（020）83781421

2015年12月10日，广东省知识产权工作会议暨专利奖表彰大会在广州市召开。广东省委书记胡春华（主席台中），广东省省长朱小丹（主席台右二），国家知识产权局局长申长雨（主席台左二），广东省常委、省委秘书长林木声（主席台右一），广东省副省长陈云贤（主席台左一）出席会议

国家知识产权局　广东省人民政府
第二轮知识产权高层次战略合作2015年度工作会议

JPO
KIPO

1 | 3
2 |

1. 2015年4月14日，国家知识产权局与广东省人民政府第二轮知识产权高层次战略合作2015年度工作会议在广州市召开。广东省省长朱小丹、国家知识产权局局长申长雨出席

2. 2015年11月17日，第15次中日韩知识产权局局长政策对话会在广州召开。中国国家知识产权局局长申长雨（中）、日本特许厅长官伊藤仁（左）、韩国特许厅厅长崔东圭（右）出席会议并讲话

3. 2015年9月18日，最高人民法院副院长陶凯元（右）、广东省副省长陈云贤（左）共同为最高人民法院知识产权司法保护与市场价值研究（广东）基地揭牌

国家知识产权示范城市
鲁 毅

第八届两岸专利论坛
2015年9月22—23日
广东·广州

1/2 | 3

1. 2015年7月24日，佛山市人民政府召开佛山市高标准建设国家知识产权示范城推进大会，会上国家知识产权局副局长贺化（左）向佛山市政府正式授予“国家知识产权示范城市”牌匾

2. 2015年9月22—23日，由中华全国专利代理人协会与台湾工业总会共同主办、广东省知识产权研究会承办的“第八届两岸专利论坛”在广州市举办。广东省副省长陈云贤会见两岸与会主要嘉宾并在开幕式上致词

3. 2015年4月27日，国家知识产权局副局长何志敏调研组一行到中山市琪朗灯饰有限公司参观考察

1 | 2/3

1. 2015年10月28日，《广东省政府深入实施知识产权战略推动创新驱动发展行动计划新闻通气会》在广州市召开

2. 2015年10月28—30日，香港特区政府知识产权署和澳门特区政府经济局知识产权厅联合举办“2015年泛珠三角区域知识产权公务人员交流活动”，广东省知识产权局、广东省工商局、省新闻出版广电局等5人组成广东代表团出席

3. 2015年8月28日，广东专利代理协会在广州举办“创新知识产权服务论坛（2015）”

版權及商標調查科

创新知识产权服务论坛(2015)
主办单位：广东专利代理协会
支持单位：国家知识产权局专利局专利审查协作广东中心
广东省知识产权局
赞助单位：广州华进联合专利商标代理有限公司
东莞市华南专利商标事务所有限公司
广州新诺专利商标事务所有限公司
广州三环专利代理有限公司
广州市华学知识产权代理有限公司
广州嘉权专利商标事务所有限公司
严小宣

1 | 2 / 3

1. 2015年10月21日，广东省知识产权局与唯品会签署了《保护知识产权战略合作协议》

2. 2015年11月26日，首届“汇桔杯”南粤知识产权创新创业大赛启动大会在广州举行

3. 2015年8月13—14日，由国家知识产权局专利局主办、广东省知识产权局承办的“专利电子申请推广培训班”在广州举行

IPIEC
创意 · 创新 · 创业
首届汇桔杯南粤知识产权创新创业大赛启动大会
1st Intellectual Property Innovation & Entrepreneurship Contest
知识产权让 创意 · 创新 · 创业 成为现实

何越峰
丛树平
黄琳

专利③
专利②
版权

1 2 | 3

1. 2015年10月26日，世界知识产权组织中国办事处主任陈宏兵一行到中山古镇调研，并参观星光联盟LED照明博览中心

2. 2015年11月，全国打击侵权假冒工作领导小组办公会会同国务院新闻办组织20家中央主要媒体和重点新闻网站对广东省“清风”行动集中采访宣传

3. 2015年6月5日，工业机器人产业专利导航研讨会在东莞举行

全省专利信息推送及知识产权贯标
服务推送活动(汕头澄海站)会议

商标品牌海外注册与维权研讨会
张晓英
刘阳
张吕宝儿

1/2 | 3

1. 2015年12月2日，全省专利信息及知识产权贯标服务推送活动在汕头澄海举行

2. 2015年11月24日下午，广东省工商局与香港特区政府知识产权署在广州共同举办“商标品牌国际注册和海外维权应对”研讨会

3. 2015年7月28日，广东省知识产权局与中华全国专利代理人协会在广州签署《贯彻企业知识产权标准合作关系议定书》。全国第一个“贯标”地方性办事机构“中规（北京）认证有限公司广州办事处”正式落户广东

2015年12月8日，广东省知识产权专家咨询委员会成立大会暨第一次咨询会议在广州举行

编辑说明

一、《广东知识产权年鉴》自2002年首卷问世以来至今已满十五周岁。她在各级领导、省知识产权局、有关主管部门以及社会各界人士的关心和支持下，正在健康成长，在此一并表示谢意。

二、《广东知识产权年鉴》是由广东省知识产权局主持，全省有关知识产权管理和执法的单位和部门，以及各地级以上市知识产权管理部门共同参与编撰的大型资料性工具书。《广东知识产权年鉴》每年出版，公开发行，其宗旨是全面、系统、详实地载录广东知识产权工作的基本情况和最新发展状况，为广东历史提供基本资料保存，为社会各界乃至海外人士了解与研究之用，也可作为企事业单位知识产权部门及有关人员的参考书。

三、《广东知识产权年鉴》采取分类编辑法，以编目、分目、条目组成框架结构的主体部分，着力满足读者的需求，方便读者查阅，体现年鉴作为知识产权工具书的现实意义。

四、《广东知识产权年鉴》以出版年号为版次名称，2016年版主要记载广东省2015年知识产权工作的基本资料，设有十二个编目：（1）特辑；（2）综述；（3）知识产权创造；（4）知识产权运用；（5）知识产权保护；（6）知识产权管理与服务；（7）知识产权交流与合作；（8）宣传、教育培训；（9）地市知识产权工作；（10）表彰奖励；（11）专题研究与工作交流；（12）附录。

五、书内所刊载的内容和数据，均由广东省内省直各厅局、高等院校、科研院所以及各地级以上市知识产权部门提供，并经过一定程序的审核。

六、本年鉴的编辑出版工作得到各供稿单位大力支持和通力合作，谨此致谢。由于时间仓促、水平有限，本书难免有疏漏之处，欢迎各界人士批评指正。

主编：唐　毅

2016年10月31日

《广东知识产权年鉴》（2016年版）

编辑委员会

目 录

特 辑

- **第二轮知识产权高层次战略合作** ……… 2

第二轮知识产权高层次战略合作 ……… 2
· 概况
· 知识产权强国建设先行地
· 知识产权改革创新
· 知识产权保护
· 知识产权运用
· 知识产权服务业
· 知识产权对外合作
· 知识产权人才队伍建设
· 知识产权管理

- **贯彻实施《珠江三角洲地区改革发展规划纲要（2008—2020年）》** ……… 6

贯彻实施《珠江三角洲地区改革发展规划纲要（2008—2020年）》……… 6
· 概况
· 知识产权创造
· 知识产权运用
· 知识产权运营体系建设
· 知识产权行政保护

- **打击侵犯知识产权和制售假冒伪劣商品工作** ……… 8

打击侵犯知识产权和制售假冒伪劣商品工作 ……… 8
· 概况
· 组织管理
· 行政执法
· 刑事司法
· “两法”衔接与司法保护
· 行政处罚案件信息公开
· 营造良好社会氛围

- **广东省政府颁布实施《广东省深入实施知识产权战略　推动创新驱动发展行动计划》** ……… 11

广东省政府颁布实施《广东省深入实施知识产权战略　推动创新驱动发展行动计划》……… 11

- **领导讲话** ……… 13

国家知识产权局局长申长雨在广东省知识产权工作会议暨专利奖励大会上的讲话 ……… 13
广东省人民政府省长朱小丹在全省知识产权工作会议暨专利奖表彰大会上的讲话 ……… 16
广东省人民政府省长朱小丹在国家知识产权局　广东省人民政府第二轮知识产权高层次战略合作2015年度工作会议上的讲话 ……… 20
广东省人民政府副省长陈云贤在第八届两岸专利论坛上的致辞 ……… 23
广东省人民政府副省长陈云贤在最高法院知识产权司法保护与市场价值研究（广东）基地揭牌仪式上的讲话 ……… 24
广东省知识产权局局长马宪民在广东省知识产权局工作总结会议上的讲话 ……… 25

综 述

- **协调机制** ……… 36

广东省人民政府知识产权办公会议 ……… 36
· 概况
· 主要职责
· 组织架构
广东省打击侵犯知识产权和制售假冒伪劣商品工作领导小组 ……… 37
· 概况
· 领导小组办公室主要职责
· 组织架构

粤港保护知识产权合作专责小组 ……38
· 概况
· 粤港知识产权合作
粤澳知识产权工作小组 ……39
· 概况
· 工作机制
泛珠三角区域知识产权合作机制 ……40
· 概况
· 泛珠三角区域知识产权合作联席会议制度
· 泛珠三角区域知识产权合作联络员制度
· 泛珠三角区域知识产权合作专题工作小组制度
职能部门工作概述 ……41
广东省人民政府知识产权办公会议成员单位 ……41
广东省发展和改革委员会 ……41
· 概况
· 全面创新改革试验
· 创新驱动发展政策环境
· 创新成果产业化
· 区域创新体系建设
· 试点示范工程建设
· 推进创业投资发展
广东省经济和信息化委员会 ……42
· 战略性新兴产业重点项目
· 科技成果产业化应用
· 企业技术中心建设
· 品牌建设
广东省教育厅 ……43
· 专利申请和授权
· 知识产权获奖
· 专利技术的实施
· 全国中小学知识产权教育试点推进
广东省科学技术厅 ……44
· 概况
· 自主创新政策环境
· 知识产权创新能力
· 知识产权战略实施
· 产学研协同创新
广东省公安厅 ……46
· 概况
· 专项推动
· 提升效能
· 加强协作
· 宣传发动
广东省司法厅 ……48
· 概况
· 版权纠纷人民调解委员会
· 开展广东省律师知识产权典型案例系列活动
· 第三届广东知识产权法律服务论坛
· 中港新三地国际版权法律研讨会
广东省农业厅 ……49
· 概况
· 科技创新
· 行业管理
· 品牌建设
广东省林业厅 ……52
· 概况
· 林业知识产权宣传与普及
· 林业植物新品种保护
· 林木种苗质量检查
· 林业植物新品种权专项行动
· 信息公开
广东省商务厅 ……53
· 广交会知识产权保护
· 知识产权战略实施
· 品牌国际化知识产权培训
· 电商领域知识产权保护交流合作
广东省文化厅 ……53
· 概况
广东省卫生和计划生育委员会 ……54
· 概况
· 科技重大专项
· 专利信息资源开发利用计划项目
广东省版权局 ……54
· 广东版权专题调研

· 作品著作权
· 版权兴业
· 护航“漫博会”
· 版权宣传
· “剑网 2015”
· 大案要案
· 软件正版化
· 粤港合作
· 服务组织机构
· 全国版权示范城市
· 国家版权示范

广东省工商行政管理局 …………………56
· 概况
· 商标注册
· 商标保护
· 商标品牌战略
· 对外合作交流

广东省质量技术监督局 …………………57
· 概况
· 名牌产品
· 地理标志工作
· 打击质量技术监督领域知识产权违法行为

广东省知识产权局 ……………………60
· 概况
· 实施知识产权战略
· 发明创造
· 专利信息资源
· 专利运营机制
· 知识产权保护
· 知识产权能力

广东省人民政府法制办公室 ……………64
· 政府立法
· 规范性文件审查

广东省食品药品监督管理局 ……………64
· 监管机构
· 假冒侵权
· 企业创新
· 药品标准

广东省人民政府知识产权办公会议特邀单位 ……………………………………65

海关总署广东分署 ……………………65
· 概况
· 专项执法行动
· 跨区域执法协作
· 宣传活动

广东省高级人民法院 …………………67
· 概述
· 审判职能
· 体制机制创新
· 监督指导

广东省人民检察院 ……………………70
· 概况
· 知识产权犯罪
· 行政执法与刑事司法相衔接机制
· 跨行政区域知识产权专门检察院
· 广东自贸区建设
· 知识产权保护宣传

知识产权创造

专利……………………………………74

专利申请及授权 ………………………74
· 概况
· 主要特点

商标……………………………………76
· 概况
· 马德里商标国际注册
· 地理标志商标注册

地理标志………………………………77

标准与地理标志 ………………………77

地理标志产品 …………………………77
· 概况
· 连平鹰嘴蜜桃
· 莞香
· 始兴石斛
· 石湾玉冰烧酒
· 高要巴戟天
· 罗浮山大米

- ·柏塘山茶
- ·观音阁花生
- ·汶朗蜜柚

农产品地理标志 …… 79
- ·概况
- ·激励机制
- ·证后监管
- ·产品宣传

植物新品种 …… 80

农业植物新品种 …… 80
- ·概况

林业植物新品种 …… 80
- ·概况

重大知识产权获奖成果 …… 81

第十七届中国专利奖 …… 81
- ·年度中国专利奖相关工作情况

2015 年广东专利奖 …… 81
- ·概况

2015 年广东省名牌产品（工业类） …… 81
- ·概况

知识产权运用

重大经济活动知识产权分析评议 …… 84

重大经济活动知识产权分析评议 …… 84
- ·分析评议试点
- ·知识产权分析评议服务示范创建
- ·重大经济科技活动知识产权评议促进计划
- ·地市评议

战略性新兴产业专利信息资源开发利用计划 …… 85

战略性新兴产业专利信息资源开发利用计划 …… 85
- ·概况
- ·主要举措
- ·主要成果

产业专利导航及分析预警 …… 85
- ·专利信息服务平台
- ·专利导航新模式
- ·广东省出口贸易专利预警分析计划

产业知识产权联盟 …… 87

产业知识产权联盟 …… 87
- ·概况
- ·主要举措
- ·广东省产业专利联盟示范培育工程
- ·专利联盟规范化、实体化发展
- ·研究成果

信息运用 …… 88

专利信息化建设及推广 …… 88
- ·广东省专利大数据应用服务系统建设
- ·中国专利法律状态数据加工
- ·产业 / 行业专题数据库建设
- ·专利信息推送服务

国家知识产权局（广东）专利信息传播利用基地 …… 89
- ·概况
- ·工作体系建设
- ·人才工作
- ·专利信息利用促进工作
- ·专利信息情报服务
- ·合作开展专利信息传播利用工作
- ·组织参加 2015 年中国专利信息年会

知识产权运营 …… 92

知识产权运营 …… 92
- ·概况
- ·重点企业、区域知识产权高端运营及创新运用
- ·广东省专利技术实施计划
- ·国家级专利产业化基地

知识产权质押及投融资 …… 94

知识产权质押及投融资 …… 94
- ·概况
- ·主要举措

广东省专利权质押登记 …… 95
- ·概况
- ·专利权质押登记特点
- ·广东省与全国及有关省市的对比情况

专利保险……97

专利保险……97

· 概况

转化……98

知识产权交易……98

· 概况

广东省专利实施许可合同备案……98

· 概况

· 广东省与全国及有关省市的对比

知识产权保护

概述……102

知识产权保护……102

· 概况

· 打击侵犯知识产权和制售假冒伪劣商品

· 专利保护

· 商标保护

· 著作权保护

· 质监知识产权保护

· 植物新品种保护

· 海关知识产权保护

· 打击侵犯知识产权犯罪

· 知识产权司法保护

行政保护……105

专利行政执法……105

· 概况

· 专项行动

· 展会保护

商标行政执法……105

· 概况

· 专项行动

· 打击侵权假冒工作

· 展会与专业市场执法监管

· 驰名商标保护

海关行政执法……106

· 概况

司法保护……107

广东省检察机关知识产权司法保护……107

· 概况

· 打击侵犯知识产权犯罪

· 民事和行政案件的法律监督

· 知识产权保护长效机制

执法协作……108

专利行政执法协作……108

· 概况

维权援助与涉外应对……109

知识产权维权援助……109

知识产权涉外应对工作……109

委局合作……110

委局合作共建……110

实例……111

2015年广东省文化厅知识产权保护主要案例……111

· 案例一：广州市 www.dj020.com 网站传播侵权音乐作品案

· 案例二：广州市“6·9”特大侵权盗版教材案

· 案例三：广州“11·27”特大淫秽盗版光盘案

· 案例四：吴某某未经批准擅自从事音像制品批发、零售经营活动

· 案例五：高某某从事非法印刷品印刷经营活动

· 案例六：肇庆市某学校侵犯著作权案

2015年广东省质量技术监督局知识产权保护案例……113

· 案例一：佛山市南海区质监局查处生产假冒伪劣服装案

· 案例二：中山市质监局查处生产冒用注册商标及认证标志的电源适配器案

2015年广东海关知识产权保护典型案例……114

· 案例一：粤港海关开展执法合作成功查获化妆品类侵权案

· 案例二：广州海关查获区域通关一体化出口轮毂案
· 案例三：广州海关查获出口假冒“苹果”“三星”等电子产品案
· 案例四：深圳海关开展粤港合作查获假冒手机系列案
· 案例五：拱北海关查获申报出口的巧克力侵犯“费列罗立体商标”商标专用权案
· 案例六：黄埔海关查获成都某进出口公司出口假冒香烟案
· 案例七：黄埔海关查获丰顺某针织服装有限公司出口侵权运动服装案
· 案例八：江门海关查获侵犯“555”商标专用权电池案

2015 年广东省法院十大知识产权案例 ··· 119

· 案例一：珠海格力电器股份有限公司诉广东美的制冷设备有限公司、珠海市泰锋电业有限公司侵害商标权纠纷案
· 案例二：皇家菲利浦有限公司诉超人集团有限公司、刘某平等侵害发明专利权纠纷案
· 案例三：广东蒙娜丽莎新型材料集团有限公司诉广州蒙娜丽莎建材有限公司、佛山市贝佳斯洁具有限公司侵害注册商标专用权纠纷案
· 案例四：南京微盟电子有限公司与泉芯电子技术（深圳）有限公司侵害集成电路布图专有权纠纷案
· 案例五：杭州市西湖区龙井茶产业协会诉广州市种茶人贸易有限公司侵害商标权纠纷案
· 案例六：广州医药集团有限公司诉广东加多宝饮料食品有限公司、彭某娟虚假宣传纠纷案
· 案例七：中山市商房网络科技有限公司诉中山市暴风科技有限公司著作权侵权纠纷一案
· 案例八：暴雪娱乐有限公司、上海网之易网络科技发展有限公司诉成都七游科技有限公司、北京分播时代网络科技有限公司、广州市动景计算机科技有限公司著作权侵权及不正当竞争纠纷诉中禁令案
· 案例九：广州市虎头电池集团有限公司、广州轻工工贸集团有限公司诉临沂华太电池有限公司擅自使用知名商品特有包装装潢纠纷
· 案例十：原告张某义不服深圳市市场监督管理局行政处理决定案

2015 年广东省检察机关知识产权保护典型案例 ··· 124

· 案例一：矽微公司、房某磊侵犯商业秘密案
· 案例二：陈某田等四人假冒注册商标案
· 案例三：梁某克等三人非法制造注册商标标识及赖某莲销售非法制造的注册商标标识案

知识产权管理与服务

广东创建知识产权服务业发展示范省规划（2013—2020 年） ··· 128

广东创建知识产权服务业发展示范省规划（2013—2020 年） ··· 128

· 概况

知识产权试点示范 ··· 129

国家知识产权试点示范城市 ··· 129

· 概况
· 国家知识产权示范城市
· 国家知识产权试点城市

国家知识产权强县工程试点示范 ··· 129

· 概况

高新区知识产权示范创建 ··· 130

· 概况

企业知识产权管理规范 ··· 131

企业知识产权管理规范 ··· 131

· “贯标”培训
· “贯标”服务体系
· 地市“贯标”
· 企业“贯标”认证
· 编写“贯标”指导书籍

专利代理管理 …… 132

专利代理管理 …… 132
· 概况
· 监管工作
· 专利代理服务能力建设
· 专利代理管理工作发展
· 专利代理行业发展

百所千企知识产权服务对接工程 …… 134

百所千企知识产权服务对接工程 …… 134
· 概况

产业专利信息服务平台 …… 135

产业专利信息服务平台 …… 135
· 概况

服务与支撑机构 …… 136

国家专利审查协作广东中心共建情况 …… 136
· 概况
国家知识产权局专利局广州代办处 …… 136
· 概况
· 专利电子申请
· 试点工作
· 公共服务
广东省知识产权研究与发展中心（广东省知识产权维权援助中心） …… 137
· 概况
· 信息服务体系
· 信息化平台
· 服务能力
· 培训服务
· 维权援助服务
· 司法鉴定服务
· 委托任务
广东省知识产权研究会 …… 141
· 概况
· 学会基础工作
· 知识产权课题研究
· 知识产权学术交流
· 承接政府项目
广东知识产权保护协会 …… 143
· 概况
· 合作项目
· 常规项目
· 承接政府工作
广东专利代理协会 …… 145
· 自律建设
· 培训交流
· 承办政府工作
广东省专利信息协会 …… 146
· 协会建设
· 机构建设
· 行业服务
广东商标协会 …… 147
· 概况
· 广东省著名商标
· 行业建设
· 宣传培训
· 服务平台
广东省版权保护联合会 …… 149
· 交流活动
· 普法与维权协作
· 承接政府项目
· 成果与荣誉
广东省知识产权研究与发展中心司法鉴定所 …… 150
· 概况
· 入册法院
· 培训教育
· 沟通交流
· 内部管理
广东省律师协会知识产权法律专业委员会 …… 150
· 典型案例评选和巡讲活动
· 第三届广东知识产权法律服务论坛举办
· 知识产权贯标

·举办中港新三地国际版权法律研讨会
·举办“知识产权管理与商业化实务研讨会”
·举办商业秘密民事诉讼实务问题讨论会
广东发明协会 …… 151
·概况
广东省法学会知识产权法学研究会 …… 153
·概况

知识产权交流与合作

■ 对外交流与合作 …… 156
知识产权对外交流与合作 …… 156
·概况
·对外交流合作体系
·广东自由贸易试验区
·“一带一路”知识产权工作
·重大外事及交流活动
·重大平台建设
·知识产权涉外应对
·对外宣传
·粤港澳台区域知识产权合作
■ 区域交流与合作 …… 159
2015 年粤港知识产权合作 …… 159
·概况
·知识产权合作机制
·知识产权执法及案件协作处理机制
·知识产权贸易和法律服务
·亚洲知识产权营商论坛
·粤港澳知识产权交流研讨
·粤港知识产权引导服务
·粤港知识产权宣传教育
2015 年粤澳知识产权合作 …… 161
·概况
·粤澳知识产权合作机制
·粤澳知识产权案件协助处理机制
·粤澳知识产权交流互访
·粤澳知识产权宣传培训
·粤澳知识产权研究
·粤港澳知识产权信息资源共享
2015 年粤台知识产权合作 …… 163
·概况
·第八届两岸专利论坛
·粤台知识产权服务机构交流
·粤台知识产权交流合作
2015 年泛珠三角区域知识产权合作 …… 163
·概况
·泛珠三角区域知识产权专题交流
·泛珠三角区域内地九省（区）专利行政执法协作
·泛珠三角区域内地九省（区）专利信息
2015 年粤喀知识产权合作 …… 164
·概况
·知识产权创造
·知识产权执法
·知识产权人才交流
·知识产权教育
·知识产权宣传培训

宣传　教育培训

■ 宣传 …… 168
广东省知识产权宣传工作 …… 168
·概况
·部署安排
·重点、热点
·宣传渠道
广东省工商行政管理系统知识产权宣传培训工作 …… 169
·概况
·商标宣传
·商标培训
■ 教育培训 …… 170
广东省知识产权人才培训工作 …… 170
·概况
国家知识产权培训（广东）基地（华南理工大学） …… 170

· 人才培养体系与师资
· 知识产权教育
· 科学研究
· 学术活动
· 社会服务
国家知识产权培训（广东）基地（广东省知识产权研究与发展中心）…… 172
· 概况
· 知识产权人才培训
· 国际交流
· 知识产权研究
广东省知识产权培训基地（暨南大学）…… 173
· 概况
· 人才培养
· 科学研究
· 学术活动
· 服务社会
广东省知识产权培训基地（深圳大学）…… 174
· 人才培养
· 学术活动
· 平台建设
广东省知识产权培训基地（汕头大学）…… 175
· 概况
· 知识产权教育
· 企业服务
广东省知识产权培训基地（惠州学院）…… 175
· 概况
· 宣传培训
· 基地教育
广东省知识产权培训基地（广东海洋大学）…… 176
· 概况
· 知识产权宣传
· 知识产权培训
广东省知识产权培训基地（顺德职业技术学院）…… 176
· 概述
· 基础建设
· 运用能力培训
· 普及培训
· 专题培训
· 知识产权上量提质活动
· 知识产权选修课
· 知识产权远程教育顺德分站
广东金融学院知识产权研究所 …… 177
· 概况
华南师范大学 …… 178
· 概况
· 宣传培训
· 创造与运用
中小学知识产权教育工作 …… 178
国家中小微企业知识产权培训（南海）基地 …… 178
· 概况
· 培训活动
· 培训管理
· 社会服务

地市知识产权工作

地市知识产权工作 …… 182
广州市 …… 182
· 示范试点工作
· 知识产权管理
· 知识产权创造
· 知识产权运用
· 知识产权保护
· 宣传培训
· 交流合作
深圳市 …… 185
· 知识产权创造
· 知识产权运用
· 知识产权保护
· 知识产权管理
· 知识产权服务
· 知识产权宣传培训

珠海市 …… 188
· 概况
汕头市 …… 188
· 知识产权创造
· 知识产权运用
· 知识产权保护
· 知识产权管理
· 知识产权宣传培训
· 知识产权交流合作
· 统计资料
佛山市 …… 194
· 知识产权创造
· 知识产权运用
· 知识产权保护
· 知识产权管理
· 知识产权服务
· 知识产权宣传
· 统计资料
韶关市 …… 199
· 知识产权创造
· 知识产权运用
· 知识产权保护
· 知识产权管理
· 知识产权宣传培训
河源市 …… 200
· 知识产权创造
· 知识产权保护
· 知识产权管理和服务
· 知识产权宣传培训
梅州市 …… 202
· 知识产权创造
· 知识产权运用
· 知识产权保护
· 知识产权管理
· 知识产权宣传培训
· 统计资料
惠州市 …… 206
· 知识产权创造
· 知识产权运用
· 知识产权保护
· 知识产权管理
· 知识产权宣传培训
· 统计资料
汕尾市 …… 210
· 知识产权创造
· 知识产权保护
· 知识产权管理
· 知识产权交流与合作
· 宣传培训
东莞市 …… 211
· 概况
· 知识产权创造
· 知识产权运用
· 知识产权保护
· 知识产权管理
· 知识产权宣传培训
· 知识产权服务
· 统计资料
中山市 …… 217
· 知识产权创造
· 知识产权运用
· 知识产权保护
· 知识产权管理
· 知识产权宣传培训
江门市 …… 219
· 知识产权创造
· 知识产权运用
· 知识产权保护
· 知识产权管理
阳江市 …… 221
· 知识产权创造
· 知识产权运用
· 知识产权保护
· 知识产权管理
· 知识产权宣传培训
湛江市 …… 222
· 概况
· 知识产权创造
· 知识产权管理
· 知识产权保护

· 知识产权宣传培训
· 统计资料
茂名市 ………………………………… 224
· 知识产权创造
· 知识产权保护
· 知识产权管理
· 知识产权宣传培训
肇庆市 ………………………………… 226
· 知识产权创造
· 知识产权运用
· 知识产权保护
· 知识产权管理与服务
· 知识产权宣传培训
清远市 ………………………………… 228
· 知识产权创造
· 知识产权保护
· 知识产权管理
· 知识产权宣传
潮州市 ………………………………… 230
· 知识产权创造
· 知识产权运用
· 知识产权保护
· 知识产权管理
· 知识产权宣传培训
揭阳市 ………………………………… 232
· 知识产权创造
· 知识产权保护
· 知识产权管理
· 宣传、教育培训
云浮市 ………………………………… 233
· 知识产权创造
· 知识产权运用
· 知识产权保护
· 知识产权管理
· 宣传、教育培训

表彰奖励

■ 表彰奖励 ………………………………… 238
2015 年全国知识产权领军人才百名高层次人才培养人选 ………………… 238
2015 年全国专利信息领军人才和师资人才名单 ………………………… 238
国家知识产权试点示范城市工作先进集体和先进个人 ……………………… 239

专题研究与工作交流

■ 专题研究报告 ……………………………… 242
广东省知识产权局软科学研究管理工作 ……………………………… 242
· 概况
关于广东省地理标志产品保护与管理工作现状的调研报告 ……………… 242
· 概况
· 广东省国家地理标志产品保护工作的基本情况
· 地理标志保护的重要意义
· 当前地理标志产品保护与管理方面存在的问题
· 下一步对策与建议
■ 工作交流 ………………………………… 246
广交会知识产权保护工作 …………… 246
· 概况
· 第 117 届广交会知识产权保护工作情况
· 第 118 届广交会知识产权保护工作情况

附 录

■ 政策法规 ………………………………… 250
广东省深入实施知识产权战略 推动创新驱动发展行动计划 …………… 250
广东省知识产权局、科技厅、经济和信息化委、商务厅、质监局、国资委印发关于全面推进《企业知识产权管理规范》国家标准的实施意见 ……………………………………… 254
地理标志产品保护规定 ……………… 257
地理标志产品保护工作细则 ………… 260

- 2015 年知识产权大事记 …… 265
- 统计资料 …… 284
  - 广东省历年专利申请情况 …… 284
  - 广东省历年专利授权情况 …… 285
  - 1986—2015 年广东省各类专利申请人三种专利申请情况 …… 286
  - 1986—2015 年广东省各类专利申请人三种专利授权情况 …… 286
  - 2010—2015 年广东省各地级以上市专利申请情况 …… 287
  - 2011—2015 年广东省各地级以上市专利授权情况 …… 288
  - 2002—2015 年全国及广东省 PCT 国际专利申请情况 …… 289
  - 2015 年广东省各地级以上市 PCT 专利申请情况 …… 289
  - 2015 年广东省各地级以上市专利行政执法统计表 …… 289
  - 广东省专利行政部门历年受理、办结专利案件情况表 …… 290
  - 2010—2015 年广东省专利案件收、结统计表 …… 290
  - 2015 年广东省专利奖名单 …… 291
  - 2015 年度广东省查处商标侵权假冒案件情况统计表 …… 296
  - 2015 年查处商标一般违法案件情况统计表 …… 297
  - 2015 年查处侵犯港澳台和外国商标注册人权益案件情况统计表 …… 298
  - 2015 年广东省林业植物新品种授权品种名录 …… 299
  - 2015 年广东省文化市场行政执法数据统计表 …… 300
  - 广东省农产品地理标志登记产品信息名录 …… 301
  - 广东省农业植物新品种授权公告名录 …… 301
  - 广东省已注册地理标志名录 …… 304
  - 2015 年广东省专利申请及授权 …… 304
- 专利代理机构 …… 308
  - 广东省专利代理机构名录 …… 308
  - 广东省专利代理机构分支机构名录 …… 311

主题索引

- 主题索引 …… 316

Contents

Feature

The Second Round of High-Level Intellectual Property Rights Strategic Cooperation ········2

The Second Round of High-Level Intellectual Property Rights Strategic Cooperation ········2

- Overview
- Construction of the Forerunner Area in the Strong Country of Intellectual Property Rights
- Reform and Innovation of Intellectual Property Rights
- Protection of Intellectual Property Rights
- Utilization of Intellectual Property Rights
- Services of Intellectual Property Rights
- Foreign cooperation of Intellectual Property Rights
- Talent Team Construction of Intellectual Property Rights
- Management of Intellectual Property Rights

Implementation of "Outline of the Reform and Development Plan of the Pearl River Delta Area (2008-2020)" ········6

Implementation of "Outline of the Reform and Development Plan of the Pearl River Delta Area (2008-2020)" ········6

- Overview
- Creation of Intellectual Property Rights
- Utilization of Intellectual Property Rights
- Operation System Construction of Intellectual Property Rights
- Administrative Protection of Intellectual Property Rights

Operations to Combating Intellectual Property Rights Infringement and the Manufacture and Sales of Counterfeit and Inferior Goods ········8

Operations to Combating Intellectual Property Rights Infringement and the Manufacture and Sales of Counterfeit and Inferior Goods ········8

- Overview
- Organizational Management
- Administrative Enforcement of Law
- Criminal Judicature
- "Bridging of Administrative Law Enforcement and Criminal Judicature" and Judicial Protection
- Disclosure of Administrative Penalty Information by Law
- Creation of Good Social Atmosphere

"Plan of Action for Deep Implementation of Intellectual Property Strategy and Pursuit of Innovation-driven Development by Guangdong Province" Promulgated and Implemented by the People's Government of Guangdong Province ········11

"Plan of Action for Deep Implementation of Intellectual Property Strategy and Pursuit of Innovation-driven Development by Guangdong Province" Promulgated and Implemented by the People's Government of Guangdong Province ········11

Contents

■Speeches by the Leaders······················· 13

Speech by Changyu Shen, Director of the State Intellectual Property Office, at the Guangdong Symposium on Intellectual Property Rights and the Guangdong Patent Awards Conference·································· 13

Speech by Xiaodan Zhu, Governor of Guangdong Province, at the Guangdong Symposium on Intellectual Property Rights and the Guangdong Patent Awards Conference ··· 16

Speech by Xiaodan Zhu, Governor of Guangdong Province, at the 2015 Symposium for the Second Round of High-Level Intellectual Property Rights Strategic Cooperation by the State Intellectual Property Office and the People's Government of Guangdong Province ·· 20

Speech by Yunxian Chen, Vice Governor of Guangdong Province, at the Eighth Across-Straits Patent Forum ································ 23

Speech by Yunxian Chen, Vice Governor of Guangdong Province, at the Opening Ceremony of Judicial Protection and Market Value Research (Guangdong) Base for Intellectual Property of Supreme People's court ·············· 24

Speech by Xianmin Ma, Director of the Intellectual Property Office of Guangdong Province, at the Work Summary Symposium of Intellectual Property Office of Guangdong Province ·· 25

General Review

■Coordination Mechanism······················· 36

The Conference of Guangdong Intellectual Property Rights Office ······························· 36

· Overview

· Main Responsibilities

· Organizational Structure

The Steering Group for Combating Intellectual Property Rights Infringement and the Manufacture and Sales of Counterfeit of Guangdong Province ······························· 37

· Overview

· Main Responsibilities of Steering Group Office

· Organizational Structure

The Joint Task Force of Guangdong and Hong Kong to Protect Intellectual Property Rights ··· 38

· Overview

· Cooperation of Intellectual Property Rights between Guangdong and Hong Kong

The Task Force of Guangdong and Macao on Intellectual Property Rights ·························· 39

· Overview

· Working Mechanism

Mechanism of Intellectual Property Cooperation of Pan-Pearl River Delta ··························· 40

· Overview

· System of Joint Conference on Intellectual Property Cooperation of Pan-Pearl River Delta

· Liaison System of Intellectual Property Cooperation of Pan-Pearl River Delta

· System of Task Force on Special Subject of Intellectual Property Cooperation of Pan-Pearl River Delta

■Overview of Works of Functional Departments ·· 41

Members of the Conference of Guangdong Intellectual Property Office·························· 41

The Guangdong Committee on Development and Reform ··· 41

· Overview

· Pilot Program of Comprehensive Innovation and Reform

· Policy Environment of Innovation-driven Development

· Industrialization of Innovation Results

· Construction of Regional Innovation System

· Construction of Pilot Demonstration Project

· Promotion of Venture Capital Investment and Development

The Guangdong Committee on Economy and Information Technology ······ 42

· Key Project of Strategic Emerging Industries

· Industrialization Application of Technological Achievements

· Construction of Technology Center for Enterprises

· Brand Construction

The Education Department of Guangdong Province ······ 43

· Patent Application and Patent Authorization

· Intellectual Property Awards

· Implementation of Patent Technology

· Promotion of Intellectual Property Education in National Primary and Secondary Pilot Schools

The Department of Science and Technology of Guangdong Province ······ 44

· Overview

· Independent Innovation of Policy Environment

· Ability of Intellectual Property Innovation

· Implementation of Intellectual Property Strategy

· Collaborative Innovation of Industry-University-Research

The Public Security Department of Guangdong Province ······ 46

· Overview

· Special Promotion

· Advancement of Efficiency

· Enhancement of Collaboration

· Launch of Propaganda

The Department of Justice of Guangdong Province ······ 48

· Overview

· People's Mediation Committee on Copyright Dispute

· Launch of a Series of Activities of Typical Cases on Intellectual Property of Guangdong Province

· The Third Legal Service Forum on Intellectual Property of Guangdong Province

· Symposia on International Copyright Laws Among Mainland, Hong Kong and Singapore

The Department of Agriculture of Guangdong Province ······ 49

· Overview

· Technological Innovation

· Industrial Management

· Brand Construction

The Department of Forestry of Guangdong Province ······ 52

· Overview

· Publicity and Popularization of Forestry Intellectual Property Rights

· Protection of New Varieties of Forestry Plants

· Quality Inspection of Forestry Plants Seedlings

· Special Action on Combating Infringement of New Varieties of Forestry Plants Rights

· Information Disclosure

The Department of Commerce of Guangdong Province ······ 53

· Intellectual Property Protection of Canton Fair

· Implementation of Intellectual Property Strategy

· Training for Intellectual Property of Brand Internationalization

· Exchange and Cooperation of Intellectual Property Protection in E-commerce

The Department of Culture of Guangdong Province ······ 53

· Overview

The Department of Health of Guangdong Province ······ 54

· Overview

· Major Projects of Science and Technology

· Project of Exploitation Plan for Patent Information Resources

The Bureau of Copyright of Guangdong Province ······ 54

· Investigation and Research on Special Subject of Copyright of Guangdong Province
· Copyright of Works
· Industrial Engineering of Copyright
· Protection for "The Diffuse Fair"
· Copyright Campaign
· "Jian Wang in 2015", the Special Law Enforcement Action on Music Copyright on Music Website
· Major and Serious Criminal Cases
· Advocation of the Use of the Genuine Software
· Cooperation between Guangdong and Hong Kong
· Service Organizations
· National Copyright Demonstration Cities
· National Copyright Demonstration
The Administrative Bureau for Industry and Commerce of Guangdong Province ················ 56
· Overview
· Trademark Registration
· Trademark Protection
· Trademark Brand Strategy
· International Exchange and Cooperation
The Bureau of Quality and Technical Supervision of Guangdong Province ································ 57
· Overview
· Famous Brand Product
· Working for Geographical Indications
· Crackdown on Intellectual Property Rights Violations in the Quality and Technology Supervision Field
The Intellectual Property Office of Guangdong Province ·· 60
· Overview
· Implementation of Intellectual Property Strategy
· Invention and Innovation
· Patent Information Resources
· Patent Operation Mechanism
· Protection of Intellectual Property
· Ability of Intellectual Property Application
The Office of Legislative Affairs of Guangdong Province ·· 64
· Government Legislation
· Review of Normative Documents
The Food and Drug Administration of Guangdong Province ·· 64
· Regulators
· Counterfeit and Infringement
· Enterprise Innovation
· Drug Standards
Specially Invited Units of the Conference of Guangdong Intellectual Property Offices ······ 65
The Guangdong Branch of the Customs Department ·· 65
· Overview
· Special Law Enforcement Operations
· Cross-regional Cooperative Enforcement
· Campaigns
The Higher People's Court of Guangdong Province ·· 67
· Overview
· Judicial Function
· Institutional Innovation
· Supervision and Guidance
The People's Procuratorate of Guangdong Province ·· 70
· Overview
· Crime of Intellectual Property Infringement
· Convergence Mechanism of Administrative Execution and Criminal Justice
· Special People's Procuratorate on Intellectual Property of Cross-administrative Regions
· Construction of China (Guangdong) Pilot Free Trade Zone
· Protection and Campaign for Intellectual Property

Intellectual Property Creation

Patent ·· 74
Patent Application and Licensing ······················ 74

· Overview
· Main Characteristics

Trademark ······ 76
· Overview
· Madrid Trademark International Registration
· Geographical Indications Trademark Registration

Geographical Indications ······ 77
Standards and Geographical Indications ······ 77
National Geographical Indications Protection Products ······ 77
· Overview
· Lianping Yingzui Nectarine
· Dongguan Aquilaria Sinensis
· Shixing Dendrobium
· Shiwan Yubing Wine
· Gaoyao Morinda officinalis How
· Luofu Mountain Rice
· Baitang Tea
· Guanyin'ge Peanut
· Wenlang Honey Pomelo
Agro-product Geographical Indications ······ 79
· Overview
· Excitation Mechanism
· Supervision after Certificate Issued
· Product Promotion

New Varieties of Plants ······ 80
New Varieties of Agricultural Plants ······ 80
· Overview
New Varieties of Forestry Plants ······ 80
· Overview

Significant Intellectual Property Awards ··· 81
The Seventeenth Chinese National Patent Award ··· 81
· Related Working Condition of Annual Chinese National Patent Award
Guangdong Patent Award in 2015 ······ 81
· Overview
Guangdong Products of Famous Brand (Industrial Products) in 2015 ······ 81
· Overview

Intellectual Property Utilization

Analysis and Evaluation on Intellectual Property of Significant Economic Activities ······ 84
Analysis and Evaluation on Intellectual Property of Significant Economic Activities ······ 84
· Analytic and Evaluative Pilot
· Demonstration Organization Construction of Analytic and Evaluative Service for Intellectual Property
· Program for Promoting Review and Evaluation on Intellectual Property of Significant Economic, Scientific and Technological Activities
· Regional Evaluation

The Plan to Develop and Utilize Patent Information Resources of Strategic Emerging Industries ······ 85
The Plan to Develop and Utilize Patent Information Resources of Strategic Emerging Industries ······ 85
· Overview
· Main Approaches
· Main Achievements
Guidance, Analysis and Forewarning of Industrial Patent ······ 85
· Service Platform of Patent Information
· New mode of Patent Guidance
· The Plan for Patent Forewarning and Analysis of Export Trade of Guangdong Province

Industrial Intellectual Property Alliance ······ 87
Industrial Intellectual Property Alliance ······ 87
· Overview
· Main Approaches
· Project for Demonstration and Cultivation of Industrial Patent Alliance of Guangdong Province

· Standardized and Substantialized Development of Patent Alliance
· Research Achievements

Application of Information ······ 88

Construction and Promotion of Patent Information Technology ······ 88
· Construction of Application Service System of Patent Big Data of Guangdong Province
· Data Processing of Chinese Patent Law Status
· Construction of Specialized Database of Industries
· Service for Pushing Patent Information

State Intellectual Property Office (Guangdong) Patent Information Dissemination and Utilization Base ······ 89
· Overview
· Construction of Working System
· Talent Management
· Work Related to Promoting the Utilization of Patent Information
· Service for Patent Information and Intelligence
· Collaboration of Promoting the Dissemination and Utilization of Patent Information
· Organizing and Participating of Patent Information Annual Conference of China in 2015

Intellectual Property Operation ······ 92

Intellectual Property Operation ······ 92
· Overview
· Premium Operation and Innovative Utilization of Intellectual Property by Key Enterprises and Regions
· Program for Implementing Patent Technology of Guangdong Province
· National Patent Industrialization Base

Pledge, Investment and Finance of Intellectual Property ······ 94

Pledge, Investment and Finance of Intellectual Property ······ 94
· Overview
· Main Approaches

Registration of Patent Rights Pledge of Guangdong Province ······ 95
· Overview
· Characteristics of Registration of Patent Rights Pledge
· Comparison on Registration of Patent Rights Pledge among Guangdong Province and Other Related Provinces in China

Patent Insurance ······ 97

Patent Insurance ······ 97
· Overview

Exploration of Patent Insurance Transformation ······ 98

Intellectual Property Trading ······ 98
· Overview

Record of Contracts on the Licensing of Patent Exploitation of Guangdong Province ······ 98
· Overview
· Comparison among Guangdong Province and Other Related Provinces in China

Intellectual Property Protection

Overview ······ 102

Intellectual Property Protection ······ 102
· Overview
· Operations to Combating Intellectual Property Rights Infringement and the Manufacture and Sales of Counterfeit and Inferior Goods
· Patent Protection
· Trademark Protection
· Copyright Protection
· Protection for Quality and Technical Supervision of Intellectual Property
· Patent Protection for New Varieties of Plants
· Protection for Intellectual Property of the Customs
· Operations to Combating Crimes of Intellectual Property Infringement
· Judicial protection for Intellectual Property

Administrative Protection ······ 105
Patent Administrative Law Enforcement ······ 105
· Overview
· Special Operation
· Protection of Exhibitions
Trademark Administrative Law Enforcement ··· 105
· Overview
· Special Action
· Combat for Infringement and Counterfeit of Copyright
· Law Enforcement and Supervision of Exhibition and Professional Market
· Well-known Trademark Protection
Customs Administrative Law Enforcement ······ 106
· Overview
Judicial Protection ······ 107
Intellectual Property Judicial Protection by Guangdong Procuratorial Authorities ······ 107
· Overview
· Combating Crimes of Intellectual Property Infringement
· Legal Supervision for Civil and Administrative Cases
· Long-Term Mechanism of Intellectual Property Protection
Cooperation on Law Enforcement ······ 108
Cooperation on Patent Administrative Enforcement of Law ······ 108
· Overview
Aids for Intellectual Property Protection and Response to Situations involving Foreign Rights Holders ······ 109
Aids for Intellectual Property Protection ······ 109
Intellectual Property Work Involving Foreign Rights Holders ······ 109
Cooperation between the Patent Reexamination Board and the Guangdong Intellectual Property Office ······ 110
Cooperative Constructions of the Patent Reexamination Board and Guangdong Intellectual Property Office ······ 110
Cases ······ 111
Major Intellectual Property Cases of the Department of Culture of Guangdong Province in 2015 ······ 111
· Case One: The Case of Infringement of Music Composition Transmission against the Website www.dj020.com in Guangzhou
· Case Two: The Specially Important Case of Infringement of Pirated Textbooks Seized on June 9th in Guangzhou
· Case Three: The Specially Important Case of Indecent and Pirated Compact Disks Seized on November 27th in Guangzhou
· Case Four: The Case of Unauthorized Wholesale and Retail of Audiovisual Products against Wu
· Case Five: The Case of Printing Operation of Illegal Publication against Gao
· Case Six: The Case of Copyright Infringement against A School in Zhaoqing
Intellectual Property Protection Cases of the Guangdong Quality and Technical Supervision Bureau in 2015 ······ 113
· Case One: The Case of Manufacturing Counterfeit and Inferior Clothing Examined and Dealt with by Quality and Technical Supervision Bureau in Nanhai District, Foshan City
· Case Two: The Case of Manufacturing Counterfeit of Registered Trademark and Certification Mark of Power Adaptor Examined and Dealt with by Quality and Technical Supervision Bureau in Zhongshan City
Typical Cases of Intellectual Property Protection of the Guangdong Customs in 2015 ······ 114

· Case One: The Case of Cosmetic Infringement Cooperated on Law enforcement and Seized Successfully by Guangdong Customs and Hong Kong Customs

· Case Two: The Case of Exporting Hub of the Regional Customs Clearance Integration Seized by Guangzhou Customs

· Case Three: The Case of Exporting Counterfeit Electronic Products Including "Apple" and "Samsung" Seized by Guangzhou Customs

· Case Four: The Series of Cases of Counterfeit Cell phone Seized by Shenzhen Customs Collaborating with Hong Kong Customs

· Case Five: The Case of Infringing Exclusive Rights of Trademark "Three-dimensional Mark of FERRERO ROCHER" against a Chocolate Declared Seized by Guangzhou Customs

· Case Six: The Case of Exporting Counterfeit Cigarette against an Import and Export Corporation of Chengdu Seized by Huangpu Customs

· Case Seven: The Case of Exporting Infringement Sportswear against a Knitting Clothing Co., Ltd. of Fengshun Seized by Huangpu Customs

· Case Eight: The Case of Infringing Exclusive Rights of Trademark "555" Battery Seized by Jiangmen Customs

Ten Typical Cases on Intellectual Property of Guangdong Court in 2015 119

· Case One: The Dispute Case of Violating the Trademark Rights against GD Midea Air-Conditioning Equipment Co., Ltd. and Taifeng Electricity Power Co., Ltd. of Zhuhai Sued by Gree Electric Appliances Inc. of Zhuhai

· Case Two: The Dispute Case of Violating the Patent Rights for Invention against China-Superman Group Co., Ltd. and Mouping Liu, etc. Sued by Royal Philips Co., Ltd.

· Case Three: The Dispute Case of Violating the Exclusive Rights of Registered Trademark against Guangzhou Monalisa Construction Material Co., Ltd. and Foshan Beijiasi Sanitary Ware Co., Ltd. Sued by Guangdong Monalisa New Material Group Co., Ltd.

· Case Four: The Dispute Case of Violating the Exclusive Rights of Layout-designs of Integrated Circuits against Nanjing Micro One Electronics Inc. and Quanxin Micro Devices (Shenzhen) Co., Ltd.

· Case Five: The Dispute Case of Violating the Trademark Rights against Guangzhou Tea Planter Trading Co., Ltd. Sued by Hangzhou Xihu Longjing Tea Industry Association

· Case Six: The Dispute Case of False Propaganda against Guangdong jiaduobao Beverage & Food Co., Ltd. and Moujuan Peng Sued by Guangzhou Pharmaceutical Holdings Limited

· Case Seven: The Dispute Case of Infringing Copyrights against Zhongshan Baofeng Technology Co., Ltd. Sued by Zhongshan Shangfang Network Technology Co., Ltd.

· Case Eight: The Injunction Case of Infringing Copyrights and Unfair Competition Disputes against Chengdu Qiyou Technology Co., Ltd., Beijing Fenbo Shidai Network Technology Co., Ltd. and Guangzhou Dongjing Computer Technology Co., Ltd. Sued by Blizzard Entertainment Co., Ltd. and Shanghai Wangzhiyi Network Technology Co., Ltd.

- Case Nine: The Dispute Case of Unauthorized Use of Specific Package and Decoration of Famous Commodity against Linyi Huatai Battery Co., Ltd. Sued by Guangzhou Tiger Head Battery Group Co., Ltd. and Guangzhou Light Industry and Trade Group Co., Ltd.
- Case Ten: The Case of Administrative Handling Decision made by Market and Quality Supervision Commission of Shenzhen Municipality and Refused to Accept by the Plaintiff Mouyi Zhang

Typical Cases on Intellectual Property Protection of Guangdong Procuratorial Authorities in 2015 ······ 124

- Case One: The Case of Infringement of Commercial Secrets against Microsis Company and Moulei Fang
- Case Two: The Case of Counterfeiting Registered Trademark against Four Persons including Moutian Chen
- Case Three: The Case of Illegal Manufacture of Registered Trademark against Three Persons including Mouke Liang and Illegal Sales of Registered Trademark against Moulian Lai

Management and Service of Intellectual Property

Overview of the "Development Project to Build into a Demonstrative Province on Intellectual Property Service Industry by Guangdong (2013–2020)" ······ 128

Overview of the "Development Project to Build into a Demonstrative Province on Intellectual Property Service Industry by Guangdong (2013–2020)" ······ 128

- Overview

Pilot and Demonstrative Programs of Intellectual Property ······ 129

National Pilot and Demonstrative Cities of Intellectual Property ······ 129

- Overview
- National Demonstrative Cities of Intellectual Property
- National Pilot Cities of Intellectual Property

National Pilot and Demonstration in the Strong Intellectual Property County Project ······ 129

- Overview

Construction of High–tech Demonstration Zone of Intellectual Property ······ 130

- Overview

Management Regulations of Enterprise Intellectual Property ······ 131

Management Regulations of Enterprise Intellectual Property ······ 131

- Training for Implementation of Standards
- Service System for Implementation of Standards
- Regional Implementation of Standards
- Implementation of Standards and Authentication for Enterprises
- Compilation of the Guidebook related to Implementation of Standards

Patent Agency Management ······ 132

Patent Agency Management ······ 132

- Overview
- Regulation of Patent Agency
- Construction of Patent Agency Service Capacity
- Development of Patent Agency Management
- Development of Patent Agency Industry

Joint Intellectual Property Project by Hundreds and Thousands of Intellectual Property Service Agency–Enterprises ······ 134

Joint Intellectual Property Project by Hundreds and Thousands of Intellectual Property Service Agency–Enterprises ······ 134

- Overview

Service Platform of Industrial Patent Information ······ 135

Service Platform of Industrial Patent Information ………… 135
· Overview
■Service and Supporting Institutions …… 136
Construction of Guangdong Patent Examination Cooperation Center ………… 136
· Overview
Guangzhou Division, State Intellectual Property Office ………… 136
· Overview
· Electronic Patent Application
· Pilot Work
· Public Service
Guangdong Intellectual Property Research and Development Center (Guangdong Intellectual Property Protection and Aids Center) ………… 137
· Overview
· Information Service System
· Information Platform
· Service Capability
· Training Service
· Service for Intellectual Property Protection and Aids
· Service for Judicial Identification
· Tasks Commissioned
Guangdong Intellectual Property Research Association ………… 141
· Overview
· Element Tasks of the Research Association
· Subject Study on Intellectual Property
· Academic Exchanges on Intellectual Property
· Undertaking of Government Programs
Guangdong Intellectual Property Protection Association ………… 143
· Overview
· Cooperation Programs
· Regular Programs
· Undertaking of Government Work
Guangdong Patent Agency Association ………… 145
· Construction of the Self-discipline
· Training and Exchanges
· Undertaking of Government Work
Guangdong Patent Information Association …… 146
· Association Construction
· Organization Construction
· Industry Service
Guangdong Trademark Association ………… 147
· Overview
· Guangdong Famous Trademarks
· Industry Construction
· Campaign and Training
· Service Platform
Guangdong Copyright Protection Association …· 149
· Interchange Activities
· Collaboration of Popularizing Law and Safeguarding Rights
· Undertaking of Government Programs
· Achievements and Honors
Judicial Appraisal Institute of Guangdong Intellectual Property Research and Development Center ………… 150
· Overview
· Registered in Court
· Training and Education
· Communication and Exchange
· Internal Management
The Committee on Intellectual Property Laws of Guangdong Lawyers Association ………… 150
· Appraisal, Election and Tour Speech of Typical Cases
· The Third Forum of Guangdong Intellectual Property Law Service Held
· Standards Implementation of Intellectual Property
· International Copyright Law Symposium among Mainland, Hong Kong and Singapore Held
· "Intellectual Property Management and Commercial Practice Symposium" Held

- The Symposium on Practical Problems of Civil Procedure of Commercial Secrets Held

Guangdong Association of Inventions ··············· 151
- Overview

Intellectual Property Law Association of Guangdong Province Law Society ················ 153
- Overview

Intellectual Property Exchange and Cooperation

Foreign Exchange and Cooperation of Intellectual Property ······························ 156

Foreign Exchange and Cooperation of Intellectual Property ·· 156
- Overview
- Foreign Exchange and Cooperation System
- China (Guangdong) Pilot Free Trade Zone
- Intellectual Property Work of the Belt and Road Initiative
- Key Foreign Affairs and Exchange Activities
- Key Platform Construction
- Efforts on Intellectual Property Rights Involving Foreign Countries
- Foreign Publicity
- Intellectual Property Cooperation among Guangdong, Hong Kong, Macao and Taiwan

Regional Exchange and Cooperation ·· 159

Cooperation on Intellectual Property between Guangdong and Hong Kong in 2015 ············ 159
- Overview
- Cooperation Mechanism of Intellectual Property
- Mechanism of Law Enforcement and Collaboration to Handle Cases of Intellectual Property
- Trade and Legal Service of Intellectual Property
- Business of Intellectual Property Asia Forum
- Exchange, Research and Discussion of Intellectual Property among Guangdong, Hong Kong and Macao
- Guidance and Service for Intellectual Property between Guangdong and Hong Kong
- Publicity and Education of Intellectual Property between Guangdong and Hong Kong

Cooperation on Intellectual Property between Guangdong and Macao in 2015 ···················· 161
- Overview
- Cooperation Mechanism of Intellectual Property between Guangdong and Macao
- Mechanism of Collaborating to Handle Intellectual Property Cases between Guangdong and Macao
- Communication and Exchange Visits of Intellectual Property between Guangdong and Macao
- Publicity and Training of Intellectual Property between Guangdong and Macao
- Research on Intellectual Property between Guangdong and Macao
- Information Resource-Sharing of Intellectual Property among Guangdong, Hong Kong and Macao

Cooperation on Intellectual Property between Guangdong and Taiwan in 2015 ···················· 163
- Overview
- The 8th Cross-Straits Patent Forum
- Communication among Intellectual Property Service Organizations between Guangdong and Taiwan
- Exchange and Cooperation on Intellectual Property between Guangdong and Taiwan

Cooperation on Intellectual Property of Pan-Pearl River Delta Regions in 2015 ·············· 163
- Overview
- Exchanges on Special Subjects of Pan-Pearl River Delta Regions
- Cooperation on Patent Administrative Enforcement of Law by Pan-Pearl River Delta Regions and Nine Provinces and Autonomous Regions in Mainland

· Patent Information of Pan-Pearl River Delta Regions and Nine Provinces and Autonomous Regions in Mainland
Cooperation on Intellectual Property between Guangdong and Kashi ······ 164
· Overview
· Intellectual Property Creation
· Law Enforce of Intellectual Property
· Personnel Exchange of Intellectual Property
· Intellectual Property Education
· Publicity and Training of Intellectual Property

Publicity & Education and Training

Publicity ······ 168

Intellectual Property Campaign in Guangdong Province ······ 168
· Overview
· Plan and Arrangement
· Emphasis and Hotspot
· Publicity Channel
Intellectual Property Campaign and Training of the Industrial and Commercial Administrative Management System of Guangdong Province ······ 169
· Overview
· Trademark Campaign
· Trademark Training

Education and Training ······ 170

Personnel Training of Intellectual Property of Guangdong Province ······ 170
· Overview
State Intellectual Property Training, Guangdong Base (South China University of Technology) ······ 170
· The System of Personnel Training and Teachers
· Education of Intellectual Property Rights
· Scientific Studies
· Academic Activities
· Social Services
National Intellectual Property Training Base of Guangdong Province (Guangdong Intellctual Property Research and Development Center) ······ 172
· Overview
· Personnel Training on Intellectual Property
· International Exchanges
· Intellectual Property Studies
Intellectual Property Training Base of Guangdong Province (Jinan University) ······ 173
· Overview
· Personnel Training
· Scientific Studies
· Academic Activities
· Social Services
Intellectual Property Training Base of Guangdong Province (Shenzhen University) ······ 174
· Personnel Training
· Academic Activities
· Platform Construction
Intellectual Property Training Base of Guangdong Province (Shantou University) ······ 175
· Overview
· Education of Intellectual Property Rights
· Service for Enterprises
Intellectual Property Training Base of Guangdong Province (Huizhou University) ······ 175
· Overview
· Campaign and Training
· Educational Base
Intellectual Property Training Base of Guangdong Province (Guangdong Ocean University) ······ 176
· Overview
· Intellectual Property Campaign
· Intellectual Property Training

Intellectual Property Training Base of Guangdong Province (Shunde Polytechnic) ······ 176
· Overview
· Infrastructure Construction
· Ability Training
· Popularization and Training
· Training on Special Subjects
· Activity of Quantity Increase and Quality Improvement of Intellectual Property
· Optional Courses of Intellectual Property
· The Shunde Branch Office of Intellectual Property Tele-education
The Research Institute of Intellectual Property of Guangdong Financial College ······ 177
· Overview
South China Normal University ······ 178
· Overview
· Campaign and Training
· Creation and Application
Intellectual Property Education for Primary and Secondary Schools ······ 178
National Intellectual Property Training Base (Nanhai) for Micro, Small and Medium Companies ······ 178
· Overview
· Training Activity
· Management of Training
· Social Service

Regional Operations on Intellectual Property

Regional Operations on Intellectual Property ······ 182
Guangzhou City ······ 182
· Pilot and Demonstrative Operations
· Intellectual Property Management
· Intellectual Property Creation
· Intellectual Property Application
· Intellectual Property Protection
· Campaign and Training
· Exchange and Cooperation
Shenzhen City ······ 185
· Intellectual Property Creation
· Intellectual Property Application
· Intellectual Property Protection
· Intellectual Property Management
· Intellectual Property Service
· Campaign and Training of Intellectual Property
Zhuhai City ······ 188
· Overview
Shantou City ······ 188
· Intellectual Property Creation
· Intellectual Property Application
· Intellectual Property Protection
· Intellectual Property Management
· Campaign and Training of Intellectual Property
· Exchange and Cooperation of Intellectual Property
· Statistical Information
Foshan City ······ 194
· Intellectual Property Creation
· Intellectual Property Application
· Intellectual Property Protection
· Intellectual Property Management
· Intellectual Property Service
· Intellectual Property Campaign
· Statistical Information
Shaoguan City ······ 199
· Intellectual Property Creation
· Intellectual Property Application
· Intellectual Property Protection
· Intellectual Property Management
· Campaign and Training of Intellectual Property
Heyuan City ······ 200
· Intellectual Property Creation
· Intellectual Property Protection
· Management and Service of Intellectual Property
· Campaign and Training of Intellectual Property
Meizhou City ······ 202
· Intellectual Property Creation

· Intellectual Property Application
· Intellectual Property Protection
· Intellectual Property Management
· Campaign and Training of Intellectual Property
· Statistical Information
Huizhou City ······ 206
· Intellectual Property Creation
· Intellectual Property Application
· Intellectual Property Protection
· Intellectual Property Management
· Campaign and Training of Intellectual Property
· Statistical Information
Shanwei City ······ 210
· Intellectual Property Creation
· Intellectual Property Protection
· Intellectual Property Management
· Exchange and Cooperation of Intellectual Property
· Campaign and Training
Dongguan City ······ 211
· Overview
· Intellectual Property Creation
· Intellectual Property Application
· Intellectual Property Protection
· Intellectual Property Management
· Campaign and Training of Intellectual Property
· Intellectual Property Service
· Statistical Information
Zhongshan City ······ 217
· Intellectual Property Creation
· Intellectual Property Application
· Intellectual Property Protection
· Intellectual Property Management
· Campaign and Training of Intellectual Property
Jiangmen City ······ 219
· Intellectual Property Creation
· Intellectual Property Application
· Intellectual Property Protection
· Intellectual Property Management
Yangjiang City ······ 221
· Intellectual Property Creation
· Intellectual Property Application
· Intellectual Property Protection
· Intellectual Property Management
· Campaign and Training of Intellectual Property
Zhanjiang City ······ 222
· Overview
· Intellectual Property Creation
· Intellectual Property Management
· Intellectual Property Protection
· Campaign and Training of Intellectual Property
· Statistical Information
Maoming City ······ 224
· Intellectual Property Creation
· Intellectual Property Protection
· Intellectual Property Management
· Campaign and Training of Intellectual Property
Zhaoqing City ······ 226
· Intellectual Property Creation
· Intellectual Property Application
· Intellectual Property Protection
· Management and Service of Intellectual Property
· Campaign and Training of Intellectual Property
Qingyuan City ······ 228
· Intellectual Property Creation
· Intellectual Property Protection
· Intellectual Property Management
· Intellectual Property Campaign
Chaozhou City ······ 230
· Intellectual Property Creation
· Intellectual Property Application
· Intellectual Property Protection
· Intellectual Property Management
· Campaign and Training of Intellectual Property
Jieyang City ······ 232
· Intellectual Property Creation
· Intellectual Property Protection
· Intellectual Property Management
· Campaign, Education and Training
Yunfu City ······ 233

- Intellectual Property Creation
- Intellectual Property Application
- Intellectual Property Protection
- Intellectual Property Management
- Campaign, Education and Training

Commendation and Awards

Commendation and Awards ·················· 238

One Hundred Cultivate High-Level Talents of National Intellectual Property Leaderships Selected in 2015 ········· 238

The List of Talents of National Patent Information Leaderships and Professionals in 2015 ········· 238

Advanced Groups and Individuals for Construction of National Pilot and Demonstrative Cities of Intellectual Property ········· 239

Monographic Research and Work Experience Exchange

Monographic Research Report ············ 242

Soft Science Research and Management of Guangdong Intellectual Property Bureau ······ 242

- Overview

Survey Report on the Status Quo of Protection and Management of National Geographical Indication Products of Guangdong Province ········· 242

- Overview
- Basic Situation of Protection of National Geographical Indication Products in Guangdong Province
- The Significance of Geographical Indication Protection
- Current Problems of Protection and Management of National Geographical Indication Products
- The Approaching Countermeasures and Suggestions

Work Experience Exchange ················ 246

Intellectual Property Protection in the China Import and Export Fair (Canton Fair) ····· 246

- Overview
- The Situation of Intellectual Property Protection in the China Import and Export Fair (the 117th Canton Fair)
- The Situation of Intellectual Property Protection in the China Import and Export Fair (the 118th Canton Fair)

Appendix

Policies and Regulations ······················ 250

Plan of Action for Deep Implementation of Intellectual Property Strategy and Pursuit of Innovation-driven Development by Guangdong Province ········· 250

Implementation Opinions on Promoting the National Standard of "Rules of Enterprise IPR Management" Comprehensively Issued by The Intellectual Property Office, Department of Science and Technology, Economic and Information Commission, Department of Commerce, Administration of Quality and Technology Supervision and State-owned Assets Supervision and Administration Commission of Guangdong Province ········· 254

Provisions for the Protection of National Geographical Indication Products ··············· 257

Implementing Rules for the Protection of National Geographical Indication Products ·· 260

Chronicle of Events about Intellectual Property in 2015 ········· 265

Statistical Information ························· 284

Patent Applications of Guangdong Province Annually ········· 284

Patent Licensing of Guangdong Province Annually ········· 285

Applications of Three Types of Patents among All Types of Patent Applicants in Guangdong Province in 1986–2015 ············ 286
Licensing of Three Types of Patents among All Types of Patent Applicants in Guangdong Province in 1986–2015 ············ 286
Patent Applications of All Cities at the Prefecture Level or Above in Guangdong Province in 2010–2015 ············ 287
Patent Licensing of All Cities at the Prefecture Level or Above in Guangdong Province in 2010–2015 ············ 288
National and Guangdong Provincial PCT International Patent Applications in 2002–2015 ············ 289
PCT International Patent Applications of All Cities at the Prefecture Level or Above in Guangdong Province in 2015 ············ 289
Statistical List of Executions of Patent Policies by All Cities of Guangdong Province at the Prefecture Level or Above in 2015 ············ 289
List of Patent Cases Accepted and Concluded by Patent Administrative Departments of Guangdong Province Annually ············ 290
Statistical List of Patent Cases Accepted and Concluded in Guangdong Province in 2010–2015 ············ 290
List of Patent Award of Guangdong Province in 2015 ············ 291
Statistical List of Investigation and Treatment in Cases of Trademark Infringement and Counterfeit in Guangdong Province in 2015 ············ 296
Statistical List of Investigation and Treatment in General Illegal Cases of Trademark in 2015 ············ 297
Statistical List of Investigation and Treatment in Infringement Cases for the Trademark Registrants of Hong Kong, Macao, Taiwan and Foreign Countries in 2015 ············ 298
Directory of New Products Authorized of Guangdong Forestry Plants in 2015 ············ 299
Statistical List of Administrative Law Enforcement of Guangdong Cultural Market in 2015 ············ 300
Information Directory of National Geographical Indication Registered by Guangdong Agro-products ············ 301
Bulletin Directory of New Products Authorized of Guangdong Agricultural Plants in 2015 ··· 301
Directory of National Geographical Indication Registered by Guangdong Products ············ 304
Guangdong Patent Application and Licensing in 2015 ············ 304
Patent Agencies ············ 308
Directory of Patent Agencies of Guangdong Province ············ 308
Directory of Branches of Patent Agencies of Guangdong Province ············ 311

Theme Index

Theme Index ············ 316

TE JI

特辑

- 第二轮知识产权高层次战略合作
- 贯彻实施《珠江三角洲地区改革发展规划纲要（2008—2020年）》
- 打击侵犯知识产权和制售假冒伪劣商品工作
- 广东省政府颁布实施《广东省深入实施知识产权战略推动创新驱动发展行动计划》
- 领导讲话

第二轮知识产权高层次战略合作

第二轮知识产权高层次战略合作

【概况】 国家知识产权局与广东省政府共同围绕广东经济结构战略性调整的总目标，坚持“服务转型升级、服务创新驱动、服务扩大内外需”，开展第二轮知识产权高层次战略合作。2013年至2015年，双方共同实施完成合作项目39个，实现合作预定的目标，发挥知识产权制度对广东创新驱动发展的助推作用。

【知识产权强国建设先行地】 2015年，广东形成《广东省深入知识产权战略推动创新驱动发展行动计划》，并以省政府名义印发实施该计划。同时，为支持强国建设先行地试点工作，广东相继出台系列支撑政策，并组建广东省知识产权专家咨询委员会。组织开展知识产权产品纳入国民经济核算体系专题研究，制订《关于运用知识产权促进产业转型升级的意见》《关于促进我省知识产权服务业发展的若干意见》《广东创建知识产权服务业发展示范省规划（2013—2020年）》，为广东探索创新实现路径、发挥知识产权对产业转型升级支撑作用奠定政策基础。

【知识产权改革创新】 合作期间，国家知识产权局与广东省政府着力通过广东知识产权改革创新试点，形成可复制可推广的经验，助推广东产业转型升级及创新驱动发展战略实施。

一是推进中新（广州）知识城为首个国家级知识产权运用和保护综合改革试点。2015年，双方稳步推进中新广州知识城知识产权运用保护综合改革试点，举行高级别会谈并签署会谈纪要，推动知识城开展国家知识产权运用和保护综合改革试验区总体方案获批实施，全面推进知识产权服务业集聚中心、知识产权法院、知识产权研究院等的高端项目在中心知识城的集聚实施，并争取在全国率先开创支撑创新型经济发展新模式。

二是国家重点布局区域的知识产权改革。制定并印发《关于加强中国（广东）自由贸易试验区知识产权工作的指导意见》，提出六项主要任务和四项保障措施。同时，配合全省自贸区建设整体任务安排，将“探索建立统一的知识产权管理和执法体制”重要政策内容纳入省政府《中国（广东）自由贸易试验区管理试行办法》、省人大《中国（广东）自由贸易试验区条例（征求意见稿）》和省编办《中国（广东）自由贸易试验区综合行政执法体制改革方案（征求意见稿）》，力争从法律层面上为加强自贸区知识产权工作提供有力支撑。

【知识产权保护】 合作期间，国家知识产权局与广东省人民政府从严开展知识产权保护，知识产权执法协作得到加强。2015年，开展电商专利保护试点项目，支持唯品会、梦芭莎等电商建立知识产权保护平台，建立专利侵权纠纷和假冒专利行为投诉处理机制，推动电子商务企业提高知识产权意识，实现专利保护有效自律。加速推进知识产权快速维权援助体系建设。知识产权快速维权中心是国家知识产权局支持广东改革突破的重点项目之一，在国家知识产权局大力支持下，广东继中山灯饰古镇设立快速维权中心后，中国东莞（家具）知识产权快速维权中心、中国顺德（家电）知识产权快速维权中心、中国广州花都（皮革皮具）知识产权快速维权中心相继落户广东。广东已设立知识产权快速维权中心4家，占全国总数的一半以上，知识产权快速维权中心服务模式日益完善，成效日益凸现，专利申请数量和质量实现双提升。

【知识产权运用】 促进知识产权运用，服务创新驱动发展是双方合作的重点内容之一，合作期间，国家知识产权局将专利导航产业发展、知识产权运营、知识产权金融等重要试点均放在广东开展，取得实效。

一是专利导航产业发展。国家知识产权局对广东开展运用专利信息导航产业高端发展给予有力的指导和支持，广东相继启动实施“珠江西岸先进装备制造产业带专利导航工程”“珠江三角洲地区产业转型升级专利导航工程”及创建“国家专利导航产业发展实验区”，推动辖区内优质知识产权服务及运营资源，围绕战略性新兴产业、智能装备、卫星通信、机械装备制造等重点产业，开展专利导航产业发展。至2015年，已形成专利分析及预警报告30份，并召开系列报告会23场，面向各相关政府部门和4200多家企事业单位发布。

二是知识产权金融创新试点。合作期间，佛山市南海区成为全国唯一的国家级“国家知识产权投融资（南海）综合试验区”，顺德区获批国家知识产权投融资服务试点，双方以佛山知识产权金融试点为抓手，全面推进知识产权金融创新。2015年，佛山市、广州经济技术开发区、增城经济技术开发区、广东自贸区深圳前海蛇口片区获批“国家知识产权投融资试点”，惠州仲恺高新区获批“国家知识产权质押融资试点”。2015年，全省专利质押融资金额近59亿元，位居全国前列。专利保险方面，广州、深圳、东莞市和佛山市禅城4市（区）开展“全国专利保险试点”，截至2015年底，四地逾200家企业已累计完成专利投保超过3000件，保费168.4万元，最高可获赔6558.3万元。中山市开展了全国首例单一行业专利保险探索，2015年投保企业13家，涉及105件专利，保费9.82万元，最高可获赔800万元。

三是知识产权运营交易市场。合作期间，国家知识产权局批准设立“全国知识产权运营公共服务横琴特色分平台”。广东省政府批准省产权交易集团成立广州知识产权交易中心。中孵网、广东金融高新区股权交易中心华南知识产权运营中心、广州汇桔网互联网知识产权金融平台、深圳7号网等知识产权交易运营服务平台发展壮大，为社会提供专业化、深层次知识产权运营服务。佛山市海科知识产权交易有限公司与银行（投行）、评估等机构建立市场化运作平台，建设广东知识产权（中山灯饰照明）运营中心、广东知识产权创新运用（顺德）试验区。中兴通讯、腾讯、中彩联等3家企业深化国家专利运营试点工作。深圳市出台全国首个企业专利运营指南地方标准（SZDB/Z 102–2014）。2015年，广东设立重点产业知识产权运营基金，以中央财政4000万元为引导资金，筹备成立总规模达30亿元、首期规模达5亿元的广东省粤科国联知识产权投资运营基金。

【知识产权服务业】 合作期间，广东率先提出创建知识产权服务业发展示范省，并于2013年出台实施《广东创建知识产权服务业发展示范省规划（2013—2020年）》及《关于促进知识产权服务业发展的若干意见》，从优化发展环境、培育服务市场、扶持服务机构等多方面下功夫，全面推动广东知识产权服务业发展。在双方共同努力下，广东知识产权服务业蓬勃发展：

一是知识产权特色服务。双方共同培育深圳市福田区、佛山市成为国家知识产权服务业集聚发展试验区，支持东莞松山湖新区、广州市越秀区、广州新区设立省级知识产权服务业集聚发展试验区，加快广东省知识产权服务业集聚中心建设立项，推动知识产权服务业聚集。

二是知识产权机构。引导资产评估公司积极参与知识产权评估，新设知识产权评估推广项目和知识产权运营机构培育试点项目，扶持服务机构发展，促进知识产权服务业集聚区建设。合作期间，广东4家知识产权服务机构入选“全国知识产权服务品牌机构培育单位”，5家机构成功挂牌“全国知识产权服务品牌机构”。双方还支持中兴通讯、腾讯、中彩联等企业和行业组织开展国家专利运营试点工作，研制和推广应用质押评估技术规范地方标准。此外，广东微生物所获批成为全国第三家具有专利菌种保藏功能的菌种保藏中心。

三是知识产权信息服务。广东深化泛珠三角区域专利信息服务（广州）中心服务，组建广东专利信息协会、引导全国知识产权服务联盟成员入粤服务等措施，构建公益服务和商用服务相融合、线上线下立体服务专利大数据利用新局面。此外，广东创新开展了中小微企业专利信息推送服务，截至2015年，面向广东省内21个地市，45个专业镇近1500家企业推送了定制的专利信息服务产品。同时，广东借力国家专利信息资源，与中国专利信息中心、知识产权出版社等国字头单位建立合作关系，分别在专利信息数据资源完善、“互联网+知识产权”全覆盖子系统建设、专利信息服务专项合作、专利信息人才培养等方面实现深入合作。

【知识产权对外合作】 国家知识产权局着重推动广东知识产权国际交流合作平台建设。广东积极构建知识产权多元国际合作试验区，累计接待国外知识产权代表团组来访87批次523人次，组织人员参加出国访问和培训33批次119人次，与美国、英国、德国、日本、韩国、新加坡、台湾等20多个国家和地区的官方机构、社会团体、企业建立广泛、深入的合作关系，同时继续加强国际知识产权交流研讨活动，举办各类国际性知识产权论坛和研讨会28场，既全面展示广东知识产权事业发展成绩，增进外方对广东省知识产权工作的了解和认识，又有效拓展知识产权国际视野，加强国际型人才培养力度。同时，知识产权活动进入“第五届粤东侨博会”，为粤东侨博会提供知识产权服务。建设“企业知识产权海外护航优势区”方面，广东围绕“21世纪海上丝绸之路”，在展会知识产权保护、行业涉外保护及重点产品专利预警分析三方面开展企业知识产权海外护航优势区建设。广东支持9家行业协会和展会主办单位开展知识产权涉外应对工作。起草企业规避海外知识产权风险指南，对粤企出现的涉外知识产权纠纷及“337调查”重点案件进行对接维权服务。

【知识产权人才队伍建设】 合作期间，国家知识产权局大力支持广东知识产权人才培养工作，批准首家国家中小微企业知识产权培训基地（南海）和首家高校以外的国家知识产权培训（广东）基地（广东省知识产权研究与发展中心）落户广东，支持广东实施“百千万知识产权人才工程”，据统计，全省共举办各类培训活动500多期，参加人数8万余人次。此外，广东相继推出“知识产权培训基地建设工程”“知识产权人才信息化工程”及“广东省知识产权人才信息管理系统建设工程”，全力打造高素质复合型的知识产权人才梯队。同时，在国家知识产权局的支持下，广东在深圳、广州试点开展了知识产权专业技术资格评审工作，深圳共有168人取得知识产权研究员系列职称，广州启动高、中级职称评审，广东启动全省知识产权专业技术资格评价工作。2015年，在暨南大学和广州市政府的大力助推下，广东省政府、广州市政府、暨南大学、北京大学、国家知识产权局、国侨办明确在暨南大学共同建设广州知识产权人才基地。据统计，广东知识产权专业人才总量已达3.6万人，23人成为国家知识产权领军人才，14位专家入选国家知识产权专家库，31人入选全国“百千万知识产权人才工程”百名高层次人才培养人选，8人入选全国专利信息领军人才、18人入选全国专利信息师资人才。

【知识产权管理】 一是《企业知识产权管理规范》贯彻实施。合作期间，双方围绕企业知识产权“贯标”，大力提升广东企业知识产权创造、运用能力。广东制定并印发了《关于全面推行〈企业知识产权管理规范〉国家标准的实施意见》，借力国家资源，与中华全国专利代理人协会签署《贯彻企业知识产权标准合作关系议定书》，全国第一个“贯标”地方性办事机构“中规（北京）认证有限公司广州办事处”于2015年落户广东。同时，加大“贯标”专业人员培养力度，组织开展“贯标”培训班11期，培训人员1600多人。实施“广东省企业知识产权管理规范推进项目”，扶持20家服务质量高、运营情况好的“贯标”服务机构，按市场化运作原则发动并辅导企业“贯标”。截至2015年底，广东31家企业通过“贯标”认证。

二是专利审查协作中心服务区域发展合作机制建立运行。为充分发挥国家知识产权局专利局专利审查协作广东中心的人才和资源优势，在国家知识产权局的指导下，国家专利审查协作广东中心与广东省签订《国家专利审查协作广东中心、广东省知识产权局2014年服务区域发展帮扶合作计划》，建立长效合作机制，面向广东逐步探索开展专利战略推进、提高专利申请质量、专利导航分析、企业知识产权管理、重大经济和科技活动知识产权评议、知识产权人才培训等服务地方经济的工作。

三是专利代办工作创新试点顺利铺开。为适应广东密集型产业知识产权快速维权需求，经国家知识产权局同意，在广州代办处开展灯饰、家具和家电等行业的外观设计专利前置服务试点工作，通过对企业提交的外观设计专利申请按照初审要求进行前置检查，对申请图片进行预先检索，及时反馈修改意见，提高申请质量，缩短授权时间，广州专利代办工作在外观设计专利前置服务方面取得新成效。

（供稿人：阳屹琴）

贯彻实施《珠江三角洲地区改革发展规划纲要（2008—2020年）》

贯彻实施《珠江三角洲地区改革发展规划纲要（2008—2020年）》

【概况】 2015年，广东省知识产权局以数量合理增长为基础，以全面提升专利申请主体的申请质量为目标，制定实施《关于提升我省专利申请数质量的若干意见》，同时，通过评选第一、二届广东省专利奖，激发社会创新积极性。珠三角地区百万人口发明专利申请量为1728件，万人发明专利拥有量为23.3件，两个指标均已超过年初设定的1295件、20件目标值。

【知识产权创造】 2015年，珠三角地区知识产权创造能力再上新台阶。珠三角地区发明专利申请量达99595件，同比增长38.24%。同时，《广东省专利奖励办法》明确规定将“广东专利奖”从部门奖提升到省政府奖的高度，极大调动了创新主体的积极性。在第十七届中国专利奖评选活动中，全省获中国专利金奖数达6项，优秀奖119项，其中，全省获金奖地市全部集中在珠三角地区，彰显珠三角地区知识产权质量新优势。

【知识产权运用】 2015年，广东省知识产权局大力促进知识产权运用。一是积极推动贯彻《企业知识产权管理规范》国家标准，中山、惠州、东莞、佛山等地相继出台了贯标扶持政策。二是扶持小微企业创新发展，建成为小微企业技术研发提供免费检索查询的知识产权综合服务平台，涵盖全球104个国家9800万条专利信息的手机专利检索平台——“专利知道”APP正式上线运行，免费服务小微企业创新发展。三是推动知识产权投融资发展，广州、东莞完成“全国知识产权质押融资试点城市”建设，佛山市南海区完成“国家知识产权投融资（南海）综合试验区”建设，佛山市顺德区完成“国家知识产权投融资服务”试点。同时，广州、深圳、东莞、佛山禅城4市（区）开展“全国专利保险试点”。截至2015年底，四地逾200家企业已累计完成专利投保超过3000件，保费168.4万元，最高可获赔6558.3万元。中山市开展全国首例单一行业专利保险探索，2015年投保企业13家，105件专利，保费9.82万元，最高可获赔800万元。

【知识产权运营体系建设】 2015年，广东省知识产权局开展国家级以市场化方式促进知识产权运营服务工作试点，成为全国承担“全国知识产权运营公共服务横琴特色试点平台”“股权投资扶持知识产权运营机构”“重点产业知识产权运营基金”“知识产权质押融资风险补偿基金”全部4项国家级试点唯一省份。建成一批国家级和省级知识产权交易、运营服务平台，扶持一批知识产权运营机构高端化发展，广州知识产权交易中心、横琴国际知识产权交易中心、广东金融高新区股权交易中心华南知识产权运营中心、汇桔网、高航网、7号网等知识产权运营机构纷纷涌现。

【知识产权行政保护】 2015年，广东省知识产权局按照国家统一部署，全面推进侵权假冒行政处罚案件信息公开、开展打击互联网侵权假冒农村和城乡结合部专项整治、车用燃油专项整治和维护中国制造海外形象的“清风行动”，大力查处专利侵权、假冒专利案件，建立健全行政执法与刑事司法衔接机制，建立完善行政保护、司法保护、行业自律的全方位、多层次的知识产权保护体系。全国首个皮具产业知识产权快速维权中心落户花都，至此，珠三角地区成为全国首个拥有灯饰、家具、家电和皮具四家快速维权援助中心的地区。

（供稿人：阳屹琴）

打击侵犯知识产权和制售假冒伪劣商品工作

打击侵犯知识产权和制售假冒伪劣商品工作

【概况】 2015年，全省各地各主要行政执法部门共立案查处侵权假冒案件29754宗，同比上年的21072宗增长41%。全省公安系统侦破侵权假冒案件4595宗（其中知识产权案件1888宗，食品药品案件2707宗），公安部8次发来贺电，广东打击侵权伪劣犯罪绩效排名位居全国公安系统前列；检察机关批捕犯罪嫌疑人8552人，起诉案件6412宗；法院系统受理相关刑事案件6243宗。

【组织管理】 广东省人民政府副省长、省打击侵权假冒工作领导小组组长陈云贤主持召开全省打击侵权假冒工作电视电话会议，传达中央精神，部署广东省工作任务。省打击侵权假冒工作领导小组办公室充分发挥组织协调作用，转发国家年度工作要点，制定印发广东省年度工作要点，组织完成2014年度绩效现场考核，制订方案并深入推动开展互联网打击侵权假冒、农村和城乡结合部、车用燃油、中国制造海外形象维护清风行动等专项整治工作。

【行政执法】 一是互联网打击侵权假冒专项整治。工商部门开展“2015红盾网剑”专项行动，严查网络交易平台、大型购物网站、团购网站和企业官网的侵权假冒行为，共网上检查网站14.4万个次，实地检查网站、网店经营者1.3万个次，删除违法商品信息669条，责令整改网站1040个，已提请关闭网站70个，查处各类网络交易违法案件794宗，罚没款971.66万元。文化系统印发了《广东省网络文化市场巡查制度》，抽调全省各地网络文化市场执法业务骨干，组建“网络文化市场巡查小组”，组织查办网络文化市场侵权假冒类案件。版权系统巡查网络经营单位3204家，主动监管本地网站800余家，查办案件35宗，行政罚款145.2万。公安系统推进打击互联网领域侵权、假冒犯罪，破案291宗，查处违规网站、电商平台230个，刑拘764人。深圳市以现代信息技术手段为依托，形成“一网一库两平台三中心”的监管执法构架，电子商务监管监测中心和网络电子证据取证中心投入使用，主动监测检查电子商务主体16781个，搜索监测网络经营交易信息4.2万条，检查网络商品交易主体6.2万家，形成涉嫌违法案件线索231件，查办各类利用电子商务市场领域违法案件189宗。

二是农村和城乡结合部侵权假冒专项整治。工商系统以农村和城乡结合部为重点区域，以农资、电器、日用消费品等商品为重点商品，开展专项整治，共检查农资经营户54023户次，检查农资商品市场664次，取缔无证无照经营49户，立案查处各类农资商品违法经营行为1284宗，案值568.42万元，罚没647.22万元，受理投诉举报63宗，为农民挽回经济损失24.89万元。质监系统共出动执法人员12994人次，检查农资生产企业和农资经营单位2396家，查办案件60宗，减少农业生产损失155.04万元。农业系统重点组织部署开展农药及农药使用、瘦肉精、生鲜乳、养殖抗菌药、生猪屠宰、农资打假等6大专项整治行动，并在全省组织开展了农资打假“夏季百日行动”。共出动执法人员188825人次，检查农资企业22404家次，整顿农资市场879个次，查获侵权假劣农资92704公斤，涉案1504台件，受理举报案件26宗，为农民挽回直接经济损失956.54万元，有力打击了制售假冒伪劣农资的违法行为，有效保障了农资市场的正常秩序、农业生产的正常开展和农产品质量安全。公安系统与相关行政执法部门开展联合执法行动次1145 次，破案869宗，捣毁窝点971个，刑拘2194人

三是车用燃油专项整治。工商系统制定了《2015年广东省流通领域车用汽油、车用柴油商品质量抽查检验实施方案》，共抽检车用燃油1946组，其中车用汽油1360组，车用柴油586组，发现不合格车用燃油66组，其中车用汽油28组，车用柴油38组。质监系统在全省范围内组织开展针对石油炼化企业的监督检查，严厉打击缺斤短两、掺杂掺假、生产劣质汽柴油等违法、违规行为。经信系统结合成品油经营企业年审工作，对不符合经营条件的企业依法要求整改，并加强对成品油市场的检查和监管，对购销台账制度不完善、证书过期、基础设施不规范的情况及时落实整改。国税系统对各地车用燃油企业进行认真筛查，重点开展税务检查工作。公安系统相关行政执法部门开展联合行动次数133次，捣毁窝点12个，破案5宗，刑拘20人。

四是海关“清风行动”。海关系统针对省内关区出口特点，采取“分阶段、有重点、逐步推进”的方式，加大对出口货物的监控力度，在“清风”行动中查扣进出口侵权货物122万件，制止侵权货物输往48个国家或地区。检验检疫部门根据广东输往非洲商品以及市场采购出口商品特点，不断深化市场采购、输非商品检验监管模式改革，积极推动市场采购出口商品检管区、输非商品检管区和公共服务平台建设。广东检验检疫局共对输非产品实施装运前检验14818批，货值52345万美元，查处进出口假冒伪劣商品案件48宗，伪造、使用假证书案7宗；移送公安机关案件3宗。

【刑事司法】 公安系统开展跨省打假集群战役55起，侦破侵犯知识产权犯罪案件1888宗，抓获5121人，刑拘4391人，逮捕2757人，移送审查起诉3698人，涉案价值约52亿元；立案食品药品案件4280宗，刑事拘留4645人，破案2707宗，逮捕4089人，公安部8次发来贺电；检察机关批捕犯罪嫌疑人8552人，起诉案件6412宗；法院系统受理相关刑事案件6243宗，持续保持对侵权假冒违法犯罪分子的强大震慑力。

【“两法”衔接与司法保护】 省公安厅、省经信委等21个省直部门联合下发《关于公安机关提前介入行政执法机关办理的案件以及联合办案制定的规定》（粤公通字〔2014〕165号），省检察院与省环保厅、省地税局等19个部门联合签发涉嫌犯罪的案件移送标准。省级两法衔接信息共享平台运转良好，全省21个地市与县区完成联网。广州、佛山、江门等10个地市年初实现行政处罚及移送案件数据的对接，打击侵权假冒数据作为省两法衔接信息共享平台的子项目成功导入。

【行政处罚案件信息公开】 全省各执法部门高度重视打击侵权假冒行政处罚案件信息公开工作，严格依照要求，及时、准确、全面地公开行政处罚案件信息。食药监系统共公开行政处罚案件15342件，占适用一般程序应当公开案件数的58.74%，公布不合格药品信息1054批，食品药品生产经营企业“黑名单”信息62条。工商系统共公示“双打”案件2320宗，发布严重违法广告的45家媒体以及信用排名后30位的媒体，通报2014年全省十大农资违法典型案例，依法认定并公告抽检的缺陷商品447款。

【营造良好社会氛围】 省新闻办会同各相关职能部门组织召开了系列新闻发布会，主动发布新闻曝光大案要案，组织正面宣传报道。各地各部门以“3·15”“4·26”等重要节点为

契机，充分利用电台、电视、报刊和网络等各类媒体，通过召开新闻发布会、开展宣传咨询、公开集中销毁侵权假冒物品和曝光典型案例等活动，宣传报道打击侵权假冒工作成果。2015年11月9日至11日，全国打击侵权假冒工作领导小组办公室会同国务院新闻办，组织中央主要外宣媒体和中央重点新闻网站来广东开展集中采访活动，共20家媒体的27名记者对广东省开展中国制造海外形象维护“清风”行动工作进行了深入采访，对广东在打击侵权假冒方面所取得的工作成绩进行了深入的宣传。

（供稿人：毕赓）

广东省政府颁布实施《广东省深入实施知识产权战略推动创新驱动发展行动计划》

广东省政府颁布实施《广东省深入实施知识产权战略推动创新驱动发展行动计划》

2015年9月24日，广东省政府印发《广东省深入实施知识产权战略推动创新驱动发展行动计划》（以下简称《行动计划》）。《行动计划》内容覆盖知识产权创造、运用、保护和服务等方面，明确新时期、新形势下广东创建知识产权强国建设先行省的总体要求和目标任务，对充分发挥知识产权制度的重要作用，全面激发创新动力和创新活力做出了一系列重要部署，为广东知识产权事业发展带来了新机遇。

《行动计划》明确了十项重点行动计划：实行严格的知识产权保护、促进发明创造增量提质、提升企业掌握核心专利能力、实施重点产业专利导航计划、推动专利技术实施转化、构建知识产权运营交易机制、大力发展知识产权金融、加快知识产权快速维权机制建设、积极开展知识产权海外护航和全面增强知识产权服务能力等。立足广东省实际，《行动计划》对未来三年广东知识产权事业发展做出全面部署，确立了创建知识产权强国建设先行省的发展目标。

《行动计划》旨在充分发挥知识产权对创新驱动发展战略的支撑引领作用。《行动计划》提出要强化保护力度，建立长效机制。将加大知识产权侵权赔偿力度，健全知识产权保护执法协作机制，在重点领域和区域开展专项行动，加强网络环境下知识产权保护，并将构建知识产权保护信用系统。《行动计划》明确要激活市场要素，推动运营交易。将建立市场化的知识产权动作模式，培育知识产权运营机构，加快全国知识产权运营公共服务横琴特色试点平台和广州知识产权交易中心建设，支持省内知识产权交易机构探索开展知识产权证券化业务。《行动计划》强调要提升运用效益，拓宽融资渠道。鼓励各地建立知识产权质押融资扶持及风险补偿机制，支持银行、证券、保险、依托及互联网金融等机构参与知识产权金融服务，鼓励保险机构开展知识产权新险种业务。《行动计划》明确要加强海外布局，推进交流合作。将建立知识产权涉外应对和援助机制，支持重点行业、企业建立知识产权海外维权联盟，构建多元知识产权国际合作平台，在中新（广州）知识城创建国家级知识产权保护和运用综合改革试验区，打造知识产权枢纽城市。《行动计划》提出要构建服务平台，加快人才培养。将搭建知识产权大数据应用平台，面向全社会免费提供基础服务，加快省知识产权服务业集聚中心建设，加大知识产权人才培养和引进，支持广州创建知识产权学院。

立足广东省实际，《行动计划》对未来三年广东知识产权事业发展做出了全面部署，确立了创建知识产权强国建设先行省的发展目标。《行动计划》提出，到2017年底，全省有效发明专利量超过16万件，万人发明专利拥有量（专利密度）达到15件，年发明专利授权量达到3万件，年均增长10%，PCT国际专利年均增长10%；全省参加贯标辅导的企业达到2000家；全省年度知识产权质押融资额达100亿元；专利信息推送覆盖产业10个、企业2万家以上，全省专利代理机构达200家、分支机构200家以上。

《行动计划》是广东实施知识产权战略的重大部署和推动创新驱动发展的重要载体，是当前和今后一个时期广东省知识产权事业改革与发展的纲领性文件，对充分发挥知识产权对经济社会发展的助推器作用，加快经济转型升级、支撑新驱动发展具有重要意义。

（供稿人：刘嵘）

领导讲话

国家知识产权局局长申长雨在广东省知识产权工作会议暨专利奖励大会上的讲话

（2015年12月10日）

尊敬的春华书记、小丹省长、云贤副省长、同志们：

今天，很高兴出席广东省知识产权工作会议暨专利奖励大会。在这里，我谨代表国家知识产权局，对大会的召开表示祝贺，向获奖的单位和个人表示敬意，向广东省知识产权战线上的同志们表示问候！同时也借这个机会，向广东省委、省政府，向春华书记、小丹省长和云贤副省长长期以来对知识产权工作的关心、重视和支持表示由衷感谢！

刚才，听了宪民局长的报告和几个部门的发言，确实很受鼓舞。过去一年，在广东省委、省政府的正确领导下，广东知识产权事业又取得了新进步、迈上了新台阶。特别是有几组数据我印象非常深刻，例如，有效发明专利拥有量已连续五年位居全国首位，PCT国际专利申请量连续十四年居全国首位，有效商标注册量连续二十年居全国首位。今年发布的《中国知识产权发展状况报告》显示，广东在知识产权综合发展指数、运用指数、保护指数、环境指数等多个方面也均居全国之首。特别是刚才，我们对获得第十七届中国专利奖的单位和个人进行了表彰，这次广东一共获得了6项金奖，115项优秀奖，同样位居全国首位，确实可喜可贺。在这里，我们也对广东省知识产权工作取得的可喜成绩表示祝贺。

为了鼓励发明创造，国家知识产权局和世界知识产权组织自1989年起，共同开展了中国专利奖评选活动，至今已成功举办了17届。十七年来，在奖励优秀专利成果的同时，我们还表彰了一大批在专利创造、运用、保护、管理等领域作出突出贡献的单位和个人。同时，中国专利奖经过十多年的探索和积淀，其公信力、权威性和影响力也日益增强，获得了各方面的广泛关注和高度重视，成为了我国知识产权事业发展水平的重要标志之一，有力地推动了我国知识产权事业由大到强、由多到优的转变。

当前，我国正处在由知识产权大国向知识产权强国迈进的关键时期。去年，全国共受理发明专利、实用新型和外观设计申请236.1万件，其中发明专利92.8万件，连续四年居世界第一。受理PCT国际专利申请2.6万件，居世界第三位。去年受理商标注册申请228.5万件，同比增长21.5%。此外，作品登记量99.2万件，计算机软件著作权登记量21.9万件，也均创历史新高。同时，我国已基本建立了符合国际通行规则，门类较为齐全的知识产权法律制度，加入了几乎所有重要的知识产权国际公约，成为世界知识产权领域不可或缺的重要力量。但同时我们也深刻地认识到，我国还不是一个知识产权强国，知识产权大而不强、多而不优的矛盾依然突出，知识产权保护效果与社会期待依然存在差距，随着企业“走出去”步伐加快，也面临着越来越多的知识产权风险，所有这些都迫切需要我们加快实现由知识产权大国向知识产权强国的转变。

长期以来，党中央、国务院高度重视知识产权工作，特别是近年来又相继作出了一系列重要决策部署，提出了一系列新的要求。去年底，国务院办公厅印发实施《国家知识产权战略实施行动计划（2014—2020年）》，明确提出了建设知识产权强国的新目标。今年3月，党中央国务院出台《关于深化体制机制改革加快实施创新驱动发展战略的若干意见》，明确提出要让知识产权制度成为激励创新的基本保障，要实行严格的知识产权保护制度。十八届五中全会提出，要深化知识产权领域改革，加强知识产权保护和交易平台建设。昨天，国务院常务会议研究确定了改革完善知识产权制度的措施，强调要用改革的办法加快建设知识产权强国，实行更加严格的知识产权保护，激励大众创业万众创新。这些都为知识产权事业发展指明了努力的方向和工作的重点，需要我们认真加以落实。国家知识产权局希望与广东省加强合作，共同开展深化知识产权领域改革、加强知识产权保护、促进知识产权运用、完善知识产权管理等方面的实践与探索，加快推动知识产权强国建设。

借此机会，我也对广东的知识产权工作提几点建议和希望。

一是希望广东认真总结知识产权方面的好经验好做法，为正在制定的国家知识产权“十三五”规划建言献策、提供参考。目前，我们国家正处在“十二五”迈向“十三五”的重要时空交接点上，国家知识产权局正在认真研究制定知识产权“十三五”规划，谋划未来一个时期知识产权事业发展。“十三五”时期不仅是全面完成国家知识产权战略纲要目标任务最后冲刺的五年，也是全面推进知识产权强国建设的第一个五年，还是深化知识产权领域改革要取得决定性成果的关键五年，所以国家知识产权局对知识产权“十三五”规划高度重视。这些年，广东在知识产权方面积累了很多好经验好做法，希望广东能够把这些好经验好做法总结好、提炼好，并积极融入国家“十三五”规划，促进国家知识产权事业更好更快发展。

二是希望广东着眼知识产权强国建设先行省的定位，积极参与国家知识产权强省建设试点。围绕知识产权强国建设，目前我们已经明确了“点线面结合、局省市联动、国内外统筹”的总体思路，并计划率先建成一批知识产权强省，以点带面推进知识产权强国建设。前不久，国家知识产权局正式印发了《加快推进知识产权强省建设工作方案》，明确到2030年，建成3—4个引领型知识产权强省、5—6个支撑型知识产权强省、4—5个特色型知识产权强省，基本形成布局合理的知识产权强省建设格局，为知识产权强国建设提供有力支撑。广东早在2012年就率先作出了建设知识产权强省的决定，并进行了积极探索，取得了可喜成绩，积累了宝贵经验。希望广东积极做好国家知识产权强省建设试点申报工作，加强与国家局的工作对接，努力在国家知识产权强省建设试点中发挥好引领示范作用。

三是希望广东发挥作为国家深化改革开放先行地的优势，积极开展知识产权综合改革试验。十八届五中全会明确提出，要深化知识产权领域改革。昨天国务院常务会也提出，要用改革的办法加快建设知识产权强国。广东省知识产权综合实力雄厚，拥有众多的国家级知识产权试验、试点、示范项目，还有国家知识产权局、广东省政府和新加坡知识产权局合作共建的中新广州知识城，这也是一个知识产权综合改革的试验区，所以广东开展知识产权综合改革试验不仅基础好、条件好，而且环境好、氛围好，希望广东积极开展知识产权综合改革试验，率先在知识产权重点难点领域和关键环节上实现突破，取得可借鉴、可复制、可推广的好经验，促进国家知识产权事业创新发展。

同志们，当前知识产权强国建设已经全面展开，知识产权深化改革业已启动，让我们进一步携起手来，加强省部会商，努力改革创新，共同推动广东知识产权强省建设，助力广东“三个定位、两个率先”总目标早日实现，为全面建成小康社会、实现第一个百年奋斗目标提供更加有力的支撑！

谢谢！

广东省人民政府省长朱小丹在全省知识产权工作会议暨专利奖表彰大会上的讲话

（2015年12月10日）

尊敬的春华书记、申长雨局长，同志们：

今天，我们在这里隆重召开全省知识产权工作会议暨专利奖表彰大会，主要任务是贯彻落实党的十八届五中全会和省委十一届五次全会精神，回顾总结去年以来我省知识产权工作，表彰获得第十六届中国专利奖及2014年广东专利奖的单位和个人，对下一步建设知识产权强国先行省工作进行部署。省委、省政府对这次会议高度重视，春华书记亲自出席大会并为获奖代表颁奖。申长雨局长在百忙之中专程莅临大会指导并作了重要讲话，充分体现了国家知识产权局对广东工作的厚爱与支持。会上，云贤同志宣读了省政府表彰通报，宪民同志作了工作报告，深圳市政府、省工商局、广州开发区管委会、珠海格力公司的负责同志分别作了发言，讲得都很好。在此，受春华书记委托，我代表广东省委、省政府，向获奖单位和个人表示热烈祝贺！并通过你们向全省知识产权工作者表示衷心感谢！希望全省各行各业都向获奖者学习，努力推出更多高质量的知识产权成果，共同为建设知识产权强国先行省作出新的贡献。

省委、省政府历来高度重视知识产权工作。近年来特别是党的十八大以来，我省把知识产权工作作为实施创新驱动发展战略、推动产业转型升级的重要任务来抓，制定实施一系列新的政策举措，注重强化部省合作，推动我省与国家知识产权局第二轮高层次战略合作不断深化，全面提升知识产权创造、运用、保护、管理和服务能力，知识产权强省建设取得新的进展和成效。全省专利申请量和拥有量稳步增长，截至今年10月，有效发明专利量达13.35万件，PCT国际专利申请量达1.24万件，均保持全国第一；累计专利授权量达140万件，居全国第二；专利密度达每万人口12.55件，为全国平均值的2.07倍。知识产权交易及运营积极推进，成立省级知识产权交易平台“广州知识产权交易中心”，知识产权服务业发展示范省建设全面启动，知识产权保护力度不断加强，企业利用知识产权提升产业核心竞争力的能力不断提高。

尤为可喜的是，近年来在部省知识产权高层次战略合作框架下，国家知识产权局与我省围绕打造知识产权服务经济结构战略性调整的创新地、知识产权服务业发展示范省开展了深入合作，国家专利审查协作广东中心、国家区域专利信息服务广东中心等运转顺畅，服务能力稳步提升。去年以来国家知识产权局先后支持我省成立中国顺德（家电）、中国花都（皮革皮具）2家知识产权快速维权中心，设立重点产业知识产权运营基金、知识产权质押融资风险补偿基金，建设广州知识产权法院、全国知识产权运营公共服务横琴特色分平台等，并在知识产权保护运用、人才建设以及国际交流合作等方面给予大力支持，为我省实施创新驱动发展战略、全面提升区域创新能力提供了重要平台和支持。对此，受春华书记委托，我代表省委、省政府，对申长雨局长和国家知识产权局长期以来对我省知识产权工作的关心支持，表示衷心的感谢！

但我们也要清醒地看到，与建设知识产权强国先行省、推动创新驱动发展的目标要求相比，当前我省知识产权工作中仍存在不少问题和薄弱环节：拥有自主知识产权的核心技术仍然不多，发明专利占比有待提高，知识产权战略推进不平衡，知识产权高端人才仍较缺乏，等等。对此，我们必须高度重视，采取有力措施认真加以解决。

当前，伴随全球新一轮科技革命和产业变革的加快孕育兴起，知识产权日益成为一个国家和地区经济社会发展的战略性资源和国家竞争力的核心要素，成为创新发展的重要支撑和掌握发展主动权的关键所在。党的十八届五中全会明确把创新发展放在五大发展的首位，提出要深入实施创新驱动发展战略，强调要把深化知识产权领域改革、加强知识产权保护，作为实施创新驱动发展战略的重要内容。省委十一届五次全会明确要求，要强化知识产权应用和保护，完善知识产权执法管理体制。加强知识产权工作，对于我省加快发展动力转换、推进经济转型升级、提升国际竞争力、建设创新驱动发展先行省，具有非常重要的意义。全省各地、各有关部门要切实将思想行动统一到中央和省委、省政府的决策部署上来，不断增强责任感和紧迫感，全面提升我省知识产权创造、运用、保护和管理服务水平，充分发挥知识产权作为创新驱动发展助推器的作用，努力打造知识产权强国建设先行省。

做好我省当前和今后一段时期的知识产权工作，要认真贯彻党中央、国务院和省委、省政府的决策部署，深入实施创新驱动发展战略和知识产权战略，以体制机制改革创新为动力，以知识产权保护和运用为重点，坚持问题导向和需求导向相统一、市场主导和政府支持相结合，着力打造一批具有知识产权核心竞争力的骨干企业，形成一批具有国际影响力的知识产权密集型产业，探索出一条知识产权推动创新驱动发展的新路径，把广东建设成为国际化知识产权创造运用中心和知识产权保护高地，成为知识产权强国建设先行省。力争到2017年，建设知识产权密集型产业集聚区10个；支持全省专利技术实施项目1000项、新增经济产值500亿元；建设知识产权运营交易服务机构20家，全省年度知识产权运营交易总额达100亿元。重点要抓好以下六个方面工作：

（一）聚焦发展，更好地运用知识产权服务经济结构战略性调整。要充分挖掘知识产权在产业链前端研发设计和后端品牌商标中的核心价值，推动产业向价值链的两端延伸，增强产业发展和创新活动的前瞻性，提高产业国际竞争力。一是围绕落实《中国制造2025》、发展战略性新兴产业、建设珠江西岸先进装备制造产业带等，深入开展专利导航、分析和预警，缩减企业研发时间和成本，引导重点产业充分运用全球知识产权战略资源。二是积极推动知识产权密集型产业发展，支持高新区和特色产业基地等园区建立专利导航产业发展工作机制，培育形成一批成长性好、附加值高的专利密集型产业。三是大力实施“版权兴业工程”，在版权产业集聚区域设立版权基层工作站，积极发展版权产业链，形成版权产业集群。引导和扶持企业积极运用版权许可和转让等手段，延伸产业链条，实现版权商品化、产业化。

（二）激励创新，促进知识产权创造扩量提质增效。要围绕大众创业、万众创新，充分激发创新主体能量和活力。一是完善创新者激励。认真落实《关于深入实施知识产权战略推动创新驱动发展行动计划》确定的各项资助、奖励政策，特别是要加强对中小微企业、高校和科研院所的支持力度。对小微企业首件发明专利授权给予申请费、代理费全额补贴。对年授权发明专利达到10件以上、增长率超过30%的中小微企业、高校和科研院所给予奖励。对维持五年以上有效发明专利和获得国外授权的发明专利给予资助。各地也要落实专利奖励配套政策，重奖发明创造者。二是全面推行企业知识产权管理规范。强化企业自主创新主体意识，提升企业知识产权管理水平。引导高新技术企业、大型骨干企业建立企业知识产权管理规范工作平台，促使创新成果尽快获得知识产权，使企业掌握一批有竞争力的核心知识产权。三是积极发展专利联盟。围绕知识产权密集型或控制型产业，支持建立一批以优势企业为龙头、技术关联机构为主体、按照产业链布局的专利联盟，构建专利池。支持联盟以知识产权共享和共同维权为纽带，实施有效的利益协调机制和发展策略，并以市场化方式重点推动一批专利联盟集聚创新资源、掌握市场话语权。

（三）注重运用，着力把知识产权更快更好转化为现实生产力。一是加快完善知识产权运营交易机制。充分发挥省知识产权运营基金的引导作用，建立市场化知识产权运作模式，培育一批知识产权运营机构。加快全国知识产权运营公共服务横琴特色试点平台和广州知识产权交易中心建设，支持省内知识产权交易机构探索开展知识产权证券化业务。二是大力发展知识产权金融。充分发挥省级知识产权质押融资扶持及风险补偿金作用，支持各地建立知识产权质押融资扶持及风险补偿机制，简化质押融资流程。支持银行、证券、保险、信托及互联网金融等相关机构参与知识产权金融服务，建设中国（广东）知识产权投融资服务平台，开展知识产权投融资项目对接活动。鼓励保险机构开展知识产权交易保险、执行保险、侵权保险、专利代理人职业保险等新险种业务。三是择优扶持一批专利项目转化运用。创新专利技术应用推广实施方法，在战略性新兴产业、未来产业和重点民生产业等领域，每年择优扶持一批核心技术专利项目和专利技术创业示范项目，促进高质量专利技术转化运用。四是实施专利资源军民融合计划及国防专利申请资助计划。探索建立军民融合专利技术试验区，搭建军民融合知识产权运营平台，争取在我省举办国防专利展示交易会，推动高质量国防专利在广东实施转化，拓展军民可转移技术的应用领域。

（四）严格保护，让知识产权制度成为激励创新的基本保障。一要依法严厉打击侵犯知识产权违法犯罪行为。推进知识产权综合行政执法，加强对重点领域、重点市场、重点产品、重点案件的查处力度。强化电子商务、互联网、展会和专业市场等领域的知识产权保护。强化打击侵权假冒“两法”衔接信息共享和行政处罚案件信息公开，完善知识产权纠纷国际仲裁机制，加大知识产权侵权赔偿力度。构建知识产权保护信用系统，将恶意侵犯知识产权等违法失信行为信息纳入社会信用记录。二要完善知识产权快速维权和知识产权纠纷快速调处机制。依托专业镇和各类重点产业聚集区加快部署知识产权快速维权中心，全面提升中山灯饰、东莞家具、顺德家电、花都皮具等知识产权快速维权中心服务能力，探索在陶瓷、刀具、珠宝等行业建立知识产权快速维权中心，逐步构建跨行业、跨区域的知识产权快速授权、确权和维权服务体系。三要实施“走出去”企业知识产权海外护航计划。设立海外知识产权维权援助中心，建设海外维权援助案例库，为企业应对海外知识产权纠纷提供必要资助，为企业提供知识产权信息、法律等服务。开展重点出口产品专利分析预警工作，及时发布预警信息。支持重点行业、企业建立知识产权海外维权联盟，助推企业加快海外知识产权布局和保护。

（五）优化服务，全面增强知识产权服务能力。围绕知识产权服务业发展示范省建设，促进知识产权服务与科技、产业、金融深度融合，推动综合服务能力不断提升。将知识产权服务业纳入高新技术企业领域。实施“互联网+知识产权”计划，加快建设知识产权大数据应用平台，以专利大数据为基础，整合相关知识产权数据资源，面向全社会免费提供基础数据，吸引各类中介、创业团队等开发者进入，推动知识产权大数据的开发利用。探索构建互联网线上线下连接的知识产权运营交易新机制。强化对企业的专利信息推送，逐步在全省范围内实现线上线下立体覆盖。加快省知识产权服务业集聚中心建设。支持广州创建知识产权学院，加快中小微企业知识产权培训基地、高端知识产权人才培育基地建设，培养和引进更多优秀的知识产权人才。鼓励专利代理机构提升服务能力和水平。

（六）深化改革，进一步释放知识产权制度红利。坚持向改革要动力，努力破除体制机制障碍，最大限度地解放和激发科技第一生产力。强化知识产权政策与科技、产业、金融政策的融合创新，形成激励创新的政策合力。强化科技创新知识产权管理，将知识产权管理纳入省科技重大专项和科技计划全过程管理，促进高校和科研院所知识产权转移转化。不断完善知识产权保护政策体系，积极探索新商业模式、新业态中的知识产权保护立法研究。适时在省级层面整合知识产权各部门相关行政管理职能，探索综合行政管理和综合执法机制，提升知识产权行政管理效率。加强对知识产权状况的监测评估，建立知识产权产业统计制度，在战略性新兴产业、重大科技专项等领域选取一定数量的企业开展知识产权数据统计，发布有关统计报告。

与此同时，我们要始终把握好部省合作的战略机遇，不断扩大合作广度和深度，深入落实省部知识产权高层次战略合作协议，主动做好与国家知识产权局的衔接配合和各项服务工作，确保省部会商建设项目顺利推进、取得实效。我们诚挚希望申长雨局长和国家知识产权局对广东工作多提宝贵意见，一如既往大力支持我省知识产权事业改革发展。

同志们，实施知识产权战略、建设知识产权强国先行省是一项系统工程。希望全省各地、各有关部门进一步加强对知识产权工作的组织领导，落实责任分工，强化督促检查，深入开展知识产权宣传普及，在全社会积极营造尊重劳动创造、尊重知识产权、自觉保护知识产权的良好社会氛围，努力把知识产权各项工作落到实处，共同为建设知识产权强国先行省、推动创新驱动发展、实现“三个定位、两个率先”目标作出新的贡献！

谢谢大家。

广东省人民政府省长朱小丹在国家知识产权局　广东省人民政府第二轮知识产权高层次战略合作2015年度工作会议上的讲话

（2015年4月14日）

尊敬的申长雨局长、贺化副局长，国家知识产权局的各位领导，同志们：

今天，我们非常高兴与国家知识产权局在这里举行第二轮知识产权高层次战略合作2015年度工作会议，总结前一阶段省部合作成效，会商下一阶段工作安排，合力推进广东知识产权事业发展。申长雨、贺化两位领导到会，充分体现了国家知识产权局对广东工作始终如一的关心和支持。在此，受春华书记委托，我谨代表广东省委、省政府向申长雨局长一行表示热烈欢迎和衷心感谢！

刚才，申长雨局长作了重要讲话，对我们第二轮知识产权高层次战略合作提出了新的希望和要求。贺化同志、云贤同志分别就2015年的合作事宜提出了具体的意见和建议，宪民同志总结了第二轮合作2014年工作情况，都讲得非常好。我们要按照这次会议精神，特别是申长雨局长的重要讲话精神，认真抓好贯彻落实，推动部省合作共建不断取得丰硕成果。

过去一年，在上一轮部省知识产权战略合作框架下，部省双方加大政策引导、项目支持和资金投入力度，多形式多领域推进部省合作，为我省推进实施创新驱动发展战略、全面提升区域创新能力提供了重要平台和新的机遇，部省高层次战略合作取得良好成效。主要表现在四个方面：一是知识产权强国建设先行地工作深入开展。2014年，在国家知识产权局的支持帮助下，我省在全国率先提出打造知识产权强国建设先行地目标，围绕这一目标组织开展了政策体系、运行体系、指标体系、保障体系以及纳入GDP核算体系的政策研究。先后出台了《广东省专利奖励办法》《关于促进我省知识产权服务业发展的若干意见》等政策法规，提供了法治和政策保障。二是稳步提升了区域自主创新能力。部省合作为社会创新活动注入了新的活力，全省知识产权创造能力稳步提升。2014年，全省专利申请量、专利授权量保持良好增长态势。其中发明专利授权量增长10.91%，有效发明专利量、PCT国际专利申请量保持全国第一。三是充分发挥了知识产权对产业发展的导向作用。通过部省合作平台，有效发挥了知识产权对产业发展的引领作用和转型升级的导向作用。珠江三角洲地区重点产业转型升级专利导航工程扎实推进，广东省级知识产权交易中心正式成立并投入运营，知识产权金融创新试点取得实效。知识产权服务业发展示范省建设深入推进，培育形成国家、省、市三级知识产权服务业集聚发展区。截至2014年底，我省建立各类产业专利联盟25个，建成战略性新兴产业专利信息资源开发利用计划专利数据库30个，全省知识产权优势企业568家、示范企业达到140家。四是有效促进了构建公平有序市场竞争环境。在部省合作有力推动下，我省知识产权保护力度不断加大，知识产权快速维权模式不断完善，华南地区专利侵权判定中心正式提供服务，企业知识产权海外护航优势区建设路径进一步明确。

实践证明，部省合作的六年，是广东知识产权工作功能不断强化、作用有效发挥的六年，也是广东知识产权工作先行先试、不断深化改革和加快创新的六年。继续坚持和加强部省合作，是我省知识产权工作紧密服务地方经济社会发展有效途径，必将为我省创新驱动、转型发展提供更加坚实有力支撑。

2015年是全面深化改革的关键之年和全面推进依法治国的开局之年，也是我省大力实施创新驱动发展战略、稳增长调结构的重要一年。今年全国“两会”后，党中央、国务院随即印发《关于深化体制机制改革加快实施创新驱动发展战略的若干意见》。这是党中央、国务院主动适应经济发展新常态，总揽改革发展全局做出的一项重大部署。《意见》把实施知识产权战略，加强知识产权保护作为文件的第一项措施，充分说明知识产权工作已经前所未有地摆在了党中央、国务院的重要议事日程上，充分说明知识产权制度是激励创新的基本保障，是创新发展和转型升级的重要支撑，也是全面推进依法治国的重要内容。因此，我们要全面把握新形势新要求，紧紧抓住改革机遇，重点围绕我省在创新驱动发展方面的薄弱环节，主动加强与国家知识产权局的沟通交流，提出更紧密、高层次、全方位的合作目标，不断扩大合作广度和深度，以扎实的成效把双方的交流合作不断推向深入，为全国知识产权工作改革创新探索新路。关于今年部省知识产权合作的具体工作，刚才双方进行了全面的对接，在此特别感谢国家局对广东工作非常具体的支持，我省将全力以赴抓好落实。这里，我想就下一步合作再提几点建议。

（一）立足当前，更加突出服务科技创新和产业转型升级。知识产权工作一头连着创新，一头连着市场，是推动实施创新驱动发展战略的核心内容。希望省部知识产权合作突出我省产业转型升级的迫切需求，更紧密结合我省新一轮重大科技专项，指导我省战略性新兴产业知识产权专项工程的实施，帮助我省突破一批核心技术，形成一批具有先进水平的自主知识产权。进一步开拓专利导航产业发展新模式，突出围绕优势产业做好专利布局规划，推动重点产业和产业集群专利池、专利联盟建设，提升产业创新驱动发展能力。推动实施“版权兴业工程”，引导和扶持更多企业积极发展版权产业链，加快形成版权产业集群。

（二）着眼长远，更加注重创新体制机制。坚持向改革要动力，大力营造有利于建设知识产权强省的政策环境、法制环境、市场环境、社会环境、文化环境，充分发挥知识产权制度作用，最大限度激发全省知识产权创造运用活力。通过深化部省合作，在突出企业创新主体地位上下功夫，大力推行“企业知识产权管理规范”，加快培植一批国家级知识产权试点、示范骨干企业。进一步加强中小微企业知识产权公共服务平台建设，拓展企业知识产权特派员试点，创新中小微企业知识产权托管服务等。特别是通过部省合作先行先试，推动各个层面完善知识产权资助和奖励办法，推动知识产权政策与科技、产业、外贸、金融等政策的衔接与融合，激励创造更多高质量的知识产权成果。

（三）突出重点，推动双方合作尽快取得可复制的经验。下一步部省知识产权合作，希望在以下这些重点方向上得到国家知识产权局的更加有力支持。一是研究做好珠三角自主创新示范区的知识产权顶层设计，在珠三角自主创新示范区中积极实践知识产权政策、模式创新。探索在中新知识城和自贸区建立专利、版权、商标“三合一”的知识产权综合行政管理和执法机制。二是强化侵权假冒领域“两法衔接”信息共享和行政处罚案件信息公开，加强对展会、电商等重点市场、重点产品、重点案件的查处力度，强化跨区域知识产权执法机制建设。三是关注和参与知识产权国际规则变革，探索建立涉外案件处理的有效途径和涉外问题的快速应对机制，不断提升海外知识产权纠纷诉讼应急能力。开展重点出口产品专利分析预警工作，为企业“走出去”保驾护航。四是突出人才作为第一资源的作用，把集聚知识产权高端人才作为建设知识产权强国先行地的重要举措，创新人才培养和引进机制，大力引进海内外知识产权高端人才，造就一支高层次创新人才队伍、高素质管理人才队伍和高技能服务人才队伍。

（四）狠抓落实，努力确保完成第二轮知识产权高层次战略合作议定事项。刚才，中国国家知识产权局、新加坡知识产权局与广东省政府三方进行了友好会谈，并签署了中国国家知识产权局与新加坡知识产权局会谈纪要，就共同推动在中新广州知识城积极探索开展知识产权运用和保护综合改革试点工作达成了很多共识。云贤同志就2015年知识产权高层次战略合作工作安排提出了12条很具体的建议。我省将全力推动议定各项合作事项的落实，促进知识产权政策创新、运用创新、保护创新、管理创新，推动双方合作走向深入，配合国家知识产权局共同把各项合作议定事项抓实并尽快抓出成效。

（五）加强领导，为深化部省合作提供坚强保障。部省知识产权合作六年来，进行了许多有益的探索，创造了许多成功的经验。但知识产权战略实施是一项系统工程，专业性、综合性都很强。建设知识产权强国先行地也是一项长期的全新的工作，没有现成的经验可供借鉴。我省将在国家知识产权局指导下，努力把握知识产权事业科学发展的规律，加强知识产权战略规划和政策制定研究，统筹处理好数量与质量、创造与保护的关系，统筹知识产权创造、运用、保护和管理各项工作。全省各地、各部门将主动做好与国家知识产权局的衔接配合和各项服务工作。我们也诚挚希望申长雨局长等各位领导和国家知识产权局对广东工作多提宝贵意见，一如既往大力支持我省知识产权事业改革发展。

我们坚信，经过双方不懈努力，广东知识产权创造、运用、保护和管理水平必将实现新的飞跃，全省知识产权事业发展必将焕发更加蓬勃的生机。让我们继续携手前进，为我省实施创新驱动发展核心战略、为全国知识产权工作改革发展作出新的更大贡献！

谢谢大家。

广东省人民政府副省长陈云贤在第八届两岸专利论坛上的致辞

（2015年9月22日）

尊敬的何志敏副局长、王美花局长，尊敬的杨梧会长、蔡练生秘书长，各位来宾，女士们、先生们，朋友们：

大家上午好！非常高兴参加第八届两岸专利论坛，这是海峡两岸加强知识产权交流合作、助推科技创新和经济社会发展的重要举措。首先，我谨代表广东省政府对论坛的举办表示热烈祝贺！对国家知识产权局、中华全国专利代理人协会等单位一直以来对广东知识产权事业的支持帮助表示衷心感谢！对出席本次论坛的两岸嘉宾朋友表示诚挚欢迎！

知识产权特别是专利制度是激励创新的重要保障，也是使科技成果向现实生产力转化的桥梁和纽带。广东高度重视专利的创造、运用和保护，近年来通过完善专利政策法规体系，加快专利转化和运用，加强专利保护，健全专利服务体系，深化专利国际交流与合作，推动专利事业实现了跨越式发展，为我省产业转型升级和实现创新驱动发展战略提供了有力支撑。截至2014年12月底，广东累计提交专利申请数量达到187.87万件，累计专利授权120.68万件。有效发明专利拥有量11.19万件，连续五年居全国第一，每万人口发明专利拥有量为10.56件。2014年，广东PCT国际专利申请受理量1.33万件，占全国受理总量的55.53%，连续十三年保持全国首位。2015年1—7月，我省专利申请量和授权量分别为178124件和131770件，同比增长33%和27%，PCT国际专利申请受理量8430件，占全国受理总量的57.18%。与此同时，粤台知识产权合作取得重要进展，双方在知识产权教育与培训、专利预警分析服务、知识产权公共服务平台建设等领域开展了深入交流与合作，培养了一批精通知识产权法律法规、熟悉知识产权国际规则，具有较高理论水平和实务技能的高层次专门人才。

当前，广东正处在大力实施创新驱动发展战略、深化改革开放、加快转型升级的关键阶段。知识产权特别是专利制度对于加快实施创新驱动发展战略，进一步激励自主创新、保护科技成果、营造公平竞争环境、支撑产业转型发展至关重要。台湾地区专利事业发达，从专利立法、行政和司法，到专利布局、研发与产业运用，都有着丰富的实践经验，值得广东乃至全国各兄弟省市学习借鉴。希望两岸专利业界专家和企业家朋友充分用好两岸专利论坛这一好平台，畅所欲言，深入交流，为推动两岸专利事业发展，深化两岸产业合作，促进两岸关系发展作出新贡献！也希望两岸专家和企业家朋友多来广东考察指导，加强与广东的互利合作，为我省实施创新驱动发展战略、建设知识产权强省和知识产权强国先行地提供新动力！

最后，祝愿2015年两岸专利论坛圆满成功！祝各位领导、各位朋友身体健康，工作顺利，万事如意！

谢谢大家。

广东省人民政府副省长陈云贤在最高法院知识产权司法保护与市场价值研究（广东）基地揭牌仪式上的讲话

（2015年9月18日）

尊敬的陶凯元副院长，同志们：

大家上午好！

非常高兴应邀出席最高人民法院知识产权司法保护与市场价值研究（广东）基地揭牌仪式，这是全国知识产权司法保护事业的一件盛事，也是助推我省实施创新驱动发展战略、建设知识产权强国先行省的一件大事。首先，受朱小丹省长委托，我谨代表广东省政府对基地的顺利揭牌表示热烈祝贺！对陶凯元副院长和最高法院一直以来对广东各项事业的关心支持表示衷心感谢！对出席揭牌仪式的各位嘉宾朋友表示诚挚欢迎！

知识产权是一个国家或地区经济社会发展的战略性资源和国家竞争力的核心要素。近年来，我省坚持“激励创造、有效运用、依法保护、科学管理”方针，积极实施知识产权强省战略，知识产权创造活力不断增强，知识产权综合发展指数、保护指数、环境指数以及发明专利授权量、有效发明专利量、PCT国际专利申请量、商标有效注册量、中国驰名商标拥有量等一系列重要指标均连续多年位居全国首位。以华为、中兴为代表的高科技企业，已经发展成为全球依靠知识产权抢占国际市场的典范。同时，我省高度重视知识产权保护工作，以维护知识产权市场化为重点，深入开展打击侵权假冒工作，有效维护了社会环境和营商环境。特别是广东法院，以不到全国十分之一的知识产权审判力量，每年办结约全国四分之一的知识产权案件，出色发挥了司法保护知识产权的职能作用。

当前，我省正处在大力实施创新驱动发展战略、加快经济社会转型升级的关键阶段。加强知识产权保护对于进一步激励自主创新、保护科技成果、营造公平竞争环境、支撑产业转型发展至关重要。此次最高法院在广东设立知识产权司法保护与市场价值研究基地，充分体现了最高法院对广东司法工作和知识产权工作的关心支持，必将进一步密切法院、知识产权行政执法部门以及学术界的合作，为知识产权保护领域的理论研究、实务交流搭建很好平台。省政府将全力支持研究基地建设和各项工作开展，切实提供必要的支持帮助。借此机会，我就进一步加强知识产权保护及理论研究，提几点建议：一是健全侵权查处机制，加强知识产权综合行政执法，完善审判工作机制，推进知识产权案件“三审合一”；二是强化行政执法与刑事司法衔接，加强行政部门与司法机关的协作配合，建立健全联席会议、案件咨询制度，及时会商复杂、疑难案件，实现执法、司法信息互通；三是建立知识产权信息开放共享和知识产权市场价值专项课题合作研究机制，争取推出一系列卓有成效的实践与研究成果，推动更多的优质知识产权资源转化为现实生产力；四是在自贸区等创新试验区域探索建立知识产权纠纷仲裁、调解、快速处理等多元解决机制，促进研究基地建设与知识产权产业配套服务业发展相衔接。

最后，祝研究基地越办越好！祝各位嘉宾朋友身体健康、工作顺利、万事如意！

谢谢大家。

广东省知识产权局局长马宪民在广东省知识产权局工作总结会议上的讲话

“十二五”时期，在省委、省政府的正确领导下，我省知识产权工作坚持围绕中心、服务大局，按照国家和省关于创新驱动发展的战略部署和产业转型升级的总体安排，扎实推进知识产权战略实施和知识产权强省建设，取得显著实效。

一、“十二五”时期全省知识产权发展情况

“十二五”时期，我省深入实施知识产权战略，全面推进知识产权创造、运用、保护、管理和服务，知识产权事业取得巨大进展，主要知识产权指标提前完成。2011年，省政府批准实施《广东省知识产权事业发展“十二五”规划》。2015年底，有效发明专利量达到138878件，居全国第一。万人发明专利拥有量从2010年的4.02件增长到2015年底的12.95件。PCT国际专利申请量从2010年的6678件增长到2015年的15190件，自2002年以来连续保持全国首位，占全国PCT国际专利受理总量的53.49%。《珠三角规划纲要》“四年大发展”监控指标和预定目标超额完成。

主要抓了以下工作：

（一）深入实施知识产权战略，推进知识产权强省建设。

省委、省政府于2012年作出《关于加快建设知识产权强省的决定》，推动我省逐步从知识产权大省向知识产权强省迈进。

一是不断完善政策法规。相继制定了《关于促进我省知识产权服务业发展的若干意见》《关于加强中国（广东）自由贸易试验区知识产权工作的指导意见》《广东省知识产权举报投诉工作规定（试行）》《广东省知识产权优势示范企业认定办法》《关于加强我省知识产权维权援助工作的指导意见》和《关于全面推进〈企业知识产权管理规范〉国家标准的实施意见》等文件，组织开展《关于推进互联网知识产权工作的指导意见》调研起草工作。2015年，省政府颁布《广东省深入实施知识产权战略推动创新驱动发展行动计划》，明确将广东建设成为国际化知识产权创造运用中心和保护高地，成为知识产权强国建设先行省的目标。

二是深入实施知识产权战略。全国地方战略实施情况中期评估成绩居全国第二位。21个市都出台了本地区的知识产权战略纲要或实施方案。广州、深圳、东莞、佛山、中山等5市成为国家知识产权示范城市，茂名等14个市（含县级市）入选国家知识产权试点城市，广州花都等5个县（区）获评国家知识产权强县工程示范县（区），广州海珠等15个县（区）入选国家知识产权强县工程试点县（区）。自2012年以来，我省知识产权综合发展指数连续三年位居全国首位。以专利战略推进计划为抓手，省市联动，推动全省工作向纵深发展。

三是持续推进高层次局省会商。京外专利审查协作广东中心、国家级区域专利信息服务（广州）中心、知识产权快速维权中心、中小微企业知识产权培训基地、专利信息传播利用基地等一批国家级重点项目落户广东，创造了众多全国第一，在知识产权强国先行地建设、产业专利导航、快速维权、知识产权服务等方面取得突破，在专利信息数据资源完善、“互联网+知识产权”全覆盖系统建设等方面开展深入合作，对广东转型升级和创新发展起到了重要支撑作用。

四是大力推进基层知识产权工作。制定《关于加强县级知识产权工作的意见》，安排专项资金支持基层知识产权工作。广州、深圳、东莞、佛山、中山、惠州先后被评为国家知识产权示范城市，珠海、湛江、潮州、江门、肇庆、茂名、顺德等12个市（含地级市和县级市）入选国家知识产权试点城市，珠三角地区实现国家试点城市全覆盖；广州花都、越秀、萝岗和佛山禅城、南海等5区获评国家知识产权局强县工程示范县（区），广州海珠、番禺、汕头澄海、惠州惠东、韶关武江、梅州梅县等15个县（区）入选国家知识产权强县工程试点县（区）。加强与各市的合作，与东莞、揭阳市人民政府建立局市会商合作关系。全省所有地级以上市设立知识产权局，市级拥有知识产权专职人员181人，8个地级以上市专项经费超千万元，10个地市超百万元，县（区）知识产权局挂牌113个，挂牌率达到93.4%。

（二）支持和鼓励发明创造，推进知识产权提质增量。

为满足创新驱动发展要求，我省采取多种措施，推动创新成果及时产权化。发明、实用新型、外观设计三类专利申请量占比从2010年的26.7：31.2：42.1调整到2015年的29.2：38.1：32.7。

一是完善发明专利激励机制。制定《关于提升我省专利申请数质量的若干意见》《发明专利申请资助办法》，建立有效专利申请监测系统。省财政每年安排资金4500万元带动各市财政资金约2亿元支持各类创新主体申请专利。全省发明专利申请量、授权量分别从2010年的40866件、13691件增长到2015年的103941件、33477件，年均增长达到18.90%和16.39%，2015年增速达38.32%和50.28%，超过“十二五”增长预期目标，实现翻番。

二是强化发明专利奖励机制。省政府颁布实施《广东省专利奖励办法》，将广东专利奖由部门奖升格为政府奖，增设发明人奖，2014—2015年两届广东专利奖共评出金奖30项，优秀奖110项，发明人奖19项。2011年以来我省在五届中国专利奖中获得金奖25项、优秀奖350项，其中，2015年第17届中国专利奖评选中，我省获金奖6个，优秀奖119个，获奖数目再创新高，金奖数目居全国第一。省政府五年共投入近2亿元重奖中国专利奖和广东专利奖获奖单位和个人。

三是探索专利申请快速通道。积极探索争取国家知识产权局支持，在部分专业镇开通专利申请、授权快速通道，大大缩短外观设计专利授权周期，从原来的3—4个月缩短至7—10天。

四是不断增强企业知识产权能力。推广《企业知识产权管理规范》，获得贯标认证企业31家，扶持贯标辅导机构20家，培训贯标人员近2000人。广州、中山、惠州、东莞、佛山等地相继出台了贯标扶持政策。强化知识产权优势示范企业培育，国家级知识产权优势和示范企业达97家，省级优势和示范企业分别达568家及160家。企业知识产权主体地位凸显，五年间，全省8.57万家企业提交专利申请67.95万件，3.46万家企业提交发明专利申请24.3万件，其中，2015年全省2.6万家企业提交专利申请20.6万件，1.15万家企业提交发明专利申请7.3万件。2015年国内企业发明专利授权量前十名的企业中有5家来自广东，2015年国内企业PCT申请受理量排名前十名的企业中有6家来自广东，华为技术有限公司和中兴通讯股份有限公司2015年PCT申请量位列全国前两名。

五是提升专利代理服务能力和审查服务。组织开展“百所千企知识产权服务对接工程”和“知识产权特派员”系列活动，每年组织代理机构与专业镇、企业对接活动多场。大力扶持专利代理机构发展，专利代理机构、分支机构以及专利代理人数分别从2010年的91家、94家、676人增长到2015年的158家、164家、1455人。组织举办了多场企业发明专利巡回审查活动，对格力、广汽、TCL、德赛、华南理工大学等创新主体开展发明专利巡回审查，加强发明人、代理人与审查员的沟通，加快专利授权进程。

（三）不断探索专利运营机制，促进知识产权转化运用。

坚持以知识产权有效运用为目的，推动专利技术转移转化。

一是设立专利技术实施专项计划。至2015年底，累计投入专项资金3905万元，安排项目518项，支持高价值专利技术转化实施。

二是推动知识产权运营机构和运营体系建设。省政府批准由广东省产权交易集团牵头组建“广州知识产权交易中心”，积极争取国家知识产权局支持在珠海设立全国知识产权运营公共服务横琴特色试点平台。培育知识产权运营机构13家，在运营能力、模式及市场开拓方面予以指导。中彩联、汇桔网、高航网、7号网、第五大发明等一批民营投资、市场化、网络化知识产权运营机构迅速涌现，知识产权转让、许可、交易市场日益活跃。2015年，专利实施许可合同备案1308项，涉及专利4104件，合同金额12.3亿元人民币和90万美元。广州、深圳、东莞、佛山等4个国家专利技术展示交易中心累计完成专利展示41250件、专利交易2085件，金额超过6亿元。

三是促进知识产权质押融资。联合印发《关于加快推进我省知识产权质押融资工作的若干意见》，编制发布知识产权质押评估技术规范地方标准，持续举办中国（广东）知识产权投融资项目对接会，有效解决中小微企业知识产权转化融资难问题。五年来先后举办先进制造、生物医药、新材料等产业领域的46个知识产权项目与创投企业对接，涉及金额7.88亿元。佛山市南海区创建国家知识产权投融资综合试验区、顺德区开展国家知识产权投融资服务试点，均取得显著成效，顺利通过验收。支持广州、中山、珠海等5市设立知识产权质押融资风险补偿基金试点。2012年至2015年，全省专利质押融资额达到175亿元，其中2015年达59亿元。

四是积极开展专利保险试点工作。支持广州、深圳、东莞和佛山市禅城区积极开展“全国专利保险试点”。截至2015年底，四地367家企业已累计完成专利投保超过2000件，保费166.7万元，最高可获赔5913.8万元。支持中山市结合该市古镇灯饰行业实际，积极开展全国首例单一行业专利保险探索，2015年该市投保企业20家，涉及219件专利，保费21.55万元，最高可获赔1061.1万元。

五是积极开展知识产权资产评估工作。扶持20家资产评估机构在专利入池、购买、许可、转让、出资及知识产权质押融资等方面，完成40份设计知识产权的资产评估报告。

（四）深度开发专利资源，强化对产业的服务和支撑。

围绕我省重点产业发展，我省积极开展产业专利分析、预警及导航。

一是开展产业专利分析预警。开展“战略性新兴产业专利信息资源开发利用专项计划”，对LED、新能源汽车、高端新型电子信息、生物医药、云计算、生物医学工程、新一代显示、集成电路等29个我省重点发展的战略性新兴产业及重点技术领域进行全球专利分析，共立项41项，形成高质量的分析预警报告30份，建立战略性新兴产业专利数据库8个，组织战略性新兴产业专利分析预警发布会23场，4200多家企业参加。培养了一批产业专利分析机构及人才，为我省知识产权服务业规模化、高端化发展提供了人才储备。

二是加强专利导航建设。实施“珠三角重点产业转型升级专利导航工程”，在工业机器人等技术领域开展深度研究，探索根据专利链布局创新链新模式。开展“珠江西岸先进装备制造产业带专利导航工程”，安排项目5项，围绕江门市轨道交通装备、肇庆市智能化成形和加工成套设备、顺德区智能装备制造、佛山市汽车制造、中山市电动汽车等5市（区）的5个先进装备制造产业，组织开展专利导航。推动广州开发区、佛山市整合区域内优质知识产权服务及运营资源，围绕智能装备、卫星通信、机械装备制造等重点产业，开展产业专利导航。实施重点出口产品专利预警分析计划，围绕3D电视、半导体照明灯具、蒸汽挂烫机、不锈钢压力锅等我省重点出口产品，组织项目50项。广州市进出口专利预警平台上线运行。深圳出台全国首个企业境外参展知识产权预警指引地方标准（SZDB/Z 72-2013）。

三是设立重点产业知识产权运营基金。以中央财政专项扶持资金为引导，筹备成立总规模达30亿元、首期规模达5亿元的广东省粤科国联知识产权投资运营基金。目前，该基金已形成2.2亿元的规模，并和中国智能制造领域第一个专利池——工业机器人专利联盟签署战略合作协议，双方将共同推动工业机器人产业领域高价值专利的培育和运营。

四是加快产业知识产权联盟建设。建立各类产业知识产权产业联盟25个，其中16个在省级知识产权职能部门备案，5个在国家知识产权局备案。

（五）不断加大知识产权保护，维护创新市场竞争秩序。

知识产权保护是发挥知识产权激励作用、实现知识产权市场价值的核心，我省高度重视。

一是严厉打击知识产权侵权行为。建立打击侵权假冒工作长效机制，建立健全行政执法与刑事司法衔接机制，组织互联网领域、农村和城乡结合部、车用燃油、皮具行业、对非出口商品、“护航”“清风”等多项专项整治行动，大力查处侵权假冒案件，知识产权保护得到强化。“十二五”时期，全省各级知识产权局共受理各类专利侵权案件8701件，结案8114件。2012年以来，广东打击侵权假冒工作在全国绩效评价中均居全国前列。

二是加强会展知识产权保护。省政府颁布实施《广东省展会专利保护办法》，在广交会、加博会、美博会等重要展会设立知识产权投诉站，维护展会知识产权市场秩序，规范展会专利投诉案件处理规程，提高展会办案质量，已经形成广东展会品牌。

三是推进电子商务知识产权保护。与唯品会签署《保护知识产权战略合作协议》，支持唯品会、梦芭莎等电商单位建设知识产权保护平台，探索建立“政府有效指导监管+知名网络平台自律保护”相结合的互联网知识产权保护措施和长效机制。着手起草电子商务领域知识产权保护和发展政策性文件。

四是建立知识产权快速维权机制。全省建设灯饰、家具、家电和皮具4个重点产业快速维权中心，占全国的一半。设立华南地区专利侵权判定中心，顺德探索建立家具专利快速调处中心。全省建设国家级维权援助中心6家；广东省知识产权维权援助中心在省内设立分中心7家、工作站31家。

（六）多措并举加强能力建设，夯实知识产权发展基础。

一是大力推进专利信息服务能力建设。完善区域专利信息服务（广州）中心服务功能，构建专利大数据服务平台，拥有全球专利信息达到1亿条。打造“互联网+专利信息”服务新模式，推出手机APP专利检索平台。开展专利信息推送服务，建立省、市、镇、企业4级服务推送工作渠道，向45个专业镇、省内外1300家中小微企业免费推送专利信息，涵盖18个技术领域。开展专利信息服务地市行活动。

二是加强知识产权人才培养。实施“百千万知识产权人才工程”，加强国家和省级知识产权人才培训基地建设。建设由知识产权学院、知识产权培训基地、知识产权培训计划、海外知识产权机构巡回演讲计划等组成的多元知识产权培养体系。推进知识产权专业技术资格评定试点工作。据不完全统计，全省各类知识产权人才达3.6万人。入选国家知识产权专家库专家14人、国家知识产权领军人才23人、“百千万知识产权人才工程”高层次人才31人、全国专利信息领军人才8人、全国专利信息师资人才18人。

三是构建多元知识产权国际交流合作平台。与20多个国家和地区的官方机构、社会团体建立合作关系。加强国际知识产权交流研讨，举办各类国际性知识产权论坛和研讨会28场。举办中、新知识产权局与广东省政府三方会谈，中、日、韩三国知识产权局长会议等重大外事活动。翻译出版《知识产权密集型产业对欧盟经济及就业的贡献》。

四是积极推进地区知识产权合作。粤港、粤澳知识产权合作分别被纳入粤港、粤澳合作框架协议，开展粤港知识产权合作项目79项，粤澳知识产权合作项目11项。粤台合作不断加强，组织赴台湾访问交流9批102人次，成功举办“第八届两岸专利论坛”。积极推进泛珠三角知识产权合作，启动新一轮知识产权援疆工作，推进粤青、粤蒙等知识产权工作合作。

五是建立高层次知识产权智库。组建广东省知识产权专家咨询委员会，组织开展知识产权软科学研究，加强对知识产权重大理论和政策问题的研究，为省的重大知识产权决策提供依据。

六是加强宣传提高公众知识产权意识。连续举办知识产权宣传周等重大宣传活动，知识产权宣传周品牌效应显著。召开年度知识产权发展状况等多场新闻发布会，及时向社会宣传知识产权工作取得的新成就，取得良好社会效果。积极拓宽宣传渠道，开通“广东知识产权”“粤知界”微信账号，利用新媒体加强知识产权宣传。开展中小学知识产权教育试点、示范工作。

主要体会和做法：

（一）坚持“围绕中心、服务大局”。

牢固树立中心意识、大局意识和服务意识，助推全省经济社会发展。“十二五”期间，省先后推出珠三角规划纲要、粤东西北振兴发展专项计划等，我们及时找到知识产权能够发挥作用的切入点和突破口，积极争取把发明专利、专利密度等重要指标纳入考核范畴。围绕省战略性新兴产业发展，很快提出开展“战略性新兴产业专利信息资源开发利用专项计划”获得批准，连续3期投入，对广东战略性新兴产业及相关技术领域作了系统专利分析，发布了一批预警报告。围绕创新驱动发展战略，及时制定《深入实施知识产权战略推动创新驱动发展行动计划》。

（二）坚持高层次推进强省建设。

省委、省政府作出《关于加快建设知识产权强省的决定》，在全国第一个确立知识产权强省目标，并相继制定多项配套政策。广东把强省建设目标纳入部省会商框架内，2014年提出创建“知识产权强国建设先行省”。每年召开部省知识产权高层次战略合作会议、全省知识产权工作会议暨专利奖表彰大会，强省建设工作得到扎实推进。

（三）坚持以改革创新推动发展。

积极推进中新广州知识城知识产权运用保护综合改革试点。顺德区建设“广东知识产权创新运用试验区”。坚持市场导向构建知识产权运营机制，开展知识产权运营分平台建设试点、知识产权运营机构试点、重点产业知识产权运营基金试点、知识产权质押融资扶持与风险补偿基金试点，促进知识产权资本和金融资本的融合。

（四）坚持以优质服务支撑发展。

全面启动知识产权服务业发展示范省建设，建设知识产权服务业聚集中心。在深圳福田、佛山国家知识产权服务业聚集发展试验区基础上，认定广州越秀、东莞松山湖、广州开发区为省级试验区。广州奥凯信息咨询有限公司、深圳中科院知识产权投资有限公司、珠海智专专利商标代理有限公司等12家服务机构成功入围“全国知识产权分析评议服务示范创建机构”。

（五）坚持以反腐倡廉保障发展。

按照中央和省委统一部署，深入开展党的群众路线教育实践活动、“三严三实”专题教育活动等。聚焦“四风”，查摆问题，认真整改。加强反腐倡廉，认真贯彻落实党风廉政建设责任制。做好廉政风险防控，加强对重点环节权力运行的监督。

在取得成绩的同时，我们也清醒地认识到，我省知识产权工作仍然存在不少困难和问题。一是企业知识产权运用能力薄弱。企业运用知识产权提高产业核心竞争力的综合能力不强；适应全球化发展的国际化高层次知识产权人才队伍缺乏。二是专利质量有待提高、转化率偏低。发明专利申请量仅占30%左右，与发达国家和地区相比存在较大差距；高校和科研院所存在不少沉睡知识产权资产。三是知识产权政策、管理体制机制需进一步完善。知识产权政策与产业、科技、金融政策的融合度不够；管理体制不完善、执法能力弱、保护力度亟待加强。四是知识产权结构和区域发展不平衡。以广州、深圳为中心的珠三角地区城市群知识产权综合发展水平远高于粤东西北地区，并且差距呈增大趋势。五是知识产权意识依然薄弱，企业、大学、科研机构、社会公众以及政府部门，知识产权意识仍有待提高，等等。这些问题和短板制约着知识产权在创新驱动发展中发挥更大作用，如何加大改革创新力度、优化治理以满足各类创新主体需求等问题，应当高度重视并加以改进。

二、“十三五”知识产权工作主要思路

“十三五”时期是我省率先全面建成小康社会的决胜阶段。做好知识产权工作对于广东实施创新发展核心战略、促进产业转型升级具有重要意义。从国际形势看，世界经济仍处于国际金融危机后的深度调整期，国际规则话语权的争夺日趋激烈，知识产权制度国际化进程加速，知识产权保护状况成为影响国际产业转移的重要因素，基于知识产权的贸易摩擦、经济纠纷将进一步加剧。作为外贸大省，我省企业在“走出去”过程中必然要面临巨大的知识产权国际压力。广东要增强产业国际竞争力，在更高层次、更大范围、更宽领域参与国际经济合作，必然需要将知识产权作为战略支撑。从国内形势看，我国经济发展呈现出新常态，中央充分认识到知识产权对创新驱动发展的重大作用，党的十八大以来，将知识产权工作提升到新的战略高度，出台了一系列涵盖知识产权在内的政策措施，国务院印发《关于新形势下加快知识产权强国建设的若干意见》，对深入实施知识产权战略、建设知识产权强国作了总体部署。在产业价值链的高端，普遍都是密集的知识产权布局，没有知识产权的推动，任何企业都难以在价值链高端有立锥之地。知识产权制度必将在创新驱动发展和产业转型升级中发挥不可或缺的支撑作用。

“十三五”时期全省知识产权工作的指导思路是，全面贯彻中央十八大以来的各项重要精神，按照国家和省的总体部署，深入贯彻落实《国务院关于新形势下加快知识产权强国建设的若干意见》，深入实施知识产权战略，深化知识产权重点领域改革，有效促进知识产权创造和运用，实行更严格的知识产权保护，优化知识产权公共服务，促进新技术、新产业、新业态蓬勃发展，着力提高企业核心竞争力，着力增强产业国际竞争力，为实施创新驱动发展战略提供有力支撑，为大众创业、万众创新提供激励和保障，为知识产权强国建设和加快实现“三个定位、两个率先”目标做出贡献。

“十三五”时期全省知识产权发展目标是，把广东建设成为国际化知识产权创造运用中心和知识产权保护高地，建成引领型知识产权强省。一是在发明创造上实现突破，发明专利申请和授权年均增长15%左右，万人发明专利拥有量达到20件。二是在运用转化上实现突破，运营交易机制得到完善，预警、导航在产业和创新中广泛运用，专利实施率达到85%。三是在保护力度上实现突破，知识产权保护、维权援助体系得到健全，侵权行为大幅度降低。四是管理体制上实现突破，管理体制机制更加有效，管理体系更加合理，贯标企业达到2000家。五是服务体系上实现突破，人才队伍大大加强，数据信息共享便捷。六是在公众意识上实现突破，宣传教育体系得到加强，尊重知识产权的社会风气基本形成。

为实现全省“十三五”知识产权发展目标，全省的知识产权工作要按照国家关于坚持战略引领、改革创新、市场主导、统筹兼顾的要求。

要坚持改革方向，在体制机制体系创新上谋突破。强化知识产权政策与科技、产业、金融政策的融合创新，形成激励创新的政策合

力。在全面创新改革试验区、珠三角自主创新示范区、广东自贸区等特定区域创新改革知识产权体制机制，加快推进有利于激发知识产权市场活力的改革，增创知识产权发展新优势。发挥市场配置创新资源的决定性作用，强化企业知识产权主体地位和主导作用，促进知识产权要素合理流动和高效配置。

要坚持需求导向，在支撑产业、服务创新上促发展。坚持战略引领。按照创新驱动发展核心战略、“一带一路”战略、珠三角规划纲要、《中国制造2025》及广东发展智能制造、发展战略性新兴产业、省重大科技专项、建设珠西先进装备制造产业带等重点任务，着力推动提升知识产权创造、运用、保护、管理和服务能力，提升知识产权质量，实现我省知识产权从大向强、从多向优的转变。

要坚持问题导向，在强化保护、共享覆盖上补短板。加强知识产权法规建设和市场监管，着力构建公平公正、开放透明的知识产权法治环境和市场环境。统筹省内外知识产权资源，形成若干知识产权领先发展区域，培育我省知识产权优势。围绕解决知识产权区域发展差距较大的突出问题，更好地统筹实施知识产权主体区规划，进一步优化空间布局，协同推进珠三角地区优化发展与粤东西北地区振兴发展。

三、2016年主要工作

（一）高层次谋划建设知识产权强国先行省。

认真贯彻落实《国务院关于新形势下加快知识产权强国建设的若干意见》和《广东省深入实施知识产权战略推动创新驱动发展行动计划》，制订全省知识产权服务创新驱动发展的指导意见，主动抓好相关任务的落实。做好《广东省专利条例》修订的前期调研、论证、修改征求意见等各项工作。编制实施广东知识产权事业发展“十三五”规划，科学设置工作目标、工作任务和工作措施。

做好专利事业发展战略推进工作。创新工作思路和推进方式，做好2016年专利战略推进计划的落实和2017年战略推进顶层设计研究，引导项目、经费、人力等资源配置。科学设定2016年《珠江三角洲规划纲要》中专利指标目标值，做好全年监控工作。继续制定并实施全省知识产权战略纲要年度实施计划，建立战略实施目标制度和报告制度。

做好第三轮省部会商筹备工作，加强省部会商合作需求及合作内容的研究，科学安排第三轮省部会商工作主要内容。加快引领型知识产权强国建设申报工作。

（二）积极推进知识产权体制机制改革。

完善知识产权管理体制。完善省知识产权办公会议制度，强化省政府知识产权办公会议制度在重点事项总体设计、统筹协调、整体推进和督促落实方面的作用，研究和解决制约知识产权事业发展的重大问题。探索省知识产权综合管理体制改革路径。

推进中新知识城知识产权综合改革试验。改革知识产权行政执法保护体制，构建多层次知识产权维权援助体系。培育多元化知识产权金融服务市场。培育全链条知识产权服务业，建立知识产权导向的创新驱动评价体系。完善知识产权行政管理体制，设立一站式知识产权综合政务服务中心。创新知识产权国际交流合作机制，建设知识城知识产权国际智库。

推进广东自贸试验区知识产权工作。完善知识产权政策法规，探索建立统一的知识产权行政管理和执法体系，建立自贸区重点产业知识产权纠纷快速处理机制，推动全国知识产权运营公共服务横琴特色试点平台建设，探索在广州南沙片区、深圳前海蛇口片区建立知识产权运营中心，改革自贸区专利申请服务。

探索珠三角国家自主创新示范区建立统一的知识产权行政管理体制和执法机制。

（三）实行严格的知识产权保护。

完善知识产权行政和司法保护机制，构建司法、行政、调解、举报投诉多元纠纷解决机制。建立知识产权保护责任制。建立重点产业重点市场知识产权保护机制和重点企业知识产权保护直通车制度。加快建设完善知识产权维权援助机制，支持高新区、专业镇等重点产业集群建立知识产权快速维权机制，培育建设省知识产权快速维权中心，争取批准建设陶瓷、刀具、珠宝等行业国家知识产权快速维权中心，形成专利快速授权、快速维权和快速确权通道。推进与国家知识产权局专利复审委员会在专利快速受理、快速确权和远程审理等方面的合作，建设复审委巡回审理庭多媒体全网管理系统。

加大知识产权犯罪打击力度。完善和规范执法程序，加强全省专利行政执法监督和指导，着力推动县区执法能力建设。开展执法专项行动，加强对重点市场、重点产品、重点案件的查处力度，集中力量查处重大和典型专利违法案件。推动建立健全跨区域执法协作工作机制，强化侵权假冒领域"两法衔接"，行政处罚案件信息公开工作。创新专利执法体制机制，加强重点领域专利行政执法，增强专利行政执法效能。加强专利行政执法监督检查，积极开展案卷评查工作。

加强新业态新领域创新成果的知识产权保护。加强互联网、电子商务、大数据等领域知识产权保护规则研究。推动出台《关于推进电子商务领域专利保护工作的指导意见》。加强电子商务领域专利案件办理和指导工作。研究电子商务领域保护深层次问题，探索建立电子商务领域专利保护长效机制。制定众创、众包、众扶、众筹的知识产权保护政策。推进行业协会知识产权自律保护工作。强化展会和专业市场知识产权保护。构建知识产权保护信用系统。

（四）高效促进知识产权创造和运用。

改革知识产权处置和收益机制，建立健全职务发明知识产权成果权益归属、奖励报酬机制和知识产权转化服务机制。

实施知识产权倍增计划。完善省市财政专利申请资助和奖励政策，逐步消除各市规模以上工业企业"零专利"现象。

提升企业掌握核心专利能力。加快推广《企业知识产权管理规范》，引导高新技术企业、大型骨干企业及国有企业等提升知识产权管理水平，使创新成果尽快获得知识产权保护，掌握一批重点产业核心专利技术。建立企业知识产权管理标准认证后补助制度。鼓励企业通过自主创新、开放合作、知识产权引进等多种途径，形成具有市场竞争力的知识产权资产组合。

推进新兴产业和重点产业建立专利联盟。支持在能源环保、生物技术等新兴产业和无人机、超材料等未来产业从事研究开发的企业，通过自主研发和知识产权运营掌握核心技术专利，形成具有控制力的专利联盟和国际标准，提升市场竞争力。

推进知识产权分析评议和专利预警导航。建立重大经济和科技活动知识产权评议制度，为投资决策提供依据。针对省战略性新兴产业、省重大科技专项、珠西先进装备制造产业及未来产业和《中国制造2025》，深入开展专利导航、分析和预警，引导重点产业优化全球知识产权战略布局，提高产业国际竞争力。围绕支持高新区、特色产业基地等园区建设专利导航产业发展试验区。

推动专利技术实施转化。围绕"大众创业、万众创新"，推动知识产权创业、孵化和产业化基地发展，在战略性新兴产业、未来产业和重点民生产业等领域，择优扶持一批核心技术专利项目和专利技术创业示范项目，促进专利技术转化，在专利产业化推进相关项目立项评审中，将专利的标准转化率作为重要评审指标。

加强专利技术军民融合。与国家国防知识产权部门的合作，探索建立知识产权军民融合高层次战略合作关系，筛选军民双方可转化专利，拓展军民可转移技术的应用领域。实施专利资源军民融合计划及国防专利申请资助计划，探索建立军民融合专利技术试验区，搭建军民融合知识产权运营平台，争取在广东举办国防专利展示交易会，推动高质量的国防专利在广东的实施转化。

加强知识产权交易平台建设，支持广州知识产权交易中心、横琴国际知识产权交易中心建设，支持社会化知识产权交易运营服务平台发展壮大，扶持广东知识产权（中山灯饰照明）运营中心、广东知识产权创新运用（顺德）试验区建设。

推动知识产权金融，稳步推进国家级知识产权质押、投融资及专利保险试点，健全政策支持体系，完善综合服务平台，促进知识产权金融工作规模化、常态化开展。建立知识产权质押融资扶持和风险补偿机制。探索设立专利保险公司，开展知识产权交易保险、执行保险、侵权保险、专利代理人职业保险等新险种业务。

（五）大幅度增强知识产权服务能力。

加快创建知识产权服务业发展示范省建设步伐。制定2016年知识产权服务业发展年度计划。探索建立规范化市场活动程序和交易行为的政策体系，推动知识产权服务业重大项目建设。加快省知识产权服务业集聚中心建设，培育5—10个国家和省知识产权服务业集聚发展试验区。继续加强对专利代理行业的执业监管，引导代理机构不断发展壮大。

加强知识产权信息开放利用。实施“互联网知识产权”服务计划，以专利大数据为基础，搭建知识产权大数据应用平台，加快建设一批重点产业专利数据库，面向全社会免费提供基础数据，实现知识产权信息利用便利化。面向中小微企业开展专利信息推送服务。推进专利大数据服务基地平台建设，探索开展广东省知识产权综合服务平台建设，开展广东省高新区、孵化器知识产权综合服务体系建设。

有序开展专利代办创新试点工作。开展外观设计专利申请前置服务试点工作，为我省重点产业专利快速授权提供咨询、检索等服务。推进专利申请优先审查、批量专利申请（专利权）法律状态出证、专利申请文件查阅等业务试点。

推动知识产权交流合作。探索建立与“一带一路”沿线国家和地区的知识产权合作机制，谋求构建深层次、广领域的合作模式。持续打造国际知识产权制度巡回演讲、国际知识产权高层次论坛等对外合作品牌。主动探索“走出去”思路，争取组织专业人士赴重点贸易伙伴国家或地区宣讲广东知识产权工作成效。加强粤港澳台知识产权合作交流，召开粤港保护知识产权合作专责小组第十五次会议和粤澳知识产权工作小组第三次会议，在知识产权保护、运用、保护、培训等领域继续推进合作项目，深化合作内容。

开展知识产权海外护航。建立知识产权涉外应对和援助机制。加快构建海外知识产权维权机制，为企业应对海外知识产权纠纷提供必要资助，为企业提供知识产权相关的信息、法律等服务。支持重点行业、企业建立知识产权海外维权联盟，指导企业加快海外知识产权布局和保护。继续开展广东省重点出口产品专利预警分析计划，支持知识产权密集型商品出口。

（六）加强知识产权人才队伍建设和知识产权文化建设。

完善知识产权人才培养体系。加快知识产权人才培养和引进，支持广州创建知识产权学院。加快中小微企业知识产权培训基地、高端知识产权人才培育基地建设。建立知识产权专业技术资格评价体系，在全省范围内开展知识产权专业职称评定工作。构建科学化的知识产权人才培训体系，完善知识产权培训课程设置、师资建设、评价方式和管理体制。鼓励社会化的知识产权培训机构发展壮大，开发市场化的知识产权培训产品，丰富知识产权培训内容。加强知识产权师资队伍建设。继续开展境外合作教学。

加强知识产权文化建设。加大对党中央、国务院和省委、省政府有关知识产权重大决策部署的宣传力度，提高知识产权宣传周等活动的品牌效应。建设“知识产权宣传（广东）中心”。实施社会大众知识产权意识普及、高校知识产权教育推广和知识产权宣传能力提升三项工程。建设知识产权宣传数据库。建立热点事件迅速响应机制和省、市、县区配合联动机制。

（七）加强党风廉政建设。

加强理论学习。落实局党组中心组理论学习制度，组织全局党员干部理论学习，举办“知识产权学习讲坛”，组织开展体验式学习教育活动。巩固“三严三实”专题教育成果，认真贯彻落实八项规定，坚持不懈反对“四风”。严格组织制度。贯彻落实《中国共产党党和国家机关基层组织工作条例》，落实党内各项制度，健全党的组织生活，加强党员的教育、管理、服务。加强权力运行监管。落实“两个责任”，开展反腐倡廉教育，进一步加强对重点环节的监督。

ZONG SHU

综 述

● 协调机制

● 职能部门工作概述

协调机制

广东省人民政府知识产权办公会议

【概况】 广东省人民政府知识产权办公会议是根据国发〔1994〕38号文和粤府〔1994〕103号文件成立的议事机构，主要目的是加强知识产权的宏观管理和统筹协调。2000年，办公会议办公室职能划入广东省知识产权局。经2002年、2006年、2010年和2014年三次调整，办公会议由省发展改革委等25家组成单位以及省委宣传部等6家特邀单位组成。

【主要职责】

1. 组织、协调、指导全省知识产权工作。

2. 贯彻执行国家有关知识产权的法律法规和方针政策；研究制定广东省有关知识产权的法规、重大政策、措施和规划，并组织实施。

3. 协调解决广东省经济、科技和文化发展中有关知识产权的重大问题，并提出政策性意见和建议。

4. 组织知识产权联合执法行动。

5. 组织大型知识产权宣传活动，普及和提高社会各界知识产权意识。

6. 建立各组成单位信息交换、情况通报制度，定期发布广东省知识产权保护状况。

【组织架构】

2015年，广东省人民政府知识产权办公会议领导和组成人员名单如下：

主持人：

广东省人民政府副省长　陈云贤

副主持人：

广东省人民政府副秘书长　李捍东

广东省知识产权局局长　马宪民

办公室主任：

广东省知识产权局局长　马宪民

办公室副主任：

广东省知识产权局副局长　唐毅

组成单位及人员：

广东省发展和改革委员会副主任（正厅级）　张军

广东省经济贸易委员会副主任　戚真理

广东省教育厅巡视员　罗远芳

广东省科学技术厅副巡视员　周木堂

广东省公安厅副厅长　何广平

广东省司法厅副厅长　余继军

广东省财政厅副巡视员　曾毓昌

广东省人力资源和社会保障厅副厅长　李长峰

广东省环境保护厅巡视员　王子葵

广东省农业厅副厅长　程萍

广东省林业厅总工程师　谭天泳

广东省商务厅副厅长　蔡勇

广东省文化厅党组成员、执法局局长　胡振国

广东省卫生和计划生育委员会副主任　江效东

广东省人民政府外事办公室副主任　罗军

广东省人民政府国有资产监督管理委员会副主任　周兴挺

广东省新闻出版广电局副局长　陈春怀

广东省统计局副局长　刘智华

广东省工商行政管理局副局长　钱永成

广东省质量技术监督局副局长　邱庄胜

广东省知识产权局副局长　唐毅

广东省人民政府法制办公室副主任　王光辉

广东省人民政府港澳事务办公室副主任

叶维园

广东省食品药品监管局副局长（正厅级） 黄绍龙

广东省人民政府发展研究中心副主任 李惠武

特邀单位及人员：

中共广东省委政策研究室副主任 吴茂芹

中共广东省委宣传部副部长（正厅级） 朱仲南

广东省人大教科文卫委员会副主任委员（正厅级） 许家瑞

海关总署广东分署副主任（正厅级） 赵民

广东省高级人民法院副院长 徐春建

广东省检察院副厅级检委会委员 李庆协

（供稿人：王一）

广东省打击侵犯知识产权和制售假冒伪劣商品工作领导小组

【概况】 2011年底，国务院下发《关于进一步做好打击侵犯知识产权和制售假冒伪劣商品工作的意见》（国发〔2011〕37号），明确打击侵权假冒是一项长期、复杂、艰巨的任务，要求各省建立健全长效机制，并设立常态化的全国打击侵权假冒工作领导小组，办公室设在商务部，领导小组现任组长为中共中央政治局委员、国务院副总理汪洋。为落实国务院的部署和要求，2012年4月23日，广东省人民政府于成立省打击侵权假冒工作领导小组（粤办函〔2012〕251号），领导小组办公室设在省知识产权局，承担领导小组日常工作。其中打击侵权工作由省知识产权局牵头负责，打击假冒伪劣工作由省质监局（打假办）牵头负责，相关部门配合。2015年，领导小组成员单位共28家，由省政府副省长陈云贤担任领导小组组长。

【领导小组办公室主要职责】

1．承担领导小组日常工作，向领导小组提出工作建议，协调、督促各地区、各成员单位落实领导小组决定事项。

2．建立打击侵权假冒案件统计制度，推动跨地区跨部门执法协作，督办侵权假冒重大案件。

3．落实打击侵权假冒领域行政执法与刑事司法衔接工作。

4．推动落实打击侵权假冒相关法律法规修订工作，推动健全检验、鉴定和其他相关标准。

5．组织推动打击侵权假冒重点领域社会信用体系建设。

6．组织协调知识产权涉外应对事项，推动建立和完善多双边执法合作机制。

7．组织打击侵权假冒宣传教育工作，承办并管理打击侵权假冒工作网站。

8．承办全国打击侵权假冒工作领导小组及办公室、省政府和省打击侵权假冒工作领导小组交办的其他事项。

【组织架构】

组长：

陈云贤 副省长

副组长：

李捍东 省政府副秘书长

马宪民 省知识产权局局长

郭元强 省商务厅厅长

任小铁 省质监局局长

成员：

蔡伏青 省委宣传部副部长

邓远强 省综治办专职副主任

张 军 省发展改革委副主任（正厅）

邹 生 省经济和信息化委副主任

黄守应 省公安厅经侦局局长

余继军 省司法厅党委委员、副厅长

钟 炜 省财政厅总会计师

李长峰 省人力资源社会保障厅副厅长

王子葵 省环境保护厅党组副书记、巡视员

程 萍 省农业厅副厅长

谭天泳　省林业厅总工程师
罗练锦　省商务厅巡视员
李剑先　省文化厅党组成员、省文化市场综合执法局局长
温伟群　省卫生计生委副巡视员
周兴挺　省国资委副主任
余振荣　省地税局稽查局局长
陈春怀　省新闻出版广电局（省版权局）党组成员、版权局专职副局长
钱永成　省工商局副局长
邱庄胜　省质监局副局长
苏盛锋　省食品药品监管局党组成员、稽查局局长
唐　毅　省知识产权局副局长
袁有楼　省知识产权局副局长
陈春生　省法制办副主任
赵　军　省法院审委会副厅级专职委员
李庆协　省检察院检委会副厅级专职委员
何　力　海关总署广东分署副主任
朱江涛　省国税局副局长
陈小帆　广东出入境检验检疫局副局长
丘　斌　人民银行广州分行副行长

联络员：

曾宝瑜　省委宣传部新闻处副调研员
陈　策　省综治办综治督导处副处长
曹　鹏　省发展改革委高技术产业处副处长
李小华　省经济和信息化委技术创新与质量处调研员
吴义来　省公安厅经侦局副局长
黄梅新　省司法厅政策法规处副处长
李广文　省财政厅行政政法处副处长
彭　力　省人力资源和社会保障厅专业技术人员管理处副处长
王大力　省环境保护厅环境监测与科技标准处副处长
李耀武　省农业厅科技教育处调研员
林　新　省林业厅科技与交流合作处调研员
彭跃进　省商务厅市场秩序与调节处副处长
杨智勇　省文化市场综合执法局副调研员
冯惠强　省卫生计生委监督处处长
林济远　省国资委规划发展处副处长
张　弟　省地税局稽查局专职纪检监察员
张同英　省新闻出版广电局（省版权局）版权管理处处长
林　方　省工商局商标管理处处长
廖家恒　省质监局稽查局副局长
刘国光　省食品药品监管局稽查局副局长
蓝伟宁　省知识产权局协调与合作处处长
陈曦帆　省知识产权局执法与监督处副处长
吴　笛　省法制办行政执法监督处调研员
谭双堰　省法院刑二庭庭办负责人
罗永忠　省检察院侦查监督一处副处级检察员
梁润超　海关总署广东分署法规处处长
李小杰　省国税局稽查局副调研员
刘科峰　广东出入境检验检疫局稽查处副处长
张学贵　人民银行广州分行货币金银处副处长

（供稿人：毕赓）

粤港保护知识产权合作专责小组

【概况】　2003年12月，“粤港保护知识产权合作专责小组”（以下简称“专责小组”）成立，并在香港召开第一次会议。粤港双方确定定期会议制度，每年定期在两地轮流召开专责小组会，确定项目合作模式。“粤港保护知识产权合作专责小组”成立以来，粤港知识产权合作全面展开并不断向前推进。截至2015年，粤港双方召开专责小组联席会议14次，在粤港合作联席会议上签署《粤港知识产权合作协议》5份，两地公安、工商、版权、海关等部门在知识产权跨境保护、交流研讨、宣传教育等领域开展178项合作。

【粤港知识产权合作】　在专责小组各成员单位的大力推动下，粤港知识产权合作机制不断

完善，内容不断丰富。截至2015年底，两地知识产权相关部门在粤港保护知识产权合作框架下，开展逾百个合作项目。

粤港知识产权跨境保护执法协作机制。粤港两地知识产权执法部门加强沟通，深化合作，进一步完善粤港知识产权跨境执法和案件协作处理机制，加大打击粤港两地海运及邮递快件渠道走私侵权物品违法活动力度。海关总署广东分署与香港海关设置粤港海关保护知识产权专职联络员，持续加大情报通报和信息交流力度。广东省公安厅、省版权局、省工商局等知识产权相关部门相继与香港海关建立知识产权联络员制度，开展知识产权保护合作。

粤港企业知识产权保护与创新促进机制。粤港知识产权部门从2003年开始联合举办“粤港知识产权与中小企业发展研讨会”。截至2015年，研讨会已在广东省内各个不同的地市（深圳、东莞、韶关、顺德、惠州、江门、湛江、珠海、汕头、中山、广州、肇庆、佛山、清远）巡回举办16次，累计数千家企业参加。

“正版正货承诺”活动。省知识产权局联合省版权局、省工商局在全省全面推广“正版正货承诺”活动，全省21个地级以上市大力推进。

“粤港澳知识产权资料库”与“粤港知识产权合作专栏”。粤港双方及时更新和丰富粤港澳三地知识产权执法的信息，增加了有关三地知识产权执法信息的英文版和知识产权贸易信息的超链接，对帮助粤港澳三地企业和公众适时掌握三地知识产权制度的最新发展发挥了积极的作用。

协助香港居民参加全国专利代理人资格考试。根据CEPA有关内地服务行业对香港开放的承诺，自2004年开始，全国专利代理人资格考试对港澳考生开放。根据国家知识产权局的安排，港澳考生统一在广东考点参加考试。广东省知识产权局与香港知识产权署合作，并协同澳门特区政府经济局知识产权厅，共同做好有关考试的咨询、报名、培训和考点准备等相关工作。

粤港知识产权交流研讨活动。举办商标、版权为主题的知识产权交流活动，持续加大广东省知识产权政策宣传力度，大力引导有产品内销的在粤港资企业申请认定广东省著名商标。

（供稿人：尹怡然）

粤澳知识产权工作小组

【概况】 2012年5月10日，《粤澳知识产权合作备忘录》签署仪式暨知识产权工作小组第一次会议在广州成功举行。会议正式成立了粤澳知识产权工作小组，并审议通过了《粤澳知识产权工作小组工作机制》，确立了粤澳知识产权工作小组会议制度，建立了粤澳知识产权合作项目制度。截至2015年，粤澳知识产权工作小组已召开两次工作会议，完成合作项目11项。

【工作机制】 组建知识产权工作小组，建立粤澳知识产权协调机制。工作小组由粤澳双方知识产权保护及管理部门组成，粤方成员包括广东省知识产权局（牵头单位）、广东省工商行政管理局、广东省版权局、广东省公安厅、海关总署广东分署；澳方成员包括澳门经济局（牵头单位）、澳门知识产权厅、澳门海关。

建立粤澳知识产权工作小组会议制度，原则上每两年召开一次会议，总结上一阶段粤澳知识产权合作计划落实情况，商讨确定下一阶段合作计划。工作会议由广东省知识产权局和澳门经济局轮流主持召开。

建立粤澳知识产权项目合作制度，由各成员单位提出粤澳知识产权合作项目及牵头落实单位建议，经粤澳知识产权工作小组会议审议确定后，由牵头单位负责组织落实。

建立粤澳知识产权合作情况通报制度，各单位联络员负责粤澳知识产权合作的联络沟通工作，及时将该单位合作项目进展情况通报各方牵头单位。

（供稿人：尹怡然）

泛珠三角区域知识产权合作机制

【概况】 为贯彻落实中共中央政治局委员、广东省委书记张德江关于开展泛珠三角区域知识产权合作的指示精神，2004年，首届泛珠三角区域知识产权合作联席会议在广州召开，全国第一个集专利、商标、版权为一体的区域合作体系形成。2005年，香港、澳门特别行政区加入泛珠合作，“9+2”区域知识产权合作平台正式建立。为确保泛珠三角区域知识产权合作工作的有效开展，各方建立以下三个合作机制。

【泛珠三角区域知识产权合作联席会议制度】 联席会议成员由泛珠三角各省（区）及特区知识产权协调机构及相关专利、商标、版权管理部门负责人组成。会议每年举行一次，研究决定合作重大事宜，必要时可召开临时联席会议。会议由协议各方轮流召集和主持，每届会议确定下届会议的主办方、时间和地点。会议设会议主席，由当年主持会议的省（区）及特区知识产权负责人担任。

【泛珠三角区域知识产权合作联络员制度】 泛珠三角各省（区）及特区确定一名联络员，负责联络、沟通和协调工作。联络员应加强跟踪、落实和情况反馈，畅通各成员单位信息交流渠道，提高工作效率，确保各项合作项目的顺利完成。

【泛珠三角区域知识产权合作专题工作小组制度】 根据每年联席会议确定的合作项目，成立相应的专题工作小组，开展具体的专项合作工作。专题工作小组成员由协议各方指定，对具体合作项目及相关事宜制订合作计划，提出工作措施，落实合作事项，并定期向联席会议报告合作项目落实情况。

（供稿人：尹怡然）

职能部门工作概述

广东省人民政府知识产权办公会议成员单位

广东省发展和改革委员会

【概况】 2015年，广东省发展改革委积极推进实施创新驱动发展战略、培育战略性新兴产业、促进高技术产业发展壮大、推进信息化建设等相关工作，推动广东省成功纳入全国全面创新改革试验区域，战略性新兴产业和高技术产业呈现加快集聚发展态势。

【全面创新改革试验】 2015年广东省被纳入全国八个全面创新改革试验区域之一。根据《中共中央办公厅 国务院办公厅关于在部分区域系统推进全面创新改革试验的总体方案》要求以及省委、省政府工作部署，广东省发展和改革委员会牵头起草了《广东系统推进全面创新改革试验加快建设创新驱动发展先行省方案》，围绕发挥市场和政府作用、促进科技与经济深度融合、激发创新者活力和动力、深化开放创新等方面，在科技管理、高等教育、人才激励、知识产权、成果转化、开放创新等领域提出了一批国家授权和省级权限改革事项，为加快实施创新驱动发展战略注入新动力。

【创新驱动发展政策环境】

推动出台《中共广东省委、广东省人民政府关于加快建设创新驱动发展先行省的意见》。贯彻落实《中共中央国务院关于深化体制机制改革加快实施创新驱动发展战略的若干意见》，牵头起草《中共广东省委、广东省人民政府关于加快建设创新驱动发展先行省的意见》。该意见于2015年10月由省委、省政府印发实施，是广东省实施创新驱动发展战略的行动纲领。

完善大众创业万众创新政策环境。贯彻落实《国务院关于大力推进大众创业万众创新若干政策措施的意见》和《国务院关于加快构建大众创业万众创新支撑平台的指导意见》，牵头起草《广东省人民政府关于大力推进大众创业万众创新的实施意见》，进一步优化创业创新环境，激发全社会创业创新活力。

推动建立创新驱动发展工作考核指标体系的意见和具体考核办法。牵头起草《关于建立创新驱动发展工作考核指标体系的意见》《广东省创新驱动发展工作考核实施办法》，将加快建设创新驱动发展先行省的目标和要求转化为可量化考核的指标，引导各地创新发展。

【创新成果产业化】

继续推进战略性新兴产业区域集聚发展试点工作。2015年顺利通过国家发展改革委、财政部组织开展的2014年战略性新兴产业区域集聚发展试点核查；研究提出了新一代显示技术、新型动力电池、蛋白类生物药及植（介）入器械等三个领域2015年实施方案，并确定2015年集聚试点支持项目。

积极争取中央投资支持。根据国家发展改革委关于组织实施新兴产业重大工程包的工作部署，积极争取7个项目获得国家批复支持，9个高技术领域项目获得国家专项建设基金支持。

启动实施重大科技成果产业化专项。牵头研究制订《广东省重大科技成果转化产业化扶持专项实施方案》，推进2015年度重大成果产业化项目遴选工作。

【区域创新体系建设】

加快国家重大科技基础设施建设。积极推进惠州加速器驱动嬗变系统研究装置和强流离子加速器装置两个国家重大科技基础设施项目前期工作，协调推进散裂中子源项目建设，积极推进江门中微子试验项目按计划顺利实施。

推进国家级创新平台建设。2015年广东省新增1家国家工程实验室、10家国家地方联合工程研究中心（工程实验室）、8家国家企业技术中心。截至2015年底，广东省共有15家国家工程实验室（工程研究中心）、78家国家认定企业技术中心、51家国家地方联合创新平台。

完善省级工程实验室体系。2015年新批复组建13家省级工程实验室，截至目前共组建59家。

【试点示范工程建设】

编制信息基础设施建设方案。会同省通信管理局等单位编制《关于加快推进广东省信息基础设施重点领域投资建设的实施方案（2015—2017年）》，研究提出了2015—2017年加快广东省光纤宽带、4G基站、三网融合及物联网示范应用、云计算和大数据中心等信息基础设施项目的建设目标、主要任务及政策建议等。

提出信息基础设施项目投资计划。将全省通信基础设施项目纳入2015年度省重点项目建设计划中，加快推进下一代互联网示范城市、物联网重大应用示范工程、超算中心等国家新一代信息技术设施项目建设。

开展信息惠民国家试点城市评价。按照国家关于组织实施信息惠民国家试点城市评价工作的部署，组织广州、深圳、佛山、东莞等信息惠民国家试点城市开展自评价和预评价工作。

【推进创业投资发展】 确定支持首批省新兴产业创投计划参股创业投资基金，根据首批省新兴产业创投计划参股创业投资基金尽职调查报告，确定支持温氏生物、广州达安京汉医疗健康、广东清大、中山市东方盛世可再生能源等4支创业投资基金。推动与广东明阳风电产业集团有限公司参股设立广东可再生能源产业基金。

（供稿人：曲延军）

广东省经济和信息化委员会

【战略性新兴产业重点项目】 贯彻落实广东省战略性新兴产业发展规划，推动重大项目建设。重点推动河源中兴通讯生产基地、华星光电二期8.5 代TFT—LCD（含氧化物半导体及AMOLED）生产线项目、惠州信利二期（6 代AMOLED 项目）、新岸线芯片产业化等项目的建设发展。加快战略性新兴产业区域集聚试点项目实施，重点围绕新一代显示产业，集聚创新要素、突出企业主体、激励多元投入，实现新一代显示领域的重点突破，培育珠三角高端新型电子信息产业集群，促进产业整体升级。发展高端新兴业态，实施中小企业云计算应用工程，深化粤港云计算合作。推动设立省集成电路产业发展专项资金，促进集成电路产业提升。组织战略性新兴产业政银企合作，运用政策优惠带动银行资金投向战略性新兴产业领域，拉动广东省战略性新兴产业投资规模上水平。

【科技成果产业化应用】 举办2015年广东省科技成果与产业对接活动。结合当前战略性新兴产业科技成果产业化现实需求，省经济和信息化委会同省科技厅、教育厅联合主办以促进战略性新兴产业科技成果转化为主题的2015年广东省科技成果与产业对接活动。省委、省政府高度重视对接活动，中共中央政治局委员、广东省委书记胡春华视察对接活动现场，副省长招玉芳出席对接活动启动仪式并见证13个合作项目签约。对接活动吸引了15家高等院校、科研院所和335家企业共600多人参会。活动期间还举办了战略性新兴产业重点科技成果展示、成果发布、人才对接等活动。一批科技成果实现了与企业对接，取得良好成效。

【企业技术中心建设】 为加快建立以企业为主体、市场为导向、产学研相结合的技术创新体系，发挥省级企业技术中心在产业优化升级的重要作用，2015 年省经济和信息化委会同财政厅、国税局、地税局、海关总署广东分署认定了第十五批117 家省级企业技术中心，省级企业技术中心总数达到831 家，组织实施省级企业技术中心创新能力建设项目，提升企业知识产权创造能力。

【品牌建设】

制订出台《关于推进我省工业品牌建设的指导意见》。《关于推进我省工业品牌建设的指导意见》提出了今后培育工业品牌的指导思想、总体目标、基本原则、主要任务措施等，集中力量培育一批拥有自主知识产权、自主核心技术的工业企业品牌，形成一批国际和国家级名牌优势企业和企业集团。

开展产业集群区域品牌建设试点示范工作。为促进工业转型升级，依托产业集群，加快培育一批知名度高、美誉度好、竞争力强、附加值高的区域品牌，省经济和信息化委组织实施产业集群区域品牌建设试点培育工作。

（供稿人：黄海丹）

广东省教育厅

【专利申请和授权】 据广东省73所高校统计，2015年广东省高校申请专利量为9271件，其中发明专利申请量为5550件，实用新型申请量为2444件。广东省高校发明专利授权量为5154件，其中发明专利授权量为2130件，实用新型授权量为1981件。广东省高校专利申请量和发明专利授权量最多的高校是华南理工大学，专利申请量为2824为件，专利授权量为1181件。

【知识产权获奖】 中山大学等4所省内高校在2015年广东省专利奖方面获得5项奖励。其中华南师范大学的邢达教授及华南理工大学的万金泉教授获得广东专利奖（发明人奖）；华南理工大学“一种高磺化度高分子量木质素基高效减水剂及其制备方法”获得广东专利奖（金奖）；中山大学的“一种化痰止咳的药物及其生产方法”和广东工业大学的“一种单轨绝对光栅尺及其图像编码方法”获得广东专利奖（优秀奖）。

【专利技术的实施】 与工厂企业生产部门签订技术转让合同405项，合同金额10189.5万元，2015年实际收入10824.2万元。其中，有107个为专利出售合同，合同金额7594.6万元，2015年实际收入1703.6万元；有55个为其他知识产权出售合同，合同金额4626.3万元，2015年实际收入4252.7万元。

【全国中小学知识产权教育试点推进】 广东省教育厅和省知识产权局联合面向全省开展了全国中小学知识产权教育试点学校的组织申报工作，推荐佛山市南海区九江镇初级中学、顺德区李伟强职业技术学校、汕头市龙湖区龙湖小学、惠州市南坛小学、东莞市莞城实验小学、阳春市第一中学等6所学校申报全国试点。最终佛山市南海区九江镇初级中学、顺德区李伟强职业技术学校2所学校被确定为首批“全国中小学知识产权教育试点学校”。

（供稿人：吴宝榆）

广东省科学技术厅

【概况】 2015年，广东省科学技术厅推动召开全省科技创新大会、全省科技企业孵化器建设工作现场会、珠三角国家自主创新示范区建设启动会等高规格会议，助力省委、省政府深入谋划部署全省科技创新工作，出台系列重大创新政策举措，优化全省创新创业环境，创新驱动发展取得重要进展。2015年，全省科技综合实力和自主创新能力稳步提升，区域创新能力综合排名连续八年位居全国第二，稳居第一梯队；科技投入不断增加，全省研发（R&D）投入占GDP比重提高到2.5%；关键核心技术不断获得突破，技术自给率达71%。

【自主创新政策环境】 2015年2月，广东省人民政府出台《广东省人民政府关于加快科技创新的若干政策意见》及系列配套实施细则（“科技创新12条”），着力构建覆盖创新链的“1+N”政策体系，包括激励企业创新投入的“普惠性”政策，完善孵化育成体系和新型研发机构扶持举措的“引导性”政策，以及激励科技人员创新积极性的“松绑性”政策等；广东省科学技术厅等有关部门先后出台8个配套文件，包括：《广东省激励企业研究开发财政补助试行方案》《广东省省级企业研究开发财政补助资金管理办法》《广东省科学技术厅 广东省财政厅关于科技创新券后补助试行方案》《广东省科学技术厅 广东省财政厅关于科技企业孵化器后补助试行办法》《广东省科学技术厅 广东省财政厅关于科技企业孵化器创业投资及信贷风险补偿资金试行细则》《关于创新产品与服务远期约定政府购买试行办法》《关于支持新型研发机构发展的试行办法》《广东省经营性领域技术入股改革实施方案》等；其中，支持企业建立研究开发准备金制度、科技企业孵化器创业投资及信贷风险补偿、创新产品与服务远期约定政府购买、经营性领域技术入股改革等政策措施均属于国内首创，对于破除广东省科技体制机制瓶颈，加快创新驱动发展具有突破性意义，是近年来广东省深化科技体制改革，深入实施创新驱动发展战略的标志性成果。同时，广东省科学技术厅积极推动各地市制定相关配套政策或实施细则，促使政策举措落实落地，为实施知识产权战略营造良好的政策环境。

【知识产权创新能力】

高新技术企业。启动实施高新技术企业培育计划，制定相关政策文件，建立高企培育后备库，大力培育发展高企。截至2015年底，全省共有3500多家企业入库培育。

科技型中小微企业。通过中小微企业创新基金、科技创新券后补助等专项资金，以及孵化育成体系、各级生产力促进中心、科技服务机构等公共服务平台，大力扶持科技型小微企业创新创业，其中，清远、中山、佛山等地已率先启动创新券补助制度。江门获批全国小微企业创新创业基地。

大型骨干企业。积极落实企业国家财税优惠政策，促进大型骨干企业提高研发投入。2015年减免企业税收超过100亿元，有力促进企业研发及涵养税源。继续鼓励和优先支持大型骨干企业牵头申报各级重大项目，安排实施智能机器人、新型印刷显示材料、可见光通信技术及标准光组件、新能源汽车电池及动力系统、3D打印技术等重大专项及一批专题科技计划引导支持企业开展研发；支持建设技术工程中心、企业研究院、院士工作站、企业科技特派员工作站等研发机构。目前，全省共有2014家工程技术研究中心，其中国家级23家，建有研发机构的企业占规上工业企业总数的12%。

实验室体系。2015年，广东省新增格力、风华高科、南方电网、东阳光制药、金发科技等5家企业国家重点实验室，截至2015年底，广东省已经形成由26家国家重点实验室、6家省部共建国家重点实验室培育基地、200家省重点实验室、54家省企业重点实验室、32家省重点科研基地组成的较为完整的实验室体系，成为广东省产业技术创新的重要平台和谋划建设国家实验室的主体支撑。

【知识产权战略实施】

珠三角国家自主创新示范区。2015年，广东省科学技术厅引导发挥广州、深圳市创新发展的龙头带动作用，联合珠海、佛山、惠州、东莞、中山、江门、肇庆市等7个地市，共同创建珠三角国家自主创新示范区。2015年9月，珠三角国家自主创新示范区获批，加上2014年6月获批的深圳国家自主创新示范区，广东形成了以深圳、广州和珠三角7个地市国家级高新区为核心的“1+1+7”自主创新新格局，成为推进全省创新驱动发展的重大平台。

高新区。截至2015年底，广东共有高新区23家，其中，国家级高新区11家、省级高新区12家，实现了21个地市省级以上高新区的全覆盖。2015年，河源、清远高新区升级为国家级高新区。2015年，广东省科学技术厅力推汕头、茂名、湛江、顺德等省级高新区升格国家级高新区，湛江高新区已经省政府批准上报国务院。2015年，全省23家高新区实现营业总收入2.66万亿元。

专业镇特色产业。2015年，广东省科学技术厅深入实施“一校一镇”“一所一镇”“科技特派团”等产学研协同创新行动计划，有力推进专业镇创新创业和传统优势产业转型升级。截至2015年底，全省已建成399个专业镇，涌现出中山小榄、中山古镇、东莞大朗、东莞横沥等一批转型升级和创新创业专业镇典型代表。2015年，全省专业镇实现地区生产总值2万亿元，占全省GDP的27%。积极引导珠三角专业镇与粤东西北专业镇进行对口合作，2015年，全省共有广州—梅州、佛山—云浮、东莞—韶关、中山—潮州等珠三角与粤东西北8对专业镇实现对接。

广东省科学院。2015年6月，广东省科学院在广州揭牌成立，着力打造广东省产业技术创新与重大成果转化的高端枢纽和平台。广东省科学技术厅按照省委、省政府的要求，加强对广东省科学院组建工作的督导检查，推动广东省科学院组建步伐不断加快。截至2015年底，广东省科学院基本完成法人变更、场地布置、资产清理划转、研究机构整合、院机关到位运作等基础工作，落实一批创新平台建设项目，引进高水平创新团队7个、领军人才10人，并于11月举行广东省科学院技术创新联盟科技成果对接会；与珠海市达成共建3个新型研发机构建设协议。

【产学研协同创新】　2015年，广东省科学技术厅继续深入推进省部院产学研合作，推进广东省与中科院、清华大学、北京大学等机构的新一轮战略合作，以及解放军信息工程大学军民技术融合发展，推动省部院产学研合作迈向纵深发展。2015年，省部院产学研合作全年实现产值2000亿元，利税200亿元。累计建成各类产学研创新平台1600多家，院士工作站109家，科技特派员工作站101家，产业技术创新联盟123家。加强与发达国家和地区的科技交流合作，揭阳中德生态金属园区、东莞中以水处理产业园区等重大科技合作平台进展顺利，汕头中以创新产业园区顺利奠基，全球优质创新资源加快集聚。2015年，广东省科技工作逐步实现从传统科技部门向驱动发展部门转变、从研发计划管理向创新服务治理转变的“两个转变”，全力推进部门协同与省市联动，加强了与省财政、发改、教育、经信、金融、农业、林业、水利、海洋渔业、食品药监、侨务等部门，以及各地市政府的沟通协调，建立起长期合作机制，形成了全省科技创新一盘棋。2015年11月，广东省科学技术厅继续与省经信、教育等部门合作举办第三届全省科技成果与产业对接会，促进646项科技成果实现落地转化。

（供稿人：严军华）

广东省公安厅

【概况】 2015年，公安机关成功组织收网跨省、跨境打假集群战役68起，占全国总数的1/3；侦破侵犯知识产权犯罪案件2036宗，占全国总数的1/10；逮捕3139人，涉案价值约56亿元，绩效考核综合排名位列全国第一名。广东省打击侵权假冒犯罪工作得到上级领导充分肯定，公安部9次发来贺电，孟庆丰、李春生等部省级领导多次批示肯定。

【专项推动】

组织领导，部署推进。公安厅党委部署开展“3+2”专项行动后，厅经侦局切实增强担当意识和责任意识，迅速成立由局长黄守应牵头的专项工作专班，建立“每周一例会、每月一总结、每季一汇报”的常态化工作机制，并研究制定信息登记台账，做到方向明确、分工细致、措施到位。同时，召开全省经侦工作会议，将打假行动作为全年中心工作进行动员部署，并多次召开局务会，专题研究专项工作，厘清目标任务、优化人员结构、完善机制建设，推动专项工作有序开展。

制定方案，考核督导。厅经侦局多次开会研究并征询各地意见，结合过去专项行动的经验做法及涉假犯罪的新情况、新特点，科学制定了打假行动工作方案及评价办法，下发具体指标任务，对重点项目进行达标考核，并建立动态通报制度，不定期向各市局主管领导、支队长短信提示进度排名及工作要求，有效引导各地工作开展。同时，制定督导工作指引，局领导分片包干、挂点包案，对12宗特重大案件挂牌督办，并多次带队分赴重点地区开展现场督导，查找薄弱环节、研究对策措施，帮助基层解决实际问题，有效推动专项行动纵深发展。

统筹安排，专项保障。厅经侦局以基础信息化、警务实战化建设为契机，大力推进“三台二站一室”建设，并按照李春生关于“强化基础信息对专项行动的服务支撑”的指示精神，将技术手段和情报信息资源重点向专项、向基层倾斜，着力解决基层专项工作中技术资源不足、侦查资源和实战需求直接对接不畅的问题。同时，专门设立了200多万元的重点案件补助经费，充分运用经济犯罪举报奖励经费，提高举报积极性，确保专项工作有力推进。

【提升效能】

情报导侦，提升破案攻坚能力。厅经侦局树立“让数据多跑腿，让民警少折腾”的理念，科学规划，精心打造具有经侦特色的一体化综合应用平台，努力实现“资源充分整合、实时碰撞比对”，提升对犯罪线索的“规模发现、深度发现、持续发现”能力。同时，抽调业务骨干成立情报作战专班，以类案情报导侦为方向，采取线上线下多种手段广泛获取情报线索，综合运用信息战、合成战、证据战等技战法，抓住信息流、资金流、物流等关键要素开展情报导侦，运用1020系统、SIS系统、I2分析软件等信息工具进行深度研判，梳理出有价值的情报交各地落地查控，形成“专班统筹协调，各市组织实施，省、市、区协同作战”的工作模式，最大限度地将信息资源转化为情报产品，将情报产品转化为打击成果，极大提升了专项打击效能。如惠州“5·13”制售假冒伪劣自行车案从举报线索入手，利用专门成立的“网上作战室”，综合运用公安大情报平台、SIS情报系统等专业情报资源，快速确认涉案嫌犯身份、落脚点、关联人员、车辆等基础信息，并针对造假窝点隐秘、很难贴靠侦查等难点，使用高清夜视仪、无人机、车辆跟踪器等先进手段锁定造假窝点、查明活动规律，成功捣毁犯罪窝点8个，抓获嫌犯42名，被评为2015年下半年全国打假十大经典战役，公安部经侦局评价该案为“情报导侦、高科技手段在打假领域综合运用，有效提升侦查效能的经典之作”。

集群战役，打击跨区涉假犯罪。厅经侦局始终抓住跨省区集群战役这一主战模式，将其列为专项行动的主要考核指标，用考核倒逼各地开展集群作战。进一步完善情报导侦条件下信息拓展、批量研判、合成联动的信息化作战机制，努力锻造“统一指挥、情报主导、合成作战、高效打击”的打击犯罪新模式。同时，组织专人采取分析立破案数据、召开座谈会、实地走访调研等方式对全省涉假犯罪形势开展深入分析研判，扎实做好集群战役线索的梳理、经营和筹备工作。针对制假售假犯罪存在明显区域化特征的情况，积极推动广州针对涉假皮具、汽配、打印耗材犯罪，深圳针对涉假手机、电子产品犯罪，佛山针对涉假日化用品、小家电犯罪，汕头、惠州针对涉假玩具、机械配件犯罪，中山、东莞针对涉假润滑油、服装、鞋类犯罪，揭阳针对假烟犯罪开展重点集群攻坚，形成题材丰富、亮点纷呈的持续性打击攻势。2015年，全省共发起并收网集群战役68起，占到全国集群战役收网总数的1/3以上，协助其他省市开展集群战役收网行动150多次，对100多个跨省犯罪团伙实现了全链条打击。如在深圳景昊科技有限公司假冒注册商标案集群战役中，广东、江西、河北、河南、湖北、浙江等6省公安机关联合出动，捣毁窝点7个，打掉犯罪团伙6个，查获假冒“先科”等品牌音响6478部，案值达7309.8万元，实现对制售假犯罪的全链条打击，被评为2015年全国首批五大经典战役。

重大行动。公安厅经侦局先后组织开展了“打假1号”、“打假2号”、打击涉烟犯罪“百日行动”三个波次的集中破案收网行动，充分保持时间、地区分布合理的战役梯次，推动各地展开有节奏、全覆盖的打击破案。一是开展“打假1号”行动。5至6月，组织开展了“打假1号”网上打假行动，共侦破网上侵犯知识产权犯罪案件152宗，涉及假冒耗材、家电、日化、玩具及箱包、服装、鞋子等多个领域，查处违规网站、电商平台127个，刑拘334人。二是开展“打假2号”行动。8至9月，针对危害生产生活安全和群众身体健康的制售假犯罪，部署开展了“打假2号”集中收网行动，共发起跨省集群战役22起，侦破大要案件395宗，逮捕583人，捣毁窝点890个。三是开展“百日行动”。11月，联合省烟草专卖局组织开展打击涉烟犯罪“百日行动”。截至2015年底，已收网跨省集群战役2起，侦破涉烟案件126宗，刑拘367人，逮捕205人，取得阶段性显著成效。

【加强协作】

部门协作。依托与工商、质监等7个行政执法机构成立的联合执法办公室，在线索移送、联合行动、联合督办等方面紧密协作，建立侵权行政处理重点人员名单库，信息量达5万多条。2015年，与相关行政执法部门在车用汽柴油专项整治、农村和城乡结合部假冒伪劣专项整治中开展联合行动1728次，捣毁窝点983个，破案874宗，刑拘2214人。

国际协作。厅经侦局高度重视涉外侵权案件线索的侦办，将国际执法合作作为打假工作重点，以合作求主动，以合作促宣传，取得一定成效。2015年，公安部交办涉及美国、意大利、波兰、韩国等国家的涉外线索16条，厅经侦局均进行了有效协查，并按时反馈结果。其中，2月至9月，公安部交办了四批共8条涉及美国的跨境制售假冒汽车气囊案件线索。厅经侦局黄守应局长亲自研究部署，并两次派人赴公安部汇报侦办情况，与美方移民海关执法局驻北京办事处人员进行案情交流。收网当日，共捣毁制售假窝点9个，抓获犯罪嫌疑人11名，涉案价值700多万元，充分彰显了广东省打击知识产权犯罪的决心和能力。

粤港澳协作。在粤港、粤澳知识产权合作框架下，厅经侦局推动深圳与香港海关，珠海、中山与澳门海关建立了情报交流机制，对跨境案件开展执法协作。2015年，先后3次派人赴香港、澳门参加粤港保护知识产权专责小组第十四次会议及跨境打击假烟犯罪协调会。5月7日，中山联合澳门海关开展跨境集群战役破案行动，查获非法经营香烟、雪茄烟价值1000万元，刑拘2人，逮捕1人。

警企协作。厅经侦局高度重视与企业协作，多次走访知识产权重点企业，收集意见、提供预警信息、接受报案，并与腾讯、华为等200多家重点企业签署协议，建立知识产权刑事保护协作机制和绿色通道，积极探索搭建全省电子商务领域打击侵犯知识产权犯罪平台。9月23日，组织召开以“加强保护民族品牌，提升警企效能联动”为主题的全省第二届公安经侦部门警企联动工作座谈会，与省内17家企业代表就加强协作打击侵犯知识产权犯罪等议题进行了广泛深入的讨论。

【宣传发动】 按照中共中央政治局委员、广东省委书记胡春华关于“公安机关打击刑事犯罪工作要大力宣传”的重要指示精神和厅党委具体部署，研究制定了专项宣传工作方案，多形式、多渠道、有节奏、有波次地开展宣传报道。截至2015年底，共在国家级媒体上宣传报道175次，省级媒体宣传报道324次，市级媒体宣传报道847次。

宣传氛围。抓住“3·15”消费者权益保护日、“4·26”世界知识产权日、“5·15”打击和防范经济犯罪宣传日等重要节点，通过召开新闻发布会、街面宣传、销毁假冒伪劣商品等多种形式掀起宣传攻势。

媒体合作。指派专人加强与《人民公安报》《南方法治报》《南方日报》等主流媒体的合作，并要求各地在积极加强与当地媒体沟通联系的同时，要向省厅提供重大新闻线索和素材，争取在更高层级媒体上进行宣传，达到最佳宣传效果。2015年，共向《人民公安报》《南方法治报》送稿50余篇，均被采纳刊出。同时，推出经侦互联网平台，发布打假宣传信息30余条，开辟出新的打假专项宣传阵地。

引导舆情。针对突出的典型案例，组织记者深入一线采写行动现场素材，及时主动开展舆情引导。如涉美假气囊案件告破后，经报公安部，并征求外交部的意见后，厅经侦局组织广州支队在习近平总书记访美期间对该案进行了集中宣传报道，社会反响热烈。

强化研判预警，服务发动群众。加强网上网下涉假犯罪信息分析研判，主动向相关执法部门和行业协会通报新型涉假犯罪手法，提出防范建议，堵塞政策漏洞。依托全省经侦部门警企联动机制，及时向重点企业发布预警信息，提升企业防范经济犯罪的意识和能力。同时，努力提升人民群众防范能力，结合典型案例，剖析犯罪伎俩，传授防假常识，使人民群众充分认识假冒伪劣犯罪可恨、可防，着力提升全民打假意识和氛围。

（供稿人：李游）

广东省司法厅

【概况】 2015年，广东省司法厅出台《2015年知识产权工作计划和知识产权宣传周活动计划》，组织律师、法制宣传、人民调解等方面的力量，推动《深入实施国家知识产权战略行动计划（2014—2020）》的落实，取得新成效。

【版权纠纷人民调解委员会】 继广州市、深圳市成立版权纠纷人民调解委员会后，2015年，佛山市、东莞市先后成立版权纠纷人民调解委员会。这种新型的专业委员会为解决日益增多的知识产权纠纷提供新的途径，有利于保护当事人的合法权益，促进知识产权事业健康发展。

【开展广东省律师知识产权典型案例系列活动】 继续发挥和扩大律师知识产权典型案例评选和巡讲活动，作为广东省知识产权宣传周重要活动之一的品牌，社会影响较大。

2015年4月17日，在“4·26”世界知识产权日来临之际，省律协知识产权专委会举办了“2014年度广东律师十大知识产权典型案例发布会”，公布了广东省律师主办的十大知识产权典型案例，部分案件被最高人民法院、广东省高级人民法院和广东省知识产权保护协会等有关单位评选为全国、全省典型案例。

典型案例公布后，省律协知产委先后与广州市律师协会、广东司法警官职业学院律师学院、佛山市律师协会知识产权专业委员会、珠海市律师协会知识产权专业委员会等单位分别在广州、佛山、珠海等地共举办5场巡回报告会，参加报告会的听众达800余人次。

9月11日，广东省律师协会知识产权法律专业委员会应湖南省律师协会知识产权法律专业委员会的邀请，派出省律协知产委律师和省知识产权讲师团成员赴湖南省湘潭市，与当地律师协会等有关单位联合举办“广东省、湖南省知识产权典型案例办案技巧巡回报告会”。湖南省100多名律师、政府部门人员到场学习和探讨。这是广东省律师首次赴外省举办的知识产权典型案例报告会。

为扩大交流学习的范围，加强典型案例的指导作用，省律协知产委从2014年、2015年征集的案例中挑选并组织编写了以案例研究为主的专业书籍《知识产权典型案例主办律师评述》，由法律出版社出版。全书一共收录38篇案例评析文章，涉及知识产权多个领域，对法学研究者、企业管理者、法律实务工作者有借鉴与指导意义。

【第三届广东知识产权法律服务论坛】 2015年11月28—29日，由省律协与佛山市律协主办，省律协知识产权专委会与佛山市律协知识产权专委会承办的“第三届广东知识产权法律服务论坛”在佛山举行。来自全国律协和江西、湖南、云南、贵州、广西、杭州、成都、宁波等省市律协知识产权专委会主任、副主任，泛珠三角九省区和港澳台地区的律师代表、企业代表等250余人参加论坛。

论坛主题为“合作、分享、锐意进取”。主论坛上，广州知识产权法院、佛山市中院知识产权庭、广东外语外贸大学法学院等知名法官、专家、学者分别以“知识产权法院运营的现状和展望”“新型机制下的知识产权审判实务问题”和“对我国知识产权法院的未来展望”为题作了演讲。分论坛上，与会人员围绕“泛珠三角区域知识产权法律服务合作与发展”“知识产权法律业务的创新与拓展”“知识产权诉讼业务技巧及典型案例分享”和“知识产权商业运营”四个议题，对文化产业知识产权法律保护、知识产权反垄断与海关保护、西南部地区知识产权法律服务的现状与发展、“两岸三地”知识产权法律业务交流与合作、“互联网+知识产权业务”的发展模式、中介机构在知识产权营运的角色与作用等内容进行了实务研讨和经验交流。此外，此届论坛还举办了优秀论文奖颁奖仪式，对广东知识产权法律服务论坛十大优秀论文的作者颁发了荣誉证书。

【中港新三地国际版权法律研讨会】 2015年6月27日，省律协知识产权专业委员会与广东知识产权保护协会在广州联合举办国际版权保护最新动态研讨会。广东省律师、实习律师、企业高管等100余人参加研讨。研讨会特邀省法院知识产权庭、广州知识产权法院、新加坡管理大学法学院、香港城市大学法学院等法官、专家、学者担任主讲嘉宾。各主讲嘉宾就著作权与言论自由的界限、著作权侵权诉讼的证据博弈与证明标准、大数据时代下著作权集体管理组织的现状及前景及现行法律框架下网游纠纷的法律保护进行了阐述和分析。

（供稿人：骆文经　唐东标）

广东省农业厅

【概况】 截至2015年底，全省累计通过省级审定的农作物品种1625个，共申请植物新品种权323个，获得授权133个，申请量和授权量分别居全国第14位和第16位；新增3个国家畜禽新品种及配套系，累计总数达到31个；12个产品获得农产品地理标志证书，有效期内有机农产品60个、绿色食品810个、无公害农产品1710个；农业类名牌产品数量达到934个，生产企业 623家。

【科技创新】 整合资金分别设立农业科技创新、推广与信息化和现代种业发展专项，着力提升现代农业科技创新能力，育成一批优质高产、抗逆性强的农作物新品种和畜禽良种；杂交稻优质化和高产育种研究与应用、畜禽和航天育种技术、重大动物疫病快速诊断与防控技术、疫苗和饲料产品等研发水平处于全国领先，部分达到国际先进水平，支撑了广东省现代农业创新驱动发展。

一是种业科技创新能力持续增强。推动落实国家和省委、省政府关于现代种业发展决策部署和政策扶持，支持育种科研机构和企业加大新品种选育及配套设施建设，实施农作物新品种区域试验、种质资源保护利用、种子质量监督检查及“育繁推”一体化建设，不断提升农作物品种研发能力，选育了一批优良品种，全年审定通过了农作物新品种有137个，其中水稻59个，玉米19个，花生1个，马铃薯4个，甘薯3个，蔬菜7个，果树12个，花卉30个，中药材2个。申请农业植物新品种权70个，获得授权51件，同比2014年增加39件，其中水稻32件，玉米4件，大豆7件，棉花4件，油菜2件，小麦和花卉各1件。

二是畜禽品种保护开发和利用稳步推进。实施国家畜牧良种补贴、畜禽良种工程和省特色畜禽品种保护开发利用等项目，扎实推进畜禽遗传资源保护，新增3家国家生猪核心育种场、总数达到11家；创建了7家国家肉鸡核心育种场和5个国家级肉鸡良种扩繁推广基地；建立了省级畜禽遗传资源保种场18个，国家级保种场总数增至10个；全国新增11个畜禽新品种配套系，广东省就有温氏WS501猪配套系、温氏青脚麻鸡2号配套系、科朗麻黄鸡配套系等3个配套系获得国家畜禽配套系证书。

三是现代农机装备科技创新加快推进。整合资源、大力推动养殖机械、设施设备、加工装备、智慧农业等农机装备科技创新力度，全年新申请专利21件，获得新授权专利18件，其中发明专利、实用新型专利、软件著作权、外观设计数量分别为1、10、6、1件。并通过涉农专利成果转化，有效降低了农产品干燥加工能耗，提高了畜牧养殖机械智能化水平和生产效率，实现了农业废弃物资源化利用，取得显著的经济效益。

【行业管理】 围绕打击制售假冒伪劣农资、农业植物新品种权保护“两大重点内容”，紧扣源头生产、加工流通、销售使用等“三个重点环节”，注重种植生产、畜禽养殖、兽药饲料、种业发展等“四大重点领域”，牢牢把握关系农业生产的种子、化肥、农药、兽药、饲料及添加剂等“五大重点产品”，主动作为，依法行政，扎实推动行业规范管理和市场准入，为保障农业知识产权的创造、运用、保护和管理发挥了积极作用。

一是强化种子质量监督管理。制定印发《2015年广东省打击侵犯品种权和制售假劣种子行为专项行动实施方案》，通过开展种子企业质量监督抽查和制种基地巡查，对广东省生产经营水稻和玉米种子的15家企业进行品种全覆盖监督抽查，并进行品种真实性鉴定，有效遏制了制售假劣种子和侵犯品种权等违法行为。全年停止推广主要农作物品种58个。

二是强化农药质量监督管理。开展春季、秋季农药监督抽查专项行动，抽查了全省22个地级以上市（顺德区）的农药经营单位，共抽查农药产品539批次。全省累计出动执法人员14942人次，检查生产经营单位6600多家，立案200件，涉案货值100多万元。惠州等地农业部门结合保护知识产权专项行动，抽检农药产品11个，经检测均合格。全年共受理农药登记初审132项、农药田间药效试验申请116项、农药续展登记112项、农药广告审查申请33项。

三是强化肥料质量监督管理。制定印发

《2015年广东省肥料打假专项治理行动实施方案》，组织开展肥料市场检查，共检查了109个肥料产品，发现并处理了少数企业产品仍然存在包装标识不符合国家标准，假冒、套用肥料登记证号，使用过期肥料登记证，更改产品名称等擅自修改标签内容以及夸大产品功效、虚假宣传误导农民的情况。依法开展农业部部级肥料登记省级初审和省级肥料登记审批工作，严格遵守审批权限、程序、条件，做好肥料产品登记工作。明确申请企业提交不存在不构成知识产权侵权行为，全年共办理260家（次）594个产品登记，其中新申请登记235个，续展登记338个，变更登记21个，没有发生有关知识产权问题的投诉情况。

四是强化饲料质量监督管理。制订了《广东省2015年饲料和饲料添加剂产品打假专项治理行动实施方案》，印发了《2015年广东省饲料产品质量安全监测方案》，省级组织开展获证企业监督检查25次，共抽查企业136家，饲料产品100%合格；累计查处饲料及饲料添加剂生产及经营企业55家，其中无证生产2家，行政立案53起，涉案金额366473元，无害化处理饲料34吨。全年核（换）发饲料和饲料添加剂生产许可证185个，核发饲料添加剂和添加剂预混合饲料产品批准文号3298个。

五是强化兽药质量监督管理。严把兽药市场准入关，重点推进兽药专项整治行动，监督抽检兽药406批次，合格400批次，合格率为98.52%，比2014年抽检合格率提高1.53%；共出动执法人员8980人次，检查生产经营企业6336家次，立案查处11起，有力打击了制售假劣兽药行为。全年核发兽药GMP证16个，核发兽药生产许可证16个，换发兽药生产许可证6个。

六是强化农机质量监督管理。制定《2015年广东省补贴机具质量跟踪调查工作实施方案》，组织和指导市、县开展农机质量监督检查，督促农机生产企业、经销商落实“三包”责任，公开全省各市县（区）农机质量监督投诉站的详细地址及投诉电话，全省共派发农机使用宣传资料4512.94万份，检查农机生产经营企业1318家，整顿市场132次，对检查中发现的安全隐患要求立即整改。

【品牌建设】 实施名牌带动战略，持续推进以农产品地理标志和无公害农产品、绿色食品和有机食品（简称“三品一标”）为主要内容的认证登记与监督管理，不断提升广东省主要特色农产品质量安全和市场竞争力。

一是推进产品认证，提升质量效益。加强“三品一标”认证时效性的规范化管理，加大申报工作力度，指导各级工作机构开展现场检查和材料审核，严把质量管理认证关口，敦促企业增强自律意识，完善管理制度，确保认证企业和申报产品符合标准。全年全省新增申报无公害农产品产地认定222个；新增绿色食品企业20多家，产品60多个；颁证公示农产品地理标志5个，4个农产品完成初审。全省已建立绿色食品和有机农产品监测面积15.8万公顷，总产量近227万吨；无公害和农产品地理标志基地面积达24万公顷；创建全国绿色食品原料标准化基地有4个县，面积近60万亩。

二是推动名牌战略，提升运用效益。继续推进广东省农业类名牌产品申报和复审工作，参考申报企业科技创新水平、产品科技含量、产品地方特色、与同类产品的比较优势及企业研发费用投入、自主知识产权数量等综合指标因素，启动2015年度名牌评价工作，经组织专家评审和广东省名牌产品（农业类）推进委员会审核，共评出2015年广东省名牌产品（农业类）364个，其中初评产品152个，到期复审产品212个。有效期内的名牌产品（农业类）达到934个，大多数品牌农产品具有一个或多个专利，农业领域知识产权运用水平得到明显提升。

三是强化品牌推介，提升产品效益。启动省名特优新农产品评选推介工作，经政府主导、专家评审、媒体宣传、群众参与相结合，层层严格审核把关，从广东省现有农业品牌中好中选优，评选推介了1000个广东省名特优新农产品并建立目录，其中具有地方特色的区域公用品牌300个，经营专用品牌700个，对其中150个区域公用品牌和150个经营专用品牌进行表彰，并在广东现代农业博览会上展示，有效提升了全省主要特色农产品的产品竞争力和产业效益。

（供稿人：刘晓治）

广东省林业厅

【概况】 2015年，广东省林业厅加强林业知识产权保护宣传，积极推进林业知识产权的创造、运用和保护，认真开展林木种苗质量抽查和打击侵犯林业植物新品种权专项行动，并依法实行行政处罚案件信息公开。

【林业知识产权宣传与普及】 采取网络媒体、书籍资料、现场咨询等多种形式积极宣传林业植物新品种保护条例等相关知识产权法律法规和政策，增强公众对林业知识产权保护相关法律法规及政策的了解，提高社会各界对打击林业植物新品种和林木种苗侵权假冒工作重要性、必要性的认识，营造良好的林木种苗发展环境。利用知识产权宣传周、科技进步活动月和科技下乡等活动，大力宣传植物新品种保护等知识，并现场发放《林业知识产权宣传手册》，提供咨询服务。

【林业植物新品种保护】 2015年，继续加强林业科技创新，加快林木花卉新品种的培育，促进林业植物新品种创造、运用和转化。全省有9个林木花卉新品种申请植物新品种权；9个新品种获得国家林业局植物新品种授权。至2015年底，广东省申请林业植物新品种权总数量达82个，授权总量达70个，申请量和授权量在全国各省（区、市）中位居前列。

【林木种苗质量检查】 为加强林木种苗质量管理，严厉打击制售和使用假冒伪劣林木种苗行为，确保林业重点工程种苗质量和建设成效，根据《中华人民共和国种子法》和《林木种子质量管理办法》规定，按照《国家林业局办公室关于开展2015年林木种苗质量抽查工作的通知》要求，在全省林业系统部署开展林木种行政执法和质量抽查工作。主要对苗圃、造林地种苗质量和种苗行政执法等情况进行检查。2015年3月下旬至4月初，广东省林业厅组织检查组对河源、梅州等14个地级市46个县（市、区）的林木种苗质量进行了抽查，共抽查29个品种、210个苗批，苗批合格率为100%。

【林业植物新品种权专项行动】 为加大打击侵权假冒工作力度，规范植物新品种交易市场，有效保护植物新品种权人的合法权益，促进林业植物新品种的培育和转化应用，根据国家林业局部署要求，广东省林业厅于2015年5月印发《2015年广东省林业厅打击侵犯林业植物新品种权专项行动方案》，在全省林业系统部署开展打击侵犯林业植物新品种权执法专项行动，主要打击未经品种权人许可，以商业目的生产或者销售林业授权品种的繁殖材料、假冒林业授权品种以及销售林业授权品种时未使用其注册登记名称的违法行为。通过对已授权林业植物新品种的单位和个人调查摸底，了解授权植物新品种的推广应用，以及侵权、假冒情况。并在摸底调查的基础上，在全省组织开展林业植物新品种权保护执法检查，重点检查授权品种的繁殖、生产、销售环节，包括苗圃、繁殖场、种苗（花卉）交易市场、经营等场所。专项行动未发现有林业植物新品种权侵权行为。

【信息公开】 广东省林业厅于2014年制定《广东省林业厅公开制售假冒伪劣商品和侵犯知识产权行政处罚案件信息工作实施管理办法》，2015年继续在全省林业系统推开行政处罚案件信息公开工作，进一步增强执法透明度，更好地震慑违法者、保护消费者。广东省林业厅在门户网站设立双打信息公开专栏，及时报道行政处罚信息公开工作动态信息。

（供稿人：叶龙华）

广东省商务厅

【广交会知识产权保护】 广东省商务厅高度重视展会业知识产权保护工作，严厉打击侵权不法行为，重点在广交会和对广东交易团大力加强知识产权保护力度。一是完善上下联动的工作机制。在各市分团（广州、深圳除外）以及选取的省属重点企业中建立了保护知识产权负责人和联系人工作机制，由分团（企业）有关领导负总责，联系人具体落实，上下联动，确保知识产权保护“有人管、管得住”。二是加强侵权案件提前介入处理力度。通过工作重心前移，在大会投诉站认定涉嫌侵权并录入电脑前，加强与投诉人、被投诉企业、投诉站、各市分团多方的沟通协调，通过调解纠纷、协调涉嫌侵权企业、投诉站专家释疑等多种方式，切实降低涉案率。

【知识产权战略实施】 广东省商务厅认真贯彻落实《广东省知识产权战略纲要（2007—2020年）》，结合2015年实施广东省知识产权战略纲要工作方案制定省商务厅2015年知识产权工作方案，采取有力措施开展商务领域知识产权保护工作。加强对展会知识产权保护、粤港保护知识产权合作以及“双打”等工作的统筹协调，全面推进商务领域知识产权工作。

【品牌国际化知识产权培训】 2015年5月20日，广东省商务厅联合省工商局、香港知识产权署共同主办了品牌国际化知识产权培训班。省知识产权局、版权局、海关总署广东分署、香港海关为支持单位，广东省各市企业代表、省纺织协会会员企业共计110多人参加了培训。这是围绕品牌国际化知识产权保护主办的第二次品牌专题培训班，重点培训广东省各类型企业在走出去海外知识产权规则和防控风险。通过专题培训，广东省企业对品牌国际化知识产权保护重要性的认识提高，掌握了国际知识产权保护的正确方法，建立了知识产权领域的联系。

【电商领域知识产权保护交流合作】 为增强粤港双方对跨境电子商务和快递业的知识产权的保护力度，经省商务厅提请，粤港保护知识产权合作专责小组第十四次会议正式将“开展电商领域知识产权保护交流合作”列为粤港保护知识产权合作项目。2015年11月20日，香港知识产权署牵头的港方代表团与省商务厅共同就重点领域、重点产业开展打造合作机制，建立风险防控工作合作进行探索。香港海关、香港电子商贸协会、香港淘宝商盟、香港电商联会、省自贸办、海关总署广东分署、省知识产权局、省跨境电商行业协会、省物流行业协会等单位代表参加了交流会议。为加大对广东自贸试验区的知识产权工作建设，省商务厅组织港方代表赴南沙自贸区与自贸区有关部门开展交流并参观风信子跨境购物体验中心考察。通过交流考察，粤港双方增进了在自贸区建设、跨境电子商务知识产权保护方面的了解，形成进一步加强相关领域知识产权保护交流合作的共识。

（供稿人：邓楷凯）

广东省文化厅

【概况】 2015年，广东省各级文化市场综合执法机构按照文化部、省委省政府有关工作部署和要求，结合工作实际，围绕“平安文化市场”创建工作，强化文化市场监管，依法严查违法违规行为，有力推进文化市场执法制度建设和队伍建设，切实履行文化市场安全生产职责，有效地保证了全省文化市场的健康、平稳、安全。据统计，2015年广东省文化市场行政执法部门共出动行政执法力量约87.7万人次，检查各类文化市场经营场所约32.6万家次；受理举报1630件，立案调查各类违法违规案件2411宗，移交案件81宗，办结案件1909宗；行政处罚违法违规文化经营单位2149家次，其中责令停业整顿93家次、吊销经营许可证12家，罚没人民币约1137万元。

（供稿人：王子尤）

广东省卫生和计划生育委员会

【概况】 2015年，广东省卫生和计划生育委员会结合卫生计生工作实际，贯彻落实《深入实施国家知识产权战略行动计划（2014—2020年）》，进一步加强医药卫生知识产权保护与管理，全面提升卫生计生行业知识产权参与竞争能力，有效推进医药卫生知识产权的创造和合理利用。2015年，全省卫生计生系统共鉴定成果448项，其中有302项成果获各级科技奖励，占67.4%，其中4项成果获国家科技进步二等奖，1项成果获国家自然科学奖二等奖，40项成果获广东省科技奖励，其中广东省科技奖励一等奖6项，占获奖总数的24%，二等奖19项，三等奖15项。出版专著755本，发表SCI收录论文6133篇，较2014年分别增长31.1%和13.2%。

【科技重大专项】 2015年，广东省承担的国家“十二五”“艾滋病和病毒性肝炎等重大传染病防治”科技重大专项项目结题工作顺利通过国家卫生计生委重大专项办预评估，同时，规范了有关项目的知识产权管理，促进创新成果的转化、利用和合理分享。

【专利信息资源开发利用计划项目】 广东省医学学术交流中心和国家知识产权局专利审查协作广东中心联合承担的广东省战略性新兴产业专利信息资源开发利用计划项目——生物医学工程产业专利分析及预警研究顺利完成。该研究从专利技术分析出发，围绕医学诊断和治疗两大主题，重点分析了医学成像设备、医用检测及监护设备、体外诊断设备、重点治疗设备以及植介入医疗器械等领域，整合成为数据量达53.84万件的生物医学工程产业专利数据库，摸清国内外生物医学工程领域处于领先地位的企业和专利，揭示产业专利分布和发展趋势，对政府部门和企事业单位科学决策具有重要的参考意义。

（供稿人：涂正杰）

广东省版权局

【广东版权专题调研】 2015年，为充分体现版权的经济特性，广东省版权局专门委托中国新闻出版研究院开展“广东省版权经济贡献率专题调研”，以权威数据为基础，利用定量方式，通过行业增加值、就业人数、出口额等指标，描述利用统计方法来定量描述版权在国民经济中的贡献率，展现版权经济属性，强化版权意识，推进版权产业发展。

“2014年广东省版权产业经济贡献”调研结果表明：2014年广东省版权产业行业增加值5691.14 亿元人民币，占全省地区生产总值的8.39%，就业人数为461.18万人，占全省就业人数的7.46%，商品出口额为891.51亿美元，占全省商品出口额的13.80%。

【作品著作权】 2015年，广东省一般作品著作权登记总量达30882件，首次突破3万件，同比增长近50%，为历年之最。计算机软件登记总量达61804件，全国排名第二，同比增长64.18%，增速全国第一。

【版权兴业】 2015年，以打造广东具备国内影响力的区域品牌、做大做强产业集群，省版权局授予斯达高瓷艺发展（深圳）有限公司等

10家企业“广东省版权兴业示范基地”称号。全省共有86家“版权兴业示范基地”。

以评促优，促进版权产业优质发展。通过评选年度“广东省最具价值版权产品”，培育版权产品品牌，提升版权产业市场竞争力，促进全省版权产业的持续发展。2015年，省版权局从全省各地版权行政部门申报的几十件作品中评选认定了计算机软件、雕塑、美术、动画片、微电影、漫画、设计图等7大类共12件作品为2014年度广东省最具价值版权产品，入选的“广州解放纪念碑”等12件版权产品创意独特，特点明显，创造出良好的社会价值和经济价值。截至2015年底，全省共有46个“最具价值版权产品”。

【护航“漫博会”】 2015年8月，第七届“漫博会”在东莞市举行。此届漫博会，“版权服务工作站”加强版权保护，版权服务得到提升，版权贸易成绩显著。“漫博会”组委会授予广东省版权局、省版权基层工作站东莞站等单位“突出贡献奖”以示嘉奖。共核发著作权来源信息登记卡1022个；受理参展作品著作权登记申请312项，比上届增长106%，工作站现场完成著作权登记并出证256宗，比上届增长30%。8月20日至23日期间，共出动执法人员89人次，开展之前处理版权投诉2宗，有效维持展会的版权秩序，连续七届“漫博会”开展期间实现侵权盗版“零投诉”。

【版权宣传】 依托“4・26版权保护宣传周”，印发《2015年广东省保护著作权宣传周活动计划》（粤权〔2015〕14号），明确宣传主题、宣传重点，通过播放版权宣传短片、赠送版权笔记本、派发《图解中华人民共和国著作权法》等宣传资料。以“4・26”活动为契机，全省文化执法部门加大巡查力度，严密布控，对全省音像经营场所、电子出版物市场、印刷厂、游商、地摊，进行全面清查。共出动执法人员8988人次，检查经营商户5273家，行动中清理取缔非法出版物地摊96个，查处违法违规经营单位3家，收缴涉嫌侵权盗版出版物101922张（册）。

【“剑网2015”】 2015年全省各地市共出动执法人员78976人次，巡查网络经营单位3204家，主动监管各地网站800余家，查办案件35宗，行政罚款145.2万元，为全省版权产业的发展提供了良好的版权保护秩序和有利的发展环境。共报送查办的网络侵权盗版案件35宗。

【大案要案】 2015年，全省各级版权行政执法监管部门切实担负起版权执法监管责任，抓住社会影响大的案件，寻求重点突破，把有限力量和行政执法资源集中到大案要案的查处和重点产业的专项治理上，查处了广州市“6・9”制售盗版教材案、广东“DJ020网”侵犯音乐作品著作权案、广东张某某销售侵权复制品案等一批大案要案，进一步巩固了广东省版权治理成果。省版权局主动作为，查处了潮州市枫溪区某花纸厂侵犯著作权案。经省版权局查证，《万寿无疆》瓷艺系列为斯达高瓷艺发展（深圳）有限公司2008年自主开发的原创作品，潮州市枫溪区某花纸厂复制了其整个系列作品的陶瓷贴花纸，并在门店公开销售以获取经济利益，侵犯了斯达高瓷艺发展（深圳）有限公司的著作权，依据《中华人民共和国著作权法》《中华人民共和国著作权法实施条例》有关条款，省版权局给予其没收侵权有关物品并罚款4万元的行政处罚。

【软件正版化】 建立软件正版化长效机制。为健全长效机制，省版权局专门印发《建立政府机关软件正版化工作长效机制实施意见》《2015年度全省推进企业使用正版软件工作督办企业名录》，巩固软件正版化工作成果。

【粤港合作】 2015年2月12日至13日，广东省版权局与香港海关、香港知识产权署联合举办的2015年粤港中学生版权知识和版权保护的交流活动在香港举行。5月6日至5月8日，广东省版权局与香港特别行政区知识产权署联合举办的2015年粤港版权产业企业交流活动在香港举行。

【服务组织机构】 2015年广东省新增作品代办机构2家，版权基层工作站2家。全省已建立了16个“版权基层工作站”和27个作品登记代办机构。版权中介机构和行业社团组织建设得到加强。基本建立起了覆盖全省的版权社会服务体系。

【全国版权示范城市】 近年来，东莞高度重视版权工作，将版权保护工作和版权产业发展纳入城市发展总体规划，版权工作机制健全、政策到位，版权服务举措不断创新，版权产业持续健康发展，软件正版化工作扎实推进，版权执法工作取得明显成效，版权保护意识整体提高。鉴于东莞版权工作的成绩，国家版权局2015年7月批复东莞市创建“全国版权示范城市”。

【国家版权示范】 为贯彻落实《国家知识产权战略纲要》和《版权工作“十二五”规划》，充分发挥版权先进典型的示范引导作用，不断提升版权创造、运用、保护和管理的整体水平，树立版权示范典型，通过版权保护工作更好为经济建设服务，凭借多年在尊重原创、保护版权与商业模式等方面取得的突出成绩，国家版权局于2015年10月授予腾讯科技（深圳）有限公司“国家版权示范单位”称号。

（供稿人：沈欣）

广东省工商行政管理局

【概况】 2015年，广东省工商系统全面落实国家知识产权战略纲要和广东省委、省政府《关于加快知识产权强省建设的决定》，围绕“一带一路”与广东自贸区建设对商标工作的需求，积极推进商标品牌战略实施，强化商标专用权保护。

【商标注册】 2015年，广东省商标注册申请量512857件，同比增长26.20%；商标注册量395601 件，同比增长77.00%。截至2015年底，全省商标有效注册量1659477件，同比增长26.27%，自1995年以来连续二十一年居全国首位。2015年度广东省马德里商标国际注册申请588件，累计有效注册量4550件，保持全国前列。

【商标保护】 商标行政执法。全省工商系统共查处商标违法案件4208件，案件总值4245.53万元，罚没金额5106.66万元，移送司法机关涉嫌商标犯罪案件35件、嫌疑人21人。其中，查处侵犯港澳台和外国商标注册人权益案2021件，案值1941.29万元，罚款金额3098.00万元，移送司法机关涉嫌商标犯罪案件22件、嫌疑人13人。

驰名商标保护。2015年，广东省获得国家工商行政管理总局认定与保护的驰名商标75件，总量715件，自2006年以来连续十年保持全国第一。

【商标品牌战略】 商标注册派出机构筹备工作。落实国家工商行政管理总局《关于支持广东加快转型升级建设幸福广东的意见》，成立商标注册派出机构广东筹备领导小组，经过调研与协调，向工商总局、广东省委省政府汇报，初步拟定筹建方案，对接筹建中的重大关键事项，商标注册派出机构筹备工作取得初步进展，并得到工商总局的肯定与支持。商标维权援助体系建设。在深圳、佛山、东莞市工商局完善商标预警平台和机制基础上，探索推进商标维权援助体系建设，建立维权援助平台和重点产业知识产权快速维权中心，开展知识产权境外护航，支持行业、企业建立商标境外维权联盟。贯彻《关于知识产权支持小微企业发展的若干意见》，强化面向小微企业的商标公共服务，提高小微企业商标注册、管理与保护能力，优化小微企业商标发展环境。支持江门市作为广东省商标品牌维权援助服务平台的建设试点单位，为江门市小微企业发展提供国内外商标法律法规、产业发展政策等信息。

【对外合作交流】 按照粤港保护知识产权合作专责小组第十三、十四次会议的要求，完善与香港海关的商标执法与案件协作制度，通过定期情报交流掌握跨境商标侵权情况。与澳门海关磋商建立商标案件线索通报、协查、联络制度。落实粤港粤澳商标合作项目。2015年1月8日，广东省工商局与香港特区政府知识产权署在香港联合举办“新《商标法》研讨会”，邀请国家工商总局等部门和企业参加。广东省工商局代表介绍了广东商标领域发展和保护情况，回顾粤港商标保护合作成果，讲解商标管理与保护方面的新规定，解答参会代表关于《商标法》新规定、维权实务等方面问题。9月17日，广东省工商局应邀参加澳门经济局在澳门举办“内地及澳门商标注册与保护座谈会”，向澳门工商业界介绍内地商标行政管理和保护制度，与澳门经济局和澳门海关就商标跨境保护粤澳合作展开交流。继续指导广东商标协会支持在粤港资、澳资企业申请认定广东省著名商标。加强与国际知识产权组织的合作，先后接待中国欧盟商会华南分会来访、出席中英广东商标研讨会，就商标保护等问题进行交流。

（供稿人：陈小冰）

广东省质量技术监督局

【概况】 2015年，广东省质量技术监督局实施以质取胜战略和名牌带动战略，探索建立以消费者认可和市场竞争力为基础的名牌评价新体系和“评”“管”分开的评价新机制，提高名牌评价和名牌产品的社会公信力。在积极开展地理标志产品保护工作以及严厉打击质量技术监督领域知识产权违法行为等方面取得新成效。

【名牌产品】

名牌评价目录。发挥名牌带动作用，科学制定名牌评价目录。2015年各地市质监局和行业协会要求新增目录343个，经认真筛选并经名推委主任会议研究确定，2015年新增名牌产品目录88个，90%以上都是国家和广东省鼓励发展的新产品目录。

名牌评价体系。贯彻省名推委主任会议意见，修改完善评价体系。根据环保部《关于改革调整上市环保核查工作制度的通知》（环发〔2014〕149号）的要求，各级环保部门不再对上市企业及各类企业开展任何形式的环保核查、不再出具环保守法证明等任何形式的类似文件。名推委会议研究同意调整省名牌产品评价通则中关于“环境保护审查”的要求，不再要求申报企业到环保部门开具环保证明，改为“申报企业自觉声明近三年内没有发生重大环境污染事件，并接受社会监督。同时，各地市质监部门统一去函本地环保局征询申报企业是否存在环保违法问题。如果申报产品生产企业存在污染物排放不达标的，或近三年内发生重大环境污染事件的，将自动失去参评资格”。同时，为构建良好的商业环境，帮助消费者清楚识别产品的质量信用，专家提出在“质量评价”评价中增加20分的“质量信用”评价指标，要求企业在产品宣传推介销售中自觉明示产品执行标准和产品主要质量安全性能指标，以及是否“重信用、守合同单位”。2015年9月，邀请行业专家根据行业发展水平研究制定名牌产品的申报条件和主要质量性能指标。10月，针对每一类产品的不同特点，请各专业权威机构分类制定名牌产品评价细则，确保评价规则更加科学具体、更具针对性和操作性。

名牌产品申报。积极开发运用名牌产品网上申报系统，促进廉洁办事，共同把好名牌产品申报关。各地市质监局对申报企业严格审核把关，并广泛征求当地进出口检验检疫、工商、国税、地税、统计等部门意见，或召开质量工作联席会议的形式对申报企业进行审查。各地市实际推荐申报产品共682个。研究院为确保申报资料真实有效、准确可靠，严格审查申报材料，并对通过初步审查的682个产品（复评302个，新申报380个）数据进行公示，广泛接受社会监督，积极处理举报投诉问题。

用户满意度调查。积极改进用户满意度调查方法，制定《广东省名牌产品评价用户满意度电话调查实施办法》和《广东省名牌产品（工业类）用户满意度评价细则》，实现用户满意度调查的制度化、规范化和科学化。广泛开展网络调查、电话调查工作。据统计，2015年共有66789用户参与了网络调查，共实施58970宗电话调查。同时，除发文征求省工商局、省出入检验检疫局等单位意见外，还征求省食药监局的意见，确保评价出来的名牌具有较高的知名度和满意度。

专家评审工作组织。2015年12月11日，从专家库中随机抽取了66名专家，组成12个评审专业委员会。12月16—18日，在省局监察室、质管处、质监处和稽查局的共同监督下，在河源国家通讯终端产品质检中心，封闭组织专家对申报的682份资料进行评审。同时，改进专家评审工作程序。各专业组分别分成3个小组（一审、二审和汇审），先由一审和二审对每一份材料进行独立打分，然后汇审组进行比较，对出现分差较大的项目提交中心和专家组组长审核裁定，对分值相近的则取其平均值，较好地保证公平公正。此外，评价期间，研究院特别邀请行业协会代表和名牌企业代表进行了全程监督观察，增加了评审工作的透明度和公正性，得到了参评专家、协会代表和名牌企业代表的称赞。

名牌评价质量。2015年12月30日，召开省名牌产品推进委员会全体会议，对卓越质量品牌研究院提交的评价结果进行认真讨论，对近三年来在监督抽查、稽查打假和举报投诉中存在突出问题的19个产品实行一票否决，积极维护广东省名牌产品的声誉。最后，省名推委综合考虑各相关部门意见、申报产品得分、产品质量监督抽查等因素，决定2015年广东省名牌产品（工业类）初选名单共593个，其中复评269个，新申报324个，总的推荐率为87%。

【地理标志工作】

地理标志产品申报。2003年年底“河源米粉”成为广东省第一个获得地理标志保护的产品，实现“零”突破，2015年有9个产品获得保护，累计数量位居全国第三，截至2015年底已有112个产品获得保护，位居全国前列。

获保护产品的经济和社会效益。据2015年广东省质监局对全省获保护产品开展的初步统计数据显示，广东省获保护的地理标志产品年总产值已达265亿元，较保护前的93.8亿元增长183%，受惠农户785813户、养殖户5915户、生产企业91006家，农民年平均收入获保护后达8965元，较获保护前的6500元增长了38%，高出全国农民年平均收入水平2800元，如新会陈皮实施保护后销售价格较保护前增长85%，企业总产值也由保护前的5000万元增至2.5亿元，增幅达180%；如端砚自2004年实施保护后，加工企业数从保护前的400家增至如今的700多家，增幅达75%。至2015年底，广东省质监系统开展的地理标志产品保护工作已惠及全省农户、养殖户达300万人，获保护产品的经济和社会效益得到显著提高，有力地促进县域经济的发展和农民的增收。

广东省农业标准化发展进程。截至2015年底，在广东省获批的地理标志产品中已经制定省地方标准（农业类）94项，已建立国家级农业标准化示范区22个，省级农业标准化示范区52个。大多数地理标志产品均实现标准化种植与生产，“地理标志产品+龙头企业+农户”的经营模式不断推广，有利于推动广东省农业标准化的发展。

地理标志产品保护的后续监管。广东省自实施地理标志产品保护工作以来，一直注重加强地理标志产品保护的后续监管，推动广东省地理标志产品生产企业和种养殖者不断提升产品质量。

一是健全规章制度。截至2015年底，广东省质监局积极推动地方政府出台了地理标志产品保护管理办法50件。如肇庆市政府出台《关于进一步加强广东省地理标志产品保护工作的意见》；江门市新会区政府发布了《新会柑、新会陈皮地理标志产品保护管理办法》《新会区维护和使用地理标志产品品牌的实施方案》等规范性文件；湛江吴川市政府出台《吴川市地理标志产品保护管理办法》；全省其余大部分地方政府对辖区内的地理标志保护产品均出台《地理标志产品保护专用标志使用管理办法》，上述规范性文件的出台，为广东省地理标志产品保护工作的开展提供了坚实的制度保障。

二是加强对地理标志保护产品所在产地及产品质量的监管。湛江吴川市质监局对吴川月饼的生产、管理行为加大监督力度，督促企业严格执行月饼企业联盟标准及相关生产技术规范、质量管理规范，建立规范的生产技术工艺，严格按标准组织生产，确保产品质量符合标准要求，并按标准要求明确标注产品质量等级。

三是加强地理标志产品专用标志管理。截至2015年底，全省质监系统90个国家地理标志产品共有150家企业使用专用标志。江门市新会区质监局依托广东省现代服务业先进标准体系试点项目平台，建立新会陈皮质量可追溯体系，实现生产记录可存储、产品流向可追踪、储运信息可查询的全过程质量信息追溯，消费者可通过扫描地理标志保护产品外包装上的二维码，登录到网络平台进行地理标志真伪辨别及质量安全追溯信息查询。

国家地理标志产品保护示范区。2015年10月25至26日，国家质检总局在江门市新会区召开国家地理标志产品保护示范区（广东新会）验收会，组织对国家地理标志产品保护示范区（广东新会）进行考核验收。考核中，国家质检总局科技司领导要求江门市质监系统要以特产产品实施地理标志保护为手段，通过打造国家地理标志产品保护示范区，做大做强高端特色名牌农业，促使新会柑、新会陈皮形成地标区域品牌。国家质检总局于2015年11月3日正式批准成立该示范区，江门市新会区成为广东省首个获批国家地理标志产品保护示范区的地区，也成为国家质检总局第一个非指定的国家地理标志产品保护示范区试点省份外的获批地区。

【打击质量技术监督领域知识产权违法行为】

2015年，广东省质监系统围绕“重点战役促进日常执法打假”工作思路，针对重点产品、重点行业和重点区域，牵头各有关部门开展各类打假治劣专项行动，与刑事司法建立刑事案件快速移送“绿色通道”，严厉查处、打击侵犯知识产权的违法案件。2015年，全省质监系统共出动执法人员117203人次，立案查处案件4349宗，捣毁窝点167个，移送公安机关案件29宗。在“双打”“质检利剑”等专项行动期间，广东省质监局针对涉嫌存在质量违法问题电子商务产品的案件线索，组织对相关生产企业进行专项执法检查，对存在违法行为的企业进行立案查处，实现从互联网销售追踪到生产企业源头的有效打击，推广“网上发现、源头追溯、落地查处”的电商执法新模式。2015年全省质监系统共出动执法人员2372人次，查处伪造、冒用他人厂名、厂址案件2855宗，并针对投诉较多的皮具、儿童用品、服装、家用电器等电商产品，检查重点生产企业775家/次，立案34宗，累计罚没58.52万元，取得了明显的工作成效。与此同时，加大知识产权案件的查处密度和曝光力度，通过典型案例，造成轰动和热点效应，努力扩大宣传覆盖面和执法影响力，普及市民的知识产权法律意识，形成良好的保护知识产权的法治环境和宣传氛围。

（供稿人：钟培敬）

广东省知识产权局

【概况】 2015年底，有效发明专利量达到138878件，居全国第一。万人发明专利拥有量从2010年的4.02件增长到2015年底的12.95件。PCT国际专利申请量从2010年的6678件增长到2015年的15190件，自2001年至2015年连续十五年保持全国首位，占全国PCT国际专利受理总量的53.49%。《珠三角规划纲要》“四年大发展”监控指标和预定目标超额完成。

【实施知识产权战略】

政策法规。2015年，省政府颁布《广东省深入实施知识产权战略推动创新驱动发展行动计划》明确将广东建设成为国际化知识产权创造运用中心和保护高地，成为知识产权强国建设先行省的目标。珠海、佛山、江门、东莞、清远等市出台支撑创新驱动发展政策。积极争取引领型知识产权强省试点。

实施工作。全国地方战略实施情况中期评估成绩居全国第二位。21个市都出台了当地区的知识产权战略纲要或实施方案。广东省知识产权综合发展指数连续三年位居全国首位。以专利战略推进计划为抓手，省市联动，推动全省工作向纵深发展。广州、深圳、东莞、佛山、中山先后评为国家知识产权示范城市，珠海、湛江、潮州、江门、肇庆、茂名、顺德等14个市（含地级市和县级市）入选国家知识产权试点城市，珠三角地区实现国家试点城市全覆盖。佛山建立市长牵头的联席会议制度并构建特色知识产权强市，东莞成立以市长为组长的市建设国家知识产权示范城市工作领导小组，中山由市长牵头推进示范城市工作。

高层次局省会商。专利审查协作广东中心、国家级区域专利信息服务（广州）中心、知识产权快速维权中心、中小微企业知识产权培训基地、专利信息传播利用基地等在知识产权强国先行地建设、产业专利导航、快速维权、知识产权服务等方面取得突破，在专利信息数据资源完善、“互联网+知识产权”全覆盖系统建设等方面开展合作，对广东转型升级和创新发展起重要支撑作用。

市县知识产权工作。广州花都、越秀、萝岗、佛山禅城、南海5区获评国家知识产权局强县工程示范县（区），广州海珠、番禺、汕头澄海、惠州惠东、韶关武江、梅州梅县等13个县（区）入选国家知识产权强县工程试点县（区）。全省所有地级以上市设立知识产权局，市级拥有知识产权专职人员190人，县（区）知识产权局挂牌113个，挂牌率达到93.4%。市级知识产权专项资金合计近6亿元，县级专项经费合计超2.5亿元。加强与各市的合作，与东莞、揭阳市人民政府建立局市会商合作关系。揭阳以市局会商为平台创建中德（揭阳）中小企业知识产权保护试验区。

【发明创造】

激励机制。省财政每年安排资金带动各市财政资金支持各类创新主体申请专利。广州、惠州、东莞、中山、阳江、湛江、云浮等完善知识产权资助政策。肇庆实施“挖潜、灭零”行动。全省发明专利申请量、授权量分别从2010年的40866件、13691件增长到2015年的103941件、33477件，年均增长达到18.90%和16.39%，2015年增速达38.32%和50.28%，超过“十二五”增长预期目标，实现翻番。

发明专利奖励机制。2015年广东专利奖共评出金奖15项，优秀奖55项，发明人奖9项。2015年第17届中国专利奖评选中，广东省获金奖6个，优秀奖119个，获奖数目再创新高，金奖数目居全国第一。省政府五年共投入近2亿元重奖中国专利奖和广东专利奖获奖单位和个人。

专利申请快速通道。争取国家知识产权局支持，在部分专业镇开通专利申请、授权快速通道，缩短外观设计专利授权周期，从原来的3—4个月缩短至7—10天。

企业知识产权。推广《企业知识产权管

理规范》，获得贯标认证企业31家，扶持贯标辅导机构20家，培训贯标人员近2000人，引进“贯标”认证机构在广东设立办事处。广州、中山、惠州、东莞、佛山等地相继出台贯标扶持政策。佛山实施“鲲鹏”“繁星”和“乘龙”计划。河源、湛江、茂名等培育优势企业。强化知识产权优势示范企业培育，国家级知识产权优势和示范企业达97家，省级优势和示范企业分别达568家及160家。企业知识产权主体地位凸显，五年间，全省8.57万家企业提交专利申请67.95万件，3.46万家企业提交发明专利申请24.3万件。2015年国内企业发明专利授权量前十名的企业中有5家来自广东，国内企业PCT申请受理量排名前十名的企业中有6家来自广东，华为技术有限公司和中兴通讯股份有限公司2015年PCT申请量位列全国前两名。

专利代理和代办服务。组织开展“百所千企知识产权服务对接工程”和“知识产权特派员”系列活动，每年组织代理机构与专业镇、企业对接活动多场。大力扶持专利代理机构发展，专利代理机构、分支机构以及专利代理人数分别从2010年的91家、94家、676人增长到2015年的158家、164家、1455人。组织多场企业发明专利巡回审查活动，加快专利授权进程。2015年，广州、深圳代办处共受理专利申请20多万件，处理专利收费超83万笔，合计金额7.66亿元；办理专利实施许可合同备案1305件；办理专利登记簿副本1.2万件；办理专利权质押登记23件，合同金额20.7亿元。

【专利信息资源】

产业专利分析预警。开展“战略性新兴产业专利信息资源开发利用专项计划”，对LED、新能源汽车、高端新型电子信息、生物医药、云计算、生物医学工程、新一代显示、集成电路等29个广东省重点发展的战略性新兴产业及重点技术领域进行全球专利分析，共立项41项，形成高质量的分析预警报告30份，建立战略性新兴产业专利数据库8个，组织战略性新兴产业专利分析预警发布会23场。培养了一批产业专利分析机构及人才，为广东省知识产权服务业规模化、高端化发展提供了人才储备。

产业专利导航。实施“珠三角重点产业转型升级专利导航工程”，在工业机器人等技术领域开展深度研究，探索根据专利链布局创新链新模式。开展“珠江西岸先进装备制造产业带专利导航工程”，围绕江门市轨道交通装备、肇庆市智能化成形和加工成套设备、顺德区智能装备制造、佛山市汽车制造、中山市电动汽车等5市（区）的5个先进装备制造产业，组织开展专利导航。广州开发区、佛山市整合区域内优质知识产权服务及运营资源，围绕智能装备、卫星通信、机械装备制造等重点产业，开展产业专利导航。广州经济技术开发区入选国家专利导航产业发展实验区，东莞开展工业机器人产业专利导航项目。实施重点出口产品专利预警分析计划，围绕3D电视、半导体照明灯具、蒸汽挂烫机、不锈钢压力锅等广东省重点出口产品，组织项目50项。广州市进出口专利预警平台上线运行。深圳出台全国首个企业境外参展知识产权预警指引地方标准。

重点产业知识产权运营基金。以中央财政专项扶持资金为引导，筹备成立总规模达30亿元、首期规模达5亿元的广东省粤科国联知识产权投资运营基金。目前，该基金已形成2.2亿元的规模，并和中国智能制造领域第一个专利池——工业机器人专利联盟签署战略合作协议，双方将共同推动工业机器人产业领域高价值专利的培育和运营。

产业知识产权联盟。实施“广东省产业专利联盟示范培育工程”，发布《产业知识产权联盟建设指南》。认定顺德电压力锅、中彩联、广东LED联合创新中心（LED）等3家联盟为省专利联盟示范单位，深圳工业机器人专利联盟、新能源标准与知识产权联盟、第三代半导体专利联盟、深圳市医疗器械行业专利联盟等4家联盟列为培育单位。顺德电压力锅专利联盟，大力建设专利和标准“双联盟”，专利池专利数量从初期46项增加至472项。中彩联建立彩电行业专利数据库及预警平台，管理2600多件彩电专利池，基于深度专利分析，使国外彩电专利收费从每台彩电41美元降到20美元以下。深圳制定《深圳市专利联盟管理办法》。全省发展各类产业知识产权产业联盟25个，其中16个在省级备案，5个在国家知识产权局备案。

专利密集型产业。实施专利密集型产业集聚区培育工程，佛山高新区、肇庆高新区顺利通过国家知识产权试点园区试点工作考核验收，东莞松山湖（生态园）高新区获批“国家知识产权试点园区”，广州开发区、深圳高新区、惠州仲恺高新区跻身“国家知识产权示范园区”行列。深圳高新区培育出7家年产值超百亿元的世界知名企业、81家上市公司，诞生了世界第一个U盘、世界第一个基因治疗药物、世界第一台3G-USB液晶电视等多项世界第一；发明专利申请量连续多年居国家级高新区第二位，PCT申请量连续多年居国家级高新区首位。

【专利运营机制】

专利技术实施。至2015年底，累计投入专项资金3905万元，安排项目518项，支持高价值专利技术转化实施。建设国家专利产业化基地，至2015年底，238家企业进驻“国家专利产业化（广州数字家庭）试点基地”，专利池容量5000多件，年产值110亿元；100余家企业进驻“国家工业设计与创意产业（顺德基地）”。发起举办首届南粤知识产权创新创业大赛。

知识产权运营体系。省政府批准由广东省产权交易集团牵头组建“广州知识产权交易中心”，国家知识产权局在珠海横琴设立全国知识产权运营公共服务特色分平台。培育知识产权运营机构13家，在运营能力、模式及市场开拓方面予以指导。中彩联、汇桔网、高航网、7号网、第五大发明等一批民营投资、市场化、网络化知识产权运营机构迅速涌现，知识产权转让、许可、交易市场日益活跃。以中央财政4000万元为引导资金，设立重点产业知识产权运营基金，筹备成立规模达5亿元的广东省粤科国联知识产权投资运营基金，培育和运营重点产业领域的高价值专利。深圳出台《企业专利运营指南》，东莞成立东莞市知识产权交易服务中心，中山建设“广东（灯饰照明）知识产权运营中心”，顺德区建设广东省知识产权创新运用试验区。广州设立运营服务专项资金。深圳搭建O2O网上交易平台。积极推进知识产权许可贸易，2015年，专利实施许可合同备案1308项，涉及专利4104件，合同金额12.3亿元人民币和90万美元。广州、深圳、东莞、佛山等4个国家专利技术展示交易中心累计完成专利展示41250件，专利交易2085件，金额超过6亿元。

知识产权质押融资。发布《知识产权质押评估技术规范》。打造中国（广东）知识产权投融资项目对接会品牌，五年来先后举办先进制造、生物医药、新材料等产业领域的46个知识产权项目与创投企业对接。佛山市南海区创建国家知识产权投融资综合试验区，东莞开展国家专利质押融资试点，顺德区开展国家知识产权投融资服务试点，均取得显著成效，顺利通过验收。佛山、广州、增城开发区、自贸区深圳前海蛇口片区获批开展“国家投融资试点”，惠州仲恺高新区获“国家质押融资试点”，珠海、惠州、江门、湛江获省质押融资试点。深圳构建质押融资再担保体系。佛山、东莞、中山等设立质押融资风险补偿基金。顺德、梅州、江门等补贴质押贷款利息。2015年全省专利质押融资额达58.9亿元。

专利保险试点。广州、深圳、东莞和佛山市禅城区积极开展“全国专利保险试点”。截至2015年底，四地367家企业已累计完成专利投保超过2000件。

知识产权资产评估。支持20家资产评估机构在专利入池、购买、许可、转让、出资及知识产权质押融资等方面，完成40份涉及知识产权的资产评估报告。启动“重大经济科技活动知识产权评议促进计划”，深圳、东莞和佛山南海、江门高新区等7个区域开展试点。广州粤高等3家机构新进入国家分析评议服务示范创建行列并纳入全国联盟。

【知识产权保护】

打击知识产权侵权。建立打击侵权假冒工作长效机制，建立健全行政执法与刑事司法衔接机制，组织互联网领域、农村和城乡结合部、车用燃油、皮具行业、对非出口商品、“护航”、“清风”等多项专项整治行动，大力查处侵权假冒案件。开展专利执法专项行动，集中办案，集中整治，加大重大、复杂案件查处力度。加大对基层执法案件的指导力度，推动全省加强重点领域执法检查。2015年，全省立案查处侵权假冒行政违法案件2.98万件，占全国总量1/6。

执法协作和联合执法。建设华南地区专利行政执法协作调中心，与兄弟省市互派人员开展联合执法，派员参加南宁中国—东盟博览会开展知识产权执法维权工作。严格履行各项协作义务，向重庆市知识产权局移送和通报了在广交会上涉嫌专利侵权的案件和企业。总结执法协作经验，建立闽粤两省沿海城市知识产权保护、九省市专利行政执法协作机制，探索通过执法协作提高执法水平和效率的新模式。东莞、桂林两市多次开展执法座谈会和联合执法行动。

会展知识产权保护。在广交会、加博会、美博会、乐器展、口腔展等重要展会设立知识产权投诉站，维护展会知识产权市场秩序，规范展会专利投诉案件处理规程，提高展会办案质量，已经形成广东展会品牌。国家专利复审委每届广交会派出6位（每期2位）专家现场指导。

电子商务知识产权保护。与唯品会签署《保护知识产权战略合作协议》，支持唯品会、梦芭莎等电商单位建设知识产权保护平台，探索建立“政府有效指导监管+知名网络平台自律保护”相结合的互联网知识产权保护措施和长效机制。着手起草电子商务领域知识产权保护和发展政策性文件。

知识产权快速维权机制。制定《关于加强我省知识产权维权援助工作的指导意见》。全省建设灯饰、家具、家电和皮具4个重点产业快速维权中心，占全国的一半。设立华南地区专利侵权判定中心，顺德探索建立家具专利快速调处中心。全省建设国家级维权援助中心6家；广东省知识产权维权援助中心在省内设立分中心7家、工作站31家。

知识产权纠纷多元解决机制。广州推进行业纠纷人民调解组织建设工作。珠海构建企业自律机制。汕头牵头粤东搭建专利异地维权机制。中山设立全省首家法院远程诉讼服务处。潮州建立纠纷多元化解决机制。珠海、阳江、清远、云浮等制修订执法规程和标准。河源开展执法巡查。汕尾等组织专项执法行动。

【知识产权能力】

专利信息服务能力。完善区域专利信息服务（广州）中心服务功能，构建专利大数据服务平台，拥有全球专利信息达到1亿条。打造“互联网+专利信息”服务新模式，推出手机APP专利检索平台。开展专利信息推送服务，建立省、市、镇、企业4级服务推送工作渠道，向45个专业镇、省内外1300家中小微企业免费推送专利信息，涵盖18个技术领域。开展专利信息服务地市行活动。汕头建设小微企业专利信息推送服务试验区。

知识产权人才培养。实施“百千万知识产权人才工程”，加强国家和省级知识产权人才培训基地建设。建设由知识产权学院、知识产权培训基地、知识产权培训计划、海外知识产权机构巡回演讲计划等组成的多元知识产权培养体系。推进知识产权专业技术资格评定试点工作。佛山成立首个民办知识产权人才学院，东莞理工学院政法学院开设了法学（知识产权方向）双学位，将开展知识产权远程教育。据不完全统计，全省各类知识产权人才达3.6万人。入选国家知识产权专家库专家14人、国家知识产权领军人才23人、“百千万知识产权人才工程”高层次人才31人、全国专利信息领军人才8人、全国专利信息师资人才18人。

知识产权国际交流合作平台。与20多个国家和地区的官方机构、社会团体建立合作关系，截至2015年，与美国、英国、德国、日本、韩国、新加坡、台湾等20多个国家和地区的官方机构、社会团体、企业建立广泛、深入的合作关系，并举办各类国际性知识产权论坛和研讨会28场。举办中、新知识产权局与广东省政府三方会谈，中日韩三国知识产权局长会议等重大外事活动。支持中山灯饰产业与国际知识产权制度接轨。

地区知识产权合作。粤港、粤澳知识产权合作分别被纳入粤港、粤澳合作框架协议。粤台合作不断加强，到2015年共组织赴台湾访问交流9批102人次，成功举办“第八届两岸专利论坛”。积极推进泛珠三角知识产权合作，推进粤疆、粤青、粤蒙等知识产权合作。

高层次知识产权智库。组建广东省知识产权专家咨询委员会，组织开展知识产权软科学研究，加强对知识产权重大理论和政策问题的研究，为省的重大知识产权决策提供依据。成立中策知识产权研究院。

知识产权意识。连续举办知识产权宣传周等重大宣传活动。召开年度知识产权发展状况等多场新闻发布会，及时向社会宣传知识产权工作取得的新成就，取得良好社会效果。拓宽宣传渠道，开通“广东知识产权”“粤知界”微信账号，利用新媒体加强知识产权宣传。佛山发布专利富豪榜和新锐榜并建立企业经理人俱乐部。梅州、韶关等持续开展“正版正货”承诺活动。东莞开展 “知识产权到企业，服务经济镇街行”等系列宣传培训。揭阳举办2015年“泰宝杯”创新创业专利设计大赛。湛江组织大学生外观设计大赛。开展中小学知识产权教育试点、示范工作。

（供稿人：徐靓薇）

广东省人民政府法制办公室

【政府立法】

修订《广东省自主创新促进条例》。该条例规定了研究开发与创造成果、成果转化与产业化、创新性建设人才与服务、激励与保障等方面的制度机制，对提高自主创新能力，推动产业转型升级，促进经济社会发展有积极促进意义。

开展《广东省科技成果转化促进条例》修订工作。该条例明确了促进科技成果转化的基本原则、工作职责和体制机制，规定了保障措施，明确了科技成果转化的“技术权益”，对促进科技成果转化为现实生产力，规范科技成果转化活动，加快实施创新驱动发展战略起积极作用。

【规范性文件审查】 审查《关于全面推进〈企业知识产权管理规范〉国家标准的实施意见》《广东省重大经济和科技活动产权分析评议暂行办法》等规范性文件，对《广东省人民政府关于知识产权服务创新驱动发展若干意见》提出审查意见，为深入实施知识产权战略，推动创新驱动发展战略实施提供制度保障。

（供稿人：林乔昕）

广东省食品药品监督管理局

【监管机构】 2015年，广东省食品药品监督管理局推进市县食品药品监管体制改革，全省21个地级以上市均已出台“三定”并履行新职，119个县（市、区）也已出台“三定”并挂牌运作，在全省1586个乡镇（街道）共设置877个食品药品监管派出机构。增加省旅游局、广州铁路（集团）公司为省食品安全委员会成员单位。一体化、专业化、广覆盖的食品药品监管和产权保护新格局更加完善。

【假冒侵权】

开展专项整治。在食品生产加工环节，开展食用植物油、婴幼儿配方谷粉、配制酒、调味面制品等重点产品的专项整治，取缔49家小作坊；在农村食品安全专项整治中，捣毁农村地区食品制假售假窝点493个；在集体食堂食品安全专项整治中，发出责令改正通知书632份；在药品研制环节，扎实推进药物临床试验数据自查核查工作；在药品生产环节，组织开展血液制品、疫苗、中药注射剂、中药饮片、特殊药品生产经营专项整治；在药品经营领域，加大对药品经营企业飞行检查力度；在医疗器械领域，组织开展“五整治”专项行动“回头看”、体外诊断试剂质量评估和综合治理、打击非法经营装饰性彩色平光隐形眼镜行为等专项检查；在保健食品领域，组织开展“打四非”专项整治；在化妆品领域，继续组织开展“四打一规”专项整治，实施省市县三级联动飞行检查。

大案要案。与省公安厅联合开展“清源行动”“秋风行动”，共同打击食品非法添加，以及肉及肉制品生产经营违法犯罪，查处了一批重大案件。2015年，全省食品药品监管系统共查办食品药品违法案件28415宗，移送公安机关1667宗，吊销生产经营许可证52张，捣毁窝点1428个。

【企业创新】 在全国率先实施医疗器械产品注册全程无纸化办理模式、推行二类创新医疗器械特别审批程序，促进创新医疗器械产品上市，注册各类医疗器械1990件，同比增长116%。坚持对创新药物和治疗重大疑难杂症的药品注册审评审批实施“绿色通道”，推动创新药早日上市，共受理1类新药20件。建立起符合药品特点及监管规律，适应新时期药品技术转让需求的工作机制，完成国家总局委托药品技术转让技术审评13个品种。发布《2014年广东省药品注册年度报告》、形成《广东省生物医药自主创新调研报告》，分析全省药品注册发展趋势，研究提出支持生物医药创新的政策。推动成立广东省生物医药创新技术协会，建立整合各方力量的平台，推进技术开发成果的转化与应用。

【药品标准】 发布《广东省中药配方颗粒标准》第二册，《广东省医疗机构制剂规范》第二册、第三册。组织对广东所有地方药材标准进行了逐一核对，经清理保留药材标准222个、饮片标准70个，更名药材标准6个，废止药材标准20个。

（供稿人：陈勇）

广东省人民政府知识产权办公会议特邀单位

海关总署广东分署

【概况】 2015年，海关总署广东分署协调广东省内海关稳步开展知识产权保护工作，加大对进出口环节侵权行为的打击力度。据“知识产权海关保护执法系统”统计（下同），2015年广东省内海关共查获进出口侵犯知识产权案件1602宗，查扣侵权嫌疑货物2953批次，涉及侵权嫌疑货物约1905万件。

【专项执法行动】

重点商品、重点领域执法。广东省内海关高度重视利用风险分析手段开展查缉工作，总结分析近年来关区查获侵权案件特点，加大对出口到发生侵权风险较高的国家或地区的货物以及侵权高发领域的商品的监控力度；将有侵权记录的企业列入重点监控名单，加强对这类企业的进出境监管；对于多次进出口侵权货物的企业加大处罚力度，从重从快进行处理；针对水客携带侵权物品进出境行为采取更加严厉的管理措施，做到有的放矢，确保监管到位。据统计，2015年广东省内海关通过风险分析手段查获的侵权货物共119批次、涉及侵权嫌疑货物逾1317万件。

专项执法。2015年广东省内海关采取“分阶段、有重点、逐步推进”的方式，开展了针对海运渠道、邮递快件渠道以及互联网领域侵权的专项执法行动；为更好维护“中国制造”的国际形象，积极推进“清风”行动开展，加强对上述重点渠道、重点进出口货物的监管，加大情报分析的力度，在重点口岸部署了专项查缉行动。自“清风”行动开展至2015年底，广东省内海关共查扣侵权出口货物1723万件，制止侵权货物输往84个国家和地区。同时，省内海关结合当地进出口情况，自行组织打击进出口侵权专项行动，强化严打高压态势，发挥示范效应，形成威慑，深化和扩大了成效。

执法合作。广东省内海关全面贯彻国务院发布的《关于做好打击侵犯知识产权和制售假冒伪劣商品工作中行政执法与刑事司法衔接的意见》，根据海关总署与公安部联合下发的《关于加强知识产权执法协作的暂行规定》，开展进出口侵权涉罪案件线索的通报和移送工作。广东分署积极落实与广东省工商局联合签署的关于加强知识产权保护合作的协议，开展与广东省工商行政管理部门在专业咨询、教育培训、专门问题研究等方面的合作。此外，广东省内各海关也在积极研究建立与专利、版权、法院等知识产权行政、司法部门合作长效机制的工作。

【跨区域执法协作】

与香港、澳门海关的知识产权保护合作。进一步完善以侵权案件情况通报为基础、以案件协查为重点、以专项联合执法行动为契机、以交流互访为助力的粤港、粤澳海关知识产权保护合作机制，加强联系配合，进一步遏制了粤港、粤澳两地进出口侵权活动。据统计，2015年，广东省内海关共查获涉及香港、澳门的侵权货物556批次，涉及侵权货物约69.7万件。

粤港、粤澳海关保护知识产权合作机制。一是发挥粤港澳知识产权专项联络员联络机制。粤港、粤澳海关专职联络员开展定期会晤和日常联络，及时交换两地海关查获的有关侵权案件信息，交流侵权案件情报，促进双方各形式、各层次的交流沟通，粤港、粤澳海关保护知识产权的联系配合更加紧密。二是以“情报”交换为基础，强化粤港澳海关信息交流和资源共享的效能。广东分署与香港、澳门海关坚持每月定期通报相互查获的涉港、涉粤侵权案件信息。广东分署要求省内有关海关对香港、澳门海关通报的侵权案件信息逐项予以核查、分析和反馈，督促对重点企业和重点口岸加强监管力度；继续尝试开展事前情报交流以及粤港、粤澳进出口侵权状况趋势性和综合性分析，以便更具针对性地加强对跨境侵犯知识产权违法行为的打击力度。2015年底，粤港海关通过即时情报交换，在广州南沙港成功查获申报出口的侵权化妆品近6万件，该案是至2015年几年间粤港海关点对点情报合作查获的最大一起侵权案件。

知识产权跨境保护。粤港、粤澳海关坚持开展集中打击重点区域、重点环节进出口侵权货物的专项联合执法行动。针对粤港两地通过邮递快件渠道进出口侵权货物情况有所蔓延发展的情况，广东分署组织省内海关与香港海关联手开展了打击邮递快件、海运和汽运渠道侵权违法活动的专项合作。2015年度与香港海关举行了2次打击侵权违法活动联合执法行动，其中，在针对邮递快件渠道专项行动中，深圳海关查获涉嫌侵权案件6宗，扣留涉嫌侵权产品1760件，涉及手机、电子屏、皮带等货物物品；在打击海运和汽运渠道输往香港和经香港去往非洲地区的侵权高发商品联合执法行动中，共查获涉嫌侵权货物8批次，涉嫌侵权物品约1.6万件，价值人民币约34.8万元。

2015年，粤澳海关在闸口及横琴口岸开展了打击以旅检以及货运渠道，经拱北海关口岸输往澳门或者经由澳门输往其他国家或者地区的侵权货物的联合执法行动。行动期间，广东有关海关将食品、药品、消费电子产品等商品列为重点监控商品，异地经营单位列为重点监控企业，现场查验布控13票；在旅检渠道方面，对多次进出境往返旅客携带的行李物品实施重点查验，加强车流分析和司乘人员流动排查。通过粤澳热线进行信息、资料互换7次。

交流研讨。粤港、粤澳海关充分利用海关联络员会议、业务联席会议、保护知识产权专题会议等制度开展各层次的会晤交流，及时沟通知识产权保护工作情况，探讨进一步合作的要点。此外，2015年6月，广东分署继续为香港海关承办第九期海关管理发展课程之中国海关考察研修班，向香港海关人员介绍广东海关知识产权执法工作。

【宣传活动】 广东省内海关以开展“清风”行动及“4·26”知识产权宣传周、“8·8”法制宣传日、全国“质量月”为契机，不断加强知识产权海关保护的宣传工作，通过互联网、政策宣讲会、新闻报道等多种形式宣传报道广东省内海关知识产权保护工作，宣讲海关知识产权法律和政策，为公众答疑解惑。在“4·26”知识产权宣传周期间，广东省内海关集中开展了针对进出口企业、进出境旅客的宣传活动以及侵权货物的销毁活动，推动了社会各界对海关打击侵权假冒工作的认知，提高了守法的自觉性。2015年11月，全国“双打”办联合中宣部外宣局，组织20家中央外宣媒体对广东省内海关开展中国制造海外形象维护“清风”行动进行了专题采访，40多家中央外宣媒体、网络媒体刊载广东省海关“清风”行动阶段性成果。

广东省内海关还依托“12360”海关统一服务热线，完善知识产权社会举报受理处置机制，鼓励社会各界人士举报进出口侵权违法行为，同时宣传海关知识产权保护规定和执法政策，回应社会各界对海关知识产权保护工作的关切。

（供稿人：刘雨）

广东省高级人民法院

【概述】 2015年，广东省高级人民法院（下称广东高院）加强知识产权司法保护，依法履行民事、刑事和行政审判职能，公正高效审理各类知识产权案件，加强知识产权审判领域改革创新，完善知识产权审判体制机制，充分发挥知识产权审判的职能作用，为全面深化改革和实施创新驱动发展战略提供了有力的司法服务和司法保障。

【审判职能】

民事审判。2015年，全省新收知识产权民事一审案件23766件，同比减少0.56%；新收二审案件6132件，同比增长11.37%。全年共审结知识产权民事一审案件20215件，同比减少18.03%，结案率为75.04%，同比下降18.13个百分点；审结知识产权民事二审案件6272件，同比增长13.32%，结案率为93.63%，同比上升2.74个百分点；二审发改案件224件，发改率为3.57%，同比上升1.06个百分点。广东高院新收各类知识产权案件827件，审结982件。

刑事审判。2015年，全省新收知识产权刑事一审案件6780件，同比增长65.20%，占全省新收一审刑事案件总数5.25%，同比上升1.30个百分点；全省审结知识产权刑事一审案件6621件，同比增长68.56%，占全省审结一审刑事案件总数5.49%，同比上升1.67个百分点。其中，审结生产、销售伪劣商品罪3255件3982人；假冒注册商标罪1047件2215人；销售假冒注册商标的商品罪649件1100人；非法制造、销售非法制造的注册商标标识罪192件319人；侵犯著作权罪248件275人；侵犯商业秘密罪11件20人。

行政审判。2015年，全省新收知识产权行政一审案件22件，审结22件，同比分别增长13.33%和10%；新收知识产权行政二审案件16件，审结18件，同比分别增长5.88%和

28.57%。在有力地促进行政执法机关充分发挥职能作用、强化知识产权行政保护的同时，又依法有效地监督行政机关依法行政。

审结情况。审结南京微盟电子有限公司诉泉芯电子技术（深圳）有限公司侵害集成电路布图设计专有权纠纷案，通过日常生活常理与行业经验的分析认定，探讨了《集成电路布图设计保护条例》第三十三条第一款不视为侵权的条件规定；审结广州医药集团有限公司诉广东加多宝饮料食品有限公司、彭某虚假宣传纠纷案，准确把握了虚假宣传判断的要件与判断的时间点，划清了客观正当行使权利与不正当竞争的界限，发挥了规范市场秩序、引导正当竞争的判例导向作用；审结珠海格力电器股份有限公司诉广东美的制冷设备有限公司、珠海市泰锋电业有限公司侵害商标权及不正当竞争纠纷案，明确注册商标未实际使用的，商标权人无权请求侵权人承担损害赔偿责任；审结广东联塑科技实业有限公司诉江苏联塑高分子材料有限公司侵害商标权及不正当竞争纠纷案，厘清商标使用行为在侵害商标权与不正当竞争中的界限和成立要件，认定将他人注册商标登记为企业名称的行为构成不正当竞争；审结广州市格风服饰有限公司诉杭州娅品贸易公司、东莞市牛尊鞋业有限公司侵害商标权纠纷案，在判断商品是否类似时，坚持避免来源混淆的基本原则，综合考虑商品的功能、用途、生产部门、销售渠道、消费群体等是否相同或者具有较大的关联性；审结顾芳诉中国南方航空股份有限公司拒绝交易纠纷案，指出航空公司取消预定航班的行为并非为了达到排除或限制竞争的目的，且我国现行的法律法规也并不禁止该行为，消费者基于拒绝交易纠纷的相关规定来主张权利不符合反垄断法的立法宗旨。2015年，全省法院有1件案件入选最高法院公布的中国法院10大知识产权案件，1件案件入选中国法院10大创新性知识产权案件，7件入选中国法院50件典型知识产权案例。

【体制机制创新】

“探索完善司法证据制度破解知识产权侵权损害赔偿难”试点工作。2014年7月，最高法院副院长陶凯元在全国法院知识产权审判工作座谈会上提出“加大损害赔偿力度，充分实现知识产权的市场价值”的要求。为贯彻最高法院这一重要司法政策和工作要求精神，广东高院以充分实现知识产权的市场价值为目标和统领，进一步加大对知识产权侵权损害赔偿数额司法认定办法的研究。在总结前期试点工作经验的基础上，2015年3月30日，广东高院下发了《关于确定广东法院“探索完善司法证据制度破解知识产权侵权损害赔偿难”第二批试点法院的通知》，扩大了“赔偿难”试点法院的范围，增加了广州知识产权、珠海、惠州、江门、肇庆等5个中级法院和广州市越秀区等12个基层法院作为试点单位。以真正实现知识产权的市场价值为目标，指导各级法院把握试点案件范围，发挥办案法官在案件审理中适用证据规则的主导作用，细化认定侵权损害赔偿数额的操作程序和法律规则，成功审结了广州格风公司与杭州娅品公司侵害商标权纠纷案等典型案件。

跨区域管辖知识产权案件。经最高法院同意，新增广州市黄埔区、阳江市江城区等2个法院管辖一般知识产权案件，至此广东省有一般知识产权案件管辖权基层法院数量增加至35个。同时深入分析全省案件增长态势和审判力量等情况，进一步向最高法院申请调整广州市越秀区、天河区和萝岗区等3个基层法院跨区域管辖第一审一般知识产权民事案件的地域范围，申请佛山市禅城区、珠海市香洲区、惠州市惠城区、肇庆市端州区、清远市清城区等5个基层法院跨区域集中管辖所在市第一审一般知识产权民事案件，并获得最高法院批复同意。基层法院跨区域集中管辖能够有效解决案多人少的矛盾，促进中级法院和基层法院知识产权审判队伍建设，集中中级法院、省法院的优质审判资源应对案情复杂、诉讼标的额较大、社会影响大的案件。

知识产权法院建设。根据最高法院关于明确广州知识产权法院定位的要求，广东高院进行研究后认为，广州知识产权法院可利用广东的优势，定位为知识产权司法保护与市场价值研究基地，建议并促成“最高人民法院知识产权司法保护与市场价值研究（广东）基地”在广州知识产权法院挂牌成立。针对广州知识产权法院在成立初期面临着许多问题和困难，广东高院根据最高法院的要求及广州知识产权法院的需求，推进广州知识产权法院的建设工作。针对珠三角部分地市及部分人大代表、政协委员提出的设立广州知识产权法院派出法庭的意见和建议，广东高院会同广州知识产权法院进行了深入调研，认为从长远来看可对专门法院设立派出法庭问题进行研究论证并在适当的时候分阶段加以推进，但是现阶段设置广州知识产权法院派出法庭的条件尚不成熟。同时，为了落实诉讼“两便”原则，广州知识产权法院在中山市古镇设立全省首家远程诉讼服务处，提供包括立案咨询、指导调解、案件查询、远程答疑、远程接访、法治宣传等在内的一系列诉讼服务功能，作为广州知识产权法院立案窗口的延伸，并进一步探索推广远程视频开庭，把司法为民落在实处。针对广州知识产权法院干警待遇较低、吸引力有限的问题，广东高院起草了《关于提高广州知识产权法院干警待遇的报告》报省委，争取在省委和省委政法委领导的支持下予以协调解决。

司法公开。推动全省法院上网公布知识产权裁判文书，建立规范化、制度化和常态化的裁判文书发布机制，广东省法院在中国知识产权裁判文书网发布裁判文书总量排名全国第一位。不断扩大庭审公开程度，邀请人大代表、政协委员、新闻媒体、专家学者、高校学生等社会各界人士旁听庭审。“新百伦”商标侵权纠纷、“奥的斯”商标侵权纠纷、“梦特娇”商标侵权纠纷、“达芙妮”商标侵权及不正当竞争纠纷等10余件社会关注度较高案件的公开开庭通过网络全程视频直播。2015年“4·26知识产权宣传周”期间，举行了广东省法院新闻发布会，发布了2014年度广东省知识产权司法保护状况白皮书和广东省十大知识产权典型案例。邀请人大代表、政协委员、高校学生团体及十余家媒体单位到庭观摩旁听美的公司与格力公司侵害商标权纠纷上诉案公开开庭，并通过广东法院网、金羊网直播庭审全过程，在现场直播过程中还由法官进行实时解说。

业务交流。全省法院注重与行政管理部门、高等院校、行业协会和国外知识产权保护机构之间的沟通交流，介绍广东知识产权审判经验，深入交流探讨专利法、商标法、著作权法的热点难点问题，就专利法第四次修改的相关工作进行座谈，并提出相关的修改意见，共同促进知识产权保护水平的提高；与知识产权司法鉴定机构进行座谈，就开展知识产权鉴定工作的情况、华南地区知识产权侵权纠纷类型和特点、广东省知识产权审判工作对司法鉴定的具体需求等内容开展交流。派出业务骨干百余人次参加最高法院、全国各法院、行政部门、高等院校及行业协会召开的高端学术研讨会和国际性交流活动，如“互联网+时代知识产权保护热点问题”研讨会、“互联网+民商事案件热点难点问题高端论坛”、第八届两岸专利论坛、第十四届互联网大会、“创新驱动发展战略背景下的知识产权司法保护高端研讨会”、“标准专利许可与反垄断规制”研讨会等。

【监督指导】

审判情况分析通报机制。运用审判情况分析通报、分类指导和沟通协调三项工作机制，依法加强审判监督指导。每季度对全省各项审判数据进行统计分析并印发《全省知识产权审判工作统计分析情况的通报》，加强对工作发展趋势的分析研判，以便提早谋划，积极应对，使监督指导工作更具科学性、前瞻性和有效性。针对广州、深圳等地存案数量较多的情况，及时进行分析并报告院党组，指导当地法院落实清理案件的工作。

沟通协调机制。随着广州知识产权法院

挂牌成立，集中管辖全省（除深圳外）的专利等技术性较强的第一审知识产权民事和行政案件，广州知识产权法院在广东知识产权审判工作中的重要性凸显。加强广东高院与广州知识产权法院之间审判业务工作的沟通协调既是提升广东法院知识产权审判质效的迫切需要，也是司法改革新形势下解决全国知识产权法院乃至各专门法院上下级沟通协调的必然要求。为此，广东高院在既维护审级独立，又有利于上级法院加强监督指导的原则下，研究出台了《关于加强与广州知识产权法院审判业务工作沟通协调的若干意见》，对广东高院和广州知识产权法院审判业务工作的沟通协调进行了规范，保障该项工作能够依法依规、规范高效地运行。在此基础上，进一步制订了《关于加强全省法院知识产权审判业务工作沟通协调的若干意见》，加强对全省知识产权审判工作的监督指导。

典型案例收集整理发布。全省法院及时收集、整理已审结的重大、疑难、复杂和新类型知识产权案件，报送到广东高院进行分析汇总，分别形成了2015年第一批和第二批典型案例，报送给最高法院并通过广东高院自媒体向全社会公开发布，对于提高全省知识产权案件审判质量和统一裁判尺度具有积极意义。

（供稿人：裘晶文）

广东省人民检察院

【概况】 2015年，广东省检察机关切实维护广大知识产权权利人和消费者的合法权益，严厉打击侵犯知识产权犯罪行为，加大行政执法与刑事司法衔接力度，充分发挥检察机关在知识产权保护中的保障和促进作用。

【知识产权犯罪】 2015年，全省检察机关共批准逮捕涉及侵犯知识产权犯罪案件1585件2876人，提起公诉2071件3823人；批准逮捕涉及生产销售伪劣商品犯罪案件2588件3615人，提起公诉3059件4059人。2015年，全省检察机关民事行政检察部门办理知识产权民事、行政诉讼监督案件6件，提出抗诉5件，依法维护知识产权人合法权益，打击侵权行为。

【行政执法与刑事司法相衔接机制】 2015年年底前实现了省直行政执法与刑事司法衔接信息共享平台与各市平台在网上信息互通，共有3059件侵犯知识产权案件录入平台。

【跨行政区域知识产权专门检察院】 2015年，深圳市检察院在《深圳市人民检察院关于加强服务保障中国（广东）自由贸易试验区前海蛇口片区和前海深港现代化服务业合作区建设的意见》中提出探索成立跨行政区知识产权专门检察院。针对珠海市知识产权刑事案件主要集中在香洲区的情况，珠海市检察院就知识产权刑事案件跨区域集中受理问题，多次与法院等相关部门进行了沟通、协调，最终由珠海市香洲区人民检察院管辖珠海市各基层检察院办理审查批捕和审查起诉的“知识产权罪”案件。2015年3月18日，珠海市检察院正式印发《珠海市人民检察院办理知识产权案件工作规则》，标志着珠海市知识产权刑事案件跨区域审理诉讼格局正式形成，保障案件的专业化办理和统一性法律适用。

【广东自贸区建设】 省检察院郑红检察长亲自主持制定《保障中国（广东）自由贸易试验区建设的若干意见》，着力服务保障创新驱动发展战略，严厉打击发生在自贸区内的侵犯知识产权犯罪，主动为自贸区内企业提供法律咨询、法律服务，促进自贸区建设营造国际化、法治化营商环境。珠海市检察院根据《2015年广东自贸试验区珠海横琴片区改革创新发展总体方案》在横琴新区人民检察院挂牌成立了“广东自贸试验区横琴片区知识产权检察工作站”，为充分发挥工作站的职能作用，珠海横琴检察院专门指定一名主任检察官负责该站的日常事务及与市检察院高新区知识产权检察室的联系工作，切实保障其工作规范有序运转，为横琴自贸片区建设提供有力的服务和支持。

【知识产权保护宣传】 全省检察机关通过加大在广播、电视、报刊、网络、微博等媒体进行知识产权法制宣传的力度，引导和促进市场主体依法诚信经营，增强其维权意识，营造全社会尊重知识产权的氛围。如中山市检察院在依法批准逮捕制假售假的相关嫌疑人后，通过《中山日报》《中山商报》《南方都市报》等报刊及相关微信平台，公布案件的办理情况，消除广大市民疑虑和恐慌，有力震慑和打击此类制假售假的犯罪。

（供稿人：刘月星）

ZHI SHI CHAN QUAN CH

知识产权创造

- 专利
- 商标
- 地理标志
- 植物新品种
- 重大知识产权获奖成果

专　利

专利申请及授权

【概况】 2015年广东省专利申请受理量、发明专利申请量、外观设计专利申请量位居全国第二位，广东省实用新型专利申请受理量居全国第三位。

1—12月份，广东省发明专利授权量居全国第二位。

2015年，PCT国际专利申请受理量居全国第一，连续十四年保持全国首位。

截至2015年12月底，广东省有效发明专利量居全国第一，每万人口发明专利拥有量居全国第四位。

【主要特点】

专利申请受理量、授权量双双呈现爆发性增长态势。2015年，广东省专利申请受理量为355939件，同比增长27.87%。比全国平均水平19.00%高8.87个百分点。专利授权量241176件，同比增长34.02%，比全国平均水平32.00%高2.02个百分点。专利申请受理量、授权量均仅次于江苏省居全国第二。

专利申请受理量累计超过两百万件。截至2015年底，广东省累计专利申请受理量为2234620件，突破专利申请两百万件大关。其中，发明专利申请受理量为550757件，实用新型专利申请受理量733638件，外观设计专利申请受理量950225件。

发明专利申请受理量首次突破十万件。2015年广东省发明专利申请受理量首次突破十万件，达103941件，同比增长38.32%，排名超过北京市、山东省重回全国第二名。数据显示，发明专利申请受理增幅比上年同期高29.39个百分点，广东省创新主体创造能力不断增强，科技创新正成为引领经济新常态的重要力量。

PCT国际专利申请受理量连续十四年领跑全国。2015年，广东省PCT国际专利申请受理量15190件，同比增长13.94%，占国内PCT国际专利申请受理总量的53.49%，连续十四年保持全国第一。2008年起，广东省PCT国际专利申请受理量连续八年稳占全国半壁江山。

有效发明专利量六年蝉联全国首位。2015年，广东省有效发明专利总量达138878件，较2014年同比增长24.13%，连续六年保持全国首位。统计数据显示，广东省有效发明专利年限主要集中在二至八年，占有效发明专利总量的81.00%。有效发明专利年限十年以上的占比10.59%，比上年同期8.93%高1.66个百分点。

企业专利申请占全省专利申请半壁江山。广东省共有25987家企业申请专利，合计为205675件，同比增长37.42%，增长超过5万件，占广东省专利申请受理量的57.78%；23866家企业获得专利授权，合计141112件，同比增长35.43%，占全省专利授权总量的58.51%。其中，11462家企业有发明专利申请，合计73243件，同比增长35.89%，占全省发明专利申请受理量的70.47%，占企业专利申请总量的35.61%；5819家企业有发明专利授权，合计26019件，占全省发明专利授权的77.72%。企业作为创新主体的地位持续稳固，在自主创新中继续发挥决定性作用。

大批中小型企业正成为专利申请的第二梯队。2015年，拥有1件专利申请的企业为6627家，同比增长27.17%；拥有2—10件专利申请的企业为15976家，合计70469件，比2014年同期增加4141家20859件；拥有11—50件专利申请的企业为3103家，合计58894件，比2014年同期增加877家15932件。由此可见，科技型中小企业专利申请呈现快速增长态势，成为2015年度专利增长的有力推手。在华为、中兴等龙头企业领跑的同时，大批中小型企业正成为专利申请的又一生力军。

全省大部分地市专利申请授权增速明显。2015年，全省20个地级以上市的专利申请保持正增长。其中，深圳等19个地级以上市发明专利申请均保持正增长，清远市增长率超过100%。值得注意的是，全省21个市的专利授权均保持正增长。其中，深圳等19个地级以上市发明专利授权均保持正增长，阳江、汕尾、茂名、清远、佛山（不含顺德区）、韶关、珠海七市的发明专利授权增长率超过100%。

珠三角区域专利实力稳步提升。2015年，珠江三角洲区域的专利申请受理量占了全省专利申请受理量的89.67%，同比增长28.27%；其中，发明专利申请受理量占全省发明专利申请受理量的95.82%，同比增长38.24%。深圳、东莞、广州、佛山四市的专利申请受理量均超过38000件，发明专利申请均超过10000件。

（供稿人：洪伟）

商 标

【概况】 2015年，广东省商标申请量512857件，占全国申请总量的19.29%；广东省商标注册量395601件，占全国年注册量的19.04%；商标有效注册量1659477件，占全国商标有效注册量的18.03%，自1995年以来连续二十一年居全国首位。2015年广东省的商标申请量创历史新高，是排名全国第二的北京市的近1.7倍，比泛珠三角区域其他8省申请量总和还多8.67万件；年度商标注册量是排名第二的浙江省的近1.88倍，比泛珠三角区域其他8省年度商标注册量总和还多4.81万件；商标有效注册量是排名第二的浙江省的1.44倍，比泛珠三角区域其他8省商标有效注册量总和还多13.29万件。

【马德里商标国际注册】 2015年，广东省马德里商标国际注册申请量588件，累计有效注册量4550件，居全国第二位。

【地理标志商标注册】 2015年，广东省新增“水东芥菜”“高州龙眼”“大埔杏花瓷”3件地理标志证明商标，全省已注册的地理标志证明商标、集体商标共38件。全省已注册地理标志证明商标、集体商标量排名前三位的地级以上市是肇庆、茂名、佛山，分别为8件、7件、5件。

（供稿人：陈小冰）

地理标志

标准与地理标志

2015年，广东省大力推进“质量强省”建设，以标准助推广东经济发展，继续推动地理标志产品保护。全年获批地理标志保护产品9个（累计112个，总量居全国第三位），获批成立的国家地理标志保护产品示范区1个（广东新会），全省质监系统90个国家地理标志产品共有150家企业使用专用标志。批准实施战略性新兴产业地方标准58项（累计364项），批准成立省级专业标准化技术委员会 3项（累计43项），制定地理标志产品省级标准（农业类）3项（累计94项），累计建立国家级农业标准化示范区22个、省级示范区52个。2015年，全省企事业单位主导或参与制修订国际标准167项（累计1041项）、国家标准254项（累计4061项）、行业标准317项（累计3385项）、地方标准289项（累计1855项），制定高于国际、国家或行业标准的企业（联盟）标准8215项（累计44862项）。

（供稿人：钟培敬）

地理标志产品

【概况】 2015年广东省获得国家地理标志保护的9个产品中，都具有鲜明的地方特色，源自特定的自然环境和人文环境，传递着浓厚的岭南文化气息。

【连平鹰嘴蜜桃】 因产于河源市连平县而得名。连平鹰嘴蜜桃是连平县最负盛名的名优特产，也是目前广东乃至中国南方最好的桃类品种，被农科专家誉为“桃之极品”。其色泽鲜亮，果大形美，肉质脆嫩，清甜爽口，风味独特且价格适宜，深受广大消费者喜爱。连平鹰嘴蜜桃至今已有三十多年的种植历史，目前种植面积达6万亩，产值约8亿元，农民净收入约6亿元，畅销珠三角、港澳地区乃至全国各地。2005年11月，连平县被中国特产之乡推荐暨宣传活动组织委员会确认为“中国鹰嘴蜜桃之乡”，2011年10月，连平鹰嘴蜜桃获得“岭南十大佳果”的称号。

【莞香】 因原产于东莞市而得名。莞香是以莞香树为载体，在特定环境及使用传统有机方法产生的含油脂的固态结晶体，是东莞市特有的珍贵特产和东莞文化的载体。莞香历史悠久，在唐宋朝开始已普遍种植，截至目前全市达到结香数龄的莞香树超过10万株，年产量约1000公斤，年产值约1亿元。莞香的应用非常广泛，可用于入药，具有行气镇痛、温中止呕、纳气平喘等功效，对于治疗腹胀、胃寒、肾虚、气喘有明显疗效，也可用于制作香料、净化空气以及雕塑等。2012年，“莞香生产与制作工艺”进入第四批广东省级非物质文化遗产名录并作为特邀项目参展了第二届中国非物质文化遗产博览会。

【始兴石斛】 始兴石斛种植历史悠久，南朝华阳隐居陶弘景在整理古代《神农本草经》中云：“今用石斛，出始兴（也就是今天的韶关市始兴县）。”始兴石斛具有较高的药用价值、经济价值和人文价值。药用可配药，作保健品，《本草纲目》记载铁皮石斛：“除痹下气，补五脏虚劳羸瘦，强阴益精，轻身延年，健阳……”吃用可煲汤、泡茶、浸酒、配菜等，还可作花卉观赏。2014年始兴县累计种植始兴石斛1250亩，年产石斛鲜条374吨，年产值1.4亿元。目前始兴石斛已畅销广东、北京、江西、四川、香港等地，成为人们馈赠亲朋好友的佳品和社会交往的珍贵礼品，享有较高的知名度，深受广大消费者的好评。

【石湾玉冰烧酒】 石湾玉冰烧酒诞生于佛山市禅城区石湾镇，因其观而玉洁冰清、闻而豉香独特、酒体醇和细腻、余味甘爽，大受当地民众欢迎，该独特的石湾玉冰烧酒酿制技艺也一直传承至今。目前主要销售分布区域是广东、广西、海南、河南、福建等省区和西安、天津、乌鲁木齐、上海、北京等主要城市，以及加拿大、美国、澳大利亚、新西兰、新加坡、马来西亚、东南亚一带和港澳等国家和地区，出口量一直名列中国白酒出口量前茅。“石湾牌玉冰烧酒”荣获2012年度广东酒类市场“畅销品牌”以及2013年度广东酒类市场“受消费者欢迎产品”和“畅销品牌”称号。

【高要巴戟天】 高要巴戟天产于肇庆市高要区。巴戟天，又名“鸡肠风”，常被简称为“巴戟”，《本草纲目》注：巴戟天根气味辛、甘、微温、无毒，主治风湿、脚气、肾虚、阳痿。据有关记载，早在清·康熙五十五年（1715年）就在高要县禄步镇大榕云碌坑有人种植，距今已有二百七十多年的历史。目前高要巴戟天种植面积达9000多亩，平均亩产2500公斤，年销售5625吨左右。高要巴戟天因其质量上乘，药用成分耐斯糖含量高，远销东南亚、台港澳以及北京、上海、四川、云南、深圳、广州等地。

【罗浮山大米】 产于惠州市博罗县，有着悠久的栽培历史，水稻的种植历史可追溯至汉代。由于罗浮山钟灵秀气，土地肥沃，水质矿物质丰富，环境极佳，种出的稻米外形晶莹洁白，米粒细长苗条，米泛丝光，口味清香，柔滑爽口，营养丰富。2014年博罗县现有参保水稻种植面积达32万亩，全年粮食总产量16.94万吨，产值约6.8亿元。由于当地政府大力重视和扶持，罗浮山大米如今已成为博罗县粮食种植和生产加工业的支柱产业之一，产品已远销至东南亚等地区。罗浮山大米于2010年获广东省名牌产品称号，2008年获得广东省粮食行业协会授予的“放心米”称号。

【柏塘山茶】 产于惠州市博罗县柏塘镇。根据《广东省志·农业志》的有关记载，自明以来，博罗便是广东较早的产茶区之一，所产罗浮山茶也是岭南四大名茶之一。由于博罗种植的山茶以柏塘镇品种最为传统、种植分布最广、茶叶品质最佳，因而柏塘山茶被公认为罗浮山茶的代表。加之柏塘镇地势群峰相连，峡谷纵横，气候温和，冬暖夏凉，雨量充沛，如自然环境与条件非常有利于茶树的发育和生长，非常有利于茶多酚和高芳香物质的形成。因此柏塘山茶具有外形紧结、色泽油润、香气天然、汤色柔亮、回味甘甜、叶底柔嫩等特征。目前柏塘镇种植山茶的农户有4000多户。2014年茶叶产值约4.8亿元，茶农人均收入达3.9万元。柏塘山茶目前已远销至港澳以及东南亚地区，成为博罗县名优特产。

【观音阁花生】 产于惠州市博罗县观音阁镇。观音阁镇种植花生至今已有三百多年的历史，其品种多为小粒种，种子一直沿用前人留下来的土种，当地人称为“百日掂”。因观音阁镇地处博罗东南沿江丘陵区，拥有丰厚的东江系土壤与谷底冲积地，因此其花生种植时间最长，且质量上乘。近年来，观音阁镇花生种植已达1.2万亩，全年总产量达到2400吨。同时，近年来当地政府致力于观音阁花生的品牌推广和经济价值提升，并利用观音阁镇得天独厚的生态环境及旅游资源，如2010年11月珠三角户外活动圈著名的“磨房@惠州60公里徒步”（第八届）在观音阁镇举行，一时间汇集了数千名来自台湾、香港、澳门、广东等地的运动员。当地政府借助此次活动平台，组织了5个专业合作社和东江原生态美食协会进行以观音阁花生为主的特色农产品展销。同年12月，“观音阁镇第一届花生美食节”在观音阁开幕。

【汶朗蜜柚】 产于肇庆市怀集县。当地农户种植该产品的历史悠久。据民间传说，清康熙年间在现汶朗镇的汶塘、草朗等地已有蜜柚种植。汶朗蜜柚保持一般柚子的基本特征，外观和风味又具有独特之处，且因其果肉甜脆无渣，生津消食，故具有宽中理气、化痰止咳等保健食疗价值。近年来当地政府十分重视汶朗蜜柚的种植与发展，通过举办推介会、种植能力大赛、产销对接签约活动和参加肇庆市举办的“肇庆金秋”经贸洽谈会等活动，大力介绍和宣传汶朗蜜柚，吸引众多新闻媒体、网络和广播电视的大量报道。美国植物学家艾伦博士于2014年9月18日前往汶朗镇蜜柚基地参观考察并品尝汶朗蜜柚后，对其独特品质赞不绝口。目前汶朗蜜柚种植面积已达1.2万亩，带动种植户2500户，年产量达8000吨，产品销往珠三角以及港澳等地区。

（供稿人：钟培敬）

农产品地理标志

【概况】 2015年，广东省新增登记农产品地理标志5个，其中完成初审农产品4个。截至2015年12月，累计登记农产品地理标志12个，对发展区域经济、打造特色品牌、增强农产品核心竞争力发挥作用。

【激励机制】 从激励政策和全力服务品牌发展入手，鼓励具有一定实力的农业技术推广部门、科研院所和协会积极开展地理标志产品登记工作，推进全省农产品地理标志组织申报。明确扶持重点，对前景良好的潜在农产品地理标志申请人每个产品给予10万元补助，加大了农产品地理标志登记的积极性。同时在指导各级工作机构和申请主体调研规划、产品检测、评估申报、现场检查、材料审核和资料编制，协助解决申报过程中的存在问题。全年新增登记农产品地理标志5个，其中大埔蜜柚列为中欧地理标志互认产品目录和创建国家级农产品地理标志示范样板，共培训核查及品牌建设人员24人次。

【证后监管】 突出抓好农产品地理标志产品的规范化管理工作。开展地理标志农产品标志使用综合检查，各市至少对2—3家有代表性的超市、农贸市场重点对标示“地理标志农产品”的产品进行了包装标识的检查。省农业厅中心组织检查组到广州、云浮和韶关市等市进行现场检查，共抽查了10家大型超市和3家农贸市场，对伪造、冒用标志、超范围用标等不规范用标行为对违规企业进行查处。

【产品宣传】 充分利用多途径多方式宣传地理标志产品，不断提升品牌效应。一是结合“3·15国际消费者权益日”活动，向广大群众派发宣传资料，提高消费者对地理标志产品的认知，维护生产者和消费者合法权益。二是发动4家农产品地理标志登记单位参加第十三届中国国际农产品交易会。三是推荐地理标志产品参加《源味中国》纪录片拍摄。四是与《农民日报》《南方农村报》等多家新闻媒体合作，广泛宣传农产品地理标志，引导绿色消费，提高人们对农产品地理标志的认知程度。五是协助江门市、新会区、大埔县和连州市成功举办了“江门凉瓜节”“新会陈皮节”“大埔蜜柚茗茶节”“连州菜心节”和广州“荔湾连州心连心”的水晶梨品尝推介会。通过宣传推介活动促进农产品地理标志事业发展和品牌保护。

（供稿人：杨艳芹）

植物新品种

农业植物新品种

【概况】 2015年，广东省审定通过农作物新品种137个，其中水稻59个，玉米19个，花生1个，马铃薯4个，甘薯3个，蔬菜7个，果树12个，花卉30个，中药材2个。申请农业植物新品种权70个，涉及水稻、玉米、花生等作物种类，获得农业植物新品种授权51件，比2014年增加39件，其中水稻32件，玉米4件，大豆7件，棉花4件，油菜2件，小麦和花卉各1件。截至2015年12月，累计申请植物新品种权323件，获得授权133件，申请量和授权量分别位列全国第14位和第16位。

（供稿人：刘凯）

林业植物新品种

【概况】 2015年，广东省林业植物新品种申请量和授权量均为9件，累计申请量和授权量分别为82件和70件。蔷薇科苹果属的红屹海棠、红雾海棠、红菱海棠，木兰科含笑属的世植2017，山茶科山茶属的红屋积香、茶香居、岭南元宝、夏梦谢作、夏日叠星共9个林木新品种申请植物新品种权；紫金牛科紫金牛属的中科紫金1号，杜鹃花科杜鹃花属的红艳艳，木兰科木莲属的镛粉、镛红，蔷薇科苹果属的红屹海棠、红雾海棠、红菱海棠，桃金娘科桉属的热桉1号、热桉2号共9个林木花卉新品种获得国家林业局植物新品种授权。

（供稿人：叶龙华）

重大知识产权获奖成果

第十七届中国专利奖

【年度中国专利奖相关工作情况】 2015年，广东开展了两项中国专利奖相关工作，一是对广东省获得第十六届中国专利奖的单位及个人实施配套奖，二是组织和推荐广东省项目参加第十七届中国专利奖评选。

第十六届中国专利奖配套奖。在第十六届中国专利奖评选中，广东省共有83项专利获奖，其中金奖项目6项、优秀奖项目77项，获奖项目总数创历史新高。2015年10月12日，省政府召开表彰大会，对广东省获奖项目单位及个人给予表彰，并给予金奖每项100万元，优秀奖每项50万元的奖励。获奖项目在《南方日报》《中国知识产权报》等媒体开辟专版、在广东省知识产权局官方网站设立专栏进行宣传报道，充分发挥奖励工作激励创新、推动知识产权成果运用和保护的积极作用。

第十七届中国专利奖组织推荐。广东省认真组织开展第十七届中国专利奖项目遴选推荐工作，广东省知识产权局按照国家知识产权局《关于评选第十七届中国专利奖的通知》要求，在全省范围内遴选优秀项目，共推荐项目30项，其中，发明专利15项、外观设计专利15项。积极鼓励、引导优秀专利项目单位通过国务院部委、行业协会、科学院院士和工程院院士等多种推荐渠道参加评选。11月，第十七届中国专利奖评选结果揭晓。广东取得历史最好成绩，共125项项目获奖，其中金奖6项，优秀奖119项。

（供稿人：阳屹琴）

2015年广东专利奖

【概况】 2015年广东专利奖评选与表彰工作于2015年3月启动，按照《广东省专利奖励办法》和《广东省专利奖励办法实施细则》组织开展，至2015年底，广东专利奖评审办公室完成2015年广东专利奖项目及人员申报、推荐、形式审查、专家评审等工作。评审办公室收到项目267项、发明人43个。经形式审查，共265个项目进入专家网评程序，265个项目采用国际专利分类号即IPC分类号进行分组，分为机械、通信、医药、光电、电学、材料、化学、外观设计8个组，经过专家网上评审、项目答辩评审、评审委员会评审等程序，评选出拟奖项目70项，其中金奖15项、优秀奖55项；43个发明人均顺利通过形式审查进入专家评审程序，并经评审委员会评审等程序，评选出拟奖发明人9个。经公示无异议，2015年11月省人民政府审核通过拟奖名单。

（供稿人：阳屹琴）

2015年广东省名牌产品（工业类）

【概况】 2015年，广东省质监局围绕名牌的培育、评价、带动、发展和保护五个中心环节，实施名牌带动战略，取得显著成绩。593个工业类产品被评为广东省名牌产品，截至2015年底，全省共有在有效期内的广东省名牌产品（工业类）1847个。593个广东省名牌产品（工业类）主要分布的地区有：广州88个、深圳54个、珠海25个、汕头28个、佛山91个、韶关8个、河源5个、梅州3个、惠州15个、汕尾1个、东莞64个、中山58个、江门20个、阳江15个、湛江3个、茂名7个、肇庆17个、清远6个、潮州14个、揭阳16个、云浮10个、顺德45个；主要辐射的行业有：电子信息、电器机械及专用设备、汽车及摩托车产业等九大支柱产业，其中合资企业、股份制企业和民营企业的名牌产品已占据半壁河山，有效促进了产品结构和企业组织结构的优化升级。广东省所获中国世界名牌中，九大支柱产业生产企业占100%。以“HUAWEI 华为”“ZTE中兴”“震雄CH”“兴发”等品牌为代表的名牌优势企业吸纳生产要素的能力不断增强，有效促进了产业结构和企业组织结构的优化升级。以名牌企业为龙头，逐步形成了深圳珠宝、佛山陶瓷、顺德家电、南海铝材、虎门服装、狮岭皮具等100多个产业集群和区域品牌。名牌产品已成为带动广东省经济发展的有生力量，不仅成为广东省经济新的增长点，还提升了广东省的产业竞争力，带来了核心技术、产业集群、经济质量的提高，优化了广东省的经济结构。

（供稿人：钟培敬）

ZHI SHI CHAN QUAN YUN YONG

知识产权运用

- 重大经济活动知识产权分析评议
- 战略性新兴产业专利信息资源开发利用计划
- 产业知识产权联盟
- 信息运用
- 知识产权运营
- 知识产权质押及投融资
- 专利保险
- 转化

重大经济活动知识产权分析评议

重大经济活动知识产权分析评议

【分析评议试点】　按省领导指示及有关部门的提请，广东省知识产权局围绕广东省“DiiVA‘数字高清互动传输接口技术’标准推广”“锂离子动力电池研发及产业化”“新一代4G LTE关键技术及网络设备开发”“固态钒动力电池”“新岸线公司芯片项目”，组织开展专利分析评议，形成评议报告，有力地支撑了广东省对项目的决策工作，护航项目的顺利实施。

【知识产权分析评议服务示范创建】　广东省知识产权局推动广州奥凯信息咨询有限公司、深圳中科院知识产权投资有限公司、珠海智专专利商标代理有限公司等12家服务机构成功入围“全国知识产权分析评议服务示范创建机构”，并加入“全国知识产权分析评议服务机构联盟”。通过推动知识产权评议服务机构与企业对接、政策宣讲、交流研讨、实务分享等形式，不断提升全省知识产权分析评议服务能力，促进全省知识产权分析评议工作深入开展。

【重大经济科技活动知识产权评议促进计划】　选择深圳、东莞市和佛山市南海区、江门市高新区等7个有一定工作基础的区域，开展知识产权评议试点，扶持有关市（区）建立该区域的知识产权评议机制；选择广东省内提供知识产权分析评议服务实力较强的2家机构，开展重大项目知识产权评议。

【地市评议】　广东省知识产权局带动地市知识产权评议工作开展。广州开发区完善科技项目知识产权审议机制，规定在项目评审过程中，对涉及知识产权的事项实行“一票否决制”。东莞市针对引进创新创业领军人才项目开展知识产权评议，为后续出台相关政策提供有力支撑。深圳市2015年起，正式实施《深圳市重大经济科技活动知识产权评议办法》，围绕心血管项目、“超材料”产业化项目，组织开展知识产权分析评议。

（供稿人：成思）

战略性新兴产业专利信息资源开发利用计划

战略性新兴产业专利信息资源开发利用计划

【概况】 2015年，为导航战略性新兴产业科学发展，促进产业高端突破，广东省知识产权局积极推动“战略性新兴产业专利信息资源开发利用计划”实施。

【主要举措】

推进第一轮、第二轮“战略性新兴产业专利信息资源开发利用计划”项目实施。2015年，根据《广东省战略性新兴产业专利信息资源开发利用计划项目合同书》，持续推进2011年立项的11个项目和2013年立项的12个项目实施。

启动第三轮“战略性新兴产业专利信息资源开发利用计划”。广东省知识产权局会同省财政厅启动实施第三轮即2015年“广东省战略性新兴产业专利信息资源开发利用计划”，围绕新一代显示技术、集成电路、风能、核电技术、高端新型电子信息材料、高性能油墨、新材料（轨道交通用铝型材）、绿色建筑材料、海洋生物及微生物、海洋渔业、海洋油气及海底矿产开发利用、海洋可再生能源开发等12个产业领域，经公开组织申报及专家评审立项实施新一批专利分析及预警项目12个。该计划深度开发利用专利信息，形成各重点产业的专利分析及预警研究成果，分析各产业专利布局，明晰广东省产业创新发展的优势劣势、方向、突破口与路径，导航产业发展。第三轮项目于2015年全面启动实施。

【主要成果】 截至2015年底，通过三轮“战略性新兴产业专利信息资源开发利用计划”，已在云计算、智能制造装备等17个产业领域深度开展专利分析及预警，建成战略性新兴产业专利数据库7个，形成专利分析及预警报告30份，并召开系列报告会23场，面向4200多家企事业单位发布。编辑出版30期《广东省战略性新兴产业知识产权工作动态》。同时，已建立运行广东省战略性新兴产业全领域专利实时监测系统、专利信息实时统计系统、专利信息资源发布系统，支持产业专利各指标的智能化统计分析，监测产业创新全景，为广东省战略性新兴产业及企业“走出去”提供高质量的专利数据支持和信息分析支撑。另一方面，广东省知识产权局通过举办培训班、工作交流会和到各项目组听取工作进展情况汇报等方式，及时了解和解决工作中存在的问题。同时，培养了大量广受企业欢迎的专利信息利用人才。目前，不少参与课题研究的人员已分布在企业、知识产权服务机构、知识产权管理部门，为广东省知识产权服务业向高端发展提供了人才储备。

（供稿人：李伟　成思）

产业专利导航及分析预警

【专利信息服务平台】 广东省知识产权局建设完善产业专利信息服务平台。其一，大力建设省级重点产业及地方特色产业专利数据库。持续依托国家知识产权局区域专利信息服务（广州）中心和省知识产权公共信息综合服务平台，建设省级重点产业及地方特色产业专利数据库，面向产业和企业提供专利信息服务。截至2015年底，已建成重点产业专利数据库14个、地方特色产业专利数据库8个。其二，大力建设广东省专利大数据应用服务平台。以海量数据为依托，充分利用大数据技术，为市场主体提供专利信息服务；开发并上线知识产权移动应用子系统“专利知道”，提供手机APP上的全文检索、标题检索、公司检索、公开号检索等多种检索方式，为用户提供便携式移动终端专利信息服务。高效集聚涵盖103个国家及地区1亿多条专利数据的权威专利信息资源，开发基于互联网模式，集专利信息检索、专利信息管理与应用、专利态势分析及预警等功能于一体的“一站式”专利信息综合服务平台。

【专利导航新模式】 广东省知识产权局积极实践专利导航产业发展新模式。其一，启动实施“珠江西岸先进装备制造产业带专利导航工程”。围绕江门市轨道交通装备、肇庆市智能化成形和加工成套设备、顺德区智能装备制造、佛山市汽车制造、中山市电动汽车等5市（区）的5个先进装备制造产业，组织开展专利导航。其二，积极探索创建“国家专利导航产业发展实验区”。推动广州开发区、佛山市整合区域内优质知识产权服务及运营资源，围绕智能装备、卫星通信、机械装备制造等重点产业，开展产业专利导航。支持广州开发区、佛山市积极探索创建“国家专利导航产业发展实验区”。

【广东省出口贸易专利预警分析计划】 其一，启动“广东省重点出口产品专利预警分析计划”。围绕3D电视、半导体照明灯具、蒸汽挂烫机、不锈钢压力锅等广东省重点出口产品，立项实施项目50个。推动广东省内专业服务机构开展专利预警分析，与省内企业直接对接，服务企业产品“走出去”，并培养广东省专利预警分析机构及人才队伍。其二，完成相关项目的验收工作。包括2014年度该计划20个项目的验收，在项目答辩及专家评审基础上，确定优秀执行项目3个。其三，开展技术性贸易壁垒专利预警分析服务试点。组织省内专业服务机构围绕4G通信技术性贸易壁垒开展专利预警分析，探索专利分析与应对技术贸易壁垒有效结合的工作机制。其四，指导地市开展专利预警工作。广州市进出口专利预警平台上线运行。全国首个企业境外参展知识产权预警指引地方标准（SZDB/Z 72-2013）在深圳市出台。

（供稿人：成思）

产业知识产权联盟

产业知识产权联盟

【概况】 截至2015年底，在广东省知识产权局备案成功的产业知识产权联盟有18家，在国家知识产权局备案成功的产业知识产权联盟有5家。

【主要举措】 引导各知识产权联盟通过知识产权信息沟通、许可交易、保护调解和优化发展机制，对内自律、对外维权，不断完善开放式知识产权创造、运用及保护体系，集成知识产权资源，催化知识产权应用，促进专利及标准有机结合。

【广东省产业专利联盟示范培育工程】 首批认定顺德电压力锅、中彩联、广东LED联合创新中心（LED）等3家联盟为广东省专利联盟示范单位；启动实施“广东省产业知识产权联盟示范培育工程”，将深圳工业机器人专利联盟、新能源标准与知识产权联盟、第三代半导体专利联盟、深圳市医疗器械行业专利联盟等4家联盟列为培育对象。顺德电压力锅专利联盟，大力建设专利和标准“双联盟”，专利池专利数量从初期46项增加至472项，联盟成员由4家发展至13家，产品占全国市场份额75%以上，该联盟主导了电压力锅产品的国际标准修订。该联盟的电压力锅国际标准修订提案，获得国际电工委（IEC）通过并发布实施。中彩联建立彩电行业专利数据库及预警平台，管理2600多件彩电专利池，正在构建立体显示和智能电视等多个专利池模块及深圳市智能电视标准联盟。中彩联基于深度专利分析，与国外巨头谈判，使得国外彩电专利收费从每台彩电41美元降到20美元以下，为国内彩电出口节约专利费支出数亿美元。

【专利联盟规范化、实体化发展】 《深圳市专利联盟管理办法》于2015年起正式实施。《广东省专利联盟管理办法》正在制订。深圳市中彩联科技有限公司，作为彩电产业专利联盟的运作实体，以风险代理的形式运营专利池的国外专利，通过反向工程实验锁定涉案目标，预期可获得数十项专利的许可收益或诉讼赔偿；顺德成立岘德知识产权运营服务有限公司，作为电压力锅专利联盟、家用榨油机专利联盟等联盟的专利运营实体。

【研究成果】 国家知识产权局立项、广东省知识产权局承担的重点软科学研究项目“战略性新兴产业专利联盟的构建及运作模式研究”于2015年初在京顺利通过结题评审，作为课题研究重要成果的书籍《战略性新兴产业专利联盟的构建及运作：理论与实践》即将出版。

（供稿人：成思）

信息运用

专利信息化建设及推广

【广东省专利大数据应用服务系统建设】 2015年，为加快知识产权公共服务体系建设，调动和优化配置知识产权服务资源，拓展小微企业知识产权服务渠道，提升知识产权服务质量，广东省知识产权局开展广东省专利大数据应用服务系统建设。系统以国家知识产权局区域专利信息服务（广州）中心、广东省知识产权公共信息综合服务平台的海量数据为依托，建立广东省专利大数据应用服务平台，充分利用数据仓库、数据安全、数据分析、数据挖掘、移动互联等大数据技术，开发功能丰富、界面友好、操作简便、维护方便的专利大数据检索分析信息服务平台，为市场各类需求者提供专利信息服务；同时，为方便用户随时随地获取专利信息资源，开发知识产权移动应用子系统，提供手机APP上的全文检索、标题检索、公司检索、公开号检索等多种检索方式，支持有不同检索需要的用户灵活进行专利检索，以大数据平台的建设为支撑，为用户提供便携式的移动终端服务，全面提升广东省知识产权局专利信息服务水平和服务效率。

【中国专利法律状态数据加工】 2015年，广东省知识产权局完成对中国近千万条专利法律状态数据进行的深加工工作，实现专利法律状态的多字段联合检索，从专利申请号、法律状态公告日、法律状态及法律状态详细信息中的一个或者多个检索入口进行检索，为企事业单位在科研项目立项、技术引进的过程中提供客观科学的参考资料，在专利权质押保全、专利实施许可中，除以上检索入口外，还可以通过专利前后权利人信息入口进行检索，进一步丰富检索手段，深入全面地了解专利权人变更信息；同时，对现有的省重点行业、战略性新兴产业及地方特色产业专利数据库法律状态信息进行更新，为社会公众提供更加全面的专利信息服务。

【产业/行业专题数据库建设】 2015年，广东省知识产权局围绕广东省产业、区域特点、重点产业及战略性新兴产业发展的方向，继续建设并完善省级重点产业/行业、战略性新兴产业专利数据库。全面完成战略性新兴产业废弃资源再生循环利用、生物医学工程及高端电子元器件产业专利数据库建设工作，同时完成了湛江家电及海洋产业等地方行业数据库的建设并整合到广东省知识产权公共信息综合服务平台（网址：www.guangdongip.gov.cn）对外提供服务。这一系列专利数据库的建设与完善提升了用户对专利信息获取的时效性，可简捷、方便地让用户实时地掌握全省战略性新兴产业及地方特色产业技术的研发、引进、吸收、专利申请等情况，对于推动广东省战略性新兴产业的技术创新能力建设起到了积极作用。

【专利信息推送服务】 为贯彻落实《广东省知识产权战略纲要（2007—2020）》及《广东省深入实施知识产权战略推动创新驱动发展行动计划》，广东省知识产权局开展了专利信息服务“地市行”以及“专业镇中小微企业专利信息推送服务”活动。活动旨在针对广东省自主创新能力和企业市场竞争力提升的需求，面向政府、企业、高校、科研院所、中介服务机构、行业协会和社会大众，推送优质的专利信息公共服务和商用化服务，力求实现专利信息服务与需求的对接，提升企事业单位利用专利信息的能力。2015年，面向全省开展了专利信息推送服务全覆盖的工作，通过获取全省小微企业专利信息服务需求，开发适合小微企业的专利信息产品，构建科学畅通的专利信息推送服务渠道，为小微企业提供专利信息推送服务。已开展的专利信息推送服务除覆盖广东省珠三角各地市外，已延伸至汕头、茂名、肇庆、清远等周边地市，覆盖超过250家企业、39个专业镇、6个高新技术开发区，涵盖49项技术或产品。在泛珠区域的推送覆盖了泛珠八个省（区），深入宣传推广了广东省面向小微企业开展的各项工作及成果，基本满足了中小微企业在生产、研发过程中对专利信息的需求，较好地协助企业解决了在研发过程中面临的难点问题，促进了企业的研发工作。同时，还面向当地企业开展涉及专利信息利用、企业专利管理等内容的培训，提供公益性知识产权服务平台和商业专利检索工具等专利信息产品，提高企业专利信息利用的意识和专利管理的水平。

（供稿人：李润聪）

国家知识产权局（广东）专利信息传播利用基地

【概况】 2015年，国家知识产权局（广东）专利信息传播利用基地（以下简称“广东基地”）多措并举，全面开展专利信息传播利用工作体系建设，构建了多元化、区域性的专利信息服务体系，实施国家知识产权局“专利信息传播利用（广东）基地工作体系建设与能力培育项目”“专利信息传播利用（广东）基地专利信息利用促进项目”，开展“广东省中小微企业专利信息推送服务活动”以及“《企业专利信息利用工作指南》和《专利文献信息服务指南》宣贯活动”。完成广东专利大数据应用服务平台系统开发及子系统建设，完成大数据APP移动应用子系统建设。继续深入推进广东省战略性新兴产业专利信息资源开发利用计划和专利信息分析及预警工作，为专利信息服务广东省经济和产业发展、服务技术创新提供了有力支撑。编写《广东省战略性新兴产业知识产权工作动态》《广东省战略性新兴产业专利信息统计简报》《广东省专利统计简报》《广东省推进知识产权战略实施简报》等期刊，为该地区专利工作提供了有价值的决策参考。与泛珠三角区域其他省区共同开展小微企业信息推送服务，组织参加“2015年中国专利信息年会”，广东专场首次亮相中国专利信息年会。

【工作体系建设】 2015年，广东基地正式组织成立“广东省专利信息协会”，并以此协会为依托，与中规（北京）认证有限公司合作设立中规（北京）认证有限公司广州办事处。目前协会会员中有76个创新主体以及6家省外服务机构作为特邀理事单位，地域上覆盖广东省全省，体制类型上覆盖公益性和商业性服务机构，服务类型上覆盖信息资源支持、信息产品开发、信息传播、信息运用等专利信息传播利用全过程。

2015年，广东基地结合“广东省专利信息服务地市行”活动，开展“专业镇中小微企业专利信息推送服务”，通过走访调研，了解需求，进一步完善专业镇中小微企业专利信息传播利用工作体系和工作机制。

2015年，广东基地与汇桔网达成全面战略合作，联合举办知识产权创新创业大赛，引导和集聚更广泛的社会资源支持创新创业，促进知识产权、金融和产业深度融合。

2015年，广东基地完成广东专利大数据应用服务平台系统开发及子系统建设，同时完成大数据APP移动应用子系统开发及各项功能设计，并已上线试运行，这为专利信息助力科技创新发展提供了信息化平台。

【人才工作】

人才培育方面。2015年广东基地入选广东省专利信息领军人才3人，分别是：广东省知识产权局李强，深圳市标准技术研究院赵涛，腾讯科技（深圳）有限公司桂燕；入选广东省专利信息师资人才7人，分别是：广州市知识产权信息中心刘承敏，国家知识产权局专利局专利审查协作广东中心杨隆鑫、钟焱鑫，中国科学院广州生物医药与健康研究院庞弘燊，深圳市威世博知识产权代理事务所何青瓦，广州市越秀区哲力专利商标事务所（普通合伙）胡拥军，中兴通讯股份有限公司文明。

人才使用方面。2015年广东基地结合国知局项目，邀请全国专利信息领军人才及专利信息师资人才等各类专家进驻基地，参与基地相关研究课题，并对基地研究人员提供面对面的指导和培训，提高基地研究团队研究水平；邀请专利信息领军人才及师资人才参与在广东基地举办的各类培训，提高基地相关培训的含金量，充分发挥人才在区域经济发展和专利信息传播利用工作中的引领和支撑作用。

人才培训方面。2015年广东基地共开展了6期专利信息培训，吸引600余人次参加此类培训，充分发挥广东基地作为人才培养中心的重要职能。

【专利信息利用促进工作】 2015年，广东基地联合和发动广州奥凯信息咨询有限公司、广州恒成智道信息科技有限公司、北京合享新创信息科技有限公司等服务机构，开展“广东省中小微企业专利信息推送服务活动”以及“《企业专利信息利用工作指南》和《专利文献信息服务指南》宣贯活动”，综合采用多种培训、宣传、培养方式，针对专业镇中小微企业和专利信息服务机构，以及各地市局、全国知识产权品牌服务机构、优势中介服务机构等重点培育对象，推送优质的专利信息公共服务和商用化服务，推送的专利信息产品覆盖了企业约12类技术或产品，培育企事业单位总数超过1000余家。

2015年，广东基地继续开展“广东省专利信息服务地市行活动”，有力地促进了企事业单位专利信息运用。广东基地结合推进企业贯标培育，在茂名市、汕头市开展了“全省专利信息推送及知识产权贯标服务推送活动”。这是专利信息推送服务首次进驻粤东西地区，首次对接高新园区。

【专利信息情报服务】

开展面向区域经济发展的专利信息情报服务。2015年，广东基地编撰发放3期《广东省战略性新兴产业专利统计简报》，6期《广东省战略性新兴产业知识产权工作动态》，面向相关政府部门、产业（或行业）、研究机构等800余家单位普及推广专利信息研究成果等。2015年，广东基地编撰发放12期《广东省专利申请授权情况简报》，该统计简报主要内容包括发布广东省专利申请和授权情况，对全省政府机构、企事业单位了解广东省专利申请和授权现状，制定专利政策具有指导意义。2015年，广东基地根据评测广东省高新技术企业专利实力状况需要，设计一套评测指标体系，并完成《2012—2014年广东省高新技术企业专利实力状况报告》，该报告较为全面地评价了广东省高新技术企业的专利实力状况，对推动企业科技创新和发展提供了借鉴和参考。2015年，广东基地接受佛山市知识产权局委托，承担并完成《佛山专利实力状况报告》，该报告从专利创造、运用、保护、管理、服务五个方面全面衡量佛山市及广东省专利工作现状，为推进佛山市知识产权建设提供了参考借鉴。

开展面向产业升级的情报服务。2015年，广东基地推进专利信息利用促进项目，开展“广州开发区基因治疗领域专利竞争情报分析”，摸清基因治疗技术领域专利布局情况，理清开发区企业与竞争对手的优势与差距，为广州开发区基因治疗行业制定知识产权战略提供了参考借鉴。

开展面向企事业单位创新及生产经营的情报服务。2015年，广东基地开展电压力锅行业的专利导航分析工作，完成《广东省电压力锅行业态势专利研究报告》。该份报告主要面向顺德电压力锅联盟的11家企业，为顺德电压力锅联盟发展进行保驾护航，促进顺德地区电压力锅行业的发展，充分发挥产业联盟集聚作用，提升联盟内企业的自主创新能力和联盟的竞争力，促进联盟行业持续优化升级。2015年，广东基地开展“广东省技术性贸易壁垒专利分析预警服务试点工作”，制定出《技术性贸易壁垒中的专利风险预警及应对指引手册》，详细分析技术性贸易壁垒中的专利风险，提出建立专利风险监控和预警机制，该手册为企业提供在遭遇技术性贸易壁垒时的风险应对及处理方法，为广东省甚至全国企业的海外贸易保驾护航。2015年，广东基地通过开展中小微企业专利信息推送服务，面向中小微企业免费派送自主编制的《企业专利信息利用一本通》《外观设计检索指南》《企业海外知识产权风险应对管理指引》，提高广东省地方政府、企事业单位及社会公众专利信息利用的能力，实现专利信息服务地方创新发展。

【合作开展专利信息传播利用工作】 广东基地接受海口市知识产权局委托开展“海口市‘十三五’知识产权发展规划研究”项目。合作完成《海口市“十三五”知识产权规划调研报告》及《海口市“十三五”知识产权发展规划》。

广东基地与福建、贵州、广西、江西、海南、云南、湖南、四川等泛珠省区共同开展小微企业信息推送服务。2015年，广东基地面向泛珠各省区举办“泛珠三角区域专利信息培训班（成都站）”培训班、“泛珠三角区域专利信息培训班（贵州站）”培训班，“泛珠三角区域专利信息培训班（海南站）”培训班，向各省区推送了广东基地近年专利信息研究成果和服务产品。

广东基地研究团队赴青海省知识产权局、广西壮族自治区和贵州省，交流专利信息化建设及服务、成果推送、专利情报研究等方面的做法和经验，并与青海省知识产权局合作搭建了太阳能光伏产业专利专题数据库，为其提供保障平台正常运行的网络、机房等基础设施，同时完成《太阳能光伏产业专利分析预警报告》。

【组织参加2015年中国专利信息年会】 2015年，广东基地再次牵头组织广东省知识产权研究与发展中心、广州奥凯信息咨询有限公司和广州恒成智道信息科技有限公司联合参加2015年中国专利信息年会，广东基地2015年新成立的广东省专利信息协会、中规认证有限公司广州办事处也加入了参展行列。此届年会广东展区的主题是：广东深化专利信息服务，携手泛珠区域创新发展。广东展区集中展示了广东基地围绕泛珠区域创新、探索跨省信息服务新模式开展的一系列工作与成效，吸引了大批参会机构和企业关注。年会期间许多企业到广东展区与广东基地人员就专利信息服务等内容进行了深入交流和研讨。展会期间，广东基地举办了“广东省知识产权局与中国专利信息中心、知识产权出版社有限责任公司战略合作协议签署仪式”，以及“广东专利信息服务研讨专题论坛”，这是中国专利信息年会举办6届以来首次为地方局举办专场活动。

（供稿人：丁长青）

知识产权运营

知识产权运营

【概况】　2015年以来，广东省积极配合财政部、国家知识产权局开展以市场化方式促进知识产权运营国家试点，试点内容包括：其一，建设全国知识产权运营公共服务横琴特色试点平台。平台获中央财政资助5000万元，珠海市配套支持2500万元，省级财政配套正在积极协调中；该平台已完成工商注册并正式挂牌成立；申请了平台服务商标“七弦琴”、知识产权股权众筹金融产品商标“智财通宝”，开发了知识产权金融产品“智财通宝一号”；启动核心业务系统平台和官网建设。其二，股权投资扶持广东省产权交易集团有限公司和深圳市精英知识产权运营服务有限公司等两家知识产权运营机构发展。两家机构各获中央财政1000万元扶持资金，正推进交易系统、托管系统、竞价系统的开发，搭建知识产权交易大数据平台，助推专利技术的转移转化。其三，设立知识产权质押融资风险补偿基金，以中央财政5000万元为引导资金，支持广州、深圳、珠海、惠州、中山5市分别设立当地知识产权质押融资风险补偿基金，各地市财政出资配套，带动社会资本投入，对中小微企业开展知识产权质押融资提供增信支持。其四，设立重点产业知识产权运营基金，以中央财政4000万元为引导资金，筹备成立总规模达30亿元、首期规模达5亿元的广东省粤科国联知识产权投资运营基金。该基金以企业为核心、以市场化为主导，委任具有国际知识产权运营经验的专业化公司来管理，专注于高档数控机床、机器人等战略性新兴产业的知识产权运营和技术转移。至2015年底，该基金已和中国智能制造领域第一个专利池——工业机器人专利联盟签署战略合作协议，双方正共同推动工业机器人产业领域高价值专利的培育和运营。广东省是全国唯一开展全部四项国家试点的省份。

【重点企业、区域知识产权高端运营及创新运用】

国家专利运营试点企业。广东省知识产权局推动深圳市中彩联科技有限公司、腾讯科技（深圳）有限公司、中兴通讯股份有限公司、广东省产权交易集团有限公司、深圳市联创知识产权服务中心、深圳中科院知识产权投资有限公司、佛山市海科知识产权交易有限公司等，不断深化国家专利运营试点企业试点工作。推荐珠海格力电器股份有限公司、深圳市朗科科技股份有限公司、广州广电运通金融电子股份有限公司、赛恩倍吉科技顾问（深圳）有限公司、深圳市精英知识产权运营服务有限公司、广州博鳌纵横网络科技有限公司、广东高航知识产权运营有限公司等7家企业入围第三批国家专利运营试点企业。

重点区域知识产权运营。广东省知识产权局引导推进重点区域知识产权运营及创新运用。指导深圳市出台《企业专利运营指南》（SZDB/Z102-2014），引导企业对专利资产加强管理和运用；支持中山市建设“广东（灯饰照明）知识产权运营中心”，推动该市运用知识产权引领灯饰照明产业转型升级及国际化发展；与顺德区共同启动建设广东省知识产权创新运用试验区，以省、区、镇三级合作方式，共同推进该试验区的运营，试验区核心载体园区——顺德知识产权创业园、佛山市知识产权培训（顺德）基地、华南理工大学知识产权学院（顺德）研究院已揭牌启动，专利导航产业发展战略合作协议、合作建设顺德区知识产权投融资平台框架协议、知识产权孵化创投项目、知识产权商业机构入驻顺德知识产权创业园等一系列协议和项目已签约启动。

【广东省专利技术实施计划】 鼓励企业和社会资本投资于专利产业化。截至2015年底，该计划累计投入3905万元，扶持了全省518个专利项目实施。

【国家级专利产业化基地】 截至2015年底，进驻“国家专利产业化（广州数字家庭）试点基地”的企业达238家，数字家庭专利池容量达5000多件，实现年产值110亿元。加强“国家工业设计与创意产业（顺德）基地”建设，基地已入驻世界各地设计公司逾100家、入园设计师逾1000名，目前已发展成为国内最大的工业设计产业园区，成为珠三角“工业设计”的代名词。

（供稿人：何社善　成思）

知识产权质押及投融资

知识产权质押及投融资

【概况】 广东省知识产权局通过构建政策体系、开展工作试点、建设服务平台、举办活动比赛、进行培训研讨等方式推进知识产权质押及投融资工作深入开展。2015年，广东省专利权质押登记169件，质押金额58.94亿元，质押金额居全国第三位。知识产权质押融资及时缓解了部分创新型中小微企业融资难的问题。

【主要举措】

构建知识产权质押融资政策支持体系。一方面，启动质押评估技术规范地方标准制订工作，组织编制《广东省知识产权质押评估技术规范》地方标准，在省质监局指导下邀请行业专家开展标准审查，依据专家意见多次进行修改完善。该标准（DB44/T 1747-2015）已于2015年12月16日由省质监局发布，2016年4月16日起开始实施。联合省发改委、经信委、财政厅、金融办等部门出台《关于加快推进我省知识产权质押融资工作的若干意见》及其实施细则，对推进全省质押融资工作进行了全面部署和规范。另一方面，支持各地市制订实施相关政策，形成政策合力。广州市《中小企业知识产权质押贷款操作指引》、深圳市《促进知识产权质押融资若干措施》、东莞市《专利权质押贷款管理办法及操作指引》、佛山市南海区《知识产权质押融资专项资金、中介机构扶持补贴及中介机构管理办法》、佛山市顺德区《知识产权反担保质押融资业务操作管理办法》和中山市、佛山市三水区、韶关市翁源县《知识产权质押贷款贴息管理办法》等知识产权质押融资政策纷纷出台实施。

推动国家级知识产权质押及投融资试点。2014年5月，在通过创建验收后，佛山市南海区启动“国家知识产权投融资（南海）综合试验区”全面建设工作，这是目前全国唯一的国家级试验区。2015年12月，佛山市、广州经济技术开发区、增城经济技术开发区、广东自贸区深圳前海蛇口片区获批开展“国家知识产权投融资试点”，惠州仲恺高新区获批开展“国家知识产权质押融资试点”。

建设“中国（广东）知识产权投融资服务平台”（www.ip2vc.com）。平台确立按行业分类指导原则，以项目风险分级信息披露为核心内容，对知识产权项目分成融资借款、股权投资、许可合作三个链条进行细化，并与各地产业平台、产业资本、私募创投对接。

举办中国（广东）知识产权投融资项目对接会。2011—2015年，连续五年举办中国（广东）知识产权投融资项目对接会。先进制造、生物医药、新材料等产业领域的46个知识产权项目与创投企业对接，涉及金额7.88亿元。2015年对接会中，17个项目与创投企业对接，合作金额1.5亿元。

启动广东省知识产权质押融资试点。2015年支持珠海、惠州、江门、湛江四市开展知识产权质押融资试点。

举办首届南粤知识产权创新创业大赛。大赛以“知识产权让创意、创新、创业成为现实”为主题，于2015年11月正式启动，逾1200个创业项目与团队报名，涉及智能家居、智能安防、移动互联网等多个前沿创新领域，大赛先后完成海选、初赛、国际知商营、知商谷论道、半决赛等环节，并于2016年1月举行了总决赛。总决赛上，格力电器董事长董明珠担任创新创业总导师，由格力、TCL、香雪制药等企业主要负责人和国内外知识产权运营界、资本投资界一批资深专家组成的评委会，对入围总决赛的十强项目予以评审和指导；整个大赛期间，由IDG资本、九鼎投资领衔的国内外上百家著名风投机构与拥有自主知识产权的创新创业团队与项目直接对接，并为优秀项目提供融资机会，其中，入围总决赛的十强项目更是得到了千万级别的投资。

（供稿人：何社善　成思）

广东省专利权质押登记

【概况】 2015年，广东省共进行专利权质押登记169件，比2014年184件下降了8.15%；质押金额58.9425亿元，比2014年46.7996亿元增长了25.95%；涉及专利1025件。2015年平均每件专利权质押登记涉及的专利量为6.07件，质押金额为3487.72万元，专利对经济社会发展的贡献度明显提高。

【专利权质押登记特点】

*专利权质押融资九成分布在珠三角地区。*按出质人地址统计，2015年，广东省专利权质押融资主要分布在珠江三角洲地区，质押登记数量为165件，占全省总数的97.63%；质押金额为53.87亿元，占全省总金额的91.39%。其中深圳市专利权质押登记数为114件，占全省质押总量的67.46%；质押金额为29.17亿元，占全省质押总金额的 49.49%。

表1　2015年广东省各地市专利权质押登记情况

地区	数量（件）	金额（万元）
深圳市	114	291710
广州市	19	39158
东莞市	13	177257
佛山市	11	22910
惠州市	3	708
江门市	3	6425
中山市	2	500
韶关市	2	3000
汕头市	1	620
潮州市	1	47137
珠海市	0	0
肇庆市	0	0
湛江市	0	0
梅州市	0	0
汕尾市	0	0
阳江市	0	0
茂名市	0	0
揭阳市	0	0
清远市	0	0
云浮市	0	0
河源市	0	0
合计	169	589425

专利权质押金额主要分布在100万至1000万元区间。统计数据表明，2015年广东省专利权质押金额主要集中在100万至1000万元区间，质押登记数127件，占全部质押登记的75.15%。其他分布有：10万元及以下，质押登记数1件，占比0.59%；10万至100万元，质押登记数8件，占比4.73%；1000万元至1亿元，质押登记数20件，占比11.83%；超过1亿元，质押登记数13件，占比7.69%。

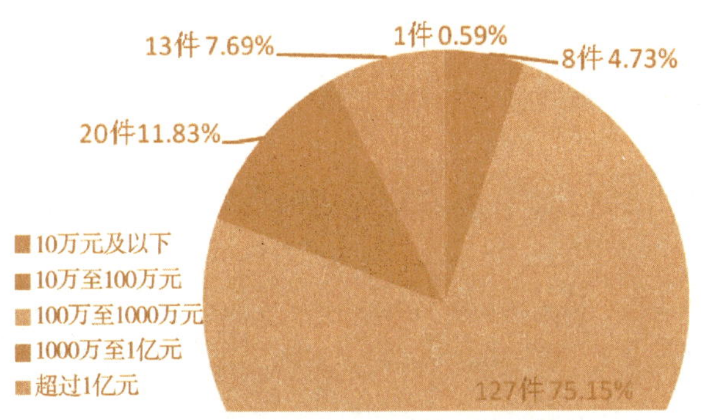

图1　2015年广东省质押登记中质押金额分布情况

专利权质押主要集中在企业。2015年，按出质人统计，企业质押登记数158件，占比93.49%，质押金额56.62亿元，占比96.06%。个人、高校、科研机构、机构团体所占甚少。

表2 2015年广东省专利权质押登记中出质人类型分布情况

出质人	数量（件）	占比	金额（万元）	占比
企业	158	93.49%	566175	96.06%
个人	5	2.96%	19832	3.36%
企业和个人共同	5	2.96%	3118	0.53%
企业和高校共同	1	0.59%	300	0.05%
合计	169	100%	589425	100%

涉及专利以发明和实用新型为主。2015年，广东省共进行专利权质押登记169件，涉及专利1025件。在明细数据中①，发明专利432件，占42.90%；实用新型专利552件，占54.82%；外观设计专利23件，占2.28%。

开展知识产权质押业务的主要是担保机构和银行。2015年，广东省专利权质押权人分别有：担保机构96件，占比56.80%；银行62件，占比36.69%；其他企业8件，占比4.73%；个人3件，占比1.78%。知识产权质押贷融资正在成为破解中小企业融资难、助力“双创”的一个重要途径。

【广东省与全国及有关省市的对比情况】

2015年，广东省专利权质押登记数量在全国各省市中排名第五，质押金额排名第三。

表3 2015年广东省专利权质押与全国及部分省市对照表

指标	数量	质押金额（人民币）	质押金额（美元）
全国总量	2133件	554.48亿元	8829.50万元
广东总量	169件	58.94亿元	0
广东占比	7.92%	10.63%	0
广东名次	5	3	–
前五名省市	浙江240件	山东80.26亿元	排名略
	陕西235件	宁夏71.46亿元	
	山东205件	广东58.94亿元	
	北京192件	辽宁41.92亿元	
	广东169件	浙江36.38亿元	

全国专利质押登记数量前三名依次是浙江、陕西、山东；质押金额前三名依次是：山东、宁夏、广东（2015年度国内采用美元合同质押登记的省市很少，故排名略去）。

（供稿人：洪伟）

①因国家知识产权局统计总数和明细的时间截点不同，涉及专利数会有差异：总数是1025件，明细是1007件。

专利保险

专利保险

【概况】 2015年，广东省知识产权局积极开展专利保险试点工作。一是支持广州、深圳、东莞市和佛山市禅城4市（区）积极开展“全国专利保险试点”。截至2015年底，四地367家企业已累计完成专利投保超过2000件，保费166.7万元，最高可获赔5913.8万元。2012年4月，全国第一例专利保险赔付案件在佛山市禅城区顺利结案，信达财产保险股份有限公司广东分公司履行保险责任，向佛山市新概念磁电设备有限公司赔付了价值2.04万元的专利保险金。二是支持中山市结合该市古镇灯饰行业实际，积极开展全国首例单一行业专利保险探索；2015年投保企业20家，涉及219件专利，保费21.55万元，最高可获赔1061.1万元。

（供稿人：何社善）

转 化

知识产权交易

【概况】 广东省知识产权局积极推进知识产权许可贸易。2013—2015年，全省专利许可合同备案量达3353件，许可合同金额达16.65亿元。广东省还建设了广州、深圳、佛山、东莞4个国家专利技术展示交易中心，截至2015年底，4个中心累计完成专利展示41250件、专利交易2085件，金额超过6亿元；并通过一年一度的"中国专利周"广东地区活动促进专利展示交易。省政府批准设立广州知识产权交易中心、横琴国际知识产权交易中心，两个中心已于2015年正式揭牌成立；同时，支持中孵网、广东金融高新区股权交易中心华南知识产权运营中心、广州汇桔网互联网知识产权金融平台、广州高航网知识产权运营平台、深圳市知识产权服务平台、深圳7号网、"第五大发明"等知识产权交易运营服务平台发展壮大，为社会提供市场化、网络化、专业化、深层次知识产权运营服务。

（供稿人：何社善　成思）

广东省专利实施许可合同备案

【概况】 2015年，广东省专利实施许可合同备案数共计1308件，同比增长28.87%；备案总金额为人民币12.2958亿元和美元90.00万元，同比增长390.82%；涉及专利4104件，同比增长126.37%。广东省专利实施许可备案数量在全国各省市中排名第一，备案金额排名第二，涉及专利数排名第一。在2015年专利实施许可合同备案明细数据中，发明专利2077件，占48.78%；实用新型专利1672件，占39.27%；外观设计专利323件，占7.59%；PCT国际申请186件，占4.37%。2015年平均每件备案涉及的专利数为3.14件，备案金额为94.00万元。

实施许可合同备案区域分布状况。由表1可以看出，按照许可人来统计，2015年广东省专利实施许可主要分布在珠三角地区，备案数量1224件，占全省的93.58%，备案金额达到12.20亿元，占全省的99.24%。

表1　2015年广东省专利实施许可合同备案区域分布状况

地区	数量（件）	金额（万元）
深圳市	346	10865
广州市	334	12439
佛山市	195	8599
中山市	151	10323
东莞市	128	72023
汕头市	45	427
珠海市	30	4753
江门市	17	0
惠州市	15	22
潮州市	10	53
肇庆市	8	3003
韶关市	7	26
湛江市	7	20
河源市	5	3
梅州市	3	73
阳江市	2	0
云浮市	2	150
揭阳市	1	1
清远市	1	180

（续上表）

地区	数量（件）	金额（万元）
汕尾市	1	1
茂名市	0	0
合计	1308	122958

实施许可备案许可人类型分布。2015年，广东省专利实施许可合同备案中，按许可人类型进行划分，个人占居超六成的比重，企业约占三成，其他类型的备案占比较少，具体见表2。

表2 2015年广东省专利实施许可备案许可人类型分布

类型	数量（件）	占比
工矿企业	396	30.28%
大专院校	76	5.81%
科研单位	12	0.92%
机关团体	2	0.15%
个人	818	62.54%
混合类型	4	0.31%

专利实施许可合同金额分布。专利许可使用费的支付方式比较多样，根据合同法的规定，专利许可使用费的支付方式可以采用一次总算、一次总付的方式或一次总算、分次支付的方式，也可以采用提成支付或提成支付加入门费的方式。如表3 所示，从合同金额来看，合同金额分布多数集中在10万元以下（含10万元），占总数比重87.77%，而其中无偿许可的比例占许可总数近六成（本文统计的数据不涉及提成支付部分）。

表3 2015年广东省专利实施许可合同备案金额规模分布

金额（元）	数量（件）	所占比重
1000万以上	14	1.07%
100万至1000万（含1000万）	30	2.29%

（续上表）

金额（元）	数量（件）	所占比重
10万至100万（含100万）	116	8.87%
1万至10万（含10万）	246	18.81%
1万以下（含1万）	154	11.77%
0	748	57.19%
合计	1308	100%

专利实施许可类型分布。按照被许可人取得的专利实施权范围，可以将专利实施许可分为：普通实施许可、独占实施许可、排他实施许可、交叉实施许可和分实施许可五种类型。2015年广东省专利实施许可主要采用独占许可的方式，此类型占总数的87.69%。

表4 2015年广东省专利实施许可备案许可类型分布

许可类型	数量（件）	所占比重
普通实施许可	137	10.47%
独占实施许可	1147	87.69%
排他实施许可	23	1.76%
其他	1	0.08%
合计	1308	100%

专利实施许可合同涉及知识产权类型分布。2015年，广东省专利实施许可合同中，合同仅涉及专利的有1299件，占99.31%；合同涉及专利和技术秘密的有9件，占0.69%；合同涉及专利和其他知识产权的0件。

【广东省与全国及有关省市的对比】

2015年广东省备案数量在全国各省市中排名第一，备案金额（人民币）排名第二。全国备案数前三名依次是广东、江苏、北京；备案金额（人民币）前三名依次是：新疆、广东、北京（2015年度国内采用美元合同备案的省市很少，故排名略去）。

表5　2015年广东省实施许可合同备案与全国及部分省市对照表

指标	数量	金额（人民币）	金额（美元）
全国总量	5759件	49.00亿元	5649.30万元
广东总量	1308件	12.30亿元	90.00万元
广东占比	22.71%	25.10%	1.60%
广东名次	1	2	–
前五名省市	广东1308件	新疆20.23亿元	排名略
	江苏783件	广东12.30亿元	
	北京468件	北京5.44亿元	
	浙江465件	江苏2.51亿元	
	山东251件	上海1.50亿元	

（供稿人：洪伟）

知识产权保护

ZHI SHI CHAN QUAN BAO HU

- 概述
- 行政保护
- 司法保护
- 执法协作
- 维权援助与涉外应对
- 委局合作
- 实例

概 述

知识产权保护

【概况】 2015年，广东省大力促进知识产权工作与创新驱动发展战略深入融合，实施严格的知识产权保护，为推动广东改革开放和现代化建设取得新成就作出积极贡献。

【打击侵犯知识产权和制售假冒伪劣商品】 2015年，全省各职能部门按照国务院和全国打击侵权假冒工作领导小组的部署要求，加强部门和区域协调，加大生产源头治理力度，加强市场监督管理，强化刑事司法打击，扎实推进诚信体系建设，建立长效治理机制，打击侵权假冒工作取得显著成效。全省各级主要行政执法部门累计立案查处侵权假冒案件29754宗，占全国案件总量的1/6。

省打击侵权假冒工作领导小组召开电视电话会议，制定年度工作要点，推进互联网打击侵权假冒、农村和城乡结合部、车用燃油专项整治，开展中国制造海外形象维护“清风行动”等专项行动，着力解决群众关注的热点、难点和市场反映的突出问题。

全省各职能部门持续完善行政执法与刑事司法衔接机制。省检察院监督行政执法机关移送涉嫌侵犯知识产权犯罪案件75件，监督公安机关立案侦办涉嫌侵权犯罪案件46件，省直行政执法与刑事司法衔接信息共享平台实现与各市平台在网上信息互通，省打击侵权假冒信息共享平台同期开通，全年共录入侵犯知识产权案件3059件，行政处罚案件信息公开及时、准确、全面。省检察院、公安厅与省文化厅、知识产权局等部门联合制定行政处罚和涉嫌犯罪案件移送标准。省公安厅与7个行政执法机构建立联合执法办公室并密切开展协作。

【专利保护】 全省各级知识产权局实施知识产权执法维权“护航”专项行动，严厉查处专利违法行为，全年共受理专利纠纷案件2492件，结案2626件，查处假冒专利案件722件。省知识产权局进驻中国进出口商品交易会（以下简称广交会）、中国国际美博会等开展专利保护工作，第117届和第118届广交会共受理专利侵权纠纷案件815宗，涉及被投诉企业1088家。省知识产权局与电商平台签署《保护知识产权战略合作协议》，构建电子商务领域专利保护新机制。2015年，新增国家知识产权快速维权中心2个，目前4个中心已覆盖灯饰、家具、家电和皮具四大行业领域。

【商标保护】 2015年，全省工商行政管理部门注册商标专用权保护长效工作机制继续完善，防范利用网络、广告、企业注册等多个端口开展侵权假冒的大市场监管合力形成，防范预警与打击惩处为一体的监管执法机制有效建立。全年共立案查处商标侵权案件3974宗，案值3600万元，罚款4893万元，移送司法机关35宗。在第117届和第118届广交会上开展商标维权保护，共受理有效侵权投诉412宗，已经作撤架处理327宗。

【著作权保护】 2015年，全省各级版权行政执法部门深入推进“剑网”专项行动，有效打击网络侵权盗版违法行为，净化版权市场。全年共出动执法人员78976人次，巡查网络经营单位3204家，主动监管本地网站800余家，查办案件35宗，行政罚款145.2万，取缔非法出版物经营户96个，查处违法经营单位3家，收缴侵权盗版出版物达10万册。省版权局继续进驻中国国际漫博会并设立“版权服务工作站”，有效维护展会版权秩序。

全省软件正版化长效机制不断完善。省版权局出台《建立政府机关软件正版化工作长效机制实施意见》《2015年度全省推进企业使用正版软件工作督办企业名录》，积极构建软件正版化工作机制。国务院检查组充分肯定广东政府机关软件正版化工作。

2015年，全省各级文化行政执法部门以音像、电影、出版物、互联网、动漫和电子游戏等领域为重点，大力开展专项整治，严厉打击文化市场侵权盗版行为。全年共出动执法人员87.8万人次，检查经营场所32.7万家次；受理举报1635件，立案查处案件2411宗，移送司法机关81宗；处罚行政违法经营单位2149家次，罚没1137万元。

【质监知识产权保护】　2015年，全省质监系统以十类产品为重点深入开展打假专项行动，出动执法人员117203人次，立案查处案件4349宗，涉案货值2.44亿元，捣毁窝点167个，罚没款9339万元，移送公安机关案件29宗。省质监局集中开展互联网侵权假冒专项整治，创建“网上发现、源头追溯、落地查实”的执法新模式。

【植物新品种保护】　2015年，全省农业和林业行政管理部门加强农林业市场监管，组织开展种子、化肥、农药、兽药、饲料、添加剂和林木种苗市场的执法检查，组织开展打击侵犯农业、林业植物新品种权专项行动。

【海关知识产权保护】　2015年，广东省内海关共查获进出口侵犯知识产权案件1602宗，查扣侵权嫌疑货物2953批次，涉及侵权货物1905万件，侵权案件主要涉及通讯设备类、服装类、鞋类等19类商品，涉及93个贸易国家（地区）。

【打击侵犯知识产权犯罪】　2015年，全省公安机关以“3+2”专项行动为抓手，以“打假1号”“打假2号”和打击涉烟犯罪“百日行动”等重大行动为牵引，深入推进打击侵犯知识产权和制售假冒伪劣商品犯罪工作。全年共立侵权假冒案件2471宗，侦破2036宗，占全国破案数的1/10，抓获犯罪嫌疑人5489名，执行逮捕3143人，移送审查起诉3998人，绩效考核综合排名全国第一，获得公安部和省政府的肯定与嘉奖。

全省公安机关强化情报导侦，通过SIS等信息分析系统对案件信息流、资金流、物流等关键要素梳理线索严格查控，侦破了一系列大要案，如惠州“5·13”制假案被评为全国打假十大经典战役。全省公安机关狠抓集群战役，打击跨区域涉假犯罪，推动广州针对涉假皮具、汽配、打印耗材犯罪，深圳针对涉假手机、电子产品犯罪，佛山针对涉假日化用品、小家电犯罪，汕头、惠州针对涉假玩具、机械配件犯罪，中山、东莞针对涉假润滑油、服装、鞋类犯罪，揭阳针对假烟犯罪开展重点集群攻坚，共发起集群战役68起，占全国1/3以上，协助其他省市开展收网行动150多次，对100多个跨省犯罪团伙实现了全链条打击。

全省公安机关重视警企协作，与腾讯、华为等200多家重点企业签署协议，建立知识产权刑事保护协作机制和绿色通道，搭建全省电子商务领域打击侵犯知识产权犯罪平台。

【知识产权司法保护】　2015年，全省检察机关依法履行各项检察职能，全年批准逮捕涉及侵犯知识产权犯罪案件1585件、2876人，提起公诉2071件、3823人；批捕涉及生产销售假冒伪劣商品犯罪案件2588件、3615人，提起公诉3059件、4059人。全省检察机关成功办理一批具有较大影响的重点案件，如珠海高新区知识产权检察室承办假冒注册商标一案入选全国检察机关年度保护知识产权十大典型案例。省检察院探索构建跨行政区域知识产权专门检察院，指导珠海建立知识产权刑事案件跨区审理诉讼格局。

2015年，全省法院系统坚持公正司法，大力推进知识产权审判工作。全年新收知识产权民事一审案件23766件，审结20215件，分别同比减少0.56%和18.1%，新收案件数量占全国总量的1/5；其中审结涉外一审案件302件，同比增长4.5%，审结涉港澳台一审案件153件，同比增长26.5%；新收二审案件6132件，审结6272件，分别同比增长11.4%和13.3%。省法院坚持打造“精品案件”理念，依法审结一批类型新颖、疑难复杂和社会关注度高的典型案件。全省法院努力通过司法调解化解知识产权纠纷，全年共调撤案件10853件，调撤率40.97%。

全省法院充分发挥行政审判职能，支持和监督行政机关依法行政，全年共新收知识产权行政一审案件22件，审结22件，分别同比增长13.33%和10%；新收二审案件16件，同比减少5.88%，审结18件，同比增长28.57%。

全省法院坚持加大对侵犯知识产权犯罪行为的打击力度，全年共受理侵犯知识产权犯罪案件和生产、销售假冒伪劣商品犯罪一审案件2016件，审结1983件，分别同比增长45.9%和51.1%；受理二审案件234件，审结222件，分别同比增长35.3%和44.2%。

全省法院深入推进“探索完善司法证据制度破解知识产权侵权损害赔偿难”试点工作，增加广州知识产权、珠海、惠州、江门、肇庆等5个中级法院和广州市越秀区等12个基层法院作为试点单位。全省法院探索基层法院跨区域集中管辖，优化知识产权案件管辖布局，经最高法院同意，新增广州市黄埔区、阳江市江城区2个法院管辖一般知识产权案件，全省有一般知识产权案件管辖权基层法院增至35个；调整广州市越秀区、天河区和萝岗区3个基层法院跨区域管辖第一审一般知识产权民事案件的地域范围，调整佛山市禅城区等5个基层法院跨区域集中管辖所在市第一审一般知识产权民事案件。积极推进广州知识产权法院建设，广州知识产权法院正式成立“最高人民法院知识产权司法保护与市场价值研究（广东）基地”，在国内率先引入技术调查官参与庭审，并在中山古镇设立全省首家远程诉讼服务处。

（供稿人：王一）

行政保护

专利行政执法

【概况】 2015年，广东省各级知识产权局共受理各类专利案件3214件，结案3348件。其中：专利纠纷侵权纠纷案件2490件（含调解展会专利侵权纠纷案件），结案2625件；调解其他专利纠纷案件2件，结案1件；查处假冒专利案件立案722件，结案722件。

【专项行动】 2015年6月，广东省知识产权局在全省开展查处假冒专利集中行动月工作，严厉打击假冒专利违法行为，规范专利标识标注行为，全省知识产权局共立案372件，涉及商家188家。

【展会保护】 2015年，广东省知识产权局共进驻第117届广交会、118届广交会等重要展会开展专利保护工作，全省知识产权局共调解展会专利侵权纠纷案件1000件左右。

2015年12月2日，受国家知识产权局委托，广东省知识产权局举办展会专利维权工作交流研讨会，邀请了来自9个省（直辖市、自治区）知识产权局系统共50余人参加，会议研讨了展会专利执法维权的疑难和共性问题，探索强化展会专利执法维权的具体举措，推动全系统共同建立健全展会专利执法维权办案机制。

（供稿人：毕赓）

商标行政执法

【概况】 2015年，广东省工商行政管理局制定下发《广东省工商行政管理局关于2015年开展打击侵权假冒工作通知》等多个文件，部署全省工商系统开展打击侵权假冒工作，并对部分地区的“双打”工作开展督查，有效保护注册商标专用权，保障消费者与生产者、经营者的合法权益，维护公平竞争的市场秩序，为市场发挥配置资源的决定性作用提供有利条件。

【专项行动】 广东省工商行政管理局先后组织“中国制造海外形象维护‘清风’行动”“保护地理标志商标专用权专项行动”“打击假冒伪劣日用品专项行动”“商标代理市场专项整治行动”和保护“迪士尼”商标专用权专项行动等专项整治，有效打击有组织、重复性的商标侵权行为，有力保护国内外驰名商标专用权。

【打击侵权假冒工作】 2015年，广东省工商行政管理系统共立案查处侵权假冒案件5972宗，案值9232.53万元，罚款8453万元，捣毁窝点84个，移送司法机关107宗，公开双打案件信息2926件。其中立案查处商标侵权案件4140宗，案值5137.48万元，罚款4541.95万元，移送司法机关77宗。

【展会与专业市场执法监管】 广东省工商行政管理局接受国家工商行政管理总局委托，派人指导广州市工商行政管理局参加第117届广交会驻场商标监管工作，广交会驻场商标维权保护共受理有效侵权投诉189件、认定不构成侵权31件、已作撤架处理158件。

【驰名商标保护】 2015年，广东省获国家工商行政管理总局认定与保护的驰名商标75件，广东省驰名商标总数715件，继续居全国首位。有关工商和市场监管部门对在查处商标违法案件程序中获得认定的29件驰名商标给予保护，着力促进知名品牌的创建。

（供稿人：陈小冰）

海关行政执法

【概况】 广东省内海关高度重视运用风险分析手段开展查缉工作，总结分析近年来关区查获侵权案件特点，加大对出口到侵权风险较高的国家或地区的货物以及侵权高发领域的商品的打击力度。2015年通过风险分析查获侵权货物达1317万件。省内海关采取“分阶段、有重点、逐步推进”的方式，开展了针对海运渠道、邮递快件渠道以及互联网领域侵权的专项执法行动，积极推进中国制造海外形象维护“清风行动”，加强对重点渠道、重点进出口货物的监管，加大情报分析力度，在重点口岸部署了专项查缉行动，至2015年底，“清风行动”共查扣侵权出口货物1723万件，制止侵权货物输往84个国家和地区。

广东省内海关强化与其他执法部门的执法衔接，形成知识产权保护合力。加强与公安机关案件线索通报和移送工作；不断落实与省工商局签署的加强知识产权保护合作协议；积极研究与专利、版权、法院等知识产权行政、司法部门建立合作长效机制。

（供稿人：王一）

司法保护

广东省检察机关知识产权司法保护

【概况】 2015年，广东省检察机关切实发挥检察职能，继续加大行政执法与刑事司法衔接力度，严厉打击侵犯知识产权的犯罪行为。

【打击侵犯知识产权犯罪】 全省检察机关充分履行批准逮捕、刑事公诉职能，坚决严厉打击侵犯知识产权犯罪活动，成功办理一批侵犯知识产权犯罪案件。如珠海市高新区知识产权检察室承办的马某军、孙某珍假冒注册商标一案入选全国检察机关2014年度保护知识产权的十大典型案例。针对社会反映强烈，涉及人民群众生命财产安全的重大案件，全省检察机关依法及时批捕、起诉，维护了广大知识产权权利人和消费者的合法利益。如深圳南山区检察院办理的刘某武等六人假冒注册商标案被中国外商投资企业协会优质品牌保护委员会评为“2014—2015年度知识产权保护最佳案例”。

【民事和行政案件的法律监督】 2015年，广东省检察院设立了知识产权监督科，专门负责办理知识产权民事、行政案件的法律监督；出台《广东省铁路检察院管辖体制改革方案》，由广州铁路运输检察分院专门对广州知识产权法院的知识产权诉讼案件进行监督。

【知识产权保护长效机制】 广东省检察机关加强与行政执法机关的联系，完善联席会议、信息通报、备案审查等工作机制，监督行政执法机关依法移送涉嫌犯罪案件，防止知识产权犯罪案件以罚代刑、降格处理。广东省检察院在省“两法衔接”平台的基础上，结合《打击侵权假冒领域行政执法与刑事司法衔接工作信息共享平台建设规范（试行）》的要求，本着统一、规范又不重复建设的原则，把省“双打”领域平台纳入省“两法衔接”平台建设二期工程，作为平台升级的一个子项目进行设计开发，建成省“双打”信息共享平台，省平台与中央平台可以通过导入进行互联互通。广东省检察院、公安厅与知识产权局等多家行政执法机关联签下发行政处罚和移送涉嫌犯罪案件的标准，规范基层执法。

（供稿人：刘月星）

执法协作

专利行政执法协作

【概况】 2015年，广东省各级知识产权局加强专利行政执法协作工作，积极强化省际、区域间、部门间的执法协作，严格履行现有协作机制的义务，全省各级知识产权局共开展各类执法协作共133次，其中：省内知识产权局协作执法60次；跨省知识产权局协作执法31次；与其他部门协作执法22次；接受其他部门移交案件20件。

2015年，广东省知识产权局共安排执法人员赴广西南宁参加第12届中国—东盟博览会知识产权保护工作，广西知识产权局安排执法人员参加第117届广交会知识产权保护工作。

广东省知识产权局向重庆市知识产权局移送和通报了在广交会上处理的涉嫌专利侵权的案件29宗，涉及企业14家。

（供稿人：毕赓）

维权援助与涉外应对

知识产权维权援助

2015年，广东省各知识产权维权援助中心共受理维权援助和举报投诉728件。详情如下：

广东省知识产权维权援助中心48件：办理维权援助申请27件，办理举报投诉案件21件。

深圳市知识产权维权援助中心24件：办理维权援助申请10件，办理举报投诉案件14件。

汕头市知识产权维权援助中心72件：办理维权援助申请26 件，办理举报投诉案件46件。

佛山市知识产权维权援助中心53件：办理维权援助申请21件，办理举报投诉案件32件。

东莞市知识产权维权援助中心68件：办理维权援助申请32件，办理举报投诉案件36件。

中国中山（灯饰）知识产权快速维权援助中心431件：专利侵权纠纷调解423件，电商领域快速维权8件。

中国东莞（家具）知识产权快速维权援助中心32件：专利侵权纠纷调解32件。

2015年7月2日，广东省知识产权局印发《关于加强我省知识产权维权援助工作的指导意见》（粤知执〔2015〕120号），推动加强广东知识产权维权援助体系建设和公共服务工作。

2015年10月，经国家知识产权局批准，中国广州（皮革皮具）知识产权快速维权中心落户花都狮岭镇。

（供稿人：毕赓）

知识产权涉外应对工作

2015年，为帮助企业提升知识产权涉外应对能力，广东省知识产权局通过知识产权涉外应对项目支持行业协（商）会组织开展企业出国参展中的知识产权保护工作。

针对中国扭扭车行业在国外遭到阻击事件，广东省知识产权局2015年12月29日派人赴深圳开展相关调研，广东产品质量监督检验研究院、深圳市标准技术研究院、广东省电动车商会以及20多家平衡车生产企业召开座谈会，针对相关专利问题进行分析讨论。

（供稿人：毕赓）

委局合作

委局合作共建

2015年，广东省知识产权局继续加强同国家知识产权局专利复审委员会的交流合作，共同推动提高地方专利行政执法工作。

2015年，国家知识产权局专利复审委员会共分5批41人次来粤对广东省专利无效和专利复审案件进行巡回审理。广东省知识产权局在做好巡回审理的保障工作的同时，组织企业、代理机构及社会公众参加旁听，提高企业和社会公众知识产权意识，扩大了社会影响，起到较好宣传效果。

在第117届、118届广交会，国家知识产权局专利复审委员会共派出12名专家分批参加广东省知识产权局的驻会专利保护工作，为专利侵权判定工作提供技术指导，大幅提高执法人员的案件处理能力和水平。

（供稿人：毕赓）

实 例

2015年广东省文化厅知识产权保护主要案例

【案例一：广州市www.dj020.com网站传播侵权音乐作品案】 2014年12月9日，广州市文化市场综合行政执法总队接到国家版权局、国家“扫黄打非”办举报材料转送单，举报反映www.dj020.com网站涉嫌传播侵权音乐作品谋利。

根据案件线索，广州市文化市场综合行政执法总队执法人员立即开展全面细致的调查取证工作。2014年12月15日，执法人员对DJ020网站进行了远程勘验，该网站是一个音乐网站，成立于2003年，主要涉嫌经营DJ舞曲音乐，兼营各类高品质唱片音乐有偿下载，网站提供近5000首歌曲试听及有偿下载，点击数已超过5万次；通过注册发展会员并通过支付宝充值、包年高级账号等提供音乐下载，营利目的明显。执法人员未发现该网站有提供任何版权授权的声明。

2015年3月，专案组赴福建莆田、厦门等地开展调查取证工作，在莆田市“扫黄打非”办、莆田市文化市场综合执法支队、莆田市公安局网络警察支队的大力支持和配合下，莆田市文化市场综合执法支队现场对服务器进行先行登记保存为案件铺开奠定了坚实的基础。2015年5月专案组再次带公安及执法人员和省人大代表、外聘见证律师接管服务器并对关键证人进行佐证，在现场律师及当地执法机构和重要证人多方见证下，实现了将重要物证直接交付进入司法鉴定中心的无缝接轨。经专案组努力，成功获取深圳市腾讯计算机系统有限公司、广州酷狗计算机科技有限公司、海洋互动（北京）文化有限公司、国际唱片业协会等四家公司出具的618首音乐作品版权声明材料，同时总队与福建中证司法鉴定中心签订了协议，委托其对涉案服务器进行鉴定并出具鉴定报告。2015年5月，顺利拿到了福建中证司法鉴定中心出具的鉴定报告。

经侦查取证，广州市文化市场综合行政执法总队成功破获这起利用互联网架设网站销售侵权音乐作品谋利的案件，现已查清该网站涉嫌侵权62286首音乐作品，成功在线支付的订单总金额为6240元，等待付款的订单总金额为257547.48元。2015年5月29日，总队对当事人莫某作出行政处罚：没收用于提供网络服务的涉案服务器，没收违法所得6240元，处以非法经营额5倍的罚款，即131.8937万元。同时由于该案已达刑事案件立案标准，移交公安机关后，当事人莫某已被检察院批准逮捕。

【案例二：广州市“6·9”特大侵权盗版教材案】 2015年6月9日10时25分至13时50分，广州市文化市场综合行政执法总队执法人员联合广州市公安局便衣支队示证到广州市白云区陈田西约南街三巷某号一楼及广州市白云区陈田东约东街一巷某号一楼三个仓库检查，现场查获《实用英语综合教程1第四版》《新编商务英语（第二版）写作教程2》《临床心理学》等涉嫌侵权盗版出版物，当事人张某华正在仓库内，总队执法人员现场对《实用英语综合教程1第四版》《新编商务英语（第二版）写作教程2》《临床心理学》等出版物共269种147640册及印刷胶片823张进行登记保存，制作《现场检查（勘验）笔录》，开具《调查询问通知书》作进一步调查。广州市公安局于6月9日进行刑事立案，对犯罪嫌疑人张某华采取刑事拘留强制措施。经广州市出版物鉴定委员会鉴定共有262种145864册为非法出版物，其中22种31694册为侵权出版物。

【案例三：广州“11·27”特大淫秽盗版光盘案】 2014年11月27日，广州市文化市场综合行政执法总队到广州市白云区增槎路湖天货运市场某档某某货运部进行执法检查。现场截获1台正在卸货的重型货车和1台接货的面包车，查获涉嫌非法音像制品53.0955万张，后经鉴定，其中250种16.9738万张涉嫌为淫秽音像制品，5524种36.1217万张为非法音像制品。由于现场无当事人，广州市文化市场综合行政执法总队将案件移交公安机关后，与广州市公安局白云区分局持续开展联合联合办案，于2015年4月16日，将10名涉案人员抓获。目前，检察机关已将档口法人陈某，货车车主等6名犯罪嫌人员批捕。

【案例四：吴某某未经批准擅自从事音像制品批发、零售经营活动】 2014年12月15日，深圳市龙岗区文体旅游局执法人员对位于深圳市龙岗区平湖街道白泥坑社区的某某音像门店进行检查，该门店为音像制品销售门店，经营者为吴某某，当事人无法提供出版物经营许可证，涉嫌未经批准擅自从事音像制品批发零售经营活动。执法人员当即责令停止违法经营行为，并依法对涉案的1600张音像制品予以扣押。2014年12月31日执法人员将该批1626张音像制品送龙岗区音像制品鉴定委员会进行鉴定。2015年1月5日，深圳市龙岗区音像制品鉴定委员会认定：送检的该批1626张音像制品为非法音像制品，并出具《音像制品鉴定意见》（深龙音鉴〔2014〕013号）。

因涉案非法音像制品数量巨大，当事人行为已触犯刑法，应当由司法机关依法追究其责任，2015年1月15日深圳市龙岗区文体旅游局依法将该案件移送公安部门进行处理。2015年1月27日，深圳市龙岗公安分局向深圳市龙岗区文体旅游局送达《立案告知书》，告知该案件已刑事立案进行处理。

【案例五：高某某从事非法印刷品印刷经营活动】 2015年4月21日下午，佛山市文化市场综合执法大队执法人员在南海区丹灶镇金沙高海工业区的某某印刷厂检查时，发现该工厂内正在进行“苹果”“最老板”“管家婆（小）”“管家婆（大）”“家中宝”“刘三姐”等多种含有六合彩内容日历芯印刷品的印刷经营活动，佛山市文化市场综合执法大队立即集中区镇两级执法人员会同南海区丹灶派出所到达案发现场迅速开展查处，并对全部涉嫌含有六合彩内容日历芯的印刷品、账本、合同、账单、生产经营用电脑主机等进行了证据先行登记保存。在该印刷厂查获含有六合彩内容日历芯印刷品成品至少有10555本，半成品有16000本，规格58厘米×80厘米的日历芯印刷品单张内页至少有5360000张，规格58厘米×80厘米的日历芯印刷品封面至少有7200张。

经向该印刷厂负责人麦某某询问得知，该印刷厂从2015年4月初开始生产，所生产的多种含有六合彩内容日历芯印刷品主要是通过网络下单销售的方式向新加坡、马来西亚、香港等境外进行出口销售。根据《印刷业管理条例》第三条的规定，由于案件经营数量巨大，佛山市文化市场综合执法大队已依法移交公安机关追究刑事责任。

【案例六：肇庆市某学校侵犯著作权案】 2014年10月15日，人民交通出版社派人到肇庆市文化广电新闻出版局举报肇庆市某学校购买、销售涉及侵害该社专有出版权的《出租汽车驾驶员从业资格考试全国公共科目培训教材》，严重侵害了该社和广大学员的合法权益，要求肇庆市文化广电新闻出版局依法查处。

肇庆市文化广电新闻出版局接到举报后，立即派出执法人员对肇庆市某学校销售盗版书籍进行核查，在该校行业培训办仓库现场查获涉嫌侵权出版物《出租汽车驾驶员从业资格考试全国公共科目培训教材》共744本并予以先行登记保存，2014年10月16日予以立案调查，经调查，肇庆市某学校所使用的涉嫌侵权图书《出租汽车驾驶员从业资格考试全国公共科目培训教材》一书是通过打电话方式与广州某文化发展有限公司业务员苗某某进行订购，通过快递方式寄到该校，该批涉案图书共订购1000本，除了现场查获的744本外，其余256本涉案图书已出售给学员用于出租汽车驾驶员从业资格培训。

涉案图书经著作权人人民交通出版社鉴定为侵权复制品（盗版图书），经肇庆市文化广电新闻出版局出版物鉴定小组鉴定为非法出版物。

根据对涉案相关人员的调查询问和案件相关证据证明，肇庆市某学校未经著作权人人民交通出版社许可，发行侵权盗版图书，没有证据证明涉案图书有合法来源，同时损害社会公共利益，违法事实清楚，证据确凿、充分。肇庆市文化广电新闻出版局于2015年1月9日向肇庆市某学校发出《行政处罚事先告知书》，拟给予“依法没收侵权盗版书籍《出租汽车驾驶员从业资格考试全国公共科目培训教材》柒佰肆拾肆本（744本），并处人民币捌万元罚款”的行政处罚。2015年1月9日，肇庆市某学校向肇庆市文化广电新闻出版局提出申请，要求就此案举行听证。

2015年2月6日，肇庆市文化广电新闻出版局应肇庆市某学校的申请，在肇庆市端州区星湖大道广电中心六楼会议室举行了公开听证会。主持人和听证员针对该案的事实和法律适用问题进行了讨论，在听取公职律师的意见后一致认为，肇庆市某学校未能提供证据证明涉案图书有合法来源，依法应当承担法律责任。该案事实清楚，证据充分，程序合法，拟作出行政处罚的自由裁量权行使得当，建议按照《行政处罚事先告知书》拟定的行政处罚决定执行。

2015年3月5日，肇庆市文化广电新闻出版局向肇庆市某学校送达《行政处罚决定书》，给予“依法没收侵权盗版书籍《出租汽车驾驶员从业资格考试全国公共科目培训教材》柒佰肆拾肆本（744本），予以销毁，处以人民币捌万元的罚款”的行政处罚。

（供稿人：王子尤）

2015年广东省质量技术监督局知识产权保护案例

【案例一：佛山市南海区质监局查处生产假冒伪劣服装案】 2015年10月22日，根据群众举报，佛山市南海区质监局行政执法人员依法对位于佛山市南海区狮山镇松岗山南工业区中区一路服装加工场进行检查，现场查获该加工场生产好的标注“ANTA”及其图案的polo衫2038件；标注LI-NING及其图案的T恤衫153件，半成品T恤衫200件；标注QIAODAN及其图案的T恤衫837件；标注“361°”的T恤衫943件。经调查，该加工场涉嫌存在生产假冒伪劣商品行为，涉案物品货值约15万元，执法人员对上述涉案物品予以扣押。

上述涉案物品经商标权利人鉴定，均系侵权的假冒伪劣产品。该加工场未经授权擅自生产上述服装产品的行为，已涉嫌构成《中华人民共和国商标法》第五十七条第（二）项规定的商标侵权行为。按照《行政执法机关移送涉嫌犯罪案件的规定》的规定，该案已于2015年10月22日移送公安机关办理。

【案例二：中山市质监局查处生产冒用注册商标及认证标志的电源适配器案】 2015年9月9日，根据举报，中山市质监局执法人员依法对位于中山市东凤镇东海二路东六街某号一电源适配器加工场进行执法检查。执法人员在该加工场内发现：（一）标称“ Designed by Apple in California UL Model NO：A1385 Made in china Input：100-240V-50/60Hz 0.15A Output：5V=1A CAUTION：For use with information technology equipment”等字样的电源适配器共15600个；（二）标称

"WWW.hippo.id UL Model No：A1385 Made By HIPPO Input：100-240V-50/60Hz 0.15A Output：5V=1A CAUTION：For use with information technology equipment Midea"等字样的电源适配器共954个；电源适配器配件一批、生产工具7台。现场该加工场未能提供工商营业执照及UL认证证书，也未能提供相关注册商标的授权委托书，执法人员依法对上述涉案物品、生产工具等采取扣押强制措施。

该加工场涉嫌生产冒用注册商标及认证标志的电源适配器这一行为属于情节严重的情形，已涉嫌构成犯罪，按照《行政执法机关移送涉嫌犯罪案件的规定》的规定，该案已于2015年9月9日移交至中山市公安局东凤分局办理。

（供稿人：钟培敬）

2015年广东海关知识产权保护典型案例

【案例一：粤港海关开展执法合作成功查获化妆品类侵权案】 2015年12月23日，香港海关通过粤港海关知识产权保护合作渠道向广东分署提供一份紧急情报，称某装有疑似侵犯"联合利华"（Unilever）、"旁氏"（Pond's）及"莱肯"（Lakme）商标货物的集装箱拟自广州南沙港经香港运往印度那瓦西瓦港。收到情报后，广东分署高度重视，迅速对情报进行分析研判，会同广州海关对在广州南沙港申报出口的该集装箱实施风险布控。2015年12月28日，成功捕获由广州市某公司以"旅游购物商品"贸易方式申报出口的涉嫌侵犯"POND'S及图形"商标的BB霜1152支，涉嫌侵犯"Unilever 联合利华"商标的粉饼、眉笔等化妆品约61176件。经权利人联合利华有限公司确认，该批化妆品为侵权产品。

典型意义：该案是近年来粤港海关通过点对点即时情报交流合作查获的最大一起侵权案件，也是广东省内海关查获的一起涉案货物数量较大的化妆品类侵权案件。长期以来，粤港海关始终保持畅顺的知识产权保护合作沟通联系渠道渠道，广泛开展情报交流、联合行动等多领域执法合作，取得显著成效。港方对于粤方此次快速行动，成功查获输港侵权案件表达了诚挚谢意。假冒伪劣化妆品严重威胁消费者的健康和安全，一直是海关总署要求从严打击的重点侵权产品。此案查获的假冒化妆品数额巨大，一旦流入国际消费市场，将会对境外消费者，特别是发展中国家人民的健康和安全造成威胁，严重损害中国的国际声誉。此案是打击利用"旅游购物商品"贸易方式出口侵权货物行为取得的成功案件。在"旅游购物商品"贸易方式出现后，侵权企业多次利用其便利通关特点，多次企图逃避海关监管。南沙海关在查办此案过程中，充分发挥了海关作为国家进出境监督管理机关的职能和优势，加强对旅游购物商品出口的日常监控，严格执行总署关于旅游购物方式的相关监管要求，并将有关情况及时通报地方商务部门建议取消企业备案资格，坚决打击旅游购物商品出口备案企业出现的侵权行为。该案的查发大大提高企业利用"旅游购物商品"贸易方式侵权违法成本，并阻止其成为侵权企业的特殊"通道"。

【案例二：广州海关查获区域通关一体化出口轮毂案】 2015年11月，广州海关隶属南沙海关接到珠海某贸易有限公司委托珠海市某报关服务有限公司向拱北海关申报的区域通关一体化报关单，该报关单被海关总署无干预随机布控，提请出口所在口岸地的南沙海关细化查验指令并实施查验。南沙海关通过审核单证，发现该票报关单货物单价异常高，货值极大，有涉嫌假冒名牌商品的重大风险，当即监控并调取该报关企业近期同一模式通关数据，对该批还未离境的已放行16个集装箱的货物追加指令予以重点查验。经查验，在申报出口至沙特阿拉伯一批货物中，发现标有"丰田图形"商标的轮毂1249个，货值高达163万元。权利人丰田汽车公司确认上述货物为侵权产品。

典型意义：此案是海关查获区域通关一体化出口侵权的典型案例。区域通关一体化是海关方便企业通关的重大改革之一，其报关单具有隐蔽性，由于有海关总署布控机制，使口岸海关能够在方便企业通关的情况下，有效监管，防止侵权货物进出口。假冒伪劣的轮毂严重威胁消费者的交通安全，一直是海关总署要求从严打击的重点侵权产品。此案查获的假冒轮毂数量巨大，一旦流入国际消费市场，将会对境外消费者，特别是发展中国家人民的交通安全造成威胁，严重损害中国的国际声誉。此案对进出口企业具有警示作用，同时也对今后海关强化区域通关一体化出口侵权的执法具有借鉴作用。

【案例三：广州海关查获出口假冒“苹果”“三星”等电子产品案】 2015年7月13日，广州海关驻萝岗办事处在陆路汽车运输渠道查获一批侵权电子产品，包括涉嫌侵权手机5811部、手机配件1523件、平板电脑521台、闪迪内存卡295件、打印硒鼓50个，涉及假冒“苹果”“三星”“小米”“MOTOROLA”“OPPO”“惠普”“SANDISK”等7个品牌商标。该批货物由广州市某有限公司以“旅游购物商品”贸易方式申报出口一批五金制品，目的地为中国香港。海关经过风险分析，认为该批申报货物有夹藏风险，遂决定对该批货物进行开箱彻底查验，经查，发现该批货物有“苹果”“三星”等品牌手机涉嫌侵权，海关立即联系七个在海关备案的权利人进行鉴定。经权利人确认，该批货物为侵权产品，涉案货物总值约400万元。广州海关根据权利人的申请对该批货物予以扣留。

典型意义：此案是海关加强风险分析有效提升旅游购物商品出口渠道知识产权执法效能的典型案例。2013年以来，海关积极支持旅游购物商品出口健康发展，为广东省促进外贸稳定发展发挥了重要作用。但在实际监管中，旅游购物商品出口品种多、种类繁杂，装载多数比较散乱，且经常存在拼单、拼货情况，个别经营企业有伪报、瞒报甚至夹藏危险品出口等走私违规行为，表明旅游购物商品出口渠道存在较大的监管风险，海关监管查验难度较大。此案对中国海关运用风险分析提高出口侵权货物的查获率，在旅游购物商品出口渠道有效遏制侵权贸易具有重要的借鉴意义。此案件影响巨大，《国际商报》、《光明日报》、“中国海关互联网站”等媒体先后对此案进行宣传报道，产生了良好的社会效果。假冒伪劣手机严重威胁消费者的健康和安全，一直是海关总署要求从严打击的重点侵权产品。此案查获的假冒手机数量巨大，一旦流入国际消费市场，将会对境外消费者，特别是发展中国家人民的健康和安全造成威胁，严重损害中国的国际声誉。

【案例四：深圳海关开展粤港合作查获假冒手机系列案】 2015年1月5日，重庆市某公司向深圳海关隶属文锦渡海关申报出口纸彩盒、灯罩等货物一批，目的地为香港。经查验发现，所申报货物均为多报少出，少出部分由9493部手机代替，涉及iPhone、SAMSUNG、BLACKBERRY、LG、SONY五个品牌，掩藏于所申报货物中，隐蔽性极强。该关立即通知有关商标权利人进行鉴定，经鉴定9493部手机全部为假冒产品。如此大量的假冒手机在陆运渠道被查获非常罕见，不同于通常“大批量、高案值侵权品经海运出口”的规律。针对该异常情况，该关立即向海关总署进行了案情通报并经总署统筹与输入地的香港海关进行了情报交换。

2015年4月，香港海关根据该关提供的情报线索，在香港查获假冒iPhone等品牌的手机及配件19196件，捣毁窝点并拘捕11人。对此次粤港海关共享信息、联合查处的成功合作，香港海关专门致函海关总署表示感谢。

自该关与香港海关相继查发假冒手机大案后，深圳海关意识到，此类假冒货物可能进行口岸转移。2015年全国开展了声势浩大的打击侵权假冒“清风行动”，第一阶段的重点是打击输往非洲、阿拉伯国家的侵权货物。由于输非、输阿均为海运航线，面临海关不断加大海运航线监控力度的形势，不法分子可能进行口岸转移，先通过陆运渠道出口至香港，再利用香港便利的贸易运输条件转运。而由于手机体积小、价值高的特点，更容易通过陆运集装箱进行藏匿和批量运输。该关有针对性地加强了对陆运输港、具有上述违法特征“杂货”的监控与分析，并在分署组织下与香港海关开展“粤港海关联合执法行动”中加大了查缉力度。

行动很快取得了成效。2015年4月，该关又查获了江西省永修县某公司、江苏省金湖县某公司通过该口岸输港的假冒手机及配件共8726件，藏匿手法与上一案件一致，均是申报出口多项货物，并将侵权手机隐藏于多种类的合法货物中，查发难度极大。2015年6月，又查获衢州市某公司出口的假冒手机2983部。截至2015年7月28日，该关已在文锦渡口岸查获侵权手机案件15宗，扣留假冒手机及其配件2.8万件，案值逾1600万元。

典型意义：该系列案是粤港海关开展深度合作、遏制侵权风险口岸转移的典型案例。香港作为国际贸易和航运中心，其便利的贸易、转运条件一直为出口侵权货物的内地不法分子所觊觎。但由于陆运输港货物受集装箱容量所限，近年来并未在该渠道发现规模性出口态势。但该系列案中，自第一宗案件发生以来，深圳海关即意识到手机等易于陆运集装箱藏匿的侵权货物存在口岸转移的风险，就此积极进行信息通报并有效开展粤港合作。通过深港两地监控，该关、香港海关均查获一系列大要案，有效遏制了此类不法行为的苗头，扼住了侵权货物陆运输港的咽喉要道。光明网、深圳特区报、文汇网等内地、香港媒体均对该系列案进行了报道，社会反响强烈。

【案例五：拱北海关查获申报出口的巧克力侵犯“费列罗立体商标”商标专用权案】 2015年8月1日，济南某贸易公司向横琴海关申报出口门闸机等货物一批，申报目的地为澳门。经海关查验，发现有未向海关申报的巧克力59箱1368盒，共210千克。上述巧克力中，有204千克共16320粒是用金色纸质包装，具有皱褶状包装效果的金黄色球状巧克力，在金色球状顶部配以印有“Chocolate”的椭圆形白底小标贴，另有各3千克共480粒分别用深红色、咖啡色纸质包装，具有皱褶状包装效果的深红色、咖啡色球状巧克力，在球状顶部配以印有“Chocolate”的椭圆形白底小标贴。上述巧克力的造型为“褶皱锡纸球状包装+顶部白底小标贴”、外包装造型为钻石包装，涉嫌侵犯费列罗有限公司在海关总署备案的“费列罗立体商标”商标专用权。经海关联系权利人费列罗有限公司，权利人书面申请对上述货物采取知识产权保护措施，海关遂于2015年8月6日依法扣留了涉案货物。

2012年5月，费列罗公司在中国核准注册了“费列罗立体商标”，并于2013年9月在海关总署进行了备案。“费列罗立体商标”是三维标志，包括锡纸等包装材质与形状、颜色的排列组合，附加在包装上的标签等等，其构成要素在图形、色彩、形状、大小等方面的排列组合具有独特性，形成了显著的整体形象，具有识别其商品来源的作用和较高的知名度。此案中，当事人在涉案巧克力上使用的“褶皱锡纸球状包装+顶部白底小标贴”包装造型与权利人备案的“费列罗立体商标”在构图、颜色和其各要素组合后的整体结构、立体形状相差不大。虽然涉案巧克力没有咖啡色纸托，但因每个巧克力被置于透明密封容器内，在包装盒内的凹槽中形成阴影折射，从整体视觉效果上看，如同具有暗色底托。从外观上看，包装造型为“褶皱锡纸球状包装+顶部白底小标贴”的巧克力，特别是金色巧克力容易对消费者视觉形成较大冲击力，易使相关公众对商品的来源产生误认，认为该批巧克力就是费列罗品牌的巧克力。鉴于此，海关认为，根据《最高人民法院关于审理商标民事纠纷案件适用法律若干问题的解释》第九条第二款规定，当事人使用的“褶皱锡纸球状包装+顶部白底小标贴”包装造型，与权利人费列罗有限公司在海关总署备案的“费列罗立体商标”构成商标近似，且“费列罗立体商标”的核定使用商品范围包括巧克力。由此海关认定，此案中当事人未经权利人的许可，在相同商品上使用了与他人注册商标相近似的商标标识，根据《中华人民共和国商标法》第五十七条第（二）项之规定，该批巧克力属于侵犯费列罗有限公司“费列罗立体商标”商标专用权的货物。当事人出口上述货物行为构成出口侵犯商标专用权货物行为。海关最终做出了没收该批侵权巧克力并处相应罚款的行政处罚决定。

典型意义：此案是拱北海关查办的首宗立体商标侵权案。立体商标，又叫三维商标，是以立体标志、商品整体外形或商品的实体包装物等以立体形象呈现的商标。立体商标的“显著性”，就是要带来超出产品属性之外的新视觉印象，让公众看到该商标就能联想到对应的商品。费列罗巧克力在中国境内市场占有率较高、广告宣传量较大、市场知名度较高，“费列罗立体商标”新颖、独具匠心的外部形状，在视觉上具有冲击力和吸引力，显著性和识别性较高，能够较好地起到区分商品来源的作用。此案作为该关查办的首宗立体商标侵权案件，具有较强的代表性和典型意义，对于今后海关系统查办立体商标侵权案件将发挥积极的借鉴和示范作用。

2015年，拱北海关认真按照总署的有关要求，在关区范围扎实组织开展“中国制造海外形象维护‘清风’行动”，并将侵权食品作为此次行动的重点监控商品之一。横琴口岸是自贸区内连接澳门的重要陆路口岸，该关立足自贸区建设的新高度，致力加强知识产权海关保护工作，重拳打击侵权假冒商品。此案的成功查办，是该关切实当好供澳物流生命线的忠实守护者和自贸经济发展的积极推动者的又一例证。

【案例六：黄埔海关查获成都某进出口公司出口假冒香烟案】 2015年1月，黄埔海关接获情报，反映有整柜假烟可能从黄埔老港码头出口。该关高度重视，迅速反应，提取分析风险要素，精确锁定嫌疑货柜，秘密控柜，张网以待。2015年1月28日，该关在黄埔老港口岸外运仓码头一举查获了成都某进出口贸易有限公司伪报成炒锅准备出口至比利时安特卫普的整柜香烟，涉嫌侵权香烟均使用了“MARLBORO及图形”及“ROYALE”商标，共计940万支。

查获的涉嫌侵权香烟中有470万支使用了“ROYALE”商标，但该商标的权利人未向海关总署申请备案保护。考虑到该批假冒香烟回流市场可能造成的危害后果，广东海关紧急启动“两法衔接”机制，对查获的涉嫌假冒香烟做出中止放行决定的同时，及时联系了地方公安局，利用司法移送制度弥补行政执法短板。为了彻底查清“ROYALE”香烟的侵权状况，办案人员经过多方查找，联系上了“ROYALE”商标的国内代理人，经权利人判定该柜出口的“ROYALE”香烟全部为假冒香烟。7月8日，该关将全案连同涉案假冒香烟一并移送至地方公安局继续侦办。

根据地方公安局的反馈情况，该案经扩线被公安部列为一级挂牌督办专案，抓获犯罪嫌疑人3人，查扣的假冒香烟市场估值超亿元。

典型意义：该案为“两法衔接”的重大案件。黄埔海关严格遵循海关公安打击侵权“两法衔接”办案程序，加强了双方的情报交流、案情通报、证据交换工作，行政执法与刑事司法无缝对接，完善案件证据体系、加大惩处力度。黄埔海关接到线索后，通过风险分析，精确布控查获侵权案件，是海关以风险管理为先导，不断积累风险分析经验，增强自身监管能力的体现。该案也是黄埔海关2015年自主查获的最大宗侵权案件。该案中“ROYALE”商标未在海关总署备案，案件调查遇到阻滞，但办案人员通过多方努力联系“ROYALE”商标的国内代理人，及时获取鉴定假冒香烟信息，固定好证据，并配合公安部门做好案件移交和涉案货物的移送。

【案例七：黄埔海关查获丰顺某针织服装有限公司出口侵权运动服装案】 2015年5月14日，丰顺某针织服装有限公司分两票报关单以一般贸易方式向黄埔老港海关申报出口棉制针织童套装、棉制针织男装长裤等45000余件到印度孟买。该关对经营单位、运输航线、出口商品等风险要素进行了分析，丰顺地处广东省东部，毗邻汕头，但该公司却舍近求远到黄埔报关出口，大量棉制针织衫裤向海关申报无品牌违反常理，且出口目的地印度又是“一带一路”沿线的主要贸易国之一，属于“清风”行动的重点保护范围。综合考虑以上因素，该出口柜商品存在较高的侵权风险。该关遂对同一货柜的两票报关单实施了布控查验。经查，该柜共装有侵权的球衣套装共28800套、男长裤5400条，涉嫌侵犯NIKE、ADIDAS、 PUMA、JAKO、DIADORA的商标权。

典型意义：该柜侵权服装的查获有赖于黄埔海关扎实有效的风险分析，选准风险要素，紧扣侵权商品特点，从纷繁芜杂的报关信息中甄别出嫌疑货柜。该案的整柜货物均涉侵权，海关一举查获的侵权服装34000余件，案值超过人民币33万元，打击了侵权货柜恶意冲关的气焰。

【案例八：江门海关查获侵犯“555”商标专用权电池案】 2015年1月7日，江门市某公司以一般贸易方式向江门海关驻外海办事处（现为“现场业务一处”）申报出口干电池120万粒，价值27000美元。申报品牌为“ROCKET 555”，运抵国为巴基斯坦。经风险分析，货物有可能分离使用商标，具有较大的侵权风险。经查验，该批电池带有“ROCKET 555”字样，但“ROCKET”“555”分离，单独突出使用了“555”商标，涉嫌侵犯“555”商标专用权。

经“555”商标专用权权利人确认，该批干电池属于侵权货物。2015年1月23日，江门海关对上述货物予以扣留。在调查该公司提供了“ROCKET”在巴基斯坦的商标注册，但无法提供使用“555”商标的使用授权。江门海关于2015年4月20日作出没收侵权电池和罚款处理。

在对没收的侵权电池实施处置时，除标拍卖的成本很高，而销毁电池要求有资质企业才能实施，还需要配额。由于上述种种困难，权利人表现出不积极配合的情绪。在这种情况下，海关考虑将侵权货物用于社会公益事业。但广东省红十字会（以下简称“省红会”）回复由于使用数量有限，很难接收大量的电池，不过同意如找到有需要的社会公益事业需求，该会可以协助转交。考虑到江门地区仍然有需要救助的贫困群众，办案人员又积极协调地方民政部门。最终地方慈善机构江门市慈善会通过省红会接收了该批侵权电池，并直接用于江门市的扶贫济困工作。省红会为此还专门发来感谢信感谢海关的工作。

典型意义：此案查获涉案货物数量、案值较大，业内影响大，惩戒效果好。电池是江门市传统出口产品，当事人在业内有较高的知名度。知名企业在知识产权方面侵权“触线”被海关处罚，表现出海关执法的公正、公平，没有因为当事人是业内的知名企业就法外施恩，真正做到“法律面前人人平等”。而且因为“知名”，对于整个行业的警示作用将会比处罚普通企业更加明显，“查获一个案件，规范一个行业”的效果也更加突出。此案是提醒企业树立知识产权意识，时时刻刻守法经营的“好教材”。当事人从原来的侵权受害者，转变为侵权者，究其原因主要是对知识产权守法意识的懈怠。接单过程中，外商改变了外包装，企业内部未进行相关的审核，疏于管理，因小失大，得不偿失，直接影响声誉，是很好的反面教材。此案是海关通过风险分析手段查获侵权货物的典型案例。江门海关法规部门主动作为，通过实时监控和风险分析，结合近年查获的侵权案件特征等手段，指引现场准确查发案件，体现了高水准的风险分析技巧。此案是海关按照环保要求依法处置侵权货物的成功范例。在处置环节权利人不配合的情况下，海关办案人员集思广益，严格依法、依规办事，创新思维，秉承环保、有效利用、低成本的理念，使侵权电池的处置物尽其用，值得推广。

（供稿人：刘雨）

2015年广东省法院十大知识产权案例

【案例一：珠海格力电器股份有限公司诉广东美的制冷设备有限公司、珠海市泰锋电业有限公司侵害商标权纠纷案】

基本案情：格力公司注册了“五谷丰登”商标。格力公司认为美的公司生产的空调器贴有“　”标识，在“美的集团官方网站”的“家电下乡产品专区”中展示有副品牌名称为“五谷丰登”空调器产品，泰锋公司销售该产品，共同侵犯其商标权，诉请法院判令美的公司、泰锋公司停止侵权，美的公司赔偿格力公司经济损失500万元以及合理维权费用5510元等。

裁判结果：一审法院认定美的公司侵犯该案商标权，判令美的公司、泰锋公司停止侵权，美的公司赔偿格力公司经济损失380万元及合理开支5510元。美的公司不服，提起上诉。二审法院判令美的公司、泰锋公司停止侵权，美的公司赔偿格力公司合理开支5510元。

典型意义：“五谷丰登”系寓意农业丰收吉祥的成语，美的公司将其作为家电下乡空调器产品的系列名称使用，是否属于“商标性使用”？法院认为美的公司在被诉侵权产品上使用“五谷丰登”标识，客观上起到了指示商品来源的作用，应认定为商标法意义上的使用。美的公司在相同商品上使用与格力公司涉案注册商标相近似的标识，侵害了格力公司注册商标权，应承担相应的侵权责任。但商标的生命力在于使用，商标法的基本要求和重要价值取向是确保注册商标的实际使用。在美的公司实施被诉侵权行为之前，格力公司注册商标没有实际使用，没有起到区分商品来源的功能，虽然美的公司侵害了格力公司注册商标专用权，但不会给格力公司造成实际损失，而且美的公司无从借用格力公司该案注册商标尚未建立起来的商誉来推销自己的产品并因此而获得利益，因此，格力公司侵权损害赔偿请求权不能成立，其请求以美的公司因侵权所获得的利益作为计算赔偿损失的依据，不应得到支持。该案在保护注册商标专用权和鼓励商标使用中取得良好平衡。

〔（2015）粤高法民三终字第145号，
承办人：邓燕辉、欧阳昊〕

【案例二：皇家菲利浦有限公司诉超人集团有限公司、刘某平等侵害发明专利权纠纷案】

基本案情：菲利浦公司系一项名为“剃须器”的发明专利的权利人。菲利浦公司认为超人公司侵犯其专利权，请求法院判令超人集团公司停止侵权，赔偿经济损失200万元，销售者刘某平停止销售侵权行为。超人公司答辩称被诉侵权的12款产品的技术特征与菲利浦公司主张的权利要求4的技术特征既不相同也不等同，未落入专利权保护范围，不构成侵权。

裁判结果：一审法院认定侵权成立，判令超人公司停止侵权并赔偿100万元，刘某平停止销售。超人公司不服，提起上诉。二审法院认为被诉技术方案在正常实施中，绝大多数情况下与专利的技术方案不同，仅偶然呈现专利所描述的结构特征，并且这种偶然状态是随机发生的，不是常态，很难规律地加以实施和运用，在专利技术方案并未限定这一特定偶然状态时，不应认定落入专利权的保护范围，遂改判驳回菲利浦公司的全部诉讼请求。

典型意义：该案系侵害发明专利权纠纷。当事人为国际和国内知名家电企业，该案争议技术方案涉及剃须刀的一项关键技术，对整个剃须刀产业影响巨大。生效裁判认为，专利的技术特征应当是明确的，其要求保护的技术方案必须能够通过科学方式加以描述，应当是正常情况下可被实施的技术方案，无规律、随机出现的偶然状态，不应被纳入专利权保护的范围，否则将导致专利权保护范围被不恰当地扩大。二审分析认定思路，既遵循了现行法律精神和原则，又进行了有益的探索和延伸，为今后立法或司法解释的补充完善提供了有价值的素材。

〔（2014）粤高法民三终字第912号，承办人：郑颖〕

【案例三：广东蒙娜丽莎新型材料集团有限公司诉广州蒙娜丽莎建材有限公司、佛山市贝佳斯洁具有限公司侵害注册商标专用权纠纷案】

基本案情：广东蒙娜丽莎公司在第19类瓷砖商品上享有“蒙娜丽莎”系列注册商标权。广州蒙娜丽莎公司在第11类卫浴装置商品上亦享有第1558842“蒙娜丽莎 Mona Lisa”注册商标。广东蒙娜丽莎公司认为广州蒙娜丽莎公司明知广东蒙娜丽莎集团“蒙娜丽莎”品牌驰名的情况，恶意将“蒙娜丽莎”登记为字号，同时，广州蒙娜丽莎公司及其经销商佛山市贝佳斯洁具公司还将“蒙娜丽莎”中文、“MONALISA”英文、蒙娜丽莎头像作为商标进行突出使用，其行为构成对广东蒙娜丽莎公司驰名商标的侵害，请求法院判令广州蒙娜丽莎公司、佛山市贝佳斯洁具公司停止侵权、消除影响及赔偿损失。

裁判结果：一审认定广州蒙娜丽莎公司及其经销商在第11类商品上使用“蒙娜丽莎”系列标识的行为和使用“蒙娜丽莎”作为企业字号的行为构成侵权，判令其停止侵权，更改企业名称并赔偿损失。广州蒙娜丽莎公司不服，提起上诉。二审改判驳回广东蒙娜丽莎公司的全部诉讼请求。

典型意义：该案涉案标识作为中国陶瓷行业的知名品牌，当事人之间的商标权互诉纠纷持续数年，案件事实复杂，社会影响力较大。该案深入分析注册商标与驰名商标之间的关系并准确界定二者的权利边界。权利人在合法获得的核准注册的商品类别上行使自己的正当权益，他人无权干涉更无权禁止。中国法律给予驰名商标的保护具有相对性，需遵循利益平衡原则，从维护市场秩序，保护信赖利益的角度出发，合理界定驰名商标禁用权的范围：驰名商标跨类保护是与其驰名程度和显著性相适应的跨类保护，不能绝对排他地禁止他人的正当、合理使用。在处理在先注册商标与驰名商标的关系问题上，应当遵守公平诚信、利益平衡的基本原则，充分考量注册商标与驰名商标的权利边界，尊重既有法律秩序与市场格局。

〔（2015）粤高法民三终字第143号，承办人：石静涵〕

【案例四：南京微盟电子有限公司与泉芯电子技术（深圳）有限公司侵害集成电路布图专有权纠纷案】

基本案情：微盟公司创作了ME6206芯片的集成电路布图设计，并获得国家知识产权局颁发的“集成电路布图设计登记证书”。微盟公司认为泉芯公司的QX6206产品侵害其集成电路布图专有权，诉请法院判令泉芯公司停止侵权，赔偿微盟公司经济损失及维权费用500万元。泉芯公司抗辩被诉QX6206芯片合法来源于京众公司并提交了对账单、送货单、增值税专用发票等证据。

裁判结果：一审法院将被诉QX6206芯片分别与微盟公司备案的ME6206芯片、京众公司的JZ6206芯片就电路布图设计的版图相似度委托鉴定，鉴定结论显示，两者的版图相似度分别为89.04%和96.91%。一审认为泉芯公司销售的芯片布图与微盟公司的电路布图设计相近似，而与京众公司的产品并非100%相同，故被诉产品并非来源于京众公司，遂认定泉芯公司构成侵权，判决停止侵权、判赔40万元。泉芯公司不服，提起上诉。二审法院撤销一审判决，改判泉芯公司不侵权。

典型意义：该案系侵害集成电路布图设计专有权纠纷，由于集成电路布图设计及相应芯片制造行业存在特有的行业规则和发展背景，对相关证据的认定应当符合日常生活经验及行业经验。二审通过深入了解行业经验和常识，纠正了一审“版权相似度不是100%即不属于同一电路布图设计”的错误认识，并综合鉴定结论、行业经验和相关交易票据，认定被诉产品符合《集成电路布图设计保护条例》第33条第1款情形，同时对“改标销售”是否属于正常商业投入进行了阐述。该案类型新颖，充分发挥了维护集成电路布图专有权权益和促进市场正常商业交易秩序的利益平衡功能，为如何结合行业背景及经验进行正确合理的司法判断起到良好示范效应。

〔（2014）粤高法民三终字第1231号，承办人：肖海棠〕

【案例五：杭州市西湖区龙井茶产业协会诉广州市种茶人贸易有限公司侵害商标权纠纷案】

基本案情：龙井茶协会是案涉“西湖龙井”地理标志证明商标在第30类商品（茶叶）上的注册人。种茶人公司在其销售的茶叶商品所使用的包装盒上印有“西湖龍井”字样的标识。龙井茶协会认为种茶人公司的上述行为侵害了其商标权，诉至法院。

裁判结果：一审法院判决被告种茶人公司立即停止销售涉案侵犯龙井茶协会享有的对第9129815号“西湖龙井”注册商标权利的茶叶，并赔偿龙井茶协会经济损失4万元。种茶人公司不服，提起上诉。二审驳回上诉，维持原判。

典型意义：生效裁判认为，该案种茶人公司侵害商标权的行为状态表现为在其制造并销售的被诉侵权产品的包装上使用了与龙井茶协会享有商标权的“西湖龙井”地理标志证明商标相近似的商标。即使种茶人公司所称的茶叶的来源地属实，其亦无权未经权利人许可擅自使用与“西湖龙井”相同或相似的证明商标。该案判决确立了销售者兼具制造以及销售侵权产品构成“叠加式”侵权形态的审理思路，进而指出此情形不适用销售者免除赔偿责任的抗辩。同时，判决深入论证作为农产品的茶叶的产地来源对于认定侵权行为的意义，进而指出该案中茶叶的产地来源对于侵权行为的构成没有影响。二审注重发挥知识产权司法保护的主导作用，针对案件反映出来的茶叶集贸市场上仿冒地理标志标识印制的监管漏洞，发出司法建议，推动监管部门开展地理标志标识印制的专项治理，促进了商标行政保护，净化了市场营商环境。

〔（2015）粤知法商民终字第2号，承办人：林广海〕

【案例六：广州医药集团有限公司诉广东加多宝饮料食品有限公司、彭某娟虚假宣传纠纷案】

基本案情：广东加多宝公司在报纸、网络和电视宣传中，发布“王老吉改名加多宝”“全国销量领先的红罐凉茶改名加多宝”等广告语，彭某娟在其经营的店铺中，使用了相关广告语进行宣传。广州医药集团有限公司认为相关行为将使相关公众误以为“王老吉”商标业已消亡，并将“王老吉”品牌上凝结的一切价值转移到“加多宝”上，广药集团为此不得不相应宣传“王老吉从未更名”以减轻负面影响，诉请法院判令被告停止虚假宣传的侵权行为、赔礼道歉，承担合理维权费用，并由加多宝公司赔偿广药集团1000万元经济损失。

裁判结果：一审判决：（1）加多宝公司立即停止使用“全国销量领先的红罐凉茶改名加多宝”“原来的红罐王老吉改名为加多宝凉茶了”广告语进行广告宣传的行为，销毁相关宣传物品；（2）彭某娟立即停止在其经营场所使用“全国销量领先的红罐凉茶改名加多宝”广告语进行广告宣传的行为，销毁相关宣传物品；（3）加多宝公司赔偿广药集团经济损失1000万元及合理费用81万元；（4）彭某娟支付合理费用2500元；（5）加多宝公司公开赔礼道歉；（6）驳回广药集团其他诉讼请求。广药集团和加多宝公司均不服，提起上诉。二审驳回上诉，维持原判。

典型意义：该案系全国首宗根据新修订的

民事诉讼法中的诉讼保全制度而采取禁令措施的不正当竞争纠纷民事案件。在程序上，根据广告宣传造成的误导效果难以挽回的特性，为及时制止被诉虚假宣传行为的持续，一审法院在受理案件后即适用新修订的民事诉讼法作出了禁令，禁止被告加多宝公司继续进行相关广告宣传，避免误导后果扩大。在实体上，该案准确把握了虚假宣传判断的要件与判断的时间点，指出是否构成虚假宣传，应当根据当时的产品情况以及相关公众认知情况来综合判断，判断的关键仍在于相关宣传信息是否产生了引人误解的效果，时间节点应当限定于根据涉案广告语发布时的相关公众认知状态来进行合理判断，从而充分维护了权利人的正当权益。

〔（2014）粤高法民三终字第482号，承办人：肖海棠〕

【案例七：中山市商房网络科技有限公司诉中山市暴风科技有限公司著作权侵权纠纷一案】

基本案情：商房网公司是微信公众号“中山商房网”的运营公司。2014年1月28日、2月6日及3月12日，商房网公司向微信用户发布了标题为《中山谁最高？利和高度将被刷新　解密中山高楼全档案》《初八后大幅度降温阴雨天气（转告朋友们注意添衣保暖哦）》《莫笑老饼　为您推介中山四大名饼（你都吃过了吗）》等三篇文章。暴风公司运营的微信公众号“最潮中山”，以发布推广信息、收取广告费谋利，该公众号于同年2月3日、2月6日及3月13日向微信用户发布了《谁是中山第一高楼？中山高楼全档案！祝全体中山人更上一层楼！与你放眼中山！》《中山下周大幅降温最低7度！你爸妈知道吗？扩散周知！》及《中山四大名饼，你都吃过了吗？中山人转走》等三篇文章。商房网公司认为暴风公司侵害了其著作权，诉请法院判令：（1）暴风公司在“最潮中山”微信公众平台及《中山日报》刊登道歉声明；（2）暴风公司向商房网公司赔偿经济损失1元。

裁判结果：一审法院认定暴风公司未经许可擅自将商房网公司在微信上发表并载明不允许其他微信公众号转载的文章《中山谁最高？利和高度将被刷新　解密中山高楼全档案》，侵犯了商房网公司享有的署名权、修改权、信息网络传播权及获得报酬等著作人身权及财产权，故判决暴风公司书面赔礼道歉、向商房网公司赔偿经济损失1元。暴风公司不服，提起上诉。二审驳回上诉，维持原判。

典型意义：该案为广东首例微信侵权纠纷案。随着微信平台的火爆，微信公众号侵权现象越来越多，不少公众号未经授权即转载或抄袭他人原创作品，借他人的智力成果提高点击量而获利。该案判决对引导相关公众尊重和保护知识产权，合法利用微信等公众平台，起到积极的导向和示范作用。

〔（2014）中中法知民终字第197号，承办人：谢劲东〕

【案例八：暴雪娱乐有限公司、上海网之易网络科技发展有限公司诉成都七游科技有限公司、北京分播时代网络科技有限公司、广州市动景计算机科技有限公司著作权侵权及不正当竞争纠纷诉中禁令案】

基本案情：原告暴雪娱乐公司是《魔兽世界》系列游戏的著作权人，原告网之易公司是该游戏在中国大陆地区的独家运营商。两原告认为，被告七游公司开发、被告分播时代公司独家运营、被告动景公司提供下载的被诉游戏《全民魔兽》（原名《酋长萨尔》）侵害了其美术作品著作权，被告分播时代公司同时构成擅自使用原告知名游戏特有名称、装潢及虚假宣传的不正当竞争行为。两原告在起诉的同时提出禁令申请，请求法院立即禁止三被告停止被诉侵权行为，并提供了1000万元的等值现金担保。

诉中禁令：广州知识产权法院在组织双方听证后作出裁定，禁止被告七游公司复制、发行及通过信息网络传播被诉游戏，禁止被告分播时代公司复制、发行、通过信息网络传播被诉游戏和实施涉案不正当竞争行为，禁止被告动景公司通过其官网传播被诉游戏。禁令效力维持至该案判决生效日止，禁令期间不影响为该游戏玩家提供余额查询及退费等服务。

典型意义：该案是广州知识产权法院成立以来颁发的第一个禁令，彰显了法院加强知识产权司法保护的决心。该案严格遵循禁令的程序要求，严格审查禁令的实体要件，整个过程规范、合法。禁令颁发后顺利执行，维护了法律的尊严和司法的权威，实现了较好的法律效果。同时，裁定特别要求被告在禁令期间应继续为游戏玩家提供余额查询及退费等服务，体现了对游戏玩家利益的考虑，实现了较好的社会效果。

〔（2015）粤知法著民初字第2-1号、（2015）粤知法商民初字第2-1号，承办人：龚麒天〕

【案例九：广州市虎头电池集团有限公司、广州轻工工贸集团有限公司诉临沂华太电池有限公司擅自使用知名商品特有包装装潢纠纷】

基本案情："虎头牌电池"以及其"红黄色"电池包装装潢是新中国成立前炎光电池厂始创，经过企业合并和商标转让，2006年9月14日广州轻工集团受让"虎头牌"商标，同年10月1日将该商标许可虎头电池公司使用。广州轻工集团和虎头电池公司主张其生产的产品的红黄颜色搭配、商标及文字组合的包装装潢系知名商品特有包装装潢，并主张华太公司生产销售被诉商品使用的包装装潢构成不正当竞争，遂起诉请求判令华太公司停止使用被诉包装装潢、赔偿损失200万元。

裁判结果：一审认定华太公司擅自使用广州轻工集团和虎头电池公司的知名商品特有包装装潢，构成不正当竞争，判令华太公司停止实施不正当竞争行为，赔偿广州轻工集团和虎头电池公司经济损失40万元。华太公司不服，提起上诉。二审法院驳回上诉，维持原判。

典型意义：该案原告是历经多次改制的老国企，生产"虎头"牌电池的历史可追溯到上世纪，社会影响较大。该案依法保护了老国企在传统行业经过长年经营沉淀积累下来的知识产权。通过司法提示社会公众，具有区别商品来源的显著特征的知名商品包装装潢，作为一项重要的知识产权可以善加运用、管理和保护。它是企业用时间、精力、信誉努力经营培育而成的，这种创造性劳动成果理应受到尊重，而市场中那些不诚信、"搭便车"式的擅自使用他人知名商品特有包装装潢的行为，应受到法律的规制。

〔（2014）粤高法民三终字第100号，承办人：郑颖〕

【案例十：原告张某义不服深圳市市场监督管理局行政处理决定案】

基本案情：张某义是一种名称为"基于客户端的停车计时方法"的发明专利权人。宜停车APP系由深圳市道路交通管理事务中心推出的用于路边停车的手机软件，可供车主下载至手机，地感埋设于停车泊位，后台服务器设置于深圳市道路交通管理事务中心。张某义认为深圳市道路交通管理事务中心侵犯其发明专利，请求深圳市市场监督管理局认定深圳市道路交通管理事务中心侵权，要求深圳市道路交通管理事务中心立即停止侵权，关闭宜停车APP下载或指向下载的链接，停止宜停车APP服务等。深圳市市场监督管理局于2015年1月28日作出《专利侵权纠纷行政处理决定》（深知稽专处字第〔2015〕001号），认为深圳市道路交通管理事务中心的行为不构成侵犯专利权。宜停车APP未落入张某义发明专利权的保护范围，深圳市道路交通管理事务中心开通的"微信"客户端和"支付宝"客户端的操作步骤和宜停车APP的操作步骤一致，亦未落入其发明专利的保护范围。张某义的全部请求及追加请求不予支持。原告张某义不服深圳市市场监督管理局行政处理决定，向法院提起行政诉讼。

裁判结果：一审认为，宜停车APP计时操作与涉案专利技术方案至少一项技术特征既不相同也不等同，故不落入涉案专利保护范围。被告作出《专利侵权纠纷行政处理决定》（深知稽专处字第［2015］001号）认定事实清楚，适用法律正确、程序合法，依法予以支持。原告张某义的诉讼请求不能成立，予以驳回。张某义不服，提起上诉。二审法院驳回上诉，维持原判。

典型意义：该案系深圳法院实行“三合一”审判以来首宗涉及专利侵权知识产权行政诉讼案件。路边停车、收费所使用APP软件系统系由深圳交通管理部门投资、招标、采用并推广，该系统软件侵权与否直接涉及这一交通市政工程能否继续顺畅实施，引起了社会及有关部门的高度关注。该案详细论证了宜停车APP计时操作与涉案专利技术方案的技术特征并进行充分比对，体现了知识产权庭审理专利行政案件的专业性，增强了司法裁判的公信力，展现了“三合一”审判改革成果。

〔（2015）深中法知行初字第1号，
承办人：陈文全〕
（供稿人：袁晶文）

2015年广东省检察机关知识产权保护典型案例

【案例一：矽某公司、房某磊侵犯商业秘密案】
珠海欧某特控制工程股份有限公司（以下简称欧某特公司）是国内具有自主知识产权的高可靠高性能嵌入式SOC芯片、立体封装SIP模块、智能图像处理及人脸识别、微型航天器、微纳卫星及星座、卫星空间信息平台、卫星大数据服务平台及系统集成供应商，其技术及产品广泛应用于民用航空航天、实时控制系统和工业控制等领域。

2003年4月，欧某特公司着手研发1553BIP核技术，用于航空航天设备的测试，该IP核由三个主要功能模块组成：总线控制器（BC）、远程终端（RT）、总线监视（BM），被告人房某磊作为该公司的技术负责人，负责研发此技术。2005年10月，被告人房某磊在1553BIP核BM模块尚未完成情况下（BC、RT等模块已研发完成），提出辞职申请，离职获批准后遂转到其妻子付某利为法定代表人的矽某公司工作。由于1553BIP核技术一直由被告人房某磊负责研发，于是在2005年12月1日，欧某特公司便与被告人房某磊签订《技术委托开发合同》，约定欧某特公司出资5万元，由被告人房某磊继续负责BM模块的研发，同时约定技术成果归欧某特公司所有，被告人房某磊负有保密义务。2006年4月11日，被告人房某磊交付了BM模块及相关技术成果，至此，欧某特公司1553BIP核整套技术已研发完成。2009年开始，被告人房某磊违反约定，披露、使用、允许他人使用其掌握的欧某特公司1553BIP核技术，以矽某公司名义，先后生产销售系列1553B测试仪17个，销售金额达800多万元，其中，在2010年至2012年期间，生产销售相关产品11个，给欧某特公司造成2568539.14元人民币经济损失。

该案于2012年11月16日由珠海市公安局以房某磊涉嫌侵犯商业秘密罪立案，并指定高新区公安分局侦查。2013年6月6日，房某磊被珠海市公安局高新分局刑事拘留，于同年7月12日被逮捕。2014年3月12日，珠海市香洲区人民检察院对该案提起公诉。同年11月6日，珠海市香洲区人民法院以侵犯商业秘密罪判处矽某公司罚金人民币250万元；判处被告人房某磊有期徒刑三年，并处罚金人民币20万元。房某磊不服，提起上诉。2015年6月15日，珠海市中级人民法院作出终审裁定：驳回上诉，维持原判。

评析意见：该案是较为罕见的侵犯上市公司技术秘密的刑事案件。由于该案涉案技术专业性强、取证难度大、审查认定难，作为承办部门，珠海市检察院高新区知识产权检察室充分利用专业办案机制优势，主动提前介入引导侦查，督促公安机关依法开展侦查，并多次就案件的检材提取、办案程序的完善、涉案技术的鉴定、产品利润的审计、损失的计算认定等问题，提出了有针对性的意见，为案件的成功办理奠定了扎实基础。同时，为提高办案质量，检察人员两次前往广州听取鉴定专家对涉案技术的讲解与分析，保障精准有力指控犯罪。案件审理过程中，加强与审判机关的沟通交流，提出的关于涉案商业秘密的损失计算方法，获得了两级法院的支持和采纳，为今后办理此类案件提供了借鉴和示范。案件办理后，检察机关主动回访被害单位，及时反馈办案中发现的知识产权风险漏洞问题，帮助企业建立健全相关制度，受到了企业和当地党委政府的高度好评。

该案历时两年半，一审五次开庭、二审三次开庭、审计鉴定达七次、侦查、审计、鉴定和专家辅助人员均先后到庭作证说明情况，案件的办理不易，彰显了中国检察机关在保护知识产权、保障服务创新驱动发展、营造法治化、市场化营商环境方面的决心和水平。

【案例二：陈某田等四人假冒注册商标案】

2013年6月，被告人陈某田在长安镇新民社区某某路22号某某工业园及乌沙社区某某路75号各承租了一个仓库分别作为其生产假冒注册商标饮料的生产地、成品存放地及原材料存放地。后陈某田在某某工业园的仓库引入生产设备并先后招聘陈某姣、周某云、陈某等人为其从事生产假冒加多宝、王老吉、红牛等注册商标饮料工作。其中陈某姣为生产流水线主要工人从事成品包装及其他协调工作，周某云为假冒饮料调剂师，陈某为假冒饮料原材料、成品运送司机。2014年7月3日，长安工商分局对某某工业园的仓库进行查处，现场查获假冒加多宝2640罐、假冒王老吉26400罐、假冒红牛18000罐（经查，每箱饮料共24罐，若按实际销售价格43元每箱计算，上述饮料共价值84280元）。经查，单是6月1日至7月2日期间的产量就有17888箱，除现场查获的假冒饮料外，其余生产的假冒饮料均以43元许一箱对外已销售。

该案由东莞市第二市区人民检察院侦查监督科通过行政执法和刑事司法衔接信息共享平台发现，东莞市工商管理局办理陈某田假冒注册商标行政案已达刑事追诉标准，东莞市第二市区人民检察院于2014年7月23日向东莞市工商管理局发出《建议移送涉嫌犯罪函》。同日，东莞市工商管理局向东莞市公安局发出《涉嫌犯罪案件移送书》。

东莞市公安局于2015年8月29日将该案被告人陈某田等四人提请批准逮捕，东莞市第二市区人民检察院于2014年9月5日以涉嫌假冒注册商标罪批准逮捕陈某田等四人。

该案于2014年11月4日移送审查起诉，2015年4月16日东莞市第二人民法院一审以假冒注册商标罪分别判决陈某田有期徒刑二年六个月并处罚金7万元、判处陈某姣有期徒刑一年六个月并处罚金6000元、判处周某云有期徒刑一年三个月并处罚金5000元、判处陈某有期徒刑一年并处罚金4000元。2015年4月16日一审判决生效。

评析意见：该案系检察机关通过与行政执法机关、公安机关建立的行政执法和刑事司法衔接信息共享机制发现立案监督线索，继而监督行政执法机关依法移送涉嫌犯罪案件线索，最终追诉了一起假冒注册商标犯罪的成功范例。该案中，东莞市第二市区人民检察院会同东莞市工商管理局以及公安机关，建立了案件咨询和信息通报制度，畅通了知情渠道，使检察机关能及时发现监督线索，并且从取证标准、搜集证据等方面给予引导，促进行政执法机关严格规范执法，有效防止了以罚代刑，增强了行政执法与司法保护协调配合，共同促进了知识产权全方位保护。

【案例三：梁某克等三人非法制造注册商标标识及赖某莲销售非法制造的注册商标标识案】

2012年3月开始，梁某克明知是非法制造他人商标标识，仍然利用深圳市某包装制品有限公司的法人代表人身份，在该公司下班后，安排陈某茂操作印刷机、许某兵操作“切料机”和“合掌机”，生产假冒的“益力”“景田”“怡宝”等知名品牌的桶装水贴标120万余张。制造上述贴标后，梁某克便通过快递销售给赖某莲，赖某莲再转卖给付某生。

2013年8月1日，民警抓获了付某生，并从其在深圳市南山区某村某平房门前停放的长安面包车内当场缴获非法制造的注册商标标识36000件，桶装水盖子12000个。上述缴获的非法制造的注册商标标识均由付某生向赖某莲购买。2014年2月24日，民警在深圳市龙华新区某村某区某号某房抓获赖某莲，并当场缴获向梁某克购买并准备销售的假冒的“景田”“益力”“怡宝”桶装水商标共计24800张，以及缴获激光打码机和桶盖压缩机各一台。同日，民警在龙岗区某路某号赖某莲父亲住处，缴获了赖某莲向梁某克购买并放在该处准备销售的假冒的“景田”“益力”“怡宝”桶装水商标共计12万张、盖子6000个，以及“乐百氏”和“怡景”商标共计3万张、盖子3200个。4月25日，民警对在深圳市龙岗区某社区某村某号某楼的深圳市某包装制品有限公司，当场缴获尚未销售的假冒的“景田”“益力”“怡宝”桶装水商标共计29500张，同时缴获印刷假冒商标标识的模具19个和大型印刷设备一套。

该案由深圳市公安局南山分局以被告人梁某克、陈某茂、许某兵、赖某莲涉嫌非法制造、销售非法制造的注册商标标识罪，于2014年7月30日向南山区检察院移送审查起诉。南山区检察院经审查后，于2014年12月22日向深圳市南山区人民法院提起公诉。经开庭审理后，南山区检察院于2015年11月10日收到深圳市南山区人民法院的判决。该判决认定梁某克、陈某茂、许某兵均犯非法制造注册商标标识罪，分别判处梁某克有期徒刑二年六个月、判处陈某茂有期徒刑二年、判处许某兵有期徒刑一年六个月，认定赖某莲犯销售非法制造的注册商标标识罪，判处有期徒刑三年，缓刑四年。

评析意见：饮用水的健康为群众基本的生活需要，一段时间内，深圳市内多发假冒桶装水事件，假冒或伪造桶装水未经过相关的消毒杀菌等技术处理，也未经过相关部门的检查，存在多种致病的可能，危害群众的身体健康，引起广泛关注。该案中涉案的益力、怡宝、景田等均系著名桶装水商标，有广大用户群体，且因其品质获得了用户的信赖。非法制造的上述标识会被用于生产伪造的桶装水，将会给上述公司带来巨大的损失。该案的成功办理，从源头上打击假冒桶装水的制假行为，遏制了假冒桶装水的商标来源，控制了该类违法犯罪行为的发生。

（供稿人：刘月星）

ZHI SHI CHAN QUAN GUAN LI

知识产权管理与服务

- 广东创建知识产权服务业发展示范省规划（2013—2020年）
- 知识产权试点示范
- 企业知识产权管理规范
- 专利代理管理
- 百所千企知识产权服务对接工程
- 产业专利信息服务平台
- 服务与支撑机构

广东创建知识产权服务业发展示范省规划（2013—2020年）

广东创建知识产权服务业发展示范省规划（2013—2020年）

【概况】 2015年，广东省知识产权局大力推进知识产权服务业发展示范省建设，知识产权服务业快速发展。福田区、佛山市加快建设国家知识产权服务业集聚发展实验区，东莞松山湖新区、广州越秀区、开发区设立省级知识产权服务业集聚发展试验区，顺德区试点建设“知识产权创新运用试验区”。加强专利信息的传播与利用。开展中小微企业专利信息推送服务，2015年，面向45个专业镇近1500家企业推送了定制的专利信息服务产品。组织实施广东省战略性新兴产业专利信息资源利用计划项目、省市重点产业专利信息分析评议项目。探索信息公益和商务服务新模式。深入开展产业专利分析预警及导航。启动实施“珠江西岸先进装备制造产业带专利导航工程”，围绕江门市轨道交通装备、肇庆市智能化成形和加工成套设备、顺德区智能装备制造、佛山市汽车制造、中山市电动汽车等5个先进装备制造产业，组织开展专利导航。实施“珠江三角洲地区产业转型升级专利导航工程”，围绕佛山市高端制造装备、东莞市工业机器人、深圳市生物医学工程、中山市海洋工程装备等4市的4个重点发展的战略性新兴产业，推进专利信息的深度开发利用，导航产业的转型升级及创新发展规划制定。推动广州开发区、佛山市整合区域内优质知识产权服务及运营资源，围绕智能装备、卫星通信、机械装备制造等重点产业，开展产业专利导航。支持广州开发区、佛山市积极探索创建“国家专利导航产业发展实验区”。启动实施“广东省重大经济科技活动知识产权评议促进计划”。深圳市、东莞市、佛山市南海区、江门市高新区等7个区域，开展知识产权评议试点，扶持有关市（区）建立本区域的知识产权评议机制。

（供稿人：阳屹琴）

知识产权试点示范

国家知识产权试点示范城市

【概况】 截至2015年底，广东省共有国家知识产权示范城市5个（广州、深圳、东莞、佛山、中山），原国家知识产权工作示范城市1个（汕头）、被认定具备国家知识产权示范城市资格1个（惠州）、地级试点城市7个（肇庆、潮州、江门、珠海、湛江、茂名、顺德）、县级试点城市5个（广州增城、肇庆四会、江门台山、茂名化州、肇庆高要）。在国家局的考评结果中，广东省知识产权局和广州、深圳等9个城市知识产权局获国家知识产权试点示范城市工作先进集体称号，全省9名个人获先进个人称号。

【国家知识产权示范城市】 2015年，国家知识产权城市试点示范工作取得良好成效。佛山、中山顺利进入国家知识产权示范城市工作序列，圆满召开佛山、中山“国家知识产权示范城市工作会谈和高标准建设国家知识产权示范城市推进大会”，促进两市不断完善示范城市建设工作机制和方案。惠州参评国家知识产权示范城市，在机构、编制、经费等方面取得重大突破，在第四批国家知识产权示范城市评定结果公示中位列地级市第四位，被认定具备国家知识产权示范城市资格。广州、深圳、东莞积极开展示范城市建设工作。广州以副省级城市第一名的成绩通过首批国家示范城市年度考核和复核，获批开展新一轮示范城市建设。深圳继续打造“深圳质量”，以企业为主体、以市场为导向、以政策为支撑，产学研相结合，努力打造创客空间，扶持企业、创客等创新主体发展。东莞召开全市科技创新大会，中共东莞市委书记徐建华、市长袁宝成等主要领导出席，表彰该市中国专利奖获得者。

【国家知识产权试点城市】 2015年，广东省知识产权局继续推进国家知识产权试点城市工作。各试点城市认真实施知识产权试点城市建设工作方案，并取得积极成效。2015年底，按照国家知识产权局的有关部署和要求，广东省知识产权局制定《2015年度国家知识产权试点（含示范培育）工作考核表（广东省）》，组织开展了2015年度试点城市（含原国家知识产权工作示范城市、具备第四批示范城市资格的城市）考核工作，所有参加考核的城市均获得优秀等级。

（供稿人：陈劼）

国家知识产权强县工程试点示范

【概况】 截至2015年底，广东省有国家知识产权强县工程示范县（区）5个，分别为：佛山市禅城区、广州市花都区、佛山市南海区、广州市越秀区、广州市萝岗区；国家知识产权强县工程试点县（区）13个，分别为：惠州市惠城区、惠州市博罗县、江门市江海区、韶关市曲江区、阳江阳东区、广州市海珠区、广州市番禺区、惠州市惠东县、汕头市澄海区、韶关市武江区、梅州市梅县区、佛山市高明区、韶关市浈江区。

2015年，国家知识产权局印发《关于做好2015年度国家知识产权强县工程、传统知识保护相关工作的函》，部署2015年度国家知识产权强县工程示范县（区）和试点县（区）考核验收和推荐工作。广东省知识产权局成立了

“广东省实施国家知识产权强县工程试点县（区）考核验收组”，对广州市越秀区、广州市萝岗区、惠州市博罗县、惠州市惠城区、韶关市曲江区、阳江市阳东区、江门市江海区等7个2013年9月之前获批开展国家知识产权强县工程试点工作的县（区）进行了考核验收，广州市越秀区、广州市萝岗区、惠州市博罗县、惠州市惠城区、阳江市阳东区、江门市江海区等6个县（区）考核成绩为优秀。同时，择优向国家知识产权局推荐县区申报国家知识产权强县工程示范县（区）、试点县（区）。

2015年12月，广州市越秀区、广州市萝岗区被确定为国家知识产权强县工程示范县（区），佛山市高明区和韶关市浈江区被确定为国家知识产权强县工程试点县（区）。各县（区）认真制定并大力实施强县工程试点示范方案，积极推动各项工作切实有效开展。

（供稿人：陈劼）

高新区知识产权示范创建

【概况】 发挥知识产权对产业集聚区的“集聚放大”效应。一是启动实施广东省专利密集型产业集聚区培育工程。扶持深圳市、佛山市南海区、惠州仲恺高新区、广州开发区、东莞松山湖高新区等产业集聚区的相关专利密集型产业创新发展。二是推动高新区知识产权示范创建。肇庆高新区顺利通过国家知识产权试点园区试点工作考核验收，东莞松山湖（生态园）高新区获批“国家知识产权试点园区”，广州开发区、深圳高新区、惠州仲恺高新区继续保持“国家知识产权示范园区”的荣誉。广州开发区积极推进国家知识产权局专利局专利审查协作广东中心和广东省知识产权服务业集聚中心建设，完善知识产权审议机制，开展生物产业等重点产业知识产权预警，培育知识产权示范企业。深圳高新区在全国率先形成了独具特色的“六个90%”，培育出7家年产值超百亿元的世界知名企业、81家上市公司，诞生了世界第一个U盘、世界第一个基因治疗药物、世界第一台3G-USB液晶电视等多项世界第一；发明专利申请量连续多年居国家级高新区第二位，PCT国际专利申请量连续多年居国家级高新区首位；落户深圳高新区的国家专利审查员实践基地已成为全国规模最大的专利审查员实践基地。

（供稿人：郑俊秋　吴瑛）

企业知识产权管理规范

企业知识产权管理规范

【“贯标”培训】 2015年，广东省知识产权局组织开展“贯标”培训班7期。各地市局也积极开展“贯标”培训，东莞、佛山、揭阳等地都举办了不同规模的“贯标”培训班。此外，省知识产权局还多次组织广东省知识产权管理及服务机构人员，参加国家知识产权局举办的“贯标”培训班；多次组织广东省服务机构参加中知（北京）认证有限公司举办的“贯标”体系认证审核员培训班；与中规（北京）认证有限公司合作组织了一期“贯标”体系认证审核员培训班。

【“贯标”服务体系】 其一，加强横向联动。省知识产权局联合省科技厅、经信委、商务厅、质监局、国资委等部门研究制定并印发了《关于全面推行〈企业知识产权管理规范〉国家标准的实施意见》。其二，推动合作共建。省知识产权局与中华全国专利代理人协会签署《贯彻企业知识产权标准合作关系议定书》，全国第一个“贯标”地方性办事机构“中规（北京）认证有限公司广州办事处”于2015年7月落户广东；中知（北京）认证有限公司与深圳市标准技术研究院建立重点合作关系，将在广东省及其周边区域积极组织社会服务资源，高质量、高效率开展企业“贯标”审核、认证工作及配套服务。其三，实施推进项目。实施2014、2015年度“广东省企业知识产权管理规范推进项目”，扶持20家服务质量高、运营情况好的“贯标”服务机构，按市场化运作原则发动并辅导企业“贯标”，项目任务要求20家机构辅导200家企业进行“贯标”。

【地市“贯标”】 发动全省市、县（区）级知识产权局结合实际，探索有效的“贯标”推行工作模式。部分地市包括广州、中山、东莞、佛山、惠州等已出台“贯标”扶持配套政策。

【企业“贯标”认证】 截至2015年底，广东省已有广州白云山制药总厂、朗科科技、国云科技、巨大音响、纽恩泰等31家企业通过认证。省知识产权局对2014年通过“贯标”认证的首批5家企业给予5万元/家的经费支持，并将继续对2015年通过“贯标”认证的企业给予经费支持。

【编写“贯标”指导书籍】 组织编写了全国第一部“贯标”工作指导专著《GB/T 29490-2013〈企业知识产权管理规范〉理解及知识产权管理体系审核指南》，并于2016年初，在东莞举办了该专著的新书发布会。

（供稿人：吴瑛）

专利代理管理

专利代理管理

【概况】 截至2015年底，广东省共有专利代理机构158家，占全国13%；专利代理人1455人，占全国12%；共有分支机构164家；专利代理机构从业人员近4200人；代理机构中，合伙制91家，公司制50家，律师事务所开办专利代理17家。

【监管工作】 广东省知识产权局按《专利代理条例》和《专利代理管理办法》，做好对代理机构设立的审核及改革前跨省分支机构的设立许可审批工作，配合省政府开展职能清理和行政审批制度改革。2015年，广东省新设代理机构15家，审核上报代理机构设立申请19家（截至10月底批准外省来广东省设立分支机构20家、撤销1家，批准本省机构向外省设立分支机构10家，直接经工商部门注册后报省知识产权局备案的本省机构在省内设立分支机构5家、撤销0家）。2015年11月取消分支机构审批后报省知识产权局备案设立分支机构4家，撤销分支备案2家。

根据行政审批制度改革的要求，专利代理机构分支机构的设立审批取消，改为备案制，监管任务更繁重，省知识产权局一是召开全省专利代理管理工作会议，总结成绩，并对专利代理行业存在的问题进行深入剖析；二是通过年度报告加强对代理机构及代理人执业监管；三是按照新修订的《专利代理管理办法》的要求，通过书面检查、实地检查和网络监测等方式综合开展专利代理机构抽查，全年共实地检查代理机构8家，书面检查30家，实现对代理机构网络监测全部覆盖；四是依据属地管理的原则，支持指导地市知识产权局加强对本地代理机构、专利代理人的执业监管。

【专利代理服务能力建设】 2015年，省政府印发《广东省深入实施知识产权战略推动创新驱动发展行动计划》，明确全面增强知识产权服务能力，提升代理机构服务能力和水平。

一是专题培训活动。2015年，广东组织了包括专利文件撰写、欧洲专利实务、PCT国际阶段电子申请及审查系统（CEPCT）培训、外观部设计相关讲座、通讯领域专利审查与代理交流培训、机电领域实务技能培训和专利电子申请推广等一系列专题培训活动，大力提升全省专利代理服务的质量和水平。

二是专利代理人实务技能培训。根据国家局《专利代理人实务技能培训工作实施方案（2011—2015）》，2015年是实务技能培训的收官之年，从2012年开始，广东共有930名专利代理人参加了此类培训，在加强代理人专业理论学习和实际操作能力锻炼的同时，提升了专利代理服务能力和水平。

三是专利代理人资格考试。2015年全国专利代理人资格考试首次采取计算机化考试方式，广州考点各项数据均为历年之最：共有3229名考生报名参加考试，比2014年增长9.46%；参考率71.82%，其中专利法科目72.14%，相关法科目71.84%，专利代理实务科目71.48%，均为全国最高；考试合格776人，通过率达31.18%，创历史新高。为进一步加大对考试工作的支持力度，吸引更多人才进入专利代理行业，广东省继续拨专款全额支持举办为期7天面向全省及港澳台考生的考前培训班，邀请国家局资深审查员授课，据统计，参加培训班的学员中通过考试93人，通过率达34.07%，成效显著。

【专利代理管理工作发展】

代理机构调研。为及时了解掌握专利代理行业发展状况及存在的问题，2015年，省知识产权局局长马宪民带队到代理机构调研，并就互联网环境下代理机构发展所面临的问题、如何进一步加强中高层次尤其是高端专利人才的培训等问题与代理机构代表进行了沟通交流；对代理机构反映的热点难点，如“营改增”对知识产权服务业带来的冲击问题，积极加强与有关方面的沟通与联系，收集、整理代理机构提供的税收资料和信息，反映到省国税局、国家局条法司及全国专利代理人协会，推动国家在“营改增”中明确免征专利代理机构官费及涉外代理增值税。

专题座谈会。2015年，省知识产权局先后两次组织专利代理机构召开座谈会，就如何在实施创新驱动发展战略、加快现代服务业发展中进一步加强专利代理服务体系和能力建设，全面推进专利代理行业又好又快发展和与会代表进行了交流。座谈会总结分析了当前国内外知识产权发展形势，通报了广东省知识产权工作特别是专利代理管理工作有关情况，听取了专利代理机构对广东省知识产权工作特别是专利代理管理的意见和建议，共同对当前专利代理行业存在的问题和下一步工作进行了探讨。

【专利代理行业发展】

引导行业规范。2015年，广东省继续引导广东专利代理协会在行业内开展“广东代理机构管理规范达标单位评选活动”和“优秀发明专利申请文件评选活动”。通过这两个活动有效推动专利代理机构加强规范管理，引导代理行业加强专利代理质量管理。

开展执业培训。支持广东专利代理协会大力开展各类针对提升专利代理人执业能力的执业培训及同业交流活动，支持、指导协会组织召开第二届创新知识产权服务论坛。

对外交流与合作。2015年，由广东专利代理协会组织全省12家规范达标单位代表赴北京参访相关代理机构、全国协会等单位；同时由协会组织相关代理机构赴港参加亚洲知识产权营商论坛，通过与国内国际同行的交流学习，提升广东省代理机构的管理及业务水平。

（供稿人：王强）

百所千企知识产权服务对接工程

百所千企知识产权服务对接工程

【概况】 “百所千企知识产权服务对接工程”2010年启动，广东省先后在东莞、中山、佛山市南海区、顺德区、禅城区等五个地区进行试点，再逐步向全省各市推进。至2015年底，绝大部分地市结合各自实际，开展形式多样的对接活动。

2015年11月至12月，广东省知识产权局分别牵头组织在茂名、四会、高要、韶关4市举行百所千企知识产权服务对接系列活动，共有26家专利代理机构、290多家企业以及多家高校、科研院所代表，市、区知识产权工作负责人300多人参加了此次系列活动。结合对接地的产业特点，分别举办“专利挖掘与申请”“专利侵权判定及规避设计”“企业知识产权管理规范”“专利电子申请及网上缴费”“企业专利申请与保护”“专利战的攻与防——空客A380登机桥发明专利侵权纠纷案”等专题讲座，通过深入企业、召开座谈会等形式，就企业如何进一步加强知识产权申请保护等相关问题进行深入的交流。

（供稿人：王强）

产业专利信息服务平台

产业专利信息服务平台

【概况】 2015年，广东省知识产权局完成广东省战略性新兴产业全领域专利实时监测系统建设，此工作旨在形成科学的专利检索策略和开发实时监测网络系统，对全球战略性新兴产业全部技术领域的专利申请、专利授权、有效专利发展情况进行实时监测，向省政府及相关部门提供及时、权威、准确的全球战略性新兴产业专利发展动态，为广东省掌握战略性新兴产业创新发展趋势、制定促进相关产业发展的政策措施提供有利支持。该项目建设利用广东省知识产权研究与发展中心现有条件，通过中心全面权威的专利信息资源（涵盖100多个国家及地区1亿多条数据）以及专业的研究队伍（涉及机械、电子、通信、医药、化学、光电、管理、计算机等多个专业领域，覆盖战略性新兴产业全领域技术），以七大新兴产业的专利数据深加工为核心，制定形成科学的专利检索策略，搭建先进实用的信息服务平台，实时监测和掌握战略性新兴产业全领域（国家发展改革委员会2013年第16号公告发布的《战略性新兴产业重点产品和服务指导目录》，确定了7个产业、24 个发展方向，并进一步细化到近 3100 项细分的产品和服务）专利发展情况，包括专利申请、专利授权、有效专利等情况，有利于促进重点产业的科学发展，加快高端突破，增强知识产权服务业的发展后劲，提升企业自主创新能力和专利制度运用能力，为产业发展和政府科学决策做好服务。

（供稿人：李润聪）

服务与支撑机构

国家专利审查协作广东中心共建情况

【概况】 2015年，国家专利审查协作广东中心（下称审协广东中心）完成第一次审查意见通知书13.9万件，完成结案12.4万件。至2015年底，永久业务用房建设项目按计划已取得国有土地使用证、建设用地规划许可证、建设工程规划许可证、建筑工程施工许可证，完成主体施工图设计，获得项目可行性研究报告、立项、概算、主体初步设计方案等批复，并进行主体施工。

2015年4月18日，国家科技部副部长曹健林、广东省副省长陈云贤到审协广东中心调研，对审协广东中心工作给予肯定，并希望审协广东中心继续支持地方自主创新，有效促进地方经济发展。

（供稿人：孟梦）

国家知识产权局专利局广州代办处

【概况】 2015年，国家知识产权局专利局广州代办处（以下简称代办处）共受理专利申请135206件，同比增长48.4%，其中，纸件专利申请2223件，电子申请人工审查132983件；收取专利费用363790笔，同比增长15.84%，金额3.12亿元，同比增长17.31%；处理远程票据110196笔，同比增长18.14%，金额8208万元，同比增长19.46%。

【专利电子申请】 电子申请推广工作注重广东工作实际，全面分析全省电子申请率提升空间，促进专利电子申请率稳步提升。一是开展系列宣传推广活动。举办多期电子申请宣传与使用培训班，普及专利电子申请知识和系统操作方法。二是及时通报电子申请推广信息。2015年每月编辑《广东省专利电子申请简报》，在省局网站和代办处受理大厅定期通报全省及各专利代理机构电子申请率，为各地市打击“黑代理”提供信息支持。三是积极做好相关服务保障工作。编印《专利电子申请使用手册》免费提供给广大申请人。通过专线电话、QQ群、上门服务等方式指导申请人使用电子申请，重点跟踪纸件申请量大的个人和未达到100%电子申请率的代理机构，帮助申请人解决在电子申请中遇到的实际困难。四是积极配合国家局复审委做好复审与无效宣告电子请求系统使用推广工作。窗口接收复审、无效宣告专利文件大幅减少，对全省电子申请推广工作起到很好的促进作用。

【试点工作】 截至2015年，共办理专利实施许可合同备案达3895件，涉及专利6346项，合同金额9.2亿元人民币；办理专利权质押登记申请59件，合同金额43.9亿元；为各有关部门和申请人出具专利登记簿副本14177件；为广交会知识产权执法工作提供专利确权信息2440件；办理专利技术合同认定231件，合同金额7.7亿元；受理向外国申请专利保密审查请求13973件；承担各类通知书对外发文及管理1012291件；扫描各类请求及相关文件73765件；办理电子申请注册18348件；代收复审无效请求20件；受理法律手续类文件144件。

【公共服务】 2014年，代办处获得“2013—2014年度国家知识产权局青年文明号”荣誉称号。为最大限度满足公众需求，给办事群众提供方便，2015年底起广州代办处服务大厅窗口对外的服务时间调整为8个小时，午休时间增设了值班岗。并在此基础上完善了一系列便民举措：一是提供高效便捷的服务环境，建立了集受理、收费、查询、政务公开、等候等五个功能区为一体的工作大厅，并提供免费直拨咨询电话和公用电脑，指导专利申请人办理相关业务。二是公开服务监督电话和业务咨询电话，更新升级业务语音咨询查询系统，提供24小时电话语音咨询服务，设置群众意见箱，认真对待投诉和咨询，自觉接受社会公众的监督。三是加强服务大厅业务指引，设置业务指引牌，为公众提供更有效和快捷的指引。并对窗口人员文明礼仪、依法解答、接待态度等方面制定相应规定，要求工作人员挂牌上岗、文明用语、微笑服务，对老弱病残等弱势群体提供优先受理、优先办理的“一站式”服务，对中小微企业和港澳台企业提供“绿色通道”。四是提供服务大厅公众无线网络WiFi上网服务，方便公众通过网络查询办理专利业务。

（供稿人：洪伟）

广东省知识产权研究与发展中心（广东省知识产权维权援助中心）

【概况】 2015年，广东省知识产权研究与发展中心（广东省知识产权维权援助中心）（以下简称“中心”）围绕专利信息传播利用和知识产权维权援助两个轴心，开展各项工作。

【信息服务体系】

构建多元化、区域性的专利信息服务体系。中心召开“泛珠三角区域九省（区）专利信息服务工作座谈会”，介绍泛珠三角区域跨省区专利信息服务项目，交流专利信息传播和利用的经验并提出跨省区专利信息服务建议以及发布广东省专利大数据应用服务情况；开展泛珠区域内专利信息推送服务及专利信息人才跨省区培育服务，面向泛珠区域省区600多家企业开展专利信息推送服务，服务涵盖技术领域22大类技术领域，与海南、四川、广西、贵州等省区联合举办多次专利信息人才培训班；围绕“区域专利信息高端服务示范工程”开展项目研究工作。

牵头开展并完成“专利信息传播利用（广东）基地专利信息利用促进项目”及“专利信息传播利用（广东）基地工作体系建设与能力培育项目”“专利信息领军人才师资人才实践项目”等任务。

依托信息传播利用基地、区域专利信息服务中心、培训基地和省综合服务平台等广东省现有专利信息化建设及运用成果，采用多种大数据及云计算应用技术，实现“打造一个服务平台，创新一种运营模式，培育一个运用市场”，探索专利信息资源市场化配置服务模式，建立公益性和商务性相结合的“专利大数据服务基地”建设思路。

牵头发起成立“广东省专利信息协会”。截至2015年12月，会员包括76个创新主体及6家省外服务机构作为特邀理事单位。参加“全国知识产权分析评议服务机构联盟”和“全国知识产权品牌服务机构联盟”。引导服务联盟成员入粤服务形成优势互补、资源共享的知识产权信息服务新方法和新模式，完善广东省知识产权分析评议和信息服务体系。

与全球领先的知识产权交易与产业升级平台——汇桔网达成全面战略合作，与汇桔网联合举办“知识产权创新创业大赛”。

以协会为依托，与中规（北京）认证有限公司合作设立中规（北京）认证有限公司广州办事处。作为全国第一个贯标地方性办事机构，举办了全省首个贯标外审员培训班，共141名学员成功通过CCAA的考试；在广东省知识产权服务地市行粤东站活动中为粤东地区120多家重点企业的300多名知识产权工作人员讲解企业知识产权管理体系认证审核实务。

【信息化平台】

广东省知识产权公共信息综合服务平台。重新策划综合服务平台首页面和栏目版面，升级改造综合平台各功能模块及数据栏目的访问效果，满足用户对海量数据快速访问需求。完成数据库的整体迁移、平台页面改版及系统功能升级等工作，且全新平台已正式对外开放使用。

广东专利大数据应用服务平台系统开发及子系统。完成平台系统检索接口开发、后台用户管理机制设计，实现专利检索、专利详情查询、专利说明书下载、专利附图下载、用户注册和登录等功能，并已上线试运行；完成大数据APP移动应用子系统建设，提供手机APP上的全文检索、标题检索、公司检索、公开号检索等多种检索方式，利用手机APP开展信息服务及移动推送，至2015年底，已完成系统开发及各项功能设计并已上线试运行。

广东省战略性新兴产业全领域专利实时监测系统。以七大新兴产业的专利数据深加工为核心，制定科学的专利检索策略，实时监测战略性新兴产业全领域专利发展情况，形成《战略性新兴产业专利检索策略汇编》和《2014年广东省战略性新兴产业专利监测分析报告》，完成专利实时监测系统开发工作，系统在2015年12月上线试运行。

广东省有效专利监控系统。方便监控和分析广东省有效专利拥有状况和发展动态，客观评估广东省创新主体的创新质量和活跃度，实现多种有效专利数据的统计、分析、监控以及输出。

湛江海洋、家电产业专题数据库。通过对专利数据的有效整合和深度加工标引，建设符合湛江市海洋、家电产业现状，同时具有国内先进水平的海洋、家电产业专利信息专题数据库。

广东省专利数据加工中心项目。建立符合广东省行业应用需求的专利信息数据平台，至2015年底，项目已完成购置深加工数据加载入库服务器及与之配套的系统软件，同时开展项目人员培训。

专利法律状态数据加工项目。对中国近千万条专利数据法律状态进行深加工，实现法律状态的多字段联合检索，从专利申请号、法律状态公告日、法律状态及法律状态详细信息中的一个或者多个检索入口进行检索，对现有省重点行业及地方特色产业专利数据库法律状态信息进行更新。

区域中心数据加载。实现著录项目类数据的同步数据更新，截至2015年11月，已完成加载的全球专利著录项目数据约1.03亿条，其中中国专利约1535万条，美国专利1505万条，日本专利2875万条，EPO 535万条，WIPO 382万条；全文图像数据约6628万份，法律状态数据约2.88亿条，总存储容量约105TB。

专利数据资源服务和运维支持。通过数据抽取和整理，形成一套中国全量专利数据资源，以提供数据资源服务。顺利保障近30个应用系统及托管网站安全运行，主要专利应用系统访问量约为100万次，是2014年的访问量30万次的3.3倍；专利检索量约为87.5万次，是2014年的检索量25万次的3.5倍。

【服务能力】

知识产权分析评议。2015年，中心继2014年首次将知识产权评议写入省委组织部“珠江人才计划”引进创新创业团队项目申报指南后，牵头完成了116家创新团队（其中10家未通过形式审查）的知识产权分析评议工作并形成评议报告。独立承担《2012—2014年广东省高新技术企业专利实力状况报告》《佛山专利实力报告》《技术性贸易壁垒中的专利风险预警及应对指引手册》《广东省专利实力状况研究》等项目，联合开展《海口市知识产权十三五规划》《区域专利信息高端服务指南研究报告》等项目研究。全面推进“广东省战略性新兴产业专利信息资源开发利用计划”专项，完成2011年项目验收及2013年项目阶段性总结工作，开展2013年项目工作，编写《广东省战略性新兴产业知识产权工作动态》6期、

《广东省战略性新兴产业专利统计简报》2期，完成“广东省战略性新兴产业专利信息成果发布系统”升级改版工作，组织开展广东省战略性新兴产业专利信息资源开发利用计划项目团队交流会和专题培训。

项目研究。开展“广州开发区基因治疗领域专利竞争情报分析”“太阳能产业专利预警分析研究”“电压力锅领域专利竞争情报分析研究”项目研究。完成广东省知识产权局2011年广东省战略性新兴产业两大专项“生物医药产业专利信息资源开发工程”“广东省战略性新兴产业专利信息运用推进工程”的结题验收材料撰写工作及“广州开发区基因治疗领域专利竞争情报分析”项目的结题验收工作，服务科技创新和产业发展。申报2015年广东省战略性新兴产业专利信息资源开发利用计划项目“广东省战略性新兴产业专利信息开发综合服务工程”“珠江西岸先进装备制造产业带——江门市轨道交通装备产业发展专利导航工程”及“海洋可再生能源开发产业专利分析及预警工程”。逐步形成以自主研究为核心的发展格局。

企业服务。推进小微企业专利信息推送服务，向东莞、中山等专业镇企业提供专利信息推送服务，编制了“国外专利外观设计检索指南”。首次开展粤东西地区“双推”活动，结合推进《企业知识产权管理规范》和企业贯标培育，在茂名市、汕头市开展“全省专利信息推送及知识产权贯标服务推送活动”，首次进驻粤东西地区，对接高新园区，吸引近90家企业代表参加。开展日常专利信息检索服务，完成交易会投诉案件专利检索及一般企业项目专利检索和广东省专利奖评选检索，针对广东省科学院下属单位的专利申请情况及法律状态统计工作，以及中科院广州分院、省科学院以及广州有色金属研究院专利申请状况比较研究，完成检索报告数十项。开放非专利科技文献信息检索账号，为广东省企业提供检索便利，提供包括中国知网系列数据库——中国期刊全文数据库、中国博士学位论文数据库、中国重要会议论文数据库等十二种数据库的子账号免费向广东省企业开放，已有近70家企业申请非专利文献系统账号，下载文献次数近2500余次，检索科技文献次数达到20000余次。

【培训服务】 2015年，中心共举办或协办各类培训（研讨）班23期，参训人员近2000人次。

培训服务体系。开展知识产权高端人才培养和小微企业专利信息利用人才培训工作，联合深圳市启创知识产权管理促进中心共同开展企业高端知识产权人才培训。成功申报“中小微企业专利信息利用能力培训班”，入册国家知识产权培训基地名录。继续开展2015年知识产权远程教育培训工作，与四个分站分拟定培训计划并指导各分站远程教育工作。

培训内容。根据新政策、新形势调整，并兼顾到知识产权创造、运用、保护、管理、服务等五方面内容，满足各行业知识产权从业人员需求。针对不同区域的需求特点，开展多区域的分类培训，新增知识产权高端人才培养和小微企业专利信息人才培训项目，为广东省知识产权事业发展储备人才。

课程设计。采取主动走出去的方式，与地方知识产权管理部门合作，解决当地师资和部分经费不足等问题，根据当地知识产权从业人员现状及需求设计合适课程。

课程内容。增加培训案例，邀请知名企业高管将理论和案例相结合，使从业人员了解实际工作中有可能遇到的重点、难点和解决问题的方式方法。

【维权援助服务】

日常维权援助与举报投诉。2015年的维权援助案件申请及举报投诉量与2014年同比明显上升，截至2015年12月中旬，共受理知识产权维权申请案件27件，结案27件；举报投诉案件28件，成功转交28件；专利侵权判定咨询委托17件，结案17件；参与5个展会知识产权保护工作。

企业知识产权海外护航政策制度研究。形成《关于提高广东省企业“走出去”知识产权保护能力的若干意见》（代拟稿）初稿；制作四本企业“走出去”知识产权风险防范和操作指引手册并整合为《企业海外知识产权风险应对管理指引》书籍出版；起草完成海外知识产权维权援助工作制度，筹备设立海外知识产权维权专家库和在维权中心网站设立“企业海外维权援助快速通道”版块，确保海外护航工作制度化、程序化。

企业知识产权海外护航帮扶。为湛江市新诺电器有限公司等多家企业提供专利技术分析与风险评估，助力海外参展；为5宗涉外知识产权风险帮扶企业提供涉外专利侵权判定咨询服务；接收金发科技股份有限公司提出的涉外维权申请，为其提供竞争对手3件专利稳定性分析报告和海外维权指引服务，金发科技据此提交专利无效请求，使竞争对手未利用该3件专利维权，其因此避免了高达500万元以上的损失。

参与维权援助政策研究与制定。着手起草《关于加强广东省知识产权维权援助工作的指导意见》，多次修改完善后形成《意见》终稿，并配合局执法处做好文件印发和相关工作准备，《意见》于2015年7月2日正式出台并向各地级以上市及顺德区知识产权局印发。

维权援助服务体系。承办由省知识产权局主办的全省知识产权维权援助工作研讨会；建立茂名、潮州、江门、惠州、揭阳和阳江6家分中心，华南理工大学、广东省日化商会等7个服务工作站，组建五邑大学知识产权保护志愿服务队和揭阳职业技术学院知识产权保护志愿服务队。

电商领域专利维权。顺利开展关于淘宝网的5起电商领域维权案件和转办10起电商领域举报投诉案件，为中山市爱贝尔日用制品有限公司的提供侵权判定咨询意见被淘宝网采纳，免除其商品撤架风险，避免了其销售旺季期间的严重损失。

专利行政执法协助。积极完成省局执法处对近两年专利侵权纠纷案件的回访回查，整理分析广交会广东参展企业被外国权利人投诉情况；协助受理广交会、美博会、口腔展、灯光音响展和中博会400多个专利侵权投诉；向花都局、惠州局、阳江局、南宁局、东莞局、深圳宝安分局提供专利侵权判定咨询服务。

【司法鉴定服务】

鉴定业务。截至2015年12月，鉴定所受理新委托的各类知识产权鉴定案件共22件，累计已完成共25件（含2014年度至2015年度完成的案件）。

内部管理。制定及修订了适用该鉴定所管理的《司法鉴定工作程序》《司法鉴定人管理规定》《鉴定所所长职责》《鉴定人职责》《特聘专家聘用办法》《知识产权软件相似性鉴定实施规范》《鉴定过错处理办法》《档案管理办法》等，推动鉴定所内部管理规范化、有序化。

入册各级法院。分别向广东省高院、广州中院、佛山中院、珠海中院共4个法院提交申报入册资料，并入选各个法院的名册。

知识产权鉴定专家团队。通过多方推荐专家、招募等方式择优组建知识产权鉴定专家团队；为鉴定提供技术支持，组织鉴定人参加省市司法管理部门举办的各类培训；为即将到期的鉴定人执业证办理延续手续，保障鉴定工作顺利开展。

树立品牌。接待广州市司法局司法鉴定管理处调研，接受华南理工大学法学院、福建工程学院法学院电话采访和调研来访，有效维护中心品牌，树立良好社会形象。

【委托任务】

完成《广东知识产权年鉴（2014）》和《广东知识产权局年报（2014）》编纂工作。在2014年版年鉴获得中国出版协会授予的第五届年鉴编纂出版质量评比综合二等奖、框架设计二等奖等奖项的基础上，进一步明确年鉴编撰目标，优化年鉴基本框架结构，规范稿件标准，拓宽发行面，发行量达到469家单位，比2014年增加300个单位。

编制《广东省专利统计手册》。多方获取统计数据，在整理、汇总、完善、核实数据方面加大推进力度，完成的《手册》较为系统、全面地反映广东省知识产权事业发展情况。

组织开展全省专利调查工作和全省知识产权服务业统计调查工作。全省专利调查总体抽样样本量为2100份，回收问卷为1454份，回收率为69.3%；全省知识产权服务业统计调查总体抽样样本量为1700份，回收问卷502份，回收率为29.5%。

（供稿人：林莺）

广东省知识产权研究会

【概况】 2015年，广东省知识产权研究会共有会员177个，其中团体会员69个，个人会员108个。新动员腾讯科技（深圳）有限公司等6家企业，以及发明人广州天网安防科技有限公司总经理邱亮南、肯尼思（中国）有限公司知识产权部总经理何炳辉等4人申请入会。

【学会基础工作】 2015年，广东省知识产权研究会网站各板块内容进一步完善。向会员编辑、发放《知识产权简讯》共6期。根据有关规定对学会进行审计及汇算清缴、社会团体收费情况自查、省级财政专项资金检查自查自纠、省级知识产权专项资金支出项目绩效自评等。先后与江苏省、浙江省知识产权研究会、深圳市专利协会进行业务交流。

【知识产权课题研究】

完成“专利制度对创新驱动发展的作用研究”。课题对专利制度与创新驱动发展辩证关系进行分析，同时开展专利制度对创新驱动发展的作用机理研究，全面探索专利制度推动创新驱动发展的路径，阐明专利制度作为重要创新驱动力，对推动创新型经济发展做出的突出贡献。

“物联网产业专利信息资源开发工程”项目进入结题阶段。2015年4月23日，组织广东省促进战略性新兴产业发展相关单位代表、各地市知识产权、经济和信息化主管部门代表、广东省物联网领域企业、行业协会和有关高校及科研机构代表、知识产权服务机构代表共156人参加“广东省战略性新兴产业——物联网产业专利分析及预警报告会”。

完成“智能制造装备产业专利分析及预警”项目的阶段性总结报告。2015年3月中旬，向广东省知识产权局提交“智能制造装备产业专利分析及预警”项目阶段性总结报告。报告利用现有的专利数据资源，对高端装备制造产业下的高档数控机床、工业机器人领域的中国和全球的专利数据进行全面检索和数据分析，并根据各领域的特点进行深度挖掘，逐层分解其关键技术与发展热点，得出各领域的专利技术构成和发展状况。

组织“物联网专利技术”和“新一代通信产业专利技术”转化应用情况调研。2015年10—12月，组织华南理工大学、华进公司等会员代表和审协北京中心等专家赴江苏、浙江、深圳等地，就“物联网专利技术”和“新一代通信产业专利技术”转化应用情况进行调研。

组织“广东省战略性新兴产业——新一代通信产业专利信息资源开发工程”项目成果发布会。2015年12月8日，组织会员及广东省促进战略性新兴产业发展相关单位代表，各地市知识产权、经济和信息化主管部门代表，广东省新一代通信产业企业、行业协会和有关高校及科研机构代表，知识产权服务机构代表等200多人参加“广东省战略性新兴产业——新一代通信产业专利信息资源开发工程”项目成果发布会。

【知识产权学术交流】 2015年1月14日，广东省知识产权研究会应华南美国商会及美国全国商会全球知识产权中心邀请，由黄玉霞副秘书长代表学会出席主题为“中国创新和知识产权保护”的专题研讨活动，并就知识产权保护问题以及知识产权宣传等问题发表意见。

3月27日，广东省知识产权研究会与日本知识产权协会联合主办“2015年中日知识产权（广州）研讨会”。日本驻广州总领馆商务领事田中朝哉出席会议。会议以沙龙模式，围绕“全球业务中的IP风险应对及IP运用战略”作深度交流。来自广东的创新企业、在华日企代表等50多位业界代表参加会议。其中，天威飞马、华为技术、腾讯科技、中兴通讯、迈瑞生物、比亚迪、炬芯科技和京信通信等8家企业作主题演讲；日本日立、索尼、松下、佳能、东丽等全球知名企业代表亦围绕主题发表演讲。

5月29日，美国知识产权法律协会会长莎伦·伊斯雷尔女士率领代表团一行19人到访广东省知识产权研究会，黄玉霞副秘书长接待来访人员，并就各专业领域知识产权研究的事务交换意见。

7月10日，澳门经济局及海关知识产权代表团一行来粤开展相关调研工作，广东省知识产权研究会派员参加接待，并就两地知识产权有关工作交换意见。

7—8月，广东省知识产权研究会组织广东省知识产权业界代表25人，前往台湾进行知识产权研习。

9月19—21日，中国知识产权法学研究会2015年年会在广州举行，年会主题是“厉行知识产权法治，保障创新驱动发展”。广东省知识产权研究会作为支持单位，在会议筹备、组织等各方面给予支持。

9月22—23日，由中华全国专利代理人协会与台湾工业总会共同主办、广东省知识产权研究会承办的第八届两岸专利论坛在广州举行。副省长陈云贤，中华全国代理人协会高级顾问、国家知识产权局副局长何志敏，台湾工业总会秘书长蔡练生，台湾工业总会智慧财产权委员会高级顾问王美花，中华全国代理人协会有关负责人出席论坛开幕式并致辞。200多名两岸专利主管机构人员和业界人士，围绕两岸专利领域最新发展、专利法制发展动态、专利审理面临的挑战与应对、专利布局与诉讼的策略和管理等主题展开热烈的交流与探讨，10余名来自两岸知识产权界的专家、学者以及企业家代表做主题发言。广东省知识产权研究会理事长马宪民在主持两岸专利领域最新发展主题时表示，知识产权对社会经济发展“顶梁柱”作用凸显，通过两岸专家学者的经验分享，充分了解了两岸专利领域的最新进展，更深刻感受到专利对社会经济的促进作用。

12月3—4日，广东省知识产权研究会组团参加由香港特别行政区政府、香港贸易发展局及香港设计中心合办的第四届“亚洲知识产权营商论坛”，并同时在论坛展示厅设展位宣传广东省知识产权研究会，代表还与参加论坛的世界各地知识产权界人士和商家就知识产权最新发展进行了交流。

【承接政府项目】 2015年，配合做好专利奖励有关工作。其中：配合组织“2014年度广东广东专利奖评审委员会会议”、制作拟奖项目介绍PPT演讲稿、对推荐项目材料审查和申报单位来询解答等；协助组织召开“2015年广东专利奖发明人奖专家评审会”“2015年广东专利奖项目答辩会”和“2015年广东专利奖评审委员会会议”等。协助广东省知识产权局举办“中国专利奖、广东专利奖奖励政策及评价指标体系解读培训会”，共组织各地市知识产权局有关业务负责人、2014年广东专利奖拟授奖项目单位代表、有关企事业单位代表共100余人参加培训会。协助筹备2015年全省专利奖励表彰大会。制作“第十六届中国专利奖”和“2014年广东专利奖”单位和个人的表彰牌匾、证书及光荣册印制等。

承接2015年广东省知识产权示范企业申报及评审等工作，制作并发放2014年广东省知识产权优势、示范企业牌匾共78块；整理2008—2014年广东知识产权优势、示范企业相关信息共490家。

承接“2015年重大经济科技活动知识产权评议试点”“2015年广东省技术性贸易壁垒专利预警分析服务试点”“2015年广东省专利密集型产业集聚区培育工程”的专家评审工作。

4月15—17日，承接国家知识产权局副局长贺化率领的调研组一行来粤就知识产权金融服务工作开展专题调研期间的“专利保险、知识产权质押融资专题座谈会”会务工作。

4月，承接面向广东省知识产权金融服务相关企业、银行、评估机构等单位，开展知识产权质押融资问卷调查工作，回收调查问卷共350份，其中评估机构18份。

5—6月，完成更新粤港超链接工作。通过将原来链接的内容重新搜索并在资料库上更新，实现所有链接点击即进入粤港知识产权网站的效果。

6月7—11日，承接国家知识产权局专利局医药生物发明审查部调研组接待工作。组织广东省医药企业、科研院所和代理机构等单位代表共14人参加“中药领域组合物申请的‘三性’评判标准研究”座谈会，并先后组织前往白云山和记黄埔中药有限公司、广州中医药大学和华进联合专利商标代理有限公司就中药领域组合物申请的“三性”评判标准问题进行实地调研。

6月15—18日，承接接待国家知识产权局专利局审查部、电学部、北京中心、广东中心、河南中心和湖北中心巡回工作审查组赴粤专利巡回审查（到广州市广州汽车集团股份有限公司、珠海市珠海格力电器股份有限公司，就20余件发明专利申请作巡回审查）接待工作。

6月25—30日，承接国家知识产权局专利局外观设计审查部调研组接待工作。组织企业、院校和服务机构等100多位从业者参加“外观设计专利制度宣讲交流会”。组织前往广州汽车集团股份有限公司汽车工程研究院、欧派家居集团股份有限公司、中山（灯饰）知识产权快速维权中心、中山琪朗灯饰有限公司和广州工业设计促进会深入开展调研交流。

8月10日，协助国家知识产权局专利局实用新型审查部赴粤调研期间，召开“实用新型专利权评价报告实务问题研究”座谈会工作，组织了相关的3家服务机构和3家企业参加会议。

8月10—12日，承接国家知识产权局专利局机械审查部调研组接待工作。调研组一行7人，由广东省知识产权研究会派员协助调研组在广东地区就有关企业在机械发明专利方面的情况实施调研。

2015年11月26日，由国家知识产权局专利管理司指导、广东省知识产权局发起、汇桔网和广东省知识产权研究与发展中心联合主办的首届“汇桔杯”南粤知识产权创新创业大赛启动，省知识产权研究会作为支持单位，提供了经费以及派员出席活动。

（供稿人：黄培辉）

广东知识产权保护协会

【概况】 2015年1月30日，在理事年会上向与会理事汇报并讨论了换届筹备工作情况，筹备工作就绪后，报经广东省民间组织管理局同意，于同年4月29日，召开换届选举大会。

第三届广东知识产权保护协会会长为朱万昌，秘书长为陈胜杰。协会分设综合管理部、项目管理部和宣传教育部，初步完成了秘书处的架构建设。

9月，协会编制协会宣传册，开通微信公众号，建设协会网站，每周通过微信群及QQ群发布最新的《知识产权·每周资讯》及活动通知，畅通与广大会员单位之间的信息沟通和往来。

11月初至2016年元月中旬，协会会长朱万昌和秘书长陈胜杰深入理事单位走访调研，听取理事单位对协会工作的意见和建议。协会全年共新增17家会员单位，包括广东联塑科技实业有限公司、广东泰宝医疗科技股份有限公司、汕头专利协会、深圳专利协会、广东海石知识产权服务有限公司等5家副会长单位，广州盘古网络科技有限公司1家常务理事单位，以及金发科技股份有限公司、东莞市三友联众电器有限公司、广东省广业科技集团有限公司、广东精英集团广州分公司、广州奥凯信息咨询有限公司、广州恒成智道信息科技有限公司、深圳中一专利商标事务所等7家理事单位，广州中大微电子有限公司、飞亚达（集团）股份有限公司、广东省柏盈律师事务所、广东新明珠陶瓷集团有限公司等4家一般会员单位。

【合作项目】

开展广东省知识产权专家咨询委员会筹备，并组织召开成立大会暨第一次咨询会议。从2015年下半年以来，协会受广东省知识产权局委托，参与调研和筹备成立广东省知识产权专家咨询委员会的相关工作，并于12月8日，举行“广东省知识产权专家咨询委员会成立大会暨第一次咨询会议”，协会会长朱万昌被聘任为第一届专家咨询委员会常务副主任兼秘书长。召开首次咨询委员会专题会议，与会专家围绕现阶段广东应当如何保持知识产权工作优势，推动广东省实施创新驱动发展战略做出积极贡献为议题。

设立中知（广州）联络办公室，推动广东知识产权体系贯标工作。2015年12月30日，与中知（北京）认证公司签署了《贯标认证合作协议》。协会将作为中知公司在广州的联络办公室，负责广东区域（除深圳外）的认证业务推广、培训和承担部分认证流程的工作。

【常规项目】

《广东知识产权》杂志改版创新，争创一流内刊。改选杂志第二届编委会，聘请省高院及广州知识产权法院和业内专家组成《广东知识产权》杂志第二届编委会；调整改进杂志栏目；扩大稿件来源；根据国家最新稿酬标准上调稿酬标准，激发通讯员投稿积极性。

“广东地区知识产权经典案例报告会”塑造品牌活动。2015年6月19日，协会在广州举行“2015年广东地区知识产权经典案例报告会”。提高企事业单位应对知识产权纠纷能力。这是协会自2005年以来，第十次举行年度知识产权典型案例报告会，共计150多人参加。

“2014年度广东省知识产权十大事件、十大案件和优秀案件”的评选活动引发关注。2015年4月，协会和广东省商标协会、广东省版权保护联合会共同举办“2014年度广东省知识产权十大事件、十大案件和优秀案件”的评选活动，评选出“华为、中兴位居全球企业PCT专利申请量第一、三位”等“十大事件”和“深圳海关连续查获侵犯朗科发明专利系列案”等“十大案件”和“深圳市腾讯计算机系统有限公司与广州酷狗计算机科技有限公司因信息网络传播权申请诉前禁令案”等20件优秀案件。

举办“电子商务领域专利保护工作培训会”。为推进电子商务领域专利保护工作，提升广大企事业单位电子专利保护能力和水平，2015年6月，协会在广州浙江大厦举办“电子商务领域专利保护工作培训会”。

举办“知识产权运营及专利诉讼培训班”。2015年10月27日，协会联合广东专利代理协会共同举办“2015年知识产权运营及专利诉讼培训班”。

组织会员单位旁听知识产权诉讼案件和国家复审委的巡回口审案件。2015年4月17日，协会应广东省高级法院民三庭邀请，组织会员单位参加“格力与美的商标侵权纠纷案”公开庭审的旁听。9月21日，协会组织会员单位参加国家专利复审委员会在广州举行的对两起涉及一种电脑硬盘托架和定位柱与螺丝柱之间设置有加强筋的电脑机箱专利无效请求案件的口头审理旁听。11月9—10日，协会组织会员单位参加国家专利复审委员在广州举行的游戏机、酒吧椅座体、门窗装饰、玩具电子琴等侵权纠纷案件口头审理旁听。

为会员企业提供个性化服务。应美的集团的要求，协会于9—10月邀请龚麒天法官、郑志柱法官分两次为该公司做“企业知识产权司法保护实务、案例分析及工作建议”专题培训，每场培训规模近100人，收到良好的培训效果。9月，协会作为支持单位，支持了由珠海天威飞马打印耗材有限公司主办的“天威杯”打印耗材创新设计与专利大赛。

【承接政府工作】 2015年6月8—9日，协会受省知识产权局委托，在广州浙江大厦举办“全省专利行政执法案例征集及撰写培训班”。增强了全省专利行政执法人员处理专利侵权纠纷案件的能力。

开展广东省知识产权局2016年度全省知识产权优势和示范企业的组织评审工作。全省21个地市级知识产权局共推荐了43家“知识产权示范企业候选单位”、89家“知识产权优势企业候选单位”，在组织专家进行评审，并报广东省知识产权局认证后，最后将评出省级知识产权示范企业20家，省级知识产权优势企业50家。

2015年12月，配合广东省知识产权局，在广州华泰宾馆举办“2015年全国专利行政执法培训班”，主要培训了专利及相关法律法规、发明与实用新型专利侵权判定，外观专利侵权判定、专利侵权纠纷案例分析、海关专利保护、模拟庭审，专利行政执法相关政策与要求等为期5天的培训，来自全国各省市执法人员90多人参加。

12月，受广东省知识产权局和国家知识产权局的委托，收集“华中、华南地区行政执法案例”，制作《案例汇编》。在广州浙江大厦举办“华中、华南地区行政执法案例与实务研讨交流会”，加强了华中、华南地区知识产权局执法办案人员的业务交流与工作联系，推动了跨区行政执法合作，区域执法办案能力水平也得到了提升。有关省（区）知识产权局及有关地级以上知识产权局的执法人员近60人参加。

协会接受广东省知识产权局委托，组织相关单位为第117、118届广交会专利行政执法案件进行纸质档案电子化处理和归档。

与相关单位合作，在《中国知识产权报》《广东科技报》连续专版报道广东开展行政执法的经验做法，起到了良好的宣传作用。

（供稿人：朱万昌）

广东专利代理协会

【自律建设】

广东专利代理协会（下称代理协会）2015年继续开展“广东专利代理机构管理规范达标单位”评选活动，以提高广东省专利代理机构管理水平和服务质量。

3月12日，代理协会开展“广东专利代理机构管理规范达标单位”开放日活动。组织全省17家代理机构参访广州三环、广州华进、广州哲力，听取有关专利代理机构管理方面的介绍，并进行有关专利代理机构规范管理经验交流座谈会。

为引导专利代理机构加强质量管理，提升专利代理水平，促进全省专利事业快速发展，代理协会继续开展2015年优秀发明专利申请文件评选活动，由国家知识产权局专利局专利审查协作广东中心资深专家组评选出10篇广东专利代理协会“第二届优秀发明专利申请文件”。获得评优的单位及相关专利代理人获得相应的表彰。

【培训交流】 2015年，代理协会主办或承办的培训交流活动共计25场次，培训时间共30天，计240个以上课时，参加培训的人员超过2000多人次。

创新知识产权论坛。8月28日在广州成功举办了协会第二届创新知识产权论坛。省高院、广州知识产权院、大型国际企业以及美国、台湾香港等知识产权界、法律界的专家学者作为主讲嘉宾参与论坛，220多人报名参加论坛，论坛的学时还被中华全国专利代理协会纳入2015年专利代理人A类年检学时。

专利代理人实务技能培训。是国家局在2012年开展为期四年的全国执业专利代理人大轮训收官之作，代理协会积极配合省局开展这项工作，7月16—18日，代理协会开展了专利代理人实务技能培训班（机、电领域），广东省共有150名专利代理人参加了此次培训，培训对提高广东省专利代理人的实务技能水平起积极作用。

机构业务能力促进培训班。国家知识产权局外观设计审查部、光电技术发明审查部2015年分别在广州、深圳开展专利代理机构业务能力促进工作。5月27—28日，代理协会承办了该项工作，共有220人参加此次培训。

座谈交流活动。6月份，代理协会组织会员单位及省局相关部门负责人参访广州知识产权法院，共有19家会员单位代表参与该项活动。

7月份，代理协会组织获得2014年“广东专利代理机构管理规范达标单位”的负责人赴北京，参访中华全国专利代理协会及北京柳沈律师事务所、中国国际贸易促进委员会专利商标事务所、康信知识产权代理公司等知名机构，就行业发展和企业经营文化等进行了深入交流，并取得了中华全国专利代理协会在培训资源及年检学时给予代理协会优先保证的支持。

12月份，协会组织会员参加在香港举办的第四届“亚洲知识产权营商论坛”。该论坛由香港特别行政区政府、香港贸易发展局及香港设计中心合办，就知识产权的最新发展互相交流。

【承办政府工作】 配合省局对专利代理机构设立申请资料的初审工作。2015年1—12月，代理协会配合省局共受理、初核19家专利代理机构设立申请资料，国家局批准15家代理机构设立申请；截至12月，全省共有 158家专利代理机构（同比上年增加15家），164家分支机构（同比上年增加26家）。

承办2015年全国专利代理人资格考试广州考点的考务工作。2015年，代理协会接受省局的委托，承办2015年全国专利代理人资格考试广州考点的考务工作。

各项数据均为历年之最：广州考点共有3229名考生报名参加考试，比2014年增长9.46%；参考率71.82%，其中专利法科目72.14%，相关法科目71.84%，专利代理实务科目71.48%，均为全国最高；考试合格776人，通过率达31.18%，创历史新高。

（供稿人：陈一忠）

广东省专利信息协会

【协会建设】

首次会员代表大会。2015年4月10日，广东省专利信息协会（下称信息协会）举办第一次会员代表大会。会议通过了协会各项制度，产生了第一届理事会。广东省知识产权局副局长谢红当选协会会长，广东省知识产权研究与发展中心、广州奥凯信息咨询有限公司、腾讯科技公司等9个机构当选副会长单位，汕头市知识产权服务中心、茂名市生产力促进中心、TCL集团股份有限公司等10个机构当选理事单位，广东省知识产权研究与发展中心副主任魏庆华当选秘书长，广东格林律师事务所合伙人、律师、知识产权部负责人杨河当选监事。正式会员包括76个创新主体以及6家省外服务机构作为特邀理事单位，共同为创新主体提供优质专利信息服务。

首次理事会议。2015年7月23日，信息协会组织召开第一次理事会议，通报了协会工作情况，决定设立“中规（北京）认证有限公司广州办事处”，选定广东省知识产权研究与发展中心主任、信息协会副会长李强为执行日常工作副会长。

【机构建设】 2015年7月28日，信息协会与中规（北京）认证有限公司合作设立的中规（北京）认证有限公司广州办事处正式挂牌成立，广州办事处负责在广东省及其周边区域积极组织社会服务资源，开展知识产权审核、认证工作及配套服务，进一步推动广东知识产权贯标工作深入广泛开展。

【行业服务】

交流活动。2015年信息协会组织会员参加“企业知识产权管理实务研讨会”“泛珠三角区域九省（区）专利信息服务工作座谈会”“中国专利信息年会”“知识产权创新创业大赛”等各类知识产权交流活动。

2015年5月22日，信息协会的副会长单位奥凯公司在协会支持下召开 “企业知识产权管理实务研讨会”。信息协会积极组织会员参与此次研讨会，为企业知识产权工作带来有效政策信息，分享知识产权实务经验及专利信息工作经验，剖析知识产权管理问题。

7月23日，协会主要副会长单位、理事单位在广州参与组织召开泛珠三角区域九省（区）专利信息服务工作座谈会。会上通报国家知识产权局区域专利信息服务（广州）中心建设情况，介绍可提供的跨省区专利信息服务项目，促进会员间交流专利信息传播和利用的经验并提出跨省区专利信息服务建议，同时发布广东省专利大数据应用服务情况。

2015中国专利信息年会（PIAC）于9月15—16日在北京举办，协会广泛发动会员参加中国专利信息年会，及时递送最新的专利信息服务资讯，同时与中规认证有限公司广州办事处加入参展行列，在年会上成功亮相。

11月，协会作为承办单位联合汇桔网举办“2015年度第一届汇桔杯·南粤知识产权创新创业大赛”。来自政府、企事业单位、创业投资界、参赛者、新闻媒体等社会各界代表500余人参加了启动大会。启动仪式后，国家和省知识产权管理部门、知识产权运营联盟、企业、投资机构等业界代表与来自全球的“创客”们进行现场交流，并对参赛者创业中遇到的困难进行答疑解惑。向全球进行海选项目征集，截至启动日有超过1200个创业项目与团队报名，涉及新材料、智能家居、智能安防、生物环保、移动互联网等多个前沿创新领域。

培训活动。2015年10月，协会与中规（北京）认证有限公司联合主办的“知识产权管理体系认证审核员培训班”在广州举办。培训后共有141位学员成功通过CCAA的考试审核，其中广东省内学员71名。

交流平台。协会秘书处积极利用会员QQ、微信群及电子邮箱，为会员提供一个及时交流沟通的统一平台。上传会员意见和建议，下达国家局、省局的最新精神及通知，积极调动会员参加各类专利信息培训、座谈会、年会、交流会等，协助及解决会员遇到的问题，充分发挥协会的桥梁纽带作用。

贯标建设。2015年，中规广州办选派协会中专业过硬的实习审核员参加企业知识产权管理体系（IPMS）实习审核工作，加强实习锻炼，至12月底已达18人次。中规广州办积极配合中规公司协调安排广东省内知识产权管理体系认证审核员（以下简称“正式审核员”）开展企业IPMS审核，至12月底已培养广东省内正式审核员2名。中规公司2015年在广东的正式审核员一共3名，均为协会的核心发起单位的优秀专业人员。

（供稿人：黄静）

广东商标协会

【概况】 2015年，广东省商标有效注册量占全国商标有效注册量的18.03%，连续二十一年居全国首位，广东省商标代理机构有3000多家，约占全国的1/4。广东商标协会通过探索完善政府引领、工商推动、企业创建、社会参与的著名商标认定工作体系，为促进广东省商标品牌战略实施发挥积极作用。同时，协会积极推广实施《商标代理服务规范》，引导和监督商标代理行业健康发展，得到国家商标局的肯定。

【广东省著名商标】 2015年度广东省著名商标评审工作于2015年6月25日正式启动，秘书处共收到认定申请575件，延续申请778件，合计1353件。2015年6月9日，省工商局印发《广东省工商行政管理局关于加大品牌培育力度支持广东省著名商标认定工作的通知》（粤工商标字〔2015〕242号），要求各地工商充分发挥工商职能，支持广东省著名商标认定工作开展，推进全省商标品牌战略的实施。按照该文要求，2015年著名商标申报渠道发生变化，由各地市工商行政管理部门（市场监督管理部门）对申请材料进行指导、核实，出具核实意见与监管意见后，代收申请材料报送秘书处受理。

为使评审工作更加客观、公平、公正，秘书处对2013年至2014年审核过程中遇到的有关问题进行归纳，在严格执行《广东省著名商标认定和管理规定》及《广东省著名商标评审委员会关于广东省著名商标认定和管理的实施细则》的前提下，一是征询74家相关行业协会意见，并根据有效的反馈意见，对现有经济指标线进行合理的调整，二是明确相关行政执法部门反馈意见的采纳规则。

截至2015年12月，广东省著名商标有效件3124件。

【行业建设】 《商标代理服务规范》（DB44/T 1579-2015）自2015年7月16日起实施。为了贯彻实施《商标代理服务规范》，广东商标协会商标代理分会组织编制了《广东商标代理服务规范审核认定实施办法》，并组建成立了广东商标代理服务规范审核认定专家小组。

根据《商标代理服务规范》和《广东商标代理服务规范审核认定实施办法》的有关规定，自2015年10月起对广东省内申报“商标代理服务规范单位”的25家商标代理机构进行现场考察核实及材料审查，并征求了广东省工商行政管理局、国家工商行政管理总局商标局和商标评审委员会等有关部门的意见，认定18家商标代理机构为广东省“商标代理服务规范单位”，于2016年2月4日在广东商标网、广东省工商行政管理局官网发布公告。2015年度广东省“商标代理服务规范单位”分别是：深圳市精英商标事务所、广州华进联合专利商标代理有限公司、广东哲力知识产权事务所有限公司、广东慧道知识产权事务所有限公司、广东永华知识产权管理有限公司、广东泽正知识产权服务有限公司、广东本色商标专利事务所有限公司、广州市商专知识产权服务有限公司、深圳市赋权知识产权代理有限公司、中山国文商标事务所有限公司、中山市世纪铭洋知识产权服务有限公司、广东一智知识产权代理有限公司、东莞市华南专利商标事务所有限公司、佛山市国方商标服务有限公司、珠海市恒益商标事务所（普通合伙）、广州粤高专利商标代理有限公司、汕头市潮汕商标事务所有限公司、普宁市鑫科商标事务所。

【宣传培训】 广东商标协会分别在2015年3—5月、8月、12月在广州、深圳、顺德等地，为会员单位组织6场有关商标业务知识、商标政策法规、商标代理行业自律管理等培训交流会议，参加人数达1000人次。

【服务平台】 为提高广东商标协会服务水平，为企业、代理机构搭建广东省商标代理行业的交流平台，广东商标协会秘书处通过广东商标网（www.gdta.com.cn）、会员QQ群、电子邮箱、现场走访等形式，进一步密切企业、协会、政府之间的关系，促进广东省品牌建设。

（供稿人：郭姝均）

广东省版权保护联合会

【交流活动】 2015年1月6日，应香港贸易发展局的邀请，广东省版权保护联合会（下称联合会）组织20多家会员单位，共计30人前往香港国际会展中心参加第13届亚洲国际授权展。

4月22日，联合会与省知识产权保护协会共同举办的“2014年度广东省知识产权十大案件和十大事件”评选结果揭晓。这是联合会继2013年后第二次参与主办此项活动。

2015年4月26日，为纪念“4·26”世界知识产权日正式生效十五周年，联合会在小洲艺术区举办 “艺术品交易与版权保护”论坛，近百名来自有关高校、法律工作者、版权产业界人士以及小洲艺术区的艺术创作人员参加此次论坛。

4月26日，联合会驻小洲艺术区“版权服务工作站”正式挂牌。此前，联合会先后与华南理工大学共同成立了“联合会驻广州大学城版权服务工作站”；与广东省皮具文化协会、广东知识产权保护协会、广州市创意经济促进会和肯尼斯（中国）有限公司等单位分别挂牌设立了“联合会作品著作权自愿登记工作站”，且已全面开展工作。

12月30日，为加强与政府版权行政管理部门的工作交流和业务沟通，联合会召开 “联合会版权保护和版权社会服务工作汇报座谈会”。省版权局领导和省版权局版权管理处负责人以及深圳、广州、佛山、东莞、江门、肇庆、中山等珠三角城市的版权局有关领导应邀出席了此次座谈会。

【普法与维权协作】 2015年5月28日至6月1日“春季广州茶博会”期间，为减少和避免广州150多户茶商因遭受杭州某行业协会恶意诉讼而造成的经济损失，联合会协同广东省茶叶协会、广东省茶文化促进会共同举办了“诚信经营茶叶产品，保护茶商的合法权益”的主题论坛，联合会牟晋军副会长和张云理事担任主讲嘉宾，回答与会茶商提出的有关知识产权问题。

【承接政府项目】 2015年12月20日，由省版权局以委托服务的方式委托联合会负责组稿编辑的《广东省版权兴业示范基地名录》画册出版。该画册详细介绍了省版权局自2005年以来认定的全省86家版权兴业基地的详细情况。

【成果与荣誉】

出版《图解中华人民共和国著作权法》。“4·26世界知识产权日”前夕，由省版权局策划、联合会组织编绘的《图解中华人民共和国著作权法》，由花城出版社出版。该书已被省内外多个城市的版权管理部门以及律师事务所列为版权普法宣传和版权知识培训的教材之一。

荣获“全省版权登记优秀代办机构”称号。2015年8月11日，省新闻出版广电局政务服务中心在珠海召开“2015年广东省版权登记工作会议”，来自全省26家版权登记代办机构负责人以及部分地级市的版权局版权管理科负责人参加了会议。会议介绍了2014年以来广东省版权登记工作情况；向荣获“2014年度全省版权登记优秀代办机构”“2014年度全省版权登记优秀工作人员”的单位和个人颁发牌匾和荣誉证书。联合会荣获“优秀代办机构称号”，这是联合会继2011年度以来第三次获得此荣誉。

代理作品著作权登记数创新高。2015年，联合会完成作品著作权登记量达到4814件（实件5200多件），与2014年度的3065件相比，增长57%，这是联合会在作品著作权登记工作方面完成数量最多、增量最大的一年。2015年全年核发企业使用CAD正版软件示范单位证书201份。提供作品版权鉴定38件。

（供稿人：梁守坚）

广东省知识产权研究与发展中心司法鉴定所

【概况】 2015年，广东省知识产权研究与发展中心司法鉴定所接受公检法和行政管理部门及企事业单位委托的鉴定案件30余件，出庭质证4件。

【入册法院】 鉴定所作为广东省首家知识产权鉴定机构，为更好服务社会，2015年，鉴定所分别向广东省高院、广州中院、佛山中院、珠海中院等4个广东地区的主要法院递交申报入册资料，并已经顺利入册上述法院名册。

【培训教育】 为提高鉴定队伍的整体素质，鉴定所分别于2015年8月20日、9月26日、12月12日组织鉴定人参加省市司法管理部门举办的各类培训，参与培训人员共计67人次。

【沟通交流】 2015年6月24日，广州市司法局司法鉴定管理处处长谭和平、副调研员刘兴京一行到鉴定所调研，鉴定所备了相关材料向调研组汇报。

为了解其他知识产权司法鉴定机构的运营状况，汲取北京知识产权司法鉴定机构在发展与管理鉴定工作方面的成功经验，鉴定所于2015年8月到北京多个知识产权司法鉴定机构进行调研。其间，鉴定所了解了北京鉴定机构的运作机制、鉴定人队伍建设与管理、出庭质证、鉴定规范和标准、质量控制体系等方面情况，并就执业过程中遇到的困难展开交流。经多年建设，该鉴定所在社会上已有知名度，树立了良好的社会形象。2015年4月，鉴定所接受了华南理工大学法学院学生的采访，回答其有关司法鉴定方面的问题。

【内部管理】 2015年，鉴定所针对自身情况，新制订了《司法鉴定工作规范》《软件相似性鉴定规范》《司法鉴定工作程序》，修缮了鉴定所内部《司法鉴定人管理规定》《鉴定人职责》《鉴定过错处理办法》《档案管理办法》等一批管理文件，并广泛征求各位鉴定人对有关管理文件的意见建议，促进了鉴定所内部管理的规范化、有序化。

（供稿人：唐硕穗）

广东省律师协会知识产权法律专业委员会

【典型案例评选和巡讲活动】 2015年继续举办了上一年度（2014年）广东省律师知识产权典型案例征集与评选活动，并在全省举办了5场巡回报告会。广东省律师知识产权典型案例评选和巡讲活动经两年努力，已连续两年被列为广东省知识产权宣传周重要活动之一。

2015年9月11日，广东省律师协会知识产权法律专业委员会（下称知产委）应湖南省律师协会知识产权法律专业委员会的邀请，赴湖南省湘潭市，与当地律师协会等有关单位联合举办了“广东省、湖南省知识产权典型案例办案技巧巡回报告会”。广东省派出了省律协知产委主任邓尧、知识产权讲师团成员程跃华、何俊律师参加报告会，湖南省律师协会副会长刘立新、湘潭市律师协会会长王莹等领导出席了报告会并讲话，100多名律师、政府部门人员参加到场学习和探讨。

为扩大交流学习的范围，加强典型案例的指导作用，知产委从2014年、2015年征集的案例中挑选并组织编写了以案例研究为主的专业书籍《知识产权典型案例主办律师评述》，并在2015年10月由法律出版社出版。

【第三届广东知识产权法律服务论坛举办】 2015年11月28—29日，由省律协与佛山市律协主办，省律协知识产权专委会与佛山市律协知识产权专委会承办的“第三届广东知识产权法律服务论坛”在佛山举行。来自全国律协和江西、湖南、云南、贵州、广西、杭州、成都、宁波等省（区）市律协知识产权专委会主任、副主任，泛珠三角九省区和港澳台地区的律师代表、企业代表等250余人参加论坛。

【知识产权贯标】 知产委于2015年12月12日在广州举办了“广东省律师从事知识产权贯标服务政策与实务专题宣讲会”，广东省知识产权局副局长谢红出席了宣讲会，来自全省90余名律师参加了宣讲会。

宣讲会后，在知产委的沟通和申请下，广东省知识产权局协调了相应培训师资和经费，于2015年12月28—30日为广东省律师举办了企业知识产权贯标咨询服务专场培训，全省100余名律师和律师辅助人员报名参加了为期三天的培训学习。

【举办中港新三地国际版权法律研讨会】 2015年6月27日，知产会与广东知识产权保护协会在广州联合举办国际版权保护最新动态研讨会。广东省律师、实习律师、企业高管等100余人参加研讨。研讨会特邀省法院知识产权庭副庭长张学军、广州知识产权法院法官郑志柱、新加坡管理大学法学院研究员王佳、香港城市大学法学院教授关伟文等担任主讲嘉宾。

【举办“知识产权管理与商业化实务研讨会”】 2015年10月16日，由知产委、华南理工大学法学院、中美知识产权协会共同主办的“华南知识产权月谈——知识产权管理与商业化实务研讨会”在广州举行。省律协知识产权专委会主任邓尧、中美知识产权协会创始会长陈伟杰、华南理工大学法学院党委书记李良成，以及来自珠三角地区律所、高校和企业的知识产权界30余位同仁参加研讨。

【举办商业秘密民事诉讼实务问题讨论会】 知产委与珠海市律协知识产权专业委员会、佛山市律师协会知识产权专业委员会于2015年12月19日在珠海市共同举办了商业秘密民事诉讼实务问题讨论会。来自广州、珠海、佛山、深圳、东莞、中山等地市的20余名律师和2名特邀法官参加此次讨论会。

（供稿人：邓尧）

广东发明协会

【概况】

参加第二十一届全国发明展览会。展览会于2015年10月24日至27日在浙江省举办。展览会以“大众创业，万众创新”为主题。广东展团组织了13个展位、40多名参展人员、58项发明成果参加展览和大会交流。在参展的58项目中，获奖39项，其中金奖13项、银奖11项、铜奖15项。此次，广东展团又被评为“优秀展团”，也是广东发明协会在全国发明展览会上连续十二届获得“优秀展团”的称号。

第十三届广东省少年儿童发明奖评选活动。2015年10月10日至11日，由广东发明协会、广东科学中心、广东省知识产权研究会、广东教育学会、广东省少先队工作学会、广东省科技馆研究会主办，广东省科学技术厅、广东省教育厅、广东省知识产权局、少先队广东省工作委员会支持举办的“第十三届广东省少年儿童发明奖优秀作品展”在广东科学中心成功举行。参加此届少年儿童发明奖优秀作品展的作品共360项，来自广东省及港澳地区101所学校。共评选出获奖作品217项，其中：一等奖20项、二等奖63项、三等奖119项，专利申请鼓励奖11项，港澳特别奖16项，组织奖30项。此届少年儿童发明奖吸引了众多港澳地区中小学生参与，对扩大两岸青少年在创新方面的交流及合作，共同发展、实现双赢起到积极作用。

参加第十一届“宋庆龄少年儿童发明奖”。第十一届宋庆龄少年儿童发明奖于2015年8月13日至17日由中国宋庆龄基金会、中国发明协会在广州市番禺区举办。由广东发明协会副秘书长施明领队的广东省展团，共10件作品参赛，获得3项金奖、2项银奖、4项铜奖。其中广州市白云区石井中学学生发明的“城市斜坡（挡土墙）坍塌自动预警系统”、广州祈福英语实验学校学生发明的“手摇发电与太阳能冷暖食物便携箱”和深圳市龙岗区实验学校学生发明的“省力楼梯”获金奖。

成功举办第九届广东省DI创新思维竞赛暨2015年广州市DI创新思维竞赛。由广东发明协会、广东教育学会、广州市教育局、广州市青少年科技教育协会主办，广州市青少年科技教育协会物理专业委员会、广州市绿翠现代实验学校、广州市第九十七中学、广州凯誉文化传播有限公司等单位承办的“第九届广东省DI®创新思维竞赛暨2015年广州市DI®创新思维竞赛”于2015年11月22日在广州市第九十七中学圆满落下帷幕。竞赛共评出广州市第六中学等23支队伍获此次竞赛一等奖，27支队伍获二等奖，20支队伍获三等奖。特别奖方面优秀组织奖25项、探索精神奖、文艺复兴奖、达芬奇奖各6项以及服务类特别奖火炬奖1项。

2015年12月7日，“2015年DI®北京国际邀请赛”在中信国安天下第一城落幕。协会副秘书长施明带领的24所学校39支代表队近350人参加2015年度DI北京国际邀请赛。广东省参赛队在比赛场上团结协作，充分发挥了自身才艺与创意解决问题的能力，共荣获一等奖5项、二等奖10项、三等奖23项，DI特别奖文艺复兴奖3项、探索精神奖2项，即时挑战第一名3项，广州市汇龙小学叶晓同学获DI全面发展奖创意奖学金。

引进“创意结构搭建”项目。广东发明协会首次引进“创意结构搭建”项目并在广东省以及全国推广。2015年7月11日至12日，由广东发明协会及广东教育学会共同主办的以“快乐搭建、筑就中国梦！”为主题的首届创意结构搭建全国邀请赛在广州育才中学举行。大赛共有来自青岛、云南等各省市师生700多人，50多支队伍参加团队赛，400多位同学参加个人赛。比赛评出最佳创意奖14项、最佳功能奖13项、最佳外观奖15项以及育才中学校长奖5项。共颁发一等奖62项、二等奖110项、三等奖141项。

创意结构搭建训练创新思维和动手能力，现已成功申请为广州市科技教育特色课程。目前在广东、黑龙江、青岛、天津、西安、重庆、云南等省市已开展教学。

参与承办第四届广东省创意机器人大赛。2015年5月23—24日，由广东发明协会参与承办的“第四届广东省创意机器人大赛”在广东科学中心举办，广东发明协会副理事长兼秘书长刘庆茂出席颁奖仪式，并为获得创意发明专项奖的学生代表颁奖。此届大赛共有来自全省各地市132所学校，317支队伍，1151名学生和344名指导老师报名参加。共评出基础组一等奖36个，二等奖51个，三等奖86项，优胜奖41个；编程组一等奖17个，二等奖24个，三等奖40个，优胜奖20个。评出园丁奖197名，最佳组织奖20个，突出贡献奖2个，优秀志愿者12名，创意发明专项奖31个。创意发明专项奖由广东发明协会首次特设。

组团参加“2015澳门国际创新发明展”。“2015澳门国际创新发明展”于2015年7月3日至5日在澳门凼仔威尼斯人会展中心举行，此届展览会主要以“创新发明”为宗旨，有来自15个国家和地区，约160件发明作品参展。由广东省推送的作品“多功能运动器材仪”“超级奶瓶”获金奖，“田径短跑比赛自动计时系统”获银奖。

加强国内科技交流。2015年3月28日，应香港发明协会邀请，广东发明协会名誉理事长周兆龙、广东发明协会副理事长兼秘书长刘庆茂参加香港发明协会迎春联欢活动并进行协会工作交流。10月27日，在参加完第21届全国发明展后，由广东发明协会副理事长兼秘书长刘庆茂为团长的广东省科技考察团继续在浙江省进行科技考察。考察团与当地科技有关部门就进一步推动科技发展、科技成果转化等问题交换经验。

网络平台与期刊建设。据统计广东发明协会网站2015年点击量25万次左右，通过互联网，能更广泛地宣传广东省的发明创造情况，联系发明人和应用单位，在全省营造发明创新氛围、提高群众性发明创新水平、建设创新型的广东服务。协会与广东科技图书馆、广东省科学研究信息服务中心一起编印了科技信息快报，全年出版24期，每期印数320份。

（供稿人：邝伯麟）

广东省法学会知识产权法学研究会

【概况】 2015年12月19日，知识产权法学研究会召开广东省法学会知识产权法学研究会换届会议暨2015年学术年会。研究会第二届理事会会长唐毅（广东省法学会知识产权法学研究会秘书长朱列玉代发言）对第二届理事会工作做了总结，对第三届理事会的工作提出建议。研究会第三届理事会会长关永红对第三届研究会工作提出了具体思路。

2015年12月19日，在广东省法学会知识产权法学研究会主办的“知识产权新常态、新机遇——知识产权与创新驱动发展”研讨会上，与会专家学者就如何把握国内外知识产权法律制度的变化及趋势，如何在知识产权新常态、新机遇背景下促进知识产权法律保护与创新驱动发展战略实施，提出了有创新性和针对性的对策建议。主要包括知识产权案例审判模式改革探讨、著作权和专利保护法律问题及对策建议两大方面。

（供稿人：薛晓光　郭晓颖）

ZHI SHI CHAN QUAN JIAO LIU

知识产权交流与合作

- 对外交流与合作
- 区域交流与合作

对外交流与合作

知识产权对外交流与合作

【概况】 2015年，广东省知识产权局全面实施知识产权战略，积极参与“丝绸之路经济带”和“21世纪海上丝绸之路”建设（以下简称“一带一路”），拓展与欧美发达国家、东盟国家的直接交流合作。

【对外交流合作体系】 本着平等、务实、互利的原则，拓展对外交流合作渠道，规范全省知识产权系统外事管理，制定出台《广东省知识产权局外事管理办法》。紧紧围绕知识产权强国先行省建设和知识产权战略纲要工作部署，拓展与“一带一路”国家和地区的知识产权交流，推动构建多元知识产权国际合作平台，积极开展知识产权海外护航，探索建立知识产权涉外应对和援助机制。贯彻落实省部第二轮知识产权高层次战略合作要求，积极构建知识产权多元国际合作试验区。加强与相关部门的沟通协作，积极举办“两岸专利论坛”“内地与港澳知识产权研讨会”“中日韩三国知识产权局长会议”等重大外事活动，大力提升全省知识产权外事工作水平，全面推进知识产权对外交流合作，构建多层次知识产权对外交流合作体系。

【广东自由贸易试验区】 广东自由贸易试验区（以下简称“自贸试验区”）的设立，对广东形成依托港澳、连接东盟、面向世界的区域开放新格局有重要推动意义。广东省知识产权局高度重视，成立了广东自贸试验区知识产权专项工作组。深入自贸试验区实地调研，认真研究推进自贸试验区知识产权各项工作。根据自贸试验区总体方案及建设实施方案的要求，广东省知识产权局联合省自贸办印发了《关于加强广东自由贸易试验区知识产权工作的指导意见》，围绕建设与国际接轨的高标准知识产权管理和保护体系等目标，提出了六大块12条任务措施，为自贸试验区知识产权工作的开展提供指引。广东省知识产权局主动与省法制办、省人大常委会法工委联系和沟通，争取将知识产权相关条款纳入《中国（广东）自由贸易试验区管理试行办法》及《中国（广东）自由贸易试验区条例》。推动自贸试验区快速维权中心和知识产权运营中心、全国知识产权运营公共服务横琴特色试点平台建设。

【“一带一路”知识产权工作】 2015年，广东省知识产权局在推进与“一带一路”沿线国家和地区知识产权交流合作的过程中，坚持共商、共建、共享原则，推动“中国创造”、中国品牌、中国文化更好地融入国际大局。拓展与“一带一路”政府机构、知名企业、研究机构、服务机构和高校的合作交流，谋求建立深层次、广领域和合作模式，在国际合作交流活动中，注重对广东省知识产权工作的宣传力度。积极推进与“一带一路”国家及地区的知识产权贸易合作，开展相关研讨活动，在12月3日第五届亚洲知识产权营商论坛上，广东省知识产权局局长马宪民受邀在论坛的“一带一路”下之知识产权机遇圆桌会议发言，向“海上丝绸之路”国家代表介绍中国及广东知识产权发展情况并分享对“一带一路”知识产权机遇的看法。论坛期间，由香港知识产权署主办，广东省知识产权局支持举办的“知识产权管理人员培训课程”圆满完成。与新加坡知识产权局主办新加坡知识产权制度巡回研讨活动，增进广东省珠三角地区企事业单位对新加坡及东盟知识产权制度的认识和了解，培养省内知识产权高端实务人才，提升企事业单位运用知识产权制度参与国际市场竞争的能力。

【重大外事及交流活动】 成功承办了“中国国家知识产权局、新加坡知识产权局与广东省政府三方会谈暨中国国家知识产权局与新加坡知识产权局会谈纪要签字仪式”“中日两国知识产权局局长会议”“中韩两国知识产权局局长会议”“中日韩三国知识产权局长政策对话会议”“中日韩知识产权研讨会”和“2015年内地与香港、澳门特别行政区知识产权研讨会”等一系列具有重大影响力的国家层面知识产权外事活动。全年接待世界知识产权组织、新加坡知识产权局、日本经济产业省及国际知识产权论坛官民实务代表团、中国欧盟商会华南分会、美国知识产权法律协会，英国、日本、韩国等国家和地区的政府部门、知识产权机构代表来访26批次，182人次，举办知识产权国际条约学习讲坛、知识产权制度巡回研讨活动等。组织局系统人员4批次13人赴荷兰、瑞士、法国、意大利、芬兰、德国等地进行访问交流和专题学习。

【重大平台建设】 推进广东重点产业园区拓展知识产权国际交流合作，推进中新广州知识城知识产权运用保护综合改革试点，大力推动“中新知识城知识产权运用和保护综合改革试验区工作”，加强沟通协调，争取国家部委对知识产权运用和保护综合改革试点工作的支持。支持揭阳中德金属生态城开展重大国际知识产权合作平台建设工程，打造国际知识产权创新型园区。

【知识产权涉外应对】 加强知识产权涉外应对和海外维权援助，全省成立了省中心以及深圳、汕头、佛山、东莞、中山6家知识产权维权援助中心，以及中国中山（灯饰）知识产权快速维权中心，中国东莞（家具）知识产权快速维权中心，中国顺德（家电）知识产权快速维权中心。支持灯饰等重点产业与国际知识产权制度接轨。10月，世界知识产权组织（WIPO）中国办事处官员赴中山、珠海市进行调研，了解企业通过《专利合作条约》进行专利国际注册、通过马德里体系进行商标国际注册、通过海牙体系进行外观设计国际注册的情况，以及外观设计保护对灯饰等重点产业发展的影响，向企业宣讲使用工业品外观设计国际注册海牙体系进行外观设计国际注册情况。WIPO中国办事处官员还访问广东省知识产权局，就进一步加强双方在知识产权公共服务、宣传、培训及资源共享等方面的合作进行了深入交流。会后，访问联瑞集团（UTC）、汇桔网等知识产权运营机构，就与WIPO开展在知识产权运营方面的相关合作进行了交流。

【对外宣传】 通过各种途径和利用各种机会开展对外宣传，增进国际社会对广东省知识产权制度运行状况的了解，树立广东省在保护知识产权方面的良好国际形象，增强外商来广东省投资的信心。4月知识产权宣传周期间，广东省知识产权局组织省政府知识产权办公会议26个成员单位及6个特邀单位，编写《2014年广东省知识产权保护状况》白皮书（中英文版），并联合省政府新闻办召开新闻发布会，向各国驻穗领事机构及境内外媒体发布了白皮书。2003年至2015年，发布会已连续十三年举办，成为广东对外宣传知识产权工作的品牌活动。2015年，广东省知识产权局先后协调邀请省公安厅、省工商局、省版权局、省质监局等知识产权相关部门共同接待“日本经济产业省及国际知识产权论坛官民实务代表团”，与来自日本经济产业省、在华日资企业知识产权保护联盟（IPG）、日本贸易振兴机构等机构约30名代表就知识产权保护相关问题进行会谈。2015年，广东省知识产权局多次协调广东省知识产权相关部门组织材料，为省委、省政府领导会见外国领事团提供参阅材料，提升广东知识产权工作的国际知名度和影响力，大大推动知识产权对外宣传工作。充分利用中国出口商品交易会（广交会）在海外的巨大影响力，通过在交易会设立投诉站、举行大型宣传活动、派发宣传资料等方式，多渠道、多途径地向参展的客商和来宾介绍会展知识产权保护的规定，以及中国政府保护知识产权的决心，树立中国尊重和保护知识产权的良好形象，取得了较好的宣传效果。

【粤港澳台区域知识产权合作】 一是大力推进粤港澳知识产权合作，圆满完成“2015粤港知识产权与中小企业发展（广州）研讨会”等年度项目19项，成功举办粤港保护知识产权合作专责小组第十四次会议，确定年度合作项目21项，将知识产权内容纳入粤港合作联席会议，签署《粤港知识产权合作协议（2015—2016）》，赴港澳参加2015年泛珠三角区域知识产权公务人员交流活动，粤港澳知识产权合作持续深化。二是大力加强粤台知识产权合作，圆满举办“第八届两岸专利论坛”。组织代表团一行15人赴台湾开展研习交流活动。三是积极推进内地区域知识产权合作，成功召开“粤青知识产权工作合作框架协议书签署仪式暨第一次工作会议”，确定年度合作项目7项；启动新一轮援疆工作，签署《广东省知识产权局 新疆喀什地区行政公署知识产权对口合作协议书》，确定5项年度工作安排。

（供稿人：尹怡然）

区域交流与合作

2015年粤港知识产权合作

【概况】 2015年，粤港两地知识产权相关部门围绕粤港保护知识产权合作专责小组第十三次会议确定的合作计划，推动完成合作项目19项。

【知识产权合作机制】 2015年8月18日，粤港保护知识产权合作专责小组第十四次会议在香港成功举行，会议总结了2014年7月到2015年7月的19个项目的落实情况，确定了2015年7月到2016年7月的21个合作项目。香港知识产权署与广东省知识产权局牵头，联同省公安厅、商务厅、工商局、版权局、海关总署广东分署及香港海关持续更新“粤港澳知识产权资料库”与“粤港知识产权合作专栏”，更新内容包括三地专利、商标、著作权及知识产权边境和刑事保护法律法规，知识产权行政管理及执法部门联系方式等各类信息，及时提供三地专利、商标、版权方面政策法规的最新动态，便利三地公众和企业查询使用。2015年9月9日，粤港合作联席会议第十八次会议在香港举行，省知识产权局局长马宪民和香港知识产权署署长梁家丽签署了《粤港知识产权合作协议（2015—2016）》，粤港知识产权合作开启崭新篇章。下一阶段，粤港双方以推进“知识产权贸易”为重点，开创粤港知识产权合作新局面。

【知识产权执法及案件协作处理机制】 粤港知识产权跨境保护执法协作机制建设方面取得了新进展，海关总署广东分署与香港海关加强海运及邮递快件物品的监管，坚持每月定期通报相互查获的涉港、涉粤侵权案件信息，双方加大打击粤港两地海运及邮递快件渠道走私侵权物品违法活动力度，联手举行了针对海运管道及邮递快件管道走私侵权物品的同步联合行动，香港海关在同步联合行动中，查获19宗案件，共48105件侵权货品，包括手袋、药物、衣服、手表、耳机、手机壳、电器、鞋及太阳眼镜等。在针对邮递快件渠道专项行动中，粤方共查验出口EMS邮件逾55万票、出口快件近4万票，查获涉嫌侵权案件14宗，涉及药品、香烟、手机等货物物品，在打击邮递快件渠道侵权活动联合执法行动中，粤方查获涉嫌侵权案件6宗，扣留涉嫌侵权产品1760件，涉及手机、电子屏、皮带等货物物品。香港海关及海关总署广东分署领导于2015年1月27日在香港进行了高层会晤，举行知识产权保护合作专题会谈，总结同步联合行动的成果及商讨下一阶段的合作重点，共同研究长期合作打击跨境侵权活动的策略。香港海关还与省公安厅、省工商局、省新闻出版广电局（版权局）保持紧密联系，不断完善情报合作机制，深化执法协作，探讨涉及两地侵权案件的合作，以及通过定期的情报交流掌握跨境商标侵权势态，全面打击粤港两地跨境侵权活动。

【知识产权贸易和法律服务】 粤港双方积极推动两地知识产权贸易的发展，包括继续在“粤港澳知识产权资料库”及各粤港知识产权合作专责小组成员网站中丰富有关知识产权贸易及法律服务信息、开展知识产权贸易研讨活动，以及支持两地社会组织、行业协会开展以知识产权贸易为题的交流，协助企业提升知识产权运用能力和水平，进一步增强企业竞争力。省知识产权局组织专家开展自由贸易环境下的粤港知识产权研究，探讨粤港在知识产权保护、运用、管理、转化及贸易等领域的现状及发展趋势，探索自由贸易环境下的粤港知识产权合作新路径。香港知识产权署于2014年6月委托顾问进行“知识产权贸易统计调查”，以了解目前香港知识产权贸易活动的情况。调查成功访问了2329间机构，收集了有关香港知识产权创造者、拥有人、使用者及知识产权中介服务机构进行知识产权贸易活动的统计数据及意见。香港知识产权署与粤方分享了“知识产权贸易统计调查”报告，以及在调查过程取得的经验，作为粤方专家小组研究工作的参考。2015年5月6日至8日，广东省版权局领导率广东省出版、动漫、软件等业界人士及关注版权的业界代表赴港开展版权产业企业交流活动，双方围绕“版权管理与知识产权贸易”主题开展座谈。座谈会后，广东省代表团到访了动漫基地、香港海关及数码港，与香港动漫画联会代表及其他版权业界代表开展交流。这次交流活动加深了两地在版权管理及贸易发展趋势方面的了解，为深化未来合作奠定良好基础。

【亚洲知识产权营商论坛】 2015年12月3日至4日，省知识产权局局长马宪民率团赴港，出席第五届亚洲知识产权营商论坛，并在“一带一路”下之知识产权机遇圆桌会议发言。此届论坛由香港特别行政区政府、香港贸易发展局（香港贸发局）及香港设计中心合办，以“知识产权：带领全球转型”为主题，旨在为知识产权业界和商界人士提供交流平台，共同探讨环球知识产权的最新发展、发掘商机。省知识产权局协助组织相关单位报名参加论坛。论坛邀请逾80位重量级演讲嘉宾，吸引超过2000位知识产权业界精英参与。受香港贸发局邀请，马宪民莅临论坛分组专题：“一带一路”下之知识产权机遇圆桌会议，并发表主题演讲，介绍中国及广东知识产权发展情况并分享对“一带一路”知识产权机遇的看法。其他受邀发言人还有以色列、越南及马来西亚等国政要。来自“一带一路”沿线国家和地区的官员以及江苏省、湖南省、四川省、山东省及重庆市知识产权局局长等30余人参加了圆桌会议，共同探讨知识产权新常态及“一带一路”为亚洲乃至全球知识产权带来的机遇和影响。论坛期间，由香港知识产权署主办，省知识产权局支持举办的“知识产权管理人员培训课程”圆满完成。该课程内容围绕知识产权贸易、内地的知识产权管理与保护，商标、专利、版权及外观设计的管理与开发等，为中小企业培训人才，提升企业的知识产权运用能力和竞争力，来自内地的企事业单位及海内外的企业百余人参加了培训。此外，论坛的展览活动汇聚各方面从事知识产权的人士，分享最新发展及信息。

【粤港澳知识产权交流研讨】 2015年内地与香港、澳门特别行政区知识产权研讨会。2015年4月28日，由国家知识产权局、香港特别行政区政府知识产权署和澳门特别行政区政府经济局联合主办的“2015年内地与香港、澳门特别行政区知识产权研讨会”在广东省中山市召开。会议由广东省知识产权局与中山市人民政府承办。国家知识产权局副局长何志敏、广东省政府副秘书长李捍东、香港特别行政区政府知识产权署署长梁家丽、澳门特别行政区政府经济局副局长戴建业出席开幕式并致辞。

“粤港知识产权与中小企业发展”研讨会。2015年6月4日，粤港双方在广州市联合举办以“知识产权运用及发展策略”为主题的“粤港知识产权与中小企业发展（广州）研讨会”。来自粤港两地的政府官员和知识产权业界专家在会上分享内地与香港知识产权制度的最新进展，并就知识产权保护、管理及商品化策略等问题进行研讨。

2015年1月8日，广东省工商局与香港知识产权署在香港举办新《中华人民共和国商标法》研讨会，邀请国家工商行政管理总局及广东省工商局代表主讲，详细解读新《商标法》的内容及探讨相关实施条例对企业的影响，以强化企业于内地的商标保护意识和管理工作。协助香港企业及商标相关服务业了解于2014年

5月1日实施的新《中华人民共和国商标法》及其实施条例。

2015年2月12—13日省版权局和香港海关、香港知识产权署共同举办“粤港中学生版权知识和版权保护交流活动”。省版权局带领广州市执信中学、广州市第十七中学及广州恒福中学师生一行26人组成的交流团赴港进行交流。4月8至9日，18名香港青少年代表回访广州市进行交流，访问了广州市版权局和知识产权业界的机构，加深了青少年对内地保护知识产权工作的认识。

2015年3月13日香港海关与香港保护知识产权大联盟共同举办“内地知识产权保护及执法研讨会”，邀请海关总署广东分署、省公安厅经济犯罪侦查局、版权局的专家出席，向香港保护知识产权大联盟的会员介绍广东省知识产权保护措施及各单位保护知识产权的执法工作。研讨会促进了香港业界对内地执法部门的了解，建立彼此的合作伙伴关系，加强了有关品牌及版权作品在内地的保护。

2015年5月20日，省商务厅、工商局与香港知识产权署联合举办了“2015品牌国际化知识产权保护培训班”。香港知识产权署、广东省知识产权局、广东省工商局、广东省版权局和粤港两地海关等单位的专家围绕品牌国际化知识产权保护作专题培训和交流，有效推进品牌国际化与知识产权保护建设。

【粤港知识产权引导服务】 一是协助香港考生参加全国专利代理人资格考试，省知识产权局继续向港方通报全国专利代理人资格考试相关培训的信息，港方宣传粤方在广东省举办的考前培训班课程，方便香港考生及时了解培训信息并参加培训。自2004年以来，香港共有50人通过全国专利代理人资格考试，目前有18人在内地执业。2015年，共有34名香港考生在粤报名参加全国专利代理人资格考试，5人通过考试。2015年，双方继续协助香港考生参加全国专利代理人资格考试广东考点的考试。二是加强对香港在粤执业专利代理人的跟进服务。2015年7月28日，香港知识产权署组织香港的专利代理人协会代表到广州与广东省知识产权局代表及广东专利代理协会代表会面。粤港双方代表于会上就通过专利代理人资格考试的香港考生在内地执业情况进行交流。三是宣传广东省著名商标认定。香港知识产权署继续把在粤港资企业获许申报广东省著名商标的有关信息向相关香港知识产权业界及商会通报宣传，并在香港贸易发展局中小企业服务中心、香港知识产权署的“知识产权管理人员培训课程”及展览会展台中宣传有关信息，鼓励企业申请广东省著名商标。广东省工商局指导广东商标协会继续履行粤港合作项目，支持在粤港资企业申请认定广东省著名商标。

【粤港知识产权宣传教育】 一是双方持续推进“正版正货承诺”活动的交流。2015年7月28日，广东省知识产权局联合广东省版权局、广东省工商局等“正版正货承诺”活动牵头单位组织广东省行业协会代表参与由香港知识产权署及香港海关在广州市共同举办的简报会。香港知识产权署及香港海关代表于会上分享在香港推行“正版正货承诺”计划的经验。二是协助港方参加审查员培训课程。省知识产权局积极与国家知识产权局专利局专利审查协作广东中心沟通，向香港知识产权署通报第十三期新任审查员培训的安排情况和课程资料。香港知识产权署于2014年8月派员参加了审协广东中心的新任审查员培训课程。三是支持香港民间组织参加广东省少年儿童发明奖。在广东省知识产权局的大力支持下，香港知识产权署资助并推动香港发明协会推荐香港学生参加第十二届“广东省少年儿童发明奖”。

（供稿人：尹怡然）

2015年粤澳知识产权合作

【概况】 2015年，粤澳知识产权合作继续推进，根据粤澳知识产权工作小组第二次会议商定的《粤澳知识产权合作计划（2014—2016年）》，粤澳双方在加强知识产权交流互访、跨境保护、宣传培训等领域开展系列合作，取得良好成效。

【粤澳知识产权合作机制】 粤澳知识产权合作有效推进，双方知识产权相关部门多次进行工作会晤，进一步完善粤澳知识产权合作工作机制，巩固粤澳知识产权协调联络机制，强化项目合作制度；深化粤澳在知识产权交流研讨、跨境保护、宣传教育及引导服务等领域的交流合作；促进粤澳知识产权服务业合作，提升粤澳两地知识产权创造、运用、保护、管理、服务水平，确保粤澳知识产权合作项目的顺利开展。

【粤澳知识产权案件协助处理机制】 在粤澳知识产权工作小组机制推动下，一是海关总署广东分署发挥粤澳海关保护知识产权专项联络员作用，与澳门海关加强沟通，积极开展情报交流与情况通报，加强粤澳海关高层互动，进一步开展打击粤澳两地跨境侵犯知识产权联合执法行动，以有代表性的个案为突破点，开展情报合作、联手调查和协调处置。两地海关在闸口和横琴口岸举行多次联合执法行动，将假冒药品、食品、汽车配件、酒类产品、手机、平板计算机等商品列为重点监控商品，并对水客携带侵权物品进出境的违法行为加大打击力度。结合横琴新区建设和港珠澳大桥落成等项目，两地海关共同研究如何在新形势下加强知识产权保护工作。二是省公安厅推动与澳门海关建立情报互通顺畅、执法交流常态、案件打击联动的跨境执法合作长效机制。结合公安部部署的“打假行动”，推动与澳门海关在情报等方面的交流，深化粤澳知识产权案件的执法协作。在打假专项行动中，以珠海市公安局经侦部门为依托，在与澳门司法警察局协作原有基础上，不断探索与澳门海关的跨境打假协作。三是省工商局与澳门海关商讨双方商标执法合作的需求评估，建立联络员制度，明确交流协作范围、具体程序等事项。四是省版权局拟建立粤澳著作权案件协作处理机制，以加快彼此信息交流及资料互换的效率，加强信息资源共享和沟通合作，共同打击两地跨境侵权盗版活动。

【粤澳知识产权交流互访】 加强两地知识产权行政管理机构的交流和联系，加大交流互访培训的力度，及时交流两地知识产权保护最新法律法规政策，相互借鉴学习有效的经验做法，提高自身能力和水平。共同组织“第十届泛珠三角区域知识产权合作联席会议暨知识产权专题交流活动”。在粤港澳三地举办“第十届泛珠三角区域知识产权合作联席会议”、泛珠三角区域知识产权公务人员交流活动，以及相关知识产权专题交流活动。开展粤澳版权产业交流活动。分享版权产业知识产权的创造、运用、保护、管理经验，研究推动两地企业版权维权合作及版权贸易发展途径。2015年7月10日，省知识产权局协助澳门经济局知识产权厅与澳门海关访问国家知识产权局专利局专利审查协作广东中心，了解中心为企业提供专利申请和保护等方面的技术和法律咨询服务情况，并实地调研专利申请实质审查的工作情况。此外，澳门方面就知识产权司法鉴定工作与省知识产权局及省知识产权研究与发展中心司法鉴定所进行了交流，并就专利侵权认定协作的可行性进行了初步探讨。

【粤澳知识产权宣传培训】 省知识产权局加大与澳门在知识产权交流研讨领域的合作，邀请在粤澳门企业参加“粤港知识产权与中小企业发展研讨会”“广州国际知识产权商业化会议”等知识产权交流研讨活动。对2013年澳门知识产权厅举办“内地商标的审查标准及品牌权益保护策略”座谈会进行跟进服务，为会后相关人员与粤澳专家的沟通搭建平台，深化研讨主题在实践中的运用。上述活动大大提高了在粤澳门企业对知识产权的认识，提升在粤澳门企业运用知识产权制度的能力。

【粤澳知识产权研究】 一是开展粤港澳自贸区知识产权政策研究。分析比较粤澳知识产权制度的差异，研究粤澳知识产权保护、维权、转化、运用制度的异同，为粤港澳自由贸易区内的知识产权机制建设提供政策依据。二是推动澳门大学与广东高校及科研机构开展中医药领域知识产权保护研究合作。通过举办交流活动，探索联合培养中医药知识产权专业人才。三是拓展粤澳知识产权服务贸易合作，开展粤澳知识产权服务业交流研讨活动，推进两地知识产权服务机构、行业协会间的交流，搭建粤澳知识产权中介服务对接平台。

【粤港澳知识产权信息资源共享】 进一步完善粤澳信息交流机制，及时通报粤澳知识产权法律法规和政策措施最新进展，持续建设粤港澳三地知识产权信息平台及“粤港澳知识产权资料库”，及时更新粤澳知识产权法律法规和政策信息，通报粤澳知识产权法律法规政策最新情况，为三地公众有效运用知识产权信息资源提供支撑。

（供稿人：尹怡然）

2015年粤台知识产权合作

【概况】 2015年，广东省不断提升与台湾的知识产权工作，积极促进粤台双方在知识产权信息运用和专业培训领域的交流合作，推进两岸专利事业发展、深化两岸产业合作、促进两岸关系发展。

【第八届两岸专利论坛】 2015年9月22—23日，由中华全国专利代理人协会与台湾工业总会共同主办、广东省知识产权研究会承办的第八届两岸专利论坛在广州开幕。副省长陈云贤、国家知识产权局副局长何志敏、台湾工业总会秘书长蔡练生、台湾工业总会智慧财产权委员会高级顾问王美花，以及中华全国代理人协会有关负责人出席论坛开幕式并致辞。来自两岸专利主管机构人员和业界人士的200余名嘉宾代表围绕着两岸专利领域最新发展、专利法制发展动态、专利审理面临的挑战与应对、专利布局与诉讼的策略和管理等主题展开交流与探讨。10余名来自两岸知识产权界的专家、学者以及企业家代表做了精彩纷呈的主题发言。

【粤台知识产权服务机构交流】 2015年10月12日，广东省知识产权局局长马宪民会见了到访的台湾与日本知识产权代表团一行，双方围绕广东、台湾及日本在知识产权合作方面的相关事宜进行了交流。台湾博拓国际智权集团（PIIP）执行长李彦庆、日本新树GLOBAL IP事务所所长村井康司等参加了会谈。马宪民表示，台湾的知识产权服务机构在推进粤台知识产权合作的过程中开展了卓有成效的工作，希望日本的知识产权服务机构也积极拓展广东业务，共同推进知识产权事业的发展。下一阶段，三方将继续加强在知识产权人才培训、运营、服务等方面的合作。

【粤台知识产权交流合作】 为构建知识产权领域的开放创新机制，助推知识产权强国先行地及知识产权服务业示范省建设，广东省知识产权局副巡视员黄光华率知识产权代表团一行15人，于2015年7月28日至8月3日赴台湾开展知识产权研习交流活动。

（供稿人：尹怡然）

2015年泛珠三角区域知识产权合作

【概况】 2015年，在各省（区、特区）知识产权职能部门的共同努力和积极推动下，泛珠三角区域知识产权合作关系不断深化，合作力度不断加强，合作环境不断优化。

【泛珠三角区域知识产权专题交流】 2015年10月28日至30日，泛珠三角区域知识产权公务人员交流活动在香港、澳门举办。参加活动的泛珠三角区域各省（区）代表根据本省（区）知识产权工作最新进展分别作了主题发言，香港特区政府知识产权署、英国皇家特许测量师学会亚洲区理事会、香港商业估值议会等机构介绍了香港知识产权保护及贸易相关情况，澳门特区政府经济局知识产权厅、澳门特区海关介绍了澳门知识产权行政管理及执法相关情况。活动期间，各省（区）代表还访问了香港海关、香港贸易发展局、澳门设计中心，并举行了多场座谈会，就知识产权保护、管理、贸易等相关问题进行了深入探讨。来自内地五省（区）知识产权局、工商局、版权局的代表、港澳官方及非官方代表约50人参加了会议。

【泛珠三角区域内地九省（区）专利行政执法协作】 2015年10月22—24日，闽粤沿海十二城市保护知识产权工作第十二次联席会议在广东省湛江市举办，会上各省（区）知识产权局代表交流了知识产权行政执法经验，探讨了电子商务领域专利侵权、假冒行为案件执法的工作机制与做法。

2015年，泛珠三角区域内地九省（区）深入贯彻《泛珠三角区域内地九省（区）专利行政执法协作协议》，不断完善专利行政执法协作机制，推进区域专利行政保护协作。广东省知识产权局与广西壮族自治区知识产权局积极落实《专利行政执法能力提升工程方案》，互派人员参加第12届中国—东盟博览会和第117届广交会的知识产权保护工作。

【泛珠三角区域内地九省（区）专利信息】 2015年7月23日，泛珠三角区域九省（区）专利信息服务工作座谈会在广东省广州市召开，广东省知识产权局通报国家知识产权局区域专利信息服务（广州）中心的建设及服务开展情况，并介绍跨省区专利信息服务项目。

2015年，泛珠三角区域内地九省（区）知识产权职能部门深入贯彻《区域专利信息服务（广州）中心发展规划（2013—2017）》，不断完善泛珠三角区域专利信息资源共享机制和服务功能，大力推动泛珠三角区域专利信息的广泛传播和有效利用。广东省知识产权局开展泛珠区域内专利信息推送服务及专利信息人才跨省区培育服务，面向泛珠区域省区600多家企业开展专利信息推送服务，服务涵盖技术领域22大类技术领域，并与海南、四川、广西、贵州等省区联合举办多次专利信息人才培训班。

（供稿人：尹怡然　陈燕）

2015年粤喀知识产权合作

【概况】 2015年，广东省知识产权局与喀什地区行政公署签署新一轮的知识产权对口合作协议，进一步扩大合作范围，共同推进多领域合作，商定下一阶段在知识产权人才交流与培训、专利技术转移与产业化、专利行政执法工作交流、专利信息交流等多个方面的合作。

【知识产权创造】 广东省知识产权局积极支持喀什地区知识产权局以实施知识产权战略纲要为抓手，以增强企业自主创新能力和核心竞争力为目标，大力提升地区知识产权创造能力和水平。喀什地区知识产权局通过广泛开展知识产权宣传和培训，不断强化公众知识产权创造意识，激发企业自主创新的积极性，促进喀什地区专利申请和授权量快速增长。2015年喀什地区专利申请量274件，专利授权量147件，申请量比2014年增加140%。

【知识产权执法】 广东省知识产权局支持喀什地区知识产权局改善专利行政执法条件，提升执法人员执法水平，推动喀什地区专利执法工作向规范化、制度化发展。喀什地区知识产权局充分利用支持资金，配备统一的执法服装和执法装备，保障执法车辆的正常运行，及时处理喀什地区境内发生的专利侵权纠纷案件，维护专利权利人的合法权益。2015年，喀什地区知识产权局被评为全疆专利行政执法工作先进集体。

【知识产权人才交流】 广东省知识产局与喀什地区知识产权局积极加强交流互访，双方领导多次带队开展实地互访考察，围绕合作项目进行现场座谈交流，了解项目开展过程中存在的问题和困难，保障合作项目的开展落到实处。2015年6月25—29日，广东省知识产权局领导率队赴喀什地区参加第11届中国新疆喀什·中亚南亚商品交易会，与新疆维吾尔自治区知识产权局、中国（新疆）知识产权维权援助中心喀什分中心工作人员联合组成第11届“喀交会”知识产权维权援助工作站，深入展区开展执法维权活动。其间，双方还召开“粤喀知识产权对口合作工作座谈会”，就启动新一轮知识产权对口合作工作交换意见并达成共识。

【知识产权教育】 广东省知识产权局积极支持喀什地区开展知识产权教育试点学校工作。喀什地区知识产权局多次联合试点学校开展知识产权知识竞赛、读报比赛、青少年创新大赛、知识产权保护千人签字仪式、知识产权讲座进学校等丰富多彩的活动，为试点学校开展知识产权教育营造良好氛围。

【知识产权宣传培训】 广东省知识产权局支持喀什地区知识产权局充分利用“3·15”“4·26”“科技周”“科普宣传周”“法律宣传周”和“宪法”宣传日等节点开展广泛的知识产权宣传活动。截至2015年底，喀什地区知识产权局投入宣传经费近30万元，接受知识产权咨询2万余次，印发宣传资料7万余份，联合电视台、电台等媒体开展宣传活动30多次，举办各类知识产权培训和讲座19期，取得了良好的社会效果。

（供稿人：陈燕）

宣传　教育培训

XUAN CHUAN JIAO YU PEI

宣传
教育培训

宣 传

广东省知识产权宣传工作

【概况】 2015年，广东省知识产权局统一部署，围绕知识产权大项任务和热点焦点工作加强知识产权宣传，大力营造尊重知识，崇尚创新、诚信守法的知识产权文化氛围，取得较好成效。

【部署安排】

整体谋划。印发全省知识产权系统年度宣传工作要点，规划年度知识产权宣传工作指导思想和主要内容。印发全省相关单位“4·26”知识产权宣传工作方案和局系统“4·26”知识产权宣传工作方案，布置“4·26”期间各相关单位宣传工作主要内容等。

重要宣传。先后利用“4·26世界知识产权日”“第八届中国专利周”等时间节点，精心设计新闻发布、论坛讲座、广场咨询、执法检查、法律维权等各种知识产权宣传活动，营造了浓厚的知识产权文化氛围。2015年知识产权宣传周期间，省知识产权局围绕“建设知识产权强国，支撑创新驱动发展”主题，对34个成员单位近60项工作进行统一协调汇总，并召开了2015年广东省知识产权宣传周活动方案暨2014年广东省知识产权保护状况新闻发布会，及时向社会公众、驻穗领馆及国内外媒体发布全省知识产权保护状况白皮书。

【重点、热点】

重大活动。省知识产权局通过各类新闻媒体广泛宣传包括省领导会见国家知识产权局局长申长雨、申长雨来广东省调研视察、第二轮省部知识产权高层次战略合作2015年度工作会议召开、全省打击侵权假冒工作电视电话会议等20余次知识产权重大活动。《科技日报》、《法制日报》、人民网、新华网、中国打击侵权假冒工作网等国家级媒体和广东电视台、《南方日报》、《羊城晚报》、《广州日报》、南方网等省内媒体，先后在主要版面刊登“共同为知识产权工作改革创新探索新路”“共推两岸专利事业进一步发展”等一系列重量级报道，取得良好效果。据不完全统计，2015年，累计在各类媒体发表文字报道350余篇，图片报道近百幅。

热点工作。先后策划《广东省专利奖励办法》系列宣传、“创建知识产权深化改革试验区——广东自贸试验区知识产权工作的思考”理论研讨会暨专题宣传、“《专利法》实施三十周年”系列宣传、《广东省深入实施知识产权战略推动创新驱动发展行动计划》系列宣传等热点工作宣传报道，并及时做好“皮革皮具知识产权快速维权中心落户花都”，省知识产权局与中国专利信息中心、知识产权出版社有限责任公司分别签署合作协议，印发“加强广东自贸区知识产权工作的指导意见”等媒体关注的焦点工作的宣传报道。其中，“创建知识产权深化改革试验区——广东自贸试验区知识产权工作的思考”研究成果在《南方日报》理论版发表，并被各大门户和财经网站转载，收到非常好的宣传效果；“《专利法》实施三十周年”专题宣传过程中，广东省知识产权工作情况被新华社、中新社、人民网、科技日报、南方日报等数十家主流媒体大篇幅报道，各大网站转载，取得了显著的宣传效果。

领导专访。2015年，先后承担副省长陈云贤接受《南方日报》《中国知识产权报》等媒体专访、副省长陈云贤发表“《专利法》实施30周年及4·26知识产权日”致辞、局长马宪民接受“南方网”新年致辞、局长马宪民接受

《南方日报》《中国知识产权报》及其他媒体的专访工作。

【宣传渠道】

《中国知识产权报·广东专刊》。在省知识产权局的努力争取下，自2013年起，《中国知识产权报》专门开设“广东专刊”专版，至2015年底，专刊共计出版近60期。2015年，专刊先后推出省部知识产权合作会商制度建设、第15届中国专利奖广东金奖、广东出台专利奖励办法、广东法院大力推动专利司法保护、广东各地实施知识产权战略成效显著、《专利法》实施30周年广东知识产权发展纪实等重点报道，并深入广东省一些知识产权工作成效显著的地市和县区进行报道，充分发挥专刊在培育知识产权宣传人才和知识产权文化传播方面的作用，扩大了广东省知识产权工作的影响力。

宣传平台。搭建成由《中国知识产权报》广东记者站、广东电视台、《南方日报》、《羊城晚报》等近20家媒体在内的QQ信息传送平台，对知识产权工作中的一些重要新闻、重大事件和工作动态、经验成就第一时间在平台上进行发布，增强了宣传工作时效性，基本实现了知识产权宣传“电视上有图像、广播上有声音、报刊上有文章、网络上有信息”的目标。

（供稿人：吴勇）

广东省工商行政管理系统知识产权宣传培训工作

【概况】　2015年，广东省工商行政管理系统创新商标宣传模式，丰富商标宣传内容，开展全省性集中培训、分片培训或专题培训，推动形成全社会重视商标、崇尚创新的良好舆论氛围。

【商标宣传】

“4·26”全国知识产权宣传周活动。广东省工商行政管理局以“保护知识产权、营造公平环境、建设品牌强省”为主题，指导全省工商系统在2015年4月20—26日开展商标宣传活动。4月23日，省工商局召开新闻发布会，通报新《商标法》实施一年来的商标工作情况。宣传周期间，全省工商系统通过各类媒体刊登宣传报道525条/篇，召开新闻发布会2次，举办现场咨询、集中销毁等活动319次，发布公益广告196.7万条/次。

商标注册与保护宣传。2015年1月8日，广东省工商局与香港特区政府知识产权署联合举办“新《商标法》研讨会”，向香港企业宣传新修订实施的《中华人民共和国商标法》及其实施条例，得到与会各方的肯定与好评。5月22日，广东省工商局、广东省商务厅与香港特区政府知识产权署在广州联合主办“品牌国际化知识产权保护培训班”，倡导运用知识产权参与国际竞争。10月16—18日，应中华商标协会邀请，广东省工商局有关领导带队参加2015中国国际商标品牌节，围绕“实施商标战略、发展品牌经济”主题，研讨引导企业加强商标品牌建设的工作，展示广东企业的良好形象，提高广东优势品牌的知名度。加强商标国际注册宣传培训。编印《商标国际注册指引》，通过广东省工商局门户网站发布，向广东省有关行业协会、企业发放，宣传主要贸易国家（地区）商标法律信息，提高企业创建国际化商标品牌的意识与能力。

【商标培训】　2015年5月18—20日，广东省工商局举办全省工商系统2015年商标业务培训班，邀请国家工商总局、广东省高级人民法院以及司法界等领域商标业务专家授课，对全省21个地市工商部门分管商标工作的局领导及业务骨干共100余人进行培训，增强商标执法责任感，提高执法办案水平，确保全省商标执法的统一与高效。9月22—24日，广东省工商局在深圳举办2015年全省工商系统商标品牌战略专题培训班。11月26日—12月2日，广东省工商局分别在汕头、湛江组织了商标执法专题分片培训班，并同期举办商标品牌战略实施培训班，全省约500家企业代表参加培训。

（供稿人：陈小冰）

教育培训

广东省知识产权人才培训工作

【概况】 2015年，广东省知识产权局大力贯彻落实国家知识产权局《2015年全国知识产权人才工作要点》，全面推进全省知识产权人才队伍建设。

一是组织完成2014年国家和省级知识产权培训基地考核评估、年度总结及2015年工作计划编制。二是创新人才培养项目管理机制，首次通过竞争性项目分配，确定一批工作能力强、基础扎实的项目承接单位，组织政府、企事业单位和中介服务机构等相关人员进行培训和研修活动，并委托国家和省培训基地，精心组织各类高层次培训班十余期，为省内从业人员提供了活跃的学习和交流平台。三是大力推进知识产权专业技术资格评价工作，联合省人社厅开展专题工作调研，与省人社厅、省工商局、省版权局座谈商讨职称评价工作任务和进度安排，召开座谈会广泛听取业界专家对未来职称工作的需求和建议，完成了职称评价工作的前期筹备。四是组织开展全国知识产权领军人才、百名高层次人才培养人选以及全国专利信息领军人才和师资人才的评选和推荐工作，并向国家知识产权专家库推荐了一批候选专家。2015年，广东省内新获评全国知识产权领军人才12人，百名高层次人才培养人选7人，全国专利信息领军人才3人、师资人才7人，高端人才队伍日益壮大。五是着力推进广东省知识产权人才信息化工程建设，建成集“人才信息库”“师资库”“培训管理系统”“培训效果评估系统”“培训需求调研系统”“人才大数据统计与分析”等功能于一体的知识产权人才信息化平台，整套系统已完成第一阶段开发建设工作，年内上线运行。六是进一步加强广东省知识产权远程教育分平台及子站建设，把线上教育与线下培训相结合，努力提升培训实效。

（供稿人：王一）

国家知识产权培训（广东）基地（华南理工大学）

【人才培养体系与师资】 华南理工大学知识产权学院形成了完整的知识产权人才培养体系，包括法学博士（民商法专业知识产权方向），法学硕士及法律硕士（知识产权方向），知识产权本科专业，知识产权双学位、双专业及专业辅修。

广东基地拥有知识产权专职教师11人，其中教授4人，副教授5人，讲师2人；具有博士学位10人，具有理工科背景3人；配备专职秘书1人。

广东基地已聘请知识产权知名学者专家担任兼职教授，如陶凯元、田力普、王景川、吴汉东、刘春田、李明德、杨建成、张玉敏、Peter K. Yu、厉宁等专家学者；聘请张家祥律师为客座教授。

【知识产权教育】 从2015年起，本科知识产权专业重启独立招生，招生对象限定为优秀的理工科考生。2015年招收30名理工科学生，明确要求学生同时辅修一个理工科专业，取得双学位，培养具有理工科知识背景的知识产权复合型人才。

2015年，华南理工大学知识产权学院共招收全日制法学硕士（知识产权方向）研究生和法律硕士（知识产权）31人，全日制法学博士（知识产权方向）1人。目前，全日制（知识产权方向）在校生共有92人，法学硕士周末班（知识产权方向）48人；民商法学专业（知识产权方向）同等学力课程进修班学员64人。全日制硕士研究生就业率达到100%。

在知识产权学院的法律硕士（JM）中，建立知识产权专业方向，单独开设知识产权班（“法硕知产班”），培养以理工科背景为主的知识产权复合型人才。法硕知产班的生源包括学校研究生部单独批准的校内各理工科学院法硕推免生和公开招考的法律硕士生，法硕知产班的生源包括学校研究生部单独批准的校内各理工科学院法律硕士推免生和公开招考的法律硕士生，每年招收约20人。知识产权专业课程强调校内教师与校外业界精英（包括企业、服务机构、司法部门及政府管理部门等业界精英）合作共建，强调对学生的知识产权基础理论、前沿实务和工作技能的全面培养与训练。在校内外联合共建课程之际，与校外机构建立良好的合作关系，为学生的专业实习和未来就业提供更多更好的机会空间。学院针对学生的理工背景，单独开班，并加大知识产权专业课程学分。

【科学研究】 2015年，华南理工大学知识产权学院共获得省部级课题6项、厅局级4项、校级3项、横向项目6项，经费总额达213.65万元。其中，申报的“申诉案件律师代理制度探索”“《视听表演北京条约》与我国著作权法的衔接问题研究”“Web3.0时代著作权授权困境与出路”分别获最高人民检察院、国家新闻出版广电总局、广东省科技厅立项；申报的“知识产权人才职业能力研究”“《广东省重大经济和科技活动知识产权分析评议暂行办法》实施问题研究”“网络安全立法的基本问题研究”分别获国家知识产权局、广东省科技厅、广州市社会科学界联合会规划办立项。

华南理工大学知识产权学院教师撰写出版专著1本，在二类期刊发表文章7篇，CSSCI刊物5篇，核心期刊发表文章1篇，一般期刊2篇。

【学术活动】 华南理工大学知识产权学院定期开展学术交流活动，如“华南知识产权月谈”“华进知识产权论坛”“罗思珠水围谷知识产权阅读共享沙龙”已成为在广东省内具有一定影响力并各具特色的学术交流活动。

华南知识产权月谈至今已举办34期。2015年，邀请了北京知识产权法院副院长陈锦川、北京大学法学院的张平教授，清华大学法学院的崔国斌教授、广州知识产权法院副院长林广海、中美知识产权协会创始会长陈伟杰博士、澳门大学胡元佳教授等专家出席月谈。

华进知识产权论坛已开展17期活动。2015年举办了一系列研讨会，包括“互联网金融与法律问题”“知识产权与反不正当竞争的交集与切割”“互联网领域不正当竞争的法律规制”“The Copy in Copyright”“知识产权管理与商业化实务研讨会”。邀请了国内外专家学者来院讲学，包括美国德州农工大学知识产权中心主任Peter Yu教授、俄罗斯著名的知识产权法专家赛宁·伊万·阿列克萨德诺维奇教授、中国平安保险董事会秘书兼首席律师姚军、华中科技大学法学院郑友德教授、广州知识产权法院副院长吴振、中山大学法学院谢晓尧教授、北京师范大学法学院刘德良教授。

国际交流方面。2015年11月13日，香港城市大学法律学院院长Geraint Howells教授，副院长陈磊副教授一行到华南理工大学知识产权学院交流调研。2015年4月28日，华南理工大学知识产权学院与香港城市大学法学院签署了院级全面合作协议以及本科生联合培养协议，开展学生交流以及科研合作项目，符合资格的法律本科生将有机会赴香港城大进行为期一学期的课程学习。2015年4月17日，由中英国知识产权局、英中贸易协会和广东英国商会联合举办的中英知识产权论坛成功举办，来自英国和中国各个领域的知识产权专家，共同探讨中国知识产权法最新发展以及中国公司如何面对近日英国和欧洲市场所带来的挑战。同时，如何在中国采取有效的手段维护知识产权也成为此次活动的一大讨论热点。

【社会服务】 2015年，国家知识产权培训（广东）基地共承办4期知识产权培训班，学员达256人，培训时间达42天。其中，2015年12月14—18日，广东基地举办上市企业高管知识产权研修班。省内企业和知识产权服务机构高级管理人员37人封闭式5天学习。

2015年4月26日，华南理工大学知识产权学院与国家版权贸易基地正式签约共建产学研基地，为社会输送版权人才、创意孵化、教育培训等。2015年4月27日，华南理工大学知识产权学院与顺德区经济和科技促进局签署合作协议，共建华南理工大学知识产权学院（顺德）研究院。2015年4月22日华南理工大学知识产权学院与佛山市知识产权局签订了知识产权战略合作框架协议，关永宏教授受聘为佛山市知识产权人才学院顾问。

（供稿人：李良成　俞涛　万小丽）

国家知识产权培训（广东）基地（广东省知识产权研究与发展中心）

【概况】 2015年，国家知识产权培训（广东）基地（下称广东基地）通过将面授培训和公益讲座网络培训相结合的培训方式，以培育一批符合时代要求、多层次、复合型和国际化的知识产权人才，培育一批知识产权高层次人才，培育一批企事业单位、中介服务机构实务人才和高水平师资为目标，共举办各级各类知识产权培训（研讨）班24期，培训各类人员2200多人次。

【知识产权人才培训】 2015年广东基地培训内容主要根据最新知识产权政策、形势要求，从广东企业、知识产权从业人员需求着手，有针对性地开设培训课程。培训内容包括：一是开设知识产权公益讲座网络培训。公益讲座网络课堂是国家知识产权局为宣传知识产权制度，普及专利文献知识产权和专利信息技能而开设的。通过远程教育，定期按不同内容主题安排系统课程，邀请资深专家授课。二是开展知识产权高端人才培训。2015年广东基地和中国企业知识产权研究院合作推出仅限企业内部知识产权高管的、专门培养企业知识产权经理人的“腾龙二期”企业知识产权高级经理人研修班。三是开展企业知识产权管理规范培训。为提高广东省企业知识产权管理水平，推动企业实现发展模式优化升级，2015年广东基地举办了4期企业知识产权管理规范培训班，培训人次近500余人，颁发培训结业证书80份，内审员证书100多份。广东省国资委、广州市工商联及广东省律协主动联系广东基地联合办班，成功提升了广东省知识产权培训服务品牌。四是开展中小微企业专利信息利用能力培训。为提升广东省企业利用专利信息的能力，充分发挥知识产权在助推产业转型升级方面的作用，实现专利信息利用效益最大化，同时提高广东基地知识产权服务的整体服务和水平，广东基地展开了一系列专利信息利用相关培训，内容涉及专利检索、专利信息挖掘、专利竞争情报研究及专利预警分析等。五是开展泛珠三角区域专利信息培训。为完善泛珠三角区域内专利信息资源共享机制和服务能力，实现区域内专利信息资源利用最大化，2015年广东基地与泛珠三角区域各省（区）签订了《泛珠三角区域内地九省（区）专利信息应用培训协议》。根据协议，2015年广东基地分别与海南、广西、贵州、成都联合举办4期专利信息应用培训班，共培训人员300余人次。

【国际交流】 2015年10月13日，为加强与澳大利亚及日本在知识产权领域的交流与合作，帮助广东省企事业单位了解并掌握澳大利亚及日本两国知识产权的规则与实务，国家知识产权培训（广东）基地与澳大利亚迈登思专利商标事务所及日本新树Global IP专利商标事务所联合举办了“澳大利亚和日本知识产权应对策略研讨会”。

【知识产权研究】 2015年，广东基地开展项目研究、验收、申报共计12项，其中申报4项、在研9项、结题2项；开展知识产权分析评议类项目共计116项；开展知识产权培训项目共计4项。

（供稿人：梅颖娟）

广东省知识产权培训基地（暨南大学）

【概况】 2015年，暨南大学知识产权学院共招收知识产权本科生20人、知识产权法学硕士专业5人、博士生1人。学院共有21名知识产权本科生毕业并获得学士学位。

【人才培养】 2015年11月，学院承办第八期政府知识产权行政管理人员研修班，邀请国内知名的知识产权专家进行授课，每个课程的主讲嘉宾都结合现实中的问题提出自己的深刻见解。研修班还组织了广东省知识产权局领导与学员座谈，充分了解知识产权工作在现实中遇到的问题及学员对知识产权知识的切实需求。来自广东省各市、区的共50名知识产权管理干部参加了培训。

【科学研究】 学院项目入选学校高水平大学建设项目。学院将新闻与传播学、公共管理学共同申报广东省高水平大学建设“国家治理创新研究”项目，设知识产权与创新驱动等方向，获学校高度认可。

【学术活动】 2015年9月19—20日，举办中国知识产权法学研究会2015年年会，来自全国高校、研究机构、法院系统及知名企业的知识产权专业人士共计500余人参会。最高人民法院副院长陶凯元、中国法学会副会长张文显、暨南大学校长胡军分别致辞。北京知识产权法院院长宿迟、上海知识产权法院院长吴偕林、广州知识产权法院院长杨宗仁分别就知识产权法院建设做主题报告。年会围绕“知识产权司法保护”“知识产权基本理论”“知识产权运营相关问题”以及“知识产权法修改”等议题展开。此次会议还密切关注中国《著作权法》和《专利法》的修订中的焦点问题，并根据社会发展需要，创造性地增加了“传统医药”及“体育赛事”相关知识产权保护问题的研讨单元。

学院共举办与知识产权有关的暨南法学论坛讲座多场。先后邀请国家发展和改革委员会价格监督检查与反垄断局副局长卢延纯（讲座题目《中国反价格垄断执法的热点问题》），新加坡国家知识产权局培训学院郑献超博士（讲座题目《从法律诉讼看企业知识产权布局与知识产权人才培养——知识产权枢纽与能力框架建立》），北京师范大学法学院教授、亚太网络法律研究中心创始人刘德良教授（讲座题目《网络安全问题及其法律规制》），华中科技大学管理学院教授、博士生导师余翔（讲座题目《欧洲专利制度新发展及对中国企业专利运营的思考》）等专家和学者莅院讲学。

【服务社会】 2015年4月21—27日，学院开展了“知识产权宣传周”系列宣传活动，广泛宣传实施知识产权战略、加强知识产权保护对于创新驱动发展的支撑作用，重点宣传在网络发展突飞猛进的今天关于网络侵权的保护问题。先后在暨南大学建阳篮球场、暨南大学社区居委会和暨南大学番禺校区广场以“知识产权风暴”校园摊位互动形式，通过图片展览、知产游戏提升师生群众对于知识产权的认识，提高对网络侵权的认识，加强网络维权意识。

同时，以社区法律青年志愿者服务站来开展各项宣传咨询服务工作，以学生党团员为主体，在专业教师指导下开展服务社会的各项活动。社区志愿者服务站已经完成了10余次知识产权咨询工作，共接访来访人员20余人次，除简单的法律咨询外，形成文字咨询案例6个，先后有30余名研究生和本科生志愿者参与其中，为社区的居民解决了一些知识产权问题。

（供稿人：杨远斌　陈慧瑛）

广东省知识产权培训基地（深圳大学）

【人才培养】　广东省知识产权培训基地（深圳大学）（以下简称基地）2013年招收第一期知识产权研究生课程进修班，2015年1月该班结业，课程内容包括知识产权基本法律及相关知识产权实务课程；老师由全国知识产权司法、行政、企业、中介机构中知名的理论和实务专家担任。2015年11月20日，第一届知识产权学院知识产权研究生课程班结业典礼在深圳大学国际会议厅举行，20余名结业同学参加了典礼，深圳大学副校长徐晨为参加结业同学颁发了结业证书。

【学术活动】　2015年5月31日，基地与深圳大学中国知识产权司法保护理论研究基地共同主办“新技术环境下的竞争法前沿问题”内部研讨会，来自最高院、湖北高院、长沙中院、深圳中院的资深法官和清华大学、深圳大学的教授参会，对新技术环境下的竞争法热点难点问题进行了深入探讨。

2015年6月3日，基地与深圳大学中国知识产权司法保护理论研究基地、最高人民法院知识产权司法保护研究中心、中国知识产权法学研究会共同主办 “创新驱动发展战略背景下的知识产权司法保护高端研讨会”。 来自北京大学、中国人民大学、西南政法大学院校的专家学者，全国部分高级人民法院、中级人民法院知识产权庭中华商标协会、腾讯、华为等机关、团体、企事业单位的代表，以及来自中国知识产权报社、《人民司法》杂志社等媒体代表，共计150余人参加了研讨会。会议围绕“知识产权司法保护主导作用的含义和实现路径”“专利法修改及专利侵权司法解释重点问题”“商标法和竞争法适用疑难问题”“知识产权行为保全”四个主题展开了深入的讨论。

2015年11月28日，基地与深圳市公标知识产权鉴定评估中心、深圳大学中国知识产权司法保护理论研究基地合办“知识产权鉴定评估研讨会”，律师、公司法务等共计150余人参加，参会嘉宾发表了“技术专家在知识产权技术事实查明中的权利和义务”“知识产权案件审理与司法鉴定”“技术秘密诉讼的证据准备”“诉前鉴定”等主题演讲。

2015年12月12日，基地与深圳大学中国知识产权司法保护理论研究基地共同举办了“标准必要专利研讨会”，来自全国部分著名高校的专家学者、法官，中兴、华为等企业代表，以及媒体代表，共计60余位嘉宾参加了研讨会，会议对“标准必要专利的界定”“FRAND（公平、合理、无歧视）承诺的法律属性”“FRAND承诺对禁令救济的影响”等问题进行了深入探讨。

开展知识产权系列讲座：网络环境下著作权的司法保护、微信公众号中的知识产权问题初探、互联网领域的不正当竞争、以知识产权推动产业升级转型。

【平台建设】　2015年11月20日下午，知识产权学院理事会会议在深圳大学国际会议厅举行，深圳大学副校长徐晨，深圳市市场监督管理局副局长夏昆山，深圳大学法学院院长黄亚英、副院长祝建军等，以及华为、中兴、腾讯、比亚迪等11个理事单位的代表参加了会议。

会议报告了知识产权学院2012—2015年的工作总结和经费开支情况，全体与会代表对新一届知识产权理事会换届事宜、理事会章程等进行了审议和表决，确定了新一届理事会的名单、章程和协议，并计划于2016年3月招收新一期知识产权研究生课程班。

（供稿人：戢荔）

广东省知识产权培训基地（汕头大学）

【概况】 2015年，广东省知识产权培训（汕头大学）基地（下称基地）开展多层次、多方位的知识产权教育培训工作。全年主办或联合举办知识产权培训班多场，共培训企事业单位人员255人次；开展知识产权知识宣传普及大型活动，受益逾1500人次。同时，基地还针对地方产业发展需求，着力加强知识产权服务，取得显著成效。

【知识产权教育】 2015年，基地围绕“4·26世界知识产权日”及“中国专利周”等大型活动，开展系列宣传活动，通过策划不同宣传主题，形式丰富多样的活动，吸引大量师生们参与，对增强全校师生的知识产权保护意识、营造良好的保护知识产权氛围，取得良好效果。基地依托中国知识产权远程教育平台，采用“线上+线下”培训模式，理论和实操两手抓，培训效果明显提升。2015年，基地还与厦门大学知识产权研究院等建立合作关系，聘请知识产权专家为基地兼职教师，增强师资力量。

【企业服务】 2015年，基地根据地方产业转型升级的需求，继续加强与行业协会（商会）的联动，组织更多对话性活动以及面向行业需求的培训。受培训对象包括汕头市知识产权专家库专家、维权援助服务网络合作单位及维权援助工作联络站人员、汕头市专利保护协会会员、汕头市化妆品行业协会会员、汕头市中小微企业和华侨试验区企业等专业人员。同时，基地还深入粤东塑料、包装和印刷机械装备特色支柱产业，针对性提供企业竞情、技术创新、人才培训等知识产权服务，并对广东科技型中小企业知识产权证券化融资机制展开研究，取得一定前期成果。

（供稿人：罗英光）

广东省知识产权培训基地（惠州学院）

【概况】 2015年，广东省知识产权（惠州学院）培训基地进一步完善知识产权工作体系，不断增强宣传培训和服务地方的能力，形成一套知识产权的管理制度和管理程序，全校师生员工的知识产权保护意识不断得到提高。“高校+政府+企业”合作办学特色不断凸显，社会效果不断彰显。基地设有管理人员3人，教育培训专职教师15人，其中教授3人，副教授5人，讲师7人；拥有专利代理人资质的兼职教师6人。

【宣传培训】 惠州学院基地开展了多种形式的知识产权宣传培训活动，努力促进知识产权保护的发展。如2015年10月14日举办《保护知识成果、驱动科技创新》专题讲座；2015年7月22—25日举办了为期四天的“惠州市专利布局与挖掘实战培训班”；10月30日举办了“惠州市专利信息检索暨WIPS Global专利数据库使用培训班”；11月24—26日举办为期3天的“广东省知识产权局管理干部研修班”等。

【基地教育】 2015年，惠州学院基地继续举办为期一年的知识产权双学位班（专利代理方向）第三期，培养校内外专利代理学员30人，总学时450学时，其中实践学时270学时。该专利代理班的培训经验得到广东省许多兄弟院校以及用人单位的认可，社会反响较好。

（供稿人：王鑫）

广东省知识产权培训基地（广东海洋大学）

【概况】 广东省知识产权培训基地（广东海洋大学）基地已配备较为完善的管理机构、管理人员和规章制度。基地办公地点设在广东海洋大学霞山校区东1幢308室，基地管理人员共7人，基地培训工作顺利开展，运行良好。

【知识产权宣传】 2015年4月21日，培训基地在广东海洋大学寸金学院教学楼CD报告厅为广大教师举办知识产权专题讲座。讲座从知识产权的概念入题，对知识产权保护对象、专利申请、纠纷的解决途径和法律责任等五个方面进行讲解。通过结合实例的方式，对发明与实用新型、专利申请的消极与积极条件、专利申请的流程进行详细讲解，提高了全院教师知识产权的保护意识和对专利申请的认识。

【知识产权培训】 培训基地在面向高校师生开展培训的同时，积极拓展与地方政府、行业协会（商会）的合作，为地方产业提供知识产权培训服务。2015年，分别举办知识产权基础法律知识讲座、企业知识产权管理及实务以及专利申请、专利侵权认定与专利诉讼等培训。培训基地建设有知识产权远程教育平台广东海洋大学分站，平台充分利用远程教育分站的资源，大力推广多种新型教学方法，努力构建新型、国际化的知识产权人才培养培训机制和多元化的培训经费投入机制，全面提升培训层次和水平，进一步增强主动发展意识，为粤西地区的振兴与发展提供知识产权人才的支撑和保障。

（供稿人：胡婧）

广东省知识产权培训基地（顺德职业技术学院）

【概述】 2015年，广东省知识产权培训（顺德）基地（下称基地）积极面向顺德职业技术学院在校学生开展知识产权基础知识教学工作，同时联合顺德区知识产权协会面向广大企业人员开展知识产权培训，包括企业专利工作者培训、专利特派员培训。

【基础建设】 为加强知识产权培训工作的规范化、科学化，保证知识产权工作的硬件条件，基地总投入经费15.83万元。其中软实力建设投入14.36万元，用于开展一系列的培训所需的费用；硬件建设1.47万元，更新了2个多媒体培训室以及1个电教室的部分桌椅及2台电脑等设备，不断完善基地培训条件。同时，电教室内配备60台先进电脑，可连接到互联网，为学员进行在线学习以及信息检索学习提供了优越的硬件环境。

【运用能力培训】 为进一步提升区内知识产权人员的实践能力，分别于2015年5月、7月、9月开展了三期活动，分别主要围绕“专利挖掘与技术交底书撰写”“海外专利申报”“知识产权战略”三大主题展开培训，共培训学员580人次，为学员往后在企业工作打下良好的知识基础。

【普及培训】 为进一步扩大知识产权基础知识的普及范围，在7—11月，基地参与组织举办了顺德区2015年创业培训班，培训对象包括顺德区10个镇街的在校学生、应届毕业生以及社会人员共652人。创业培训课程内容包括商标法、专利法等与企业经营有关的知识产权法律知识，帮助学员了解知识产权的基本知识，并为其往后开办企业打下良好的知识基础。

【专题培训】 为了给区域产业提供知识产权的前沿信息，培养知识产权专业人才，基地协同区知识产权协会，分别于2015年9月以及11月，举办了两期“企业专利工作者培训班”，培训时间每期3天。课程内容主要涉及专利信息传播、检索、分析、创新运用，国内外专利信息资源、数据库介绍和应用等，并通过详细的案例分享与解读，实操与考试，使学员进一步掌握知识产权保护的核心知识和技能。企业专利工作者培训班已连续多年举办，深受顺德区企业专利工作人员的青睐。2015年度共有100位学员参加了专利工作者培训班，并全部通过考试后取得课程结业证书。

【知识产权上量提质活动】 为充分发挥顺德区知识产权特派员工作机制对提升企业知识产权创造、运用、保护和管理水平的作用，并结合部分企业申请高企入库的专利问题，10月15日在大良街道办事处3楼会议室举办了一场“2015年大良街道知识产权上量提质对接会”活动。共50人参与，通过此次对接活动，较全面地了解到意向入库企业存在的专利问题，增强了企业对专利申请的信心。后续协会和特派员将通过走访企业方式，重点帮助企业突破专利不达标的困境。扎实推进顺德区高新技术企业入库培育工作、提高科技创新能力，对加快顺德区高新技术产业发展具有积极意义。此外，在龙江镇政府举办了一场“2015年龙江镇知识产权‘上量提质’及贯标工作对接会”活动，共50人参与，通过此次对接活动，搭建了企业与协会、特派员团队、质押融资公司桥梁，畅通了企业的信息渠道，加强企业对发明专利授权的信心，有力推动龙江专利工作的开展，同时扩大龙江镇家具快速维权中心知名度，为下一步企业知识产权服务积累了坚实的基础。

【知识产权选修课】 为进一步扩大知识产权基础知识在校内的普及范围，将《专利信息检索》《知识产权法律基础》，纳入学生的选修课。该课程每学期安排一次教学，总课时为16学时，学生人数为每学期60人（该年度各开展了两期）。课程主要目的讲授“专利信息检索”和“知识产权法律基础”相关基础知识，课程采用老师讲解、教学视频展示以及经典案例分析相结合的方式进行，充分调动学生的学习积极性。学生通过该课程的学习，可初步掌握知识产权的相关法律法规，同时让学生基本掌握并具备使用因特网进行专利文献的实际检索的能力，以及形成基本的知识产权保护和利用意识，进而理解和掌握保护知识产权成果的方法。

【知识产权远程教育顺德分站】 为了不断强化广大企业科技人员、政府机关人员以及高校师生知识产权保护意识，进一步提高区域知识产权创造、运用、管理能力和水平，基地依托“中国知识产权远程教育广东省子平台”，设立“顺德职业技术学院知识产权远程教育顺德分站”，具备上线运营的条件，向顺德技术学院的学生开展了教学工作。

（供稿人：卢永辉）

广东金融学院知识产权研究所

【概况】 继续加强经济发展与知识产权制度方向校级重点学科建设与知识产权人才培养。学院自《经济法学》被正式批准成为校级重点学科后，经济发展与知识产权制度作为其中的重点方向之一，在2015年继续加大其建设的力度。同时，继续高度重视知识产权人才培养，2015年，共有101名知识产权专业方向的毕业生走向社会，同时招收100名知识产权专业方向新生。广东金融学院被确定为广东省贯彻高校知识产权管理规范试点单位。

知识产权论文。2015年，知识产权团队在《知识产权》等各种刊物上发表学术论文12篇，其中《版权法激励作用的博弈论分析》

《关键字推广商标侵权问题研究——以关键字推广服务提供者的义务中心》等较有影响力。

课题研究。2015年9月和10月，研究所所长吴国平等与广东工业大学合作申请广东省知识产权局2015年软科学重点项目成功，获准立项。2015年9月，教授安雪梅主持申报的教育部人文社会科学研究项目《知识产权交叉案件合一审判模式的司法公信力研究》申报结项。安雪梅教授主持申报的广州市知识产权局招标项目——“广州市知识产权行政诉讼、复议预警机制研究”获准结项。各位项目负责人都展开了对项目的深入调研。

学院知识产权宣传活动。为响应国家实施创新驱动发展战略及建设知识产权强国的号召，保护知识产权，鼓励创新发展，广东金融学院知识产权专业方向的广大学生于2015年4月开展了知识产权宣传周活动。4月26日第15个世界知识产权日当天还举办了大型宣传活动。

（供稿人：吴国平）

华南师范大学

【概况】 2015年，华南师范大学知识产权工作体系进一步完善，在知识产权的管理、创造、运用、保护以及宣传等方面开展了较有成效的工作，构建学校知识产权管理体系，形成一套知识产权的管理制度和管理程序，全校师生员工的知识产权保护意识不断得到提高。

【宣传培训】 为了响应国家“建设知识产权强国，支撑创新驱动发展”号召，帮助学校师生更好地了解相关政策、法规，及时保护科研成果，华南师范大学开展了多种形式的知识产权宣传培训活动，努力促进知识产权保护的发展。6月11日学校举办了“科研成果的专利保护问题”知识产权讲座。针对目前高校科研成果的内容与形式，介绍科研成果的专利挖掘以及如何快捷地申请保护。

【创造与运用】 2015年华南师范大学申请专利287项（其中PCT国际专利4项，国内发明240项，实用新型43项），比2014年增长20%；获得授权专利164项（国内发明专利授权109项，实用新型授权55项）。计算机软件著作权88项，比2014年增长79.6%。学校被广东省知识产权局、广东省教育厅确定为“广东省高校知识产权管理规范试点单位”。

（供稿人：张雯）

中小学知识产权教育工作

2015年，国家知识产权局和教育部联合制定《全国中小学知识产权教育试点、示范工作方案（试行）》，共同认定首批全国中小学知识产权教育试点学校30所。

广东省知识产权局联合省教育厅面向全省开展试点学校的组织申报工作，全省共有9个地市（包括顺德区）推荐12所中小学校参加此次评选。经评审，佛山市南海区九江镇初级中学和顺德区李伟强职业技术学校入选全国首批试点学校。两所学校结合实际认真制定试点工作方案，推进试点工作，取得积极成效。

（供稿人：张璟）

国家中小微企业知识产权培训（南海）基地

【概况】 2013年5月，佛山市南海区政府与中国知识产权培训中心合作开展“企业专利管理师千人培训计划”以“中国知识产权培训中心远程教育南海分站”的在线课程为理论学习平台，线下开展实务培训和面授辅导，并提供企业专利管理实践活动。2013年12月5日，国家知识产权局批复同意设立“国家中小微企业知识产权培训（南海）基地”。南海区政府专门成立国家中小微企业知识产权培训（南海）基地建设工作领导小组，统筹南海区知识产权局、教育局、人社局、人才办、镇街经济促进局以及知识产权协会，共同开展知识产权教育培训教材开发、大中专知识产权职业教育、企业专利管理师培训及水平评价、知识产权人才实践和服务等工作。通过构筑中小学知识产权启蒙教育、大中专知识产权职业教育、企业知识产权继续教育“三位一体”的培育体系，不断提升企业知识产权创造、运用、保护、管理能力。

【培训活动】 2015年，累计举办12期企业专利管理师培训班，参与企业664家，培训人数1469人次。在培训中始终贯彻行业分类指导模式，结合地方专业镇和企业主营的技术领域特点，一是把培训班开到镇街、开到企业门口，就近、免费为在职员工提供能力培训。二是从知识产权服务机构中选拔了一批“专利特派员”，按行业特长为企业学员提供专业辅导，让培训成为中小微企业与知识产权服务业的对接平台。三是注重企业管理实践，面授和在线学习后要进行理论考核，还须参加6个月的企业实践活动对实践报告进行评价考核。

同时还多次组织企业知识产权经验分享会、政策解读座谈会等多种形式，开展各类企业、行业专题培训，有效传播知识产权信息和文化。另外，受国家、省、市（区）委托举办了专利代理人培训班、企业知识产权管理规范培训班、专利价值分析培训班、专利特派员培训班、基层培训班等，相关培训活动每年超过6场，培训人数500人以上。

【培训管理】 根据企业、学员的实际需求和培训反馈意见，南海基地开展中小微企业专利管理实务教材的开发工作，经过两年多的撰写修改，已通过国家知识产权局专家评审，并纳入国家知识产权局系列教材，教材内容包括中小微企业专利管理、专利文献与信息利用、专利申请管理、专利权维持与运用、专利侵权纠纷处理等实务内容。

南海基地与中国知识产权培训中心、专利局审查协作广东中心、多所高校开展紧密合作，拥有“千百万知识产权人才”百名高层次人才2名。还制定了实务型师资的选拔机制，组建了42人的培训教学师资库，通过主题培训、实践评价等手段提升整体授课教学水平。

在区知识产权局、人社局、教育局协助下，南海基地开展职业人才评价的探索工作，举办了专利管理师技能标准研究会议，到知识产权优势、示范企业进行调研，到先进地区学习知识产权职称评定以及院校知识产权专业学科管理、教学组织、师资建设、教材题库、学员管理等具体实务经验。研究完成国家知识产权局软科学研究项目“中小微企业知识产权人才培养模式”。

南海基地建立了知识产权人才信息管理系统，实现学员信息登记、条码生产识别、成绩登记、考勤管理、证书打印、实践报告网络评审、培训师资管理、专利特派员辅导等电子化管理功能，通过应用系统规范了管理，提升了效率。

【社会服务】 南海基地将专利管理师、专利特派员及镇街商协会作为搭建知识产权综合服务平台三大有机结合体，充分利用资源优势、政策优势、平台优势，形成人才培养——个性服务——解决需求——监督管理的“一条龙”服务。

借助平台资源（镇街属地管理职能、商协会会员企业、场地设施等）开展企业专利管理师培训。南海区13家商协会组织设立知识产权服务平台，引入20家省内外知识产权服务机构合作开展服务，为当地企业解决知识产权实际疑难问题。南海基地协助实施“知识产权服务百千对接工程”及“专利清零行动”，将企业专利数量与质量、知识产权管理能力、知识产权运用及保护能力的提升纳入专利管理师实践考核内容，对协助企业申请发明专利的专利管理师给予每件500元的奖励，每期培训班评出“优秀企业专利管理师”并授予奖状和奖金。

（供稿人：陈秋长　蔡锦琪）

DI SHI ZHI SHI CHAN QUAN GONG

地市知识产权工作

● 地市知识产权工作

地市知识产权工作

广 州 市

【示范试点工作】 广州市以副省级城市第一名的成绩通过首批国家知识产权示范城市年度考核和三年复核，获批开展新一轮示范城市建设，并被认定为首批国家知识产权区域布局试点城市。越秀区、黄埔区被国家知识产权局授予“2015年国家知识产权强县工程示范区”，广州开发区和增城开发区获批国家知识产权投融资试点，广州开发区获批省知识产权服务业集聚发展试验区。全市培育和扶持市级知识产权示范企业、服务试点园区、行业协会、展会、电子商务试点示范等42家。

【知识产权管理】 2015年，广州市知识产权局制定《广州建设知识产权枢纽城市工作方案》，并提出其实现路径研究报告，为制定“十三五”规划奠定基础；积极推动重大项目建设，配合国家、省开展广东自贸试验区南沙新区片区知识产权体制机制改革创新工作；出台《广州市专利工作专项资金管理办法》，投入专利工作专项资金7256万元。

【知识产权创造】 广州市获中国专利金奖1项、优秀奖23项；获广东专利奖发明人奖3项、金奖7项、优秀奖14项。

专利。2015年，专利申请量63366件，同比增长36.8%，增长率是2014年的两倍多，其中发明20087件，同比增长37.7%，增长率在全国19个副省级以上城市中排名第2位（仅次于重庆）；实用新型24778件；外观设计18501件。专利授权量39834件，同比增长41.6%。其中发明6626件，同比增长44.4%；实用新型17259件，外观设计15949件。PCT国际专利申请627件，同比增长13.2%。截至2015年底，全市有效发明专利量24142件，同比增长27.1%，每万人发明专利拥有量17.9件。

商标。广州市著名商标认定新申请材料107件，延续申请218件，公示认定86件，延续认定211件；向上级部门推荐认定广东省著名商标新申请材料109件，延续申请132件，截至2015年底，广州市共拥有中国驰名商标123件，比上年增长9.8%，广东省著名商标483件，广州市著名商标829件。全市商标申请量、注册量均居全国副省级城市和计划单列市首位。

版权及科技成果登记作品著作权25440件（含计算机软件）。登记科技成果741项，同比增长137.5%。

植物新品种 1个玉米品种、1个水稻品种、2个蔬菜品种、5个花卉品种和1个果树品种通过省农作物品种审定。

【知识产权运用】

知识产权产业化。市财政投入2030万元资金扶持专利产业化项目60项，比2014年增加了一倍。市发改委重点支持具有自主知识产权项目的建设，组织9个项目申报全省科技成果产业化扶持专项资金，推动了一批具有自主知识产权的科技成果实现产业化。市农业局围绕农业发展需求，遴选立项10多项农业科技和技术推广项目，有效促进了农业新技术、新品种的运用和产业化。

质押融资和保险。推进设立知识产权质押融资风险补偿基金，获中央财政引导资金1000万元支持，市财政配套3000万元，对中小微科技型企业开展知识产权质押融资提供重点支持，16家企业、98件专利质押共获融资3.64亿元，6家企业、115件专利投保专利保险，保额462.88万元。举办面向企业的商标质押融资专题培训，企业办理商标质押融资1.5亿元。

【知识产权保护】

专利行政执法。市知识产权局受理专利侵权纠纷案件203件；查处假冒专利案件358件。全市专利行政执法办案总量927件，其中立案查处假冒专利案件量较上年增长49.4%；进驻中国进出口商品交易会、广州国际家具展、广州国际照明展等大型展会开展专利维权工作，共处理各种专利侵权投诉328件。起草《互联网专利保护工作指引》，打击电子商务领域侵权假冒行为；推进知识产权保护规范化市场培育工作，指导2个专业市场成功申报国家级市场培育，首次培育市级市场7个、扶持企事业单位专利维权项目12个；市知识产权局与市司法局、广州知识产权仲裁院、广州海关和黄埔海关联合签署《关于共同推进行业知识产权纠纷调解人民组织建设的合作协议》；“中国广州花都（皮革皮具）知识产权快速维权中心”获国家知识产权局批准成立。市知识产权局专利行政诉讼无一败诉，被评为依法行政示范创建单位，在市法治广州检查考核中综合测评为优秀。

商标行政执法。市工商局立案查办各类商标侵权和假冒伪劣商品案件1106宗，办结案件956宗，案值1110.63万元，罚款1987.99万元，移送司法机关案件13宗，捣毁侵权假冒窝点21个；在第117、118届广交会上共处理商标投诉417宗，较2014年上升19%；查处案件数据全省工商系统首位。查处的某某会商标违法案件被《中国工商报》列入中国电商十大违法典型案件；清理整顿商标代理机构，经实地查无的商标代理机构22家。

版权行政执法。市文广新局在“剑网2015”专项行动中，共出动执法人员837人次，巡查网站721家，查办案件18宗，其中2宗申请国家版权局督办案件，罚款人民币145.20万元。在第117、118届广交会、中国（广州）国际家具博览会、第八届中国国际漫画节驻场开展版权保护工作，受理版权投诉案件122件，结案率100%。

海关行政执法。广州海关共查获涉嫌侵权案件411宗，同比增长16.76%；涉及货物共116.18件，同比减少39.49%；案值近1788.32万元人民币，同比增长59.84%。驻萝岗办事处查获涉嫌侵权手机6360部、手机配件1574件、平板电脑552台、打印硒鼓49个，涉案货物总值近400万元人民币，涉及“PHONE”“SAMSUNG”“HUAWEI”“HP”等10个知名商标；共销毁侵权货物45万件，转交侵权货物17.3万件，估值746万元；在知识产权边境保护中，共实施风险布控25宗，有效查获7宗，公布进出口侵犯知识产权货物行政处罚案件信息25宗。

黄埔海关采取知识产权保护措施220次，中止放行货物约541万件，货值约693万元；深入开展“清风”行动，采取布控措施52次，捕中装载侵权货物的集装箱18个，知识产权布控有效率达34.6%；相继查获假冒香烟470万支，侵权手机、移动电源、耳机等电子类消费产品2万余件，侵权汽车配件类产品2.5万件，侵权鞋、服装类产品25万余件；以无害化处理方式销毁侵权货物约48万件。

刑事保护。市公安局共立涉假案件1098宗，破案1006宗，依法刑事拘留2106人，逮捕1126人，捣毁制假售假窝点925个，主动发起全国集群战役24起，协助外地公安机关收网集群战役21起，先后摧毁跨省跨境产业链条30个，打掉职业性制售假犯罪团伙42个，收缴假人民币600多万元，缴获作案工具、假冒知名品牌商品等涉案物品一大批。

司法保护。市检察院共审查批准逮捕“双打”案件779件1357人，其中批准逮捕制假售假案件193件330人，批准逮捕侵犯知识产权案件586件1027人，审查起诉“双打”案件989件1751人，其起诉制假售假案件261件397人，起诉侵犯知识产权案件728件1354人。

广州知识产权法院受理各类知识产权案

件4862件，其中民事案件4843件，行政案件19件；一审案件2820件，二审案件2035件，再审案件7件。审结3238件，其中一审案件1317件，二审案件1914件，再审案件7件。结案率66.6%，主审法官人均结案249件，法定审限内结案率100%。

仲裁保护。广州知识产权仲裁院共受理知识产权纠纷148件，涉及标的达1.3亿元。涉及的纠纷类型包含委托创作合同纠纷、技术合作开发合同纠纷、技术服务合同纠纷、特许经营合同纠纷等，涉及的行业或专业领域包括计算机软件、动漫、网络技术、通讯设备、图书出版、光电技术、新能源开发、商标及专利的代理、企业加盟等。

长效机制建设。市知识产权局起草《互联网专利保护工作指引》，打击电子商务领域侵权假冒行为；推进知识产权保护规范化市场培育工作，指导2个专业市场成功申报国家级市场培育，首次培育市级市场7个、扶持企事业单位专利维权项目12个；与市司法局、广州知识产权仲裁院、广州海关和黄埔海关联合签署《关于共同推进行业知识产权纠纷调解人民组织建设的合作协议》，先行先试推动知识产权纠纷人民调解工作。“中国广州花都（皮革皮具）知识产权快速维权中心”获国家知识产权局批准成立。

【宣传培训】

社会宣传。创设广州知识产权大讲堂，邀请国内外知名专家授课，并成功举办3期。围绕“世界知识产权日”“中国专利周”等时间节点，开展“2015年知识产权宣传周黄埔海关开放日”等各类主题活动。通过召开新闻发布会、报纸专版宣传、公交公益广告、巡回宣讲、网站、微信、微博等方式，广泛运用多种形式开展知识产权宣传。累计派发新商标法宣传单张2万份；通过全市公交、机场、水上巴士、出租车、政务楼宇、写字楼、大型商场等公共场所近3万多幅LED电子显示屏，每天12小时滚动播放《商标法》宣传片达120次。

专业培训。举办“广州市总部企业知识产权管理贯标培训班”“专利创造工作巡回培训班”等24个专利工作培训班，累计培训7800余人，承办国家知识产权局“知识产权走基层，服务经济万里行”广州站活动；举办省、市著名商标申报培训班，知识产权诉讼与维权培训班，狮岭品牌企业交流座谈会等大型商标专题活动，培训企业人员达900余人次；组织100名科技教师参加“2015年广州市科技教师知识产权培训班”，培养了一批知识产权教育专家骨干。

人才培训。完成广州市首次知识产权职称评审工作；广州知识产权人才基地建设列入省部会商项目并落户暨南大学，基建项目资金已获市政府常务会议通过；广州大学法学本科专业设置知识产权法方向（四年制），招收培养本科生40—50人；在非法学专业二年级学生中增设法学专业（知识产权法方向）第二学位班，每届招收100—120人。

青少年教育。开展 “2015年（第二届）广州市中小学生知识产权教育活动”，全市2000多名师生参与漫画创作比赛、知识产权征文比赛和科技创意作品比赛；组织第31届广州市青少年科技创新大赛活动，全市共有10万多名中小学生参与；开展认定了“2015年广州市知识产权教育试点学校”5所。

【交流合作】

专利交流。举办“2015粤港知识产权与中小企业发展（广州）研讨会”，派员参加在香港举办的“亚洲知识产权营商论坛”，进一步推动粤港知识产权的紧密合作；组团考察新加坡知识产权工作，参加新加坡知识产权周开幕式、“2015第五届全球知识产权论坛”和“中国近年在知识产权保护和执行方面的发展趋势分论坛”；协助组织由中华全国专利代理人协会和台湾工业总会联合举办的第八届两岸专利论坛。

版权交流。派员赴青岛参加“全国版权

示范城市联盟成立大会”和“第二届青岛·东北亚版权创意精品展示交易会暨正版优秀图书展”；开展粤港中学生版权交流活动，3所中学25名师生代表赴香港开展版权交流活动，接待香港海关、知识产权署、中学生代表23人来穗开展版权交流活动；派员赴香港参加“出版物市场管理与版权保护”交流、内地知识产权保护及执法研讨会、粤港版权产业交流活动、第五届亚洲知识产权营商论坛等。

（供稿人：陈文浩）

深圳市

【知识产权创造】 2015年，深圳市国内专利申请总量 105480件，同比增长28.2%，其中发明专利申请40028件，同比增长28.7%；国内专利授权72126件，同比增长34.4%，其中发明专利授权16956件，同比增长40.9%；有效发明专利 83905件，同比增长18.4%，每万人口发明专利拥有量为73.7件（按照2015年年底常住人口数1137.89万人计算），约为全国平均水平（6.3件）的12倍；PCT国际专利申请13308件，同比增长14.3%，占全国申请总量46.9%，连续十二年居全国各大中城市的首位。截至2015年底，深圳市有效注册商标总量累计392096件，累计拥有驰名商标159件，广东省著名商标472件，深圳区域品牌的影响力进一步提升。2015年，深圳市计算机软件著作权登记量36157件，同比大幅增长57.2%，占全国登记总量（292360件）的12.4%。

【知识产权运用】

质押融资。深圳市进一步完善知识产权质押融资激励政策，建立知识产权质押融资风险补偿机制，设立知识产权质押融资风险补偿基金，由基金出资人、资金管理人、合作方三方共同参与设立。深圳市知识产权局代表深圳市政府作为基金出资人，引导资金的使用方向；受托管理机构为基金管理人，负责基金的日常运作，保障资金的有效使用；银行、担保公司等金融机构作为基金合作方，采用公开遴选方式产生，负责为中小微企业知识产权质押融资提供担保、贷款等服务。据不完全统计，2015年深圳市知识产权质押融资贷款额度为5.66亿元。

运营机构。近年来，深圳市知识产权运营工作取得新进展，构建起“1+1+5+N”的知识产权运营深圳模式：第一个“1”指的是在自贸区前海蛇口片区建立南方知识产权运营中心，打造全国知识产权运营大平台（航母）；第二个“1”指的是设立知识产权运营基金，初步规模在20亿元左右（核动力）；“5”指的是培育5家国家级知识产权运营机构（护航舰）；“N”指的是培育交易、评估、咨询、投融资、保险、证券、互联网+、保护等不同类型的知识产权运营服务新业态（战舰）。此外，深圳市知识产权运营机构不断发展，国家级的知识产权运营试点机构有深圳市中彩联科技有限公司、深圳市联创知识产权服务中心、深圳中科院知识产权投资有限公司。新近崛起的知识产权运营机构有塞恩倍吉、七号网、安盾网、精英、智汇远见、崇德广业、智衡技术、中兴达、国新南方、派富等。

交易市场。深圳市知识产权交易市场日益活跃，国家专利技术深圳展示交易中心（位于南山数字文化产业基地）成立至2015年底已接待超过2800人次/单位的展示申请，知识产权交易等相关业务咨询2160起。2015年，深圳市专利展示交易平台共展出专利技术产品140件，其中发明专利75件、实用新型42件、外观设计23件，完成专利交易189件，达成交易金额358万元。

专利保险工作试点。2015年，深圳市知识产权专项资金安排30万元工作经费建设专利保险分析预警平台，推进专利保险工作。2015年，深圳市共有29家企业与专利保险预警分析平台签订了专利保险意向书。截至2015年底，专利保险试点企业中已有4家企业出险报案，多项专利发生保险事故，合计报损金额在30万元以上。

【知识产权保护】

知识产权执法体系。一是出台贯彻落实《中共中央国务院关于深化体制机制改革加快实施创新驱动发展战略的若干意见》的若干措施，从严格知识产权保护等五个方面提出了共17项具体措施。二是推动修订《深圳经济特区加强知识产权保护工作若干规定》，探索在提高执法维权效率、降低维权成本方面先行先试，借鉴欧美等发达国家制度优势和国际惯例，完成修订草案的初稿。三是构建知识产权保护社会参与机制，以政府购买服务的形式引入社会专业力量，建设“深圳市互联网知识产权保护综合监测平台”，对互联网知识产权状况进行监测。四是探索自贸区知识产权维权援助机制建设，提出在自贸区前海蛇口片区建立集中统一的知识产权执法体系、知识产权维权体系和知识产权服务体系的工作目标。五是依托市、区、街道构建三级联动的大知识产权执法体系，强化执法业务培训打造专业化执法力量，积极开展知识产权执法维权“护航”“剑网”“电子商务领域专利执法维权”等专项行动。

知识产权专项执法。2015年4—9月，深圳市知识产权局在全市范围内开展知识产权执法维权“护航”专项行动。2015年3月18日，深圳市知识产权局印发《关于印发2015年知识产权执法维权“护航”专项行动实施方案的通知》（深市质〔2015〕59号），明确了专项行动的工作目标、工作重点和具体措施等内容。“护航”专项行动期间，深圳市知识产权局发挥“大市场、大监管”体制优势，对食品药品、数码通讯产品、农资用品等民生重点领域，推行案件线索双向溯源机制，加大专利执法办案力度。全市共查办各类专利行政案件140宗，其中处理专利侵权纠纷案件90宗，查处假冒专利案件43宗，调处展会专利纠纷6宗，查处专利代理违法案件1宗，调解赔偿金额5万元，行政处罚金额5799.2元；全市共处理专利侵权涉外纠纷案件6件，其中涉及韩国2件，涉及美国、以色列、意大利、比利时各1件。

【知识产权管理】

专利联盟。截至2015年底，深圳已有在新能源、超材料、生物医药、LED、彩电、车联网、3D显示、工业机器人、北斗导航、平衡车、无人机等战略性新兴产业领域成立13家专利联盟。专利联盟以“专利信息共享，降低海外知识产权风险”为目标，积极提升联盟企业的知识产权创造、运用、管理和保护水平，增强企业自主创新能力。同时，专利联盟还致力于产业知识产权应急及预警公共平台建设，帮助企业建立专利战略体系和知识产权保护体系，集体应对国外专利权人的许可谈判或专利诉讼，解决跨国知名企业、非专利实施主体（NPE）对深圳企业发出的专利挑战。

知识产权标准体系。2015年，深圳市先后制定并发布《专利代理机构品牌创建指引》（SZDB/Z 135-2015）、《专利信息分析与利用指南》（SZDB/Z 136-2015）和《专利许可指南》（SZDB/Z 137-2015）等三个地方标准，促进深圳市知识产权、标准与市场的紧密融合，以上标准于2015年3月20日发布，自2015年5月1日起正式实施。

《企业知识产权管理规范》。截至2015年底，深圳市共有60家企业参与贯标试点，其中已有7家企业通过了国家贯标认证。2015年初，为进一步推进贯标工作，深圳市知识产权局以国家知识产权示范城市工作领导小组的名义，要求各区组织开展贯标工作，部分区已出台相应的推进工作方案和资助政策。2015年3月31日，深圳市知识产权局组织召开全市企业知识产权管理规范推进会议，邀请全市100家知识产权优势企业、各区贯标负责人参加，现场有12家企业表达了参与贯标的意愿。

【知识产权服务】

服务体系。一是制定促进知识产权服务

业发展的资助奖励政策，扶持本地代理机构发展，将代理机构纳入了知识产权优势企业评定范围。二是制定专利代理机构服务规范，明确了专利代理机构的业务范围，对从业人员的资格、专利代理机构的信息化建设、人才培训与培养、流程管理、案件质量控制、客户服务、执业规范与监管等多方面进行规范。三是制定深圳市发展知识产权服务业行动计划，从优化知识产权服务业政策环境、加强知识产权宣传培训、实施《专利代理机构服务规范》、加强知识产权服务市场监管、壮大知识产权服务业人才队伍、培育品牌知识产权服务机构、推动知识产权运营工作、促进知识产权信息服务业发展、建设知识产权服务业集聚发展试验区等九个方面来推动知识产权服务业的发展。四是推进国家知识产权服务业集聚发展试验区建设，通过打造“一个平台、三个中心”（“一个平台”即知识产权综合服务平台，“三个中心”即知识产权运营中心、知识产权保护中心、知识产权人才培训中心），全面完善知识产权服务体系，提升知识产权服务业的竞争力，全力打造“国家知识产权服务业集聚发展试验区”。五是积极做好知识产权公共服务。2015年深圳共计发放知识产权专项资金3.2亿元，知识产权专项资金的引导和杠杆作用进一步凸显，激发深圳企业的知识产权创造热情。

专利信息分析与利用。开展深圳市重点产业知识产权分析预警以及广东省重点出口产品专利预警分析计划，围绕深圳产业发展政策，2015年共安排300万元开展知识产权分析预警，涉及北斗卫星导航、工业机器人、新能源汽车、多肽药物技术、生物医药、智能交通、激光投影等多个重点产业领域，通过加强专利信息分析与利用，促进知识产权与技术、产业发展的紧密结合，引导深圳企业加强知识产权战略层面的思考与布局。继续推动工业机器人、医疗器械产业探索专利导航工程，导航产业转型升级。依托国家知识产权局数据资源，建设多种类型、多层次的专利信息数据库，提供更专业化的专利信息服务，方便企业更有针对性地运用专利信息。截至2015年底，深圳市已建成并维护的数据库及公共服务网站系统，包括中外专利数据库检索平台、深圳市知识产权公共服务网站、深圳市专利信息服务平台等，同时加快升级改造深圳市专利资助在线申报系统，推出信息服务微信公众号，努力提升服务能力，使信息服务更贴近产业发展需求。

【知识产权宣传培训】

知识产权宣传。邀请《深圳特区报》《深圳商报》《深圳晚报》《深圳晶报》《国家知识产权报》《国家质量报》等多家媒体，报道2015年深圳市知识产权工作会议，围绕工作会议内容发布多条重要新闻。如《深圳特区报》在重要版面发表评论员文章《创新已成为驱动深圳发展的新“引擎”》，《深圳商报》《深圳晚报》发表《深圳有效发明专利密度全国居首》《深圳每150人就有一项发明专利》《深圳每万人拥有65.75件发明专利全国居首》《深圳知识产权指标漂亮得一塌糊涂》等文章，宣传深圳市知识产权工作过去一年取得的成绩。

知识产权培训。深圳市每年在知识产权专项资金拿出300万元用于知识产权专题培训，主要面向企业知识产权管理人员、知识产权服务机构人员等群体，按照企业和受训群体的不同，专题培训分成初、中、高三个层次，全年开展专题培训近50场，受训人数近万人。结合“双创”工作举办“知识产权服务创客”活动，培养创客知识产权保护意识。开展企业知识产权运营实务高级培训，围绕企业专利运营实务、品牌运营战略与规划、企业海外发展等知识产权热点、难点问题，结合实际案例进行研讨交流。

对外合作与交流。2015年，深圳市知识产权局接待了两批世界知识产权组织（WIPO）官员来访，配合国家知识产权局与WIPO开展专利合作条约巡回活动。2015年3月3—5日，深圳市知识产权局还接待了由国家知识产权局陪同法国工业产权局驻华知识产权专员让·巴普蒂斯特·巴比耶先生到深圳进行调研和工作访问。其间与深圳市知识产权局、深圳海关、深圳市公安局经济侦查局参会人员座谈，交流网络知识产权保护的相关问题。2015年6月，国家知识产权局国际合作司司长吴凯带队亲自陪同WIPO法律司的副司长到深圳走访重点企业，召开用户座谈会，听取了企业使用PCT的经验和建议，解答了企业代表对PCT制度的疑问，宣讲WIPO对于PCT制度的持续改进，更好地服务和满足深圳创新主体的需求。

（供稿人：黄远辉）

珠 海 市

【概况】 2015年，珠海市专利申请11334件，比上年增长25.96%，其中发明专利申请4420件，增长39.34%；实用新型申请5377件，增长29.19%；外观设计申请1537件。专利授权6790件，其中发明专利授权1240件，实用新型授权4021件，外观设计授权1529件，年末有效发明专利3667件。2015年珠海市每百万人均发明专利申请量2712件，比上年增长37.27%，排名全省第2位。珠海市每万人口所拥有的有效发明专利量22.5件，增长47.83%，排名全省第2位。1家企业获得中国专利金奖，6家企业获得中国专利优秀奖，截至2015年，共获中国专利奖获奖企业27家。

2015年，制定并印发了《珠海市深入实施知识产权战略　推动创新驱动发展三年行动计划（2015—2017 年）》《2016年珠海市知识产权战略实施推进计划》《珠海市知识产权局2015年专利执法维权工作方案》《珠海市知识产权局处理侵犯专利权纠纷操作规程》《珠海市知识产权局查处假冒专利行为操作规程》等规范性文件。

全年受理专利纠纷和涉嫌假冒专利案件3件，结案3件，结案率100%。有2家企业通过国家知识产权优势企业认定，截至2015年底，有国家知识产权优势企业4家；2家企业通过省知识产权示范企业认定，至2015年底有省知识产权示范企业12家；8家企业通过市知识产权优势企业认定，至2015年底有市知识产权优势企业75家。资助发明专利491件，其中国内发明专利470件，国外发明专利21件。

组织开展系列专利宣传与培训活动15场，培训2600人次，派发资料3000份；通过特区报等媒体进行宣传，营造尊重和保护知识产权的浓厚氛围。

（供稿人：权超）

汕 头 市

【知识产权创造】 2015年，汕头市新增专利申请9827件，同比增长8.02%，其中发明专利申请1043件，同比增长17.99%；新增专利授权7651件，同比增长18.25%，其中授权发明专利328件，同比增长42.61%；新增PCT专利申请52件，同比增长185.71%。2015年，汕头市有7个项目获得中国专利奖优秀奖，有5个项目获得省专利奖优秀奖，获奖数量再创历史新高，位居全省地级市前列。截至2015年年底，汕头市累计获得中国专利金奖1项，中国专利优秀奖31项，中国外观设计优秀奖4项。第七届汕头市专利奖共评选出市专利金奖4项、外观设计专利金奖2项、专利优秀奖7项、外观设计专利优秀奖4项、优秀专利发明人10名。新申请商标注册21764件，新增注册商标24261件；新认定驰名商标3件，广东省著名商标10件，申报认定广东省著名商标17件。扶持发展行业区域品牌和农业特色品牌，指导龙湖区输配电设备行业协会、龙湖区潮织商会、潮阳河溪优品种养专业合作社申请集体商标3件。新增作品著作权登记1430件，居全省地级市前列。全市企事业单位主导或参与制修订国家标准6项、行业标准16项、地方标准2项，全市重点工业产品164项采用国际标准或国外先进标准进行生产，备案企业产品标准669项；有2家企业被确认为4A级标准化良好行为企业、10家企业复审通过标准化良好行为企业。

【知识产权运用】

专利技术实施。2015年，广东达诚机械有限公司的“全自动多工位正负压热成型机组”、汕头东方科技有限公司的“圆周编码定位系统”、广东名臣有限公司的“控油化妆品组合物专利技术实施孵化”、广东壮丽彩印股份有限公司的“环保型镭射卡纸包装片材生产工艺关键技术研究及应用”、骅威科技股份有限公司的“新型智能飞行模型设计与开发”、广东爱华新光电科技有限公司的“LED灯芯片封装透明胶的方法”、广东轻工机械二厂有限公司的“自动装箱机”、广东英联包装股份有限公司的“超薄环保安全便捷易拉盖关键技术研究及其产业化”等8个项目被汕头市知识产权局确定为市专利技术实施孵化项目。

优势企业培育。2015年，广东天际电器股份有限公司、汕头市超声仪器研究所有限公司、广东潮宏基实业股份有限公司、广东夏野日用电器有限公司、汕头市华莎驰家具家饰有限公司、广东太安堂药业股份有限公司、汕头华兴冶金设备股份有限公司、汕头东风印刷股份有限公司、广东邦宝益智玩具股份有限公司等9家企业被国家知识产权局确定为国家知识产权优势企业。广东柏亚化妆品有限公司、广东树业环保科技股份有限公司、广东嘉达早教科技股份有限公司、汕头市丽盛实业有限公司、广东汇群中药饮片股份有限公司、广东正超电气有限公司、广东金源科技股份有限公司、汕头市新青罐机有限公司、广东宝贝儿婴童用品实业有限公司、汕头经济特区和通电讯有限公司等10家企业被汕头市知识产权局确定为市知识产权优势培育企业。

【知识产权保护】

行政执法。（1）专利。2015年，汕头市知识产权局扎实开展“护航”“闪电”等专项行动，全年共立案处理专利侵权纠纷案件38宗，其中涉外案件3宗；立案查处假冒专利案件35宗；接受外地知识产权局移送涉嫌假冒专利案件线索28条。

（2）商标。汕头市工商行政管理系统继续保持打击侵权假冒高压态势，突出重点商标专项保护、涉农地区、涉农商标侵权专项整治和重点商品专项整治，全年共立案查处各类侵权假冒案件193宗，其中侵犯商标权案件169宗，制售假冒伪劣商品案件24宗，罚没金额349万元。

（3）版权。汕头市文化市场综合执法部门严厉打击文化市场侵犯知识产权违法行为，全年共出动执法人员9960人次，检查经营场所1245家次，立案查处侵权假冒案件14宗，清理非法出版物地摊58个，收缴非法出版物895本（张）。

（4）质监。汕头市质监系统共出动执法人员1555人次，检查企业280家，立案查处涉假案件45宗，办结案件44宗，捣毁制假窝点6个，涉案货值约46.23万元。

（5）海关。汕头海关继续加强进出口货运渠道、行邮旅检渠道重点敏感商品和侵权商品查缉工作，全年全关共采取知识产权海关保护措施26批次，查获侵权案件8宗，查获货物118420件，案值约61.87万元。全年共为粤东关区的出口企业提供授权“预先审核”服务40宗次，有效防范企业受外商利用造成非主观侵权，同时为守法企业化解了不必要的侵权法律风险。

刑事执法。汕头市各级公安机关坚持突出重点区域整治、重点领域打击和重点案件办理，积极加强与行政执法部门的协作形成打击合力，全年共破获涉假案件120宗，刑拘涉假人员134名，逮捕71名，涉案金额3651.17万元。其中，公安机关与各执法部门联合行动70次，破案43宗。发起全国集群战役3宗，收网3宗，查获查扣侵权假冒物品和制假设备一大批，排名全省前列。

司法保护。2015年，汕头市两级检察机关批准逮捕各类侵犯知识产权刑事犯罪案件22宗28人，其中假冒注册商标案件7宗8人，销售假冒注册商标案件7宗10人，侵犯商业秘密案件3宗3人；共起诉53宗116人。汕头中级人民法院坚持实行严格的知识产权保护，依法公正审理各种知识产权民事、刑事案件，确保审判程序的高效进行和审判结果的公平正义。全年，市两级法院共受理侵权假冒刑事案件101宗、审结80宗，对141名犯罪分子予以判决；新收知识产权民事案件32件、审结53件（含旧存24件），结案率95%，调撤率达58%。

知识产权维权援助。2015年4月22日，由市知识产权局、市中级人民法院主办，潮南区知识产权局、中国（汕头）知识产权维权援助中心、汕头市北大工商管理硕士企业家协会协办的“知识产权维权保护咨询活动”在潮南区华南广场成功举行。4月24日下午，在汕头市庆祝第15个“4·26”世界知识产权日主题大会上，中国（汕头）知识产权维权援助中心汕头电商领域专利维权援助分中心举行揭牌仪式，广东省知识产权局局长马宪民和汕头市委副书记孙光辉亲自为分中心揭牌。8月20日中国（汕头）知识产权维权援助中心与粤东地区的市级中心揭阳市知识产权维权援助中心签署知识产权维权与保护协作备忘录，扶持该区域市级中心建设，加强双方信息交流协作，促进双方知识产权执法和服务能力的提高。全年，汕头中心共受理维权援助案件15宗；举报投诉案件46宗，其中移送汕头市知识产权局44宗，移送其他省、市维权中心2宗；专利侵权纠纷立案36宗。

侵权假冒。2015年，汕头市打击侵权假冒工作领导小组组织召开全市打击侵权假冒工作会议，总结交流经验，部署推进年度重点专项整治任务；领导小组办公室印发《2015年汕头市打击侵权假冒工作要点》和《关于落实省打击侵权假冒工作督查组意见，进一步推动打击侵权假冒工作的通知》，并组织协调各成员单位重点开展了互联网领域侵权假冒、农村和城乡结合部市场、车用燃油、“清风”等专项整治行动。据不完全统计，2015年市知识产权局、工商局、文广新（版权）局、质监局、药监局、农业局等主要行政执法部门共立案查处侵权假冒案件近千宗，有效规范市场秩序，净化市场环境。在推进专项整治和加强日常执法工作的同时，领导小组各成员单位还推进长效工作机制建设，取得了新进展。其中：市领导小组办公室及时根据工作需要和人员变动情况，组织对市领导小组成员单位和人员进行调整，新增市商务局为副组长单位，健全了领导机构，加强了领导力量。市食品药品监督管理局与市公安局联合制定了《汕头市公安局、汕头市食品药品监督管理局打击制售假劣食品药品违法犯罪工作机制》，并设立了联合执法办公室；市知识产权局与市信息服务和软件行业协会、市电子商务协会和柏亚电子商务产业园联合成立汕头电商领域专利维权分中心，建立了制止电商领域专利侵权假冒行为的协作机制。市国税局积极推进纳税信用体系建设，建立落实税收“黑名单”制度，主动协调相关单位签订《合作备忘录》，共制定实施了对违法行为的联合惩戒措施。

【知识产权管理】 2015年，汕头市知识产权局着力营造有助于技术创新和经济发展的知识产权环境。一是编制全市“十三五”知识产权事业发展规划。为明晰“十三五”期间汕头知识产权事业发展目标和思路，使规划编制更具科学性、实效性和可操作性，汕头市知识产权局多次深入区县、服务对象和服务机构等开展调研，组织编写《汕头市“十三五”知识产权事业规划方案》和《汕头市“十三五”知识产权事业发展思路研究报告》，在此基础上，起草了《汕头市知识产权事业发展“十三五”规划》草案并正在征求政府各部门意见。二是推进实施专利事业发展战略推进计划。根据全省统一部署，结合汕头地方实际，制订了《汕头市2015年专利事业发展战略推进计划组织实施方案》，提出专利制度创新、专利制度运行保障体系建设以及专利支撑经济社会发展等三大主体任务、31项具体工作措施和目标，并积极采取措施加以落实。截至2015年底，各项任务已基本完成，为助推全市自主创新和产业升级发挥了积极作用。三是稳步推进知识产权战略深入实施。市政府知识产权办公会议办公室牵头起草并报经市政府审核同意，以市政府知识产权办公会议名义印发了《汕头市2015—2016年贯彻实施国家和省知识产权战略纲要工作方案》，深入推进国家和省知识产权战略纲要实施。在“4・26”世界知识产权日活动期间，汕头以市政府知识产权办公会议名义召开了“汕头市庆祝第十五个‘4・26’世界知识产权日主题大会”，省知识产权局局长马宪民和市委副书记孙光辉出席会议并作重要讲话。会议发布了《汕头市2014年知识产权保护状况》和《汕头市2014年知识产权典型案例》，举行了省、市知识产权示范优势企业及“正版正货承诺”企业授牌、专利奖颁奖、市专利案件口审室揭牌仪式等，开通汕头知识产权公众微信号，向社会各界展示全市知识产权工作新成果。

【知识产权宣传培训】 2015年，汕头市知识产权局把知识产权宣传教育工作与扶持培育、执法等工作相结合，营造“尊重知识、崇尚创新、诚信守法”的良好知识产权文化氛围。一是结合知识产权人才培养和企业发展需求，制定出台了《2015年汕头市知识产权宣传培训工作方案》，对全年知识产权宣传培训工作作出部署，并先后组织举办了“中国及广东专利奖申报辅导班”“电商企业专利保护培训班”“企业专利保护专题培训班”“汕头市知识产权专家库专家业务提升培训班”“专利维权保护志愿者专题培训班”等专题培训16场次，培训各类人员2000多人。二是坚持以宣传普及知识产权知识为先导，注重通过网络、电视、广播、报纸等各种媒体宣传知识产权知识、典型案例及知识产权工作成效等，全年在各类媒体发表报道52篇次，在全市营造了良好的知识产权保护和发展氛围。

【知识产权交流合作】 2015年4月24日，汕头市知识产权局牵头举办了粤东企业专利异地维权对接研讨会，与汕尾、潮州、梅州、揭阳、惠州、河源等市知识产权管理部门就企业专利异地维权进行共同商讨并达成一致协议，为粤东企业异地维权开辟了绿色通道。

【统计资料】

（一）2015年汕头市专利奖获奖项目

表1　第七届汕头市专利奖金奖项目（4项）

专利号	项目名称	申报单位
201110332668.2	一种防静电单片式电容触摸屏	汕头超声显示器（二厂）有限公司
200910214390.1	富含天然类胡萝卜素的华贵栉孔扇贝金色新品系的培育方法	汕头大学
201020026905.3	用于防火玻璃幕墙的钢铝型材	广东金刚玻璃科技股份有限公司
201010246800.3	自粘膜吹膜法生产设备和生产方法	广东金明精机股份有限公司

表2　第七届汕头市专利奖优秀奖项目（7项）

专利号	项目名称	申报单位
200910192801.1	去屑洗发组合物	名臣健康用品股份有限公司
201210014573.0	一种高精度局部转移镀铝层生产工艺	广东壮丽彩印股份有限公司

（续上表）

专利号	项目名称	申报单位
201210276709.5	一种无线通信天线馈线的制造方法	汕头市金桥电缆有限公司
200810157198.9	一种白芨中草药牙膏	广东康王日化有限公司
201210419605.5	一种高速离心雾化装置	广东东方锆业科技股份有限公司
201220733909.4	一种无拉绳式窗帘	汕头市荣达新材料有限公司
201110380628.5	一种高强高导铜合金材料	汕头华兴冶金设备股份有限公司

表3　第七届汕头市外观设计金奖项目（2项）

专利号	项目名称	申报单位
201230251370.4	彩色多普勒超声诊断仪（推车式）	汕头市超声仪器研究所有限公司
201330603940.6	工艺摆件“金兰花”	广东潮宏基实业股份有限公司

表4　第七届汕头市外观设计优秀奖项目（4项）

专利号	项目名称	申报单位
201430207931.X	玩具机器人（3合1）	广东奥飞动漫文化股份有限公司
201330084717.5	积木玩具	汕头市大树玩具有限公司
201430146187.7	挂钟（B8151）	汕头市丽盛实业有限公司
201430047731.2	玩具飞行器（感应飞船）	广东飞轮科技股份有限公司

表5　第七届汕头市专利奖优秀发明人奖（10人）

姓　名	申报单位
李　君	汕头市东方科技有限公司
李　飚	广东金玉兰包装机械有限公司
郭境峰	汕头市超声仪器研究所有限公司
吴川中	广东南洋电缆集团股份有限公司
汤树海	广东壮丽彩印股份有限公司
谢庆坚	广东可逸智膜科技有限公司
张志宾	广东宝贝儿婴童用品实业有限公司
翁伟武	广东英联包装股份有限公司
陈祉浩	广东超力微电机有限公司
陈远平	汕头市信一塑机制造有限公司

（二）2015年度汕头市三种专利申请比例

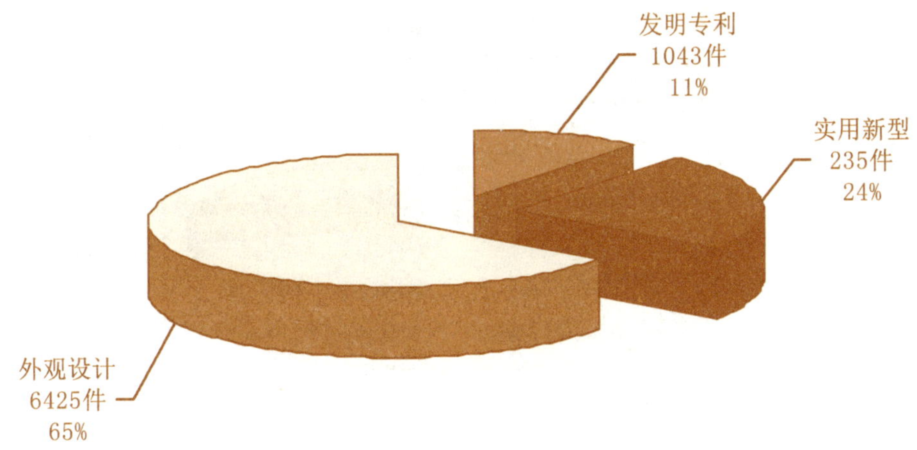

图1 2015年汕头市三种专利申请统计图

（三）2015年度汕头市三种专利授权比例

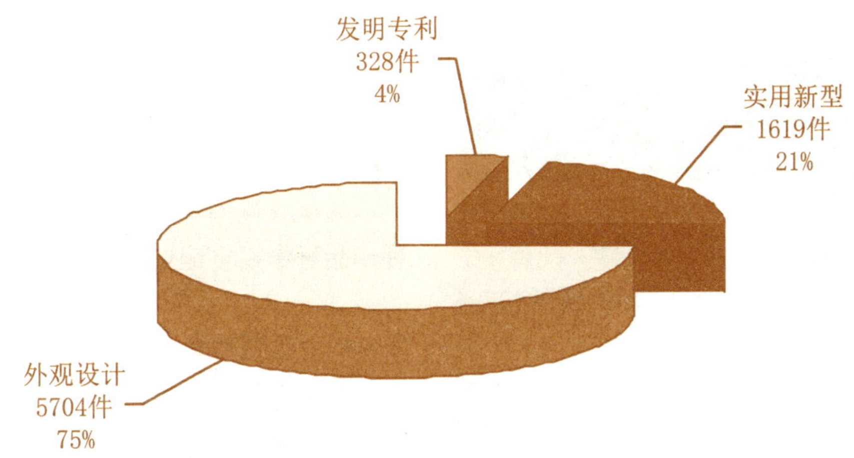

图2 2015年汕头市三种专利授权统计图

（四）2015年度汕头市各区县专利申请统计

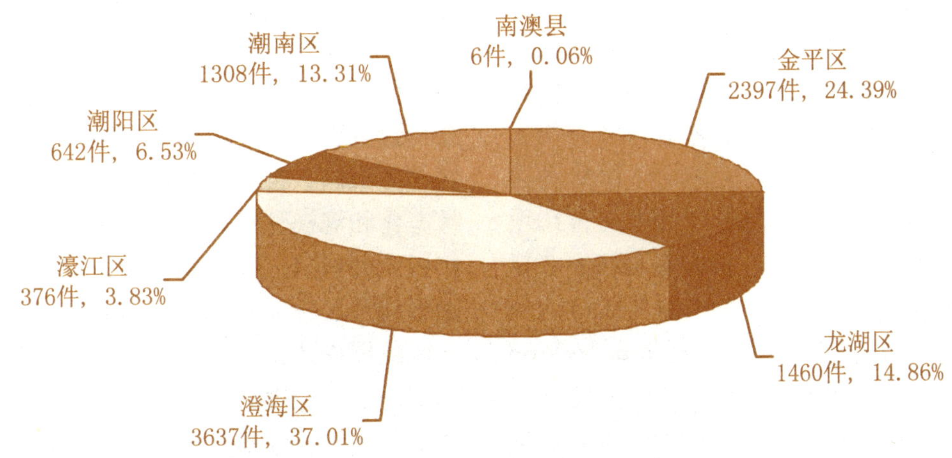

图3 2015年汕头市各区县专利申请统计图

（五）2015年度汕头市各区县专利授权统计

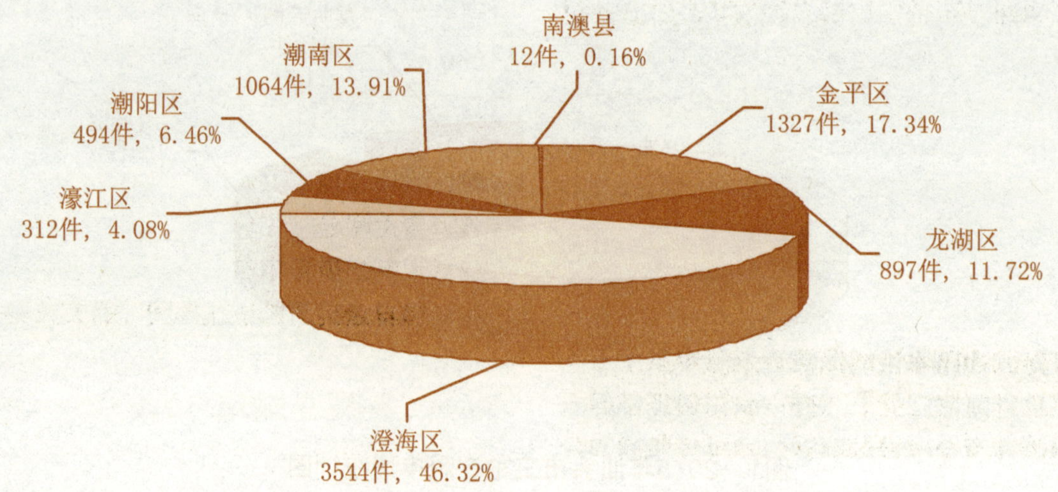

图4 2015年汕头市各区县专利授权统计图

（供稿人：黄蔚昇）

佛山市

【知识产权创造】

专利。2015年，佛山市专利申请量39796件，居全省第三，同比增长33.96%，其中发明专利申请量11507件，居全省第三，增长率高达58.48%。专利授权量27523件，居全省第三，同比增长26.79%，其中发明专利授权量2150件，同比增长93.87%，增长率大幅提升，为佛山历年最高。全市百万人口发明专利申请量1565 件，万人有效发明专利拥有量9.61件，超额完成省下达的考核指标。PCT国际专利申请306件，同比增长56.92%。知识产权数量和质量提升，佛山创新驱动成效显著。

2015年，7项专利获得中国专利奖优秀奖，8项专利获得中国外观设计优秀奖，10项专利获得广东专利优秀奖，两位专利权人获得广东省发明人奖。

商标。佛山市拥有有效注册商标160563件，位列全国大中城市第十一位，中国驰名商标共146件，广东省著名商标共467件。截至2015年12月31日，广东省的马德里国际商标注册总量4707件，占全国马德里国际商标注册总量的22.3%，排名全国第一。佛山马德里国际注册商标数量排名全省第三位，占全省总量的9.9%。

版权。佛山市版权服务登记中心2015年办理作品著作权登记1535件，居全省第三。

【知识产权运用】

示范培育。2015年佛山市成功申报国家知识产权投融资试点和国家专利导航产业发展实验区，积极组织和推荐优势知识产权企业申报国家和省级项目，6家企业被评为国家知识产权优势企业，3家企业被评为广东省知识产权示范企业。

专利交易。佛山市把金融与知识产权融合发展作为知识产权工作创新发展的新引擎，建立与投资、信贷、担保等相结合的多元化多层次服务机制，推动知识产权金融服务市场化、常态化和规模化。设立不少于6000万元的知识产权质押融资风险补偿资金，代偿银行及类金融机构开展企业知识产权质押融资时产生的部分风险损失。银行等金融机构按比例放大提供信贷额度，保险公司为信贷提供保险支持，全面推动知识产权质押融资，激发企业知识产权创造和运用。2015年，全市新增18家企业知识产权质押融资，实现融资额3.4亿元。OTC科技板实现挂牌36家，并成功举办第5届中国（广东）知识产权投融资项目对接会，意向金额1.7亿元。

专利保险。2015年佛山市禅城区参加专利保险的企业共51家，投保专利349件（其中发明135件，实用新型118件，外观96件），保费为241000元，保额为7299000元。政府支付给企业专利保险补贴共13.5万元。结合2015年企业申报专利技术实施计划项目和专利优势项目实地考察的契机，区、镇（街道）两级知识产权部门深入到申报项目的50多家企业，向企业宣讲专利保险补贴等政策，引导企业真正把专利技术作为核心价值加以保护和运用。联合各工业园区、协会、商会等组织举办各种各类的培训班、论坛和讲座，开展专利保险专题培训，宣传专利保险在科技创新、保护知识产权的积极作用，介绍专利保险的投保方案和理赔细则，引导和鼓励企业积极参保。在企业申报区“知识产权示范企业”“专利技术实施计划项目”和“专利优势项目”时，把专利保险作为其中一项考核指标，提高企业参保积极性。

【知识产权保护】

专利保护。实施“清风”计划，不断完善行政执法工作体系，加强知识产权执法人员教育，持续系统地对执法骨干队伍进行培训；加大专利、商标、版权等多部门的行政执法协作力度，形成高效的知识产权保护协作机制。建立健全司法保护体系，深入推进知识产权“三合一”审判机制，推进专家证人、专家辅助人等机制创新。健全知识产权维权援助体系，加快推进家电、家具、陶瓷等领域知识产权快速维权中心建设。全年共处理各类专利案件共83件，其中受理专利侵权纠纷案件22件，结案25件，调解或撤诉结案20件，做出处理决定结案5件，判定侵权案件3件，驳回请求案件2件；处理假冒专利案件56件，结案56件；展会处理案件5件；开展专利执法专项行动13次，出动执法人员480余人次，检查商品达10000多件。

商标保护。开展“武动传承——佛山武术文化品牌体验活动”，让市民了解佛山本土特色文化，共同保护佛山武术文化品牌。为加强佛山装备制造企业品牌保护，市工商局依托全国首个商标预警监测系统，将183家高新型装备制造企业的商标纳入预警监测系统，及时向相关企业发出预警通知书，公布装备制造业商标抢注典型案例，提醒相关企业关注该商标的注册进程，并建议相关企业采取更有力的措施，有效帮助企业预防因商标无效而影响企业品牌发展。

知识产权执法维权“护航”专项行动。制定《佛山市2015年知识产权执法维权“护航”专项行动实施方案》，以大型商场及商品批发集散地等流通环节为重点环节，以儿童用品、通讯器材产品、药品和日化用品、箱包皮具、汽车配件、小家电等关系民生商品为重点对象，联合市工商局、市质监局共同制定了《2015年汽车配筋、润滑油、车用燃油打假专项行动工作方案》《佛山市2015年儿童用品、通讯器材产品打假专项行动实施方案》和《佛山市2015年汽车配件打假专项行动实施方案》，加强专业市场和城乡结合部商贸中心的巡查力度，大力开展查处假冒专利行为，进一步规范和整顿市场秩序，提高人民群众对知识产权执法维权的满意度。

【知识产权管理】

完善知识产权政策。2015年以佛山市人民政府的名义出台了《佛山市深入实施知识产权战略加快创新驱动发展行动计划》（佛府办函〔2015〕772号）（以下简称《行动计划》），《行动计划》明确了新常态下佛山特色知识产权强市、建设广东知识产权强省先行地的总体思路和主要目标，通过多部门配合工作，加强宏观指导，促进知识产权对经济社会发展的积极作用，加快佛山的产业转型升级。起草《佛山市知识产权质押融资信贷风险补偿资金管理试行办法》《佛山市促进知识产权服务业集聚发展资助试行办法》，其中《佛山市知识产权质押融资信贷风险补偿资金管理试行办法》促进企业保护和运用知识产权，拓展更多融资渠道，每个风险补偿项目扶持金额最高可达1000万元；《佛山市促进知识产权服务业集聚发展资助试行办法》对知识产权服务业资助覆盖知识产权战略全流程，专利交易、股权化等最高资助100万元。

为提高佛山企业注册国际商标的积极性，引导具有自主知识产权和自主品牌的出口企业努力创建品牌、经营品牌、延伸品牌，提升佛山品牌国际化水平，形成一批具有国际竞争力的知名品牌，佛山市人民政府正式印发实施《佛山市商标国际注册资助办法》。该办法坚持以企业为主体，政府资助为辅的原则，企业根据其发展的需要主动申请国际注册，政府作适当资助，鼓励和扶持企业发展。

商标预警监测。通过商标预警服务对全市企业新申请商标的商标初审公告预警通知、对佛山重点企业以及公共资源商标抢注预警通知以及对全市企业的商标续展预报通知，在2015年商标预警服务中心开展商标预警服务的情况如下：

预警项目名称	监测预警事项的数量（件数）	发出预警通知书的数量（份数）
商标初步审定公告	29020	15309
抢注预警	1945	1003
续展预报	2865	920

【知识产权服务】

知识产权服务机构。大力引进培育知识产权服务机构，吸引一批知识产权服务机构落户，创办专利代理人协会。2015年新增8家专利代理机构和多家评估、交易服务机构进驻，目前佛山共有34家专利代理机构，数量仍在不断增长中。推进“1+5”佛山市知识产权协会服务联盟建设，制定统一服务流程和标准，实现市、区两级知识产权协会资源共享、人才交流、服务范围和服务能力的全面提升。继续发布“专利富豪榜”和“专利新锐榜”，带动一批专利“富豪企业”和“新秀企业”的诞生和成长，扩大全国首个以专利为标准编制的佛山企业排行榜的影响力。

知识产权人才。实施“英才”计划，以国家中小微企业知识产权培训（南海）基地（以下简称“南海基地”）为基础，建立覆盖全市五区的佛山市知识产权培训基地。成立佛山市知识产权人才学院，推动高校设立知识产权学院，开设知识产权相关课程，打造多维知识产权人才培训体系，壮大知识产权人才队伍。开展专利特派员工作，选派一批特派员，深入企业和园区创新一线，提供“一对一”专业化服务。承办国家局专利挖掘与布局和专利分析实战培训班，培养专业人才队伍。2015年全市共开展60多场培训，累计培训人数超5400人次。建立企业IP经理人俱乐部，引导企业制定IP经理人管理和培养制度，完善IP经理职业晋升发展通道。

南海区启动了第二个专利管理师千人培训计划，承接国家、省、市（区）举办各类培训5场次，组建了专利管理师教学师资库，并制定师资选拔考核相应机制。完成国家知识产权局“中小微企业知识产权人才培养模式研究”的软课题，完成企业专利管理初级培训教材开发。

【知识产权宣传】

2015年佛山市知识产权局建立“佛知界”微信公众号，及时传递国家、省、市的知识产权动态，以及各行业知识产权的发展动向、专利运用和保护等资讯。

市商标战略办、市工商局与佛山电视台联合举办以“文化传承与品牌保护”为主题的热线面对面宣传活动。活动采用情景剧宣传形式，选择社会上较关心的商标抢注问题、商标注册程序等内容进行演出，每一个情景剧表演完之后，主持人均邀请佛山市知名学者、市工商局商广科负责人、相关公共资源权属单位代表和商标代理人上台对情景剧进行专业点评。从商标的角度出发，让在场市民了解佛山公共资源商标保护的现状和重要性，进一步提高公共资源商标保护意识。

【统计资料】

表1　2015年佛山市专利申请情况表

单位：件

各区	发明	实用新型	外观设计	合计	2014年	增长
禅城	2280	1473	1453	5206	3882	34.11%
南海	2441	4568	3434	10443	7238	44.28%
顺德	4727	8490	6559	19776	15562	27.08%
高明	863	914	266	2043	1511	35.21%
三水	1193	817	312	2322	1508	53.98%
合计	11504	16262	12024	39790	29701	33.97%
2014年	7259	11842	10600	29701		
增长	58.48%	37.32%	13.43%	33.97%		

表2　2015年佛山市专利授权情况表

单位：件

各区	发明	实用新型	外观设计	合计	2014年	增长
禅城	477	1167	1373	3017	2523	19.58%
南海	475	3618	3089	7182	5193	38.30%
顺德	828	7638	6443	14909	12305	21.16%
高明	186	785	253	1224	917	33.48%
三水	183	699	309	1191	769	54.88%
合计	2149	13907	11467	27523	21707	26.79%
2014年	1109	11208	9390	21707		
增长	93.78%	24.08%	22.12%	26.79%		

表3　2015年佛山市专利奖获奖项目

申报单位	项目名称
佛山市金辉高科光电材料有限公司	一种聚烯烃微多孔膜的制作方法
广东一方制药有限公司	一种将超临界二氧化碳萃取物固体粉末化的方法
广东兴发铝业有限公司	铝型材表面制备Al-Mo-Mn-Re四元复合钝化膜的处理液及其使用方法
广东美芝制冷设备有限公司	旋转式压缩机
广东溢达纺织有限公司	织物免烫整理方法、连续式织物压烫装置及压烫整理机
广东志高空调有限公司	一种太阳能复合能源空调热水装置
万峰石材科技股份有限公司	一种仿大理石莎安娜高档品种图案之人造石的制备方法及其制备的人造石
佛山市日丰企业有限公司	一种含石墨烯的增强耐磨材料组合物、增强耐磨材料及制法
国药集团冯了性（佛山）药业有限公司	一种治疗风热感冒的中药组合物及其制备方法

（续上表）

申报单位	项目名称
广东华声电器股份有限公司	一种耐低温电缆料
佛山市海天调味食品股份有限公司	调味品中大肠菌群的快速检测方法
广东博德精工建材有限公司	高逼真度仿玉微晶玻璃陶瓷复合板制备方法
佛山华盛昌陶瓷有限公司	一种抛光废渣回用于抛光砖生产的方法及设备
国药集团德众（佛山）药业有限公司	治疗乳腺增生的口服类中药组合物及其制备方法
广东三水大鸿制釉有限公司	一种可发生负离子的釉料及其制备和应用方法
广东美涂士建材股份有限公司	一种耐酸雨水性外墙底漆
广东环球制药有限公司	一种化州柚黄酮提取物的膜分离制备方法
广东美的厨房电器制造有限公司	半导体微波炉
广东美的制冷设备有限公司	变频空调器的节能控制方法及装置
美的集团股份有限公司	一种油烟净化装置的离心风机蜗壳
广东健博通科技股份有限公司	一种2.4/5.8GHz双频MIMO全向天线
佛山市川东磁电股份有限公司	一种防水型温控器
佛山市金凯地过滤设备有限公司	卧式弹簧滤板压榨机
佛山市新东方电子技术工程有限公司	声频触发报警系统及方法
广东申菱空调设备有限公司	高精度节能型恒温恒湿空调机及其控制方法
佛山市中格威电子有限公司	一种空调的节能方法及用于空调的节能器
广东小熊电器有限公司	一种浸泡式家用芽菜机及其控制方法
佛山市富士宝电器科技股份有限公司	风扇头的摆动机构
佛山市浪鲸洁具有限公司	浴缸（WHALE）

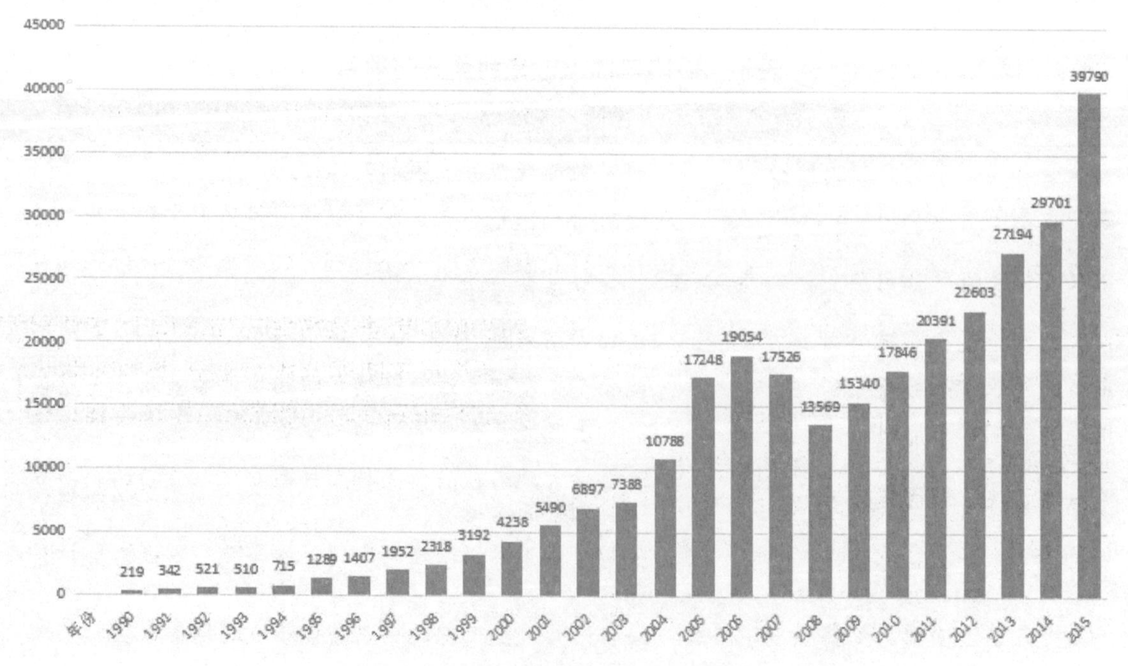

图1 1990—2015年佛山市历年专利申请量图示（单位：件）

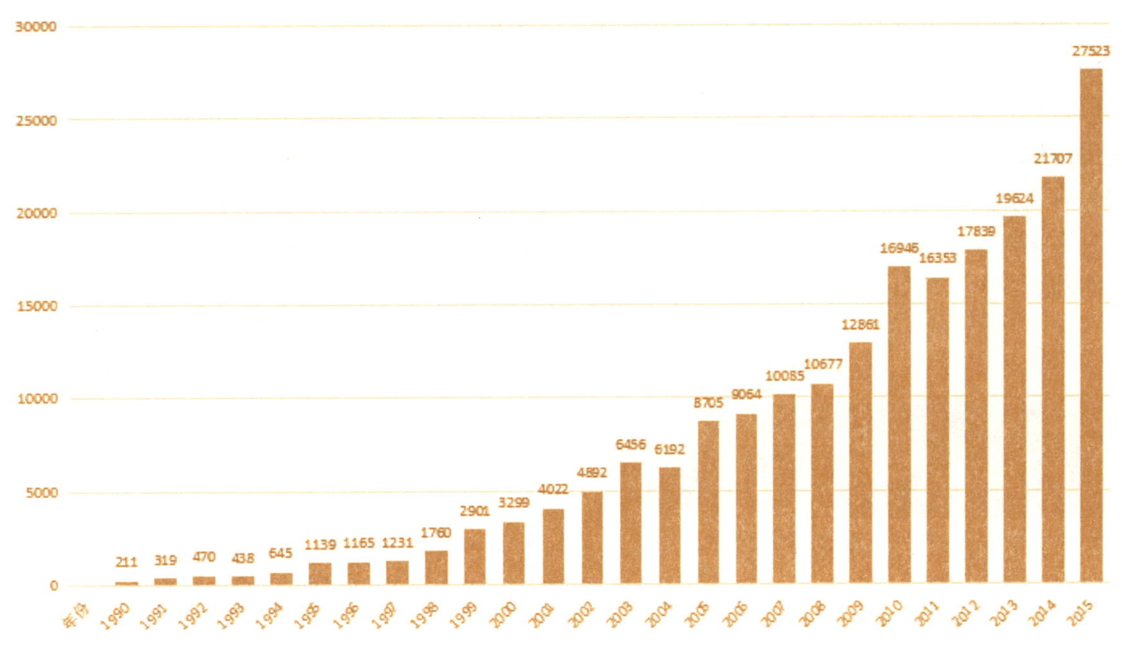

图2　1990—2015年佛山市历年专利授权量图示（单位：件）

（供稿人：潘绮雯）

韶　关　市

【知识产权创造】　2015年，韶关市专利申请量3101，同比增长31.73%，其中发明和实用新型专利申请1899件，发明和实用新型专利申请量占专利申请总量61.24%，专利授权量2107件，同比增长33.02%，发明专利授权量108件，同比增长107.69%。

【知识产权运用】

专利技术产业化。乳源东阳光精箔有限公司的“一种电解电容器高压阳极用铝箔的制造方法”项目获得省专利技术实施计划重点项目。韶关仁化县丹源水果农民专业合作社的“低蔗糖型馅饼专利技术在粤北特产深加工中的应用”项目获得市专利技术实施计划重点项目。

【知识产权保护】　2015年4月24日，韶关市开展“4·26”知识产权联合执法行动，市知识产权局联合工商局、文广新局、公安局等部门对市区商场、书店多家经营单位进行了执法检查，现场查处了专利标识不规范、假冒商标等知识产权违法行为，并对经营者进行了专利标识规范、假冒专利辨识、假冒商标认定、盗版书籍认定等知识产权法律法规宣传教育，提高了经营商家和公众的知识产权保护意识。

【知识产权管理】

知识产权试点示范。2015年，浈江区被列为“国家知识产权强县工程试点区”，截至2015年底，全市拥有国家级知识产权试点县（区）3个、省级知识产权试点县（区）4个、省级知识产权优势企业11家、省级知识产权试点事业单位2个、省级中小学知识产权教育试点（示范）学校10所，省知识产权战略试点企业一家，广东省知识产权示范企业一家。

【知识产权宣传培训】　2015年4月26日，韶关市政府知识产权办公会议办公室牵头，市知识产权局、工商局、文广新局联合在市区西河全民健身广场开展了以专利、商标、版权为主的知识产权宣传活动。活动现场向群众派发宣传资料300多份，并接受群众关于知识产权保护方面的咨询。12月23日，举办了1期企业知识产权管理及实务培训班。培训对象为全市企事业单位代表、各县（市、区）知识产权管理部门等有关人员，培训人数70多人，培训班讲解专利申请、企业专利运用、知识产权贯标等方面的知识。

（供稿人：冯瑞麟）

河 源 市

【知识产权创造】

专利。2015年河源市专利申请量1511件，同比增长77.14%，增长率居全省第二，其中发明专利207件，同比增长42.76%，增长率居全省第十二；实用新型专利764件，外观设计专利540件。专利授权量832件，同比增长46.22%，其中发明专利30件，同比增长25%。截至2015年底，河源市共有国家驰名商标2件、省著名商标16件。

【知识产权保护】

专利行政执法。2015年，河源市知识产权局专利行政巡查执法中，立案处理案件1件。该年度的专利执法案件，主要针对专利标注不规范、专利未授权、专利终止等问题进行查处。对涉嫌假冒专利产品，将依法作出立案处理，努力在全社会营造一个保护知识产权的良好氛围，为专利产品保驾护航。

商标行政执法。开展农村和城乡结合部市场假冒伪劣、车用燃油、空气和饮用水净化类生活用品、红盾网剑、保护“赣南脐橙及图”、“若羌红枣RUO QIANG HONG ZAO及图”地理标志、“松板”注册商标专用权、商标代理市场和打击假冒伪劣日用品专项行动等各专项整治行动，以查办涉及“食品、民生、高危、重害”等案件为重点，查处箱包皮具、烟酒、玩具、家用电器、建材、涉农消费品等领域的商标侵权、仿冒他人知名商品特有名称、包装装潢等侵权假冒违法行为，维护公平有序竞争环境。河源市工商系统共出动执法人员1639人次，检查大型商场、超市、商店等各类经营主体2732户，查处商标侵权假冒案件86宗，罚没金额24.23万元，案值11.19万元。其中：销售明知是假冒注册商标的商品的6宗，销售侵权注册商标专用权的商品的74宗，侵犯驰名商标权益的6宗。“4·26”期间共出动执法人员921人次，执法车辆238辆次，检查经营主体2315户，检查专业市场113个次，立案3宗，案值0.2万元，罚款0.62万元。

版权行政执法。2015年4月26日，在全市范围内开展市场执法检查。全市各级版权执法部门分别组织力量对市场进行了全面清查。全市联合执法6次，共出动执法人员168人次，检查各类印刷复制单位、发行单位、计算机经营单位232家次，收缴侵权盗版等非法电子出版物212张，盗版电脑软件138张，盗版书报刊3567份（册）；取缔无证经营地摊档口7家。并举行销毁侵权盗版产品大行动。市和各县区每年都分别举行了对侵权盗版及其他非法出版物集中销毁活动。有关单位领导、出版物经营单位从业人员及市民踊跃参与活动。据统计，2015年，全市在对侵权盗版及其他非法出版物集中销毁活动中，共销毁非法电子出版物967张，盗版光盘盗版电脑软件234张，盗版书报刊5667份（册）。

专项治理“剑网行动”。2015年在全市范围内开展打击网络侵权盗版专项行动，加大对非法网络的取缔力度，依法查处通过互联网非法传播音乐、电影、软件、图书等作品的网络侵权盗版行为，突出重点、加强监管、部门联动、齐抓共管，取得较好的成效。在该项行动中，全市共出动执法人员1000多人次，检查网吧500多家次，给予行政处罚的网吧22家，责令改正17家，警告21家，责令停业整顿5家。通过专项治理行动，帮助各经营业主树立保护版权、“先授权、后传播”的法律意识，增强广大市民和经营者自觉抵制侵权盗版的意识，进一步净化了网络版权保护环境的目标，收到了较好的效果。

“扫黄打非”“清源”行动。加大对出版物市场日常监管力度，对电脑城、繁华街区、旅游景点、车站周边等重点地区和部位进行了重点监控，严厉查处各类非法出版物、盗版音像制品和非法书报刊。开展印刷企业大清查，以“印刷企业五项制度”为抓手，对印刷企业集中地区、有出版物印刷资质的企业和有违规记录的企业进行了重点清查，从源头上查处非法印刷侵权盗版出版物等违法违规经营行为，从严打击违法违规印刷活动。行动以来，共出动执法人员765人次，检查各类出版物类经营场所100余家（次）、印刷企业160家次，查缴非法出版物1200余册，盗版光盘1345张，取缔无证经营的游商地摊5个。

专项治理“秋风”行动。对书报刊批发市场、繁华街区、车站等的报刊零售摊点及游商进行反复集中清查，坚决收缴涉及时政、军事、党史、宗教、医疗等各类非法报刊，集中打击非法报刊机构和假记者，深入整治违法违规编印传播的内部资料性出版物、固定形式印刷品广告，2015年共出动执法人员65人次，检查出版物零售店及报刊亭125家，收缴非法书报刊42册。

盗版专项行动。春秋两季先后组织人员开展打击盗版教材教辅读物专项行动，排查各中小学校订购、使用教材教辅的情况，打击非法出版、印刷、发行、采购盗版教材教辅读物行为，进一步规范教材、教辅读物经营秩序，营造健康、稳定、规范的出版物市场环境。

软件正版化。河源市建立市推进使用正版软件工作联席会议制度。建立由分管副市长担任总召集人、市府各有关部门主要领导人为成员的河源市推进使用正版软件工作联席会议制度。并且由主管副市长分别与各县区主要负责人签订了政府机关软件正版化工作目标责任状，同时对市县两级政府机关软件正版化工作进行督查。按照省推进正版软件联席会议的部署，河源市已完成了政府机关使用正版软件工作。河源市软件正版化领导小组要求各有关部门将软件作为资产纳入部门资产管理体系，制订软件资产管理制度，并认真做好软件购买、安装、更换、使用、报废等日常管理工作，并继续组织督查组对市政府各直属单位和各县区政府机关软件正版化工作进行检查。同时实施正版软件工作年度报告制度，每年向省推进使用正版软件联席工作会议报告河源市正版软件工作情况，不断巩固河源市软件正版化工作成果。

【知识产权管理和服务】

专利实施。2015年，在开展河源市中小学知识产权教育试点和示范学校认定工作中，通过认定审核工作，最终确定3所知识产权教育示范学校，4所知识产权教育试点学校。2015年12月4日，河源市知识产权局举办全市企业知识产权贯标专题培训班。2015年开展的河源市市级知识产权优势企业认定及市级专利技术实施计划项目申报工作中，5家企业被认定为河源市知识产权优势企业，4个项目被认定为市级专利技术实施计划项目。

知识产权代理服务。引进广州凯东知识产权代理有限公司在河源市设立分支机构，方便河源市企事业单位专利申请等工作。一是办理专利申请费用资助；二是办理专利申请费用减缓证明；三是配合省知识产权局每年的各地知识产权状况调查。

企业诚信信息。根据河源市文明办《河源市诚信“红黑榜”发布制度》的规定，河源市工商局制定的《河源市企业诚信经营和信用信息“红黑榜”发布制度》于2015年10月20日颁布实施。该制度主要是褒扬诚信、惩戒失信，大力推进社会信用监管，致力于营造“奖励诚信、约束失信”“守信光荣、失信可耻”的社会氛围。被认定为中国驰名商标和广东省著名商标的企业可以列入诚信经营“红榜”，10月底，河源市工商局向河源市市政府报送推荐企业名单，驰名商标企业“广东霸王花食品有限公司”进入首批河源市诚信“红榜”并得到河源市市政府的表彰。

商标评定。发挥市县区所四级联动、政企互动的商标品牌培育机制，扶持企业争创驰、著、知名商标。本着“择优推强、量质并举”的原则，做好广东省著名商标的推荐申报和认定工作，指导、帮扶企业积极申报新一轮的省著名商标评定，并对申报材料予以初审和考查。对“万绿湖”“龙乡贡”“古客风”“汇源”等4家企业进行针对性的上门指导服务，规范其商标使用，指导其争创驰名、著名商标。

【知识产权宣传培训】 通过广播电视、网络媒体、报纸杂志介绍河源市知识产权现状，播出知识产权公益广告；开展联合科技下乡活动；向河源市市内知识产权教育试点示范学校赠送《中小学知识产权教育读本》；组织中介服务机构人员深入企业进行点对点服务宣传；举办知识产权各类讲座、培训班；多次深入学校、企业开展调研工作。

“4·26”宣传周。全市按2015年的宣传主题“保护知识产权，营造公平环境建设品牌强市”，在宣传周活动期间，充分利用公共宣传资源，既充分发挥报纸、广播、电视等传统媒体优势，又利用网络、微信、微博等新兴媒体特点，创新商标宣传形式，拓展商标宣传载体，丰富商标宣传内容，扩大活动覆盖面。其间，全市共举办现场宣传咨询活动6场次，接受群众咨询1000多人次，派发商标相关宣传资料2730多份，印发宣传材料4030册，媒体相关报道6条次，发布公益广告53条次，设立商标法知识宣传专栏16个。

2015年4月26日，在全市范围内开展“保护著作权宣传周”活动。开展保护著作权户外宣传活动。由河源市扫黄打非办牵头，全市版权、专利、工商、公安、海关等部门联合举行保护知识产权户外宣传和咨询活动。河源市文广新局共计派发著作权保护宣传资料4000多份。另外，全市各级版权行政部门还组织力量分别在市区及各县城繁华地段悬挂“保护版权，促进创新发展”“拒绝盗版，从我做起”等宣传标语20多幅，在市内各新闻媒体刊播“保护版权，促进创新发展”“拒绝盗版，从我做起”等公益广告和反盗版举报电话60多条（版）次。

（供稿人：黄鹏）

梅州市

【知识产权创造】 2015年，梅州市专利申请受理量3133件，同比增长37.96%，其中发明专利申请受理量为163件，同比下降6.32%，实用新型专利申请受理量2244件，同比增长70.52%，外观设计专利申请受理量726件，同比下降7.04%；专利授权量2985件，同比增长85.52%，其中发明专利授权量46件，同比下降43.2%，实用新型专利授权量2204件，同比增长105.21%，外观设计专利授权量735件，同比增长61.89%。专利申请受理量增幅在全省地级市中居第五位，专利授权量增幅在全省地级市中居第二位。

2015年，梅州市在《商标公告》上被核准公告的商标共772件。至2015年12月底，梅州市注册商标累计数9148件，其中中国驰名商标2件，广东省著名商标65件。

2015年，梅州市文化广电新闻出版局推进“版权兴业工程”，大埔县陶艺文化创意产业园被省版权局授予“广东省版权兴业示范基地”称号，获颁证书和牌匾；盛唐动漫文化传播有限公司制作的少儿漫画系列《客家童谣》被省版权局认定为广东省最具价值版权产品。

【知识产权运用】 梅州市知识产权局选取“国家知识产权强县工程试点区”梅县区作为推进知识产权质押融资工作试点区，梅县区出台了《梅县区企业贷款贴息扶持实施办法（试行）》，对首次获得知识产权质押融资的企业补贴50%的利息，上限不超过30万元；企业获得知识产权质押融资自第二次起，利息补贴比例为20%，上限不超过15万元。2015年，梅县客家村镇银行已发放2920万元质押融资贷款。

【知识产权保护】

专利保护。2015年，梅州市知识产权系统开展跨区域、跨部门联合执法检查，加强打击假冒专利行为。（1）梅州市知识产权局联合市工商局、市文广新局，开展多次打击假冒专利执法行动、专项行动累计出动执法人员100多人次，检查商场、药店等经营场所200家次，检查药品、保健品、化妆品、电子产品等商品3000件。（2）加强案卷规范管理，及时将案卷情况报送国家和省知识产权局。同时，每季度向梅州市打假办报送打假工作情况分析报告。

商标保护。2015年，梅州市工商系统共出动执法人员1968人次，检查各类经营主体3920户，检查批发市场和集贸市场65个次，重点整治区域9处，查处商标侵权假冒案件166宗，案值55.83万元，罚款67.93万元；为权利人挽回经济损失5万多元。

软件正版化。2015年，梅州市文化广电新闻出版局按照省局的工作要求，采取“试点推进、逐步覆盖”的方式，重点督办梅州市（市、区）8个企业使用正版软件，稳步推进国有、民营企业使用正版软件工作，扩大企业使用正版软件范围。

“正版正货”承诺活动。2015年，梅州市21家企业和商家参与“正版正货”承诺活动。截至2015年底，全市共有46家企业和商家获得“正版正货”授牌。

【知识产权管理】

企事业知识产权。2015年8月，博敏电子股份有限公司获得了知识产权管理体系认证证书，成为粤东地区首家通过《企业知识产权管理规范》的认证企业。广东科伦药业有限公司被认定为2015年广东省知识产权示范企业。广东嘉元科技股份有限公司的“电解铜箔生产废水处理工艺”、广东华威化工集团有限公司的“一种高威力乳化炸药及其制备方法”等2个项目获得2016年广东专利优秀奖。

专利资助。2015年，梅州市知识产权局共办理2014年授权的专利资助792件。其中，梅县区共办理授权的专利补助413件；丰顺县办理申请费和授权专利资助203件；大埔县发放专利奖励71件。

【知识产权宣传培训】 在第15个世界“知识产权日”期间，紧紧围绕“建设知识产权强国，支撑创新驱动发展”主题，组织开展“知识产权宣传周”系列活动。活动期间，举办知识产权专题培训3场次，280多位企业代表参加培训；播（刊）相关宣传信息达50多条次，持续一周播放“正版正货”公益广告片，在城区主要街道张贴宣传标语20多条。2015年，梅州市知识产权局开展各类知识产权培训班5场次，参加培训人员达到270人次。其中，梅县区举2场次培训班，梅江区、大埔县、五华县各举办1场次培训班。

【统计资料】

表1　2015年1—12月梅州市各类专利申请人三种专利申请情况

单位：件

类型	发明	实用新型	外观设计	合计
个　　人	37	389	534	960
工矿企业	114	1839	190	2143
大专院校	6	8	0	14
科研单位	1	0	2	3
机关团体	5	8	0	13
合　　计	163	2244	726	3133

表2　2015年1—12月梅州市各类专利申请人三种专利授权情况

单位：件

类型	发明	实用新型	外观设计	合计
个　人	10	254	435	699
工矿企业	33	1933	295	2261
大专院校	3	7	3	13
科研单位	0	10	2	12
机关团体	0	0	0	0
合　计	46	2204	735	2985

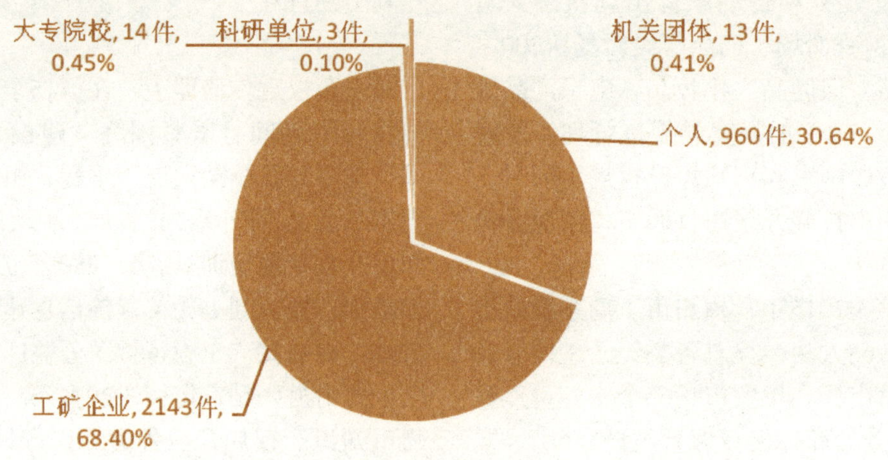

图1　2015年1—12月梅州市专利申请人类型状况图示

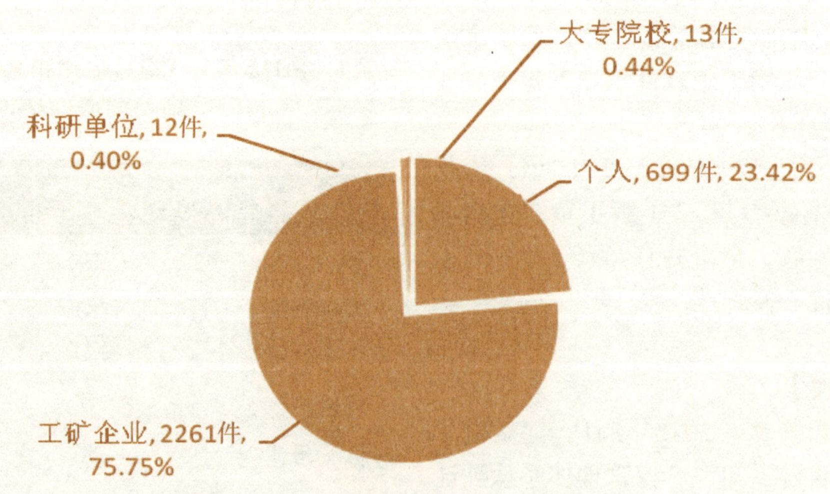

图2　2015年1—12月梅州市授权专利权人类型状况图示

表3 2015年1—12月各县（市、区）专利申请量和授权量排名情况表

单位：件

排名	县级名称	申请量						排名	县级名称	授权量					
		发明	实用新型	外观设计	小计	上年同期	比增			发明	实用新型	外观设计	小计	上年同期	比增
1	蕉岭	9	27	41	77	25	208.00%	1	平远	4	26	38	68	28	142.86%
2	兴宁	23	183	161	367	201	82.59%	2	大埔	2	34	279	315	136	131.62%
3	平远	12	40	35	87	50	74.00%	3	梅县	14	1645	77	1736	794	118.64%
4	梅县	47	1417	90	1554	1040	49.42%	4	丰顺	6	176	67	249	143	74.13%
5	市直、梅江区	47	239	38	324	230	40.87%	5	兴宁	4	111	121	236	150	57.33%
6	丰顺	6	164	96	266	197	35.03%	6	五华	3	39	109	151	118	27.97%
7	五华	6	108	108	222	237	−6.33%	7	市直、梅江区	11	162	29	2022	194	4.12%
8	大埔	13	66	157	236	291	−18.90%	8	蕉岭	2	11	15	28	46	−39.13%
	合计	163	2244	726	3133	2271	37.96%		合计	46	2204	735	2985	1609	85.52%

注：1. 以上数据以专利申请人及授权时专利权人地址为统计口径。

2. 专利申请数据为按各县区专利申请同比增长率排序。

3. 专利授权数据为按各县区专利授权同比增长率排序。

表4 2015年1—12月梅州各县(市、区)五种申请人专利申请授权情况

单位：件

县级名称	申请						授权					
	个人	大专院校	科研单位	工矿企业	机关团体	合计	个人	大专院校	科研单位	工矿企业	机关团体	合计
市直、梅江区	101	14		196	13	324	56	13	10	123		202
梅县区	184			1370		1554	123			1613		1736
兴宁市	229			138		367	140			96		236
大埔县	97		3	136		236	76		2	237		315
丰顺县	110			156		266	129			120		249
五华县	127			95		222	120			31		151
平远县	63			24		87	39			29		68
蕉岭县	49			28		77	16			12		28
合计	960	14	3	2143		3133	699	13	12	2261		2985

（供稿人：刘瑜凤　陈军忠　涂志军）

惠州市

【知识产权创造】 2015年，惠州市专利申请量21408件，同比增长16.6%，其中发明专利申请量4600件，同比增长37.4%；专利授权量9797件，同比增长32.5%，其中发明专利授权868件；有效发明专利达2500件，专利密度（万人有效发明专利量）为5.3件，PCT专利申请174件；电子申请率97.34%，全省排名第二。全市新增注册商标7629件，新增中国驰名商标3件，累计有效注册商标35581件、中国驰名商标19件、广东省著名商标97件、集体商标4件；全年新认定广东省知识产权示范企业1家，惠州市知识产权优势企业5家。

在第十七届中国专利奖的评审中，惠州市昌亿科技股份有限公司的“一种耐寒智能电表壳体用聚碳酸酯/ABS合金及其制备方法”项目获得第十七届中国专利优秀奖。

【知识产权运用】

专利技术产业化。2015年，惠州市知识产权局推进本地专利技术产业化进程，扶持了胜宏科技（惠州）股份有限公司专利技术“高端HDI线路板埋塞孔技术”等4个项目产业化，扶持资金60万元。

专利权质押融资风险补偿。2015年，国家财政部和国家知识产权局为贯彻落实《中共中央 国务院关于深化体制机制改革 加快实施创新驱动发展战略的若干意见》，启动设立了知识产权质押融资风险补偿基金试点工作。惠州市被列为首批试点城市，获得中央财政1000万元专项经费支持，市财政配套2000万元设立了知识产权质押融资风险补偿基金，开展风险补偿试点工作。惠州市知识产权局起草了《惠州市知识产权质押融资信贷风险补偿基金管理办法》上报市政府审批印发实施。

【知识产权保护】

打击侵权假冒工作。2015年，惠州市深入开展打击侵权假冒工作，严厉打击侵权假冒违法犯罪行为。惠州市主要行政执法部门查处案件1800宗，查处窝点128个，假冒伪劣商品货值32391.63万元，移送公安案件227宗，抓获犯罪嫌疑人506人，判刑188人。全市检察机关已批捕相关案件164件290人，起诉相关案件195件283人。共立案查处案件1489宗，涉案金额近亿元，其中重大案件10宗，涉案金额5000多万元，移送司法机关案件115件，捣毁窝点10个。

2015年，惠州市打击侵犯知识产权和假冒伪劣商品工作领导小组办公室组织各成员单位参加了全国2015年打击侵权假冒工作电视电话会议，召开了全市打击侵权假冒工作会议，发动各成员单位开展“中国制造海外形象维护‘清风’行动”，同时转发《2015年全国打击侵犯知识产权和制售假冒伪劣商品工作要点》等文件，要求各成员单位结合自身职责积极开展“双打”工作。

行政保护。

（1）专利行政执法。2015年，惠州市知识产权部门开展了知识产权“执法护航”行动和集中查处假冒专利“百日”专项行动，全年共开展专利专项执法活动26次，专项联合执法10次，检查各类商场、药店500家次，出动执法人员120多人次，共立案受理了专利侵权纠纷案件11件，同比增长37.5%，已结案9件；立案查处假冒专利立案129件，同比增长25%，已结案129件，并已全部公开行政处罚案件信息；惠州市专利执法工作在2014年度全国专利执法维权工作绩效考核评价工作排名广东省地级市第1名。

（2）商标行政执法。惠州市工商行政管理部门共出动执法人员6315人（次），检查经营主体5212户（次），检查批发零售市场、集贸市场等各类市场812个（次），共立案查处商标侵权和制售假冒伪劣商品等案件70宗，涉案案值56.79万元，罚没53.49万元，收缴和销毁侵权商标标识6527件、侵权商品9416件。

（3）版权行政执法。惠州市文化广电新闻出版部门开展了元旦、春节期间文化市场及出版物市场、网吧、印刷企业、广播影视行业等专项整治行动，全市文化市场综合执法机构共出动执法人员20192人次，执法车辆4125车次，检查经营单位7974家次，立案处罚127宗，罚款数额35万元。2015年4月23日，惠州市举行2015年“扫黄打非”、保护知识产权宣传周系列活动启动仪式暨非法出版物现场销毁活动，惠州市政府副市长、市“扫黄打非”工作领导小组副组长刘冠贤致辞并启动活动。活动现场展示出来的包括淫秽书籍、淫秽色情音像制品、盗版书籍等大量非法出版物在惠州市县区代表、市直成员单位代表、学生代表及业主代表约300人的见证下进行集中销毁。

（4）质监行政执法。惠州市质量技术监督部门组织围绕民众热议、关系民生的问题，开展了互联网领域、农村市场、车用燃油、建筑材料、儿童玩具、“清风”行动等10个专项整治行动，共出动执法人员980人次，检查企业327家次，立案48宗，其中假冒伪劣案件5宗，全年共办结案64宗，罚没到位数96.6万元。

（5）食药行政执法。惠州市食品药品监管部门共查处各类案件共1018宗，罚没款共计236万元，移送公安机关案件24宗，抓获犯罪嫌疑人145名；联合公安机关办案235宗，捣毁无证生产经营食品药品地下窝点21个；做好信息公开和“黑名单”有关工作，及时公开行政处罚案件信息，在局政务网站建立“黑名单”专栏，同时链接至市政府门户网“惠州市重点领域信息公开”页面，将符合规定的全部纳入“黑名单”管理并在专栏公布。

（6）农业行政执法。惠州市农业部门组织开展了“春季农资打假保春耕”“夏季百日行动”和“秋冬季农资打假促增收”等一系列农资打假专项行动和农资市场专项检查行动，共出动执法人员2800多人次，执法车辆500多辆次，检查生产、销售、仓储等单位2000多家次，立案147宗，结案132宗，涉案产品货值达20多万元。

刑事保护。惠州市公安机关开展了对互联网领域、农村市场、车用燃油等领域侵权假冒犯罪的打击工作，共开展联合行动275次，破获互联网领域侵权假冒案件2宗、查处违规网站1个，破获农村市场和车用燃油领域侵权假冒案件52宗、捣毁窝点6个、刑拘99人，有效打击侵权假冒犯罪。

司法保护。惠州市检察机关履行批捕、起诉职能，精挑骨干力量组成专门的办案组，不断加大审查逮捕、审查起诉工作力度，及时批捕、起诉一批侵犯知识产权和制售假冒伪劣商品犯罪分子。2015年已批捕相关案件164件290人，其中侵犯知识产权案件30件76人、制售假冒伪劣商品案件134件214人；起诉相关案件195件283人，其中侵犯知识产权案件80件111人，制售假冒伪劣商品案件115件172人。

惠州市两级法院共审查备案材料105件，行政执法机关向公安机关移交案件125件136人，公安机关接移交后立案侦查69件81人，监督公安机关立案侦查1件1人，批捕31件44人，起诉11件21人，有罪判决5件10人。

会展知识产权保护。2015年11月1—3日，在惠州市举行的“2015中国惠州物联网·云计算技术应用博览会”上，大会组委会设立了知识产权服务咨询点，惠州市知识产权相关部门安排执法人员进行执法检查，行动中共检查参展设备近400余件，对有专利和注册商标标识的展位与产品共30余项进行了登记备案，对专利标识不规范的企业进行了纠正，向参展商与参观人员进行知识产权知识的普及和宣传。展会中共接待知识产权服务咨询200余人次，向咨询人员发放《专利法》《商标法》《专利标识标注办法》等有关资料、宣传册近2000余份。

知识产权维权援助。中国（广东）知识产权维权援助中心惠州分中心积极开展知识产权保护培训、咨询服务和知识产权维权咨询服务，举办2期知识产权保护培训，培训60多人次，共接受现场咨询、服务交流约45人次，接听知识产权保护咨询热线60多人次、维权援助咨询电话48人次，为12家企业和个人提供了专利侵权判定及理赔咨询、维权指导意见，受理举报案件6件，协助知识产权行政管理部门调处专利侵权纠纷案件1起，为学校师生参加省、市青少年创新大赛提供知识产权法律状态查询、加强知识产权保护建议20宗。

【知识产权管理】

政策法规。2015年4月，中共惠州市委惠州市政府出台《关于实施创新驱动发展战略加快建设创新型城市的意见》，为全面实施创新驱动发展战略绘出了“路线图”、列出了“时间表”，提出了2017年建成国家知识产权示范城市。

7月，惠州市政府出台了《惠州市创新驱动发展“六大行动”实施方案》，提出了强化“数量布局、质量取胜”知识产权战略，做好专利区域布局，推进专利工作从注重数量向注重质量转变，建立财政对知识产权投入的持续增长机制，优化财政资金使用，市本级知识产权专项资金40%以上用于专利信息分析与导航、公共专利信息服务平台建设、优秀专利代理机构的培育与扶持、知识产权托管等专项运用。

惠州市知识产权局惠州市财政局联合印发了《惠州市知识产权专项资金管理办法》，惠州市知识产权局修订了《关于推进惠州市专利工作的实施意见》上报市政府审批印发，惠州市知识产权局印发了《惠州市重大经济科技活动知识产权评议管理办法》和《惠州市关于推进惠州市专利工作实施意见的操作规程补充规定》。

创建国家知识产权示范城市。2015年，惠州市第十一届人民代表大会第五次会议把创建国家知识产权示范市列入惠州市政府2015年度重点工作。惠州市政府多次召开政府常务会议研究部署创建工作。一是2015年5月惠州市政府麦教猛市长带队到国家知识产权局进行了创建示范城市专题汇报；二是加大经费投入，2015年市级知识产权专项资金预算达1700万元；三是调整惠州市知识产权局机构设置，独立设置专利执法科，增加1个科长职位；四是增加惠州市知识产权局工作人员，通过政府购买服务方式增加3名工作人员；五是在专利导航、信息分析、专利托管方面，安排专项经费，组织实施了一批项目；六是在专利代理服务业方面，建立了专利服务机构考核评价体系和优秀代理机构奖励制度，5月惠州市首家本地专利代理机构获批成立。2015年11月，惠州市已通过国家知识产权示范城市综合测试，被认定具备国家知识产权示范城市资格。

知识产权试点、示范企业。惠州市知识产权局根据企业的不同需求，开展知识产权分类指导服务，加大专利示范试点企业培育力度，培育一批国家、省、市知识产权试点示范企业。同时在知识产权优势、示范企业的基础上，组织企业参与 “企业知识产权管理规范”贯标工作，更好地助推企业创新发展。2015年，惠州亿纬锂能股份有限公司获批2015年国家知识产权优势企业，天宝电子（惠州）有限公司获批2015年广东省知识产权示范企业。惠州市知识产权局认定了4家惠州市知识产权优势企业。

企业知识产权贯标。2015年惠州市知识产权局继续推广《企业知识产权管理规范》（GB/T 29490-2013），企业知识产权管理水平得以提升。联合惠州市财政局发布《企业知识产权管理规范试点项目申报指南》，全市共有26家企业申报，经专家评审和现场考评，确定24家企业为贯标试点单位，安排专项经费支持。截至2015年底，惠州市有47家企业启动了贯标工作，其中12家进入试运行，6家提出了认证申请，2家企业通过认证。

专利电子申请。2015年，惠州市知识产权局通过宣传和培训，重点对省市知识产权试点示范企业、高新技术企业、民营科技企业和高校等单位电子申请的普及工作；同时把电子申请率作为市专利实施项目、市专利奖、市知识产权优势示范企业评选、专利资助经费等工作开展的一个重要指标参数。

开展集体商标和地理标志证明商标创建。惠州市工商行政管理局坚持“全面指导，重点帮扶”的原则，通过择优扶强，定向培育，跟踪服务，务求实效，打造具有地方优势、彰显地方特色的“农字号”名牌群，以取得集群和规模效应，推广成功运用“公司+农户+商标”经营模式的典型经验。指导符合条件的农业龙头企业和行业组织申请原产地证明商标或集体商标，引导和支持他们生产、经营证明商标农产品，对符合原产地证明商标或集体商标注册条件的农产品，加强与注册主体、农业职能机构进行沟通协调，协助做好商标注册申请的具体事宜，着力提升品牌效益。

【知识产权宣传培训】

知识产权宣传。2015年，惠州市知识产权局利用“4·26”知识产权宣传周，“中国专利周”等重大节日宣传活动，围绕“保护知识产权，促进创新发展”等主题，组织了内容丰富、形式多样的系列活动，在《惠州日报》、惠州市政府门户网站、惠州电视台开辟知识产权专栏及在《中国知识产权报》专版宣传惠州市知识产权工作；通过知识产权服务机构与学校联合创建知识产权试点示范学校，在中小学校举办知识产权讲座，在公共场所举办知识产权专题展览，针对特定人群举办专题培训，集中销毁侵权盗版产品等多渠道、多层次宣传普及知识产权知识，增强知识产权意识。各县区也结合自身实际，开展了广场咨询、专场培训等贴近实际、内容丰富的宣传活动，增强社会的知识产权保护意识。据统计，全年共向各报社媒体供稿40多篇，发表新闻信息100多条次；继续向400名骨干企业负责人、研发机构负责人、企事业单位领导、“双打”成员单位、各级党政班子领导成员赠送《中国知识产权报》。

惠州市工商行政管理局贯彻学习新《商标法》及其实施细则，推动县（区）工商行政管理局和工商行政管理分局开展商标法规的培训与宣传，充分利用“4·26”知识产权周活动，大力开展新《商标法》的学习宣传，利用广播、报纸、电视、宣传车等形式宣传新《商标法》，印制16000余份宣传手册，在“3·15国际消费者权益日”“4·26世界知识产权日”宣传活动中，向前来咨询的企业和群众免费发放。

知识产权培训。2015年，惠州市知识产权局承办了“广东省知识产权局管理干部研修班”；惠州市继续在惠州学院广东省知识产权培训基地开展知识产权双学位人才培养；与国家知识产权局专利局专利审查协作广东中心、广州奥凯信息咨询有限公司等机构合作举办了“企业高管知识产权培训班”“出口产品知识产权风险防控与纠纷应对策略培训班”“知识产权项目管理培训班”“惠州市WIPS Global专利数据库实战培训班”等10多场专题培训班，培训知识产权工作者1800多人次。在国家知识产权局的指导下，举办了惠州市专利布局与挖掘实战培训班，国家知识产权局选派4位专家现场授课辅导，针对专利挖掘务实、专利布局、专利分级、技术交底撰写、现有技术检索技巧、专利申请文件撰写、审查意见答复技巧等内容进行了手把手教学。

惠州市工商行政管理局与惠州市商标协会联合举办培育驰名、著名商标重点企业调研座谈会5次，参加人员达200人次，通过座谈会听取培育企业在争创驰名商标过程中遇到的问题、困难、需求和建议，帮助企业分析原因，寻找对策，鼓励企业积极争创品牌商标，按照培育商标企业一户一档的要求，逐步建立商标培育企业档案，掌握企业基本资料，及时了解申报工作进度情况。

【统计资料】

2015年惠州市县区专利申请和PCT专利申请统计表

单位：件

县区	发明	实用新型	外观设计	合计	2014年合计	同比增长	PCT申请
惠城区	993	1504	2585	5082	4209	20.7%	13
惠阳区	399	686	1910	2995	2534	18.2%	4
博罗县	382	642	2234	3258	2778	17.3%	9
惠东县	118	170	1426	1714	1513	13.3%	0
龙门县	83	170	163	416	321	29.6%	1
大亚湾区	289	689	461	1439	1119	28.6%	1
仲恺高新区	2336	2128	2038	6502	5882	10.5%	146
校正值	0	2	0	2	3		0
合计	4600	5991	10817	21408	18359	16.61%	174

2015年惠州市县区专利授权和有效发明统计表

单位：件

县区	发明	实用新型	外观设计	合计	2014年合计	同比增长	有效发明
惠城区	195	895	616	1706	1547	10.3%	704
惠阳区	57	418	881	1356	1006	34.8%	213
博罗县	43	548	1211	1802	527	241.9%	199
惠东县	15	203	566	784	559	40.3%	51
龙门县	22	102	94	218	103	111.7%	28
大亚湾区	40	613	151	804	630	27.6%	102
仲恺高新区	494	1853	778	3125	3023	3.4%	1202
校正值	2	0	0	2	1		1
合计	868	4632	4297	9797	7396	32.5%	2500

（供稿人：纪智敏）

汕 尾 市

【知识产权创造】 2015年，汕尾市专利申请量928件，同比增长56%，其中发明101件，实用新型340件，外观487件；专利授权量652件，同比增长42%，其中发明49件，实用新型153件，外观450件。商标注册新增400多件，累计注册商标达16000件。

【知识产权保护】 汕尾市知识产权局联合汕尾市公安、工商、文广新、质监和汕尾海关有关部门，开展“知识产权宣传周”联合执法和“雷雨”“天网”专项执法行动，重点对大型超市、百货商场等经营日常用品、食品、药品、烟酒、音像制品进行检查，对侵权假冒和伪劣商品进行查处。4月“知识产权宣传周”和6月在县（市、区）开展的专项执法行动中，执法队伍依法检查各类商品、药品300多件，查处涉嫌假冒专利案件8宗，并全部结案。

汕尾市工商行政管理局2015年立案查处侵权和假冒伪劣商品案件总数41宗，案值37.5万元，罚没金额38万元。其中查处商标侵权假冒案件39宗，案值29.23万元，案件罚没金额36万元（查处侵犯驰名商标权益案件7宗，案值2.77万元，案件罚没4.5万元；查处侵犯涉外商标专用权案件17宗，案值20.24万元，案件罚没20.70万元）；查处假冒伪劣商品案件2宗，案值8.27万元，案件罚没2万元。

汕尾市文化广电新闻出版局2015年出动文化行政执法人员7713人次，检查文化经营单位5453家次，立案调查32宗，已办结案件32宗（其中市大队办结案件21宗），责令整改32家，停业整顿8家，收缴非法出版物650册，非法音像制品597张，依法取缔兜售各类非法出版物地摊11家，有效打击文化市场违法违规经营行为，确保文化市场健康稳定发展。

【知识产权管理】 2015年汕尾市奖励汕尾展辉实业有限公司发明专利实施奖励项目（一种改性塑钢共聚物复合板材）一项，奖金10万元；资助汕尾市柏林电子有限公司专利申请费用减缓4件；海丰县圣洁木艺实业有限公司向国家知识产权局专利局提出专利费用减缓请求6件，汕尾市知识产权局为海丰县圣洁木艺实业有限公司开具费减证明6份。

【知识产权交流与合作】 2015年9月18日，以“知识产权部门在实施创新驱动发展战略中如何发挥作用”为主题的粤东第十四次知识产权局长联席会议在汕尾市召开。来自汕头、潮州、揭阳、梅州、河源、惠州、汕尾七市的代表出席了会议。广东省知识产权局副局长袁有楼应邀到会并作重要讲话，对粤东各市所取得的成效予以充分肯定，要求粤东各市知识产权管理部门一定要适应新的形势发展要求，紧紧围绕创新驱动发展战略的主题，在知识产权的创造、运用、保护和管理等工作中大胆探索，求新求特，结合各地实际，创造出具有鲜明地方特色的知识产权工作新经验。

【宣传培训】 2015年4月22日，汕尾市知识产权局联合市工商、文广新局、汕尾海关相关单位，出动工作人员20人次，在汕尾市区通港路开展主题为“建设知识产权强国，支撑创新驱动发展”的宣传咨询活动。活动现场派发《知识产权ABC》宣传册子、海关知识产权宣传册子、知识产权法规读物、报刊500多份，接受群众咨询200多人次，现场解答群众有关专利、商标、版权和进出口贸易等知识产权相关的问题，汕尾电视台对此次活动进行了报道。

汕尾市工商行政管理局开展2015年知识产权宣传活动，悬挂横幅、张贴标语32条，出动宣传车辆56车次，发放宣传资料860多份。

（供稿人：袁劭翊）

东莞市

【概况】 2015年，东莞市围绕“争创广东知识产权强省建设先行市”核心目标，高标准建设国家知识产权示范城市，2014年度示范城市工作考核结果名列全国地级市第八名，被国家知识产权局评为2014年度国家知识产权示范城市工作先进集体；被国家版权局评为“全国版权示范城市”；松山湖（生态园）被认定为国家知识产权试点园区；虎门镇、长安镇分别获全国服装、五金模具知名品牌创建示范区称号；东莞市版权协会正式在松山湖成立。

【知识产权创造】 2015年，东莞市专利申请量38094件，专利授权量26820件，均位居全省第四；发明专利申请量11166件，同比增长61.55%，占专利申请总量的比例达29.31%，位居全省第四；发明专利授权量2795件，同比增长72.11%，位居全省第三；PCT国际专利申请量299件，位居全省第三；截至2015年12月，有效发明专利量7890件，比2014年底新增2464件，有效发明专利量排名全省第三位。全市新增驰名商标7件，累计达69件，著名商标

283件，新注册商标2.4万件，同比增长51%，累计有效商标12.4万件，同比增长28%。开展国家专利奖、广东省专利奖推荐和市专利奖评选工作，共有2个项目获得第十七届中国专利奖，6个项目获得2015年广东省专利奖；评选出2014年度东莞市专利奖30项，其中专利金奖5项，专利优秀奖25项。

【知识产权运用】

企业知识产权工作。积极组织和推荐优秀知识产权企业申报国家和省级知识产权项目，2015年，东莞市共有5家企业被认定为国家知识产权优势企业，1家企业被认定为国家知识产权示范企业，4家企业被认定为广东省知识产权示范企业，1家企业获省知识产权管理规范推进项目立项。积极开展东莞市专利优势企业认定工作，30家企业被认定为2015年度东莞市专利优势企业。

企业贯标工作。东莞市共有15家企业通过《企业知识产权管理规范》（GB/T 29490-2013）认证，在全省排名第一。此外，有6家企业已提交认证申请等待评审，37家企业正在国标贯标辅导期。2015年，东莞市对2015年8月30日前获贯标认证的10家企业给予每家10万元资助，共资助100万元。举办第二期企业知识产权管理规范贯标实战培训班，共培训企业人员194名，其中培养出内审员149名。

专利质押融资及保险。2015年，东莞市与建设银行东莞分公司达成战略合作协议，共同组建科技型企业贷款风险补偿基金池，承诺未来三年向科技型企业授予知识产权质押融资额不少于5亿元的贷款。成功引入东莞邮政储蓄银行，开展专利质押融资业务的银行增加至8家。2015年，专利质押融资共发放7笔贷款，贷款额1760万元，全市纯专利质押融资累计达到1.34亿元；共有45家企业投保（其中4家续保），参保专利55项（其中续保专利8项），总保额1180万元，全市累计专利投保企业达到98家次，参保专利达到157项，总保费40多万元，总保额2000多万元。

专利导航。东莞市已完成第三代半导体专利导航项目，建成第三代半导体专利导航与创新服务平台和半导体产业专利数据库，完成导航项目分析报告。由第三代半导体专利联盟、常平镇政府以及北京大学东莞光电研究院共同成立的东莞燕园知识产权服务公司负责项目完成后的长期运营工作。东莞市工业机器人产业转型升级专利导航项目已完成专利数据的检索、去噪、深加工以及分析的工作，并形成了初步报告。2015年6月5日，东莞市成功举办工业机器人产业专利导航研讨会，来自东莞工业机器人产业的企业代表100余人共同探讨了工业机器人产业的创新规划和专利联盟建设。

专利信息运用。东莞市知识产权局联合广东省知识产权研究与发展中心向东莞市寮步、常平等5个镇街的知识产权部门和10家企业开展了专利信息推送服务。2015年，共开展了4期专利信息推送工作，合计推送专利数据近万条。2015年4月至12月在国家知识产权局的支持下，东莞市知识产权局举办了专利分析实战中级班，培养专利检索、分析运用能力强的企业知识产权中级人才20多名。

知识产权预警。2015年，东莞市工商行政管理局将19430件重点企业商标纳入了商标预警保护系统，占全市累计有效注册商标的15.65%，并积极开展商标预警保护，对“清溪”“横沥”等公共商标资源分别被四川、广东企业和个人抢注情况及时提出预警，保护公共商标资源。

【知识产权保护】

行政保护。2015年，东莞市知识产权局共受理专利侵权纠纷案件34宗，结案33宗；查处假冒专利案件2宗，当事人均积极配合调查并主动采取整改措施，上述案件未涉及处罚；全市工商系统共立案查处商标违法案件367宗，案值400.1万元，罚没414.9万元；捣毁制假窝点10个，立案查处“双打”案件547宗，其中移送公安机关7宗，涉案金额182.84万元，查处傍名牌门店47间，查扣假冒伪劣、高仿机、无合法来源手机共600台，手机配件435件，在相关新闻媒体对整治行动进行报道49次；全市文化执法机构共出动文化执法人员17万多人次，检查各类文化经营场所8万多间次；查处违规经营书店129 间次，违规经营音像店48间次，非法安装卫星电视接收用户6个；收缴翻版盗版音像制品4万多张，非法书籍12218本，非法报刊 2076份，色情淫秽光盘1994张，非法博彩类报纸7267份，电视机、VCD机、DVD机等播放设备56台/套。利用网聚平台巡查网络关键词32个、网站97012个，查处违规网站8家；处理行政处罚案件586宗，包含网络案件1宗。

刑事保护。全市公安机关立案侦查侵犯知识产权和生产、销售伪劣食品药品案件1035宗，破案797宗，刑事拘留犯罪嫌疑人1170人，逮捕957人，移送起诉928人，缴获假冒侵权商品、食品、药品和商标标识、制假机器设备一大批，价值人民币3.8亿元。

司法保护。东莞两级法院充分发挥知识产权审判职能，依法从严惩处一批犯罪分子，有力地打击和遏制侵犯知识产权和制售假冒伪劣商品犯罪行为。民事审判方面新收涉嫌侵犯著作权、商标权纠纷的民事案件共计136宗，其中涉嫌侵犯著作权纠纷案件为90宗，涉嫌侵犯商标权纠纷案件46宗，共审结涉嫌侵犯著作权、商标权纠纷的民事案件128宗，其中审结侵犯著作权纠纷的民事案件82宗，审结侵犯商标权纠纷的民事案件46宗。刑事审判方面新收涉嫌侵权知识产权犯罪案件24宗，其中非法经营罪1宗，非法制造、销售非法制造注册商标标识罪1宗，非法制造注册商标标识罪1宗，假冒注册商标罪15宗，生产、销售假药罪1宗，生产销售伪劣产品罪1宗，销售假冒注册商标的商品罪3宗。

展会保护。东莞市知识产权局共进驻4家展会开展展会专利维权工作，累计派出专家76人次，接受各类咨询268次，处理专利纠纷案件35宗，派发知识产权宣传资料900余份。

维权援助。2015年，东莞市知识产权维权援助中心通过“12345”政府服务热线受理专利类咨询工单共计37宗，来访咨询专利侵权纠纷立案流程共计68宗，通过微信平台回复各类咨询15宗，平台关注人数已达1242人。进一步探索快速维权援助机制，积极推进专利侵权判定咨询机制和专利快速调解机制的有关建设工作，完善维权援助及举报投诉转移交机制及相关工作流程。同时，进一步完善案件档案管理制度和专家库管理制度，及时更新专家库信息，为全国家具行业领域的专利行政执法案件提供专利侵权判定咨询公共服务。中国东莞（家具）知识产权快速维权援助中心积极推进知识产权快速维权工作。2015年累计受理调解侵权纠纷37宗；成功受理企业提交专利快速预审案件743宗，预审合格并提交国知局案件683宗，已获得授权668宗；协助市中院开庭审理家具侵权案件2次，审理案件5宗。

【知识产权管理】

示范城市。2015年，东莞市配合国家知识产权局完成2014年度国家知识产权示范城市的考核工作，并落实2015年度示范城市工作计划和全国专利事业发展战略推进计划实施方案，部署和开展全年各项知识产权工作。制订东莞市知识产权工作十三五规划，已完成初稿。3月24日，东莞市召开了全市科技创新大会，部署全市科技和知识产权工作。市委书记徐建华、市长袁宝成、市政协主席李毓全、市人大常委会常务副主任甄瑞潮等四套班子主要领导，市建设国家知识产权示范城市领导小组成员、市直副处以上单位和各镇街（园区）的党政主要领导等共800多人参会。省知识产权局马宪民局长应邀出席并做讲话，还对东莞市获得第十六届中国专利奖的5个项目进行了颁奖。

政策体系。东莞市知识产权局修订《东莞市专利促进项目资助办法》。东莞市版权局经市政府同意，制定并下发了《关于进一步推进东莞市版权工作的意见》，以及《东莞市版权示范单位和示范园区（基地）认定扶持办法（试行）》《东莞市优秀版权作品资助办法（试行）》和《东莞市作品著作权登记资助管理办法（试行）》等版权工作“1+3”政策文件，在明确提出版权工作“一个城市”“四个目标”具体工作任务的同时，由市财政每年安排280万元“版权专项扶持经费”，在全市认定扶持一批版权示范单位、示范园区（基地）和优秀版权作品，并对东莞市企业和个人的著作权登记进行资助。

商标（品牌）战略。东莞市工商行政管理局加强东莞市商标（品牌）战略，继续开展新《商标法》宣传和培训，在企业中普及对新《商标法》的认识，提高全社会的商标保护意识和能力。市质量技术监督管理局大力实施名牌带动战略，推动虎门、长安分获全国服装、五金模具知名品牌创建示范区，指导企业申报名牌目录及产品，推动64个产品获评2015年省名牌，指导2家企业荣获2015年省政府质量奖，占全省总数的2/9。目前东莞市有168家企业获得广东省名牌产品（工业类）195个，名牌产品数量位居全省第三。

版权兴业工程。2015年7月27日，国家版权局正式下发了《关于同意东莞市创建全国版权示范城市的批复》。围绕“创建全国版权示范城市”这一核心任务，由唯美陶瓷有限公司等东莞市具备全国影响力的版权产业龙头企业共同发起，于2015年4月成立了东莞市版权协会，并吸纳东莞市律师协会等版权服务提供单位入会，为东莞市版权产业企业提供法务咨询、企业维权、内部交流等服务。2015年，成功推荐东莞市天成动漫有限公司和东莞铭辉动漫科技有限公司获得“2014年广东省版权兴业示范基地”称号，广东艾力达动漫文化娱乐有限公司“激战奇轮”系列动漫作品获得“2014年度广东省最具价值版权产品”，全市版权优势企业和知名版权产品不断涌现。

【知识产权宣传培训】

知识产权宣传。东莞市建设国家知识产权示范城市工作领导小组各成员单位以“4·26世界知识产权日”为重点，以专题报道、举行论坛、播放宣传广告、制作户外广告、创办专栏等形式，广泛开展知识产权宣传活动，全市知识产权氛围日益浓厚。东莞市知识产权局在2015年7月31日联合商务局举办了“东莞市涉外企业知识产权宣讲会”；10月15日联合市民主建国会东莞市委会举办第九期“建华课堂——企业知识产权运用与融资”讲座；11月12日，联合东莞市机器人产业协会、广州华进联合专利商标代理有限公司举办了工业机器人产业知识产权专项培训；11月18日，联合市人大常委会举办了知识产权战略与专利法解读培训，邀请国家知识产权局专利管理司原司长、中国专利保护协会秘书长马维野就“知识产权战略与专利法解读”进行专题讲座；市工商局在东莞日报以5个版面的篇幅宣传东莞市驰名商标企业，以专刊的形式公布2014年度10大商标侵权典型案例；东莞中院评选出“东莞2014年最受媒体关注十大知识产权刑事案例”；市版权局在第七届漫博会上设立“版权服务工作站”，负责在漫博会期间版权维权、版权执法、版权法规知识宣传；市教育局将知识产权教育列入学校教育活动的内容，利用“科普知识讲座”、“知识产权宣传周”、“模拟法庭”、校园“小创作、小发明”活动、校园科技节、科普大篷车进校园活动等平台开展知识产权进学校的普法推广活动。

知识产权培训。4月至6月，东莞市知识产权局在全市开展了“知识产权到企业，服务经济镇街行”活动，组织专家宣讲团队深入各镇街（园区），根据镇街实际需求开展知识产权宣讲活动，在23个镇街（园区）共举办25场，培训企业知识产权工作人员1500多人。2015年，东莞市知识产权局举办了企业知识产权管理规范贯标实战培训班、专利布局初级实战班、专利分析初级实战班、专利分析中级实战班等4个培训班，累计培训企业和知识产权服务机构人员近400人次。市版权局举办企业软件正版化培训班，推进企业使用正版软件。市司法局先后举办了“网络知识产权及侵权之法律服务”讲座、“‘一带一路’和自贸区背景下的广东律师法治机遇”研讨会和知识产权贯标服务培训解读会，组织律师参加由一、二、三期中国涉外律师领军人才主办的“‘一带一路’与中国企业‘走出去’法律研讨会”等，不断提高东莞市法律服务人才知识产权综合实力。

【知识产权服务】

服务平台。松山湖（生态园）高新区稳步推进广东省知识产权服务业集聚发展试验区建设，成立了松山湖（生态园）广东省知识产权服务业集聚发展试验区工作领导小组和办公室；制定了松山湖（生态园）专利资助奖励办法、知识产权服务业扶持政策；引进知识产权服务机构1家和知识产权咨询服务公司5家入驻园区；举办了系列知识产权及科技创新公益讲座6场；2015年园区新增国家知识产权示范企业1家、国家知识产权优势企业3家。推动东莞市知识产权交易服务中心和运营公司建设，交易服务中心已完成工商注册、章程起草、选址及申请无编制事业单位等工作。推动建设知识产权领域信用体系，已经完成281家企业的知识产权征信评级工作，建立了企业信用台账。东莞市中级人民法院松山湖知识产权巡回法庭在松山湖图书馆、东莞理工学院、东莞中学松山湖学校举行3场公开庭审。东莞市版权协会已在松山湖（生态园）注册成立，版权服务由市版权协会积极开展。积极推动松山湖（生态园）知识产权网上服务平台建设，已经征集了3家公司的知识产权网上服务平台建设方案，目前正积极推动流程的进行，以尽快开展知识产权网上服务平台程序构建工作。

服务对接。2015年12月12日，由广东省知识产权局主办，东莞市知识产权局承办的2015年广东省知识产权服务“地市行”东莞站活动在东莞国际会展中心知识产权服务业展区成功举办，230人次企业代表参加了活动。广东省知识产权局副局长谢红，东莞市政府党组成员、松山湖（生态园）党工委书记、管委会主任殷焕明出席活动并在开幕式上致辞，省知识产权局规划发展处徐宇发处长主持开幕式。

服务机构。东莞市知识产权局新引进了3家专利代理机构，全市专利代理机构总数达到44家。

【统计资料】

2015年东莞市专利申请及授权情况

表1　2015年东莞市三种专利同比2014年同期增长情况表

		2014年	2015年	增长率
申请	发明	6913	11166	61.55%
	实用新型	11980	17567	46.64%
	外观设计	9540	9361	-1.88%
	总计	28432	38094	33.98%
授权	发明	1624	2795	72.11%
	实用新型	10585	14074	32.96%
	外观设计	8131	9951	22.38%
	总计	20340	26820	31.86%

表2 2015年东莞市五类申请人国内专利申请授权情况表

		2014年	2015年	增长率
申请	大专院校	174	259	48.85%
	个人	9818	10222	4.11%
	工矿企业	18168	27244	49.96%
	机关团体	90	137	52.22%
	科研单位	182	232	27.47%
	总计	28432	38094	33.98%
授权	大专院校	102	177	14.61%
	个人	7574	8033	−15.55%
	工矿企业	12522	18425	−6.48%
	机关团体	34	53	−8.11%
	科研单位	108	132	−1.82%
	总计	20340	26820	31.86%

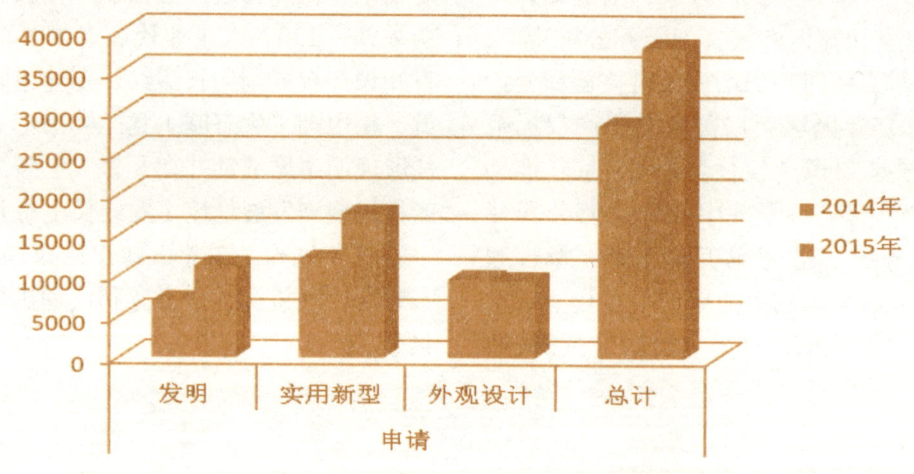

图1 2015年三种专利申请与2014年申请比较图（单位：件）

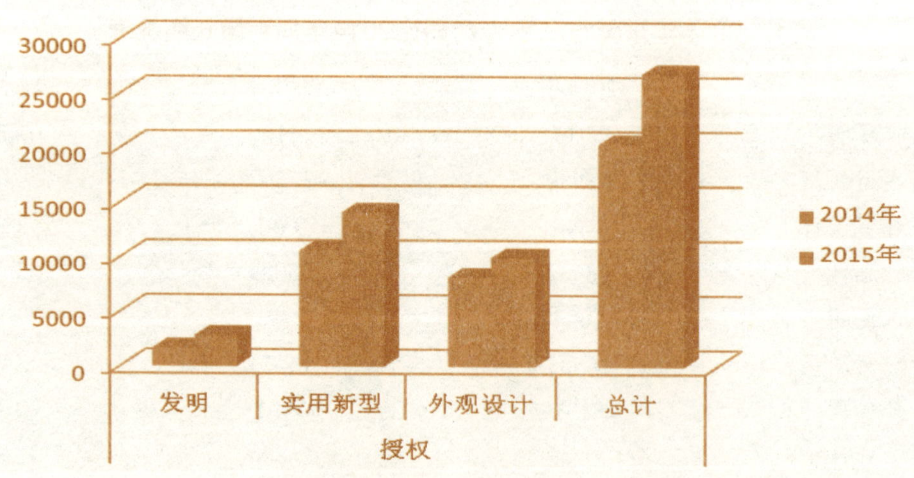

图2 2015年三种专利授权与2014年授权比较图（单位：件）

（供稿人：唐静）

中山市

【知识产权创造】 2015年，中山市专利申请量27864件，同比增长13.19%；专利授权量22198件，同比增长47.51%（其中发明专利申请量4867件，同比增长45.28%，发明专利授权量992件，同比增长为96.44%）；每百万人发明专利申请量1516件，每万人发明专利拥有量9.13件，专利结构得到进一步优化；PCT国际专利申请101件，同比增长38.36%；全市新增国家、省专利优秀奖3项、市专利金奖10项、市专利优秀奖24项，实现专利数量与质量双提升。截至2015年年底，全市注册商标76105件，拥有有效著名商标244件，新增“大洋电机”“宝宝好”“明阳电气”等，驰名商标累计达59件，新增“阿诗丹顿”“厚福”，本土品牌效应日渐显现。2015年，中山市版权登记服务中心受理版权作品登记数量达400余件，古镇快速维权中心受理版权作品登记229件，同比增长377%。

【知识产权运用】

专利导航工程。2015年，中山市围绕专业镇产业集群特色，以战略性新兴产业和传统支柱产业为重点，依托多个知识产权服务公司立项开展可穿戴式健康医疗设备、3D打印、电动汽车产业、小榄镇锁具产业集群共4个专利导航工程项目，发挥专利信息对产业研发方向、路线选择的导向作用，明晰产业竞争格局和产业发展重点，推进专利技术与产业发展深度融合。

知识产权金融。探索建立知识产权质押融资贷款风险补偿机制，研究建立知识产权质押融资风险补偿基金，起草《中山市科技企业知识产权质押融资贷款风险补偿办法》及基金运作方案；开展专利保险业务宣传培训，鼓励企业购买专利保险，2015年全年全市有5家企业92件专利购买保险，保费9.66万元，实现政府保费补贴2.898万元。

专利交易。支持两家知识产权服务机构落户在火炬开发区，为各类知识产权成果提供多样化展示交易平台和多层次融资平台，帮助企业盘活、配置、交易优质的专利技术。2015年全市实现专利交易720余件，专利交易金额超过700万元，有效促进企业、专利和资本深度融合。

专利信息分析利用。2015年，继续运用Thomson信息平台，围绕战略性新兴产业、重点行业开展专利分析和战略研究，全年共编制12期行业专利分析简报，为企业提供专利检索服务173次；利用“中国外观设计专利智能检索系统”为企业提供检索服务，实现检索与研发、检索与产品、检索与侵权诉讼的紧密对接，全年共为519家灯饰企业提供检索服务3527次。

【知识产权保护】

行政保护。

（1）专利行政执法。2015年，全市共受理专利侵权纠纷案件471宗，同比增长74%，已办结案件455宗，结案率为96.6%，成功调解案件302宗，涉及专利侵权调解金额83.44万元。查处假冒专利案件5宗，结案率100%，立案处理电子商务领域专利违法案件14宗，结案100%。共出动执法人员1794人次，检查企业、门市476家，涉及灯饰、家电、五金、家具等多个领域。举办“现场销毁侵犯知识产权产品活动”，集中销毁2011—2013年期间收缴的409件侵犯知识产权产品，涉案数439宗。协调开展“清风”行动，打击出口商品侵权假冒行为，维护“中国制造”海外形象。中山市知识产权局被国家知识产权局和公安部授予2015年度全国知识产权系统和公安机关知识产权执法工作成绩突出集体。

（2）商标行政执法。2015年，中山市工商局共查处各类商标违法案件316宗，案值284万元，其中涉外商标案件逾百宗，没收大批侵权假冒产品，涉及商标包括“GUCCI”“PRADA”

"HUGO BOSS"等奢侈品牌。先后组织开展保护"赣南脐橙""若羌红枣"地理标志和"松板"注册商标专用权的专项行动，以及农村和城乡结合部市场假冒伪劣专项整治行动、打击假冒伪劣日用品专项行动、互联网打击侵权假冒专项行动。

（3）版权行政执法。2015年，中山市版权局依法调解未经许可商业使用计算机软件版权纠纷20余宗，联合中山市工商局、经信局组成联合检查组，对上年中山市8家企业软件正版化工作情况进行复查，对3家企业下发整改通知书。协助公安部门开展侵权盗版认定工作，出具侵权盗版认定函10余份，协助执法支队开展"剑网""双打"相关版权案件执法行动等。

快速维权。一是推广中国中山（灯饰）知识产权快速维权中心建设经验，在黄圃镇设立市级跨镇区的中山市家电知识产权快速维权中心，将专利维权设在产业集聚区的"家门口"，打破行政区域限制，解决基层执法难的问题；二是在中山古镇设立全省首家远程诉讼服务处——广州知识产权法院远程诉讼服务处，通过视频接待，提供包括立案咨询、指导调解、案件查询、远程答疑、远程接访、法治宣传等在内的系列诉讼服务，突破诉讼维权地域限制；三是在中山古镇灯饰专业市场建立第四个知识产权保护示范基地，通过场内管理者与商家签订知识产权保护承诺书，以及场内设立知识产权维权援助服务工作站的方式，形成专业市场内部商家的知识产权自律机制。

展会保护。在2015年参与广交会维权工作，在春、秋两季"中国·古镇国际灯饰博览会"设立专利投诉站，进驻现场开展展会维权活动，展会期间现场快速处理了5宗涉嫌侵犯知识产权的投诉。

【知识产权管理】

国家知识产权示范城市建设。一是成立以中山市政府主要领导为组长，分管领导为副组长，知识产权相关管理部门负责人为成员的中山市建设国家知识产权示范城市工作领导小组，统筹全市知识产权工作。二是由中山市政府印发《中山市建设国家知识产权示范城市工作方案》（中府〔2015〕60号），明确未来三年全市知识产权工作目标、任务和保障措施，引导全市知识产权事业发展方向。三是加大知识产权投入。在中山市知识产权局新增3名人员专职从事知识产权工作，同时安排知识产权专项经费投入2368万元，同比增长48%，为知识产权工作开展提供了强有力的保障。

政策制度。一是启动编制全市知识产权工作"十三五"规划，已完成初稿撰写工作，为中山市未来五年谋划知识产权创造、运用、保护、管理和服务等方面的发展；二是修订并印发《中山市专利专项资金使用办法》（中科发〔2015〕96号），突出对发明专利的倾斜支持，增加发明专利年费资助、专利导航工程资助项目，提高发明专利授权、专利执法、企业知识产权贯标的资助额度，引导知识产权聚焦产业发展；三是制定《中山市2015年专利执法维权工作方案》《中山市电子商务领域专利保护工作意见》，积极推动中山市专利行政执法规范化，重点打击灯饰、家电行业电子商务领域专利侵权和假冒专利行为。

企业知识产权。通过推进企业知识产权管理规范制度建设，发掘和培育了一批具有自主知识产权和市场竞争优势的优质企业。2015年，中山市新增国家知识产权优势企业1家、省知识产权示范企业1家、通过企业知识产权管理规范国家标准认证和广东省标准认证的企业各1家、市知识产权优势企业10家；为鼓励知识产权服务机构广泛开展"百所千企"知识产权服务对接活动，对市内代理专利数量多、积极对接企事业单位及承办培训的17家知识产权服务机构进行资助，资助总额达15万元。

【知识产权宣传培训】

宣传推广。一是抓住"4·26"世界知识产权日的契机，举办了知识产权宣传周系列活动。根据市依法治市工作领导小组工作部署，组织举办“12·4”法制宣传日活动。二是开展知识产权进校园工作，培育知识产权教育试点学校，包括制作知识产权宣传栏，发放知识产权宣传册子及读本，开展知识讲座等。同时，与灯饰设计学院开展版权登记对接服务，免费为学院的作品进行版权登记。三是举办中山古镇首届创意灯饰外观设计专利评比大赛，吸引了2万多人次关注，访问量达33万次，共投票13.9万张。

人才培养。一是加大对基层专利执法人员培训，通过组织镇区专利执法人员参加知识产权管理研修班、强化跟班锻炼和挂职学习、高校研修等，实现对25个镇区专利工作人员脱产培训全覆盖；二是加强企业专业人才队伍建设，举办专利分析和布局实战培训、企业知识产权贯标培训、知识产权运营、软件正版化培训等有针对性的培训约40场次，培训人员约5000多人次，提升企业知识产权工作者综合能力。

交流与合作。举办2015灯饰行业知识产权研讨会，承办全省知识产权维权援助工作研讨会，2015年内地与香港、澳门特别行政区知识产权研讨会，2015年珠三角地区版权工作联席会议等重要活动，与港澳、珠三角各市共同分享知识产权工作经验。

（供稿人：张梦诗）

江门市

【知识产权创造】

专利。2015年江门市专利申请9555件，同比增长14.5%，其中发明专利申请2438件，同比增长26%；专利授权6384件，同比增长15.3%，其中发明专利授权508件，同比大幅增长65.5%；江门市PCT专利申请50件，同比增长高达66.7%。

商标。2015年1月29日，江门市植保有限公司的“图形”商标、广东华艺卫浴实业有限公司的“华艺”商标等企业的10件商标被广东省商标协会认定为广东省著名商标，江门市澳新食品有限公司的“十月初五”商标、广东闽江水族实业有限公司的“闽江”商标等企业的32件商标也被延续认定为广东省著名商标。截至2015年12月底，江门市共有驰（著）名商标125件，其中驰名商标22件（行政认定）、广东省著名商标103件。

版权。2015年，江门市作品著作权自愿登记代办机构共办理作品登记19件；广东省版权兴业示范基地有4家，分别是广东亿业科技有限公司、广东色色婚纱摄影有限公司、江门市新会区古典家具行业、广东缤果集团有限公司；广东省最具价值版权产品有5件。

地理标志。2015年11月3日，新会区获国家质检总局批准成为全省首个获批国家地理标志产品保护示范区的地区。2015年共有11家企业取得新会柑、新会陈皮地理标志产品专用标志，申请使用专用标志2.2万个。示范区内地理标志产品保护专用标志规范使用率达90%，推广使用情况在省内位居前列。

【知识产权运用】

知识产权质押融资。修改完善《江门市科学技术局　江门市财政局　江门市人民政府金融工作局关于江门市科技金融专项扶持资金操作细则》，将“专利质押融资专利评估费资助”条款列入细则，对以专利权质押形成的科技贷款，按项目当年发生贷款额的4%进行贴息（比一般科技贷款高一个百分点），对实现专利质押融资的企业，按项目当年发生贷款额的1%对其专利评估费用进行资助。通过制定完善知识产权质押融资和专利评估的扶持政策，积极组织企业申报年度知识产权质押融资项目备案。2015年，备案知识产权质押贷款项目10项，贷款需求5720万元，江门市企业成功实现专利质押融资贷款1740万元，知识产权质押贷款规模和拟贴息金额较上年增长约14%。

专利运营平台。不断建设完善“中国技术交易所江门工作站”和“广东省科技金融综合服务中心江门分中心”，通过整合科技支行、担保、小贷、创投、股权交易等科技金融资源，实现科技资源和金融资源的对接和共享，为科技企业提供一站式、个性化服务，加速科技成果和专利技术转化及产业化。

【知识产权保护】

行政保护。

（1）专利行政执法。2015年共调处专利侵权纠纷案件8件，通过开展箱包皮具打假专项行动、互联网领域专利侵权假冒专项治理、农村和城乡结合部侵权假冒专项整治、查处假冒专利集中行动月等一系列的专项行动，打击严重的假冒专利违法行为，在行动中核查经营单位40余家，查处案件6件。

（2）商标行政执法。2015年江门市工商系统共立案查处商标侵权案件162件，案值149.35万元，切实保护了商标专用权人和消费者的合法权益。

（3）海关行政执法。江门海关全年共采取知识产权海关保护措施28批次，货值417.5万元，货物数量975万件；立案6宗，案值129.4万元，涉案货物120.6万件；依法将总值16.74万元的120万件侵权货物移交省红十字会用于社会公益事业。

司法保护。2015年，江门两级法院共受理知识产权案694件，审结378件，结案率为54%。中级法院收案157件，审结119件，19件中止。结案率为75.6%。一是继续推进知识产权“三合一”审理工作，进一步统一知识产权民事、行政、刑事案件的诉讼程序、证据规则以及裁判标准，确保两法顺利衔接。市中级法院由民三庭统一负责“三合一”审理，共审结知识产权民事、行政、刑事案件119件。二是加强对注册商标专用权的保护力度，依法审理涉及美的、惠普、雅马哈、丽宫陈皮月饼等知名商标的侵权案件，及时制止了商标侵权行为。三是加强对假冒伪劣产品和假冒注册商标的打击力度，依法追究4名被告人的刑事责任。四是加大知识产权调解工作力度，妥善调解中国中铁股份有限公司“江门大道BT工程第四标段工程”侵犯发明专利权纠纷三案，确保了江门大道施工的顺利进程。

知识产权维权援助。江门市成立了省知识产权维权援助中心江门分中心，深入了解企业维权存在的问题，开展知识产权法律法规、保护程序等咨询，强化涉外维权指导，通过各种形式的维权援助切实维护权利人的合法权益。2015年，在五邑大学成立了江门市首支“保护知识产权志愿者服务队”，利用高校资源，强化知识产权文化建设，推进维权工作。

【知识产权管理】

政策体系。2015年，江门市结合《中共江门市委 江门市人民政府关于实施创新驱动发展战略加快创新型城市建设的意见》，印发了《江门市创建国家知识产权试点城市2015年度推进计划》和《2015年江门专利事业发展推进计划》，在知识产权运用和提高专利对促进经济发展上取得新突破，全面推动江门知识产权事业发展。2015年10月，江门市结合小微“双创”工作，出台了“1+15”政策（即1个政策总纲《江门市支持小微企业创业创新若干政策措施》和15个扶持政策和管理办法），其中《江门市知识产权局科技型小微企业专利创造扶持办法》在对科技型小微企业、专利服务机构和加强政府服务等方面加大工作力度，推动科技型小微企业的创新发展。

企业知识产权。积极组织骨干企业申报各级各类知识产权项目，以项目导向引导企业加强实施知识产权战略。为提升专利推动产业融合发展和加速创新的作用，江门市向省知识产权局申报江门市轨道交通产业专利导航等项目并获得立项，共得到228万元的资金支持；鹤山同方照明科技有限公司获得2015年广东省专利优秀奖；培育认定10家江门市级知识产权示范企业。

企业知识产权管理规范。通过实施企业知识产权管理规范推进项目，努力提高企业管理和运用知识产权水平，发挥贯标对促进企业实施专利战略的作用。2015年确定了天地壹号为江门市贯彻企业知识产权管理规范试点单位，目前已确定两批江门市贯彻企业知识产权管理规范试点单位，无限极等4家企业正开展贯标辅导工作。其中广明源光科技股份有限公司已经进行《企业知识产权管理规范》管理体系认证外审，这是江门市首家申请外审认证的企业，有望实现江门市“国标”认证零的突破。同时积极推动瑞荣、长优、同方照明等企业开展“贯标”工作，不断扩大参与贯标工作的企业群。通过开展贯标工作，对全市企业贯彻《企业知识产权管理规范》国家标准起到示范引领作用。

（供稿人：黄学敏）

阳 江 市

【知识产权创造】 2015年，阳江市专利申请量1724件，其中发明专利76件。专利授权量1437件。全市有效注册商标累计10254件。著名商标52件，驰名商标3件，地理标志证明商标2件。

【知识产权运用】 2015年，被认定为省级知识产权示范企业1家，被认定市级知识产权优势企业2家，扶持2项市级专利技术实施计划项目、3项专利孵化培育计划项目。

【知识产权保护】

行政保护。

（1）专利行政执法。2015年共受理专利侵权案件32宗，其中涉外案件7宗，电子商务案件1宗，会展案件3宗；共立假冒专利案件11宗。全部已结案。

（2）商标行政执法。阳江市工商局在全系统开展“双打”专项行动，严厉打击侵犯商标权利违法行为，开展了车用燃油专项整治、农村和城乡结合部市场假冒假劣、“赣南脐橙”注册商标专用权等专项执法行动。2015年，全市工商系统共查处商标违法案件51宗，罚款45.53万元，没收销毁侵权商品标识4646件。

（3）版权行政执法。2015年，阳江市文化广播新闻出版局（阳江市版权局）开展执法检查，共出动执法人员7922人次，检查文化经营场所2156家次，巡查网站56家次，开展文化市场联合执法检查7次，立案查处7宗，行政罚款4.4万元，收缴非法出版物800多册（张）。

执法能力建设。阳江市知识产权局选派10名工作人员参加阳江市法制局专利执法培训班，考取了行政执法证，统一了执法着装，并支持县区知识产权管理部门购置了一批专利行政执法设备，整体提高全市专利行政执法水平。

知识产权执法试点。根据《广东省专利条例》第五条第一款“县级以上人民政府专利行政部门负责本行政区域内的专利保护和管理工作”的规定，阳江市知识产权局在2014年将阳东区知识产权局列为首批专利行政执法试点单位基础上，2015年继续向全市推广，逐步推行由县区专利行政部门负责辖区内的专利行政执法工作。

“双打”专项行动。阳江市“双打”办（设在阳江市知识产权局）牵头组织公安、检察、法院、经信、工商、文广新、质监、药监、卫生、农业、林业、商务、物价、海关、烟草等部门开展联合打击行动、燃油专项打假行动、“清风”行动，出动执法人员8201人次，检查各类经营场所5632家次，查处各类违法案件331宗，涉案金额4118万元，接待咨询人员182人次，派发宣传资料13500份。

展会知识产权保护。2015年10月20—23日，第14届中国（阳江）国际五金刀剪博览会在阳江国际五金刀剪商贸城举办。阳江市知识产权局联合阳江市五金刀剪产业知识产权快速维权中心、各县区知识产权局，组织了18名执法人员进驻会场，设立知识产权投诉摊位。开展巡查、宣传和接受投诉处理等知识产权保护工作，发放《专利法》《广东省专利条例》

《广东省展会专利保护条例》等宣传资料近1000份，接受参展商及群众咨询200多人次，调处会展案件3宗。

专利快速维权服务平台。2015年8月，“阳江市五金刀剪产业知识产权快速维权中心”挂牌成立。2015年10月，经广东省知识产权维权援助中心同意在阳江市五金刀剪产业知识产权快速维权中心设立“广东省知识产权维权援助中心阳江分中心”。初步建成一个适合地方产业特色的知识产权多功能一站式服务平台。

【知识产权管理】

知识产权政策。2015年，阳江市印发《2015年实施阳江市知识产权战略纲要工作方案》，重新修订《阳江市知识产权局行政处罚自由裁量量化标准》和《阳江市专利申请费用资助暂行办法》，完善知识产权的工作机制，营造有利于知识产权发展的政策环境。

商标品牌培育。阳江市工商局以实施商标战略作为切入点，深入企业走访调研，指导企业规范管理使用商标，动员企业争创著名商标、驰名商标，形成商标品牌培育梯队。深入乡镇调研特色农产品商标培育工作，推动商标富农工作。2015年，先后走访信得安珠宝、乔士服装、恒力刀剪等多家企业，深入乡镇指导“双滘沙姜”“程村蚝”等地理标志商标培育。

【知识产权宣传培训】

知识产权宣传。2015年，阳江市知识产权局坚持日常宣传与专项宣传、普及宣传与重点宣传相结合，举办了“4·26”知识产权宣传周、中国专利周、知识产权进校园活动。通过网站、报刊等媒体，多形式、多渠道、多角度宣传知识产权知识和法律法规政策。在全市范围内开展宣传活动6场次，派发宣传资料10000多份，刊登知识产权专题特刊1期，发布知识产权政务信息20多篇。

2015年，阳江市工商局依托“3·15”“4·26”宣传日，在阳江电视台、电台分时段播出66条次商标宣传标语，在阳江日报开辟1期宣传专题专栏和刊登1篇商标调研文章，微博发布宣传知识16条次，向全市手机用户发布宣传提示，在主要道路户外电子显示屏播放标语2300多条次，分发宣传资料2700多份，接受咨询220余人次。

知识产权培训。2015年，阳江市知识产权局邀请了广东省知识产权局、广东省知识产权研究会和华南理工大学的专家先后举办了5场次知识产权培训讲座，累计培训相关人员1000多人次。

企业贯标。2015年，阳江市知识产权局印发了《关于推行企业知识产权管理规范工作的通知》（阳知通〔2015〕4号），发动了3家企业报名参加广东省知识产权局举办的企业知识产权管理规范培训班，扶持了4项企业知识产权管理规范实施项目，逐步推动《企业知识产权管理规范》（GB/T29490-2013）国家标准在本地企业的贯彻实施。

（供稿人：梁耀辉）

湛江市

【概况】 2015年，湛江市围绕“南方海谷”建设，以创建国家知识产权试点城市为抓手，在知识产权政策、投入、专利申请（授权）量、专利奖（国家、省）和知识产权机构设置上实现了突破。经批准增设知识产权政策法规科（执法科）；重新修订《湛江市科学技术局（知识产权局）专利资助办法》（湛知〔2014〕20号）并于2015年1月1日起正式实施；在知识产权计划项目中单列专利技术转化产业化项目12项，投入项目资金240万元。

【知识产权创造】 2015年，湛江市专利申请受理量3235件，同比增长54.42%，授权量2486件，同比增长92.12%，PCT申请总量6

件；广东诺科冷暖设备有限公司获评广东省专利优秀奖。

【知识产权管理】 2015年，湛江市政府出台《湛江市人民政府关于加快科技创新的若干政策意见》，其中规定：对获得国家专利金奖和专利优秀奖的项目，分别给予奖励50万元和30万元；对获得省专利金奖和专利优秀奖的项目，分别给予奖励20万元和10万元；对获得《企业知识产权管理规范》认证的企业给予奖励8万元；对获得国家级和省级知识产权示范企业，分别给予奖励20万元和10万元。2015年湛江市共资助专利申请1524件。在年度财政资金科技专项竞争性分配项目中单列了“创建国家知识产权试点城市”计划专项，其中设立12个专利技术产业化示范项目，扶持经费240万元；设立4个知识产权培训基地和服务机构建设项目。专项经费共计280万元。开展“湛江市专利奖”评选活动，2015年评出金奖6名，优秀奖18名，同时对获奖的专利产业化后税利达到500万元和1000万元的再另外奖励10万至20万元，奖金总额达96万元。

【知识产权保护】 2015年经批准，在湛江市知识产权局增设知识产权政策法规科（执法科），强化执法力量。湛江市知识产权局发挥湛江市打击侵犯知识产权和制售假冒伪劣商品工作领导小组作用，组织开展联合宣传、执法活动，部署开展“两建”“清风行动”和知识产权执法维权“护航”等专项行动。2015年由湛江市知识产权局牵头，联合市工商、公安、海关等成员单位开展专项行动，查处、移送、审结了一批知识产权案件，直接立案、查处专利侵权假冒案件12宗（侵权案件8宗，假冒案件4宗），办结率100%。

【知识产权宣传培训】 2015年，联合宣传、工商、版权、公安、质监、海关等部门，利用“3·15”保护消费者权益日、“4·26”世界知识产权日、“5·15”全国打击和防范经济犯罪宣传日、“12·4”全国法制宣传日，通过悬挂横额、出版墙报、组织知识产权活动一条街、派发知识产权宣传资料、开展行政执法等活动开展宣传。在《湛江日报》、《湛江晚报》、湛江人民广播电台、湛江电视台及《图读湛江》、市政府官方微博等媒介上，专题报道知识产权知识、专利资助、知识产权政策、知识产权相关信息。组织并指导了部分县（市、区）知识产权局、广东海洋大学和岭南师范学院开展培训，共培训企业负责人、科研人员、管理人员、老师学生等2000多人次。翻印《中华人民共和国专利法》《广东省专利条例》上万册并向社会发放。2015年6月5日，湛江市知识产权局与宝山钢铁股份有限公司科技发展部知识产权室开展对接活动。

专利设计大赛。2015年，围绕湛江市“六大产业链”，突出“南方海谷”的设计主题，由湛江市知识产权局主办，联合岭南师范学院、广东海洋大学，开展了以“新思维、新创意”“蓝色概念”等为设计主题的大学生外观设计大赛活动。湛江市对优秀设计作品进行奖励并全额资助申请国家专利。

2015年10月13日，由国家海洋局宣教中心、广东省科技厅指导，由湛江市人民政府主办的2015首届中国（湛江）“南方海谷杯”海洋科技创新创业大赛正式启动。宣讲会首先从广东海洋大学开始，其后在湛江、深圳、上海、青岛的大学、创客中心和海洋协会相继举办了20多场宣讲会和4场大型创赛训练营，共有2000多人接受了大赛组委会专业讲师的创新创业训练，共461个项目参赛。

2015年，湛江市知识产权局与湛江市旅游局联合开展旅游纪念品（商品）设计大赛活动。对参赛的优秀设计作品，湛江市知识产权局全部资助申报国家专利，并在湛江召开的“中国海洋经济博览会”上进行实物展示和多媒体演示。

交流合作。2015年10月，成功举办了第十二届闽粤沿海十二城市保护知识产权工作联席会议，开展专利执法跨省、跨区域交流与合作，共同探讨跨区域的专利执法协作。12月15—17日，参加在茂名举办的粤西四市专利行政执法合作联席会议。

【统计资料】

表1　2015年湛江市三种类型专利申请同比增长情况

单位：件

	2015年	2014年	同比增长
发明	495	343	44.31%
实用新型	1303	721	80.72%
外观设计	1437	1031	39.38%
合计	3235	2095	54.42%

表2　2015年湛江市三种类型专利授权同比增长情况

单位：件

	2015年	2014年	同比增长
发明	144	115	25.22%
实用新型	947	547	73.13%
外观设计	1395	632	120.73%
合计	2486	1294	92.12%

表3　2015年湛江市五种专利申请人申请专利同比增长情况

单位：件

	2015年	2014年	增长率
个人	1714	1240	38.23%
大专院校	872	325	168.31%
科研机构	118	123	-4.07%
企业	502	386	30.05%
机关团体	29	21	38.10%
合计	3235	2095	54.42%

2015年湛江市五种专利申请人专利授权同比增长情况

单位：件

	2015年	2014年	增长率
个人	1262	737	71.23%
大专院校	614	96	539.58%
科研机构	97	88	10.23%
企业	413	314	31.53%
机关团体	100	59	69.49%
合计	2486	1294	92.12%

（供稿人：戴辰）

茂名市

【知识产权创造】　2015年，茂名市专利申请受理3538件，连续四年列粤西第一位，同比增长32.56%，增幅列粤东西北第三位，其中发明专利650件，增长率71.96%，增幅列全省第三位；全市专利授权量1991件，同比增长68.87%，增幅列全省第三位，其中发明专利授权128件，同比增长141.51%，增长率名列全省第三位。

全市共有有效注册商标18700件，中国驰名商标1件，广东省著名商标50件，地理标志证明商标5件。

【知识产权保护】

专利保护。茂名市印发《茂名市专利行政执法专项行动实施方案》。茂名市知识产权系统从2015年6月23日至7月22日，开展了为期一个月的查处假冒专利专项行动，集中查处、严厉打击假冒专利违法行为，规范全市专利标识标注行为，营造健康有序的市场经济环境。2015年10月，省、市两级知识产权局在茂名联合开展了专利行政执法检查活动。12月，茂名市举办第八届粤西四市专利行政执法合作联席会议。来自湛江、阳江、云浮、茂名四市知识产权局的领导及相关科室业务骨干共20多人参加了此次会议，四市共同探讨知识产权行政执法问题，加强区域专利行政执法协作。2015年全市开展专利联合行政执法50余次，立案处理假冒专利案件5件。

商标保护。2015年，茂名市工商部门以“食品、民生、高危、重害”案件作为重点打击对象，加强对食品、农资、建筑材料、汽车配件等行业的执法检查，加强对涉外商标、驰名商标、地理标志的侵权假冒行为、仿冒知名商品特有名称、包装、装潢等不正当竞争行为的执法力度。全市共立案查处商标侵权、不正当竞争和制售假冒伪劣商品各类案件98件，案值119.4万元，罚款42.84万元，移送公安机关1件；没收、销毁侵权商品3111件，没收、销毁侵权商标标识4149件。

版权保护。2015年茂名市组织开展了打击网络侵权盗版“剑网2015”专项行动。专项行动期间，先后出动执法人员918人次，检查网络经营单位、网吧630家次，处置各类有害、低俗信息16000多条，关停违法微博账号5个、微博话题3个、属地微信公众号15个。开展出版物市场整治行动。以火车站、汽车站、文化广场、批发市场等出版物主要集散地为重点区域，对游商、地摊兜售非法出版物进行治理和查处；全面检查校园周边门店，严厉查处盗版教材教辅、有害卡通画册和淫秽色情“口袋本”等读物，净化校园周边文化环境，切实保护未成年人的合法权益。坚决打击政治性非法出版物和有害信息，严肃查处侵权盗版活动。集中整治音像市场。全面清理有证经营场所，发现盗版压缩音像制品全部收缴，对销售黄色、淫秽光盘的给予坚决打击。

【知识产权管理】

知识产权政策。2015年茂名市出台了《2015年关于激励专利申请的通知》、《茂名市知识产权系统专利执法专项行动实施方案》等一系列政策措施，把知识产权工作作为各级政府的一项重点工作，不断加大领导和政策引导推动力度。

国家知识产权试点城市。2015年是茂名市开展国家知识产权试点城市建设的第一年，茂名市按照国家知识产权试点城市建设的要求，扎实推进试点城市建设。2015年4月15日首次召开了全市知识产权工作会议暨推进国家知识产权试点城市建设动员会，对全市知识产权工作和国家知识产权试点城市建设工作进行了部署和安排。成立茂名市创建国家知识产权试点城市工作领导小组，出台《茂名市创建国家知识产权试点城市工作方案》和责任分工安排。按任务和计划进度推进创建国家知识产权试点城市各项工作。

企业知识产权工作。依据《茂名市知识产权优势、示范企业认定管理办法（试行）》，印发了《关于组织申报2015年度市知识产权优势、示范企业的通知》，组织申报、认定2015年茂名市知识产权示范企业9家，优势企业15家。截至2015年底，全市拥有省知识产权优势企业9家，市知识产权优势企业30家，示范企业20家。茂名市企业专利申请授权量占全市60%以上，逐步体现企业创新主体地位。

“百所千企”对接。茂名市分别于2015年1月、11月举办了两次“茂名市百所千企知识产权服务对接系列活动”，共有18家省内知名专利代理机构资深专家，130多家企业及高校、科研院所代表180多人参加活动，为服务机构与企事业单位搭建联系桥梁。

商标管理。实施商标带动战略，为企业提供帮扶指导。组织人员对2015年符合省著名商标申报条件的6家企业，申请延续的14家企业进行实地考查，形成监管意见，连同申请材料按时报送省著名商标评审委员会，并做好跟踪服务，确保申请成功率。对市政府交办的“粤西农批”申请商标注册的有关问题，提出了《关于对注册“粤西农批”商标相关问题的建议》。指导茂名市电白区羊角镇奇味花生食品厂对被异议的“口然香”商标进行答辩，并成功获得商标注册。针对茂名市企业商标被他人恶意抢注的情况，指导广东粮丰园食品有限公司向商标局申请恶意抢注的“羊角粮丰园”商标无效，并成功注册了“粮丰园之月”“粮丰园月”“刘仕粮丰园”“粮丰源”等10多件商标，使该企业多年创下的商标品牌得到了有效保护。指导茂名市驰（著）名商标企业和大型龙头企业在“一带一路”沿线国家及世界上的重要国家和地区注册商标。为化州化橘红药材发展有限公司联系有丰富境外商标注册经验的商标代理机构提供相关业务咨询，支持企业提前布局，实施走出去战略。

地理标志证明商标。2015年“高州荔枝”“化橘红”“化州橘红”地理标志证明商标获得注册，截至年末，茂名市已有地理标志证明商标5件。

【知识产权宣传培训】

知识产权宣传。制作专门宣传片，利用手机短信、“科技信息网”门户网站、《茂名日报》、茂名电视台、茂名电台等各类媒体进行广泛宣传，尤其是“知识产权宣传周”、第九届中国专利周活动期间，利用电视、广播和网站开展密集宣传。在全市范围内举办各种形式的培训班，包括 “企业专利信息利用培训班”“专利电子申请培训班”“粤西片区专利行政执法培训班”“全省专利信息推送及知识产权贯标服务推送活动（茂名站）”“知识产权维权援助培训班”。

开展“商标带动战略宣传月”活动，通过新闻媒体、户外、宣传车、印发商标知识小册子、设置商标专栏以及举办商标带动战略座谈会等形式，向广大经营者、消费者广泛开展商标法律法规宣传，提高全民商标意识。同时通过上门指导及即时通讯工具等方式指导企业申请商标注册，协助企业解决在申请过程中遇到的问题，指导企业加强对注册商标的使用和管理，运用商标策略开拓市场，提高品牌竞争力。

在“保护著作权宣传周”活动、“剑网2015”专项行动期间，茂名市利用报纸、广播、电视等传统媒体和新闻网站、手机报等新媒体，开展了版权知识宣传活动。

知识产权教育试点。2015年认定6家中、小学校为茂名市知识产权教育试点学校，截至年末，全市已认定中小学知识产权教育试点学校21家。

（供稿人：高鹏）

肇庆市

【知识产权创造】　2015年，肇庆市专利申请量2344件，同比增长31.61%，其中发明专利494件，实用新型1135件，外观设计715件。专利授权量1726件，同比增长19.12%，其中发明专利165件，实用新型885件，外观设计676件。PCT国际专利申请量13件。截至12月底，全市有效发明专利拥有量694件，万人发明专利拥有量1.56件；百万人口发明专利申请量120件，超额完成《珠三角规划纲要》考核指标。评出“肇庆专利奖”17项，资助发明专利申请308项。肇庆大华农生物药品有限公司的“一种病毒释放缓冲液的制备及其应用”获得广东专利奖金奖。

全市注册商标数量13652件，驰名商标16件，广东省著名商标77件，地理标志证明商标8件，集体商标1件。全市登记著作权作品420件，完成了20家企业的软件正版化工作，其中省重点督办企业8家。

【知识产权运用】　2015年，肇庆市知识产权局积极开展专利运营试点工作，探索专利成果转化运用的有效途径，推进知识产权运用能力提升。设立了“知识产权专项”。评出“肇庆专利奖”17项，有16个专利获得2015年“肇庆市科技计划项目”的立项，有308项专利获得资助专利申请。实施专利信息运用计划，支持企业开展专利检索，建设专利信息分析平台，支持企业、院校与服务机构联合申报或共同承担专利分析导航和专利预警项目。全市有14个项目列入省知识产权专项项目。

【知识产权保护】

专利保护。2015年，肇庆市知识产权局成为“肇庆市行政执法与刑事司法信息共享平台”“肇庆市12345投诉举报平台”上线单位，“专利举报投诉电话”全年开通，专利行政执法案件信息公开工作正常推进。跨地区、跨部门行政执法协作机制、两法衔接工作机制、专利预警机制正在进一步制订和完善。首个“知识产权维权援助工作站”在高要区建成并运作。市知识产权局还组织人员参加了“2015年春节期间应节商品集中联合打假执法”“全省知识产权局系统查处假冒专利集中行动月”“第117届广交会知识产权执法维权工作”“肇庆市10部门联合开展打击和防范经济犯罪宣传”等执法行动和宣传活动。2015年立案处理假冒专利案件2件，结案2件；立案处理侵权案件8件，结案8件。

商标保护。肇庆市工商局大力查处商标侵权案件，开展保护注册商标专用权行动，打击商标侵权行为。一是以“食品、民生、高危、重害”案件作为重点，查处仿冒他人知名商品特有名称、包装装潢等假冒侵权行为。2015年全市共查处双打案件64宗，案值60多万元，其中移送司法机关案件3宗，案值30万元。二是开展保护地理标志商标专用权专项行动。三是开展打击互联网领域商标侵权行动，积极探索网络交易市场监管方式和长效机制，推动行业自律。四是重点开展中国制造海外形象维护“清风”行动，对出口到非洲、阿拉伯、拉美和“一带一路”沿线国家和地区的重点商品及领域进行梳理，加强对生产、流通源头监管。五是组织开展打假专项行动，开展汽车配件、箱包皮具、农资、建材、日用品、卷烟等重点行业整治及专项打假行动。

版权保护。肇庆市版权局加大对版权保护工作的检查监督和执法力度，继续开展打击网络侵权盗版“剑网行动”。2015年，市版权局查办了一宗学校发行盗版教辅案，没收侵权盗版教辅书籍744本，并对该学校罚款人民币8万元。

【知识产权管理与服务】

专利。2015年，肇庆市知识产权局建立和完善知识产权举报投诉、维权援助、“两法”衔接、联合执法等制度和机制，进一步优化管理和服务工作。一是推动企业贯彻实施GB/T 29490-2013《企业知识产权管理规范》和DB44/T797-2010《创新知识企业知识产权管理通用规范》。二是企业管理创新取得新进展。高新区的广东玛西尔电动科技有限公司与辅导服务机构正式签订了贯彻GB/T 29490-2013《企业知识产权管理规范》的合作协议。三是配合省知识产权局创建知识产权服务业发展示范省，肇庆市成功引进深圳市合道英联专利事务所在肇庆市设立分所，为全市企业专利申请、商标注册和版权备案等提供咨询和服务。四是实施“微创新+微创业”计划，推动大学科技园、企业孵化器内的创新创业团队利用获得的智慧成果进行创业。五是实施专利技术产业化计划。承担广东省专利技术实施计划1项，组织实施肇庆市专利技术产业化计划4项。六是2015年肇庆市“百千对接工程”的对接活动在四会市和高要区举办，有14家代理服务机构和99家企业的250多人参加对接活动。

商标。肇庆市工商局推进商标品牌战略取得良好成效。一是企业商标意识增强，注册商标数量大幅增加。2015年全市商标注册量3400多件，2015年全市注册商标总量共13652件。二是指导企业创驰名商标工作。2015年全市新增2件驰名商标，全市的驰名商标总量共16件。三是广东省著名商标评审认定工作。2015年全市有效广东省著名商标有77件，有15家企业的15件商标提交了认定申请。四是开展地理标志商标与区域经济发展专题调研，推进商标富农工程。五是切实落实政府驰（著）名商标奖励工作政策。2015年6月，市政府出台《肇庆市人民政府关于扶持与促进实体经济发展的20条政策措施的通知》，对全市2013—2014年度获驰（著）名商标的企业进行奖励。

版权。2015年，市版权局积极引导版权综合服务平台发挥创新驱动发展功能，中国端砚文化村、四会市玉雕专业镇、广宁县广绿玉步行街和广宁宝锭山实业发展有限公司的4个版权兴业示范基地获得省财政局140万元的扶持资金。肇庆市左岸动漫科技有限公司设计的《肇庆城市风景明信片》被认定为广东省最具价值版权产品奖。

软件正版化。市版权局对市直和各县级政府机关有关负责人进行政策和业务培训，增强政府机关的版权意识，大力推进企业使用正版软件工作。2015年共完成了20家企业的软件正版化工作，其中省重点督办企业8家。

国家知识产权试点城市建设　2015年，肇庆市、四会市和高要区顺利通过“2014年度国家知识产权试点城市”考核，肇庆市获考核优秀等次，四会市获考核优秀等次以及工作先进集体表扬。肇庆高新区顺利通过国家知识产权试点园区的考核验收。

【知识产权宣传培训】　市知识产权局组织人员参加了“‘科技进步活动月’启动仪式暨大型科普集市”“广东省2015年百千知识产权服务对接活动”等大型活动和在广东工商职业学院举办的《专利的挖掘与申报》专题培训班。

2015年4月17日，市版权局联合鼎湖区版权局在鼎湖实验中学举行“2015年肇庆市著作权宣传周活动启动仪式”，现场派发《版权知识笔记本》5000本，参加活动的学生在“拒绝盗版、从我做起”宣传版画上签名，共同承诺“拒绝盗版、从我做起”。

（供稿人：胡淑妍）

清　远　市

【知识产权创造】

专利。2015年，清远市专利申请受理量为1569件，其中发明专利申请受理量346件，分别同比增长77.89%和116.25%；专利授权量1017件，其中发明专利授权量110件，分别同比增长61.43%和111.54%。2015年底全市发明专利拥有量为305件。获第十七届中国专利优秀奖1项，2015年广东专利优秀奖2项。取得了专利申请数量与质量双提升。

商标。截至2015年底，清远市共有广东省著名商标47件，中国驰名商标11件，地理标志证明商标3件，累计有效注册商标8059件，比上年增加1650件，增长25.74%。2015年，清远市佳的美电子科技有限公司的“GADMEI”等4件商标被认定为广东省著名商标，广东豪美铝业股份有限公司的“HAOMEI”等6件商标被延续为广东省著名商标；清远市冠星王陶瓷有限公司的“冠星王及图”注册商标被认定为中国驰名商标。

地理标志。2015年，清远市共有15个产品获批地理标志产品保护，分别是清远鸡、清远乌鬃鹅、清新冰糖桔、英石、英德红茶、西牛麻竹笋、西牛麻竹叶、星子红葱、东陂腊味、连州溪黄草、连南无核柠檬、连南瑶山茶油、佛冈竹山粉葛、连山大米和阳山淮山。全市获批准使用国家地理标志专用标识的企业共有40个。其中，西牛麻竹笋获批准使用专用标志的企业4个；英德红茶获批准使用专业标志的企业有15个，英德红茶也被国家质检总局推荐参加中欧地理标志合作协定拟交换名单。

名牌产品。2015年，清远市4家工业企业的6个产品获得“广东省名牌产品”称号，全市共有广东省名牌产品（工业类）32个。

【知识产权保护】

行政保护。2015年清远市知识产权局完善和规范了专利行政执法程序，添置执法设备，参加省知识产权局主办的“广东省专利行政执法提高班”等执法培训班3场。同时加强专利行政执法工作力度，对药品、医疗器械、车用燃油、小家电等重点领域和义乌商贸城等商品集散地开展专利行政执法检查12次，检查商店（铺）100多家，共立案5宗，撤案1宗，已全部结案。

2015年，清远市工商局共立案侵权假冒

案件351宗，办结313宗，案值199万元，罚没金额154.93万元。同比分别下降31.17%、27.88%、2.45%、44.71%。其中，查处商标违法案件141件，案值123.69万元，罚没金额79.37万元，同比分别下降36.48%、27.41%和58.67%。

刑事保护。2015年，清远市公安机关共立侵犯知识产权犯罪案件15起，破案8起，刑事拘留18人，逮捕10人，摧毁犯罪团伙3个，捣毁生产、销售窝点8个，涉案总价值约1000多万元。

司法保护。2015年清远市两级检察院共受理知识产权审查批捕逮捕案件6件9人，批准逮捕3件5人，其中，假冒注册商标案件2件3人，销售假冒注册商标的商品案件2件2人；受理移送审查起诉案件7件16人，提起公诉案件9件27人。审查办理的案件主要涉及蓄电池、酒类、知名皮具、名牌服装、手袋等多个知识产权的创造和运用领域。

【知识产权管理】

政策制度。制定出台《中共清远市委 清远市人民政府关于加快实施创新驱动发展战略的意见》《清远市推进专利工作实施办法》和《清远高新区科技专项资金管理暂行办法》等系列政策文件。政策文件从专利代理机构培育、专利的申请和授权、企业“灭零”“倍增”“贯标”认定、专利标准制定等方面给予重点资助，进一步激发全市创新积极性。

专利技术实施计划。2015年清远市知识产权局积极推进该地专利技术产业化进程，扶持广东先导半导体材料有限公司的“LED衬底材料砷化镓 ”等5个专利项目产业化，共扶持资金85万元。

企业知识产权管理规范。推动企业贯彻“企业知识产权管理规范”，开展贯标辅导工作企业3家。积极开展知识产权优势、示范企业培育工作，广东先导稀材股份有限公司被认定为国家知识产权优势企业，广东家美陶瓷有限公司等3家企业被认定为2015年清远市知识产权优势企业。

软件正版化。2015年市版权局完成市一级企业的软件正版化工作，市属6家市一级国有企业均已完成软件正版化，共采购139套操作系统软件和130套办公软件。

【知识产权宣传】

专利宣传。2015年全市各级知识产权管理部门坚持把知识产权宣传培训与扶持培育、执法等工作相结合，通过网络、报刊、电视台及深入校园、企业等渠道开展形式多样、丰富多彩的系列宣传活动。制定了《2015年清远市“知识产权宣传周”活动方案》《第九届中国专利周清远地区活动工作方案》，在《清远日报》开设知识产权宣传周专栏3期，举办知识产权宣传培训班7期，发放知识产权宣传资料2800多份等，取得较好宣传效果，营造了尊重和保护知识产权的良好氛围。

知识产权创新创业大赛。组织清远市4个项目参加“2015年首届汇桔杯·南粤知识产权创新创业大赛”。3个项目闯进25强，2个项目闯进10强。其中，广东埃力生高新科技有限公司的“气凝胶绝热材料”项目获得大赛季军，同时还获得优秀奖和最佳人气奖；清远市精旺环保设备有限公司“氢水燃料工业应用整体解决方案”项目获得优秀奖。

商标宣传。市工商局加强新《商标法》和《商标法实施条例》的宣传和培训工作。围绕商标法律法规开展了一系列的宣传活动。通过在电视台播放节目、在报纸及网站开设专栏、举办培训班、向广大群众和经营者派发宣传资料等多种渠道开展宣传。全市共发放宣传资料9120份，悬挂新《商标法》宣传横幅40多条，共组织了4期商标相关知识培训班，宣传新《商标法》、商标业务、企业工商登记管理实务等知识，参加人员达622人。

版权宣传。市文化广电新闻出版局开展了以“人人使用正版，个个参与创建国家文明城市”为宣传主题的版权宣传周活动。2015年4月23日至24日，市版权局牵头，联合市公安局、教育局、团委、法院、总工会、文化市场综合执法大队等单位在清远职业技术学院第一饭堂门口开展现场咨询宣传活动。现场展示了一年来收缴的部分侵权盗版音像制品、非法出版物等千余张（本），向广大师生派发了2000余份有关著作权、版权登记、正版软件知识小册子，重点宣传国家知识产权法律法规和如何识别计算机软件正版与否等基本知识，增强全社会版权意识，促进清远市版权产业的发展，为青少年健康成长创造良好的社会文化氛围。

（供稿人：林成辉）

潮 州 市

【知识产权创造】 2015年潮州市专利申请量为3450件，排名居全省第十二位；授权量3303件，排名居全省第十位。

2015年潮州市共有四个企业的5项专利获第17届中国专利奖，其中发明专利2项。

潮州市版权保护登记机构2015年共受理版权保护作品自愿登记156件。

【知识产权运用】 知识产权与金融资源融合。发挥知识产权对经济发展的支撑作用。全市专利质押融资金额累计47137.26万元。

【知识产权保护】

专利执法。2015年5月和7月，潮州市知识产权局联合相关部门集中开展多场次的打击假冒专利专项行动，现场查处假冒专利行为，要求有关商场对销售专利标识不规范的商品进行下架整改，对构成假冒专利行为则进行立案处理，并对商户进行知识产权保护的宣传教育。同时积极开展专利侵权案件调处工作，加快案件处理进度。截至2015年底，已立案侵权案件14宗，结转案件16宗，经过潮州市知识产权局调解工作的积极开展，共结案14宗；仍有未结案件15宗，其中中止3宗，12宗正在调处中。假冒案件立案23宗，均已结案。

商标执法。以“食品、民生、高危、重害”案件作为重点打击对象，查处箱包皮具、烟酒、玩具、家用电器、建材、涉农消费品等领域的商标侵权、仿冒他人知名商品特有名称、包装装潢等侵权假冒行为，严查药品、医疗、食品等关系人民群众健康安全领域中的虚假违法广告，组织流通领域商品质量抽检，抓好网络市场监管，加强对第三方交易平台经营者责任义务落实的指导监督，强化对经营性网站合同格式条款的监管，严惩各种网络侵权假冒行为。根据潮州市实际，确定以潮安区的生产销售侵权卫浴洁具和饶平县非法印制假冒注册商标卷烟标识违法行为作为打击重点，认真开展专项行动。2015年共组织农村和城乡结合部市场假冒伪劣专项整治行动、车用燃油专项整治、保护地理标志商标专用权专项整治等专项行动7场次，全市工商系统共出动执法人员1939人次，出动执法车辆608车次，检查各种经营主体2105户次，检查批发零售市场、集贸市场86个次，抽检16类商品共263批次，其中成品油40批次。在对重点对象的打击中，共查处捣毁印制假冒注册商标卷烟标识窝点3个，3宗印制假冒注册商标卷烟标识均已移送公安机关。

版权执法。潮州市采取联合检查、错时检查、暗访检查等方式，全面加大对出版物市场的监管，2015年共出动执法人员789人次，检查印刷复制、音像、书报刊等文化经营单位166家次，取缔无证经营场所及游商地摊5处，收缴非法音像制品光盘300张、书报刊30本。把“双打”工作与日常专项整治部署联合起来，5—6月份开展网络文化市场专项整治、4—5月份，开展校园周边专项整治、7—8月份开展暑期专项整治；下半年开展的无证专项整治期间共取缔无证书店3宗、游商2处，收缴光盘300张、书报刊30本。

知识产权维权援助。一方面积极推进广东省知识产权维权援助中心潮州（陶瓷）分中心的规范化建设步伐，另一方面依托行业协会实现专利纠纷多元化解决机制的建立，以鼓励对行业协会会员单位专利纠纷的内部调解，先由协会组织当事双方，进行以调解为主、按协会章程处理为辅的快速维权方式，力争将侵权纠纷在协会内部自行解决，减少当事双方诉累，达到快速维权的目的。

潮州市知识产权保护协会。在潮州市知识产权局的推动下，潮州市知识产权保护协会成立大会于9月15日成功举行，140多个企业和专利权人成为首批会员，协会的成立将有效提高我市知识产权创造、运用、保护及管理水平。

【知识产权管理】

知识产权机制。2015年8月27日，成立潮州市人民政府知识产权办公会议，由市知识产权局、市公安局等27个单位组成，有利于充分发挥办公会议成员单位职能作用，增强知识产权工作合力，逐步形成统一管理、协调有序、联动发展的知识产权工作格局。

企业知识产权管理规范。实施“企业知识产权管理规范推进项目”，支持开展企业贯标辅导。潮州三环（集团）股份有限公司、广东海利集团有限公司已启动贯标辅导工作流程。举办知识产权贯标培训班，全市各有关企业共200余人参加培训，为潮州市推动贯标工作打下良好的基础。

企业知识产权优势示范。知识产权示范和优势企业已成为潮州市企业专利创新的中坚力量，有效发挥示范带动作用。广东海利集团被认定为潮州市第一家国家知识产权示范企业，三环（集团）、博宇公司同时获评国家知识产权优势企业殊荣。

专利代理。进一步加强专利代理服务体系和能力建设，开展专利代理人职业道德教育。加强对打击非法从事专利代理行为适用法律法规、操作规程的研究和实践。

版权管理。积极帮助和推进潮州市版权保护登记机构的建设，引导版权保护登记机构改变工作方式，变被动服务为主动服务，免费上门整理、指导、准备登记资料，提高版权登记数量。版权保护登记机构加强与潮州市中天知识产权代理有限公司、潮州市开天知识产权咨询服务有限公司、广东粤高商标代理有限公司潮州分公司等代理公司合作，建立共同开展版权保护的合作伙伴关系。

【知识产权宣传培训】

知识产权宣传。在市区户外LED屏投放科技创新和国家知识产权试点城市系列宣传口号，提高知识产权创新社会影响力，营造国家知识产权试点城市良好氛围。

“4·26”期间，在市文化长廊举办了打击侵犯知识产权和制售假冒伪劣商品成果展览及现场知识产权咨询活动，相关单位领导以及有关企业、协会、机构的代表共200多人出席“双打”成果展，营造保护知识产权的良好氛围。

做好2014年潮州市青少年科技创新大赛的总结表彰工作。潮州市对获得2014年潮州市青少年科技创新大赛的学生作品申请专利的部分费用按规定给予资助。

商标宣传。在“4·26”世界知识产权日，开展商标宣传咨询活动，接受群众咨询解答疑问，现场发放宣传资料350份，新商标法解读小册子300份。以及对查处商标侵权案件进行展示，并在市区的LED电子显示屏开展商标法宣传1560条次，进一步扩大社会宣传面。

版权宣传。以潮州文化网等相关网站为依托，加强著作权保护和版权产业发展的宣传，并向在文化网等刊登了多条相关信息。通过知识产权宣传咨询和“双打”成果展示活动，向公众宣传普及保护版权的基本知识。深入书报刊经营单位、印刷企业等开展著作权法律法规宣传活动，引导企业开展作品登记、版权保护等工作，提高全社会的著作权保护意识。

知识产权培训。中小学知识产权教育试点工作。至2015年，已累计认定省级中小学知识产权教育示范学校2所，省级试点学校8所；累计认定市级中小学知识产权教育试点学校13

所，组织开展教师培训85人次，累计受教育学生达12560人次，开设知识产权教育课程286班次，开设各种知识产权实践活动78次数，学生作品申请专利12项。

（供稿人：吴家德）

揭 阳 市

【知识产权创造】 2015年，揭阳市专利申请量3726件，同比增长20.33%，授权2807件，同比增长35.47%。其中发明申请177件，同比增长43.90%。PCT专利申请10件，同比增长900%。全市新增注册商标13754件，累计有效注册商标76493件，其中"广东省著名商标"85件，受驰名商标认定保护的商标15件。共受理作品版权登记454件，新增1家"广东省版权兴业示范基地"，全市广东省版权兴业示范基地达到3家。

【知识产权保护】 创建中德（揭阳）中小企业知识产权保护试验区获省知识产权局批准，国家知识产权局副局长廖涛出席首届中德中小企业合作交流会启动仪式并调研揭阳市知识产权工作，省知识产权局副局长袁有楼为中德（揭阳）中小企业知识产权保护试验区授牌。开展交流会知识产权保护工作，制定首届中德中小企业合作交流会知识产权保护规定、专利纠纷处理规则、专利纠纷投诉与处理流程，牵头组织市工商局、市文广新局、揭阳海关在服务处开展知识产权宣传活动并接受咨询投诉，为交流会营造良好的知识产权保护环境，省知识产权局派业务骨干指导。

专利执法。2015年揭阳市知识产局立案查处假冒专利案件2宗，移送假冒专利案件1宗，作出行政处罚2宗；累计出动专利行政执法人员30余人次，接受电话及来访专利纠纷咨询6次。继续在"军埔村"微信公众号设立"电商维权"专栏，宣传知识产权保护相关内容。

商标执法。工商系统组织开展车用燃油专项整治、查处侵犯农资、建筑材料、汽车配件等侵犯注册商标专用权行动、农村和城乡结合部市场假冒伪劣专项整治、落实中国制造海外形象维护"清风"行动等工作。全市各级工商部门共查处案件158宗，案值127.06万元，罚没款179.66万元。在揭阳工商红盾网公开市局查办的"双打"案件信息23宗。查处的一宗违法使用"驰名商标"字样案件，在2015年4月被国家工商行政管理总局商标局列为2014年度工商、市场监管部门查处商标侵权和商标违法使用十二个典型案例之一。

版权执法。市版权系统组织开展文化市场检查共出动执法人员350人次，检查印刷复制企业50家次，各类出版物市场90家次、网吧75家次，娱乐场所50家次，收缴非法出版物500多张（册）。组织开展打击网络侵权盗版"剑网2015"专项行动，专项行动共出动文化执法人员600多人次，重点围绕文字、影视、音乐、游戏、软件等作品的数字版权保护，加大对互联网网站、网络销售平台、移动智能终端应用软件商店的监管力度，严厉打击各种网络侵权盗版行为，并向社会公布举报投诉电话"12318"。

知识产权维权援助。申报广东省知识产权维权援助中心揭阳分中心获省局授牌，进一步缓解揭阳市维权援助力量不足的困境。创新知识产权维权援助方式，在揭阳市知识产权工作条件较成熟的揭阳市高新技术企业协会设立知识产权维权工作站，进一步扩大揭阳市知识产权维权援助的覆盖面和社会影响力。联合揭阳职业技术学院组建"揭阳职业技术学院保护知识产权志愿服务队"，充分发挥高校专业知识优势，通过组织和参与知识产权相关的公益活动，宣传、普及知识产权知识。

【知识产权管理】

政策体系。揭阳市印发《揭阳市知识产权局落实〈国家知识产权局关于知识产权支持小微企业发展的若干意见〉工作方案》等政策文件。

管理机制。建立小微企业与专利代理机构对接机制，实施小微企业专利清零计划，开展专利信息推送，支持小微企业创新成果及时获权。建立健全软件正版化责任人数据库。在原政府机关使用软件正版化信息员名录的基础上，建立健全《揭阳市市直机关软件正版化工作责任部门及责任人信息表》，并要求各县（市、区）相应建立信息库。

企业知识产权工作。揭阳市知识产权局加强对高新技术企业、知识产权优势示范企业专利工作的服务和指导，推荐申报广东省专利奖11项，申报省知识产权优势、示范企业各1家，申报省专利技术实施计划项目4项。广东海兴塑胶有限公司的“水壶（2）”项目获得2015年广东专利奖优秀奖项目。以“贯标”为抓手，引导和鼓励企业通过实施知识产权管理规范，提升企业知识产权管理水平和核心竞争力，促进专利申请的数量和质量。2015年，广东泰宝科技股份有限公司为揭阳市首家通过“贯标”认证的企业。

知识产权服务。揭阳市知识产权局培育和发展知识产权服务业，引进南粤专利商标事务所在市区设立办事处，进一步提升揭阳市的知识产权服务水平。揭阳市版权局指导揭阳市的版权基层工作站及作品登记代办机构进驻军埔村，在军埔电商村设立作品登记、咨询服务点，普及版权知识，举办专题培训班，及时引导电商企业懂得版权保护、版权维权，自觉抵制销售假冒伪劣产品，让“电商村”走可持续发展之路。

【宣传、教育培训】

知识产权宣传。借助“4·26”宣传周活动，在市区、各县（市）区开展内容丰富、形式多样的“知识产权宣传周”活动。2015年4月23日，与市文广新局（版权局）到军埔电商村开展知识产权现场咨询宣传活动，现场接受咨询30多人次，发放宣传资料100多份。市工商各级部门共张贴宣传标语横幅58条，到企业开展专项指导10场次210户次，印发《商标常识问答》等学习宣传资料266份，派发宣传资料2100多份。市版权局积极参与“感知身边的网络安全”公众体验展活动，并免费发放《版权知识笔记本》、宣传单500多份（册）。通过市区交警LED宣传屏播放宣传标语。开展知识产权进企业活动，到广东达华节水科技股份有限公司、揭阳中诚集团有限公司举行知识产权宣传活动，为企业在专利申请、维护合法权益等方面提供指导服务，不断增强企业的知识产权保护意识。

知识产权培训。举办揭阳市2015年知识产权与创新培训班，培育一批科技创新人才，帮助企业有效运用知识产权资源，提升企业知识产权创造、运用和管理能力，共100多人参加培训。由揭阳市知识产权局发起，市经信局、教育局联合举办揭阳市2015年“泰宝杯”创新创业专利设计大赛，为揭阳市企业、社会个人、学生挖掘创意、申请专利搭建平台，营造“大众创业、万众创新”的社会氛围。其间承办单位广州粤高专利商标代理有限公司揭阳分公司在揭阳职业技术学院、普宁市新世纪职业学院、普宁、蓝城、空港等8个单位和地区举办7场大型的辅导培训活动，共有1400多名学生青年和170多家企业参加赛前辅导培训。

（供稿人：陈纯佳）

云浮市

【知识产权创造】

专利。2015年，全市专利申请916件，同比增长36.11%，其中发明专利申请113件；专利授权645件，同比增长34.38%，其中发明专利授权45件。PCT（国际专利）申请1件。

商标。2015年成功新申报认定广东省著名商标数量为8件，截至2015年底，全市拥有中国驰名商标2件，广东省著名商标33件，集体商标2件，地理标志证明商标2件。

【知识产权运用】 推动企业转型升级、带动专利技术产业化，组织企业开展市知识产权优势企业评选活动，提升企业知识产权创造和运用能力。其中，广东温氏食品集团股份有限公司、广东南牧机械设备有限公司、广东森宇林产化工有限公司、罗定市星光化工有限公司4家企业被评定为市知识产权优势企业。

【知识产权保护】

打击侵权假冒。市“双打”领导小组各成员单位深入开展专项整治，打击侵犯知识产权和制售假冒伪劣商品工作取得良好成效。着重抓好推进两法衔接平台建设、侵权假冒行政处罚案件信息公开、互联网侵权假冒专项整治、加强诚信体系建设、开展宣传教育等方面工作。全市“两法衔接”信息平台全部实现网上互联互通，共计接入单位170家，录入案件2289件。各行政执法职能单位建立和完善了网上行政处罚案件信息公开栏目。据统计，全市各级行政机关开展专项行动42场次，出动执法人员4万余人次，检查企业、门店13000多家，共查处案件784宗，涉案金额536万多元，公安机关刑事侦查立案制假售假案件15件，抓获犯罪嫌疑人11人。查获销毁假农药化肥、假烟酒、假药品、有害有毒食品、假冒名牌服装等一批，涉案价值260多万元。

专利行政执法。对案件审理室进行升级改造，并完善现场快速执法设备，购置便携式手提计算机、录音笔、应急电源等执法设备。推动县区开展专利行政执法工作，加强执法业务培训，先后多次组织市、县两级执法人员共同参与开展省的专项执法行动。深入开展2015年“护航”专项执法行动和省局部署的查处假冒专利集中行动月行动，同时，根据《2015年云浮市打假工作方案》，确定以食品、药品、医疗机械等为打击重点，加强与工商、质监、公安、检察等部门的协调沟通，采取联合执法，加强对制假售假违法行为的打击力度。在6月23日的全省统一执法行动中，查处销售假冒专利产品的销售企业3家，查获假冒专利产品11盒。据统计，2015年共计组织开展知识产权保护宣传活动1场，出动执法人员105人次，检查专利商品3000余件，查处假冒专利案件5宗，未发生侵权投诉案件。

商标行政执法。2015年，立案查处案件158宗，罚没款172.76万元（其中商标侵权案件32宗，罚没金额9.92万元，查处假冒伪劣商品立案案件有126宗，罚没金额162.84万元）。

【知识产权管理】

专利申请资助。落实专利申请资助政策，对符合条件的专利申请进行审核资助，激励社会创造热情，2015年共计资助专利297件。

知识产权服务。通过组织发动，出台相关优惠政策，推动省内专利代理服务机构进驻云浮市。2014年，广州科粤专利商标代理有限公司正式派驻人员到云浮市设立办事机构并开始日常运作，并于2014年9月21日成立云浮市科粤知识产权服务有限公司，为云浮市企业和个人提供便捷、高效的知识产权服务。截至2015年底，该机构已为云浮市代理申请专利共计200余件。

【宣传、教育培训】

“4·26”知识产权宣传周。围绕“实施知识产权战略，支撑创新驱动发展”主题，增强广大企业和市民的知识产权意识，营造良好的知识产权社会环境，针对云浮市的产业特点，于2015年4月30日在新兴县举办了“不锈钢制品企业专利知识讲座”，进一步提高企业创新创造和保护知识产权的能力。组织开展校园知识产权宣传活动，在新兴县试验中学举办知识产权游园活动，通过课堂对知识产权的讲解和宣传，并对知识产权专题黑板报进行了奖评，树立学生们尊重和保护知识产权的理念。

科技进步月活动。结合群众路线教育实践活动的开展，举办2015年科技（知识产权、地震）下乡活动。邀请省有关专家教授开展培训讲座，传授云浮市农村、农企需要适用的知识技术，并组织一批图书和科普挂图，免费发放给农村科普基地、农技协会、农家书屋、学校及农民群众使用，把知识送到了群众家门口。

品牌商标宣传活动。开展“3·15”国际消费者权益日和“4·26”知识产权宣传周活动，派送商标注册、维权等方面的资料，并进行了咨询解答，采用广东邮政的手机网页发送平台，悬挂宣传标语，接受群众咨询，派发宣传资料9377份，电视播放商标宣传公益广告，开辟商标知识宣传栏，共出动执法人员601人次，检查各类商店、超市、专营专卖店、药店、生产厂家1787户次。4月份，新兴县工商局举办了全县实施商标战略培训班暨广东省著名商标申报动员会，组织全县驰名、著名商标企业以及20多家重点企业负责人参加会议。特邀商标专业老师就商标品牌知识进行了专题讲座，从商标申请与注册、著名商标认定与保护等方面进行了详细解读，并就出口型企业和贴牌生产型企业所遇到的热点、难点问题等方面进行阐述和讲解。突出新《商标法》的宣传贯彻落实。到相关企业调研，与企业相关人员沟通、座谈，指导新形势下商标的使用、管理、保护，上门送法，通过开展一系列宣传活动，提高社会、企业、人民群众的商标品牌意识，为实施商标战略下一步目标、进一步推动全市“双打”专项行动的深入开展奠定基础。

（供稿人：陈怡莹）

表彰奖励

● 表彰奖励

BIAO ZHANG JIA

表彰奖励

2015年全国知识产权领军人才百名高层次人才培养人选

2014年12月31日，国家知识产权局印发《关于公布第二批全国知识产权领军人才和第四批百千万知识产权人才工程百名高层次人才培养人选的通知》（国知发人函字〔2014〕155号）认定了新一批全国知识产权领军人才和百名高层次人才培养人选，其中广东省人才和人选名单如下：

一、全国知识产权领军人才

知识产权行政管理与执法人才类：

广东省知识产权局　袁有楼

深圳市中级人民法院　祝建军

企业知识产权人才类：

华为技术有限公司　成绪新

中兴通讯股份有限公司　郭小明

腾讯科技（深圳）有限公司　李富山

深圳日海通讯技术股份有限公司　王冰

珠海格力电器股份有限公司　肖彪

广州白云山制药股份有限公司广州白云山制药总厂　许淑文

华为技术有限公司　张仲卿

知识产权服务业人才类：

珠海智专专利商标代理有限公司　段淑华

广州华进联合专利商标代理有限公司　胡杰

高等院校及科研机构知识产权人才类：

华南理工大学　关永红

二、百千万知识产权人才工程百名高层次人才培养人选

中兴通讯股份有限公司　沈剑锋

金发科技股份有限公司　王鹏

南方电网科学研究院　王庆红

广东省知识产权研究与发展中心　陈宇萍

广东天胜律师事务所　杜国明

深圳市智汇远见知识产权管理有限公司　李俊

广州市华学知识产权代理有限公司　李卫东

（供稿人：王一）

2015年全国专利信息领军人才和师资人才名单

2015年7月22日，国家知识产权局办公室印发《关于公布2015年全国专利信息领军人才和师资人才名单的通知》（国知办函办字〔2015〕419号）认定了新一批全国专利信息领军人才和师资人才，其中广东省入选人才名单如下：

一、全国专利信息领军人才

广东省知识产权研究与发展中心　李强

深圳市标准技术研究院　赵涛

腾讯科技（深圳）有限公司　桂燕

二、全国专利信息师资人才

中兴通讯股份有限公司　文明

广州市知识产权信息中心　刘承敏

深圳市威世博知识产权代理事务所　何青瓦

国家知识产权局专利局专利审查协作广东中心　杨隆鑫

中国科学院广州生物医药与健康研究院　庞弘燊

广州市越秀区哲力专利商标事务所（普通合伙） 胡拥军

国家知识产权局专利局专利审查协作广东中心 钟焱鑫

广州市华学知识产权代理有限公司 李卫东

（供稿人：王一）

国家知识产权试点示范城市工作先进集体和先进个人

2015年，国家知识产权局组织开展2014年度国家知识产权试点示范城市工作先进集体和先进个人评选表扬活动。经推荐、评审，广东省知识产权局、广州市、深圳市（副省级示范城市）、东莞市（地级示范城市）、中山市、佛山市、惠州市（地级试点城市）、广州增城市、江门四会市（县级试点城市）获得“国家知识产权试点示范城市工作先进集体”称号。广东省知识产权局陈燕、广州市知识产权局邓群英、深圳市知识产权局叶雪辉、东莞市知识产权局罗广林、中山市知识产权局焦学军、佛山市知识产权局何倩琨、惠州市知识产权局陈洪、广州增城市知识产权局潘正焕、江门四会市知识产权局潘海健获“国家知识产权试点示范城市工作先进个人”称号。

（供稿人：张璟）

ZHUAN TI YAN JIU YU GONG ZUO

专题研究与工作交流

- 专题研究报告
- 工作交流

专题研究报告

广东省知识产权局软科学研究管理工作

【概况】 2015年，广东省知识产权局进一步加强知识产权软科学研究计划项目的规范化、制度化管理，以满足加快建设知识产权强省对高质量、高水平软课题研究成果的需求为导向，继续通过网上项目申报系统面向全省申报单位开展项目申请，共收到符合条件的项目申报52项，经专家评审、批准立项21项，其中，重点9项，一般项目12项。同时，围绕创新驱动发展这一核心战略，组织开展了知识产权支撑广东创新驱动发展重大问题研究项目软课题申报和评审工作，确定4项重点项目。

组织全省6个项目申报2015年度国家知识产权局软科学研究项目，《知识产权人才职业能力研究》项目获得国家知识产权局立项。

（供稿人：赵飞）

关于广东省地理标志产品保护与管理工作现状的调研报告

【概况】 2015年10月至12月，广东省质监局成立调研工作组，对广东省国家地理标志工作现状进行了专项调研。调研组分别走访揭阳、梅州、茂名、阳江、韶关、清远、东莞、珠海等部分机关企事业单位及农户，实地考察国家地理标志保护产品生产企业和农户种植养殖基地。调研情况汇报如下：

【广东省国家地理标志产品保护工作的基本情况】 广东省质监部门将地理标志产品保护工作作为贯彻落实省委、省政府“三促进一保持”战略部署，促进广东省区域协调发展，有效服务“三农”，推动广东省农业产业化进程的重要抓手，一方面努力抓好新产品申报，另一方面充分发挥获批产品社会经济效益，取得了良好的效果。

（一）地理标志产品保护意识初步形成，产品申报工作驶入快车道。2003年年底“河源米粉”成为广东省第一个获得地理标志保护的产品，实现“零”突破，2008年有10个产品获得保护；2010年有19个产品获得保护；2012年有9个产品获得保护；2014年有13个产品获得保护，累计数量位居全国第三；截至2015年12月底已有112个产品获得保护，位居全国前列。

（二）充分发挥地理标志产品保护制度对经济发展的推动作用，促进农业增产、农民增收。根据省质监局近年来对全省获保护的地理标志产品开展的普查数据显示，广东省获保护的地理标志产品年总产值已达225.4亿元，较保护前的93.8亿元增长56%，受惠农户764813户、养殖户5805户、生产企业986家，农民年平均收入获保护后达8685元，较获保护前的6500元增长了55%。如新会陈皮实施保护后销售价格较保护前增长85%；端砚自2004年实施保护后，加工企业数从保护前的400家增至600多家，增幅达60%，企业总产值由保护前的9000万元增至2.8亿元，增幅达180%。截至2015年底，广东省质监系统开展的地理标志产品保护工作已惠及全省农户及养殖户，获保护产品的经济和社会效益得到显著提高，有力地促进县域经济发展和农民增收。

（三）充分发挥地理标志产品保护制度的名牌带动作用，推进县（区）域经济发展。广东省积极实施地理标志保护，提升产品的知名度，大力推进名牌带动战略。广州市政府出台《广州市质量技术监督局地理标志产品保护工作指引（试行）》、清远市政府对辖区内的13个地理标志保护产品均出台《地理标志产品保护管理办法》和《地理标志产品保护专用标志使用管理办法》等，为广东省地理标志保护工作的开展提供了坚实的法制保障；韶关市质监局对辖区内的养殖户以及生产加工企业使用专用标志的情况建立了可溯源可核查的台账，促进产品生产、加工、流通的各个阶段的实施主体在其产品上显示专用标志等相关信息；江门市新会区推进地理标志产品深加工，制定并颁布《新会陈皮普洱茶》等相关产品联盟标准，并申报筹建“广东省陈皮及相关产品技术标准化委员会”，积极推动陈皮衍生服务业升级标准化示范点建设，为广东省打造区域品牌、提高相关企业产品质量和信誉、促进县域经济发展、推动广东省城乡与区域协调发展发挥了积极作用。

（四）有力地推进了广东省农业标准化的发展进程。截至2015年底，广东省获批的地理标志产品中已经制定省地方标准（农业类）91项，已建立国家级农业标准化示范区22个，省级农业标准化示范区52个。大多数地理标志产品均推行全过程标准化种植与生产，“地理标志产品+龙头企业+农户”的经营模式不断推广，农业标准化与开发、培育品牌农产品、无公害农产品和绿色食品等实现了有机结合，有利于推动广东省农业标准化的发展，对新时期实现广东农业和农村经济结构性和战略性调整，对推动城乡经济与社会的协调发展具有重要的现实意义。

（五）充分发挥地理标志产品保护制度的文化促进作用，服务文化大省建设。

2009年11月1日，国家科学技术部、商务部、农业部、国家质检总局等十几个部委与陕西省人民政府联合主办第十六届中国杨凌农业高科技成果博览会（简称“农高会”）在陕西杨凌举行。广东省质监部门组织13家企业参展具有岭南特色的端砚、马坝油粘米、南雄板鸭、化橘红、普宁青梅、新会陈皮、流沙南珠等7个产品，很好地对外宣传了广东的风情、风貌和南粤文化，省质监局被组委会授予“最佳组织奖”。

广东新会既是广东省第一个获批筹建的国家级地理标志产品保护示范区，也是全国首个非试点省份成功获批筹建的国家级地理标志产品保护示范区。2015年10月25至26日，国家质检总局在江门市新会区召开国家地理标志产品保护示范区（ ）验收会，对国家地理标志产品保护示范区进行考核验收。国家质检总局科技司副巡视员裴晓颖对示范区地理标志产品保护推进工作给予充分肯定，强调江门市质监系统要以特产产品实施地理标志保护为手段，通过打造国家地理标志产品保护示范区，做大做强高端特色名牌农业，健全体系、规范程序、强化监管，积极引导符合地理标志保护的特色产品实施知识产权战略，不断提高产品质量和信誉，促使新会柑、新会陈皮形成地标区域品牌，促进江门经济社会全面发展。

【地理标志保护的重要意义】 发展地理标志保护产品落实党中央、国务院“三农”工作战略部署的重要举措。

（一）地理标志提高了农产品市场化组织能力。目前，农产品市场化主要体现在“地理标志+龙头企业+农户”的农业产业化经营模式，即一个地理标志产品通过几个龙头企业来带动的多龙头带动机制，较好地将政府资源、企业资源和农户资源优化组合起来的，具有强大生命力的模式。地理标志将分散的农户以地理标志知识产权为纽带、以龙头企业为通道连接到市场，使农户可以分享生产和销售的整个市场的利益。

（二）地理标志提升了我国农产品的竞争力。地理标志有力提高产品在国内国际市场的竞争力和价格水平。中国第一个受到保护的地理标志产品“绍兴酒”，曾经在国际市场2/3的份额被产自日本、中国台湾等的“绍兴酒”所挤占。得到保护后，绍兴古越龙山酒厂销往日本的绍兴酒比上年增长14%，塔牌绍兴酒销量整体翻一番，女儿红黄酒利税比上年增长18.07%，东风酒厂出口日本的绍兴酒比上年增长1倍以上。

（三）地理标志促进和保障了农产品市场秩序。中央电视台《每周质量报告》曝光个别厂家的金华火腿、龙口粉丝、山西陈醋、平遥牛肉、镇江香醋假冒伪劣事件，严重影响到整个地理标志行业的声誉。实施地理标志保护，加强管理，改进市场秩序，保护品牌，防止任何滥用、伪造和其他误导公众对产品真实产地信息认知的行为。

（四）地理标志帮助了消费者认清产品产地，做出最优消费选择。提高经济效益，生产出受到消费者认可的品质优良的产品，是地理标志产品凭着鲜明的原产地特性与突出的品质特色，切实帮助消费者清晰地辨别产地，从而作出最优的消费选择。

（五）地理标志提升了产品的知名度，促进地方经济发展。地理标志产品从标准生产的角度规范和提升产品的质量，通过实施地理标志保护，提升产品的知名度。广东省一直注重提升产品信誉和品牌影响力。江门市新会区积极推进地理标志产品深加工，制定并颁布了《新会陈皮普洱茶》等相关产品联盟标准，并申报筹建“广东省陈皮及相关产品技术标准化委员会”，积极推动陈皮衍生服务业升级标准化示范点建设。这些后续监管及品牌、技术标准推进措施，为广东省打造区域品牌、提高相关企业产品质量和信誉、促进县域经济发展、推动广东省城乡与区域协调发展发挥了积极作用。

【当前地理标志产品保护与管理方面存在的问题】

（一）管理体制上存在不协调。行政管理部门之间的管理权限的冲突和碰撞状况，给实际工作带来了明显的消极影响，使工作部门、申报单位感到十分困惑。

（二）保护意识淡薄、认识和措施不到位。

一是对地理标志保护产品的概念界定不清，缺乏足够的地理标志产品保护意识。政府与企业、企业与部门间的责任主体不明，对相关产品的监管、维权保护、政府营销等相关配套措施未能跟上。

二是对地理标志产品保护工作重要性的认识不到位。

三是知识产权意识不强，缺乏知识产权发展战略。忽视地理标志所涵盖的价值，品牌和质量意识淡薄。

四是消费者对地理标志产品的认识也还较陌生，对地理标志产品的消费没有形成主动意识。

（三）政府经费投入不足。部分市县政府由于财力不足，在该项工作中没有匹配相应的经费与补助。

（四）申报工作在程序上较之商标注册与农产品地理标志登记优势不强。质监部门管理的地理标志产品登记申报工作程序在时间与环节方面还没有优势，且申报成本也相对较高。

【下一步对策与建议】 针对广东省目前地理标志产品保护工作的现状和存在的问题，今后在继续充分发挥广东省质监系统地理标志产品申报保护的职能作用的基础上，一手抓申报，一手抓申报后综合效益尤其是经济效益的发挥，真正做到“申报一个产品，带动一个产业，带富一方百姓”。

（一）加大地理标志产品保护工作资金投入和政策扶持力度。一是每年由省财政安排广东省国家地理标志保护产品专项工作经费，加大资金投入和政策扶持力度。二是将产品培育、申报、保护、标准制定、宣传培训等经费列入省财政预算并督促落实到位。

（二）推动地理标志立法进度。省人大尽快率先出台《广东省地理标志产品保护条例》，规范、统一用语，明确统一构成要素和审批标准及管理部门及职能，终结多部门共同管理的混乱局面，保护更多名优特产品。

（三）简化地理标志产品申报程序。简化申报程序、缩短申报周期、降低申报工作成本。推进专用标志申请使用自我声明制度改革和推进地标产品在线申报、发布、查询制度改革。给予专项工作经费的支持。

（四）加强地理标志协调的督查。完善保护工作的政策和措施，加强与各级质监、农业、工商等部门的沟通与交流，加大对食品、农产品生产者伪造、冒用地理标志等违法行为的执法与督查和处罚力度；加强信息共享。

（五）广泛宣传地理标志产品保护制度。省质监局拟在南方网和局网站上开设地标专栏、在广东质监学习论坛举办一期地标专题学习讲座、出版广东省已获批地标产品的宣传画册。

（六）抓好后续监管。积极探索建立健全地理标志产品质量溯源体系和监管制度，健全完善企业产品标准及质量检验体系，严把产品出厂质量安全关。一是督促企业建立规范的生产技术工艺组织生产，确保产品质量符合标准，明确标注产品质量等级。二是对各辖区内的养殖户以及生产加工企业建立可溯源可核查的台账，明确和锁定产品的来源与流向。

（七）树立政府营销的先进理念。将发展地理标志产品特色经济提升至整体营销的高度，广泛开展政府营销活动，促进招商引资，同时进一步扩大岭南地区地理标志产品的影响力，为地方经济的长足发展奠定坚实基础。

（供稿人：钟培敬）

工作交流

广交会知识产权保护工作

【概况】 第117届广交会于2015年4月15日至5月5日在广州举办，第118届广交会于2015年10月15日至11月4日在广州举办。两届广交会期间，广东省知识产权局组织50余人的省市专利联合执法队伍驻会开展专利保护工作。在广交会业务办的统筹下，与商标、版权等职能部门共处理知识产权投诉1134宗，其中：专利类投诉 815宗，商标类投诉197宗，版权类投诉122宗。

【第117届广交会知识产权保护工作情况】 此届广交会投诉接待站受理知识产权投诉案件总量为531宗，比上届增加5宗，增幅1.0%；被投诉企业663家，比上届增加37家，增幅5.9%；最终认定涉嫌侵权企业370家，比上届增加41家，增幅12.5%，占被投诉企业总数的55.8%。

知识产权投诉涉及行业相对集中。此届广交会按电子及家电、照明、车辆及配件、机械、五金工具、建材等16大类商品设置50个展区，与往届情况相同，知识产权投诉商品涉及的行业相对集中，被投诉企业主要集中在家用电器（61家）、摩托车（57家）和家居用品（50家）等行业。

专利投诉占知识产权总投诉比例最大。知识产权投诉案件中，与往届相同，专利类投诉仍然数量最多，共受理396宗（被投诉企业460家），占知识产权投诉案件总数的74.6%；商标类投诉99宗（被投诉企业189家），占18.6%；版权类投诉36宗（被投诉企业26家），占6.8%。在专利类投诉案件中，外观设计295宗，占74.5%；另外实用新型83宗，发明18宗。

三类投诉认定涉嫌侵权企业数均有所上升。专利类认定涉嫌侵权企业数为214家，比上届的203家增加5.4%；商标类认定涉嫌侵权企业数为138家，比上届的117家增加17.9%；版权类认定涉嫌侵权企业数为18家，比上届的15家增加20.0%。

经济活跃的省份涉嫌侵权企业较多。此届68个交易团（含中央企业各分团）共有21931家参展企业，其中49个交易团的350家参展企业被最终认定涉嫌侵权。涉嫌侵权企业较多的交易团分别为：深圳团39家、浙江团37家、江苏团32家、广东团24家、宁波团22家。

群体性侵权案件时有发生。此届广交会，群体性侵权投诉案件（即同一知识产权权属号投诉10家以上参展企业）共9宗，涉及被投诉企业69家。投诉人有：杭州骑客智能科技有限公司、本田技研工业株式会社、三丽鸥股份有限公司。

商标类投诉主要为涉外权利人。在99宗商标类投诉中，有94宗是由国外权利人提起，且全部由专业的中介机构代理投诉，涉外案件比例高达94.9%。投诉人主要有三丽鸥股份有限公司、大众汽车股份有限公司、本田技研工业株式会社和泰莱白兰德公司等。

【第118届广交会知识产权保护工作情况】 此届广交会投诉接待站受理知识产权投诉案件总量为603宗，比上届增加72宗，增幅13.6%；被投诉企业800家，比上届增加197家，增幅29.7%；最终认定涉嫌侵权企业408家，比上届增加38家，增幅10.2%，占被投诉企业总数的47.4%。

知识产权投诉涉及行业相对集中。此届

广交会按电子及家电、照明、车辆及配件、机械、五金工具、建材等16大类商品设置50个展区，与往届情况相同，知识产权投诉商品涉及的行业相对集中，被投诉企业主要集中在家用电器（87家）、家居用品（75家）和摩托车（72家）等行业。

专利投诉占知识产权总投诉比例最大。知识产权投诉案件中，与往届相同，专利类投诉仍然数量最多，共受理419宗（被投诉企业460家），占知识产权投诉案件总数的69.5%；商标类投诉98宗（被投诉企业628家），占16.3%；版权类投诉86宗（被投诉企业25家），占14.3%。在专利类投诉案件中，外观设计298宗，占71.1%；另外实用新型103宗，发明18宗。

三类投诉认定涉嫌侵权企业数均有所上升。专利类认定涉嫌侵权企业数为219家，比上届的214家增加2.3%；商标类认定涉嫌侵权企业数为172家，比上届的138家增加24.6%；版权类认定涉嫌侵权企业数为19家，比上届的18家增加5.6%。

经济活跃的省份涉嫌侵权企业较多。此届68个交易团（含中央企业各分团）共有24700家参展企业，其中49个交易团的408家参展企业被最终认定涉嫌侵权。涉嫌侵权企业较多的交易团分别为：浙江团47家、宁波团33家、福建团32家、广东团29家、深圳团29家。

群体性侵权案件时有发生。此届广交会，群体性侵权投诉案件（即同一知识产权权属号投诉10家以上参展企业）共18宗，涉及被投诉企业190家。投诉人有：杭州骑客智能科技有限公司、ABBS.P.A、本田技研工业株式会社、三丽鸥股份有限公司等。

商标类投诉主要为涉外权利人。在98宗商标类投诉中，有94宗是由国外权利人提起，且全部由专业的中介机构代理投诉，涉外案件比例高达95.9%。投诉人主要有三丽鸥股份有限公司、株式会社爱世克私、ABBS.P.A和泰莱白兰德公司等。

（供稿人：毕赓）

FU LU

附录

- 政策法规
- 知识产权大事记
- 统计资料

政策法规

广东省深入实施知识产权战略推动创新驱动发展行动计划

为贯彻落实《中共广东省委广东省人民政府关于全面深化科技体制改革加快创新驱动发展的决定》（粤发〔2014〕12号）精神，深入实施知识产权战略，推动创新驱动发展战略实施，特制定本行动计划。

一、总体要求

按照党中央、国务院和省委、省政府的决策部署，以体制机制改革创新为动力，以知识产权保护和运用为重点，坚持问题导向和需求导向相统一、市场主导和政府支持相结合，深入实施知识产权战略，推动创新驱动发展战略实施，大力促进产业转型升级和提升企业核心竞争力，着力打造一批具有知识产权核心竞争力的企业，形成一批具有国际影响力的知识产权密集型产业，探索出一条知识产权推动创新驱动发展的新路径，把广东建设成为国际化知识产权创造运用中心和知识产权保护高地，成为知识产权强国建设先行省，为加快实现“三个定位、两个率先”总目标做出努力。

二、重点行动计划

（一）实行严格的知识产权保护。

完善知识产权行政和司法保护机制。发挥广州知识产权法院优势，完善知识产权纠纷审判机制，加大知识产权侵权赔偿力度。加强各级知识产权执法队伍建设，推进知识产权综合行政执法，改善执法条件。健全知识产权保护行政执法机关与公安、海关的协作机制，提高行政执法效率。强化行政执法与刑事司法保护有机衔接，依法打击侵犯知识产权犯罪行为。完善知识产权纠纷国际仲裁机制。在知识产权侵权易发的重点领域、重点区域定期开展专项查处行动。加强网络环境下知识产权保护，加大电子商务和互联网领域的知识产权执法力度。强化展会和专业市场知识产权保护。构建知识产权保护信用系统，将恶意侵犯知识产权等违法失信行为信息纳入社会信用记录。（省知识产权局牵头，省法院、省检察院、省公安厅、省工商局、省版权局、省编办、海关总署广东分署、广州知识产权法院配合）

（二）促进发明创造增量提质。

对小微企业首件发明专利授权给予申请费、代理费全额补贴。对年授权发明专利达10件以上、增长率超过30%的中小微企业、高校和科研院所给予奖励。对维持五年以上有效发明专利和获得国外授权的发明专利给予资助。每年选取部分重点行业和一批重点企业组织发明专利优先审查和巡回审查。鼓励各地落实专利奖励配套政策，重奖发明创造者，并根据实际情况加大知识产权创新补助。（省知识产权局牵头，省财政厅、省科技厅、省教育厅、各地级以上市配合）

到2017年底，全省有效发明专利量超过16万件；万人发明专利拥有量（专利密度）达到15件；年发明专利授权量达到3万件，年均增长10%；PCT国际专利年均增长10%。

（三）提升企业掌握核心专利能力。

推广运用《企业知识产权管理规范》，引

导高新技术企业、大型骨干企业及国有企业等提升知识产权管理水平，使创新成果尽快获得知识产权保护，掌握一批重点产业核心专利技术。鼓励企业通过自主创新、开放合作、知识产权引进等多种途径，形成具有市场竞争力的知识产权资产组合。加强高等学校、科研院所的知识产权管理，明确所属技术转移机构的功能定位，落实知识产权管理规范，强化知识产权申请和运营权责。加强企业贯标辅导培育，吸引认证机构落户广东并予以扶持发展，大力培养辅导认证审查专业人才。（省知识产权局牵头，省经济和信息化委、省科技厅、省教育厅、省国资委配合）

到2017年底，全省参加贯标辅导的企业达到2000家，通过《企业知识产权管理规范》认证的企业达到500家。全省开展知识产权管理规范试点的高校和科研院所达到20家。

（四）实施重点产业专利导航计划。

围绕省战略性新兴产业、省重大科技专项、珠江西岸先进装备制造产业、珠江东岸电子信息及未来产业和《中国制造2025》，深入开展专利导航、分析和预警，引导重点产业优化全球知识产权战略布局，提高产业国际竞争力。支持高新区、特色产业基地等园区建设专利导航产业发展试验区。构建重大经济科技活动知识产权审查评议机制，制定并实施知识产权评议办法。实施科技项目知识产权全过程管理。围绕战略性新兴产业和高新技术产业，加强专利技术攻关和集成创新，在主要技术领域创造一批具有战略储备价值的核心专利，推动高价值专利在产业链上下游之间的协同运用和价值实现，培育形成一批成长性好、附加值高的专利密集型产业。（省知识产权局牵头，省发展改革委、省经济和信息化委、省科技厅配合）

到2017年，完成10个以上重点产业和20个以上重点领域的专利导航。建设知识产权密集型产业集聚区10个。

（五）推动专利技术实施转化。

围绕“大众创业、万众创新”，推动知识产权创业、孵化和产业化基地发展，在战略性新兴产业、未来产业和重点民生产业等领域，每年择优扶持100项核心技术专利项目和200项专利技术创业示范项目，促进专利技术转化，在专利产业化推进相关项目立项评审中，将专利的标准转化率作为重要评审指标。加强省知识产权局与国家国防知识产权部门的合作，探索建立知识产权军民融合高层次战略合作关系，筛选军民双方可转化专利，拓展军民可转移技术的应用领域。实施专利资源军民融合计划及国防专利申请资助计划，探索建立军民融合专利技术试验区，搭建军民融合知识产权运营平台，争取在广东举办国防专利展示交易会，推动高质量的国防专利在广东的实施转化。（省知识产权局牵头，省经济和信息化委、省科技厅、省商务厅、省质监局配合）

到2017年，支持全省专利技术实施项目1000项，新增经济产值500亿元；支持建设专利技术创业孵化器10个；引进军民融合专利技术不少于500项。

（六）构建知识产权运营交易机制。

充分发挥省知识产权运营基金的引导作用，积极向社会募集资金，不断扩大基金规模。建立市场化的知识产权运作模式，围绕知识产权密集型或控制型产业，支持建立一批以优势企业为龙头、技术关联机构为主体、按照产业链布局的专利联盟，构建专利池。培育一批知识产权运营机构，以市场化方式重点推动一批专利联盟集聚创新资源、掌握市场话语权。加快全国知识产权运营公共服务横琴特色试点平台和广州知识产权交易中心建设。支持省内知识产权交易机构探索开展知识产权证券化业务。（省知识产权局牵头，省财政厅、省金融办配合）

到2017年，全省建设知识产权运营交易服务机构20家，年度运营交易专利数达5000项，运营交易总额达100亿元，形成有较强区域竞争力的专利联盟30个。

（七）大力发展知识产权金融。

发挥省级知识产权质押融资扶持及风险

补偿金作用，支持各地建立知识产权质押融资扶持及风险补偿机制，简化知识产权质押融资流程，对知识产权质押贷款提供重点支持。支持银行、证券、保险、信托及互联网金融等相关机构参与知识产权金融服务，建设中国（广东）知识产权投融资服务平台，推动知识产权投融资项目对接活动开展。鼓励保险机构开展知识产权交易保险、执行保险、侵权保险、专利代理人职业保险等新险种业务。（省知识产权局牵头，省财政厅、省金融办、人民银行广州分行、广东银监局、广东证监局、广东保监局配合）

到2017年，全省年度知识产权质押融资额达100亿元。

（八）加快知识产权快速维权机制建设。

围绕广东专业镇加快部署知识产权快速维权中心，不断完善快速维权中心的机制和功能。全面提升中山灯饰、东莞家具、顺德家电知识产权快速维权中心服务能力，探索在陶瓷、刀具、皮具、珠宝等行业建立知识产权快速维权中心。依托现有资源，探索建立广东重点产业知识产权快速维权机制，构建跨行业、跨区域的知识产权快速授权、确权和维权服务体系。（省知识产权局牵头，相关地级以上市配合）

到2017年底，争取国家支持新设立一批知识产权快速维权中心，省级以上知识产权维权援助中心及分支机构达30家以上。

（九）积极开展知识产权海外护航。

建立知识产权涉外应对和援助机制。加快构建海外知识产权维权机制，为企业应对海外知识产权纠纷提供必要资助，为企业提供知识产权相关的信息、法律等服务。支持重点行业、企业建立知识产权海外维权联盟，指导企业加快海外知识产权布局和保护。探索推动世界知识产权组织仲裁与调解中心（WIPOAMC）依托广州知识产权仲裁院设立分支或办事机构。聚焦21世纪海上丝绸之路建设，加强与相关国家知识产权领域交流合作，推动知识产权多元合作，构建多元知识产权国际合作平台。在中新（广州）知识城创建国家级知识产权保护和运用综合改革试验区，打造知识产权枢纽城市。（省知识产权局牵头，省商务厅、省编办、相关地级以上市配合）

（十）全面增强知识产权服务能力。

实施“互联网知识产权”计划，以专利大数据为基础，搭建知识产权大数据应用平台，加快建设一批重点产业专利数据库，面向全社会免费提供基础数据，实现知识产权信息利用便利化。面向中小微企业开展专利信息推送服务。实施《广东创建知识产权服务业发展示范省规划（2013—2020年）》，加快省知识产权服务业集聚中心建设，培育5—10个国家和省知识产权服务业集聚发展试验区。加快知识产权人才培养和引进，支持广州创建知识产权学院。加快中小微企业知识产权培训基地、高端知识产权人才培育基地建设。增强专利代理机构服务能力和水平。（省知识产权局牵头，省发展改革委、省经济和信息化委、省科技厅、省农业厅、省教育厅、省人力资源社会保障厅、省工商局、省版权局、相关地级以上市配合）

到2017年，专利信息推送覆盖产业10个、企业2万家以上，在全省范围内实现线上线下立体覆盖；全省专利代理机构达200家、分支机构200家以上。

三、保障措施

（一）加强组织领导。

省政府知识产权办公会议负责组织实施本行动计划。省知识产权局要发挥牵头作用，建立完善相互支持、密切协作、运转顺畅的工作机制。深化省政府与国家知识产权局高层次战略合作，加强省部会商项目实施的条件保障，确保项目建设顺利推进。

（二）完善政策法规。

不断完善知识产权保护政策体系，积极探索新商业模式、新业态方面知识产权保护立法研究。强化知识产权政策与科技、产业、金融政策的融合，形成激励创新的政策合力。大力开展知识产权宣传普及，提高全民知识产权意识。

（三）强化资金保障。

省财政整合知识产权工作相关资金，对专利导航及专利联盟发展、知识产权运营及金融服务、企业贯标和维权援助、专利申请和实施转化、专业镇快速维权中心建设及企业海外知识产权护航等工作提供专项支持。引导省产业发展资金和科技专项资金向知识产权产业化倾斜。加强财政资金使用的监督管理和绩效评价，确保财政资金发挥效能。

（四）加强监测统计。

加强对知识产权状况的监测评估，建立知识产权产业统计制度，在战略性新兴产业、重大科技专项、珠江东西两岸等选取一定数量的企业开展知识产权方面数据统计，按国家规定发布有关统计报告。

广东省知识产权局、科技厅、经济和信息化委、商务厅、质监局、国资委印发关于全面推进《企业知识产权管理规范》国家标准的实施意见

为贯彻落实国家知识产权局等八部委《关于全面推行〈企业知识产权管理规范〉国家标准的指导意见》（国知发管字〔2015〕44号），全面推动《企业知识产权管理规范》（国家标准GB/T 29490-2013）（以下简称《规范》）在我省的贯彻实施（以下简称“贯标”），指导企业建立科学、系统的知识产权管理体系，增强企业核心竞争力，服务创新驱动发展，现结合我省实际，提出以下实施意见。

一、充分认识贯标工作的重要意义

推行《规范》是指通过指导企业策划、实施、检查、改进四个环节，建立科学、规范的知识产权管理体系，持续提高企业知识产权管理水平的系统工程。加快推进实施《规范》，有利于提升企业自身价值，巩固市场竞争地位；有利于激励企业自主创新，增强企业核心竞争力；有利于聚焦产业转型升级，服务创新驱动发展。各级各有关部门要充分认识贯标工作的重要性和紧迫性，凝聚共识，加大力度，全力推进《规范》在我省的深入实施。

二、指导思想、基本原则和主要目标

（一）指导思想。

按照党的十八大和十八届三中、四中全会关于加强知识产权运用和保护、健全技术创新激励机制的总体要求，紧密结合我省产业转型升级需要，以促进企业技术创新为目标，以提升企业知识产权制度运用能力为导向，以规范企业知识产权管理为重点，坚持政府引导、市场运作、统筹协调、全面推进的原则，强化政策引导体系，提升服务机构能力，加强认证体系建设，推动企业实现创新驱动发展，为将我省建设成为知识产权强国先行地提供支撑。

（二）基本原则。

政府引导，市场运作。充分发挥政府在政策制定、社会管理、公共服务和环境营造等方面的作用，有效整合和聚集社会资源，引导企业积极参与实施《规范》。发挥市场在资源配置、知识产权制度运用中的基础性作用，健全市场导向机制，通过实施《规范》，增强企业市场竞争力。

政策扶持，企业参与。加强各级政策的衔接和联动，充分发挥政策的导向和激励作用，通过强化宣传、辅导培训、资金引导等多种方式，引导、鼓励和支持企业广泛开展《规范》贯彻实施工作。

统筹协调，全面推进。建立省和地市有关部门上下联动的工作机制，形成横向协调、纵向联动的工作局面。综合考虑企业特点、产业结构和区域状况，坚持分类指导。

（三）主要目标。

通过推行《规范》，引导企业建立科学、规范的知识产权管理体系，全面提升企业核心竞争力。到2017年底，培育一批优质的贯标咨询服务机构，培养一支专业的贯标人才队伍，全省参加开展贯标辅导的企业达到2000家，通过贯标认证的企业争取达到500家，实现省知识产权优势示范企业贯标全覆盖。到2020年，在全省范围内建立符合创新驱动发展需求的贯

标工作政策引导体系，构建市场秩序规范的咨询服务体系，形成遵循市场化机制的第三方认证体系，企业知识产权管理水平大幅提升，企业的知识产权竞争优势显著增强，创新驱动发展水平明显提高。

三、重点任务

（一）优化企业知识产权管理体系。

推动各类企业贯彻实施《规范》，建立与经营发展相协调的知识产权管理体系，引导企业加强知识产权机构、制度和人才队伍建设，将知识产权管理贯穿生产经营全流程。引导大型骨干企业、省属国有企业、高新技术企业、知识产权试点示范企业等实施《规范》。深入实施中小企业知识产权战略推进工程，鼓励和支持中小企业贯彻实施《规范》。探索开展军民知识产权融合工作，引导军工企业规范知识产权管理。

（二）构建贯标咨询服务体系。

出台激励措施，吸引各类知识产权咨询服务机构参与推行《规范》，建立健全内部管理制度和辅导工作流程，提高服务质量和效率，培育一批高质量的贯标咨询服务机构，形成竞争有序的服务市场。

（三）加强认证体系建设。

按照国家认证认可监督管理委员会、国家知识产权局的相关要求，吸引或培育若干认证机构落户广东，加快推进企业知识产权管理体系认证工作。稳步推进中规（北京）认证有限公司广州办事处建设，推动办事处高质量、高标准、高效率开展审核认证工作。鼓励各地方创造条件吸引其他认证机构在广东设立办事机构。

（四）加大贯标人才队伍培养。

充分发挥各类知识产权培训机构和贯标辅导服务机构的作用，建立《规范》培训业务体系，分层次对政府、服务机构、企业相关人员开展《规范》教育培训，培养一批了解标准化与认证管理、熟悉企业知识产权管理的专业人才队伍。加快知识产权管理标准审核员队伍建设，不断提高我省贯标认证审核水平。

（五）整合部门政策资源。

围绕产业转型升级和创新驱动发展，综合运用财政、税收、金融等政策引导企业完善知识产权管理体系，调动企业实施《规范》的积极性。积极推动企业知识产权管理体系认证与高新技术企业政策的衔接，完善高新技术企业认定管理办法，将认证情况作为高新技术企业认定的重要参考条件。对通过贯标认证的企业，在申报国家技术发明奖、中国专利金奖、广东专利奖以及国家科技重大专项、高新技术产业化项目和省知识产权优势示范企业等奖项或项目时实行政策倾斜，在同等条件下优先立项。

（六）强化贯标工作机制建设。

建立省和地市各级有关部门共同推行《规范》的工作机制，鼓励各地市结合各自实际，出台推进本地区贯标工作的政策措施和工作方案。创新工作模式，试点在广州、深圳、东莞、佛山等需求量大的地市开展批量认证审核工作。建立定期沟通机制，搭建交流平台，积极推进政府部门、服务机构和企业的沟通。深入开展《规范》宣贯、专家辅导、意见征询等活动，推动典型经验的信息共享和交流。

四、保障措施

（一）完善领导和协调机制。

各地、各部门要高度重视贯标工作，按照各自职责对贯标企业给予业务指导和支持。省、市两级知识产权管理部门要完善贯标工作领导体制和工作机制，制定实施专项规划，强化知识产权贯标政策与科教、经贸、质监等领域政策的紧密衔接。

（二）加大政策扶持力度。

省各级知识产权、科技、经济和信息化、商务、质监、财政等管理部门要根据经济社会发展需要，逐步加大财政、税收、金融等政策对企业贯彻《规范》的扶持力度。省知识产权局将采取后补助方式，对贯彻《规范》并通过认证的企业及其辅导机构给予一定的资金补助。各市、县（市、区）知识产权管理部门要结合实际，通过直接投入、后补助等方式，促进本行政区域内贯标工作的深入开展。

（三）狠抓贯彻落实。

各相关部门要把推行《规范》作为提升企业核心竞争力、推动全省企业产业转型升级的重要抓手，加强沟通联系和协作配合，积极做好资源共享、信息交流等工作，共同推进贯标工作任务的有效落实。要开展形式多样、内容广泛的宣传活动，增强企业对贯标工作的了解和支持，营造良好的贯标社会氛围。

（四）强化督查考评。

省知识产权局将每年贯标任务分解到各地级以上市知识产权局，加强推进和完成情况的督查、考核。各地级以上市知识产权局要制定年度推进计划，明确时间进度，确保年度贯标目标的实现。

地理标志产品保护规定

（2005年6月7日国家质量监督检验检疫总局令第78号公布）

第一章 总 则

第一条 为了有效保护我国的地理标志产品，规范地理标志产品名称和专用标志的使用，保证地理标志产品的质量和特色，根据《中华人民共和国产品质量法》、《中华人民共和国标准化法》、《中华人民共和国进出口商品检验法》等有关规定，制定本规定。

第二条 本规定所称地理标志产品，是指产自特定地域，所具有的质量、声誉或其他特性本质上取决于该产地的自然因素和人文因素，经审核批准以地理名称进行命名的产品。地理标志产品包括：

（一）来自本地区的种植、养殖产品。

（二）原材料全部来自本地区或部分来自其他地区，并在本地区按照特定工艺生产和加工的产品。

第三条 本规定适用于对地理标志产品的申请受理、审核批准、地理标志专用标志注册登记和监督管理工作。

第四条 国家质量监督检验检疫总局（以下简称“国家质检总局”）统一管理全国的地理标志产品保护工作。各地出入境检验检疫局和质量技术监督局（以下简称各地质检机构）依照职能开展地理标志产品保护工作。

第五条 申请地理标志产品保护，应依照本规定经审核批准。使用地理标志产品专用标志，必须依照本规定经注册登记，并接受监督管理。

第六条 地理标志产品保护遵循申请自愿，受理及批准公开的原则。

第七条 申请地理标志保护的产品应当符合安全、卫生、环保的要求，对环境、生态、资源可能产生危害的产品，不予受理和保护。

第二章 申请及受理

第八条 地理标志产品保护申请，由当地县级以上人民政府指定的地理标志产品保护申请机构或人民政府认定的协会和企业（以下简称申请人）提出，并征求相关部门意见。

第九条 申请保护的产品在县域范围内的，由县级人民政府提出产地范围的建议；跨县域范围的，由地市级人民政府提出产地范围的建议；跨地市范围的，由省级人民政府提出产地范围的建议。

第十条 申请人应提交以下资料：

（一）有关地方政府关于划定地理标志产品产地范围的建议。

（二）有关地方政府成立申请机构或认定协会、企业作为申请人的文件。

（三）地理标志产品的证明材料，包括：

1. 地理标志产品保护申请书；

2. 产品名称、类别、产地范围及地理特征的说明；

3. 产品的理化、感官等质量特色及其与产地的自然因素和人文因素之间关系的说明；

4. 产品生产技术规范（包括产品加工工艺、安全卫生要求、加工设备的技术要求等）；

5. 产品的知名度，产品生产、销售情况及历史渊源的说明；

（四）拟申请的地理标志产品的技术标准。

第十一条 出口企业的地理标志产品的保护申请向本辖区内出入境检验检疫部门提出；按地域提出的地理标志产品的保护申请和其他地理标志产品的保护申请向当地（县级或县级以上）质量技术监督部门提出。

第十二条 省级质量技术监督局和直属出入境检验检疫局，按照分工，分别负责对拟申报的地理标志产品的保护申请提出初审意见，并将相关文件、资料上报国家质检总局。

第三章 审核及批准

第十三条 国家质检总局对收到的申请进行形式审查。审查合格的，由国家质检总局在国家质检总局公报、政府网站等媒体上向社会发布受理公告；审查不合格的，应书面告知申请人。

第十四条 有关单位和个人对申请有异议的，可在公告后的2个月内向国家质检总局提出。

第十五条 国家质检总局按照地理标志产品的特点设立相应的专家审查委员会，负责地理标志产品保护申请的技术审查工作。

第十六条 国家质检总局组织专家审查委员会对没有异议或者有异议但被驳回的申请进行技术审查，审查合格的，由国家质检总局发布批准该产品获得地理标志产品保护的公告。

第四章 标准制订及专用标志使用

第十七条 拟保护的地理标志产品，应根据产品的类别、范围、知名度、产品的生产销售等方面的因素，分别制订相应的国家标准、地方标准或管理规范。

第十八条 国家标准化行政主管部门组织草拟并发布地理标志保护产品的国家标准；省级地方人民政府标准化行政主管部门组织草拟并发布地理标志保护产品的地方标准。

第十九条 地理标志保护产品的质量检验由省级质量技术监督部门、直属出入境检验检疫部门指定的检验机构承担。必要时，国家质检总局将组织予以复检。

第二十条 地理标志产品产地范围内的生产者使用地理标志产品专用标志，应向当地质量技术监督局或出入境检验检疫局提出申请，并提交以下资料：

（一）地理标志产品专用标志使用申请书。

（二）由当地政府主管部门出具的产品产自特定地域的证明。

（三）有关产品质量检验机构出具的检验报告。

上述申请经省级质量技术监督局或直属出入境检验检疫局审核，并经国家质检总局审查合格注册登记后，发布公告，生产者即可在其产品上使用地理标志产品专用标志，获得地理标志产品保护。

第五章 保护和监督

第二十一条 各地质检机构依法对地理标志保护产品实施保护。对于擅自使用或伪造地理标志名称及专用标志的；不符合地理标志产品标准和管理规范要求而使用该地理标志产品的名称的；或者使用与专用标志相近、易产生误解的名称或标识及可能误导消费者的文字或图案标志，使消费者将该产品误认为地理标志保护产品的行为，质量技术监督部门和出入境检验检疫部门将依法进行查处。社会团体、企业和个人可监督、举报。

第二十二条 各地质检机构对地理标志产品的产地范围，产品名称，原材料，生产技术工艺，质量特色，质量等级、数量、包装、标识，产品专用标志的印刷、发放、数量、使用情况，产品生产环境、生产设备，产品的标准符合性等方面进行日常监督管理。

第二十三条 获准使用地理标志产品专用标志资格的生产者，未按相应标准和管理规范组织生产的，或者在两年内未在受保护的地理标志产品上使用专用标志的，国家质检总局将注销其地理标志产品专用标志使用注册登记，停止其使用地理标志产品专用标志并对外公告。

第二十四条 违反本规定的，由质量技术监督行政部门和出入境检验检疫部门依据《中华人民共和国产品质量法》、《中华人民共和国标准化法》、《中华人民共和国进出口商品检验法》等有关法律予以行政处罚。

第二十五条 从事地理标志产品保护工作的人员应忠于职守，秉公办事，不得滥用职权、以权谋私，不得泄露技术秘密。违反以上规定的，予以行政纪律处分；构成犯罪的依法追究刑事责任。

第六章 附 则

第二十六条 国家质检总局接受国外地理标志产品在中华人民共和国的注册并实施保护。具体办法另外规定。

第二十七条 本规定由国家质检总局负责解释。

第二十八条 本规定自2005年7月15日起施行。原国家质量技术监督局公布的《原产地域产品保护规定》同时废止。原国家出入境检验检疫局公布的《原产地标记管理规定》、《原产地标记管理规定实施办法》中关于地理标志的内容与本规定不一致的，以本规定为准。

（供稿人：钟培敬）

地理标志产品保护工作细则

国质检科〔2009〕222号

第一条 为更好地贯彻实施《地理标志产品保护规定》，进一步推动地理标志产品保护工作，特制定本工作细则。

第二条 以下产品可以经申请批准为地理标志保护产品：

（一）在特定地域种植、养殖的产品，决定该产品特殊品质、特色和声誉的主要是当地的自然因素；

（二）在产品产地采用特定工艺生产加工，原材料全部来自产品产地，当地的自然环境和生产该产品所采用的特定工艺中的人文因素决定了该产品的特殊品质、特色质量和声誉；

（三）在产品产地采用特定工艺生产加工，原材料部分来自其他地区，该产品产地的自然环境和生产该产品所采用的特定工艺中的人文因素决定了该产品的特殊品质、特色质量和声誉。

第三条 国家质量监督检验检疫总局（以下简称国家质检总局）在地理标志产品保护管理工作中的主要职责是：

（一）配合立法部门，开展地理标志保护法律法规的调研、起草；

（二）制定、发布地理标志产品保护规章、制度；

（三）制定地理标志发展规划、计划并组织实施；

（三）组织协调和指导地理标志保护的行政执法活动；

（四）负责地理标志产品保护申请的形式审查；

（五）办理地理标志产品保护申请的受理事项，发布受理公告；

（六）组织对地理标志产品保护申请的异议协调；

（七）组织和管理专家技术队伍开展技术审查；

（八）办理、发布地理标志产品保护的批准公告；

（九）核准地理标志保护产品专用标志的使用申请；

（十）组织开展地理标志产品保护的宣传和培训；

（十一）组织开展和参加地理标志保护国际合作与交流活动；代表国家参加WTO地理标志谈判；

（十二）办理国外地理标志保护注册申请，组织开展互认合作。

第四条 各直属出入境检验检疫局和省级质量技术监督局（以下简称“省级质检机构”）的主要职责是：

（一）按照分工指导、协调本辖区的地理标志产品保护工作；

（二）按照分工负责本辖区地理标志产品保护申请的初审；

（三）负责指定地理标志保护产品的检验机构；

（四）负责审核生产者使用地理标志产品专用标志的申请；

（五）负责指导地理标志产品保护技术文件的制定；

（六）负责查处本辖区发生的地理标志产

品的违法行为。

第五条 关于当地质检机构。申请保护的产品产地在县域范围内的，地理标志保护的当地质检机构为县质量技术监督局或辖区内出入境检验检疫分支机构（无出入境检验检疫分支机构的，由直属出入境检验检疫局负责）；申请保护的产品产地跨县域范围的，当地质检机构为地、市、（州）质量技术监督局或辖区内出入境检验检疫分支机构（无出入境检验检疫分支机构的，由直属出入境检验检疫局负责）；申请保护的产地跨地市范围的，当地质检机构为直属出入境检验检疫局或省（自治区、直辖市）质量技术监督局。当地质检机构的主要职责是：

（一）协助申请人进行地理标志产品保护的申请；

（二）负责对生产者申请使用专用标志进行初审，监督管理专用标志的印制、发放和使用；

（三）负责地理标志保护产品的日常监督管理工作；

（四）负责草拟地理标志产品省级地方标准，组织制定地理标志产品生产过程的技术规范或标准；

（五）负责查处产地范围内发生的地理标志产品的侵权行为。

第六条 经申请、批准，以地理名称命名的产品方能称为地理标志保护产品。地理标志名称由具有地理指示功能的名称和反映产品真实属性的产品通用名称构成。地理标志名称必须是商业或日常用语，或是长久以来使用的名称，并具有一定知名度。

第七条 地理标志产品保护遵循申请自愿的原则。地理标志产品保护申请的受理、审核与批准坚持公开、公平、公正的原则。

第八条 申请产品出现下列情况之一的，不能给予地理标志产品保护：

（一）对环境、生态、资源可能造成破坏或对健康可能产生危害的；

（二）产品名称已成为通用名称的；

（三）产品的质量特色与当地自然因素和人文因素缺乏关联性的；

（四）地域范围难以界定，或申请保护的地域范围与实际产地范围不符的。

第九条 地理标志产品保护申请，由当地县级以上人民政府（含县级，以下同）指定的地理标志产品保护申请机构或人民政府认定的协会和企业（以下简称申请人）提出，由申请人负责准备有关的申请资料。申请人为当地县级以上人民政府的，可成立地理标志产品保护领导小组，负责地理标志保护相关工作。

第十条 申请人应填写《地理标志产品保护申请书》，并提供以下资料：

（一）当地县级以上人民政府关于成立申报机构或指定协会、企业作为申请人的文件。

（二）当地县级以上人民政府关于划定申报产品保护地域范围的公函，保护范围一般具体到乡镇一级；水产品养殖范围一般以自然水域界定。

（三）所申报产品现行有效的专用标准或管理规范。

（四）证明产品特性的材料，包括：

1. 能够说明产品名称、产地范围及地理特征的；

2. 能够说明产品的历史渊源、知名度和产品生产、销售情况的；

3. 能够说明产品的理化、感官指标等质量特色及其与产地自然因素和人文因素之间关联性的；

4. 规定产品生产技术的，包括生产所用原材料、生产工艺、流程、安全卫生要求、主要质量特性、加工设备技术要求等；

5. 其它证明资料，如地方志、获奖证明、检测报告等。

第十一条 省级质检机构负责对申请进行初审。初审不组织召开专家审查会。初审合格的，向国家质检总局提出初审意见，并将相关文件、资料上报国家质检总局。

第十二条 国家质检总局负责对通过初审的申请进行形式审查。对于形式要件不齐全或不符合规定要求的，国家质检总局在30个工作日内向省级质检机构发出形式审查意见通知书。形式审查合格的，通过国家质检总局公报、官方网站发布受理公告。

第十三条 自受理公告发布之日起2个月为异议期。异议协调一般遵循属地原则。在异议期内如收到异议：

（一）异议仅限于本省的，由国家质检总局授权有关省级质检机构进行处理，并及时反馈异议处理结果。必要时，国家质检总局可应省级质检机构的要求，听取专家意见并组织协调。

（二）跨省的异议由国家质检总局负责组织协调。

第十四条 技术审查准备。受理公告发布后，申请人应着手准备专家技术审查会的相关文件，包括：1. 申报产品的陈述报告；2. 申报产品的质量技术要求。

陈述报告是对申请资料的概括和总结，应重点陈述产品的名称、知名度、质量特色及其与产地的自然因素和人文因素的关联性，拟采取的后续监管措施等。

质量技术要求作为国家质检总局批准公告的基础，是对原有标准或技术规范中决定质量特色的关键因素的提炼和总结，具有强制性。内容包括产品名称、产地保护范围、为保证产品特色而必须强制执行的环境条件、生产过程规范以及产品的感官特色和理化指标等。

第十五条 对公告无异议或异议已处理，且已完成技术审查准备的，由省级质检机构向国家质检总局提出召开技术审查会的建议。国家质检总局成立地理标志产品专家审查委员会，并根据专业领域和产品类别下设分委员会。专家审查委员会根据需要聘请专家召开技术审查会。专家组成一般包括法律、专业技术、质量检验、标准化、管理等方面的人员。组成人数为奇数，一般为7人以上，但不超过11人。

第十六条 专家技术审查内容包括：

（一）听取申请人代表所作的陈述报告。

（二）审查产品的申请资料和证明材料。

（三）围绕产品名称、知名度、与当地的自然因素和人文因素之间的关联性等方面进行技术讨论。

（四）形成会议纪要。

（五）提出地理标志产品保护的建议，包括：

1. 是否应对申报产品实施地理标志保护；

2. 所存在的问题和处理建议。

（六）讨论产品的质量技术要求。

第十七条 技术审查合格的，由国家质检总局发布该产品获得地理标志产品保护的公告。颁发《地理标志产品保护证书》（有关事项另行规定）。

第十八条 申请人应在申请资料中提供现行有效的产品专用标准或管理规范，作为地理标志保护产品批准公告和综合标准的基础。

批准公告发布后，省级质检机构应在3—6个月内，组织申请人在批准公告中“质量技术要求”的框架下，在原有专用标准或技术规范的基础上，完善地理标志产品的标准体系，一般应以省级地方标准的形式发布，并报国家质检总局委托的技术机构审核备案。

第十九条 地理标志产品产地范围内的生产者需要使用地理标志产品专用标志的，应向批准公告中确定的当地质检机构提出申请，并提交以下资料：

（一）《地理标志产品专用标志使用申请书》；

（二）产地主管部门出具的产品产自特定地域范围的证明；

（三）指定的质量检验机构出具的检验报告。

第二十条 省级质检机构对生产者使用专用标志的申请进行审核，并将相关信息和专用标志使用汇总表分别以书面方式和电子版报国家质检总局，由国家质检总局发布核准企业使用地理标志保护产品专用标志的公告。

第二十一条 印制地理标志保护产品专用标志按照国家质检总局2006年第109号公告的

要求执行。

第二十二条 专用标志的标示方法有：

（一）加贴或吊挂在产品或包装物上；

（二）直接印刷在产品标签或包装物上；

（三）应申请人的要求或根据实际情况，采用相应的标示方法。

直接印刷在产品标签或包装物上的，由当地质检机构监督管理，并将印刷数量登记备案。

国家质检总局批准公告中明确的当地质检机构须控制专用标志的使用数量，建立产品的溯源体系。

第二十三条 获得专用标志使用资格的生产者，应在产品包装标识上标明“国家地理标志保护产品”字样，并在标识显著位置标明地理标志保护产品名称，同时，应执行国家对产品包装标识的强制性规定。

第二十四条 使用专用标志的，应同时标注国家质检总局批准公告号以及所执行的地理标志产品标准号以及该产品的通用标准等。

第二十五条 各地质检机构依法对地理标志保护产品实施保护。应组织完善地理标志产品综合标准体系，以保护产品质量特色的稳定性和一致性；应完善地理标志产品检验检测体系，有效打击假冒侵权行为；应完善质量保证体系，健全过程管理措施，以保护地理标志产品的质量信誉不受损害；应依法组织打击侵权行为，以净化生产流通环境，保护地理标志产品生产者的知识产权。

第二十六条 地理标志产品的质量检验由指定的法定检验机构承担。必要时，国家质检总局组织复检。

第二十七条 各地质检机构对地理标志保护产品进行以下日常监督管理：

1. 对产品名称进行保护，监督此方面的侵权行为，以依法采取保护措施；

2. 对产品是否符合地理标志产品保护公告和标准等方面进行监督，以保证受保护产品在特定地域内规范生产；

3. 对产品生产环境、生产设备和产品的标准符合性等方面进行现场检查，以防止随意变更生产条件，影响产品的质量特色；

4. 对原材料实行进厂检验把关，生产者须将进货发票、检验数据等存档以便溯源；

5. 对生产技术工艺进行监督，生产者不得随意更改传统工艺流程，而对产品的质量特色造成损害；

6. 对质量等级、产量等进行监控，生产者不得随意改变等级标准或超额生产；

7. 对包装标识和地理标志产品专用标志的印制、发放及使用情况进行监管，建立台账，防止滥用或其它不按照要求使用的行为发生。

第二十八条 国家质检总局每年安排一定数量的地理标志保护产品列入监督抽查目录，重点检查产品名称、质量、产量、包装、标识及专用标志使用等。省级质量技术监督局每年须将本省一定数量的地理标志保护产品列入地方监督抽查目录；直属出入境检验检疫局每年须对辖区内一定数量的出口地理标志保护产品进行检验抽查。各级质检机构依照职能，对假冒地理标志保护产品的行为进行查处。

对于擅自使用或伪造地理标志名称及专用标志的；不符合地理标志产品标准和管理规范要求而使用该地理标志产品的名称的；或者使用与专用标志相近、易产生误解的名称或标识及可能误导消费者的文字或图案标志，使消费者将该产品误认为地理标志保护产品的行为，质量技术监督部门和出入境检验检疫部门将依法进行查处。消费者、社会团体、企业、个人可监督、举报。

第二十九条 省级质检机构每年3月底前将上一年本辖区地理标志产品保护的情况及专用标志的使用情况报国家质检总局。

第三十条 从事地理标志产品保护工作的人员应忠于职守，秉公办事。要认真学习宣传地理标志产品保护制度，指导申请人进行申请，及时向申请人反馈上一级主管部门的审核意见，履行有关的地理标志产品保护职责。不得滥用职权，以权谋私，增加申请人负担，损害质检系统声誉；不得泄露技术秘密，使生产者蒙受损失。违反以上规定的，予以行政纪律处分；构成犯罪的，依法追究刑事责任。

第三十一条 各级质检机构不得向地理标志产品保护的申请人收取任何费用。

第三十二条 上报国家质检总局的申请资料一式两份，印刷装订。申报资料及申请表格的电子版同时发送至国家质检总局。

第三十三条 本工作细则所规定的表格式样由国家质检总局统一制定，各地质检机构可在国家质检总局网站上自行下载、印刷。

（供稿人：钟培敬）

2015年知识产权大事记

1月

7—9日 省知识产权局副巡视员黄光华率筹建组及省知识产权研究院相关人员赴北京，就省知识产权服务业集聚中心支撑项目建设等问题开展专题调研。

8日 省工商局与香港特区政府知识产权署举办的“新《商标法》研讨会”在香港圆满结束。省工商局代表讲解了商标管理与保护方面的新规定，对参会代表关于《商标法》新规定、维权实务等方面的问题进行解答。

12日 “广东省知识产权局、青海省知识产权局知识产权工作合作框架协议书签署仪式暨第一次工作会议”在广州召开。省知识产权局局长马宪民、青海省科技厅副厅长邢小方出席会议并讲话，省知识产权局副局长唐毅与青海省知识产权局局长许淳分别代表粤青双方签署协议。

14日 省知识产权局局长马宪民带领广州市越秀区、东莞市松山湖高新技术产业开发区两个广东省知识产权服务业聚集发展试验区知识产权局负责人，赴北京市中关村知识产权服务业聚集发展试验区，调研学习知识产权服务业聚集发展工作经验。

15日 全国知识产权局局长会议在北京召开，省知识产权局局长马宪民出席会议。根据会议安排，马宪民在会上作了《改革创新，争创“知识产权强国建设先行地”》的经验交流。

21—23日 省知识产权局副局长谢红率队赴河南和湖北两省，开展专利导航产业发展工作专题调研。深圳、佛山、东莞、中山市知识产权局等“珠江三角洲地区重点产业转型升级专利导航工程”项目承担单位的有关负责人参加了调研。

26—28日 中华商标协会在北京举办部分商标协会会长及专家座谈会，省工商局副局长钱永成参会。

27—28日 国家知识产权局专利管理司副司长曹冬根率全国打击侵权假冒绩效考核第十二考核组对广东省打击侵权假冒工作进行检查考核。

28日 省知识产权局副巡视员黄光华率国家知识产权局专利局广州代办处有关人员赴浙江省杭州市参加国家知识产权局专利局代办处（华东区）发展恳谈会。

28日 省知识产权局局长马宪民带队赴中国南方电网公司，就大型企业专利管理工作进行调研。

2月

4日 省知识产权局局长马宪民，纪检组长、监察专员严小宜，带队赴河源市紫金县龙窝镇高坑村和琴星村，进行春节扶贫慰问，为贫困户、老党员等送上慰问金和慰问品。

5日 省知识产权局召开制定知识产权强国建设先行地政策专题会议。研究贯彻落实《深入实施国家知识产权战略行动计划（2014—2020年）》和讨论制定《创建知识产权强国建设先行地行动纲要》。局长马宪民，纪检组长、监察专员严小宜出席会议并讲话。

6日 “创建知识产权深化改革试验区——广东自贸区知识产权工作的思考”理论研讨会在广州召开。省知识产权局副局长袁有楼出席会议并讲话。

9日 省知识产权局召开局党组（扩大）会议，学习贯彻中央纪委十八届五次全会和省纪委十一届四次全会精神。

10日 广东省知识产权维权援助中心江

门分中心揭牌仪式在江门市科学馆举行，省知识产权局副局长谢红出席并讲话。

12日 省知识产权局副局长唐毅会见来访的新加坡国际企业发展局中国司副司长陈雅丽一行7人。

12日 国家知识产权局专利管理司与财政部经济建设司，在北京联合召开知识产权运营服务试点工作座谈会。省知识产权局副局长谢红参会，并就广东知识产权运营工作进展作重点发言。

26日 省知识产权局召开制定知识产权强国建设先行地政策专题研究会议，讨论修改《广东省深入实施知识产权战略创建知识产权强国建设先行地行动计划（2014—2020年）》。局长马宪民，纪检组长、监察专员严小宜出席会议。

28日 省检察院党组会议研究决定在省检察院民事行政检察处增设知识产权监督科。其主要职能：办理对省法院知识产权民事、行政生效判决、裁定、调解的监督案件以及审判程序中审判人员违法行为监督案件；办理各地级以上市院、广铁分院提请抗诉的知识产权民事、行政案件；办理各地级以上市院、广铁分院知识产权民事、行政请示案件；备案审查各地级以上市院、广铁分院的知识产权抗诉、再审检察建议案件；指导全省知识产权民事、行政检察工作等。

28日 省工商局局长、商标注册派出机构广东筹备领导小组（下简领导小组）组长朱泽君在广州开发区管委会主持召开商标注册派出机构广东筹备领导小组第一次工作会议，讨论由领导小组办公室提交的《关于商标注册派出机构筹建工作有关问题的请示》，研究确定下一步工作安排。广州市委常委、广州开发区管委会主任、中新广州知识城管委会主任陈志英，广州市工商局局长、商标注册派出机构广东筹备领导小组常务副组长兼办公室主任张建华，省工商局副局长、商标注册派出机构广东筹备领导小组副组长钱永成等有关负责人参加会议。

3月

3日 省知识产权局局长马宪民、副局长唐毅会见揭阳市副市长张时义一行，双方就首届中德中小企业合作交流会相关事宜进行了深入交流。

6日 省知识产权局副局长谢红赴佛山市南海区就广东省半导体照明产业联合创新中心工作开展调研。

9日 省知识产权局组织召开广东专利事业战略推进计划征求意见会，听取各地市知识产权局有关负责人意见和建议。副局长袁有楼出席会议并讲话。

9—11日 由广东省美容美发化妆品行业协会主办，全国工商联美容化妆品业商会协办的第42届广东国际美博会在广州琶洲展馆B馆举办。省知识产权局派员全程参与驻会，提供知识产权咨询服务，配合主办方开展专利投诉案件的受理和处理工作。此届美博会展览面积超过14万平方米，设13大专业展馆，增加了电商采购区，来自中国大部分省份及亚洲、欧洲、美洲、大洋洲的企业参展。

12日 全国打击侵权假冒办调研组来粤就农村市场假冒伪劣、互联网领域侵权假冒和车用燃油三个专项整治的情况进行调研。

13日 广东省人民政府副省长陈云贤在北京拜会国家知识产权局局长申长雨。双方围绕经济新常态下广东知识产权工作面临的战略机遇及挑战开展了深入探讨，对广东开展知识产权强国建设先行地的政策创新、路径规划、工作思路及重点任务进行了商讨，并对下一步广东与国家知识产权局开展知识产权战略合作相关工作交换了意见。

17日 全省知识产权局局长会议在广州召开。会议传达了全国知识产权局局长会议精神，总结了2014年全省知识产权工作情况，并对2015年重点工作进行了部署。

17—19日 省工商局分别在惠州、江门市组织召开广东省著名商标认定职能转移评估工作研讨会，对近两年的著名商标认定工作进行评估，对下一步如何开展好著名商标认定及评估工作提出意见建议。省工商局副局长钱永成参加研讨会。

18日 全国打击侵权假冒工作电视电话会议在北京召开。会议结束后，广东省政府接着召开全省打击侵权假冒工作电视电话会议，贯彻落实全国会议精神，部署打击侵权假冒工作。副省长、省打击侵权假冒工作领导小组组长陈云贤出席会议并讲话，省打击侵权假冒工作领导小组副组长、办公室主任、省知识产权局局长马宪民通报2014年全省打击侵权假冒工作情况，会议由省打击侵权假冒工作领导小组副组长、省政府副秘书长李捍东主持。

18日 省知识产权局召开座谈会，欢迎国家知识产权局专利复审委员会行政诉讼处主任科员刘新蕾来省知识产权局挂职。会议由省知识产权局副局长袁有楼主持，国家知识产权局专利复审委员会人事教育处和行政诉讼处等相关部门领导参加了会议。

18日 珠海市检察院正式印发《珠海市人民检察院办理知识产权案件工作规则》，标志着珠海市知识产权刑事案件跨区域审理诉讼格局正式形成，保障案件的专业化办理和统一性法律适用。

19日 省知识产权局副局长谢红带队赴深圳市中彩联科技有限公司、深圳中科院知识产权投资有限公司、深圳市联创知识产权服务中心等单位调研。

19—20日 湖南省知识产权局副局长刘中杰一行来粤调研专利行政执法工作，省知识产权局副局长袁有楼出席座谈会并介绍有关情况。

19—21日 由国家知识产权局主办，省知识产权局承办，省知识产权研究与发展中心、国家知识产权培训（广东）基地协办的“享受专利代理人资格考试试点扶持政策人员培训班”在广州举行。

20日 由省半导体照明产业联合创新中心、省知识产权维权援助中心和深圳大学光电工程学院联合主办，LED产业专利联盟（LPA）承办的2015·美国“337调查”紧箍咒下的中国LED企业生存之道研讨会在深圳大学举行。省知识产权局副局长谢红与深圳大学副校长徐晨出席会议并发表讲话。

20日 《广东知识产权年鉴》编撰及图片采集技巧培训班在广州举办。省直相关单位和部分地市知识产权局的特约编辑近50人参加培训。《广东知识产权年鉴》（2014年版）参加由中国出版协会主办的第五届年鉴编纂出版质量评比活动，荣获综合二等奖、框架设计二等奖、条目编写一等奖、装帧设计二等奖。这是《广东知识产权年鉴》首次参加全国专业性年鉴评比并获奖。该奖项为中国地方志系统年鉴评比最高奖，是与中国韬奋出版奖并列为中国出版协会主办的两个全国性评比奖项，每五年举行一次，此次参评年鉴近400部。

23—24日 国家知识产权局专利复审委员会派电学申诉一处、光电申诉一处12名审查员来粤开展专利权无效案件头审理。此次口头审理，案件共8件。案件审理期间，省知识产权局组织了相关单位30余人旁听。

24日 应东莞市委、市政府邀请，省知识产权局局长马宪民出席了东莞市科技创新大会并讲话。

24日 省知识产权局副局长唐毅带队赴中国（广东）自由贸易试验区广州南沙新区开展知识产权工作调研，广州市知识产权局局长邓佑满陪同。

24日 全省专利代理管理工作会议在广州召开。省知识产权局局长马宪民，纪检组长、监察专员严小宜出席会议并讲话。来自全省各地级以上市知识产权局分管领导及相关工作人员、全省专利代理机构及分支负责人共170余人参加了会议。

25日 省知识产权局局长马宪民率领局领导班子成员及部分处室负责人拜会省科技厅，省科技厅的领导班子成员及相关处室负责人出席了座谈会。

26日 中国专利信息中心主任张东亮一行到省知识产权局就专利信息服务地方专题开

展调研。省知识产权局局长马宪民、副局长谢红出席调研座谈会。

26—29日 福建省德化县知识产权局组织县知识产权局、教育局、中小学校代表30人，到广州参加青少年知识产权教育普及师资培训班。

27日 省知识产权局局长马宪民率领部分局领导班子成员及相关处室负责人拜会广州知识产权法院，广州知识产权法院院长杨宗仁、副院长吴振及相关部门负责人出席了座谈会。双方围绕如何进一步健全知识产权侵权查处机制、强化行政执法与司法衔接等问题，进行深入探讨。

28日 “资本与知识产权运营”研讨会暨广东中策知识产权研究院成立仪式在广州举行。省人民政府副省长陈云贤作主题演讲并为研究院成立揭牌，国家知识产权局协调保护司副司长武晓明、省知识产权局局长马宪民、副局长谢红、副巡视员黄光华参加成立仪式。

28日至4月2日 2015年知识产权服务高端实务培训班在广州举办。此次培训由国家知识产权局主办，广东省知识产权局、广东中策知识产权研究院承办。国家知识产权局规划发展司司长龚亚麟、副司长刘菊芳，省知识产权局局长马宪民、副巡视员黄光华出席培训班。全国知识产权服务品牌机构培育单位高层管理人员和知识产权服务集聚发展试验区相关负责人共计80余人参加培训。

4月

1日 省知识产权局在广州召开新闻通气会，局长马宪民向与会媒体介绍了广东实施专利法三十年以来的工作情况和取得的成效。

1日 省知识产权局副局长唐毅会见来访的韩国知识产权委员会知识产权振兴局局长权圭佑（Kwun Kui Wou）一行6人。

1日 由国家知识产权局专利复审委员会主办、省知识产权局承办的巡回审理庭管理使用培训班在广州举办，省知识产权局副局长袁有楼出席开班仪式并致辞。

1日 惠州市仲恺高新区举行“一个服务大厅、四个中心”的揭牌仪式。作为该中心重要组成部分——省知识产权维权援助中心惠州分中心正式挂牌成立。

2—3日 省知识产权局局长马宪民、副局长唐毅率队赴深圳和珠海调研中国（广东）自由贸易试验区知识产权工作。

5—8日 由广东国际科技贸易展览公司主办的第13届中国（广州）国际专业灯光音响暨乐器展览会在琶洲展馆A馆举办。省知识产权局派员驻会期间，共调解专利侵权纠纷案件25件。

5—8日 由广东国际科技贸易展览公司主办的第20届华南国际口腔展览会在广州琶洲展馆C馆举办。省知识产权局派员驻会期间，共调解专利投诉案件3件。

8日 省知识产权局副局长谢红应邀出席江门市知识产权暨国家知识产权试点城市建设工作会议并讲话。

9日 国家知识产权局专利局南京代办处一行六人到广州代办处开展调研活动。省知识产权局副巡视员黄光华出席座谈会。

10日 “广东省专利信息协会成立暨第一次会员代表大会”在广州隆重举行。省知识产权局局长马宪民、省民政厅等单位负责人出席了会议并讲话，会议由副局长谢红主持。来自近80个会员单位、省市知识产权局相关部门和其他社会机构代表120多人参加会议。

13日 佛山、中山获评为国家知识产权示范城市。

14日 广东省政府与国家知识产权局在广州举行第二轮知识产权高层次战略合作2015年度工作会议，共同议定年度战略合作事项。广东省政府省长朱小丹、国家知识产权局局长申长雨出席会议并讲话。省政府副省长陈云贤主持会议。国家知识产权局副局长贺化、省知识产权局局长马宪民出席会议。

14日 中国国家知识产权局、新加坡知识产权局与广东省政府三方会谈暨中国国家知识产权局与新加坡知识产权局会谈纪要签字仪式在广州举行。国家知识产权局局长申长雨、新加坡知识产权局局长陈一山、广东省政府副省长陈云贤出席会议并讲话，省政府副秘书长李捍东主持会议。省知识产权局局长马宪民、审协广东中心主任毕囡参加三方会谈。

15日 省知识产权局局长马宪民会见来访的新加坡知识产权局局长陈一山一行7人，双方围绕中新知识城知识产权工作及下一阶段合作展开深入交流，省知识产权局副局长唐毅参加会见。

15日 国家知识产权局副局长贺化率国家知识产权局专利管理司、银监会、人保财险总公司、交通银行、国家知识产权局发展研究中心等一行9人，来广东调研知识产权金融服务工作。

15日至5月5日 国家知识产权局专利局广州代办处派员进驻第117届广交会，协助广交会知识产权投诉站核实投诉专利的法律状态，并为参展企业当事人提供专利信息查询和副本出证服务。

15日至5月5日 第117届广交会在广州举办。省知识产权局组织省市专利联合执法队伍驻会开展知识产权保护工作，联合执法队共有60余人。其间，投诉站共受理专利侵权纠纷396宗，涉及被投诉企业460家，占知识产权投诉案件总数的74.6%；其中，发明18宗，实用新型83宗，外观设计295宗。

16日 《商标代理服务规范》（DB44/T 1579-2015）地方标准于2015年4月16日发布公告，自2015年7月16日起正式实施。这是全国首部商标代理行业的地方标准，内容结合国内外商标代理行业的经验及专业知识，明确服务范围及服务资质，规范细化服务流程，并规定服务质量要求，对执业规范、信息化建设、监督管理等服务质量方面提出明确标准，适用于在广东省内从事商标代理服务的机构。

17日 “2014年知识产权保护状况及2015年知识产权宣传周活动方案”新闻发布会在广州召开。广东省人民政府知识产权办公会议副主持人、省知识产权局局长马宪民发布2014年广东省知识产权保护状况，省人民政府知识产权办公会议办公室副主任、省知识产权局副局长唐毅发布2015年广东省知识产权宣传周活动方案。其间，马宪民就有关问题回答记者提问。发布会由广东省政府新闻办副主任王永清主持。省政府知识产权办公会议成员单位代表，各国驻广州领事馆代表，境外及港澳驻穗新闻媒体代表，中央驻粤和广东各新闻单位代表共100余人参加发布会。

17日 国家工商总局召开2015年工商行政管理系统打击侵权假冒工作电视电话会议，贯彻落实全国打击侵权假冒工作电视电话会议精神，交流各地打击侵权假冒工作经验，部署下一阶段工作。省工商局副局长钱永成在广东分会场出席会议，并代表广东省工商局作大会交流发言。

18日 省知识产权局局长马宪民在副局长袁有楼、广交会知识产权投诉站负责人梅灵的陪同下，赴第117届广交会展馆，检查知识产权局系统驻会专利保护工作。马宪民对广交会近年来在知识产权工作方面取得的成绩予以充分肯定，对广交会的知识产权保护工作得到商务部和国家知识产权局的高度认可表示赞许。并指出，实施创新驱动发展需要知识产权的支撑，创新成果的知识产权保护工作日益重要。同时，马宪民强调下一步应加强与商务厅合作交流，为广东大型出口外贸企业提供更多的知识产权保护服务，促进企业自主创新能力和涉外应对能力的提高。

20日 省知识产权研究与发展中心与汇桔网达成全面战略合作，暨全国首家知识产权金融平台启动新闻发布会在广州召开。广州市工商联主席袁志敏、省知识产权局局长马宪民以及国家知识产权局市场产业处处长王双龙到会并致辞。发布会由广州市委统战部副部长、市工商联党组书记张镜初主持。

21日 省知识产权局赴河源市紫金县龙窝镇高坑村调研新一轮扶贫开发“双到”工作，并指导完成第三批（2015年）与第二批

（2014年）新一轮驻村干部工作交接。

21日 国家知识产权局专利局广州代办处派员赴茂名市开展电子专利申请业务宣讲活动，并为“电白区企业专利申请培训班”授课。茂名市知识产权局、电白区科工商务局相关人员、26家企业的负责人、技术骨干共50多人参加培训。

21日 省知识产权局副巡视员黄光华带队赴安徽省合肥市参加国家知识产权局专利局2015年代办工作会议。

22日 省知识产权局局长马宪民应邀出席广州市知识产权局举办的“广州知识产权大讲堂启动仪式暨首期专题讲座”，并作为首期嘉宾作了《知识产权制度是创新驱动发展的基本保障》的主题讲座。

23日 省知识产权局副局长唐毅会见韩国特许厅专利商标审判院院长诸大植（JEH Daeshik）一行7人。

23日 省政府参事室一行9人来省知识产权局开展“加强知识产权保护，促进创新驱动”专题调研。省知识产权局纪检组长、监察专员严小宜，副局长袁有楼出席座谈会。

23日 应国家知识产权局专利局审查协作广东中心的邀请，省知识产权局局长马宪民为该中心作了《发挥知识产权制度对创新驱动发展的基本保障作用》的专题报告。该中心共170余名领导干部和业务骨干听取了报告。

23日 省知识产权局与省经济和信息化委员会，在广州联合举办“广东省战略性新兴产业——物联网产业专利分析及预警报告会”。省知识产权局副局长谢红、省经济和信息化委员会总工程师谢时超出席会议并致辞。

24日 广汽集团举办首届“4·26”世界知识产权日活动，省知识产权局袁有楼副局长出席活动并讲话。

26—30日 国家知识产权局副局长何志敏赴广州、深圳调研知识产权国际合作工作。

27日 省国资委、省知识产权局联合举办省属企业知识产权管理规范培训班，省国资委周兴挺副主任、省知识产权局谢红副局长出席开班仪式并讲话。

27日 “省区共建广东知识产权创新运用试验区启动暨顺德科技支行成立大会”在顺德举行。省知识产权局局长马宪民、佛山市常务副市长黄志豪出席大会并讲话。

28日 由国家知识产权局、香港特别行政区知识产权署和澳门特别行政区经济局联合主办的“2015年内地与香港、澳门特别行政区知识产权研讨会”在中山市召开。国家知识产权局副局长何志敏、广东省政府副秘书长李捍东、香港特别行政区政府知识产权署署长梁家丽、澳门特别行政区政府经济局副局长戴建业出席开幕式并致辞。省知识产权局局长马宪民、中山市副市长吴月霞等参加相关活动。

29日 省知识产权局副局长谢红受邀参加2015格力电器知识产权工作研讨会，并发表《让知识产权成为创新驱动发展的核心推动力》的主题演讲。

29日 省政府研究室主任张爱军一行4人到省知识产权局开展知识产权强国建设先行地专题调研。局长马宪民，纪检组长、监察专员严小宜出席座谈会。

29日 广东知识产权保护协会在广州举行第三次会员代表大会暨三届一次会议。省知识产权局局长马宪民、纪检组长、监察专员严小宜出席会议并讲话。

5月

5日 省委政研室一行4人到省知识产权局开展知识产权强国建设先行地专题调研。省知识产权局局长马宪民出席调研座谈会。

5日 省人大常委会法制工作委员会召开立法协调会。省知识产权局副局长袁有楼出席会议。

6日 广东省政府参事室索健元参事一行8人到广东省工商局调研商标知识产权保护问题。省工商局局领导以及相关业务处室负责人参加调研座谈。

11—15日 国家知识产权局专利复审委

员会化学申诉一处一行10人来粤开展专利无效案件口头审理。

12日 省委办公厅召开胡春华同志督办提案办理工作第一次协调会。省知识产权局副局长袁有楼出席会议。

12日 省知识产权局局长马宪民会见来访的广州市花都区区长林中坚一行，双方就花都区争取设立广州（皮革皮具）知识产权快速维权中心相关事宜进行座谈。

12日 知识产权区域布局研讨暨推进工作会在国家知识产权局召开，省知识产权局副局长谢红带队参会。

14日 省发改委召开实施创新驱动发展战略开展全面创新改革试验工作座谈会。省知识产权局副局长袁有楼出席。

16日 国家知识产权局副局长廖涛、省知识产权局副局长袁有楼赴揭阳出席首届中德中小企业合作交流会启动仪式。在启动仪式上，袁有楼副局长为中德（揭阳）中小企业知识产权保护试验区授牌。首届中德中小企业合作交流会是在中德政府磋商机制及工业和信息化部与德国经济和能源部中德中小企业政策磋商机制下举办的，以“一带一路，携手共赢”为主题，来自中德两国政府领导、嘉宾和企业家共150多人参加会议。

18—20日 全省工商系统2015年商标业务培训班在广州召开。各地级以上市工商（市场监管）局分管商标工作的副局长、商标科（处）长和业务骨干，以及省工商局有关处室人员，共126人参加了培训。省工商局副局长钱永成出席开班仪式并作动员讲话。

18—21日 省知识产权局副局长谢红一行7人赴青海省开展知识产权调研交流活动。

20日 共青团广东省委员会副书记张志华一行拜访省知识产权局，双方就如何让知识产权制度成为广东青年创新的基本保障等议题进行了探讨。省知识产权局局长马宪民、纪检组长严小宜参加了座谈。

20日 由国家知识产权局专利局广州代办处承办的PCT国际阶段电子申请及审查系统（CEPCT）广东站培训班在广州举办。来自本省各专利代理机构的代表共100余人参加了培训。

22日 省委政法委员会召开省法学会八届二次理事会暨广州市区级法学会建设现场会。省知识产权局纪检组长、监察专员严小宜出席会议。

22日 由国家知识产权局组织召开的产业知识产权联盟建设工作座谈会在北京举行。司长雷筱云出席会议并讲话。来自北京、天津、吉林、上海、江苏、浙江、山东、河南、湖北、湖南、广东、四川、陕西和深圳等省（市）知识产权局的相关负责人以及国家专利协同运用试点单位中的全国性行业协会相关负责人约50人与会。省知识产权局副局长谢红带队参会。

22—23日 陕西省工商局在西安召开第十九届中国东西部合作与投资贸易洽谈会暨丝绸之路国际博览会，省工商局副局长钱永成应邀带队出席。其间还参加了国家工商总局商标局与陕西省工商局共同承办的“丝绸之路经济带品牌（商标）建设与经济发展合作交流大会”。

23日 第十七届中国科协年会在广州市举行。省知识产权局局长马宪民出席会议。

24—29日 国家知识产权局专利复审委员会材料工程二处一行6人来粤开展专利无效案件口头审理。

26日 省知识产权局召开制定知识产权强国建设先行地政策专题研讨会，讨论修改《关于深入实施知识产权战略推动创新驱动发展行动计划》。局长马宪民，纪检组长、监察专员严小宜，副局长袁有楼，副局长谢红，副巡视员黄光华出席会议。

28日 省政府依法行政考评第七组一行五人到省知识产权局进行实地考评。省知识产权局纪检组长、监察专员严小宜出席座谈会。

28—29日 国家知识产权局专利检索咨询中心副主任杜军一行4人到广东开展发明专利申请优先审查检索专题调研活动。

28—29日 由国家知识产权局主办、省知识产权局承办的2015年专利代理机构业务能力促进培训（广州班）在广州举办。省知识产权局副局长袁有楼出席开班式并讲话。来自全省39家代理机构185名专利代理人参加了培训。

29日 省知识产权局党组召开“三严三实”专题教育动员会，学习贯彻省委“三严三实”专题教育工作会议精神，并对省知识产权局下一步开展“三严三实”专题教育进行部署。

29日 “2015年广东省专利调查工作动员会”在省知识产权局召开。参与专利调查的广州、深圳、珠海、佛山、惠州、东莞、中山、江门等八市知识产权局的有关人员参加了动员会。

29日 美国知识产权法律协会代表团一行访问省知识产权局。

6月

1日 省知识产权局副局长谢红带队赴广州奥凯信息咨询有限公司调研。

4日 由省知识产权局、广州市人民政府、香港特别行政区政府知识产权署、香港贸发局联合主办，广州市知识产权局承办的“2015粤港知识产权与中小企业发展（广州）研讨会”在广州市举行，会议主题为“知识产权运用及发展策略”。省知识产权局副局长唐毅、广州市人民政府副秘书长冯军、香港特区政府知识产权署副署长李秀江、香港贸易发展局制造业拓展部高级经理朱启华出席研讨会并致辞。

4—5日 省知识产权局副局长袁有楼带队会同广州知识产权法院副院长吴振一行6人，先后到中国中山(灯饰)知识产权快速维权中心和中国东莞(家具)知识产权快速维权中心开展知识产权快速维权工作专项调研活动。

5日 工业机器人产业专利导航研讨会在东莞市举行。省知识产权局副局长谢红出席会议并致辞。国家知识产权局保护协调司、知识产权发展研究中心相关部门负责人，深圳、佛山、东莞等地知识产权部门及产业发展部门的负责人，以及珠三角各地与工业机器人产业相关的“产、学、研、金、介、用”等各相关单位共100余人参加了会议。

8—11日 国家知识产权局专利局外观设计审查部来粤开展专利法第四次修改专题调研。

10日 由省知识产权局、省教育厅、省科学院联合举办的“大专院校、科研院所知识产权转化和产业化专题培训班”在广州举办。广东省各大专院校、科研机构负责人、科研骨干共150人参加了培训。

10—12日 国家知识产权培训基地研讨班在浙江温州举办。广东省知识产权局副局长唐毅率领省3家国家知识产权培训基地代表参加会议并作发言。

12日 广州市天河区检察院与华南理工大学法学院（知识产权学院）举行共建“金融犯罪研究中心”暨“教学实践示范基地”挂牌仪式。天河区委常委、政法委书记谢伟，广州市检察院法律政策研究室副主任钟琦等领导出席会议。天河区检察院检察长刘志民、华工法学院院长徐松林及天河区院、华工法学院双方入选金融犯罪研究中心的老师和干警们参加了会议。

15日 省知识产权局举办“三严三实”专题教育党课，党组书记、局长马宪民以《把“三严三实”专题教育活动落实到推进知识产权事业发展实践中》为主题，为局系统全体人员上党课。

16日 省知识产权局印发《广东省知识产权局开展“四重温四增强”活动和服务创新驱动发展战略“共产党员先锋岗”创建活动实施方案》，在全局系统开展“四重温四增强”活动和服务创新驱动发展战略“共产党员先锋岗”创建活动。

16—19日 省知识产权局副局长唐毅赴汕头、潮州、揭阳、汕尾等粤东四市调研知识产权工作。

17日 省知识产权局召开制定知识产权强国建设先行地政策专题研讨会，讨论修改《关于深入实施知识产权战略 推动创新驱动发展行动计划》。局长马宪民，纪检组长、监察专员严小宜，副局长谢红，副巡视员黄光华出席会议。

24日 省知识产权局组织“三严三实”专题教育第一专题学习研讨会。

25—29日 省知识产权局副局长唐毅带队赴新疆喀什参加第十一届中国新疆喀什·中亚南亚商品交易会并开展知识产权交流调研活动。

26日 省知识产权局局长马宪民会见来访的新加坡知识产权局企业服务组高级司长胡耀宗（WOO Yew Chung）一行10人。

26日 省知识产权局机关党委组织局系统党员开展“四重温四增强”体验活动和庆祝“七一”建党94周年活动。

29日 省知识产权局局长马宪民，纪检组长、监察专员严小宜带队到局对口帮扶的河源市紫金县龙窝镇高坑村调研指导驻村扶贫工作。

30日至7月1日 由中华全国专利代理人协会与国家知识产权局专利局通信审查部组织的通信领域专利审查与代理交流培训班在广州举办。来自国家知识产权局专利局及各审查协作中心的通信领域的专家、全国各专利代理机构专利代理人共100余人参加交流培训班。省知识产权局纪检组长、监察专员严小宜出席开幕式并致词。

6月 省知识产权局组织开展查处假冒专利集中行动月活动。活动共立案372件，涉及商家188家。

6月 省工商局开展2015红盾网剑专项行动。重点整治网络交易平台、大型购物网站、团购网站和企业官网，重点监管电子产品、儿童用品、汽车配件、服装和农资等商品，重点保护驰（著）名商标、涉外商标、守合同重信用企业，查处各类网络销售侵权假冒伪劣商品违法行为，加大网络市场监管力度，规范网络市场秩序。

6月至8月 国家工商总局认定了广东省62件商标为驰名商标，广东省驰名商标总数达702件。

7月

3日 省知识产权局局长马宪民出席省全面深化改革加快实施创新驱动发展战略领导小组第一次会议。

9—10日 省知识产权局副局长袁有楼带队赴山东调研知识产权保护工作。

16日 中知认证公司派出审核组在白云山中药公司召开了贯标认证现场审查第一次会议，省知识产权局副局长谢红出席会议并致辞。

16日 省知识产权局局长马宪民出席省委全面深化改革领导小组第十一次会议。

17—19日 2015年专利代理人实务技能培训班在广州举办。国家知识产权局的资深审查员及专利代理机构资深代理人组成师资队伍、全省专利代理人共100余人参加培训。

17—20日 省知识产权局副巡视员黄光华率队赴青海省调研，粤青双方就加强代办处交流挂职、优势产业专利信息分析等项目进行了深入交流。

23日 省知识产权局组织召开“2015年泛珠三角区域九省（区）专利信息服务工作座谈会”。国家知识产权局自动化部部长钱红缨、省知识产权局局长马宪民出席会议并致辞。会议由省知识产权局副局长谢红主持，泛珠三角区域各省（区）知识产权局分管领导及信息服务机构负责人共30余人参加会议。

23日 中山市召开国家知识产权示范城市工作会谈和高标准建设国家知识产权示范城市推进大会。国家知识产权局副局长贺化、专利管理司副司长张宏、省知识产权局局长马宪民、副局长袁有楼、中山市市委书记薛晓峰、中山市市长陈良贤、副市长吴月霞等出席会议。

23日 由省知识产权局主办，省知识产权研究与发展中心承办的“2015年广东省专利大数据应用服务发布会”在广州举行。副局长谢红出席并致辞，泛珠三角区域内地八省（区）知识产权局领导以及信息服务机构的负责人，省信委等部门、各地市知识产权局、相关行业协会和企事业单位以及媒体代表等180多人参加会议。

24日 佛山市召开国家知识产权示范城市工作会谈和高标准建设国家知识产权示范城市推进大会。国家知识产权局副局长贺化、专利管理司副司长张宏、省知识产权局局长马宪民、副局长袁有楼、佛山市市长鲁毅、副市长黄志豪等领导出席会议。

24日 “广东省战略性新兴产业专利信息资源开发利用计划项目阶段性总结工作会”在省知识产权局举行。来自2013年“广东省战略性新兴产业专利信息资源开发利用计划”项目共12个研究团队负责人和核心研究人员50余人参加了交流会，省知识产权局副局长谢红出席会议并讲话。

28日 中华全国专利代理人协会、省知识产权局在广州联合举行“促进企业贯标工作合作协议签署仪式”。中华全国专利代理人协会会长杨梧、省知识产权局局长马宪民出席签署仪式并致辞，签署仪式由省知识产权局副局长谢红主持。来自广东省企业、知识产权服务机构、大专院校、科研院所等200多名代表出席仪式。

28日 粤港保护知识产权合作专责小组第十四次会议预备会在广州举行。省知识产权局局长马宪民与香港知识产权署署长梁家丽分别率两地代表出席会议。

28日至8月3日 省知识产权局副巡视员黄光华率知识产权代表团一行15人赴台湾开展知识产权研习交流活动。

29—30日 国家知识产权局专利局审查业务部调研组一行5人来粤检查指导知识产权快速维权工作。

30日 省知识产权局局长马宪民会见新加坡知识产权局局长陈一山一行，交流粤新知识产权工作及合作推进事宜。

30—31日 2015年国家知识产权局“知识产权走基层服务经济万里行”在广州市举办首站活动。此次活动由国家知识产权局主办，省知识产权局和广州市知识产权局协办。国家知识产权局专利局副局长徐治江，广东省政府副秘书长林积，省知识产权局局长马宪民、副局长谢红，广州市政府副秘书长冯军，广州市知识产权局局长邓佑满等出席活动，徐治江、林积等在启动会上致辞。来自国家知识产权局、国家知识产权局专利局、国家知识产权局专利局专利审查协作广东中心的相关部门领导和专利审查员，广东有关省直部门、广州市的企事业单位、知识产权服务机构代表共220多人参加活动。

31日 省知识产权局召开军转干部和退伍人员座谈会，局长马宪民、副局长唐毅出席会议。

8月

6日 省知识产权局召开2015年纪律教育学习月活动动员大会。局党组书记、局长马宪民作动员讲话，局党组成员、纪检组长严小宜主持会议。

6日 省知识产权局副局长谢红带队赴广州高航知识产权咨询有限公司开展调研。

10日 省知识产权局纪检组长、监察专员严小宜参加省人大组织的2015年“百名法学家百场报告会”省直机关专场暨南粤法治报告会第九讲专题辅导报告会。

11日 国家知识产权局专利局机械发明审查部部长王澄带队，前往广州汽车集团开展巡回审查工作。省知识产权局副局长谢红、广汽集团副总经理蒋平出席活动。

12日 省知识产权局局长马宪民带队到广州科粤专利商标代理有限公司、广州新诺专利商标事务所有限公司和广州三环专利代理有限公司开展调研。

13日 省知识产权局组织“三严三实”专题教育第二专题学习研讨会。

13—14日 由国家知识产权局专利局主办、省知识产权局承办的“专利电子申请推广培训班”在广州举办。国家知识产权局专利局副部长何越峰、省知识产权局副巡视员黄光华出席开班仪式并讲话，来自全省的专利代理机构、企事业单位共120余人参加了此次培训。

14—15日 国家知识产权局专利管理司司长雷筱云一行5人赴广东开展专题调研。省财厅、深圳市知识产权局、广州知识产权交易中心、横琴国际知识产权交易中心、中彩联等单位参加座谈会，省知识产权局局长马宪民主持会议。

18日 粤港保护知识产权合作专责小组第十四次会议暨记者招待会在香港成功举行。省知识产权局局长马宪民，香港知识产权署署长梁家丽分别率领粤港双方代表团出席会议。

18日 省知识产权研究与发展中心与海南省知识产权局在海口联合举办首个“泛珠三角区域专利信息培训班”。

20—22日 全国知识产权人才工作交流会在青海省西宁市召开。省知识产权局副局长唐毅率队参会。

22日 由汇桔网与中国企业联合会共同举办的“2015中国500强企业高峰会知商论坛”，在广西南宁成功举办。省知识产权局副局长谢红应邀出席知商论坛，并就开放式环境下的知识产权运营与广东省知识产权运营工作进行了专题演讲。中国企业联合会、中国企业家协会驻会副会长李明星出席论坛并致辞，世界知识产权组织（WIPO）驻中国办事处主任陈宏兵出席论坛并演讲。

26日 省知识产权局召开专题研讨会，讨论修改《关于深入实施知识产权战略 推动创新驱动发展行动计划》。局长马宪民，纪检组长、监察专员严小宜，副局长谢红出席会议。

27日 全国知识产权系统政务工作会议在江西南昌召开。会议总结了2015年全国知识产权系统政务工作情况，对下一阶段如何进一步提升知识产权政务工作水平作出具体部署。国家知识产权局副局长廖涛出席会议并讲话，国家知识产权局专利局副局长徐聪作会议总结。省知识产权局副局长唐毅出席会议并就知识产权政务工作作交流发言。

28日 省知识产权局纪检组长、监察专员严小宜出席2015年创新知识产权服务论坛并致辞。

28日 省知识产权局召开“高校知识产权管理座谈会”。副局长谢红出席会议，中山大学、华南理工大学、华南农业大学等十所高校参加座谈。

31日 广东省政府副省长陈云贤在广州会见了国家知识产权局副局长何志敏，双方围绕经济新常态下广东知识产权工作面临的战略机遇及挑战开展了深入探讨，并对下一步广东与国家知识产权局专利局专利审查协作广东中心开展知识产权战略合作相关工作交流了意见。

9月

1日 省知识产权局邀请相关企业、学校代表召开促进互联网知识产权发展座谈会，为互联网知识产权发展建言献策。

4—6日 由广东省美容美发化妆品行业协会主办，全国工商联美容化妆品业商会协办的第43届广东国际美博会在广州举办。省知识产权局派员全程参与驻会，提供知识产权咨询服务，开展专利投诉案件的受理和处理工作。

7—8日 省知识产权研究与发展中心在广州举办“中小微企业专利信息利用能力培训班”。来自企事业单位、科研院所、服务机构近160人参加培训。

9日 粤港合作联席会议在香港举行。省知识产权局局长马宪民与香港知识产权署署长梁家丽签署《粤港知识产权合作协议（2015—

2016）》。

9—11日 国家知识产权局一行来粤开展知识产权区域布局试点工作方案对接调研。

10日 省知识产权局副局长袁有楼带队赴局对口帮扶的高坑村检查指导驻村帮扶工作，就驻村帮扶工作情况与县、镇政府有关领导及村两委进行交流，并出席该村举行的奖教奖学暨庆祝第31个教师节活动。

11日 省知识产权局副局长谢红出席省发改委召开的全面创新改革试验工作座谈会。

11日 中国欧盟商会华南分会代表团访问省知识产权局。双方围绕专利行政保护等领域的问题开展了交流，并互赠了《欧盟企业在华建议书》和《广东省知识产权保护状况》。

11日 中山市副市长吴月霞率市知识产权局一行到省知识产权局汇报工作，局长马宪民出席并主持召开汇报会，纪检组长严小宜参加会议。

11日 省律师协会知识产权法律专业委员会应湖南省律师协会知识产权法律专业委员会的邀请，赴湖南省湘潭市，与当地律师协会等有关单位联合举办“广东省、湖南省知识产权典型案例办案技巧巡回报告会”。100多名律师、政府部门人员到场学习和探讨。包括当地电视台在内的多家媒体进行宣传报道。

15日 中国专利信息年会(PIAC)在北京召开，来自海内外近百名嘉宾以及中外专利行业1500余名代表出席主论坛、分论坛、展示交流等活动。会议期间，举行了“广东省知识产权局与中国专利信息中心、知识产权出版社有限责任公司战略合作协议签署仪式”。

16日 新加坡知识产权局和新加坡知识产权局中国代表处一行4人访问省知识产权局。

17—24日 省知识产权局副局长唐毅一行6人赴瑞士、荷兰开展专题调研和交流合作。

18日 第14次粤东七市知识产权局长联席会议在汕尾召开，省知识产权局副局长袁有楼参加了会议。

18日 最高人民法院知识产权司法保护与市场价值研究（广东）基地在广州知识产权法院挂牌成立，最高人民法院副院长陶凯元、广东省人民政府副省长陈云贤、省高级人民法院院长郑鄂等领导出席了揭牌仪式。该基地是解决知识产权维权成本高、赔偿额度小的难题和推进司法改革、知识产权司法保护制度改革的重要平台。

18—21日 省知识产权局、广州市知识产权局、东莞市知识产权局组成工作组，赴南宁参加第十二届中国—东盟博览会知识产权执法维权工作并进行调研。博览会期间工作组共开展专项巡查11次，调处展会专利侵权纠纷案件2件，查处假冒专利案件8件。

19日 省知识产权局局长马宪民和副局长谢红出席中国知识产权法学研究会2015年年会开幕式。

20—25日 国家知识产权局专利复审委员会电学申诉二处一行6人来粤开展专利无效案件口头审理。

22—23日 由中华全国专利代理人协会与台湾工业总会共同主办、省知识产权研究会承办的第八届两岸专利论坛在广州举办。广东省政府副省长陈云贤，中华全国代理人协会高级顾问、国家知识产权局副局长何志敏，省知识产权局局长马宪民，台湾工业总会秘书长蔡练生，台湾工业总会智慧财产权委员会高级顾问王美花，中华全国代理人协会有关负责人出席论坛开幕式并致辞。10余名来自两岸知识产权界的专家、学者以及企业家代表做了主题发言，200多名两岸专利主管机构人员和业界人士，围绕两岸专利领域最新发展、专利法制发展动态、专利审理面临的挑战与应对、专利布局与诉讼的策略与管理等主题展开深入交流与探讨。

23日 省知识产权局纪检组长、监察专员严小宜出席国家知识产权局召开的知识产权系统落实全面创新改革试验工作会议。

24日 “2015年专利信息传播利用（广东）基地工作体系建设与能力培育项目暨专利信息人才实践项目中期评审会”在省知识产权

局召开，国家知识产权局文献部部长张鹏率队莅临指导工作。省知识产权局副局长谢红出席会议并讲话。

28日 省知识产权局副局长谢红出席省发改委召开的全面创新改革试验工作第二次座谈会。

28日 中国知识产权报社全国通联工作会议在哈尔滨市召开。国家知识产权局副局长廖涛出席会议并讲话，中国知识产权报社社长曹冬根作工作报告。省知识产权局副局长袁有楼参加会议。

29日 省知识产权局、省自贸办联合印发《加强中国（广东）自由贸易试验区知识产权工作的指导意见》。

10月

8日 广东自贸试验区横琴片区知识产权检察工作站在横琴检察院举行揭牌仪式，珠海市检察院党组书记、市检察长向少良和市检察院高新区知识产权检察室主任曾宇欢共同为工作站揭牌，珠海市院班子成员、部门负责人、主任检察官及其他干警参加了揭牌仪式。设立广东自贸试验区横琴片区知识产权检察工作站，其主要履行职责：一是受理横琴公安分局立案侦查并移送审查逮捕、移送审查起诉的“侵犯知识产权罪”的刑事案件；二是对横琴新区内涉及知识产权的控告、举报、申诉进行审查处理，立案查处横琴新区内涉及知识产权的职务犯罪案件；三是对横琴新区知识产权领域“两法衔接”工作情况实施监督；四是结合办案在横琴新区内开展知识产权领域的法制宣传工作。

8—11日 国家知识产权局在新疆乌鲁木齐召开专利执法维权业务交流及案例研讨会，专利管理司司长雷筱云、副司长赵梅生出席会议并讲话。广东省知识产权局副局长袁有楼参加会议并作交流发言。

10日 福建省知识产权局副局长郑敏姜一行就知识产权“十三五”规划编制工作到广东省知识产权局调研。广东省知识产权局局长马宪民出席座谈会。

12日 省知识产权局纪检组长、监察专员严小宜出席省委办公厅召开的“加快实施我省创新驱动发展战略系列提案办理工作协调会”。

12日 省知识产权局局长马宪民会见来访的台湾与日本知识产权代表团一行。台湾博拓国际智权集团（PIIP）执行长李彦庆、日本新树GLOBAL IP事务所所长村井康司等参加了会谈。

13日 省知识产权局副局长唐毅参加国家知识产权局举办的知识产权领域专项改革工作研讨会。

13日 省知识产权局局长马宪民带队上线广东“民声热线”节目，与参加节目的特邀嘉宾、媒体和企业代表进行互动交流，现场接受广大听众的评议和监督。

13日 由广东省知识产权研究与发展中心、国家知识产权培训（广东）基地主办，澳大利亚迈登思专利商标事务所及日本新树Global IP专利商标事务所共同协办的“澳大利亚和日本知识产权应对策略研讨会”在广州举行。

14—20日 广东省工商局副局长钱永成带队赴湛江、海南开展广告商标调研工作。

15日 广州开发区科技创新和知识产权局副局长蓝伟锋一行到省知识产权研究与发展中心开展调研。

15日至11月4日 第118届广交会在广州举办。省知识产权局组织全省知识产权局系统60多人的专利执法队伍驻会，国家知识产权局专利复审委员会先后派出6位专家现场指导。

16—19日 应中华商标协会邀请，省工商局副局长钱永成带队参加在海口举办的2015中国国际商标品牌节。其间，钱永成一行拜访了国家工商总局副局长刘俊臣，汇报了广东商标工作有关情况。

17日 省知识产权局副局长唐毅参加知识产权强国建设与知识产权人才培养研讨班。

19—22日 由省专利信息协会、中规（北京）认证有限公司主办的“知识产权管理体系认证审核员培训班”在广州举办，省知识产权局副局长谢红、中规(北京)认证有限公司总经理郭亮出席开班仪式，来自全国各地知识产权服务机构、科研院所、律师事务所、企业共150人参加培训。

20日 省知识产权局副局长袁有楼参加上线广东“民声热线”节目。

20日 国家质检总局科技司副巡视员裴晓颖，省质监局党组成员、副局长丘瑞清带队，对江门市新会区国家地理标志保护示范区进行实地考察，调研该示范区地理标志产品保护推进情况。

21日 在唯品会（中国）有限公司总部，举行了省知识产权局与唯品会（中国）有限公司保护知识产权战略合作协议签署仪式。省知识产权局副局长袁有楼、唯品会（中国）有限公司副总裁冯佳路，作为双方代表共同签署了《保护知识产权战略合作协议》。根据协议，双方将建立全方位战略合作关系并共同快速有效遏制和打击电子商务领域专利侵权假冒行为。

21日 省知识产权局副局长袁有楼在中山古镇出席广州知识产权法院中山诉讼服务处揭牌仪式暨2015灯饰行业知识产权保护研讨会。

22日 第16届中国·古镇灯饰博览会开幕，中国中山（灯饰）知识产权快速维权中心驻会开展知识产权保护工作，省知识产权局副局长袁有楼一行赴现场指导。

22—24日 2015年闽粤沿海十二城市保护知识产权工作第十二次联席会议在湛江召开，湛江市副市长庄晓东、省知识产权局副局长袁有楼出席会议并讲话，来自福建和广东沿海12个城市30多名代表参加会议。

23日 2015年省知识产权评估和运营培训班在广州举办，来自省内30家知识产权服务机构、52家资产评估机构、30家科研院所和企业的知识产权从业人员共191人参加培训。

26日 省知识产权局组织“三严三实”专题教育第三专题学习研讨。

26日 全省知识产权专业技术资格评价工作座谈会在广州召开，省知识产权局副局长唐毅出席会议并讲话。

27日 新加坡知识产权局和新加坡知识产权局中国代表处一行2人访问省知识产权局。

28日 省知识产权局局长马宪民会见来访的世界知识产权组织（WIPO）中国办事处主任陈宏兵、副主任吕国良一行。省知识产权局副局长谢红陪同陈宏兵、吕国良一行访问联瑞集团（UTC）、汇桔网等知识产权运营机构。

28日 省知识产权局举办贯彻落实《广东省深入实施知识产权战略推动创新驱动发展行动计划》培训班。培训班由局长马宪民主讲，纪检组长、监察专员严小宜主持。各地级以上市、顺德区知识产权局的分管领导及相关工作人员、省知识产权局机关各处室和局属单位有关人员共90多人参加了培训。

28日 省知识产权局召开新闻通气会，局长马宪民就省政府印发的《广东省深入实施知识产权战略推动创新驱动发展行动计划》相关内容和近期全省知识产权建设的主要工作成效向媒体作了介绍。

28日 黑龙江省知识产权局副局长吴忠安一行4人来广东省知识产权局调研交流，广东省知识产权局副局长谢红主持会议。

28—30日 泛珠三角区域知识产权公务人员交流活动分别在香港和澳门举办。来自广东、云南、四川、江西、贵州、湖南、福建、澳门、香港共9个省（区）的27名人员参加。省知识产权局副局长唐毅率领省工商局、省版权局代表一行5人参加会议。

30日 省知识产权局举办知识产权学习讲坛。局长马宪民出席。

30日 省知识产权局副局长谢红带队赴对口帮扶的高坑村检查指导驻村帮扶工作。

10月 省律师协会主编的《知识产权典型案例主办律师评述》公开出版。

11月

3日 省知识产权局副局长唐毅接待来访的青海省知识产权局副局长史军放一行7人。

3日 国家质检总局正式批准成立国家地理标志产品保护示范区（广东新会），江门市新会区成为广东省首个获批国家地理标志产品保护示范区的地区，也成为国家质检总局第一个非指定的国家地理标志产品保护示范区试点省份外的获批地区。

3—4日 省质监局党组成员、副局长丘瑞清到阳江市调研地理标志保护产品工作。丘瑞清一行到阳西县程村镇红光村调研拟申报的地理标志保护产品——程村红心鸭蛋的申报情况。

3—10日 省知识产权局纪检组长、监察专员严小宜一行6人赴法国、意大利进行知识产权专题访问和交流活动。

4日 新加坡知识产权局和新加坡知识产权局中国代表处一行6人访问省知识产权局。

4日 日本知识产权协会(JIPA)海外研修F5访问团一行22人访问省知识产权局。

5日 省质监局党组成员、副局长丘瑞清带领省局科技处有关人员到云浮调研指导国家地理标志产品保护工作，并受邀参加“2015广东云浮·罗定稻米节”开幕式，为罗定第一批获准使用罗定稻米地标专用标志的3家企业颁授罗定稻米地标产品专用标志牌匾。

7—8日 由国家知识产权局组织的全国专利代理人资格考试在全国24个城市同时举行，广州考点考试工作由省知识产权局承办。考试期间，省知识产权局局长马宪民、副局长袁有楼亲临广州考场指导。据统计，2015年广州考点共有3229人参加考试，为全国第三大考点。

8日 香港特区政府知识产权署和澳门特区政府经济局知识产权厅联合举办了2015年泛珠三角区域知识产权公务人员交流活动。香港特区政府知识产权署署长梁家丽、澳门特区政府经济局知识产权厅厅长郑晓敏、澳门特区海关副关务总长殷镇玄分别出席了在香港和澳门举办的会议，来自内地五省（区）知识产权局、工商局、版权局的代表，港澳官方及非官方代表约50人参加了会议。省知识产权局副局长唐毅和省工商局、省新闻出版广电局（版权局）有关领导等5人组成广东代表团出席了会议。此次会议的主题是知识产权保护、管理及贸易。

8—14日 国家知识产权局专利复审委员会外观设计申诉处一行9人来粤开展专利复审或无效案件进行口头审理。

9日 省知识产权局举办知识产权国际条约学习讲坛，邀请了欧洲知识产权联盟（AIPEX）专家Anne Laarman女士、Sander Vermeulen先生作“工业品外观设计国际注册海牙体系”专题讲座。

9—11日 全国打击侵权假冒工作领导小组办公室会同国务院新闻办，组织中央主要外宣媒体和中央重点新闻网站共20家媒体的27名记者，对广东省开展中国制造海外形象维护“清风”行动工作进行深入采访。

10日 日本知识产权协会参事竹本一志一行6人访问省知识产权局。

10—12日 由省知识产权局主办、华南理工大学知识产权学院承办的“广东省专利行政执法提高班”在国家知识产权培训（广东）基地举办，省知识产权局副局长袁有楼出席开班仪式并讲话。

12—13日 省知识产权局副局长袁有楼带队赴石家庄参加九省市专利行政执法协作年度研讨会并讲话。

13日 中国人民解放军总装备部国防知识产权局局长蔡镭一行来省知识产权局调研交流，省知识产权局局长马宪民出席并主持会议。

14—15日 国家质检总局科技司副巡视员裴晓颖率队到梅州调研地理标志产品保护工作，省质监局党组成员、副局长丘瑞清陪同调研。调研组一行先后到梅县、蕉岭两地，了解近年来梅州地理标志产品保护工作情况，查摆存在的问题并提出指导意见。

16日 省知识产权局机关党委在全局系统党员中开展“学党章守纪律当先锋”主题教育活动。

16日 2015年中日韩知识产权局局长系列会议在广州召开。会议期间，省长朱小丹会见中国国家知识产权局局长申长雨、日本特许厅长官伊藤仁、韩国特许厅厅长崔东圭等来粤出席会议的嘉宾。副省长陈云贤、省政府秘书长李锋、省知识产权局局长马宪民等参加会见。

18日 新加坡知识产权制度巡回研讨活动在广州举办。

19日 省知识产权局组织全局党员干部学习党的十八届五中全会精神。

20日 省知识产权局纪检组长、监察专员严小宜出席省委办公厅召开的“加快实施我省创新驱动发展战略”系列提案办理工作专题研究会议。

20日 全省知识产权维权援助工作研讨会在中山古镇举行。全省6个国家级中心、4个快速维权中心和4个广东中心分中心的代表参加会议。省知识产权局副局长袁有楼出席会议。

20日 省知识产权局与广东工业大学在广州大学城广东科学中心举行协议签署仪式，副局长谢红与副校长陈卓武出席仪式并代表双方签署了《广东省知识产权局 广东工业大学关于共同创建知识产权示范高校框架协议》。

20日 省知识产权局研究与发展中心在广州市举办专利竞争情报与专利预警分析培训班。省企业、服务机构、大专院校、科研院所等100余人参加了培训。

24日 省工商局与香港特区政府知识产权署在广州开展“粤港两地商标业界交流”活动，并共同举办“商标品牌国际注册和海外维权应对”研讨会，深化粤港商标品牌保护与运用方面的合作，助力实施国家“一带一路”发展战略，推动“广东制造”向“广东品牌”转变。标志着粤港两地商标工作由分散式合作上升为全局性合作。

24—26日 2015年广东省知识产权局管理干部研修班在省知识产权培训（惠州学院）基地举办。局长马宪民，纪检组长、监察专员严小宜出席开班式并作专题报告。省知识产权局、惠州市知识产权局和惠州学院共40多人参加了培训。

25日 由省知识产权局主办，中知（北京）认证有限公司、国家中小微企业知识产权培训（南海）基地承办的2015年第五期企业知识产权管理规范培训班（企业类）在佛山南海举办。中国知识产权保护协会副秘书长顾晓莉、省知识产权局副局长谢红、佛山市知识产权局副局长李钜镇、中知（北京）认证有限公司总经理卢潮流出席开班仪式，会议由南海中小微培训基地负责人姜新主持。

25—27日 国家工商总局商标审查协作中心主任姜瑞斌一行到广东调研考察商标注册派出机构筹建工作，省工商局副局长钱永成陪同调研。

26日 由国家知识产权局专利管理司指导、省知识产权局发起、汇桔网和省知识产权研究与发展中心联合主办的首届“汇桔杯”南粤知识产权创新创业大赛启动大会，在广州举行。广东省政府副省长陈云贤向大会发来书面致辞，国家知识产权局专利管理司副司长张宏、省知识产权局局长马宪民出席活动并致辞。世界知识产权组织前副总干事James Pooley为大赛发来视频致辞。来自政府、企事业单位、创业投资、参赛者、新闻媒体等社会各界代表500余人参加了启动大会。

26日 省废弃资源再生循环利用产业专利分析及预警报告会，在广州市广东迎宾馆举行。省知识产权局副局长谢红、省经济和信息化委副主任林位超、专利审协广东中心副主任王启北出席会议并致辞。

26日 省质监局党组成员、副局长丘瑞清到韶关调研“张溪香芋”“北乡马蹄”等国家地理标志产品保护情况，并与韶关市局相关负责人座谈交流。

26日至12月2日 省工商局分别在汕头、

湛江组织商标执法专题分片培训班。各地级以上市工商（市场监督管理）局商标、经检部门及广东省工商局打击侵权假冒领导小组成员单位的业务骨干130余人参加了培训。同期广东省工商局还分别在汕头、湛江举办商标品牌战略实施培训班，全省约500家企业代表参加培训。

27日 《中国知识产权报》社长曹冬根一行来省知识产权局调研，局长马宪民出席座谈会。双方就新形势下知识产权宣传工作进行了深入交流。纪检组长、监察专员严小宜参加会议。

27日 省政协主席王荣带队深入广州数控设备有限公司、广州达意隆包装机械股份有限公司和广州瑞松北斗汽车装备有限公司等智能制造相关企业调研，现场督办推进“加快发展智能制造，引领广东制造业转型升级”重点提案。省政协秘书长杨懂，省政协提案委员会主任周義及省政府办公厅、省直相关部门负责人一同参加调研。省知识产权局副局长谢红参加调研。

27日 广西壮族自治区知识产权局局长李昌华一行来广东省知识产权局调研交流，广东省知识产权局局长马宪民出席并主持会议。双方知识产权“十三五”规划等问题进行深入交流。

27日 省知识产权局机关党委组队参加省直机关工委举办的“广东省直机关第二届趣味运动会”。

27日 广州市越秀区、广州市萝岗区被确定为国家知识产权强县工程示范区，佛山市高明区、韶关市浈江区被确定为国家知识产权强县工程试点区。

28日 省律师协会举办首届泛珠三角区域知识产权法律服务合作与发展论坛。来自广东、江西、湖南、云南、贵州、广西、四川、海南、福建泛珠三角区域省市律协知识产权专委会主任、副主任和港澳台地区的律师代表参加了论坛，讨论区域知识产权法律服务的发展与合作问题。

28—29日 由国家知识产权局发展研究中心和省知识产权局支持、北京合享新创信息科技有限公司主办的“合享新创”知识产权论坛在广州举行。国家知识产权局发展研究中心主任韩秀成、省知识产权局局长马宪民出席论坛并致辞。

28—29日 第三届广东知识产权法律服务论坛在佛山市召开，来自省内外及美国、澳大利亚及港澳台地区知识产权人士250余人参加论坛。

29日至12月1日 国家工商总局和世界知识产权组织在上海市举办第二届中国商标金奖颁奖大会，表彰全国在商标创新、运用、保护和有效利用马德里商标国际注册体系四个项目取得突出成绩的单位和个人。广东获奖数占全国25个奖项总数的16%，凸显广东商标大省的地位。省工商局党组书记、局长凌锋，副局长钱永成出席颁奖大会。其间，国家工商总局局长张茅专门会见了凌锋一行，凌锋向张茅汇报了广东省工商局在商事制度改革、市场监管立法、两建和商标派出机构筹备工作等情况。

12月

1日 “广东省知识产权服务地市行粤东站活动”在汕头市龙湖宾馆举办，省知识产权局副局长谢红，汕头市委常委、常务副市长郑通声出席活动并致辞。

1—5日 由国家知识产权局主办、省知识产权局承办的“全国专利行政执法培训班”在广州举办。省知识产权局副局长袁有楼出席开班仪式并讲话。

2日 受国家知识产权局委托，省知识产权局分别组织召开执法案例与实务研讨交流会、展会专利维权工作交流研讨会。国家知识产权局专利管理司执法处安亚磊参加会议。

2日 省知识产权研究与发展中心与汕头市知识产权局联合开展专利信息及知识产权贯标推送活动。省知识产权局副局长谢红参加活动。

2日 省知识产权局副局长谢红带队赴揭阳市调研。

3—4日 省知识产权局局长马宪民率团赴港参加第五届亚洲知识产权营商论坛并在“一带一路”下之知识产权机遇圆桌会议发言。

3—4日 香港特别行政区政府与香港贸易发展局、香港设计中心在香港联合举办“第五届亚洲知识产权营商论坛”。省工商局副局长钱永成带团参加此届论坛。其间，钱永成与香港特别行政区政府知识产权署代表就粤港商标品牌保护与运用方面的合作进行了交流与沟通。

4日 受国家知识产权局委托，省知识产权局组成以副局长谢红为组长的专家组，对肇庆高新技术产业开发区国家知识产权试点园区工作进行考核验收。肇庆市委常委、高新区区委书记关鹏，区委专职副书记关键，区委副书记、市科技局局长陈建中，市科技局副局长谢炳权，区经济贸易和科技局副局长罗盛斌等参加了验收工作会议。

7—10日 国家知识产权局专利局审查业务管理部副部长马昊一行8人赴广东开展“优化授权制度、提升专利质量”的专题调研。省知识产权局组织专利代理服务机构相关代表参加座谈会，省知识产权局副巡视员黄光华出席会议。

8日 广东省新一代通信产业专利分析及预警报告会，在广东大厦举行。报告会由省知识产权局、省经济和信息化委员会共同主办，省知识产权研究会承办、省通信行业协会协办。省知识产权局副局长谢红、省经济和信息化委总工程师神志雄出席会议并致辞。

8日 省知识产权局在广州举行广东省知识产权专家咨询委员会成立大会暨第一次咨询会议。局长马宪民、副局长唐毅、纪检组长严小宜、副局长袁有楼、副局长谢红出席会议。首届省知识产权专家咨询委员会的主任和委员共20人参加。

9日 省知识产权局机关党委组织党员干部参加省直工委等四部门举办的以“抓落实、促发展”为主题的省直单位第三届工作技能大赛，赵飞获优秀点子奖，省知识产权局获“优秀组织奖”。

9日 英国知识产权局约翰·阿尔蒂局长一行10人考察国家知识产权局专利局专利审查协作广东中心，并举行英国专利审查情况报告会。省知识产权局局长马宪民，审协广东中心主任曾志华、副主任王启北、副主任邱绛雯出席座谈会。

10日 全省知识产权工作会议暨专利奖表彰大会在广州召开。省委书记胡春华出席会议并为获奖代表颁奖。省长朱小丹、国家知识产权局局长申长雨出席会议并讲话。省委常委、秘书长林木声出席会议。副省长陈云贤主持会议。省知识产权局局长马宪民参加会议并作工作报告。会议表彰广东省获得第十六届中国专利奖和2014年广东专利奖的单位和个人。

11日 由北京大学东莞光电研究院、第三代半导体专利联盟、东莞燕园知识产权服务有限公司共同筹办的第三代半导体产业知识产权论坛在东莞举行，省知识产权局副局长谢红出席论坛并致辞。

11日 由汇桔网与中国商业联合会共同举办的“2015知商大会”在广州举行，来自全国各地的千余家知商企业参会。中国商业联合会秘书长王民、省知识产权局副局长谢红、美国知识产权所有人协会董事会主席Wayne Sobon、汇桔网董事长谢旭辉出席大会并致辞。

11—13日 “2015中国（东莞）国际科技合作周”在东莞国际会展中心举办。省知识产权局副局长谢红出席活动。

12日 “广东省知识产权服务地市行东莞活动”在东莞市国际会展中心举办，省知识产权局副局长谢红，松山湖生态园党工委书记、管委会主任殷焕明出席活动并致辞。

12日 省司法厅在广州举办“广东省律师从事知识产权贯标服务政策与实务专题宣讲

会”，省知识产权局谢红副局长出席宣讲会，来自全省90余名律师参加宣讲会。

16日 2015年第五届中国（广东）知识产权投融资项目对接会在佛山市南海区举行。来自全省各地41个项目与58个风投机构在现场进行对接。省知识产权局副局长谢红出席对接会并致辞。

22日 日本贸易振兴机构北京代表处知识产权部部长本间友孝一行4人访问省知识产权局。

23日 省发展和改革委员会蔡木灵副主任带队到省知识产权局开展创新发展工作专题调研。省知识产权局局长马宪民、纪检组长严小宜、副局长谢红出席座谈会。

24日 伊朗伊斯兰共和国驻广州总领事馆领事阿弗辛·雷米先生一行3人访问省知识产权局。

25日 专利费用减缴备案系统培训班在深圳市举办，国家知识产权局专利局审查业务管理部副部长冯小兵带队来粤授课，省知识产权局副巡视员黄光华出席了开班仪式并致辞。来自广东、广西、海南三省（自治区）负责费减工作的主管领导及地级以上市知识产权局拟承担费减备案审核的工作人员、国家知识产权局专利局广州代办处、深圳代办处派人员参加了培训。

28—30日 广东省企业知识产权管理规范培训班在广州举办。

28—30日 省律师协会协调省知识产权局为广东省律师举办了企业知识产权贯标咨询服务专场培训，全省100余名律师和律师辅助人员报名参加了培训学习。

29日 全省知识产权局系统政务信息工作会议在广州召开。省知识产权局副局长唐毅出席会议并讲话。

30日 省知识产权局局长马宪民，纪检组长、监察专员严小宜等一行5人，赴广东高航知识产权运营有限公司、广州市华学知识产权代理有限公司开展知识产权服务业专题调研。

统计资料

广东省历年专利申请情况

类别/年份	小计	专利种类构成						专利申请人构成									
		发明		实用新型		外观设计		企业		高校		科研单位		机关团体		个人	
		件	%	件	%	件	%	件	%	件	%	件	%	件	%	件	%
1985—1990	5928	910	15.4	3385	57.1	1633	27.5	1713	28.9	214	3.6	313	5.3	568	9.6	3120	52.6
1991	2997	322	10.7	1371	45.7	1304	43.5	924	30.8	36	1.2	60	2.0	514	17.2	1463	48.8
1992	4656	476	10.2	1640	35.2	2540	54.6	1554	33.4	39	0.8	64	1.4	932	20.0	2067	44.4
1993	5020	603	12.0	2002	39.9	2415	48.1	1494	29.8	65	1.3	74	1.5	958	19.1	2429	48.4
1994	5883	605	10.3	1960	33.3	3318	56.4	1334	22.7	48	0.8	49	0.8	1687	28.7	2765	47.0
1995	7729	463	6.0	2367	30.6	4899	63.4	3017	39.0	65	0.8	50	0.6	1186	15.3	3411	44.1
1996	9946	510	5.1	2798	28.1	6638	66.7	5442	54.7	47	0.5	54	0.5	87	0.9	4316	43.4
1997	12858	680	5.3	3173	24.7	9005	70.0	7084	55.1	62	0.5	102	0.8	17	0.1	5593	43.5
1998	13473	753	5.6	3621	26.9	9099	67.5	7230	53.7	88	0.7	115	0.9	40	0.3	6000	44.5
1999	16802	1127	6.7	4561	27.1	11114	66.1	8372	49.8	175	1.0	147	0.9	57	0.3	8051	47.9
2000	21123	1760	8.3	6033	28.6	13330	63.1	9988	47.3	237	1.1	194	0.9	27	0.1	10677	50.5
2001	27596	2549	9.2	8144	29.5	16903	61.3	10882	39.4	305	1.1	276	1.0	51	0.2	16082	58.3
2002	34352	3819	11.1	9972	29.0	20561	59.9	11769	34.3	384	1.1	194	0.6	59	0.2	21946	63.9
2003	43186	6181	14.3	12985	30.1	24020	55.6	14510	33.6	532	1.2	299	0.7	86	0.2	27759	64.3
2004	52201	8093	15.5	14682	28.1	29426	56.4	17222	33.0	671	1.3	227	0.4	113	0.2	33968	65.1
2005	72220	12887	17.8	18951	26.2	40382	55.9	23999	33.2	1070	1.5	371	0.5	96	0.1	46684	64.6
2006	90886	21351	23.5	23886	26.3	45649	50.2	33737	37.1	1537	1.7	429	0.5	174	0.2	55009	60.5
2007	102449	26692	26.1	25389	24.8	50368	49.2	42701	41.7	1593	1.6	500	0.5	194	0.2	57461	56.1
2008	103883	28099	27.0	28883	27.8	46901	45.1	47954	46.2	2322	2.2	783	0.8	165	0.2	52659	50.7
2009	125673	32247	25.7	39027	31.1	54399	43.3	60450	48.1	3029	2.4	1068	0.8	250	0.2	60876	48.4
2010	152907	40866	26.7	47706	31.2	64335	42.1	78119	51.1	4696	3.1	1412	0.9	484	0.3	68196	44.6
2011	196275	52012	26.5	67336	34.3	76927	39.2	107806	54.9	5165	2.6	3347	1.7	1028	0.5	78929	40.2
2012	229514	60448	26.3	78731	34.3	90335	39.4	125503	54.7	6191	2.7	2730	1.2	1321	0.6	93769	40.9
2013	264265	68990	26.1	93592	35.4	101683	38.5	136713	51.7	7533	2.9	3976	1.5	1947	0.7	114096	43.2
2014	278351	75148	27.0	96136	34.5	107067	38.5	149670	53.8	9432	3.4	3926	1.4	2077	0.7	113246	40.7
2015	355939	103941	29.2	135717	38.1	116281	32.7	205675	57.8	12179	3.4	4523	1.3	3384	1.0	130178	36.6
扣除不规范专利申请	1492	775		410		307		2								1490	
合计	2234620	550757	24.6	733638	32.8	950225	42.5	1114860	49.89	57715	2.58	25283	1.13	17502	0.78	1019260	45.61

广东省历年专利授权情况

类别/年份	小计	专利种类构成						专利申请人构成									
		发明		实用新型		外观设计		企业		高校		科研单位		机关团体		个人	
		件	%	件	%	件	%	件	%	件	%	件	%	件	%	件	%
1985—1990	2212	104	4.7	1517	68.6	591	26.7	754	34.1	96	4.3	131	5.9	129	5.8	1102	49.8
1991	1348	30	2.2	661	49.0	657	48.7	597	44.3	25	1.9	42	3.1	174	12.9	510	37.8
1992	1708	34	2.0	891	52.2	783	45.8	580	34.0	28	1.6	39	2.3	294	17.2	767	44.9
1993	4546	96	2.1	1822	40.1	2628	57.8	1556	34.2	55	1.2	67	1.5	966	21.2	1902	41.8
1994	3149	63	2.0	1440	45.7	1646	52.3	909	28.9	44	1.4	34	1.1	783	24.9	1379	43.8
1995	4611	56	1.2	1447	31.4	3108	67.4	1277	27.7	30	0.7	33	0.7	1423	30.9	1848	40.1
1996	5273	57	1.1	1399	26.5	3817	72.4	2412	45.7	46	0.9	37	0.7	726	13.8	2052	38.9
1997	7173	49	0.7	1606	22.4	5518	76.9	4340	60.5	22	0.3	30	0.4	88	1.2	2693	37.5
1998	10707	77	0.7	1992	18.6	8638	80.7	6503	60.7	45	0.4	71	0.7	28	0.3	4060	37.9
1999	14328	123	0.9	3897	27.2	10308	71.9	7697	53.7	80	0.6	89	0.6	50	0.3	6412	44.8
2000	15799	261	1.7	4797	30.4	10741	68.0	7937	50.2	132	0.8	118	0.7	41	0.3	7571	47.9
2001	18259	301	1.6	5246	28.7	12712	69.6	8354	45.8	130	0.7	108	0.6	29	0.2	9638	52.8
2002	22761	352	1.5	6395	28.1	16014	70.4	8612	37.8	135	0.6	135	0.6	26	0.1	13853	60.9
2003	29235	953	3.3	7921	27.1	20361	69.6	9467	32.4	233	0.8	196	0.7	46	0.2	19293	66.0
2004	31446	1941	6.2	9307	29.6	20198	64.2	9899	31.5	382	1.2	224	0.7	58	0.2	20883	66.4
2005	36894	1876	5.1	11017	29.9	24001	65.1	11518	31.2	393	1.1	206	0.6	45	0.1	24732	67.0
2006	43516	2441	5.6	15644	35.9	25431	58.4	13801	31.7	503	1.2	283	0.7	72	0.2	28857	66.3
2007	56451	3714	6.6	21636	38.3	31101	55.1	19776	35.0	759	1.3	272	0.5	109	0.2	35535	62.9
2008	62031	7604	12.3	25072	40.4	29355	47.3	25703	41.4	984	1.6	327	0.5	119	0.2	34898	56.3
2009	83621	11355	13.6	27438	32.8	44828	53.6	36706	43.9	1419	1.7	525	0.6	158	0.2	44813	53.6
2010	119346	13691	11.5	43901	36.8	61754	51.7	56334	47.2	1926	1.6	767	0.6	258	0.2	60061	50.3
2011	128415	18242	14.2	51402	40.0	58771	45.8	68914	53.7	2946	2.3	1121	0.9	539	0.4	54895	42.7
2012	153598	22153	14.4	65946	42.9	65499	42.6	85375	55.6	3084	2.0	1555	1.0	2357	1.5	61227	39.9
2013	170430	20084	11.8	77503	45.5	72843	42.7	92717	54.4	4241	2.5	1644	1.0	774	0.5	71054	41.7
2014	179953	22276	12.4	83202	46.2	74475	41.4	104193	57.9	4300	2.4	1786	1.0	766	0.4	68908	38.3
2015	241176	33477	13.9	105254	43.6	102445	42.5	141112	58.5	6539	2.7	2678	1.1	1434	0.6	89413	37.1
合计	1447986	161410	11.1	578353	39.9	708223	48.9	727043	50.2	28577	2.0	12518	0.9	11492	0.8	668356	46.2

1986—2015年广东省各类专利申请人三种专利申请情况

单位：件

申请人	类别 \ 年份	1986—1999年	2000年	2001年	2002年	2003年	2004年	2005年	2006年	2007年	2008年	2009年	2010年	2011年	2012年	2013年	2014年	2015年	扣除非正常专利	合计
企业	发明	1285	665	1058	1973	3508	5032	8677	15455	20296	21282	24151	30226	37770	45774	49801	53898	73243		394094
	实用新型	6681	2245	2845	3239	4089	4898	6667	8671	10843	14068	21352	29206	44375	52470	58355	63125	92384	2	425511
	外观设计	30144	7078	6979	6557	6913	7292	8655	9611	11562	12604	14947	18687	25661	27259	28557	32647	40048		295201
高校	发明	381	154	204	271	389	495	811	1188	1254	1663	1944	2566	2988	3294	4247	5086	6769		33704
	实用新型	370	80	97	111	138	170	256	314	331	473	594	785	1204	1301	1776	2216	3687		13903
	外观设计	46	3	4	2	5	6	3	35	8	186	491	1345	973	1596	1510	2130	1723		10066
科研单位	发明	404	112	203	134	215	174	265	292	355	515	708	950	2419	1875	2822	2825	3066		17334
	实用新型	418	55	61	55	76	43	89	105	126	246	293	398	803	696	1062	973	1390		6889
	外观设计	177	27	12	5	8	10	17	32	19	24	67	64	125	159	92	128	67		1033
机关团体	发明	401	13	24	20	48	47	55	83	84	91	106	163	369	430	767	790	1063		4554
	实用新型	1421	10	24	19	33	47	38	64	61	57	103	231	591	759	992	1176	2259		7885
	外观设计	4211	4	3	20	5	19	3	27	49	15	41	90	68	132	188	111	62		5048
个人	发明	3850	816	1057	1421	2021	2345	3079	4333	4703	4548	5338	6961	8466	9075	11353	12549	19800	775	100940
	实用新型	17852	3643	5117	6548	8649	9524	11901	14732	14028	14039	16685	17086	20363	23505	31407	28646	35997	408	279314
	外观设计	17365	6218	9908	13977	17089	22099	31704	35944	38730	34072	38853	44149	50100	61189	71336	72051	74381	307	638858
合计		85006	21123	27596	34352	43186	52201	72220	90886	102449	103883	125673	152907	196275	229514	264265	278351	355939	1492	2234334

注：1985年数据缺，本表未列入。

1986—2015年广东省各类专利申请人三种专利授权情况

单位：件

申请人	类别 \ 年份	1986—1998年	1999年	2000年	2001年	2002年	2003年	2004年	2005年	2006年	2007年	2008年	2009年	2010年	2011年	2012年	2013年	2014年	2015年	合计
企业	发明	74	27	54	72	123	434	1033	1024	1366	2443	5807	8839	10814	14117	17226	15455	17416	26019	122343
	实用新型	2841	1428	1904	2068	2386	2869	3176	4173	6215	9235	11962	14808	26096	34112	45067	53045	59837	77663	358885
	外观设计	14032	6242	5979	6214	6103	6164	5690	6321	6220	8098	7934	13059	19424	20685	23082	24217	26940	37430	243834
高校	发明	124	21	36	52	56	117	266	240	283	395	566	770	946	1477	1708	1667	1823	2423	12970
	实用新型	248	51	90	74	78	111	116	149	215	346	416	469	629	893	1148	1465	1974	2601	11073
	外观设计	22	8	6	4	1	5	0	4	5	18	2	180	351	576	228	1109	503	1515	4537
科研单位	发明	104	12	32	39	57	127	172	145	178	139	168	220	318	463	645	738	823	1613	5993
	实用新型	290	48	45	57	63	59	44	51	80	119	146	270	355	548	682	745	924	988	5514
	外观设计	90	29	41	12	15	10	8	10	25	14	13	35	94	110	228	161	39	77	1011
机关团体	发明	57	8	17	14	5	8	13	11	25	30	19	36	57	76	184	77	129	158	924
	实用新型	1074	28	20	12	18	24	35	23	43	54	62	60	163	347	1405	646	568	1126	5708
	外观设计	3509	14	4	3	3	14	10	11	4	25	38	62	38	116	768	51	69	150	4889
个人	发明	207	55	122	124	111	267	457	456	589	707	1044	1490	1556	2109	2390	2147	2085	3264	19180
	实用新型	8321	2342	2738	3035	3850	4858	5936	6621	9091	11882	12486	11831	16658	15502	17644	21602	19899	22876	197172
	外观设计	9733	4015	4711	6479	9892	14168	14490	17655	19177	22946	21368	31492	41847	37284	41193	47305	46924	63273	453952
合计		40726	14328	15799	18259	22761	29235	31446	36894	43516	56451	62031	83621	119346	128415	153598	170430	179953	241176	1447985

注：1985年数据缺，本表未列入。

2011—2015年广东省各地级以上市专利申请情况

单位：件

地区＼类别	2011年				2012年				2013年				2014年				2015年			
	发明	实用新型	外观设计	合计	发明	实用新型	外观设计	合计	发明	实用新型	外观设计	合计	发明	实用新型	外观设计	合计	发明	实用新型	外观设计	合计
广州	8173	10219	9705	28097	9815	11824	11748	33387	12157	14575	13019	39751	14587	15784	15941	46312	20071	24723	18501	63295
深圳	28823	21196	13503	63522	31068	23706	18335	73109	32211	28109	20337	80657	31077	30455	20723	82255	40032	41641	23826	105499
珠海	1484	2706	1404	5594	2287	3513	1297	7097	2729	3895	1393	8017	3172	4162	1664	8998	4420	5377	1537	11334
汕头	1423	1452	9796	12671	1638	2130	6620	10388	1692	2431	6877	11000	884	1670	6543	9097	1043	2359	6425	9827
韶关	179	428	638	1245	274	757	783	1814	316	1107	843	2266	420	874	1060	2354	726	1173	1202	3101
河源	147	151	191	489	125	229	216	570	194	545	359	1098	145	391	317	853	207	764	540	1511
梅州	111	317	560	988	126	401	618	1145	122	795	769	1686	174	1316	782	2272	163	2244	726	3133
惠州	1296	2236	2497	6029	1676	2614	5604	9894	2466	3830	8872	15168	3347	4853	10159	18359	4600	5991	10817	21408
汕尾	69	86	187	342	93	166	501	760	79	521	576	1176	81	127	387	595	101	340	482	923
东莞	4214	10821	9419	24454	5568	13167	10464	29199	6454	12746	9812	29012	6913	11977	9541	28431	11166	17567	9361	38094
中山	1289	4162	8684	14135	1816	5067	11518	18401	2432	5885	13501	21818	3350	6106	15162	24618	4867	8169	14827	27863
江门	821	2100	4776	7697	1259	2322	4585	8166	1634	2373	4432	8439	1935	2399	4014	8348	2438	3098	3988	9524
佛山	2758	8424	9191	20373	3310	9514	9780	22604	4674	11537	10988	27199	7261	11844	10602	29707	11507	16265	12024	39796
阳江	73	250	1009	1332	47	272	938	1257	41	381	1077	1499	69	308	996	1373	76	312	1336	1724
湛江	225	426	401	1052	263	373	516	1152	289	598	601	1488	343	721	1031	2095	495	1303	1437	3235
茂名	109	293	506	908	172	398	1026	1596	392	725	1413	2530	378	627	1664	2669	650	833	2055	3538
肇庆	266	805	395	1466	323	824	404	1551	295	964	518	1777	402	864	515	1781	494	1135	715	2344
清远	115	337	355	807	127	290	333	750	187	331	320	838	160	371	351	882	346	631	592	1569
潮州	282	497	2259	3038	251	606	2671	3528	389	1234	2941	4564	238	639	2597	3474	221	623	2606	3450
揭阳	97	330	1256	1683	142	344	2043	2529	143	768	2667	3578	123	385	2591	3099	177	755	2794	3726
云浮	58	98	195	351	55	167	284	506	79	175	315	569	71	214	388	673	113	355	448	916
校正值	0	2	0	2	13	47	51	111	15	67	53	135	18	49	39	106	28	59	42	129
合计	52012	67336	76927	196275	60448	78731	90335	229514	68990	93592	101683	264265	75148	96136	107067	278351	103941	135717	116281	355939

2011—2015年广东省各地级以上市专利授权情况

单位：件

类别/地区	2011年				2012年				2013年				2014年				2015年			
	发明	实用新型	外观设计	合计	发明	实用新型	外观设计	合计	发明	实用新型	外观设计	合计	发明	实用新型	外观设计	合计	发明	实用新型	外观设计	合计
广州	3146	8032	7168	18346	4027	9692	8278	21997	4055	12098	10003	26156	4590	13512	10036	28138	6619	17266	15949	39834
深圳	11824	16309	11230	39363	13143	20799	14919	48861	10988	23233	15545	49766	12041	25419	16221	53681	16957	33107	22055	72119
珠海	323	1999	1368	3690	503	3198	1235	4936	482	3214	1109	4805	608	4230	1420	6258	1240	4021	1529	6790
汕头	149	979	3243	4371	179	1451	4953	6583	211	1804	4818	6833	230	1414	4826	6470	328	1619	5705	7652
韶关	29	258	381	668	39	536	856	1431	61	932	445	1438	52	722	810	1584	108	787	1212	2107
河源	5	209	158	372	19	139	168	326	23	281	217	521	24	304	241	569	30	381	421	832
梅州	29	225	438	692	57	372	486	915	44	632	590	1266	81	1074	454	1609	46	2204	735	2985
惠州	117	1577	1223	2917	313	2227	1553	4093	467	2577	2870	5914	522	3563	3311	7396	868	4632	4297	9797
汕尾	4	60	163	227	21	139	342	502	24	364	430	818	16	188	254	458	49	160	443	652
东莞	758	7976	10618	19352	1381	10667	8852	20900	1495	12080	9020	22595	1624	10582	8130	20336	2795	14074	9951	26820
中山	355	3400	6272	10027	465	3822	6591	10878	464	4941	8815	14220	505	5235	9309	15049	992	6338	14868	22198
江门	213	1549	3547	5309	362	1917	2991	5270	272	1973	3101	5346	307	2226	3005	5538	508	2404	3474	6386
佛山	974	6651	8715	16340	1152	8131	8535	17818	1012	9717	8897	19626	1109	11211	9393	21713	2150	13912	11468	27530
阳江	10	204	641	855	17	239	656	912	4	252	924	1180	5	298	832	1135	25	262	1150	1437
湛江	110	329	308	747	144	382	375	901	117	473	498	1088	115	547	632	1294	144	947	1395	2486
茂名	23	197	176	396	39	239	416	694	41	457	591	1089	53	465	661	1179	128	528	1335	1991
肇庆	56	492	341	889	98	758	317	1173	116	790	382	1288	146	889	414	1449	165	885	676	1726
清远	13	233	151	397	51	290	328	669	43	266	300	609	52	292	286	630	110	491	416	1017
潮州	47	365	1465	1877	63	480	1859	2402	85	622	2250	2957	107	422	2313	2842	98	558	2646	3302
揭阳	43	286	1011	1340	59	317	1537	1913	51	580	1766	2397	63	408	1601	2072	66	440	2301	2807
云浮	12	69	154	235	19	125	225	369	28	178	255	461	26	160	294	480	45	203	397	645
校正值	2	3	0	3	2	26	27	55	1	39	17	57	0	41	32	73	6	35	22	63
合计	18242	51402	58771	128413	22153	65946	65499	153598	20084	77503	72843	170430	22276	83202	74475	179953	33477	105254	102445	241176

2002—2015年全国及广东省PCT国际专利申请情况

年份	全国		广东		广东占全国比例（%）
	数量（件）	增长率（%）	数量（件）	增长率（%）	
2002年	951	/	200	/	21.03
2003年	1146	20.50	287	43.50	25.04
2004年	1592	38.92	467	62.72	29.33
2005年	2438	53.14	989	111.78	40.57
2006年	3826	56.93	1731	75.03	45.24
2007年	5401	41.17	2646	52.86	48.99
2008年	5853	8.37	3120	17.91	53.31
2009年	8000	36.68	4418	41.60	55.23
2010年	12016	50.20	6678	51.15	55.58
2011年	16089	33.90	8941	33.89	55.57
2012年	18145	12.78	9211	3.02	50.76
2013年	20897	15.17	11525	25.12	55.15
2014年	24007	14.88	13332	15.68	55.53
2015年	28399	18.29	15190	13.94	53.49

2015年广东省各地级以上市PCT专利申请情况

单位：件

地级以上市	数量	地级以上市	数量	地级以上市	数量
广州	627	惠州	174	湛江	6
深圳	13308	汕尾	7	茂名	5
珠海	150	东莞	336	肇庆	13
汕头	52	中山	101	清远	2
韶关	29	江门	50	潮州	3
河源	0	佛山	306	揭阳	10
梅州	5	阳江	5	云浮	1

2015年广东省各地级以上市专利行政执法统计表

单位：宗

执法部门	专利纠纷案件情况									查处假冒专利行为		涉外案件（受理）
	纠纷案件受理						纠纷案件结案					
	合计	专利种类			纠纷种类		合计	纠纷类型		假冒立案	假冒结案	
		发明	实用新型	外观设计	侵权	其他		侵权	其他			
广东省知识产权局	1406				1406	0	1406	1406	0	0	0	
广州市知识产权局	234				232	2	249	248	1	369	369	
韶关市知识产权局	0				0	0	0	0	0	0	0	
深圳市知识产权局	74				74	0	50	50	0	27	27	
珠海市知识产权局	2				2	0	2	2	0	1	1	
汕头市知识产权局	38				38	0	22	22	0	35	35	
佛山市知识产权局	26				26	0	29	29	0	57	57	
江门市知识产权局	8				8	0	28	28	0	6	6	
湛江市知识产权局	8				8	0	8	8	0	4	4	
茂名市知识产权局	0				0	0	0	0	0	5	5	
肇庆市知识产权局	8				8	0	8	8	0	2	2	
惠州市知识产权局	11				11	0	13	13	0	130	130	
梅州市知识产权局	0				0	0	0	0	0	0	0	
汕尾市知识产权局	0				0	0	0	0	0	8	8	
河源市知识产权局	0				0	0	0	0	0	0	0	
阳江市知识产权局	32				32	0	51	51	0	11	11	
清远市知识产权局	0				0	0	0	0	0	5	5	
东莞市知识产权局	62				62	0	55	55	0	2	2	
中山市知识产权局	537				537	0	679	679	0	6	6	
潮州市知识产权局	15				15	0	12	12	0	23	23	
揭阳市知识产权局	0				0	0	0	0	0	2	2	
云浮市知识产权局	0				0	0	0	0	0	5	5	
佛山市顺德区知识产权局	31				31	0	14	14	0	24	24	
合　计	2492	142	533	1817	2490	2	2626	2625	1	722	722	348

注：数据源自全国专利执法办案报送系统。统计时间节点为2015年1月1日—2015年12月31日。

广东省专利行政部门历年受理、办结专利案件情况表

单位：件

执法部门			1985—1991年	1992年	1993年	1994年	1995年	1996年	1997年	1998年	1999年	2000年	2001年	2002年	2003年	2004年	2005年	2006年	2007年	2008年	2009年	2010年	2011年	2012年	2013年	2014年	2015年	合计
专利纠纷	广东省知识产权局	受理	35	11	0	18	45	83	102	72	96	97	57	44	6	29	23	42	23	23	22	33	0	5	1115	1085	1406	4472
		办结	30	6	7	12	32	56	80	56	93	83	75	55	23	13	25	20	33	26	13	33	10	8	1106	1084	1406	4385
	其他地级以上市知识产权局	受理	67	5	2	16	22	78	99	115	113	221	240	374	350	347	307	194	233	176	122	112	220	484	742	731	1086	6456
		办结	49	16	7	9	12	55	81	76	75	210	173	265	269	267	252	180	181	172	79	74	137	410	468	718	1220	5455
	小计	受理	102	16	2	34	67	161	201	187	209	318	297	418	356	376	330	236	256	199	144	145	220	489	1857	1816	2492	10928
		办结	79	22	14	21	44	111	161	132	168	293	248	320	292	280	277	200	214	198	92	107	147	418	1574	1802	2626	9840
假冒专利	广东省知识产权局	受理												0	0	0	0	1	4	16	0	0	0	7	0	0	0	28
		办结												0	0	0	0	0	0	20	1	0	0	7	0	0	0	28
	其他地级以上市知识产权局	受理												69	200	83	83	63	86	24	14	36	41	627	435	739	722	3222
		办结												61	196	69	79	46	78	25	14	29	23	544	435	739	722	3060
	小计	受理												69	200	83	83	64	90	40	14	36	41	634	435	739	722	3250
		办结												61	196	69	79	46	78	45	15	29	23	551	435	739	722	3080

2010—2015年广东省专利案件收、结统计表

单位：件

	收案						结案					
	2010年	2011年	2012年	2013年	2014年	2015年	2010年	2011年	2012年	2013年	2014年	2015年
一审	1646	2608	3726	3096	3154	4589	1441	2241	3354	3193	3179	3491
二审	541	562	690	892	1166	886	571	559	698	771	1087	994
合计	2187	3170	4416	3988	4320	5475	2012	2800	4052	3964	4266	4485

2015年广东省专利奖名单

一、2015年广东专利奖名单

（一）广东专利金奖（15项）

序号	项目名称	专利号	申报单位
1	陶瓷颗粒局部定位增强耐磨复合材料的制造方法	ZL201410183449.2	广州有色金属研究院
2	一种采用固体酸催化剂和活塞流反应器连续生产生物柴油的方法	ZL200610036419.8	中国科学院广州能源研究所
3	一种高磺化度高分子量木质素基高效减水剂及其制备方法	ZL 200910040399.5	华南理工大学
4	一种带有转接盘总成的混合动力汽车	ZL 200810185949.8	比亚迪股份有限公司
5	一种汽车车身前部结构的设计方法及其汽车的设计方法	ZL 201210269508.2	广州汽车集团股份有限公司
6	一种加密键盘	ZL 200910192854.3	广州广电运通金融电子股份有限公司
7	永磁同步电机	ZL 201110223492.7	珠海格力节能环保制冷技术研究中心有限公司
8	具有自我调节功能的心脏间隔缺损封堵器	ZL 200510032924.0	先健科技（深圳）有限公司
9	一种具备多个功能层的纳米人工硬脑膜及其制备方法	ZL 200910037736.5	广州迈普再生医学科技有限公司
10	一种桥接转发技术	ZL 200510112882.1	华为技术有限公司
11	一种媒体修改方法及系统	ZL 200910093943.2	中兴通讯股份有限公司
12	一种病毒释放缓冲液的制备及其应用	ZL 201210049094.2	肇庆大华农生物药品有限公司， 广东大华农动物保健品股份有限公司
13	制备抗病毒口服液的方法	ZL 200610122442.9	广州市香雪制药股份有限公司
14	飞行器	ZL 201430178384.7	深圳市大疆创新科技有限公司
15	空调机（落地式13-04）	ZL 201330299065.7	珠海格力电器股份有限公司

（二）广东专利优秀奖（55项）

序号	项目名称	专利号	申报单位
1	一种太阳能复合能源空调热水装置	ZL 200910143725.5	广东志高空调有限公司
2	三管制热回收多联机及其控制方法	ZL 201110186993.2	广东美的暖通设备有限公司
3	模块化多联机组及其冷冻机油均衡控制方法	ZL 200910041723.5	珠海格力电器股份有限公司
4	一种高效冷凝式热交换器	ZL 200910194321.9	广东诺科冷暖设备有限公司
5	空调器制冷剂的自动调节方法及系统	ZL 201110452321.1	TCL空调器（中山）有限公司
6	变频空调器的节能控制方法及装置	ZL 201210236422.X	广东美的制冷设备有限公司
7	一种高纯度高聚合度水不溶性结晶II型聚磷酸铵的制备方法	ZL 201110038999.5	清远市普塞呋磷化学有限公司
8	一种车辆搬运装置	ZL 200810009284.5	深圳中集天达空港设备有限公司
9	一种火法氧化铋生产方法	ZL 201010548257.2	广东先导稀材股份有限公司
10	一种含有改性聚苯醚的无卤阻燃高抗冲聚苯乙烯/聚苯醚复合物及其制备方法	ZL 03113673.7	金发科技股份有限公司
11	冷缩式电力硅橡胶套管的制备方法及其用途	ZL 200810026977.5	广东标美硅氟新材料有限公司
12	钢管防腐涂层用茂金属聚丙烯改性材料及其制备方法和应用	ZL 200910038211.3	广州鹿山新材料股份有限公司
13	一种聚酰胺6复合材料及其制备方法	ZL 201010543462.X	金发科技股份有限公司
14	污泥堆肥生产有机铁肥的方法	ZL 201010589432.2	广东省生态环境与土壤研究所
15	多级制冷压缩机及其中间补气结构	ZL 201110326821.0	珠海格力电器股份有限公司
16	双缸式旋转压缩机	ZL 201110044857.X	广东美芝制冷设备有限公司
17	全自动喷涂设备	ZL 201110168001.3	东莞丰裕电机有限公司
18	编码器控制的重型自动封边机	ZL 201010578150.2	东莞市南兴家具装备制造股份有限公司
19	直插式快接管件及取管套筒	ZL 201210269272.2	佛山市日丰企业有限公司
20	轴流风轮	ZL 200710026747.4	广东美的制冷设备有限公司
21	一种海量文件的存储方法及系统	ZL 200610061328.X	腾讯科技（深圳）有限公司
22	一种智能闭锁系统及其工作方法	ZL 200910193955.2	珠海优特电力科技股份有限公司
23	一种直流无刷电机控制方法	ZL 200910038187.3	中山大洋电机股份有限公司
24	一种降低在矢量图形填充过程中对CPU耗费的方法及装置	ZL 200910203728.3	炬芯（珠海）科技有限公司
25	一种红外触摸屏触摸点识别方法和装置	ZL 201110206718.2	广州视睿电子科技有限公司
26	电缆免调挤塑装置、其安装方法及电缆护套的加工方法	ZL 201210280855.5	广州广日电气设备有限公司
27	应用于城市轨道交通的弱电综合UPS电源系统及供电方法	ZL 201110074888.X	广州地铁设计研究院有限公司
28	一种单轨绝对光栅尺及其图像编码方法	ZL 201210165294.4	广东工业大学
29	具有防止泡沫溢出功能的电饭煲及其防止方法	ZL 201210056310.6	美的集团股份有限公司
30	一种软管灯改良结构	ZL 200410054742.9	鹤山同方照明科技有限公司
31	电源控制器	ZL 200710031504.X	珠海格力电器股份有限公司
32	化验检测判定设备及方法	ZL 201110223436.3	广州万孚生物技术股份有限公司
33	液面检测装置及加样系统	ZL 200910106574.6	深圳迈瑞生物医疗电子股份有限公司
34	用于检测挥发性有机物的检测系统及湿度检测方法	ZL 201010192127.X	东莞市升微机电设备科技有限公司
35	一种预编码方法、系统及预编码码本的构造方法	ZL 200910163676.1	中兴通讯股份有限公司
36	超宽带双频合路器	ZL 200710027110.7	京信通信系统（中国）有限公司
37	一种用于数据处理系统的无线数据通信方法及装置	ZL 02114797.3	深圳市朗科科技股份有限公司
38	调制电磁波辐射方向图的器件及天线	ZL 201210447826.3	深圳光启创新技术有限公司

（续上表）

序号	项目名称	专利号	申报单位
39	一种带低频磁通信的射频SIM卡冲突检测方法	ZL 201010138492.2	国民技术股份有限公司
40	一种治疗子宫肌瘤的中成药和制备、质量控制方法	ZL 200510036468.7	广州白云山潘高寿药业股份有限公司
41	一种制浆机的制浆方法	ZL 200810029349.2	美的集团股份有限公司
42	调味品中大肠菌群的快速检测方法	ZL 201010173244.1	佛山市海天调味食品股份有限公司
43	一种优化改良的耐高温植酸酶PHYTH及其基因和应用	ZL 201010566261.1	广东溢多利生物科技有限公司
44	含有中药本草植物的去屑养发组合物、洗发露及其制备方法	ZL 201210264457.4	拉芳家化股份有限公司
45	一种化痰止咳的药物及其生产方法	ZL 02114847.3	中山大学
46	整车	ZL 201230059657.7	比亚迪股份有限公司
47	OLED电视（E980S）	ZL 201430138630.6	深圳创维-RGB电子有限公司
48	洗地车（WOLF-1）	ZL 201230560162.2	东莞威霸清洁器材有限公司
49	灯臂（12009018）	ZL 201330463433.7	中山市琪朗灯饰厂有限公司
50	超声成像检测仪	ZL 201230613827.1	汕头市超声仪器研究所有限公司
51	水壶（2）	ZL 201230649851.0	广东海兴塑胶有限公司
52	蓝牙耳机（CN-1000B）	ZL 201230115512.4	广东佳禾声学科技有限公司
53	玩具推车（381-2）	ZL 201130434572.8	东莞市智乐堡儿童玩具有限公司
54	微波炉（TH0AGX6-BRN）	ZL 201230472489.4	美的集团股份有限公司
55	GPS追踪器	ZL 201330220969.6	广州视源电子科技股份有限公司

（三）广东发明人奖（9人）

序号	发明人	单 位
1	李金波	广东美的制冷设备有限公司
2	张 辉	珠海格力电器股份有限公司
3	方李明	华为技术有限公司
4	陈孙艺	茂名重力石化机械制造有限公司
5	戴 博	中兴通讯股份有限公司
6	万金泉	华南理工大学
7	邢 达	华南师范大学
8	裴端卿	中国科学院广州生物医药与健康研究院
9	吴育林	广东凯西欧照明有限公司

二、第十七届中国专利奖配套奖名单

（一）中国专利金奖（4项）

序号	专利号	专利名称	专利权人	发明人
1	ZL200510109483.X	一种绑定即时通信识别码与无线通信识别码的方法	腾讯科技（深圳）有限公司	吴宵光、陈泱、黄业钧、马化腾、曾李青
2	ZL200610063151.7	氯吡格雷硫酸盐的固体制剂及其制备方法	深圳信立泰药业股份有限公司	叶澄海
3	ZL200810094545.8	一种物理上行控制信道干扰随机化的方法	中兴通讯股份有限公司	夏树强、梁春丽、戴博、郝鹏
4	ZL200810185950.0	一种混合动力驱动系统及采用该系统的汽车	比亚迪股份有限公司	罗红斌、周旭光、汤小华、张鑫鑫、罗霆

（二）中国外观设计金奖（2项）

序号	专利号	专利名称	专利权人	发明人
1	ZL201330103179.X	分体式壁挂机壳体（13-01）	珠海格力电器股份有限公司	徐康泉、王洁、易东昌、谭云龙、周仁春、伍雪乔、王莹、董明珠、张辉、吴欢龙、李亮、古汤汤、张华中
2	ZL201430221358.8	金融终端（A-009）	广州广电运通金融电子股份有限公司	丁迎峰、陈瑶、朱聃、邓庆科

（三）中国专利优秀奖（97项）

序号	专利号	专利名称	专利权人	发明人
1	ZL02108386.X	一种移动终端及其用户识别模块	华为技术有限公司	熊伟
2	ZL02114797.3	一种用于数据处理系统的无线数据通信方法及装置	深圳市朗科科技股份有限公司	邓国顺、成晓华、向锋
3	ZL03146863.2	采用内导管定位的钢管对接装置及应用	李勇、陈宜言	李勇、陈宜言、聂建国、余志武
4	ZL200410054742.9	一种软管灯改良结构	鹤山同方照明科技有限公司	樊邦弘
5	ZL200410077693.0	压滤工艺分离人血浆蛋白的方法	广东双林生物制药有限公司	朱光祖、梅伟伶
6	ZL200510036344.9	液体硅橡胶基础胶料、液体硅橡胶材料及其它们的制备方法	广州天赐有机硅科技有限公司	张利萍
7	ZL200510036468.7	一种主治子宫肌瘤的中成药和制备、质量控制方法	广州白云山潘高寿药业股份有限公司	魏大华、罗国器、莫国强、黎彤、陈洁标、陈世斌、龙成、黎佩红、黄洁

（续上表）

序号	专利号	专利名称	专利权人	发明人
8	ZL200510037077.7	一种治疗消化性溃疡的中成药及其制备方法	广州白云山中一药业有限公司	冯所安、药凤荷、邹章、郑尧新、龙丽娜、钟趣宜、张一萍、赵春梅
9	ZL200510100860.3	一种登机桥行走机构的控制方法	中国国际海运集装箱（集团）股份有限公司、深圳中集天达空港设备有限公司	向卫
10	ZL200510107867.8	一种中药组合物及其制备方法	扬子江药业集团广州海瑞药业有限公司	施猛
11	ZL200510120801.2	除颤双相波的波形产生装置	深圳迈瑞生物医疗电子股份有限公司	安敏、许伟、李新胜
12	ZL200610035301.3	一种多晶硅生产过程中的副产物的综合利用方法	广州吉必盛科技实业有限公司	刘莉、王跃林、龙成坤、吴利民
13	ZL200610037167.0	一种淀粉预处理方法	华南理工大学	黄强、扶雄、罗发兴、何小维、李琳
14	ZL200610082274.5	无源光网络用户终端	华为技术有限公司	高海、董英华
15	ZL200710006801.9	一种立体孔洞装饰陶瓷砖的制备方法及其产品	广东东鹏陶瓷股份有限公司、广东东鹏控股股份有限公司	钟保民、王正旺、姜安宁、王金凤
16	ZL200710026747.4	轴流风轮	广东美的制冷设备有限公司	游斌、伍光辉、程志明、向运明
17	ZL200710031144.3	宽频带环状双极化辐射单元及线阵天线	京信通信系统（中国）有限公司	卜斌龙、刘培涛、孙善球、范颂东、苏小兵
18	ZL200710031314.8	导引包数据协议激活的方法及通用分组无线业务系统	中国移动通信集团广东有限公司	舒波、王峻、赵武、邹学农、麦晓念、夏玉青、董越、黄勤禄、吴栩欣
19	ZL200710031504.X	电源控制器	珠海格力电器股份有限公司	朱江洪、张辉、钟明生、李文灿、游剑波
20	ZL200710076841.0	扣片式散热器及其制造方法	深圳市超频三科技股份有限公司	杜建军
21	ZL200710105707.9	一种电子数据表的函数收集方法和装置	金蝶软件（中国）有限公司	乔昕明
22	ZL200720063970.1	电力、电子（通信）设备及网络大接地电阻接地分配装置	深圳远征技术有限公司	张庭炎
23	ZL200810027879.3	大跨度悬索桥先导索火箭抛送装置和方法	中交路桥华南工程有限公司、中国人民解放军理工大学工程兵工程学院	赵天法、顾文彬、李德钦、唐勇、王崇旭、刘建清、唐世进、郑向平、鲜正洪
24	ZL200810029096.9	夏桑菊制剂的制备方法	广州白云山星群（药业）股份有限公司	孙维广、谭银合、方铁铮、苏广丰、姚江雄、许招懂、符素平
25	ZL200810030191.0	移动终端及获得上网信息的方法	宇龙计算机通信科技（深圳）有限公司	倪燕
26	ZL200810066721.7	一种交叉路口的导航方法及使用了此导航方法的导航系统	深圳市凯立德科技股份有限公司	张文星
27	ZL200810067071.8	动态物理屏蔽净化器、制作方法及专用夹具	深圳厨之道空气净化设备有限公司	胡瑞志
28	ZL200810098373.1	用户识别卡初始化方法、感知用户识别卡动作方法及终端	华为终端有限公司	兰娟
29	ZL200810216864.1	血液检测试剂和方法	深圳迈瑞生物医疗电子股份有限公司	匡玉吉、张宝华、徐兵、邵建辉、雷霆、张丽
30	ZL200810217292.9	一种手表	深圳市飞亚达精密计时制造有限公司	李北、陈杰、陈恭谦、鲍贤勇、唐海元、严明
31	ZL200810217300.X	直流复合支柱绝缘子及其伞裙结构	中国南方电网有限责任公司电网技术研究中心、清华大学深圳研究生院	张福增、王黎明、关志成、赵杰、饶宏、黎小林、罗兵、彭功茂、赵锋、杨皓麟
32	ZL200810219260.2	数据包转发方法、系统及设备	华为技术有限公司	蒋胜
33	ZL200810219753.6	基于全息谱技术的不平衡方位估计方法	广东省电力工业局试验研究所	刘石、廖与禾、沈玉娣
34	ZL200810239451.5	信号编码、解码方法及装置、编解码系统	华为技术有限公司	苗磊、刘泽新、陈龙吟、胡晨、肖玮、哈维·米希尔·塔迪、张清
35	ZL200820044240.1	一种拼插式玩具的插接结构	广东邦宝益智玩具股份有限公司	吴锭辉
36	ZL200820135995.2	用于曲面胶印机的多独立交流伺服电机同步驱动系统	王贤淮、王昌佑	王贤淮、王昌佑
37	ZL200820188592.4	采砂动态监管装置	广东华南水电高新技术开发有限公司	陈军强、钟道清
38	ZL200910000313.6	一种压榨连续生产线	佛山市海天调味食品股份有限公司、佛山市海天（高明）调味食品有限公司	黎旭晖、王力展、郭罗江、陈军阳、宾跃
39	ZL200910041239.2	应用于城市轨道交通的火灾联动控制系统及方法	广州地铁设计研究院有限公司	陈小林、史海欧、毛宇丰、王迪军、贺利工、胡竞、郭莉、梁东升、韩瑶、湛维昭、黄永波、李万略、熊晓锋、向东
40	ZL200910041723.5	模块化多联机组及其冷冻机油均衡控制方法	珠海格力电器股份有限公司	张龙、刘煜、宋培刚、黄春、张仕强、武连发、王成
41	ZL200910093513.0	一种以太环网保护中防止地址表重复刷新的方法及系统	中兴通讯股份有限公司	吴少勇、甘玉玺、杨理、王红五
42	ZL200910110354.0	一种固相氧化环合合成特利加压素的方法	深圳翰宇药业股份有限公司	刘建、李红玲、马亚平、袁建成
43	ZL200910110751.8	一种具有扫描链的集成电路	炬芯（珠海）科技有限公司	谢武洪
44	ZL200910136165.0	一种用于平衡电网负荷的电池储能电站	比亚迪股份有限公司	罗红斌、廖云浩、张子峰、王营辉、邓林旺、尹韶文、陈东红、汤小华、徐娟
45	ZL200910163676.1	一种预编码方法、系统及预编码码本的构造方法	中兴通讯股份有限公司	陈艺戬、郁光辉、戴博、杨勖
46	ZL200910174452.0	一种中药及其制备方法	广东太安堂药业股份有限公司	柯树泉、柯少彬
47	ZL200910189941.3	一种核电站生产过程回放的方法和系统	中广核工程有限公司、中国广东核电集团有限公司	王婷、刘高俊、张砚、倪立功、何大宇、史觊、张焕欣、江国进
48	ZL200910203771.X	一种嵌入式系统中的异常处理方法及装置	中兴通讯股份有限公司	王继刚、谢世波
49	ZL200910217242.5	一种对多个业务进行融合的业务云系统及业务实现方法	中兴通讯股份有限公司	周士俊
50	ZL200910249910.2	一种用于反应堆保护系统的组态系统	北京广利核系统工程有限公司、中国广核集团有限公司	张智慧、齐敏、余佳、任保华、王毅璇、程建明
51	ZL200910250430.8	一种射频装置和射频读卡器以及相关通信系统和通信方法	国民技术股份有限公司	余运波、朱杉、欧阳立
52	ZL201010124327.1	移动射频装置、射频IC卡及射频存储卡	国民技术股份有限公司	沈爱民、余运波
53	ZL201010131653.5	旋转式压缩机	广东美芝制冷设备有限公司	高斌
54	ZL201010179084.1	一种不饱和聚酯树脂复合材料及其制备方法	厦门大学、汕头市华莎驰家具家饰有限公司	戴李宗、张良俊、黄茂荣、许一婷、肖永钦、余洪涛、罗伟昂
55	ZL201010266765.1	一种汽车用低TVOC聚丙烯组合物及其制备方法	金发科技股份有限公司、上海金发科技发展有限公司、绵阳东方特种工程塑料有限公司	杨波、李永华、陈广强、杨燕、罗忠富

（续上表）

序号	专利号	专利名称	专利权人	发明人
56	ZL201010299936.0	一种一体化防伪防窜标识制备工艺	广东正迪科技股份有限公司	王建程
57	ZL201010529180.4	一种核电站安全级设备监控方法及系统	中广核工程有限公司、中国广东核电集团有限公司	张学刚、徐晓梅、刘伟、吴官寅、江国进、史觊
58	ZL201010529889.4	双光学放大倍率图像采集装置及图像采集控制处理系统	华南理工大学	张宪民、贺振兴、梁经伦、欧阳高飞、邝泳聪
59	ZL201010531970.6	含芘共轭高分子荧光传感薄膜的制备方法及其应用	深圳中物安防科技有限公司	房喻、何刚、崔红、王红月、曹源、丁立平
60	ZL201010538725.8	一种陶瓷电容器的电介质及其制备方法	汕头高新区松田实业有限公司	李言、黄瑞南、林榕
61	ZL201010543462.X	一种聚酰胺6复合材料及其制备方法	金发科技股份有限公司、上海金发科技发展有限公司	孙雅杰、梁惠强、姜苏俊、陈大华、郑一泉、刘奇祥
62	ZL201010548269.5	一种亚硒酸钠生产方法	广东先导稀材股份有限公司	朱世会、朱世明、朱刘
63	ZL201010548863.4	一种视频码流加、解密方法、装置及通信、存储终端	腾讯科技（深圳）有限公司	谷沉沉
64	ZL201010557614.1	一种USB设备及其检测方法	炬芯（珠海）科技有限公司	余静、黄少彬、杜夔
65	ZL201010581609.4	一种电池模组	比亚迪股份有限公司	曾志亮、郑卫鑫、朱建华
66	ZL201010610953.1	一种艾普拉唑肠溶片剂及其制备方法	丽珠医药集团股份有限公司	侯雪梅、陆文岐、孔祥生、金鑫、陈乔柏、张丽
67	ZL201010614697.3	人干细胞生长因子在化妆品中的应用	广州赛莱拉干细胞科技股份有限公司	王一飞、陈海佳、彭鑫磊、钱垂文、杨柯、李久香、任哲、舒辉萍
68	ZL201110099641.3	一种应用服务扩展系统	深圳创维-RGB电子有限公司	王志国
69	ZL201110142765.5	基于斜坐标系的红外触摸屏触摸定位方法及装置	广州视睿电子科技有限公司	黄安麒、胡隽鹏
70	ZL201110163812.4	一种星轮盘传动机构及其装配方法	广州达意隆包装机械股份有限公司	宋俊杰、张聪敏
71	ZL201110188106.5	一种耐寒智能电表壳体用聚碳酸酯/ABS合金及其制备方法	惠州市昌亿科技股份有限公司	杜崇铭、林湖彬
72	ZL201110196551.6	半潜式起重生活平台	烟台中集来福士海洋工程有限公司、中国国际海运集装箱（集团）股份有限公司	章立人、滕瑶、李磊、兰公英、于斌、王骁勇、张辉、韩华伟、徐刚
73	ZL201110215344.0	一种建筑模板体系及其施工方法	深圳汇林达科技有限公司	胡云芳、张旭晖、谢仁甫、彭冬菊
74	ZL201110233280.7	多色发光装置	深圳市绎立锐光科技开发有限公司	李屹、杨毅
75	ZL201110237662.7	一种核电站用1E级K1类无卤阻燃热缩管及其制备方法	长园集团股份有限公司	赵成刚、尹沾松、曾志安、王进
76	ZL201120239904.1	一种基于音频接口的智能密码钥匙	国民技术股份有限公司	李华强
77	ZL201180067286.X	胎儿遗传异常的无创性检测	深圳华大基因股份有限公司	蒋馥蔓、陈会飞、柴相花、袁玉英、张秀清、陈芳
78	ZL201210032848.3	多联式空调机组的控制方法	广东美的暖通设备有限公司	李宏伟、许永锋、梁伯启、李洪生、冯伟
79	ZL201210044533.0	发光装置、发光装置组件及相关投影系统	深圳市光峰光电技术有限公司	吴希亮、胡飞
80	ZL201210049094.2	一种病毒释放缓冲液的制备及其应用	肇庆大华农生物药品有限公司、广东大华农动物保健品股份有限公司	陈瑞爱、徐家华、施维松、张东霞、汤钦
81	ZL201210094142.X	基于自耦移相变压器和双六脉波整流的UPS电源	广东易事特电源股份有限公司	徐海波、张胜发、汪家荣
82	ZL201210109959.X	一种曲面印刷机的接料叠料装置	王昌佑	王贤淮、潘悦坤
83	ZL201210132741.6	网页浏览方法、WebApp框架、执行JavaScript方法及装置、移动终端	广州市动景计算机科技有限公司	梁捷、马妙魁
84	ZL201210187944.5	实现受控设备地址分配的电连接器	广东夏野日用电器有限公司	陈梓平
85	ZL201210234027.8	九节茶提取物在降低流感病毒易感性上的应用	广州白云山敬修堂药业股份有限公司	何蓉蓉、曹会娟、李怡芳、栗原博、严志标、彭红英、陆颂规、江涛、陈雪华
86	ZL201210236422.X	变频空调器的节能控制方法及装置	广东美的制冷设备有限公司	李强、张治国、李金波、曾祥兵、潘新运、郑水胜、戚文端、陈首敏、王磊、卢海生、朱良红、黄灿彬、罗凌
87	ZL201210242065.8	超高空屋顶超长天线提升施工方法及系统	广州建筑股份有限公司	王龙、高俊岳、魏威、邵泉、娄峰、温建明、严仕基、陈德磊
88	ZL201210247969.X	一种水性砂浆改性剂及其制备方法与应用	中科院广州化学有限公司	吴昆、胡文光、吕满庚、练锦添
89	ZL201210250616.5	对终端进行控制的方法、装置及终端	腾讯科技（深圳）有限公司	袁灿材
90	ZL201210281020.1	一种大截面高效节能型燃气隧道窑	广东四通集团股份有限公司、潮州市索力德机电设备有限公司	郭俊平、蔡镇城、蔡镇锋、伍武
91	ZL201220724019.7	吸油烟机和用于其的热清洗系统	美的集团股份有限公司	李子锋、黎本锋、凌飞、覃有升、晋海彬、李星
92	ZL201310039923.3	一种前纵梁的设计方法	广州汽车集团股份有限公司	王玉超、黄向东、岳鹏、陈琪
93	ZL201320113215.5	一种用于保护产品的壳体	深圳市浪尖设计有限公司	陈汉良
94	ZL201320170866.8	直流电源	广东省智源工程抗震科技公司、广东省地震监测中心	郭德顺、李敢、谢剑波、张政平
95	ZL201320424003.9	一种柜式超声波微波紫外光组合反应系统	南京先欧仪器制造有限公司、深圳市厚生医疗有限公司	高文华、唐少春、朱健、朱马光、张平会、尹青堂、杨娟、赵勋
96	ZL201320880335.8	一种超声探头	深圳市一体医疗科技有限公司	吴睿
97	ZL201420444755.6	一种全新风印刷烘干机	广东芬尼克兹节能设备有限公司	向光富、高翔、刘远辉

（四）中国外观设计优秀奖（22项）

序号	专利号	专利名称	专利权人	发明人
1	ZL200730058929.0	浴缸（WHALE）	霍成基	霍成基
2	ZL200930341896.X	数控皮革切割机（RZCUT-2510）	郭华忠	郭华忠
3	ZL201030200669.8	LED路灯	东莞勤上光电股份有限公司	吴洪戈
4	ZL201030542469.0	手表（5523-01）	珠海罗西尼表业有限公司	王永宁
5	ZL201130175932.7	智能型隔水炖盅（GSD-22F）	广东天际电器股份有限公司	詹文杰

（续上表）

序号	专利号	专利名称	专利权人	发明人
6	ZL201130268437.0	泡茶机（聚宝盆自吸加水智能电磁泡茶机）	陈俊平	陈俊平
7	ZL201130365035.2	咖啡机主机（CM4681）	广东新宝电器股份有限公司	郭建刚、陈志艺
8	ZL201230059657.7	整车	比亚迪股份有限公司	廉玉波、但卡、刘长久、唐文全、上官长树、范吉晗
9	ZL201230082763.7	投射天花嵌灯	吴育林	吴育林
10	ZL201230382188.2	自助终端	广东金赋信息科技有限公司	任泳谊、薛立徽、徐升、刘丹
11	ZL201230522469.3	静息心电图机（BeneHeart R3）	深圳迈瑞生物医疗电子股份有限公司	周文辉、罗申、陆海荣
12	ZL201230622591.8	罐（8322）	广东顺祥陶瓷有限公司	林伟河
13	ZL201330010863.3	水龙头（ZS16375）	冯松展	冯松展
14	ZL201330133804.5	计时类手表（Z12059G）	飞亚达（集团）股份有限公司、深圳市飞亚达精密计时制造有限公司	孙磊、高仍东
15	ZL201330174872.6	电饭煲	美的集团股份有限公司、佛山市顺德区美的电热电器制造有限公司	陈倩妮、尹逊兰
16	ZL201330220969.6	GPS追踪器	广州视源电子科技股份有限公司	胡方龙
17	ZL201330277300.0	电压力锅	美的集团股份有限公司、广东美的生活电器制造有限公司	冯锦棠
18	ZL201330307070.8	玻璃十字对开冰箱（B1381）	海信容声（广东）冰箱有限公司	王少林、张添棋、徐贤辉
19	ZL201330417925.2	天线自动调谐器	广州海格通信集团股份有限公司	张源
20	ZL201330620408.5	加密移动硬盘	深圳市朗科科技股份有限公司	李向明、陈俊安、余珊珊
21	ZL201430138630.6	OLED电视（E980S）	深圳创维-RGB电子有限公司	高华明、盛瑜岚
22	ZL201430221301.8	四轴多旋翼飞行器	深圳市嘉兰图设计有限公司	郭胜荣、袁攀、赵耀东、陈浩

2015年度广东省查处商标侵权假冒案件情况统计表

项目		机器编号	案件总数（件）合计	案件总数（件）其中：投诉案件	其中：涉外案件 小计	其中：涉外案件 其中：投诉案件	案值（万元）	罚没金额（万元）	其中：立案查处（件，万元）小计	其中：立案查处 其中：投诉案件	其中：立案查处 处罚程度 罚款10万至100万元	其中：立案查处 处罚程度 罚款100万元以上	其中：立案查处（件，万元）利用互联网实施侵权假冒案件 案件数	其中：立案查处 利用互联网实施侵权假冒案件 案值	没收、销毁侵权商品（件）	没收、销毁侵权商标标识（件）	没收、销毁专门用于制造侵权商品和伪造注册商标标识的工具（件）	移送司法机关（件，人）案件数 合计	移送司法机关 案件数 其中：投诉案件	移送司法机关 案件数 人数	移送司法机关 其中：涉外案件 合计	移送司法机关 其中：涉外案件 其中：投诉案件	移送司法机关 其中：涉外案件 人数
甲		乙	1	2	3	4	5	6	7	8	9	10	11	12	13	14	15	16	17	18	19	20	21
合计		1	3974	2222	2021	1353	3600.25	4893.28	3546	2032	48	0	10	25.99	3039249	840312	1526	—	—	—	—	—	—
假冒商标	小计	2	790	455	458	324	858.79	1402.76	734	427	15	0	1	3.50	487071	361024	692	35	20	21	16	9	9
	未经注册商标所有人的许可，在相同商品上使用与其注册商标相同的商标的	3	440	257	270	180	527.67	778.32	422	247	7	0	0	0.00	407391	67668	38	26	14	16	11	5	6
	伪造、擅自制造他人注册商标标识或者销售伪造、擅自制造的注册商标标识的	4	106	42	58	34	68.00	190.15	101	38	0	0	1	3.50	34625	293356	654	5	5	3	4	4	2
	销售明知是假冒注册商标的商品的	5	244	156	130	110	263.12	434.29	211	142	8	0	0	0.00	45055	0	0	4	1	2	1	0	1
商标侵权	小计	6	3184	1767	1563	1029	2741.46	3490.52	2812	1605	33	0	9	22.49	2552178	479288	834	—	—	—	—	—	—
	未经注册商标所有人的许可，在相同商品上使用与其注册商标近似的商标或在类似商品上使用与其注册商标相同或近似的商标的	7	715	303	371	191	921.31	1127.70	671	283	6	0	0	0.00	1134669	163451	640	—	—	—	—	—	—
	销售侵犯注册商标专用权的商品的	8	2356	1412	1142	810	1787.22	2236.50	2036	1272	25	0	9	22.49	1358293	130034	130	—	—	—	—	—	—
	在同一种或类似商品上，将与他人注册商标相同或近似的标志作为商品名称或者商品装潢使用，误导公众的	9	55	20	13	7	25.55	56.88	47	19	0	0	0	0.00	8238	912	63	—	—	—	—	—	—
	故意为侵犯他人注册商标专用权行为提供仓储、运输、邮寄、隐匿便利条件的	10	12	6	8	3	0.99	22.81	12	7	0	0	0	0.00	6471	10205	0	—	—	—	—	—	—
	未经商标注册人同意更换其注册商标并将该更换商标的商品又投入市场的	11	1	1	1	1	0.00	0.20	1	1	0	0	0	0.00	200	0	0	—	—	—	—	—	—
	给他人注册商标专用权造成其他损害的	12	25	18	21	16	5.03	21.12	25	16	0	0	0	0.00	44246	174686	1	—	—	—	—	—	—
侵犯地理标志专用权的		13	0	0	0	0	0.00	0.00	0	0	0	0	0	0.00	0	0	0	—	—	—	—	—	—
侵犯特殊标志所有权的		14	3	3	0	0	0.00	1.50	3	3	0	0	0	0.00	0	0	0	0	0	0	0	0	0
侵犯驰名商标权益的		15	17	4	7	1	1.36	23.81	17	4	2	0	0	0.00	61	0	0	—	—	—	—	—	—

2015年查处商标一般违法案件情况统计表

单位：件、万元

项目		机器编号	案件总数（件）		其中：涉外案件		案值（万元）	罚没金额（万元）	其中：立案查处（件）				收缴和销毁商标标识（件）	销毁物品（件）
			合计	其中：投诉案件	合计	其中：投诉案件			小计	其中：投诉案件	罚款10–100万元	罚款100万元以上		
甲		乙	1	2	3	4	5	6	7	8	9	10	11	12
合计		1	234	77	7	1	645.28	213.38	207	71	0	0	362	664
注册商标使用的管理	自行改变注册商标的	2	5	0	0	0	2.00	—	5	0	—	—	—	—
	自行改变注册商标注册人名义、地址或其他注册事项的	3	1	0	0	0	0.35	—	1	0	—	—	—	—
	自行转让注册商标的	4	0	0	0	0	0.00	—	0	0	—	—	—	—
	商品粗制滥造、以次充好、欺骗消费者的	5	0	0	0	0	0.00	0.00	0	0	0	0	—	—
未注册商标使用的管理	冒充注册商标的	6	176	57	4	0	596.47	174.70	159	51	0	0	—	—
	商品粗制滥造、以次充好、欺骗消费者的	7	0	0	0	0	0.00	0.00	0	0	0	0	—	—
	违反《商标法》第六条规定的	8	4	0	0	0	0.34	0.43	1	0	0	0	—	—
	违反《商标法》第十条规定的	9	0	0	0	0	0.00	0.00	0	0	0	0	—	—
违反《商标法》第四十条第二款规定的		10	0	0	0	0	0.00	—	0	0	—	—	0	0
违反《商标法》第十三条规定的		11	0	0	0	0	0.00	—	0	0	—	—	0	0
违反《商标印制管理办法》规定的		12	45	20	3	1	43.65	37.37	39	20	0	0	362	664
违法使用地理标志的		13	0	0	0	0	0.00	0.00	0	0	0	0	0	0
违法使用地理标志产品专用标志的		14	0	0	0	0	0.00	0.00	0	0	0	0	0	0
违法使用特殊标志的		15	3	0	0	0	2.47	0.88	2	0	0	0	0	0

2015年查处侵犯港澳台和外国商标注册人权益案件情况统计表

（有效期至2016年3月）

国别（地区）	机器编码	案件总数（件）		案值（万元）	罚款金额（万元）	其中：立案查处（件，万元）										没收、销毁侵权商品（件）	没收、销毁侵权商标标识（件）	没收、销毁专门用于制造侵权商品和伪造注册商标标识的工具（件）	移送案件（件，人）		
		合计	其中：投诉案件			小计	其中：投诉案件	处罚程度		假冒商标案件			商标侵权案件						案件数	其中：投诉案件	人数
								罚款10–100万元	罚款100万元以上	案件数	其中：投诉案件	案值	案件数	其中：投诉案件	案值						
甲	乙	1	2	3	4	5	6	7	8	9	10	11	12	13	14	15	16	17	18	19	20
合计	1	2021	1353	1941.29	3098.00	1988	1317	28	0	442	311	389.62	1546	1006	1428.25	2151091	574871	210	22	14	13
美国	2	683	444	690.64	1023.85	668	423	6	0	126	75	128.04	542	348	513.07	1321376	79360	17	13	9	7
日本	3	282	210	271.17	414.84	276	204	10	0	42	32	35.24	234	172	235.18	301909	190040	1	2	1	0
德国	4	128	78	132.40	219.81	127	78	2	0	45	28	51.63	82	50	76.48	57706	61807	7	0	0	0
英国	5	92	47	66.61	128.66	91	47	0	0	18	10	17.46	73	37	48.33	51891	37810	7	0	0	0
法国	6	295	195	234.97	489.82	293	193	5	0	87	71	75.78	206	122	147.44	147285	93564	3	0	0	0
俄罗斯	7	1	0	1.22	2.00	1	0	0	0	0	0	0.00	1	0	1.22	16	0	0	0	0	0
瑞士	8	118	100	95.63	191.43	118	100	2	0	32	28	9.60	86	72	73.00	94883	17397	0	2	2	2
韩国	9	58	41	28.41	71.81	56	41	0	0	8	3	1.62	48	38	26.40	45353	3590	8	1	0	1
意大利	10	107	58	107.90	138.61	106	58	1	0	23	17	12.25	83	41	95.65	27911	21286	1	2	0	1
新加坡	11	33	28	8.58	15.12	33	28	0	0	7	7	2.28	26	21	4.95	2907	0	0	0	0	0
维尔京	12	3	1	2.82	2.60	3	1	0	0	1	0	1.23	2	1	1.59	988	0	0	0	0	0
澳大利亚	13	3	0	5.84	7.18	3	0	0	0	1	0	0.50	2	0	5.34	452	19	0	0	0	0
瑞典	14	11	3	21.96	23.24	10	2	0	0	0	0	0.00	10	2	1.04	180	0	0	0	0	0
加拿大	15	4	2	3.47	6.20	4	2	0	0	1	0	2.00	3	2	1.47	62	0	0	0	0	0
芬兰	16	13	2	16.39	23.55	13	2	0	0	0	0	0.00	13	2	16.17	51838	27388	0	0	0	0
泰国	17	5	5	0.18	0.90	5	5	0	0	0	0	0.00	5	5	0.18	167	156	0	1	1	1
比、荷、卢	18	64	45	78.42	176.54	63	44	2	0	16	15	28.16	47	29	49.83	16480	34316	116	0	0	0
丹麦	19	21	17	17.87	22.77	21	17	0	0	7	4	0.70	14	13	15.97	12226	0	50	0	0	0
西班牙	20	8	5	2.46	7.10	8	5	0	0	4	3	1.11	4	2	1.35	1727	0	0	0	0	0
马来西亚	21	4	3	2.49	7.01	4	3	0	0	0	0	0.00	4	3	2.49	512	0	0	0	0	0
香港	22	48	41	92.98	54.73	48	40	0	0	12	11	3.74	36	29	70.50	4550	6174	0	0	0	0
澳门	23	0	0	0.00	0.00	0	0	0	0	0	0	0.00	0	0	0.00	0	0	0	0	0	0
台湾	24	9	8	28.19	40.18	9	8	0	0	0	0	0.00	9	8	28.19	2608	0	0	0	0	0
哈萨克斯坦	25	0	0	0.00	0.00	0	0	0	0	0	0	0.00	0	0	0.00	0	0	0	0	0	0
冰岛	26	0	0	0.00	0.00	0	0	0	0	0	0	0.00	0	0	0.00	0	0	0	0	0	0
越南	27	0	0	0.00	0.00	0	0	0	0	0	0	0.00	0	0	0.00	0	0	0	0	0	0
蒙古	28	0	0	0.00	0.00	0	0	0	0	0	0	0.00	0	0	0.00	0	0	0	0	0	0
罗马尼亚	29	0	0	0.00	0.00	0	0	0	0	0	0	0.00	0	0	0.00	0	0	0	0	0	0
新西兰	30	0	0	0.00	0.00	0	0	0	0	0	0	0.00	0	0	0.00	0	0	0	0	0	0
其他	31	31	20	30.69	30.05	28	16	0	0	12	7	18.28	16	9	12.41	8064	1964	0	1	1	1

2015年广东省林业植物新品种授权品种名录

序号	品种名	所属的属（种）	品种权人	品种权号
1	中科紫金1号	紫金牛属	中国科学院华南植物园	20150027
2	红艳艳	杜鹃花属	中国科学院华南植物园	20150030
3	镛粉	木莲属	中国科学院华南植物园	20150045
4	镛红	木莲属	中国科学院华南植物园	20150046
5	红屹海棠	苹果属	山东农业大学 棕榈园林股份有限公司	20150052
6	红雾海棠	苹果属	棕榈园林股份有限公司 山东农业大学	20150053
7	红菱海棠	苹果属	山东农业大学 棕榈园林股份有限公司	20150054
8	热桉1号	桉属	中国林业科学研究院热带林业研究所 漳州市速生丰产林基地管理中心 福建省龙海九龙岭国有林场	20150173
9	热桉2号	桉属	中国林业科学研究院热带林业研究所 漳州市速生丰产林基地管理中心 福建省龙海九龙岭国有林场	20150174

（供稿人：叶龙华）

2015年广东省文化市场行政执法数据统计表

省份	日常检查			案件查办				行政处罚				
	出动检查（人次）	检查经营单位（家次）	责令改正（家次）	受理举报（件）	立案调查（件）	移交案件（件）	办结案件（件）	警告（家次）	罚款（元）	责令停业整顿（家次）	吊销许可证（家）	没收违法所得（元）
演出市场	10,325	2,032	48	23	18	5	13	14	26,800.00	0	0	0
艺术品市场	1,165	317	16	2	0	0	0	0	0	0	0	0
游艺娱乐场所	48,363	15,200	212	13	43	0	36	59	54,101.00	0	3	0
歌舞娱乐场所	156,847	57,821	768	99	428	5	294	199	1,258,126.00	15	1	126,370.00
互联网上网服务营业场所	284,355	119,074	1,513	496	1,133	30	935	679	4,243,307.80	50	0	20,500.00
互联网文化经营单位	8,706	4,756	102	512	113	2	119	59	1,995,867.12	1	0	603,930.32
电影发行放映单位	20,324	4,917	85	4	0	1	0	8	0	1	0	0
广播电视、地面卫星接收设施	9,092	2,605	230	41	46	0	38	36	71,000.00	0	0	0
互联网视听节目服务单位	3,030	1,025	16	21	22	0	24	2	347,771.00	0	0	0
互联网出版机构	658	199	0	0	0	0	2	1	30,000.00	0	0	0
书报刊经营单位	120,171	49,398	812	28	90	2	74	594	62,002.00	0	0	33,251.00
音像（电子）出版物经营单位	50,843	16,246	189	50	111	17	73	144	93,786.00	0	0	5,603.00
印刷经营单位	109,428	35,322	569	29	228	5	171	167	699,110.00	9	0	22,392.00
文物	21,847	7,365	99	12	21	1	18	10	190,000.00	0	0	0
其他	33,019	10,495	452	305	152	13	110	71	1,481,808.00	17	8	12,508.00
合计	878,173	326,772	5,111	1,635	2,405	81	1,907	2,043	10,553,678.92	93	12	824,554.32

广东省农产品地理标志登记产品信息名录

序号	产品名称	所在地域	申请人	划定的产地保护范围	质量控制技术规范编号	生产规模（公顷）	养殖规模（万头、万只、万羽）	年产量（吨）
1	大埔蜜柚	梅州市大埔县	大埔县蜜柚行业协会	地域范围大埔县县城内，包括大埔县现辖下的湖寮、百侯、枫朗、大东、光德、桃源、高陂、大麻、三河、洲瑞、银江、茶阳、西河、青溪、丰溪林场等15个镇（场），在东经116° 18′—116° 56′，北纬24° 01′—24° 41′。	AGI2015-03-1765	13256		22.1019
2	恩平簕菜	江门市恩平	恩平市大人山簕菜专业合作社	恩平市全境，包括恩平市现辖下的恩城街道办事处、沙湖镇、牛江镇、君堂镇、东成镇、良西镇、圣堂镇、大田镇、大槐镇、横陂镇和那吉镇等11个镇（办事处）及米仓、沙栏、河湾、石联、石泉、禄平、那西、北合、下湖、上湖等151条村。区域地理坐标东经112° 31′—112° 46′，北纬22° 13′—22° 41′。	AGI2015-03-1766	71306		78.9
3	鹤山红茶	江门市鹤山	鹤山市农产品质量监督检验测试中心	鹤山红茶保护区域包括雅瑶镇的南靖，古劳镇的茶山、丽水，龙口镇的福迳、那白，桃源镇的中心、龙溪、蟠光，鹤城镇的坑尾、城西、五星、万和、坪山，共和镇的来苏、新连，址山镇的云新，宅梧镇的白带、荷村、泗云和双合镇的合成、先庆等21个村委会。地理坐标位于东经112° 28′ —113° 2′ ，北纬22° 28′ —22° 51′ 。	AGI2015-03-1767	333.33		500吨
4	连州水晶梨	清远	连州市水果技术推广总站	连州市区域内，主要以星子、龙坪、西江、大路边四个镇为主；地理坐标为东经112° 7′—112° 47′，北纬24° 37′—25° 12′ 。	公示结束，待发布	3333		60000
5	台山大米	江门	台山市粮食行业协会	台山市辖下的台城街道办、大江镇、水步镇、白沙镇、三合镇、四九镇、冲蒌镇、斗山镇、都斛镇、赤溪镇、端芬镇、广海镇、海宴镇、汶村镇，北陡镇、深井镇、川岛镇、海宴华侨农场，共18个镇（街、场）。地理坐标东经112° 18′—113° 03′，北纬21° 34′—22° 27′。	公示结束，待发布	35800		250000
6	连州菜心	清远	连州市农作物技术推广站	连州市的大路边、星子、龙坪、西江、九陂、连州、西岸、东陂、丰阳、保安、瑶安、三水等12个乡镇。地理坐标为东经112° 07′ 00″—112° 48′ 00″，北纬24° 37′ 00″—25° 12′ 00″。	AGI2014-01-1419	8000		17
7	炭步槟榔香芋	广州	广州市花都区炭步镇农业技术推广站	广州市花都区炭步镇所辖的炭步居委、民主村、鸭一村、鸭湖村、平岭头村、水口村、步云村、石湖村、石南村、红峰村、布溪村等27个村。地理坐标为东经113° 06′ 00″—113° 10′ 00″，北纬23° 15′ 00″—23° 22′ 00″。	AGI2014-01-1420	11333		3150
8	岭头单丛茶	潮州	饶平县浮滨镇兴农茶叶专业合作社	饶平县浮滨、东山、汤溪、新塘、三饶、韩江林场、新丰、上饶、饶洋、建饶、樟溪等11个镇（场）。地理坐标为东经116° 35′ 00″—116° 58′ 00″，北纬23° 45′ 00″—24° 14′ 00″。	AGI2013-01-1151	3333.3		5000
9	杜阮凉瓜	江门市	江门市蓬江区杜阮镇农业服务中心	江门市蓬江区杜阮镇中和、龙溪、亭园、双楼、井根、子绵、松岭、龙眠、龙安、龙榜、杜阮、杜臂、上巷、松园、瑶村、北芦、南芦、长乔、木朗、贯溪20个村委会和中心、新河、金朗3个社区居委会。地理坐标为东经112° 54′ 55″— 113° 04′ 01″，北纬22° 33′ 07″—22° 39′ 06″。	AGI2013-03-1328	533		9500
10	马冈肉鹅	江门市	开平市禽业协会	开平市所辖的15个街道办事处和乡镇，226个村民委员会。地理坐标为东经112° 13′ 00″—112° 48′ 00″，北纬21° 56′ 00″—22° 39′ 00″。	AGI2013-02-1216		447	7872
11	饶平狮头鹅	潮州	饶平县农业技术推广中心	浮滨镇、浮山镇、联饶镇、高堂镇、樟溪镇、钱东镇、黄冈镇等中片和沿海淡水资源丰富的乡镇。地理坐标为东经116° 35′ 00″—117° 11′ 00″，北纬23° 28′ 00″—24° 14′ 00″。	AGI2012-02-938		180	10800
12	高堂菜脯	潮州	饶平县高堂菜脯加工企业协会	饶平县高堂、钱东、樟溪、黄冈、联饶、所城等6个镇。地理坐标为东经116° 45′ 00″—117° 08′ 00″，北纬23° 35′ 00″—23° 48′ 00″。	AGI2011-03-00690	1000		22500

（供稿人：杨艳芹）

广东省农业植物新品种授权公告名录

序号	申请号	植物种类	品种名称	申请日	申请/品种权人	授权公告号	授权年份
1	20110667.7	水稻	恒丰A	2011/9/19	广东粤良种业有限公司	CNA005807G	2015
2	20110641.8	甘蓝型油菜	创杂油9号	2011/8/30	创世纪转基因技术有限公司	CNA006055G	2015
3	20110357.2	秋海棠属	红绒	2011/5/18	中国科学院华南植物园	CNA005595G	2015
4	20110287.7	水稻	华恢625	2011/4/15	华南农业大学	CNA005785G	2015
5	20110212.7	水稻	竹香4号	2011/3/20	梅州金竹农业科技有限公司	CNA005782G	2015
6	20110069.1	大豆	华春1号	2011/1/21	华南农业大学	CNA005499G	2015
7	20110070.8	大豆	华春3号	2011/1/21	华南农业大学	CNA005500G	2015
8	20110055.7	水稻	黄秀占	2011/1/13	广东省农业科学院水稻研究所	CNA005205G	2015
9	20110056.6	水稻	黄软占	2011/1/13	广东省农业科学院水稻研究所	CNA005206G	2015
10	20101171.5	水稻	华小红2号	2010/12/27	华南农业大学	CNA005774G	2015
11	20101172.4	水稻	华小黑4号	2010/12/27	华南农业大学	CNA005775G	2015
12	20101173.3	水稻	华标5号	2010/12/27	华南农业大学	CNA005776G	2015
13	20101155.5	大豆	华夏1号	2010/12/23	华南农业大学	CNA006036G	2015
14	20101157.3	大豆	华夏5号	2010/12/23	华南农业大学	CNA006037G	2015

（续上表）

序号	申请号	植物种类	品种名称	申请日	申请/品种权人	授权公告号	授权年份
15	20101158.2	大豆	华春2号	2010/12/23	华南农业大学	CNA006038G	2015
16	20101159.1	大豆	华春5号	2010/12/23	华南农业大学	CNA006039G	2015
17	20101160.8	大豆	华春6号	2010/12/23	华南农业大学	CNA006040G	2015
18	20100813.1	水稻	早丰优402	2010/9/28	广东省农业科学院水稻研究所	CNA005728G	2015
19	20100719.6	水稻	合美占	2010/9/2	广东省农业科学院水稻研究所	CNA005715G	2015
20	20100685.6	甘蓝型油菜	川油36	2010/8/27	创世纪转基因技术有限公司	CNA005512G	2015
21	20100557.1	水稻	植A	2010/7/16	中国科学院华南植物园	CNA005677G	2015
22	20100492.9	棉属	创鲁1号	2010/6/18	创世纪转基因技术有限公司	CNA006082G	2015
23	20100238.8	水稻	化感稻3号	2010/4/2	华南农业大学	CNA005347G	2015
24	20100169.1	水稻	Y两优5867	2010/3/12	国家杂交水稻工程技术研究中心清华深圳龙岗研究所	CNA005342G	2015
25	20100119.2	水稻	五优华占	2010/2/11	广东省农业科学院水稻研究所	CNA005661G	2015
26	20100097.8	水稻	R8086	2010/2/10	深圳市兆农农业科技有限公司	CNA005092G	2015
27	20100098.7	水稻	R7116	2010/2/10	深圳市兆农农业科技有限公司	CNA005093G	2015
28	20100064.7	水稻	粤晶1S	2010/1/22	广东省农业科学院水稻研究所	CNA005087G	2015
29	20090983.8	水稻	粤晶丝苗2号	2009/12/30	广东省农业科学院水稻研究所	CNA004890G	2015
30	20090831.2	水稻	五山丝苗	2009/12/12	广东省农业科学院水稻研究所	CNA005192G	2015
31	20090686.8	玉米	珠甜3号	2009/11/13	广东省农业科学院蔬菜研究所	CNA005392G	2015
32	20090671.5	棉属	创杂棉28	2009/11/3	创世纪转基因技术有限公司	CNA006081G	2015
33	20090583.2	棉属	冀创18F1	2009/10/16	创世纪转基因技术有限公司	CNA005178G	2015
34	20090486	水稻	华新占	2009/9/8	广东省农业科学院水稻研究所	CNA004880G	2015
35	20090487.9	水稻	黄莉占	2009/9/8	广东省农业科学院水稻研究所	CNA004881G	2015
36	20090275.5	水稻	深优2200	2009/5/7	国家杂交水稻工程技术研究中心清华深圳龙岗研究所	CNA005053G	2015
37	20090276.4	水稻	深95A	2009/5/7	国家杂交水稻工程研究中心清华深圳龙岗研究所	CNA004874G	2015
38	20090277.3	水稻	深优9798	2009/5/7	国家杂交水稻工程研究中心清华深圳龙岗研究所	CNA004875G	2015
39	20090288	水稻	RGD7S	2009/5/4	广东省农业科学院水稻研究所	CNA005055G	2015
40	20090289.9	水稻	泰丰A	2009/5/4	广东省农业科学院水稻研究所	CNA004876G	2015
41	20090254	棉属	创杂棉21号	2009/4/20	创世纪种业有限公司	CNA006079G	2015
42	20090173.8	水稻	花香占	2009/3/23	华南农业大学	CNA005637G	2015
43	20090174.7	水稻	N68S	2009/3/23	华南农业大学	CNA005638G	2015
44	20080516.9	水稻	华标1号	2008/10/12	华南农业大学	CNA005185G	2015
45	20080415.4	水稻	深两优58香油占	2008/8/6	国家杂交水稻工程技术研究中心清华深圳龙岗研究所	CNA005635G	2015
46	20080405.7	普通小麦	华糯1号	2008/7/28	华南农业大学	CNA005950G	2015
47	20080176.7	水稻	培杂软香	2008/3/28	华南农业大学	CNA004847G	2015
48	20080177.5	水稻	华恢336	2008/3/28	华南农业大学	CNA004848G	2015
49	20080127.9	玉米	百绿珍玉18	2008/3/6	深圳百绿生物科技有限公司	CNA004897G	2015
50	20070520.2	玉米	百绿珍玉216	2007/10/17	深圳市百绿生物科技有限公司	CNA004895G	2015
51	20070151.7	玉米	田蜜2号	2007/3/16	梁耿文	CNA004893G	2015
52	20100830	水稻	建优115	2010/10/14	广东源泰农业科技有限公司	CNA004611G	2014
53	20100811.3	水稻	建优795	2010/9/29	广东源泰农业科技有限公司	CNA004610G	2014
54	20100547.4	水稻	华恢8166	2010/7/12	华南农业大学	CNA004608G	2014
55	20090529.9	水稻	星A	2009/9/25	湛江神禾生物技术有限公司	CNA004594G	2014
56	20090337.1	桑属	粤椹28	2009/6/11	广东省农业科学院蚕业与农产品加工研究所	CNA004844G	2014
57	20090138.2	桑属	粤椹74	2009/3/20	广东省农业科学院蚕业与农产品加工研究所	CNA004843G	2014
58	20090055.1	水稻	特优816	2009/2/6	广东田联种业有限公司	CNA004590G	2014
59	20080814.1	水稻	黄丝占	2008/12/16	广东省农科院水稻研究所	CNA004040G	2014
60	20080517.7	水稻	华小黑2号	2008/10/12	华南农业大学	CNA004220G	2014
61	20080502.9	花生	航花1号	2008/10/8	广东省农业科学院作物研究所	CNA004112G	2014
62	20080414.6	水稻	准两优312	2008/8/6	国家杂交水稻工程技术研究中心清华深圳龙岗研究所	CNA004030G	2014
63	20070647	玉米	正甜68	2007/12/11	广东省农科集团良种苗木中心	CNA004617G	2014
64	20090561.8	水稻	弘恢248	2009/10/12	广东天弘种业有限公司	CNA003913G	2013
65	20090530.6	水稻	宏A	2009/9/25	湛江神禾生物技术有限公司	CNA003910G	2013
66	20090531.5	水稻	建A	2009/9/25	湛江神禾生物技术有限公司	CNA003911G	2013
67	20080535.5	水稻	七桂A	2008/10/17	杨清华	CNA003899G	2013
68	20080501	花生	珍珠红1号	2008/10/8	广东省农业科学院作物研究所	CNA003996G	2013
69	20080503.7	花生	粤油7号	2008/10/8	广东省农业科学院作物研究所	CNA003997G	2013
70	20080504.5	花生	粤油40	2008/10/8	广东省农业科学院作物研究所	CNA003998G	2013
71	20070808.2	水稻	228S	2007/12/29	广东华茂高科种业有限公司	CNA003510G	2012
72	20070610.1	水稻	粤恢3008	2007/11/23	广东粤良种业有限公司	CNA003716G	2012
73	20070565.2	花生	粤油13	2007/11/9	广东省农业科学院作物研究所	CNA003569G	2012
74	20070467.2	水稻	丙4114	2007/9/26	国家杂交水稻工程技术研究中心清华深圳龙岗研究所	CNA003490G	2012
75	20070469.9	水稻	R2134	2007/9/26	国家杂交水稻工程技术研究中心清华深圳龙岗研究所	CNA003491G	2012
76	20070470.2	水稻	R152	2007/9/26	国家杂交水稻工程技术研究中心清华深圳龙岗研究所	CNA003492G	2012
77	20070184.3	玉米	新美408	2007/4/6	珠海市鲜美种苗发展有限公司	CNA003528G	2012
78	20070465.6	水稻	深两优5814	2007/9/26	国家杂交水稻工程技术研究中心清华深圳龙岗研究所	CNA3538G	2011
79	20070466.4	水稻	深优9734	2007/9/26	国家杂交水稻工程技术研究中心清华深圳龙岗研究所	CNA003539G	2011

（续上表）

序号	申请号	植物种类	品种名称	申请日	申请/品种权人	授权公告号	授权年份
80	20070468	水稻	准两优2号	2007/9/26	国家杂交水稻工程技术研究中心清华深圳龙岗研究所	CNA003684G	2011
81	20070201.7	水稻	深97A	2007/4/18	国家杂交水稻工程技术研究中心清华深圳龙岗研究所	CNA003526G	2011
82	20060475.9	水稻	美香占2号	2006/9/1	广东省农业科学院水稻研究所	CNA003254G	2010
83	20060371.X	玉米	百绿珍珠49	2006/6/25	深圳市百绿生物科技有限公司	CNA002866G	2010
84	20060309.4	水稻	华小黑1号	2006/5/22	华南农业大学	CNA002991G	2010
85	20060310.8	水稻	华粳籼1号	2006/5/22	华南农业大学	CNA002992G	2010
86	20060832	水稻	丰优大占	2006/12/21	广东省农业科学院水稻研究所	CNA002552G	2009
87	20060287.X	水稻	黄华占	2006/4/25	广东省农业科学院水稻研究所	CNA002266G	2009
88	20060169.5	水稻	荣丰A	2006/3/16	广东省农业科学院水稻研究所	CNA002260G	2009
89	20060088.5	水稻	培杂35	2006/2/27	华南农业大学	CNA002681G	2009
90	20060062.1	水稻	粤泰B	2006/2/15	广东省农业科学院水稻研究所	CNA002518G	2009
91	20060036.2	水稻	广恢398	2006/1/24	广东省农业科学院水稻研究所	CNA002675G	2009
92	20060021.4	水稻	粤恢648	2006/1/12	广东省农业科学院水稻研究所	CNA002672G	2009
93	20050943.8	水稻	华优638	2005/12/30	肇庆市农业科学研究所	CNA002662G	2009
94	20050944.6	水稻	R268	2005/12/30	肇庆市农业科学研究所	CNA002663G	2009
95	20050945.4	水稻	R263	2005/12/30	肇庆市农业科学研究所	CNA002664G	2009
96	20050946.2	水稻	R239	2005/12/30	肇庆市农业科学研究所	CNA002665G	2009
97	20050820.2	水稻	金恢138	2005/12/13	广东省金稻种业有限公司	CNA002097G	2009
98	20050785	玉米	粤甜13号	2005/12/2	广东省农业科学院作物研究所	CNA002134G	2009
99	20050493.2	水稻	博优691	2005/8/26	汕头市农业科学研究所	CNA001868G	2009
100	20050920.9	水稻	N2S	2005/12/31	华南农业大学	CNA001794G	2008
101	20050921.7	水稻	N28S	2005/12/31	华南农业大学	CNA001795G	2008
102	20050922.5	水稻	华恢305	2005/12/31	华南农业大学	CNA001796G	2008
103	20050923.3	水稻	N39S	2005/12/31	华南农业大学	CNA001797G	2008
104	20050924.1	水稻	N9S	2005/12/31	华南农业大学	CNA001798G	2008
105	20050639	水稻	航恢八号	2005/11/4	华南农业大学	CNA001781G	2008
106	20050640.4	水稻	航恢88	2005/11/4	华南农业大学	CNA001782G	2008
107	20050642	水稻	胜巴丝苗	2005/11/4	华南农业大学	CNA001783G	2008
108	20050527	水稻	华粳籼74	2005/9/13	华南农业大学	CNA001779G	2008
109	20050202.6	水稻	湛A	2005/4/4	湛江海洋大学	CNA001670G	2008
110	20050203.4	水稻	万金A	2005/4/4	湛江海洋大学	CNA001671G	2008
111	20050051.1	水稻	龙A	2005/1/18	广东农作物杂种优势开发利用中心	CNA001651G	2008
112	20040725.2	水稻	汕恢316	2004/12/30	汕头市农业科学研究所	CNA001457G	2008
113	20040696.5	水稻	粤光S	2004/12/29	广东省农业科学院水稻研究所	CNA001241G	2007
114	20040697.3	水稻	天优838	2004/12/29	广东省农业科学院水稻研究所	CNA001242G	2007
115	20040554.3	水稻	龙优673	2004/12/2	广东农作物杂种优势开发利用中心	CNA001278G	2007
116	20040535.7	水稻	龙优665	2004/11/26	广东农作物杂种优势开发利用中心	CNA001277G	2007
117	20040225	水稻	华航一号	2004/5/11	华南农业大学	CNA001216G	2007
118	20040226.9	水稻	航恢七号	2004/5/11	华南农业大学	CNA001217G	2007
119	20040227.7	水稻	华航丝苗	2004/5/11	华南农业大学	CNA001218G	2007
120	20040228.5	水稻	泰丰占	2004/5/11	华南农业大学	CNA001219G	2007
121	20040186.6	水稻	广恢290	2004/4/6	广东省农业科学院水稻研究所	CNA001213G	2007
122	20040120.3	水稻	广恢368	2004/3/10	广东省农业科学院水稻研究所	CNA001210G	2007
123	20040109.2	水稻	振丰A	2004/2/19	广东省农业科学院水稻研究所	CNA001209G	2007
124	20030469	水稻	中9优288	2003/11/24	广东省农作物杂种优势利用站	CNA000940G	2007
125	20030541.7	水稻	穗丰A	2003/12/25	广东省农业科学院水稻研究所	CNA000776G	2006
126	20030542.5	水稻	天丰A	2003/12/25	广东省农业科学院水稻研究所	CNA000777G	2006
127	20030488.7	水稻	广恢308	2003/12/8	广东省农业科学院水稻研究所	CNA000898G	2006
128	20030165.9	水稻	粤泰A	2003/5/23	广东省农业科学院水稻研究所	CNA000578G	2005
129	20010226.5	水稻	粤丰A	2001/12/27	广东省农业科学院水稻研究所	CNA000584G	2005
130	20010216.8	水稻	广恢998	2001/12/24	广东省农业科学院水稻研究所	CNA000474G	2004
131	20010222.2	水稻	GD-1S	2001/12/26	广东省农业科学院水稻研究所	CNA000230G	2003
132	20010178.1	玉米	粤甜3号	2001/9/12	广东省农业科学院作物研究所	CNA000256G	2003
133	20010018.1	水稻	Y华农A	2001/3/2	华南农业大学	CNA000282G	2003

（供稿人：刘凯）

广东省已注册地理标志名录

（2014年1月1日 至2015年12月31日）

序号	商标名称	注册人	注册证号	商品	类别	注册日期	地区	
1	高州荔枝	高州市荔枝协会	13477512	荔枝	31	2014年8月14日	茂名市	
2	水东芥菜	电白县水东芥菜协会	10941061	菜	31	2015年3月14日	茂名市	证明商标
3	大埔杏花瓷	大埔县陶瓷行业协会	14578363	日用瓷器（包括盆、碗、盘、壶、餐具、缸、坛、罐），瓷器，瓷、陶瓷艺术品	21	2015年11月7日	梅州市	证明商标
4	高州龙眼	高州市荔枝协会	15023898	龙眼	31	2015年11月7日	茂名市	证明商标

（供稿人：陈小冰）

2015年广东省专利申请及授权

广东省专利申请受理、授权情况图示

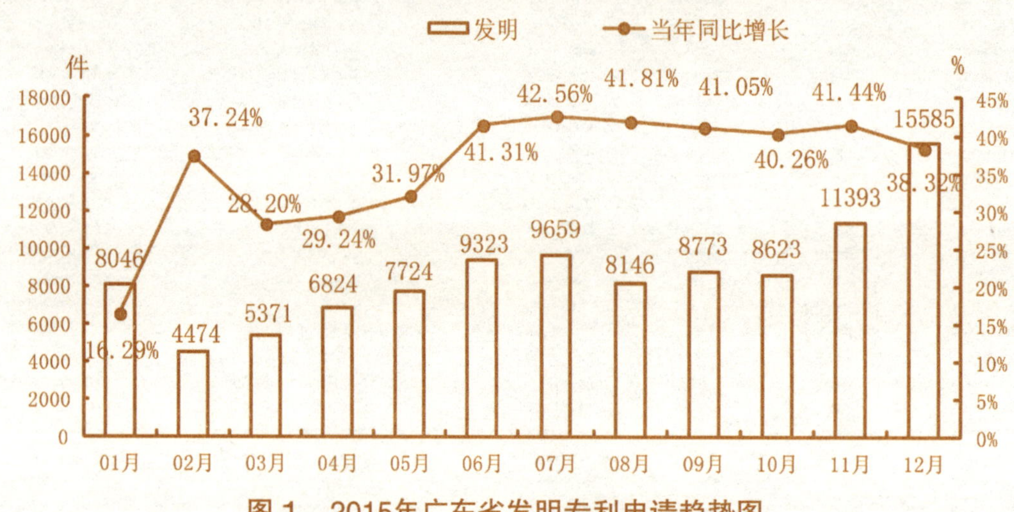

图1　2015年广东省发明专利申请趋势图

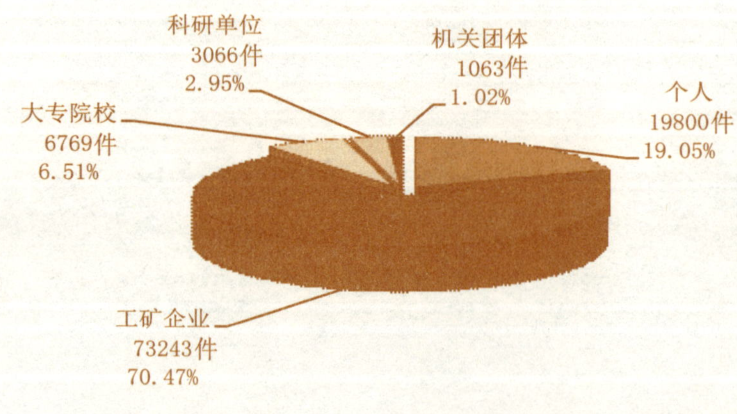

图2　2015年广东省发明专利申请人类型状况图示

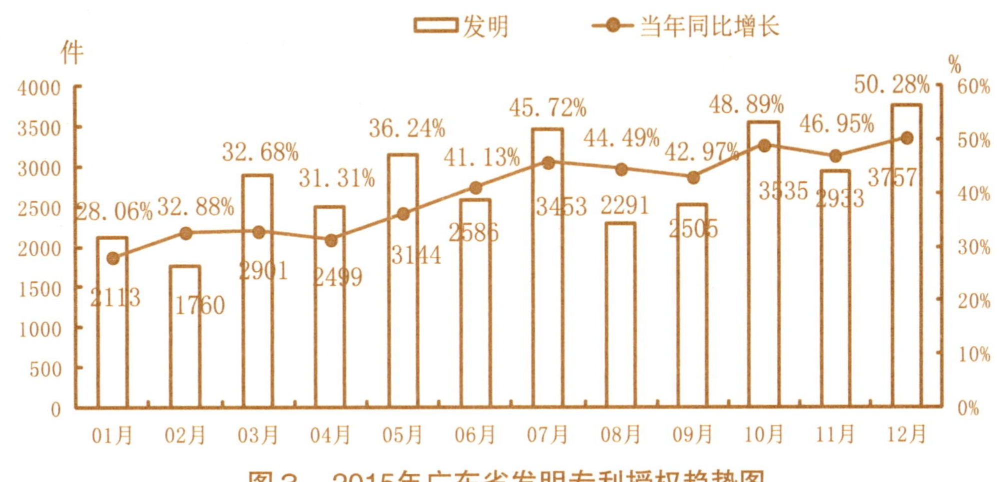

图3　2015年广东省发明专利授权趋势图

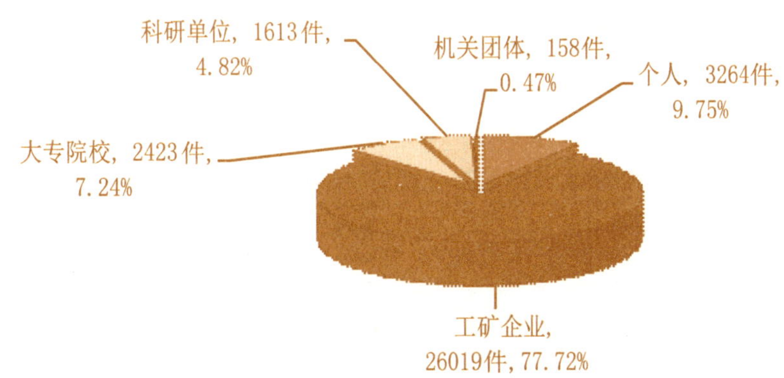

图4　2015年广东省发明授权专利权人类型状况图示

广东省专利申请及授权情况表

表1　2015年广东省各类专利申请人三种专利申请情况

单位：件

身份类型	发明	实用新型	外观设计	合计
个　人	19800	35997	74381	130178
工矿企业	73243	92384	40048	205675
大专院校	6769	3687	1723	12179
科研单位	3066	1390	67	4523
机关团体	1063	2259	62	3384
合计	103941	135717	116281	355939

表2　2015年广东省各类专利权人三种专利授权情况

单位：件

身份类型	发明	实用新型	外观设计	合计
个　人	3264	22876	63273	89413
工矿企业	26019	77663	37430	141112
大专院校	2423	2601	1515	6539
科研单位	1613	988	77	2678
机关团体	158	1126	150	1434
合计	33477	105254	102445	241176

表3 2015年广东省企业专利申请情况

	今年企业申请量（件）	去年企业申请量（件）	增长率（%）
发 明	73243	53898	35.89
实用新型	92384	63125	46.35
外观设计	40048	32647	22.67
合 计	205675	149670	37.42

表4 2015年广东省各地级以上市PCT国际专利申请情况

地级市	数量（件）	占全省比例（%）	地级市	数量（件）	占全省比例（%）
深圳市	13308	87.61	揭阳市	10	0.07
广州市	627	4.13	汕尾市	7	0.05
东莞市	336	2.21	湛江市	6	0.04
佛山市	306	2.01	茂名市	5	0.03
惠州市	174	1.15	梅州市	5	0.03
珠海市	150	0.99	阳江市	5	0.03
中山市	101	0.66	潮州市	3	0.02
汕头市	52	0.34	清远市	2	0.01
江门市	50	0.33	云浮市	1	0.01
韶关市	29	0.19	河源市	0	0.00
肇庆市	13	0.09	修正	0	0.00

表5 截至2015年12月广东省各地级以上市有效发明专利情况

（地市人口以2015年广东省统计年鉴公布的2014年底常住人口为准）

地级市	总量（件）	占全省比例（%）	万人拥有量（件）	地级市（%）	总量（件）	占全省比例（%）	万人拥有量（件）
深圳市	83903	60.41	77.84	潮州市	439	0.32	1.61
广州市	24143	17.38	18.46	揭阳市	383	0.28	0.63
东莞市	7890	5.68	9.46	韶关市	361	0.26	1.24
佛山市	7067	5.09	9.61	梅州市	331	0.24	0.77
珠海市	3667	2.64	22.72	清远市	305	0.22	0.80
中山市	2931	2.11	9.18	茂名市	282	0.20	0.47
惠州市	2500	1.80	5.29	汕尾市	135	0.10	0.45
江门市	1691	1.22	3.75	云浮市	129	0.09	0.53
汕头市	1275	0.92	2.31	河源市	122	0.09	0.40
肇庆市	649	0.47	1.61	阳江市	94	0.07	0.38
湛江市	581	0.42	0.81				

表6 2015年广东省企业专利授权前十名

单位：件

排序	单位名称	授权量				城市
		发明	实用新型	外观设计	总数量	
1	中兴通讯股份有限公司	2672	163	164	2999	深圳市
2	华为技术有限公司	2413	35	102	2550	深圳市
3	珠海格力电器股份有限公司	448	1206	389	2043	珠海市
4	佛山市顺德区美的电热电器制造有限公司	2	1039	160	1201	佛山市
5	广东美的制冷设备有限公司	53	854	257	1164	佛山市
6	广东梅雁吉祥水电股份有限公司	1	1056	0	1057	梅州市
7	腾讯科技（深圳）有限公司	598	4	446	1048	深圳市
8	比亚迪股份有限公司	509	388	89	986	深圳市
9	深圳市华星光电技术有限公司	728	0	3	731	深圳市
10	广东欧珀移动通信有限公司	377	158	54	589	东莞市

表7 2015年广东省大专院校专利授权前五名

单位：件

排序	院校名称	授权量				城市
		发明	实用新型	外观设计	总数量	
1	华南理工大学	871	544	42	1457	广州市
2	岭南师范学院	0	61	377	438	湛江市
3	广东工业大学	129	268	28	425	广州市
4	广东石油化工学院	13	53	286	352	茂名市
5	中山大学	293	29	7	329	广州市

表8　2015年广东省科研机构专利授权前五名

单位：件

排序	科研机构	授权量				城市
		发明	实用新型	外观设计	总数量	
1	深圳光启高等理工研究院	340	90	7	437	深圳市
2	中国科学院深圳先进技术研究院	199	32	2	233	深圳市
3	深圳先进技术研究院	194	21	1	216	深圳市
4	中国科学院广州能源研究所	80	31	0	111	广州市
5	中国水产科学研究院南海水产研究所	29	61	0	90	广州市

表9　2015年广东省地级以上市电子申请率排名统计表

单位：件

排名	地级市	电子申请率	排名	地级市	电子申请率
1	东莞市	97.61%	12	深圳市	93.35%
2	惠州市	97.34%	13	云浮市	92.98%
3	韶关市	96.54%	14	湛江市	92.41%
4	清远市	96.18%	15	揭阳市	90.52%
5	中山市	96.07%	16	阳江市	88.53%
6	佛山市	95.92%	17	肇庆市	88.46%
7	珠海市	95.82%	18	潮州市	86.55%
8	广州市	95.36%	19	汕尾市	85.78%
9	梅州市	94.63%	20	汕头市	85.49%
10	茂名市	94.04%	21	河源市	81.52%
11	江门市	93.59%			

（供稿人：洪伟）

专利代理机构

广东省专利代理机构名录

（2015年12月）

序号	代码	机构名称	地址	负责人	电话	传真	设立日期
1	44001	广州科粤专利商标代理有限公司	广州市先烈中路100号大院23-1栋616室	莫瑶江	020-87688146	020-87683303	（改制）2001.6
2	44100	广州新诺专利商标事务所有限公司	广东省广州市越秀区先烈中路81号之一301A、B自编01房	罗毅萍	020-83565354	020-83631275	（改制）2001.12
3	44101	深圳市中知专利商标代理有限公司	深圳市福田区下梅林二街6号颂德国际大厦办公楼805室	孙　皓	0755-83699465	0755-83699700	（改制）2001.12
4	44102	广州粤高专利商标代理有限公司	广州市天河区体育西路中石化大厦B塔3912室	林德纬	020-38922329	020-38922322	（改制）2001.6
5	44103	汕头市高科专利事务所	汕头市金砂路86号友谊国际大厦写字楼7楼C单元	丁楚浩	0754-8981161	0754-88608236	（改制）2001.6
6	44104	广州知友专利商标代理有限公司	广州市东风东路555号粤海集团大厦26楼2604室	刘小敏	020-87685310	020-87687207	（改制）2001.6
7	44106	茂名市穗海专利事务所	茂名市油城6路5号大院207	李好琚	0668-2870299	0668-2283413	（改制）2001.8
8	44202	广州三环专利代理有限公司	广州市先烈中路80号汇华商贸大厦1508	温　旭	020-37616191	020-37616451	（改制）2002.2
9	44203	湛江市三强专利事务所	湛江市霞山人民南路30号	庞爱英	0759-2231844	0759-2218471	（改制）2001.12
10	44205	广州嘉权专利商标事务所有限公司	广州市黄埔大道西100号富力盈泰广场A栋910	喻新学	020-38061202	020-38061201	（改制）2001.9
11	44206	佛山市永裕信专利代理有限公司	佛山市汾江中路217号佛山市工商大厦第六层604室	朱永忠	0757-82281605	0757-82238752	（改制）2001.2
12	44209	深圳市睿智专利事务所	深圳市南山区科技园科苑路6号科技大厦501A	郭文姬	0755-26614184	0755-26636489	1993.5
13	44210	广州华创源专利事务所有限公司	广东省广州市番禺区市桥盛泰路盛兴大街31号厂商会大厦十层103室	钟武平	020-28655962	020-28655963	（改制）2001.6
14	44211	中山市科创专利代理有限公司	中山市东区岐关西路55号朗晴假日园7幢二层1号	尹文涛	0760-88326997	0760-88330074	（改制）2001.4
15	44214	广州红荔专利代理有限公司	广州市东山区竹丝岗二马路37号617室	李彦孚	020-87695086	020-87626409	（改制）2001.6
16	44215	东莞市华南专利商标事务所有限公司	东莞市南城区胜和路华凯大厦601	张　明	0769-22800788	0769-89032550	（改制）2002.3
17	44216	广东世纪专利事务所	广州市天河区黄埔大道201号金泽大厦2109房	刘　卉	020-87502863	020-87567115	1997.9
18	44217	深圳市顺天达专利商标代理有限公司	深圳市福田区深南大道7008号阳光高尔夫大厦八楼	蔡晓红	0755-82872707	0755-82873034	1999.1
19	44218	深圳市千纳专利代理有限公司	深圳市福田区深南中路新城大厦西座601-605	胡　坚	0755-25987001	0755-25986996	2000.8
20	44219	汕头新星专利事务所	汕头市天山路绿园大厦17层C单元	林希南	0754-88167379	0754-86328655	2000.3
21	44220	广州市一新专利商标事务所有限公司	广州市天河区天河北路892号7楼自编705单元	王德祥	020-38289945	020-38288563	2001.3
22	44221	广东国欣律师事务所	深圳市红岭中路1010号国际信托大厦一、六楼	廖耀雄	0755-82117575	0755-25564216	2002.7
23	44222	江门创颖专利事务所（普通合伙）	江门市蓬江区港口一路13号-2之10F	刘晓雪	0750-3826226	0750-3826116	2002.1
24	44223	深圳新创友知识产权代理有限公司	广东省深圳市福田区南园街道上步南路东南园路北佳兆业中心A2314	江耀纯	0755-83671888	0755-83671968	2002.11
25	44224	广州华进联合专利商标代理有限公司	广州市天河区花城大道85号3901房	胡　杰	020-87323188	020-87320273	2002.9
26	44225	佛山市南海智维专利代理有限公司	佛山市南海区桂城街道深海路17号瀚天科技城A区8号楼十四楼I116室	梁国杰	0757-86224095	0757-81211785	2002.11
27	44226	韶关市雷门专利事务所	韶关市新华北路科技中心大楼3楼	周胜明	0751-8611923	0751-8611923	2002.9
28	44227	广州三辰专利事务所（普通合伙）	广州市越秀区中山三路11号越秀区工商联大厦十一楼1102室	范钦正	020-83874231	020-83874231	2002.11
29	44228	广州市南锋专利事务所有限公司	广州市先烈中路100号高技术中心实验楼二楼	刘　媖	020-87688686	020-87682576	2002.1
30	44229	广州市深研专利事务所	广州市先烈中路100号黄花岗科贸街C栋305室	陈雅平	020-87685380	020-87688087	2002.12
31	44230	汕头市潮睿专利事务有限公司	广东省汕头市大华路8号1号楼楼下	林天普	0754-88985533	0754-88280803	2003.11
32	44231	东莞市中正知识产权事务所	东莞市东城大道23号骏达商业中心901室	瞿友胜	0769-22366800	0769-22366878	2003.2
33	44232	深圳市隆天联鼎知识产权代理有限公司	广东省深圳市福田区南园路70号上田综合楼4楼A单元	刘　耿	0755-83752268	0755-82077567	2003.6
34	44233	深圳市毅颖专利商标事务所	深圳市福田区八卦四路先科机电大厦534室	张艺影	0755-83626954	0755-25841694	2003.3
35	44235	珠海市威派特专利事务所	珠海市香洲区凤凰路2088号珠都国际广场B座801室	张　润	0756-2237259	0756-2237258	2003.5
36	44236	广州弘邦专利商标事务所有限公司	广州市天河区黄埔大道西路638号富力科讯大厦902室	张钇斌	020-37883640	020-37884462	2003.5
37	44237	深圳中一专利商标事务所	深圳市福田区深南中路1014号深圳报春大厦四楼西面	张全文	0755-82094718	0755-82100908	2003.5
38	44238	深圳汇智容达专利商标事务所（普通合伙）	深圳市福田区深南中路求是大厦东座2709、2710、2711	潘中毅	0755-23968600	0755-82290360	2003.7
39	44239	广州中瀚专利商标事务所	广州市越秀区先烈中路100号大院23-1栋203室	黄　洋	020-87688195	020-37656478	2003.7
40	44240	深圳市百瑞专利商标事务所（普通合伙）	深圳市福田区竹子林益华综合楼A栋205	金　辉	0755-83581881	0755-83860058	2003.7
41	44241	深圳市智科友专利商标事务所	深圳市罗湖区太宁路85号罗湖科技大厦615室	曲家彬	0755-25599215	0755-25572914	2003.8
42	44242	深圳市精英专利事务所	深圳市福田区深南中路6009号绿景广场B栋二十层B	刘贻盛	0755-82073938	0755-82073295	2003.9

（续上表）

序号	代码	机构名称	地址	负责人	电话	传真	设立日期
43	44244	广州市天河庐阳专利事务所	广州市天河东路242号802之一室	胡济元	020-85260125	020-87531786	2003.10
44	44245	广州市华学知识产权代理有限公司	广州市天河区五山路381号华南理工大学物资大楼首层	李卫东	020-22237100	020-38744550	2004.1
45	44246	深圳市兴力桥知识产权事务所	深圳市人民南路国商大厦东座401室	董洪波	0755-82175903	0755-82175766	2004.3
46	44247	深圳市康弘知识产权代理有限公司	深圳市福田区彩田路5015号中银花园办公楼A栋6C1	胡朝阳	0755-83509309	0755-83509045	2004.3
47	44248	深圳市科吉华烽知识产权事务所（普通合伙）	深圳市南山区深南西路深南花园裙楼A区402	胡吉科	0755-83900889	0755-83089268	2004.3
48	44249	东莞市创益专利事务所	东莞市体育路二号鸿禧中心5楼B15	李卫平	0769-22806686	0769-22806676	2004.9
49	44250	佛山市科顺专利事务所	佛山市顺德区大良国际商业城A区四座三楼108	梁红缨	0757-22619500	0757-22619501	2004.10
50	44251	东莞市神州众达专利商标事务所（普通合伙）	东莞市莞城东城西路138号泰丰大厦701室	王　敏	0769-22337256	0769-22386465	2004.12
51	44252	揭阳市博佳专利代理事务所	揭阳市东山区8号街东侧沿江路北侧立康花园E幢102号	黄少松	0663-8125608	0663-8125608	2005.01
52	44253	广州致信伟盛知识产权代理有限公司	广州市东风东路767号东宝大厦1501-1502	郭晓桂	020-38210518	020-38210535	2005.2
53	44254	广州中浚雄杰知识产权代理有限责任公司	广州市花都区新华街天贵路88号A座112房	周永强	020-36998272	020-36987762	2005.6
54	44255	中山市汉通知识产权代理事务所（普通合伙）	广东省中山市石岐区岐头新村龙凤街8号A幢三层305-308	田子荣	0760-88803655	0760-88801595	2005.5
55	44256	深圳市凯达知识产权事务所	深圳市南山区科技南十二路011号方大大厦609室	刘大弯	0755-83065409	0755-83922352	2005.7
56	44257	深圳市汇力通专利商标代理有限公司	深圳市福田区振中路6号雍怡阁大厦（玮鹏花园4栋）13A	王锁林	0755-83989263	0755-83288438	2005.7
57	44258	深圳市港湾知识产权代理有限公司	深圳市南山区南头街道南山大道3838号深圳设计产业园金栋219-223	微　嘉	0755—25935856	0755-25935816	2005.7
58	44259	广州凯东知识产权代理有限公司	广州市越秀区东风东路750号十六楼1601-1606房	姚迎新	020-87663569	020-87656030	2005.8
59	44260	深圳市兴科达知识产权代理有限公司	深圳市南山区科技园高新南一道008号创维大厦A座西602室022信箱	王　翀	0755-86116996	0755-83925316	2005.8
60	44261	广州广信知识产权代理有限公司	广东省广州市越秀区先烈中路102号华盛大厦南塔1202、1203房	张文雄	020-87682813	020-87680381	2005.8
61	44262	珠海智专专利商标代理有限公司	珠海市南屏坪岚路南屏企业大厦第六层	段淑华	0756-8813895	0756-8813896	2005.9
62	44263	广东星辰律师事务所	深圳市深南大道田面村城市大厦二十四层	郭星亚	0755-82813366	0755-82816855	2005.11
63	44264	佛山市粤顺知识产权代理事务所	佛山市顺德区大良国际商业城A区四座三楼411号	唐强熙	0757-22616777	0757-22615389	2006.1
64	44265	深圳市德力知识产权代理事务所	深圳市福田区上步中路深勘大厦15E	林才桂	13922803955	0755-82092120	2006.3
65	44266	广东国晖律师事务所	深圳市福田区莲花支路1001号公交大厦主楼三层	孙智峰	0755-83033000	0755-83033022	2006.3
66	44267	深圳冠华专利事务所（普通合伙）	深圳市福田区滨河大道与一田路交界东南皇都广场1号楼3304	诸兰芬	0755-83037378	0755-83037018	2006.5
67	44268	深圳市君胜知识产权代理事务所	深圳市南山区麒麟路1号南山科技创业服务中心308，309	王永文	0755-26406581	0755-26406587	2006.5
68	44269	深圳市维邦知识产权事务所	深圳市南山区科苑路6号科技园工业大厦东706室	黄　莉	0755-83635730	0755-83655056	2006.6
69	44270	深圳市启明专利代理事务所（普通合伙）	深圳市福田区深南中路北方大厦1119号	张信宽	0755-83279101	0755-83278318	2006.9
70	44271	深圳市惠邦知识产权代理事务所	深圳市南山区科发路8号金融服务技术创新基地1栋5C01	满　群	0755-26506289	0755-26584255-802	2006.9
71	44272	东莞市冠诚知识产权代理有限公司	东莞市东城区御景大厦2001号	杨正坤	0769-22505815	0769-22505895	2006.11.2
72	44273	深圳市嘉宏博知识产权代理事务所	深圳市福田区南园街道南园路68号上步大厦十二楼C单元	杨　敏	13510470976	0755-83256786	2007.1.11
73	44274	深圳市中联专利代理有限公司	深圳市罗湖区东门南路办公楼1栋（食品大厦）605房	李　俊	0755-82228908	0755-82250395	2007.2.6
74	44275	深圳市博锐专利事务所	深圳市福田区梅林街道福田国际电子商务产业园科技楼1002	张　明	0755-82078127	0755-82078121	2007.3.28
75	44276	深圳市远航专利商标事务所（普通合伙）	深圳市福田区福田路深圳国际文化大厦1019	田志远	0755-82897199	0755-83981901	2007.7.13
76	44277	广东中亿律师事务所	中山市孙文东路639号	罗春宝	0760-88223838	0760-88223188	2007.7.13
77	44279	深圳市万商天勤知识产权事务所（普通合伙）	深圳市福田区深南大道4013号兴业银行大厦2107—C	王志明	0755-83024062	0755-83026990	2007.12
78	44280	深圳市威世博知识产权代理事务所（普通合伙）	深圳市南山区高新区南区粤兴三道8号中国地质大学产学研基地中地大楼A806	何青瓦	0755-82839168	0755-25335968	2008.4.18
79	44281	深圳鼎合诚知识产权代理有限公司	深圳市福田区金田路与福华路交汇处现代商务大厦2201	彭家恩	0755-33335533	0755-33335558	2008.6.
80	44282	珠海市英华知识产权代理事务所（普通合伙）	广东省珠海市吉大九洲大道东1023号怡海楼1102室	王　军	0756-3370193	0756-3370903	2008.6.
81	44283	佛山市中迪知识产权代理事务所（普通合伙）	广东省佛山市顺德区大良连新路22街1号地下B室	薛家驹	0757-22276980	0757-22276980	2008.7
82	44284	东莞市科安知识产权代理事务所	广东省东莞市城区八达路124号九楼A3单位	周后俊	0769-89810916	0769-89810916	2008.8
83	44285	深圳市深佳知识产权代理事务所（普通合伙）	深圳市罗湖区人民南路国贸大厦4013-4018室	李文红	0755-89530474	0755-82211322	2008.9
84	44286	中山市铭洋专利商标事务所（普通合伙）	中山市火炬开发区孙文东路濠头科益大厦四楼A区	邹常友	0760-88283758	0760-88387438	2009.1
85	44287	深圳市世纪恒程知识产权代理事务所	深圳市南山区南山大道3838号设计产业园金栋二层210—212（原南头城工业村11栋）	胡海国	0755-86218128	0755-26470166	2009.2
86	44288	广州市越秀区哲力专利商标事务所（普通合伙）	广州市越秀区东风中路300号之一东侧602房	李　悦	020-83646322	020-83646388	2009.6
87	44289	深圳市中原力和专利商标事务所（普通合伙）	深圳市南山区科技园科技路9号桑达科技工业大厦223单元	罗小辉	0755-82266719	0755-82266719	2009.12
88	44290	深圳市钧含知识产权代理有限公司	深圳市福田区新闻路1号中电信息大厦西座610室	符立新	0755-82947277	0755-82948234	2009.12
89	44291	广东秉德律师事务所	珠海市吉大路63号新怡发商贸大厦一、七楼	闵晓军	0756-3222483	0756-3222732	2009.12
90	44293	佛山市名诚专利商标事务所（普通合伙）	佛山市顺德区大良街道办事处金榜居委会凤山西路21号四楼之二	卢志文	0757-22385005	0757-22385009	2010.7.26
91	44294	广州天河互易知识产权代理事务所（普通合伙）	广州市天河区体育西路107号B座三楼A室	鲍子玉	020-22081000	020-22087610	2011.4.19
92	44295	广州市越秀区海心联合专利代理事务所（普通合伙）	广东省广州市先烈中路80号汇华商贸大厦2713室	黄　为	020-83516393	020-83516553	2011.4.19
93	44296	深圳市国科知识产权代理事务所（普通合伙）	深圳市福田区深南中路3007号国际科技大厦2505	陈永辉	0755-83789455	0755-83789448	2011.5.6
94	44297	深圳市金笔知识产权代理事务所（特殊普通合伙）	深圳市罗湖区笋岗东路2121号华凯大厦1405	胡清方	0755-25936787	0755-25936787-808	2011.5.13
95	44298	广东广和律师事务所	深圳市福田区福虹路世贸广场A座二十层	童　新	0755-89802529	0755-83679694	2011.6.3
96	44299	广州天河恒华智信专利代理事务所（普通合伙）	广州市天河北路689号1307自编02号	姜宗华	020-38351581	020-38351585	2011.6.22
97	44300	深圳翼盛智成知识产权事务所（普通合伙）	深圳市福田区深南大道南泰然九路西喜年中心A座1709.1710.1711	黄　威	0755-82879626	0755-86621781	2011.6.22
98	44301	汕头市南粤专利商标事务所（特殊普通合伙）	汕头市碧霞庄北区1幢汇泉大厦601之7	林逸平	0754-86731088	0754-86731089	2011.6.22
99	44302	广州圣理华知识产权代理有限公司	广东省广州市天河区五山路科华街251号之22-24栋自编7012、7016房	顿海舟	020-29026305	020-29026305-818	2011.6.22

（续上表）

序号	代码	机构名称	地 址	负责人	电 话	传 真	设立日期
100	44303	深圳市盈方知识产权事务所（普通合伙）	深圳市福田区福虹路9号世贸广场C座705室	朱晓江	0755-82979900	0755-82976600	2011.8.3
101	44304	深圳市铭粤知识产权代理有限公司	广东省深圳市南山区登良路21号南油第二工业区206栋六层611室（恒裕中心B座）	孙伟峰	0755-86599991	0755-86599995	2011.8.3
102	44305	广东卓建律师事务所	深圳市福田区深南中路1099号平安银行大厦三层全层	张 斌	0755-33029968	0755-33002996	2011.8.16
103	44306	深圳市携众至远知识产权代理事务所（普通合伙）	深圳市龙岗区中海康城花园（二期）26栋2单元19B	成义生	0755-86508030	0755-86508265	2011.9.19
104	44307	佛山东平知识产权事务所（普通合伙）	广东省佛山市禅城区岭南大道北123号慧港国际一座1508室	詹仲国	0757-83394427	0757-83394376	2011.9.27
105	44308	东莞市展智知识产权代理事务所（普通合伙）	广东省东莞松山湖高新技术产业开发区松科苑9号楼215室	冯卫东	0769-33211185	0769-27226785	2011.9.27
106	44309	深圳市合道英联专利事务所（普通合伙）	广东省深圳市福田区石厦北二街新天世纪商务中心1栋B座1207	廉红果	0755-88300116	0755-88300116	2011.10.26
107	44310	广东赋权律师事务所	广东省深圳市龙岗区坂田街道雪岗路2018号天安云谷产业园一期3栋D座二十层2006-A单元	张 松	0755-22214568	0755-82682466	2012.2.20
108	44311	深圳市鼎言知识产权代理有限公司	深圳市龙华新区龙观路与东环二路交汇处 荣群大厦十楼	郑海威	0755-29270865	0755-23156686	2012.2.20
109	44312	深圳市恒申知识产权事务所（普通合伙）	广东省深圳市福田区南园路68号上步大厦十楼H单元	陈 健	0755-83468251	0755-82910622	2012.7.3
110	44313	深圳力拓知识产权代理有限公司	深圳市南山区深南大道10128#南山软件园东塔1701	龚 健	0755-82209322	0755-82228011	2012.7.24
111	44314	深圳市瑞方达知识产权事务所（普通合伙）	深圳南山区科兴路11号深南花园裙楼B区二层208室	张秋红	0755-61372510	0755-61372511	2012.7.24
112	44315	深圳市君盈知识产权事务所（普通合伙）	深圳市福田区深南大道与泰然九路交界东南本元大厦9A-1	叶志频	0755-82074410	0755-82075899	2012.7.24
113	44316	深圳市科进知识产权代理事务所（普通合伙）	深圳市南山区工业六路创业壹号大楼D栋210B	郝明琴	13590119889	0755-86350180	2012.9.13
114	44317	广东安国律师事务所	广东省广州市越秀区环市东路339号广东国际大酒店A附楼十七楼A座	谢乐安	020-22372906	020-22372906	2013.2.28
115	44318	广东祁增颢律师事务所	广东省广州市越秀区先烈中路100号大院60号楼210室	曾 琦	020-87687583	020-87687583	2013.3.15
116	44319	深圳市华优知识产权代理事务所（普通合伙）	深圳市南山区高新区北区北环大道9116号富华科技大厦B栋四层405室	李丽君	0755-26562251	0755-26562251	2013.4.17
117	44320	深圳市翼智博知识产权事务所（普通合伙）	广东省深圳市福田区车公庙泰然九路皇冠科技园2栋三楼3A05	聂 智	0755-33203919	0755-33203919	2013.5.2
118	44321	深圳市硕法知识产权代理事务所（普通合伙）	深圳市福田区深南中路2070号电子科技大厦C座37E	李 姝	0755-83551188-823	0755-83671591	2013.8.2
119	44322	广东德而赛律师事务所	广东省深圳市福田区上步中路南方日报大厦二楼	叶秀进	0755-23890737	0755-23996456	2013.8.9
120	44323	广东前海律师事务所	广东省深圳市南山区高新区中区科研路9号比克科技大厦2001-E	许志兵	0755-86331083	0755-86331083	2013.9.24
121	44324	深圳市神州联合知识产权代理事务所（普通合伙）	深圳市南山区高新中区麻雀岭M-2栋三楼301房	王志强	0755-66806635	0755-85290385	2013.10.30
122	44325	深圳众鼎专利商标代理事务所（普通合伙）	深圳市龙岗区龙城街道中心城清林路546号城投商务中心四层/B	黄章辉	0755-28363699	0755-29363699	2013.10.30
123	44326	广州番禺容大专利代理事务所（普通合伙）	广州市番禺区市桥街光明南路199号2号楼414、416室	刘新年	020-83646290	020-83646291	2013.10.30
124	44327	中山市捷凯专利商标代理事务所（特殊普通合伙）	广东省中山市石岐区民科西路2号民营科技园管理大厦402室	杨连华	0760-88701600	0760-88701600	2013.10.30
125	44328	深圳华奇信诺专利代理事务所（普通合伙）	深圳市南山区南头关口二路智恒战略性新兴产业园29栋三楼B5-01	曲卫涛	0755-61613095	0755-61613092	2014.1.9
126	44329	广东广信君达律师事务所	广州市天河区珠江东路30号广州银行大厦七层	王晓华	020-37181234	020-83510021	2014.1.9
127	44330	东莞市说文知识产权代理事务所（普通合伙）	广东省东莞市南城区宏伟路33号凯旋公馆18-2-603	程修华	0769-22000462	0769-22000462	2014.1.21
128	44331	深圳壹舟知识产权代理事务所（普通合伙）	深圳市南山区南山街道南海大道2251号西海岸大厦8E	吴 娟	0755-26521906	0755-26737833	2014.1.21
129	44332	广东莞信律师事务所	广东省东莞市东城中路南81号辉煌商务大厦六楼	麦金惠	0769-22339298	0769-22339298	2014.2.20
130	44333	深圳盛德大业知识产权代理事务所（普通合伙）	深圳市福田区车公庙绿景纪元大厦44层44A.44C-145室	贾振勇	0755-86644258	0755-86644203	2014.3.31
131	44334	深圳市赛恩倍吉知识产权代理有限公司	深圳市龙华新区龙观路与东环二路交汇处荣群大厦九楼	谢志为	0755-29270808	0755-29270808	2014.4.29
132	44335	深圳市舜立知识产权代理事务所（普通合伙）	深圳市罗湖区人民南路国际贸易中心大厦B1905室	李亚萍	0755-82481788	0755-82481788	2014.4.29
133	44336	深圳市诺正专利商标代理事务所（普通合伙）	深圳市龙华新区民治街道民治大道展滔科技大厦B座十三层1310室	邹蓝	0755-86021008	0755-86020965	2014.5.27
134	44337	中山市科企联知识产权代理事务所（普通合伙）	中山市西区富华道383号柏景台3幢17A房	杨立铭	0760-85750937	0760-85750937	2014.5.29
135	44338	深圳市深软鸿皓知识产权代理有限公司	深圳市南山区高新区深圳市软件产业基地第5栋A座六层02室	朱 民	0755-83468306	0755-83468306	2014.6.12
136	44339	佛山市广盈专利商标事务所（普通合伙）	广东省佛山市顺德区大良新宁路76号503	杨乐兵	0757-22271269	0757-22271269	2014.7.4
137	44340	深圳瑞天谨诚知识产权代理有限公司	广东省深圳市南山区高新中四道30号龙泰利大厦六楼626号	张 佳	0755-26582209	0755-26582209	2014.7.9
138	44341	深圳市爱迪森知识产权代理事务所（普通合伙）	深圳市南山区南海大道4050号上汽大厦703-704室	何 婷	0755-88274088	0755-88273968	2014.7.9
139	44342	广东知恒律师事务所	广东省深圳市福田区深南中路2010号东风大厦二十一楼2101-2113全层	任 杰	0755-88890066	0755-88890066	2014.7.9
140	44343	深圳市明日今典知识产权代理事务所（普通合伙）	深圳市南山区粤海街道后海大道以东天利中央商务广场（二期）C座2016-04室	罗志强	0755-86262200	0755-86262200	2014.8.6
141	44344	深圳市龙成联合专利代理有限公司	深圳市南山区南海大道海王大厦住宅楼27E	周 雷	0755-86210250	0755-86210250	2014.9.23
142	44345	中山市兴华粤专利代理有限公司	广东省中山市火炬开发区大庙街225号东镇广场11卡之一	吴剑锋	0760-88616610	0760-88616620	2014.11.21
143	44346	中山市高端专利代理事务所（特殊普通合伙）	广东省中山市火炬开发区康乐大道33号创业大厦236号房	钟作亮	0760-28139297	0760-28139296	2014.12.8
144	44347	深圳市沃德知识产权代理事务所（普通合伙）	深圳市福田区泰然六路泰然苍松大厦北座1901-36	高 杰	0755-88640583	0755-86117790	2014.12.30
145	44348	广州市天河区倪律专利代理事务所（普通合伙）	广东省广州市天河区思成路23号607	倪小敏	020-85167676	020-38966120	2015.1.12
146	44349	惠州市超越知识产权代理事务所（普通合伙）	广东省惠州市江北云山西路4号德威大厦十二层06号	鲁慧波	0752-2555851	0752-2300771	2015.1.29
147	44350	深圳青年人专利商标代理有限公司	广东省深圳市罗湖区深南东路5045号深业中心大厦2502-2503	傅俏梅	0755-33963929	0755-33963929	2015.3.30
148	44351	深圳市智圈知识产权代理事务所（普通合伙）	广东省深圳市南山区粤海街道科苑路15号科兴科学园B1栋701-60	韩绍君	0755-23180314	0755-23180314	2015.4.29
149	44352	深圳市德锦知识产权代理有限公司	深圳市南山区粤海街道高新南环路29号留学生创业大厦602	丁敬伟	0755-88280972	0755-88281230	2015.4.29
150	44353	广东荆紫律师事务所	佛山市禅城区绿景二路11号保利天玺二座1栋812-819室	汪新明	0757-82362828	0757-82363499	2015.4.29
151	44354	深圳市博太联众专利代理事务所（特殊普通合伙）	深圳市南山区南海大道保利大厦1501室	任转英	0755-86672419-8004	0755-86670753-8060	2015.7.27
152	44355	深圳市科冠知识产权代理有限公司	广东省深圳市南山区南海大道东华园5栋303	李艳丽	0755-86664020	0755-25603885	2015.9.19

（续上表）

序号	代码	机构名称	地　址	负责人	电　话	传　真	设立日期
153	44356	深圳市壹品专利代理事务所（普通合伙）	深圳市南山区南头街道南山大道3838号设计产业园土栋一层112-113	邓 荣	0755-86645236	0755-86645236	2015.11.2
154	44357	深圳市览众联合专利商标事务所（普通合伙）	深圳市福田区华富街道田面新村20栋201	赵文曲	0755-33162918	0755-33162918	2015.11.2
155	44358	广东凯行律师事务所	广东省中山市石岐区博爱三路9号4幢第四层403-412卡	朱志强	0760-88869997	0760-88869995	2015.11.9
156	44359	佛山市顺德区荣粤专利代理事务所（普通合伙）	广东省佛山市顺德区容桂街道办事处卫红居委会泰和路1号	王玉梅	0757-28815636	0757-28815632	2015.11.9
157	44360	深圳市道臻知识产权代理有限公司	深圳市福田区莲花街道红荔西路7058号市政大厦304室	陈琳	0755-83223345	0755-83223345	2015.11.30
158	44361	深圳市智享知识产权代理有限公司	深圳市龙华新区民治街道创业花园177栋淘景大厦1308	王琴	0755-32903098	0755-85293613	2015.11.30

广东省专利代理机构分支机构名录

（含广东省代理机构在省外设立分支机构）

（2015年12月）

序号	代码	机构名称	分支机构	负责人	地　址	电　话	传　真	设立时间
1	44001	广州科粤专利商标代理有限公司	云浮办事处	黄培智	云浮市育华区市科技馆一楼	0766-8806636	0766-8921262	2003.7
2			佛山办事处	莫瑶江	佛山市南海桂城南桂东路38号房地产发展大厦主楼六楼24号	0757-86323236	0757-86237605	2012.1.19
3			贺州办事处	张新球	广西贺州市八步区建设中路25号八步区科学技术局大楼402房	0774-5282257	0774--5282257	2012.4.13
4			东莞分公司	谭一兵	东莞市莞城区东城大道金澳花园B座（方中大厦）708号	0769-22808700	0769-22808700	2014.7.30
5	44100	广州新诺专利商标事务所有限公司	江门新会办事处	黎伟虹	江门市新会区会城圭峰路科学馆内	0750-6196750	0750-6186768	2003.7
6			湛江办事处	胡　武	湛江市赤坎区海田装饰材料市场灯饰行15-18号三楼	0759-3164202	0759-3164202	2003.6
7			江门台山办事处	关静芬	台山市石花路科学馆	0750-5504184	0750-3161915	2003.7
8			江门分公司	华　辉	江门市港口一路13号之二 二十九楼H单元（中远大厦远景阁）	0750-3161915	0750-3161915	2007.3
9			佛山分公司	罗毅萍	佛山市顺德区大良新桂南路18号五楼9号单元	0757-23808575	0757-22913991	2008.2
10			阳江分公司	曹爱红	阳江市江城区东门路东安小区11号	0662-3661772	0662-3503380	2009.4
11			广州科学城办事处	罗庆西	广州市萝岗区科学城科汇发展中心（自编J-1栋）715房	020-83564153	020-83631275	2010.3.10
12			韶关分公司	许英伟	韶关市新华北路32号科技局办公楼首层101号房	0751-8762001	0751-8762001	2011.8.18
13			佛山高明分公司	李德魁	佛山市高明区荷城街道跃华路284号6座七层701室	0757-88219688	0757-88280028	2013.5.6
14	44102	广州粤高专利商标代理有限公司	惠州分公司	苏共练	惠州市江北云山西路十二号德赛大厦十八楼1806室	0752-2818976	0752-2833631	2002.4
15			阳江分公司	陈　卫	阳江市江城区安宁路富华小区A7号六楼	0662-3287575	0662-3222023	2004.12
16			东莞分公司	罗晓林	东莞市南城区鸿禧中心A座901	0769-22993790	0769-22993799	2006.7
17			中山分公司	林新中	中山市东区兴龙街27号地下	0760-88363611	0760-88363612	2007.4
18			江门分公司	禹小明	江门市港口路72号江门市科技创业中心大楼十楼1006室	0750-3861201	0750-3861201	2007.4
19			清远分公司	汤立文	清远市新城东18号区科技生活服务区二层	0763-3361715	0763-3361715	2008.2
20			汕头分公司	张月光	汕头市龙湖区长平路123号朝阳庄广海大厦801室之二	020-38922301	020-38922322	2010.9.6
21			潮州分公司	张爱武	潮州市潮州大道中物花园二幢303号	0768-3299664	0768-2268685	2011.1.19
22			湛江分公司	林伟斌	湛江市霞山区人民大道南53号国贸大厦B座3幢十四层B01房	0759-2360690	0759-2678729	2012.4.17
23			揭阳分公司	郑永泉	普宁国际商品城商贸中心南区5楼502号	0663-2666593	0663-2666583	2013.12.11
24			开发区分公司	邱奕才	广州高新技术产业开发区科学城科学大道245号总部经济区A6栋第七层705室	020-82037781	020-82037781	2013.9.6
25			天河分公司	凌衍芬	广州市天河区瘦狗岭路561号905房	020-28075830	020-28075830	2013.10.18
26			深圳分公司	邓义华	深圳市龙岗区龙城街道黄阁路天安数码新城三号楼四楼F11-12	0755-82398885	0755-82398885	2013.9.5
27	44103	汕头市高科专利事务所	汕头澄海办事处	黄河长	汕头市澄海区文冠路金冠园三幢B梯204单元	0754-88632248	0754-88608236	2003.5
28	44104	广州知友专利商标代理有限公司	顺德办事处	刘小敏	广东省佛山市顺德区北滘镇三乐路北1号	020-87684470	020-87687207	2009.11.15
29			深圳办事处	宣国华	深圳市南山区南海大道海王大厦写字楼12F2	020-87685310	020-87687207	2009.3
30	44202	广州三环专利代理有限公司	中山分公司	温　乾	中山市南头镇华辉花园环安三路二号	0760-23118002	0760-23118002	2001.11
31			东莞分公司	张艳美	东莞市南城区鸿福路108号中盛商务大厦705-708	0769-22458956	0769-22496842	2001.11
32			顺德分公司	何兆华	佛山市顺德区大良新宁路76号弘升大楼507室	0757-22269440	0757-22259770	2001.11
33			深圳分公司	熊永强	深圳市南山区科技园科苑路15号科兴科学园A栋4单元1703	0755-82734660	0755-82734662	2002.11
34			珠海分公司	温镜满	珠海市香洲区人民东路313号1栋901-902室	0756-2316632	0756-2316630	2002.11
35			汕头分公司	张泽思	汕头市高新区科技东路亨泽大厦十五楼1508	0754-88272584	0754-88980990	2002.11
36			佛山分公司	胡　枫	佛山市禅城区华宝南路13号佛山国家火炬创新创业园B2-3	0757-82500236	0757-82500236	2002.11
37			增城分公司	王会龙	增城市荔城接华丰西路6号104	020-82441689	020-82441689	2010.9
38			江门分公司	陈国平	江门市蓬江区港口路72号创业中心二期902	0750-3962186	0750-3962186	2003.7
39			北京分公司	郝传鑫	北京市海淀区北四环中路238号柏彦大厦1703	010-82334622	010-82334872	2008.4
40			温州办事处	唐　娇	温州市矮凳桥228号10幢705室	0577-88808255	0577-88809255	2009.1
41			潮州办事处	朱信贵	潮州市枫春路枫荫亭凤新大厦西侧五层3号办公楼5010单元	0768-2135555	0768-2135555	2009.4
42			惠州分公司	刘孟斌	广东省惠州市惠城区东江二路一号富力丽港中心公寓1座十四层01号	0752-2222039	0752-2222026	2012.8.24
43			厦门分公司	陈进芳	福建省厦门市思明区湖滨南路388号27C3单元	0592-5869500	0592-5166901	2013.8.21
44			柳州分公司	梁顺宜	广西壮族自治区柳州市桂中大道南端2号阳光100城市广场2号写字楼20-9室	0772-3166801	0772-3166802	2013.10.31
45			海口分公司	郭俊艳	海南省海口市蓝天路31号名门广场C栋1901-2号房	0898-68535549	0898-68535564	2014.3.7
46			苏州分公司	付　静	苏州市高新区学森路9号知识产权集聚区5号楼-9-906	0512-65360512	0512-65363055	2015.3.3

（续上表）

序号	代码	机构名称	分支机构	负责人	地 址	电 话	传 真	设立时间
47	44205	广州嘉权专利商标事务所有限公司	中山分公司	张海文	广东省中山市西区彩虹大道11号美银国际大厦2幢1101卡	0760-88809855	0760-88924555	2005.6
48			佛山分公司	谭英强	佛山市禅城区文华北路60号707房	0757-82135920	0757-82135910	2005.6
49			佛山顺德分公司	张 萍	佛山市顺德大良凤翔路创意产业园A105	0757-22213626	0757-22210236	2006.6
50			江门分公司	冯剑明	江门市港口路183号新隆基大厦301	0750-3124468	0750-3101083	2010.5
51			珠海分公司	谭志强	珠海市水湾头红塔大厦第七楼703室	0756-3330699	0756-3332444	2010.7
52			深圳分公司	唐致明	深圳市南山区高新北区朗山路7号航空电子工程研发大厦八楼803	0755-86587393	0755-86587392	2012.7.23
53	44211	中山市科创专利代理有限公司	小榄分公司	丁湘俊	中山市小榄镇民安北路东华居一期5号	0760-22269859	0760-22282024	2004
54	44214	广州红荔专利代理有限公司	珠海分公司	王贤义	珠海市香洲人民东路125号工商大厦1512房	0756-2620838	0756-2620899	2002.4
55			广州东山分公司	黄大宇	广州市越秀区德政北路401-409号801房	020-83379501	020-83636966	2004.12
56			东莞分公司	吴世民	东莞市东城区鳌峙塘连塘9号A07	0769-22302599	0769-22300598	2008.3
57			南宁分公司	李 珊	广西南宁市民族大道38-2号泰安大厦第1栋写字楼第十二层12号房	0771-5852191	0771-5880312	2013.8.6
58			深圳分公司	柴 燕	深圳市南山区南山街道桃园路北常兴路东常兴广场东座8M	0755-26398982	0755-26398982	2014.7.4
59			佛山分公司	彭姣平	广东省佛山市文庆路2号三层A9室	0757-82802656	0757-82802656	2014.9.29
60	44215	东莞市华南专利商标事务所有限公司	广州分公司	张 明	广东省广州市越秀区先烈中路83号802、803房	020-87685843	020-87685847	2009.6
61	44217	深圳市顺天达专利商标代理有限公司	武汉分公司	郭伟刚	湖北省武汉市东湖开发区珞瑜路727号星光无限4栋八层02号	027-86648182	027-86648182	2012.9.6
62			惠州分公司	柯夏荷	惠州市仲恺高新区陈江五一住宅小区A1-1、A1-2、A1-3栋613房	0755-82872707	0752-3161177	2014.6.30
63	44218	深圳市千纳专利代理有限公司	东莞分公司	易朝晖	东莞市莞城汇峰路1号汇峰中心E区701A	0769-89810333	0769-89810198	2008.11
64			梅州分公司	李开盛	广东省梅州市梅县新城办事处广梅路顺风客运站侧二楼	0753-2510300	0753-2510300	2010.4
65			醴陵分公司	夏兴友	湖南省醴陵市西山办事处碧山村委	0731-23452777	0731-23452777	2010.7
66			惠州分公司	练南星	惠州市演达大道11号港惠新天地商业广场1座二十三层05号房	0752-2885005	0752-2157309	2010.8
67			日照分公司	卜令涛	山东省日照市新市泰安路南、威海路西日照市海正置业商住楼001栋902室	0633-8781949	0633-8781949	2012.5.25
68	44219	汕头新星专利事务所	汕头澄海办事处	许映扬	汕头市澄海区文祠东路34号	0754-85732817	0754-86328655	2003.3
69	44220	广州市一新专利商标事务所有限公司	东莞分公司	王德祥	东莞市莞城区旗峰路159号东远大厦四楼407	0769-23395029	0769-23395092	2012.8.30
70			桂林分公司	滕杰锋	桂林市象山区环城南二路12号7栋601房	0773-2673785	0773-2673785	2015.5.21
71	44223	深圳新创友知识产权代理有限公司	南宁办事处	江耀纯	广西南宁市东葛路29-1号荣和中央公园1号楼2512号	0771-5670771	0755-83671968	2014.2.24
72			罗湖分公司	江耀锋	深圳市罗湖区桂园街道深南东路5002号地王大厦708室	0755-83671889	0755-83671968	2013.4.12
73	44224	广州华进联合专利商标代理有限公司	北京分公司	郑小粤	北京市海淀区学清路9号汇智大厦B座801-805室	010-82736868	010-82737016	2003.8
74			深圳分公司	邓云鹏	深圳市南山区高新区南区粤兴三道8号中国地质大学产学研基地中地大楼A803	0755-33012323	0755-33012322	2003.3
75			珠海分公司	王 昕	珠海市九洲大道东1248号九洲假日公寓1单元815房	0756-3895351	0756-3837667	2003.3
76			东莞分公司	吴 平	东莞市南城区胜和路3号胜和广场C座12楼F单元	0769-22220357	0769-22225317	2003.1
77			顺德分公司	潘雯瑛	佛山市顺德区大良新桂路明日广场一座403办公室	020-87323188	020-87320273	2011.6.22
78			惠州分公司	何 平	惠州市江北东江二路二号富力丽港中心酒店二十二层11号	0752-2169621	0752-2169621	2011.10.20
79			长沙分公司	邓云鹏	湖南省长沙市雨花区芙蓉中路二段359号佳天大厦北栋1701室	0731-85060391	0731-85060392	2013.1.17
80			苏州分公司	唐清凯	苏州工业园区星湖街328号创意产业园10-303单元	0512-82285112	0512-82285133	2013.7.22
81	44228	广州市南锋专利事务所有限公司	东莞分公司	罗晓聪	东莞市南城区鸿福路鸿福广场A座1703	0769-22824580	0769-22824580	2003.4
82			东莞办事处	李永庆	广东省东莞市南城区新城元美东路东侧东莞市商业中心A2320号	0769-23024178	0769-23024178	2011.5.9
83			肇庆办事处	梁哲文	肇庆市莲湖中路7号陶然居21卡（即湖滨派出所对面）	0758-2820823	0758-2906926	2005.6
84			湛江办事处	袁周珠	湛江市赤坎区军民路19号（荣基大厦）723房	0759-3289879	0759-3133855	2006.11
85			河源办事处	何海帆	河源市新市旺源路润宏居A栋A3-401	0762-3100361	0762-3100088	2009.2
86			潮州办事处	沈悦涛	潮州市枫春路中段潮州日报社办公楼十二层西	0768-2355511	0768-2355511	2011.12.8
87			清远办事处	罗凯梅	清远市清城区B38#洲心工业园清远铜交易中心三楼	0763-3509740	0763-3509741	2012.3.15
88			茂名办事处	何本谦	茂名市茂南区河东油城六路5号科委大院附属楼群三楼309室	0668-5115120	0668-5115120	2014.5.6
89			惠州博罗分公司	蔡蔚毅	惠州市博罗县园洲镇佛岭村	0752-6625998	0752-6625998	2014.9.26
90			深圳分公司	郑学伟	深圳市南山区南海大道西海岸大厦10F	0755-26946200	0755-26423050	2015.5.12
91	44231	东莞市中正知识产权事务所	佛山分所	成 伟	佛山市顺德区大良国际商业城B区3座103室	0757-22661119	0757-22661112	2004.7
92			中山分所	侯来旺	中山市古镇镇新兴中路88号邮电大楼七楼	0760-22323635	0760-22320995	2005.11
93			惠州分所	张汉青	惠州市惠城区演达大道2号海信金融曼哈顿广场九层913号	0752-2275834	0752-2275235	2009.6
94			贵阳分所	徐 康	贵州省贵阳市云岩区中华北路53号美佳大厦2单元十四层4号	0851—5834308	0851—5834308	2012.6.1
95	44245	广州市华学知识产权代理有限公司	中山分公司	袁 晖	中山市石岐区莲塘东路8号422房	0760-88868163	0760-88331801	2006.12
96			东莞分公司	李盛洪	东莞市莞城东纵大道地王广场写字楼七层10号	0769-22320685	0769-86220326	2007.11
97			南海分公司	梁 莹	佛山市南海区桂城海辉路2号十楼1003室	0757-86131499	020-38744550	2009.3
98			萝岗分公司	郭炜绵	广州市高新技术产业开发区科学城科学大道111号科学城信息大厦主楼第十层1001-7单元	020-62800736	020-38744550	2009.3
99			增城分公司	盛佩珍	广州市增城新塘镇荔新十二路96号14 幢117 号	020-32168663	020-38744550	2009.5
100			惠州分公司	李卫东	惠州市惠台工业园区54号小区（厂房）（308-A）号房	0752-2622020	020-38744550	2009.7
101			番禺分公司	陈燕娴	广州市番禺区市桥大北路150号华兴商贸大厦1510号	020-87113553	020-38744550	2012.3.12
102			江门分公司	付茵茵	江门市蓬江区港口路72号904	0750-3902876	0750-3902876	2013.1.6
103			东阳分公司	张金刚	浙江省东阳市吴宁东路57号科技楼2#办公楼2-205	0579-86823185	0579-86823185	2013.12.24
104			韶关分公司	谢静娜	韶关市浈江区十里亭镇五里亭良村公路2号韶关碧桂园翠林山语1街13座1403	020-38743199	020-38744550	2015.3.24
105			南宁分公司	黄 磊	广西省南宁市西乡塘区大学东路98号世贸西城广场B区A座705号	0771-2796689	0771-2796689	2015.5.21

（续上表）

序号	代码	机构名称	分支机构	负责人	地址	电话	传真	设立时间
106	44248	深圳市科吉华烽知识产权事务所	东莞分所	朱晓光	东莞市莞城区东城南路东升大厦1011室	0769-23360190	0769-23360190	2008.8
107			成都分所	陈本发	成都市青羊区大安西路56-58号11栋1单元五楼2号	028-6959590	0769-23360190	2009.2
108			广州分所	孙伟	广州市天河区华强路2号409房	020-38678810	020-38678267	2010.4
109			柳州分所	刘显扬	广西壮族自治区柳州市桂中大道南端2号阳光壹佰城市广场9栋11-12	0772-2624302	0772-2624302	2013.7.19
110	44253	广州致信伟盛知识产权代理有限公司	东莞分公司	伍嘉陵	东莞市莞城区运河东二路20号二楼B室	0769-22119785	0769-22214155	2008.2
111	44260	深圳市兴科达知识产权代理有限公司	南宁分公司	袁士林	南宁市科园大道东四路2号厂房第四层4A17号场地	0771-3214839	0771-3214839	2014.7.11
112	44268	深圳市君胜知识产权代理事务所	佛山分所	刘文求	禅城区张槎新媒体产业园4座606	0757-88034113	0757-88034113-608	2014.11.12
113	44271	深圳市惠邦知识产权代理事务所	东莞分所	满群	东莞市南城区体育路2号鸿禧中心B117单元	0755-26506289-802	0755-26506289-802	2012.10.23
114	44275	深圳市博锐专利事务所	厦门办事处	张明	福建省厦门市思明区莲前西路2号莲富大厦F15B	0592-5814556	0592-5814556	2012.6.5
115	44280	深圳市威世博知识产权代理事务所（普通合伙）	郑州分所	李庆波	郑州市管城回族区华盛街65号2单元十五层1505号	0755-61675839	0755-61675839	2014.12.5
116	44281	深圳鼎合诚知识产权代理有限公司	东莞分公司	彭家恩	东莞市松山湖高新技术产业开发区总部二路9号东莞市依时利科技办公楼-研发楼B3-03	0769-89099567	0755-33335558	2014.6.5
117			汕尾分公司	陈俊斌	汕尾市区文德路汕尾职业技术学院我A区实训中心大楼二楼213室	0755-33335533	0755-33335558	2014.7.15
118	44287	深圳市世纪恒程知识产权代理事务所	武汉分所	胡海国	湖北省武汉市东湖开发区关山大道1号软件产业三期A3栋六层03号	027-87522600	027-87522600	2013.1.31
119			佛山分所	赵爱蓉	佛山市禅城区张槎一路127号1座三层01	0755-86218128	0755-26470166	2015.5.29
120	44288	广州市越秀区哲力专利商标事务所（普通合伙）	佛山分所	贺红星	佛山市禅城区季华五路2号一座804室	0757-82369001	0757-83289348	2013.1.4
121			深圳分所	张鹏	深圳市福田区深南大道与泰然九路交界本元大厦9B-2	0755-83005234	0755-83827902	2013.1.30
122			东莞分所	罗伟添	东莞市南城区鸿福西路81号国际商会大厦十二层06A室	0769-22825599	0769-22825101	2013.1.14
123			中山分所	刘兴彬	中山市西区富华道10号西苑广场富华阁8C房	0760-88624868	0760-88614833	2013.3.4
124	44295	广州市越秀区海心联合专利代理事务所（普通合伙）	梧州分所	蔡国	广西壮族自治区梧州市蝶山一路拉船里4号	0774-3894849	0774-3894849	2013.10.31
125			玉林分所	王洪娟	广西壮族自治区玉林市玉东新区高新技术产业区中小企为创业园综合大楼二楼2A1房	0775-2806355	0775-2806355	2014.4.10
126			梅州分所	罗振国	广东省梅州市梅县区扶大园区花园城侧A-2号	0753-2880872	0753-2880872	2014.7.2
127	44302	广州圣理华知识产权代理有限公司	顺德分公司	陈业胜	佛山市顺德区凤翔路41号创意产业园B栋309	020-37636018	020-37636018-818	2013.4.15
128	44309	深圳市合道英联专利事务所（普通合伙）	广州分所	廉红果	广州市天河区车陂龙口大街7号2A03房	020-82529125	020-82529231	2014.1.7
129			东莞分所	何国涛	东莞市南城区簪花路华凯豪庭办公楼活力中心1003号	0769-38931870	0769-38931870	2015.11.1
130			肇庆分所	廉红果	肇庆市康乐北路九层综合楼五楼503房	0755-88300116	0755-88300116	2015.11.1
131	11006	北京市律诚同业知识产权代理有限公司	深圳办事处	黄韧敏	深圳市福田区深南中路2008号华联大厦1411-1413室	0755-83667462	0755-83668754	2004.7
132	35203	厦门市新华专利商标代理有限公司	东莞分公司	朱凌	东莞市东城西路181号金澳大厦6座302室	0769-22495526	0769-22504005	2008.5
133			广州分公司	李宁	广州市越秀区先烈中路92号大院8号8238房	020-37617125	020-37617125	2006.7
134	11246	北京众合诚成知识产权代理有限公司	东莞办事处	连平	东莞市南城区元美路华凯广场A1716	0769-23186866	0769-23182369	2007.7
135	11221	北京捷诚信通专利事务所	深圳办事处	杨竹清	深圳市福田区彩田南路海天大厦1928室	0755-83461499	0755-83460428	2007.7
136	11290	北京信慧永光知识产权代理有限责任公司	佛山办事处	艾持平	佛山市禅城区惠景三街40号502房	0757-82328308	0757-83120342	2007.8
137	11212	北京轻创知识产权代理有限公司	东莞分公司	吴英彬	东莞市南城区第一国际百安居A幢508	0769-23023265	0769-23182100	2008.9
138			深圳分公司	王新生	深圳市福田区彩田路瑰丽福景大厦3#楼1708室	0755-83005980	0755-53695132	2014.12.3
139	11285	北京北翔知识产权代理有限公司	深圳分公司	钟守期	深圳市宝安区新安办创业西路富源商贸大厦1栋D座604室	0755-29075489	0755-61624078	2008.7
140	12201	天津市北洋有限责任专利代理事务所	东莞分所	曹玉平	东莞市南城区鸿福西路南城商务大厦1210室	0769-23020555	0769-23020555	2009.2
141	11227	北京集佳知识产权代理有限公司	广州分公司	陈剑华	广州市天河路351号广东外经贸大厦二十一楼2109室	020-38816190	020-38806446	2009.1
142			东莞分公司	张浩	东莞市南城区元美东路东侧商业中心F座1508号	0769-22020278	0769-22020248	2010.5
143	11279	北京中誉威圣知识产权代理有限公司	东莞分公司	丛芳	广东省东莞市东城区岗贝雍华庭都市E站902号房	0769-22309696	0769-28200800	2009.6
144	11234	中国商标专利事务所有限公司	东莞办事处	桑丽茹	广东省东莞市东城区育兴路84号	0769-22609984	0769-22295542	2010.3
145	11335	北京汇信合知识产权代理有限公司	东莞分公司	王维新	广东省东莞市莞城区东纵路2号地王广场二十四层2A	0769-22482526	0769-22087052	2010.7
146	11330	北京市立方（广州）律师事务所	广州分所	刘延喜	广州市天河区珠江东路16号3801房之自编06单元	020-85561566	020-87583005	2011.1
147	11332	北京品源专利代理有限公司	东莞分公司	胡彬	东莞市南城区鸿福路76号南城商务大厦办公楼603号	0769-23033956	0769-23033595	2011.4.19
148			深圳分公司	邓猛烈	广东省深圳市福田区彩田路彩福大厦D座嘉福阁7G	0755-61547960	0755-61547961	2011.3
149			佛山分公司	吕琳	佛山市禅城区文华北路60号1911房	0757-88778186	0757-83309422	2013.9.24
150			广州分公司	钟锦舜	广东省广州市天河区林和西路157号A栋1001单元	020-22020285	020-22020286	2014.7.16
151	11350	北京科亿知识产权代理事务所（普通合伙）	东莞分所	陈正兴	东莞市莞城区东城大道23号骏达商业中心七楼10号	0769-89810940	0769-89810908	2012.7.11
152			中山分所	孙海英	中山市石岐区中山二路48号六楼623室	0760-85757870	0760-85757870	2012.8.30
153			佛山分所	肖平安	广东省佛山市高明区荷城街道沿江路463号3座1703之5	0757-88660999	0757-88660999	2013.5.23
154			深圳分所	许娆	深圳市宝安区九区宝民一路广场大厦九层913	0755-32936055	0755-32936055	2014.6.20
155			广州分所	赵蕊红	广州市天河区燕都路80号之一301房	020-87034461	020-87034461	2015.11.1

（续上表）

序号	代码	机构名称	分支机构	负责人	地　址	电　话	传　真	设立时间
156	11282	北京中海智圣知识产权代理有限公司	东莞办事处	白凤武	东莞市南城区莞太路鸿福路段63号鸿福广场A座1802C号	0769-22024556	0769-22024559	2012.7.24
157	11340	北京天奇智新知识产权代理有限公司	深圳分公司	汪琳琳	深圳市福田区彩田南路中深花园A座1612室	0755-83475145	0755-83475145	2012.8.30
158	11111	北京万慧达知识产权代理有限公司	广州分公司	杨　颖	广州市天河区林和西路3-15号耀中广场3901-03单元	020-81362728	020-81364186	2012.12.22
159			深圳分公司	王　虎	深圳市福田区香林路富春东方大厦1506	0755-82762920	0755-82762920	2014.12.3
160	11369	北京远大卓悦知识产权代理事务所（普通合伙）	江门办事处	张　清	江门市蓬江区港口路中远大厦17楼E座	0750-3963376	0750-3963376	2012.12.22
161	11129	北京海虹嘉诚知识产权代理有限公司	汕头办事处	吴小灿	广东省汕头市金砂路106号国际商业大厦B座24F	0754-88944447	0754-88484447	2013.1.8
162			东莞办事处	李正清	广东省东莞市莞城旗峰路中侨大厦B座803	0769-33326068	0769-33326067	2013.5.17
163	11201	北京清亦华知识产权代理事务所（普通合伙）	深圳分所	李志东	深圳市福田区华强北路长盛大厦1319-1320室	0755-33008005	0755-33008006	2013.4.23
164			佛山分所	宋融冰	佛山市顺德区大良镇锦龙路12号顺利德商业大厦511号	0757-26909450	0757-26909450	2015.10.8
165	11042	北京乾诚五洲知识产权代理有限责任公司	东莞办事处	杨玉荣	广东省东莞市华凯豪庭办公楼707	0769-22028595	0769-22029555	2013.8.2
166	11250	北京三聚阳光知识产权代理有限公司	深圳分公司	张　杰	深圳市福田区益田路江苏大厦B1401室	0755-22159684	0755-83547388	2013.8.2
167	11403	北京风雅颂专利代理有限公司	东莞分公司	刘　冰	广东省东莞市南城区元美东路东侧商业中心D座1711（A）号	0769-22036235	0769-22036230	2014.2.27
168			广州分公司	于晓霞	广东省广州市天河区五山路371-1号	020-66690144	020-39167076	2015.3.16
169	11400	北京商专永信知识产权代理事务所（普通合伙）	广州分所	许春兰	广州市越秀区环市中路205号自编B312	020-86669887	020-86672612	2014.9.18
170			佛山分所	高之波	佛山市禅城区金源街8号第六层（自编606室之二）	0757-83209888	0757-88359808	2014.10.31
171			东莞分所	莫莉萍	东莞市南城区商业中心二期百安中心A座1805（B）	0769-23183301	0769-23183302	2015.1.6
172			深圳分所	王　鹏	广东省深圳市福田区福虹路世界贸易广场B座26B1	0755-83980110	0755-83981109	2015.7.7
173			中山分所	李　波	广东省中山市西区富华道35号邮政大楼二层217之二	0760-87867201	0760-88336207	2015.8.20
174	11319	北京润泽恒知识产权代理有限公司	广州办事处	赵　娟	广州市天河区珠江新城华强路3号富力盈力大厦南塔1404室	020-87385717	020-87380321	2014.10.10
175			深圳分公司	王　洪	深圳市笋岗东路2121号华凯大厦二十四楼2411号	010-68118728	010-68118728-8016	2015.1.23
176	11421	北京天盾知识产权代理有限公司东莞分公司	东莞分公司	林晓宏	东莞市南城区体育路28号嘉信大厦九楼6号	0769-21682609	0769-21682609	2014.10.31
177	31253	上海精晟知识产权代理有限公司	中山办事处	黄佳丽	广东省中山市石岐区颐和山庄颐和中心1012号房-2	0760-85116777	0760-85116777	2015.1.16
178	11411	北京联瑞联丰知识产权代理事务所（普通合伙）	广州分所	曾少丽	广东省广州市天河区体育西路103号维多利广场B塔2901室	020-38199300	020-38769195	2015.1.29
179	31264	上海波拓知识产权代理有限公司	深圳办事处	李爱华	广东省深圳市罗湖区南湖街道嘉宾路城市天地广场东座裙楼I、III区8028	0755-82642081	021-51780379	2015.4.24
180	11002	北京路浩知识产权代理有限公司	深圳分公司	张　晶	广东省深圳市南山区田厦国际中心B座1835-1836	010-62196988	010-62198011	2015.5.6
181	43205	长沙星耀专利事务所	佛山办事处	赵静华	广东省佛山市禅城区同华东一路40号二层之十	0757-63974388	0757-63974388	2015.5.29
182	11372	北京聿宏知识产权代理有限公司	深圳分公司	朱　绘	深圳市福田区天然居二区A902	010-66412868	010-66412482	2015.7.7
183	11315	北京国昊天诚知识产权代理有限公司	惠州分公司	刘　戈	惠州市惠城区江北文昌一路7号华贸大厦2单元七层03号	0752-7778508	0752-7778508	2015.7.23
184	11316	北京一格知识产权代理事务所（普通合伙）	东莞办事处	李双胜	广东省南城区元美路22号黄金花园丰硕广场办公2308	0769-22322669	0769-22322669	2015.7.23
185	11429	北京中济纬天专利代理有限公司	佛山分公司	李嘉怡	佛山市顺德区大良凤翔路41号顺德创意产业园A栋F015号	0757-22251180	0757-22251180	2015.8.3
186	11344	北京市盈科律师事务所	广州分所	牟晋军	广东省广州市广州大道中289号南方传媒大厦B座十五至十八层	020-66837199	020-66857289	2015.8.20
187	11228	北京汇泽知识产权代理有限公司	深圳分公司	亓　赢	深圳市福田区深南大道与泰然九路交界东南（深南大道6017号）都市阳光名苑1栋6B	0755-82529943	0755-82529943	2015.8.31
188	11331	北京康盛知识产权代理有限公司	深圳分公司	翟　磊	深圳市南山区科兴路11号深南花园裙楼C区四层417	010-64419316	010-64415179	2015.10.8
189	11371	北京超凡志成知识产权代理事务所（普通合伙）	深圳分所	王玉桂	深圳市福田区滨河路爱地大厦办公楼十四层1413	0755-83338010	0755-83338020	2015.10.8
190	11390	北京和信华成知识产权代理事务所（普通合伙）	深圳分所	龚春娟	广东省深圳市福田八卦四路先科机电大厦1339	0755-82267965	0755-82267965	2015.10.21
191	11394	北京卓恒知识产权代理事务所	佛山分所	张绮丽	广东省佛山市顺德区容桂街道办事处红星社区居委会文明西路42号领德大厦1009号之二	0757-28801011	0757-28801011	2015.12.30

主题索引

ZHU TI SUO YIN

主题索引

说　明

一、本索引采用主题分析方法，款目按汉语拼音字母（同音字按声调）顺序排列。

二、本索引一般摘录各篇的节题、目及小目作索引条目。

三、索引款目后的数字表示内容所在的页码，数字后的拉丁字母（a、b）表示栏别（即版面的1、2栏）。

四、同一主题的内容在文中多处出现的，在其款目后用不同的页码标明。

五、本索引对《附录》等篇不作内容主题分析。

2015年泛珠三角区域知识产权合作　163b
2015年广东海关知识产权保护典型案例　114a
2015年广东省法院十大知识产权案例　119a
2015年广东省检察机关知识产权保护典型案例　124a
2015年广东省名牌产品（工业类）　81b
2015年广东省文化厅知识产权保护主要案例　111a
2015年广东省质量技术监督局知识产权保护案例　113b
2015年广东专利奖　81b
2015年全国知识产权领军人才百名高层次人才培养人选　238a
2015年全国专利信息领军人才和师资人才名单　238b
2015年粤澳知识产权合作　161b
2015年粤港知识产权合作　159a
2015年粤喀知识产权合作　164b
2015年粤台知识产权合作　163a

A

案例八：暴雪娱乐有限公司、上海网之易网络科技发展有限公司诉成都七游科技有限公司、北京分播时代网络科技有限公司、广州市动景计算机科技有限公司著作权侵权及不正当竞争纠纷诉中禁令案　122b
案例八：江门海关查获侵犯“555”商标专用权电池案　118a
案例二：陈某田等四人假冒注册商标案　125a
案例二：广州海关查获区域通关一体化出口轮毂案　114b
案例二：广州市“6·9”特大侵权盗版教材案　111b
案例二：皇家菲利浦有限公司诉超人集团有限公司、刘某平等侵害发明专利权纠纷案　119b
案例二：中山市质监局查处生产冒用注册商标及认证标志的电源适配器案　113b

案例九：广州市虎头电池集团有限公司、广州轻工工贸集团有限公司诉临沂华太电池有限公司擅自使用知名商品特有包装装潢纠纷　123a
案例六：广州医药集团有限公司诉广东加多宝饮料食品有限公司、彭某娟虚假宣传纠纷案　121b
案例六：黄埔海关查获成都某进出口公司出口假冒香烟案　117b
案例六：肇庆市某学校侵犯著作权案　112b
案例七：黄埔海关查获丰顺某针织服装有限公司出口侵权运动服装案　118a
案例七：中山市商房网络科技有限公司诉中山市暴风科技有限公司著作权侵权纠纷一案　122a
案例三：广东蒙娜丽莎新型材料集团有限公司诉广州蒙娜丽莎建材有限公司、佛山市贝佳斯洁具有限公司侵害注册商标专用权纠纷案　120a
案例三：广州“11·27”特大淫秽盗版光盘案　112a
案例三：广州海关查获出口假冒“苹果”“三星”等电子产品案　115a
案例三：梁某克等三人非法制造注册商标标识及赖某莲销售非法制造的注册商标标识案　125b
案例十：原告张某义不服深圳市市场监督管理局行政处理决定案　123b
案例四：南京微盟电子有限公司与泉芯电子技术（深圳）有限公司侵害集成电路布图专有权纠纷案　120b
案例四：深圳海关开展粤港合作查获假冒手机系列案　115b
案例四：吴某某未经批准擅自从事音像制品批发、零售经营活动　112a
案例五：高某某从事非法印刷品印刷经营活动　112b
案例五：拱北海关查获申报出口的巧克力侵犯“费列罗立体商标”商标专用权案　116a
案例五：杭州市西湖区龙井茶产业协会诉广州市种茶人贸易有限公司侵害商标权纠纷案　121a
案例一：佛山市南海区质监局查处生产假冒伪劣服装案　113b
案例一：广州市www.dj020.com网站传播侵权音乐作品案　111a
案例一：矽微公司、房某磊侵犯商业秘密案　124a
案例一：粤港海关开展执法合作成功查获化妆品类侵权案　114a
案例一：珠海格力电器股份有限公司诉广东美的制冷设备有限公司、珠海市泰锋电业有限公司侵害商标权纠纷案　119a

B

百所千企知识产权服务对接工程　134、134a
柏塘山茶　78b
版权纠纷人民调解委员会　48b
版权兴业　54b
版权宣传　55a
编写“贯标”指导书籍　131b
标准与地理标志　77a
表彰奖励　238
部署安排　168a

C

产品宣传　79b
产学研协同创新　45b
产业/行业专题数据库建设　88b
产业知识产权联盟　87、87a
产业专利导航及分析预警　85b
产业专利信息服务平台　135、135a
常规项目　144a
潮州市　230a
成果与荣誉　149b
承办政府工作　146a
承接政府工作　145a

承接政府项目 142b、149b
驰名商标保护 105b
创新成果产业化 41b
创新驱动发展政策环境 41a
创造与运用 178b

D

打击侵犯知识产权犯罪 103a、107a
打击侵犯知识产权和制售假冒伪劣商品 102a
打击侵犯知识产权和制售假冒伪劣商品工作 8、8a
打击侵权假冒工作 105b
打击质量技术监督领域知识产权违法行为 59b
大案要案 55b
当前地理标志产品保护与管理方面存在的问题 244a
地理标志 77
地理标志保护的重要意义 243b
地理标志产品 77a
地理标志工作 58b
地理标志商标注册 76b
地市“贯标” 131b
地市评议 84b
地市知识产权工作 182
第117届广交会知识产权保护工作情况 246a
第118届广交会知识产权保护工作情况 246b
第八届两岸专利论坛 163a
第二轮知识产权高层次战略合作 2、2a
第三届广东知识产权法律服务论坛 49a
第三届广东知识产权法律服务论坛举办 150b
第十七届中国专利奖 81a
典型案例评选和巡讲活动 150b
电商领域知识产权保护交流合作 53b
东莞市 211b
对外合作交流 57a
对外交流合作体系 156a
对外交流与合作 156
对外宣传 157b

F

发明创造 60b
泛珠三角区域内地九省（区）专利信息 164a
泛珠三角区域内地九省（区）专利行政执法协作 164a
泛珠三角区域知识产权合作机制 40a
泛珠三角区域知识产权合作联络员制度 40b
泛珠三角区域知识产权合作联席会议制度 40a
泛珠三角区域知识产权合作专题工作小组制度 40b
泛珠三角区域知识产权专题交流 164a
分析评议试点 84a
佛山市 194a
服务能力 138b
服务平台 148b
服务社会 173b
服务与支撑机构 136
服务组织机构 56a

G

概述 102
高新区知识产权示范创建 130a
高要巴戟天 78a
工作机制 39b
工作交流 246
工作体系建设 89b
公共服务 136b
沟通交流 150a
关于广东省地理标志产品保护与管理工作现状的调研报告 242a
观音阁花生 78b
“贯标”服务体系 131a
“贯标”培训 131a
贯彻实施《珠江三角洲地区改革发展规划纲要（2008—2020年）》 6、6a
广东版权专题调研 54b
广东创建知识产权服务业发展示范省规划（2013—2020年） 128、128a

广东发明协会　151b
广东金融学院知识产权研究所　177b
广东商标协会　147b
广东省版权保护联合会　149a
广东省版权局　54b
广东省产业专利联盟示范培育工程　87a
广东省出口贸易专利预警分析计划　86b
广东省打击侵犯知识产权和制售假冒伪劣商品工作领导小组　37a
广东省发展和改革委员会　41a
广东省法学会知识产权法学研究会　153a
广东省高级人民法院　67b
广东省工商行政管理局　56a
广东省工商行政管理系统知识产权宣传培训工作　169a
广东省公安厅　46a
广东省国家地理标志产品保护工作的基本情况　242b
广东省检察机关知识产权司法保护　107a
广东省教育厅　43a
广东省经济和信息化委员会　42b
广东省科学技术厅　44a
广东省林业厅　52a
广东省律师协会知识产权法律专业委员会　150b
广东省农业厅　49b
广东省人民检察院　70a
广东省人民政府法制办公室　64b
广东省人民政府副省长陈云贤在第八届两岸专利论坛上的致辞　23
广东省人民政府副省长陈云贤在最高法院知识产权司法保护与市场价值研究（广东）基地揭牌仪式上的讲话　24
广东省人民政府省长朱小丹在国家知识产权局　广东省人民政府第二轮知识产权高层次战略合作2015年度工作会议上的讲话　20
广东省人民政府省长朱小丹在全省知识产权工作会议暨专利奖表彰大会上的讲话　16
广东省人民政府知识产权办公会议　36a
广东省人民政府知识产权办公会议成员单位　41a
广东省人民政府知识产权办公会议特邀单位　65b
广东省商务厅　53a
广东省食品药品监督管理局　64b
广东省司法厅　48b
广东省卫生和计划生育委员会　54a
广东省文化厅　53b
广东省与全国及有关省市的对比　99b
广东省与全国及有关省市的对比情况　96b
广东省政府颁布实施《广东省深入实施知识产权战略　推动创新驱动发展行动计划》　11、11a
广东省知识产权局　60a
广东省知识产权局局长马宪民在广东省知识产权局工作总结会议上的讲话　25
广东省知识产权局软科学研究管理工作　242a
广东省知识产权培训基地（广东海洋大学）　176a
广东省知识产权培训基地（惠州学院）　175b
广东省知识产权培训基地（暨南大学）　173a
广东省知识产权培训基地（汕头大学）　175a
广东省知识产权培训基地（深圳大学）　174a
广东省知识产权培训基地（顺德职业技术学院）　176b
广东省知识产权人才培训工作　170a
广东省知识产权宣传工作　168a
广东省知识产权研究会　141a
广东省知识产权研究与发展中心（广东省知识产权维权援助中心）　137a
广东省知识产权研究与发展中心司法鉴定所　150a
广东省质量技术监督局　57a
广东省著名商标　148a
广东省专利大数据应用服务系统建设　88a
广东省专利技术实施计划　93a
广东省专利权质押登记　95a
广东省专利实施许可合同备案　98a
广东省专利信息协会　146b
广东知识产权保护协会　143b
广东专利代理协会　145b

广东自贸区建设　70b
广东自由贸易试验区　156a
广交会知识产权保护　53a
广交会知识产权保护工作　246a
广州市　182a
规范性文件审查　64b
国际交流　172b
国家版权示范　56a
国家级专利产业化基地　93a
国家知识产权局（广东）专利信息传播利用基地　89a
国家知识产权局局长申长雨在广东省知识产权工作会议暨专利奖励大会上的讲话　13
国家知识产权局专利局广州代办处　136a
国家知识产权培训（广东）基地（广东省知识产权研究与发展中心）　172a
国家知识产权培训（广东）基地（华南理工大学）　170b
国家知识产权强县工程试点示范　129b
国家知识产权示范城市　129a
国家知识产权试点城市　129b
国家知识产权试点示范城市　129a
国家知识产权试点示范城市工作先进集体和先进个人　239a
国家中小微企业知识产权培训（南海）基地　178b
国家专利审查协作广东中心共建情况　136a

H

海关行政执法　106a
海关知识产权保护　103a
海关总署广东分署　65b
行业服务　147a
行业管理　50b
行业建设　148a
合作开展专利信息传播利用工作　91a
合作项目　144a
河源市　200a
护航“漫博会”　55a
华南师范大学　178a
惠州市　206a

J

机构建设　147a
基础建设　176b
基地教育　175b
激励机制　79a
加强协作　47b
假冒侵权　65a
监督指导　69b
监管工作　132a
监管机构　64b
“剑网2015”　55b
江门市　219a
交流合作　184b
交流活动　149a
教育培训　170
揭阳市　232a
举办商业秘密民事诉讼实务问题讨论会　151a
举办“知识产权管理与商业化实务研讨会”　151a
举办中港新三地国际版权法律研讨会　151a

K

开展广东省律师知识产权典型案例系列活动　48b
科技成果产业化应用　42b
科技创新　50a
科技重大专项　54a
科学研究　171a、173a
跨区域执法协作　66a
跨行政区域知识产权专门检察院　70b

L

连平鹰嘴蜜桃　77a
“两法”衔接与司法保护　9b

林木种苗质量检查 52a
林业知识产权宣传与普及 52a
林业植物新品种 80b
林业植物新品种保护 52a
林业植物新品种权专项行动 52b
领导讲话 13
领导小组办公室主要职责 37a
罗浮山大米 78a

M

马德里商标国际注册 76b
茂名市 224b
梅州市 202b
民事和行政案件的法律监督 107a
名牌产品 57b

N

内部管理 150a
年度中国专利奖相关工作情况 81a
农产品地理标志 79a
农业植物新品种 80a

P

培训服务 139b
培训管理 179a
培训活动 179a
培训交流 145b
培训教育 150a
品牌国际化知识产权培训 53a
品牌建设 43a、51b
平台建设 174b
普法与维权协作 149a
普及培训 176b

Q

企业创新 65a
企业服务 175a
企业“贯标”认证 131b
企业技术中心建设 43a
企业知识产权管理规范 131、131a
清远市 228a
区域创新体系建设 42a
区域交流与合作 159
全国版权示范城市 56a
全国中小学知识产权教育试点推进 43b
全面创新改革试验 41a

R

人才工作 89b
人才培养 173a、174a
人才培养体系与师资 170b
入册法院 150a
软件正版化 55b

S

汕头市 188b
汕尾市 210a
商标 76
商标保护 102b、56b
商标培训 169b
商标品牌战略 56b
商标行政执法 105a
商标宣传 169a
商标注册 56b
韶关市 199a
社会服务 172a、179b
深圳市 185a
审判职能 67b
石湾玉冰烧酒 78a
实例 111
实施知识产权战略 60a
始兴石斛 77b
示范试点工作 182a
试点工作 136b
试点示范工程建设 42a

司法保护　107
司法鉴定服务　140b

T

提升效能　46b
体制机制创新　68b
统计资料　191b、197、203b、210、215、224a
推进创业投资发展　42a

W

莞香　77b
维权援助服务　139b
维权援助与涉外应对　109
委局合作　110
委局合作共建　110a
委托任务　140b
汶朗蜜柚　79a

X

下一步对策与建议　244b
协调机制　36
协会建设　146b
信息服务体系　137a
信息公开　52b
信息化平台　138a
信息运用　88
刑事司法　9b
行政保护　105
行政处罚案件信息公开　9b
行政执法　8a
行政执法与刑事司法相衔接机制　70b
宣传　168
宣传发动　48a
宣传活动　67a
宣传、教育培训　233a、234b
宣传培训　148b、175b、178a、184a、211a
宣传渠道　169a
学会基础工作　141a
学术活动　171b、173a、174a

Y

亚洲知识产权营商论坛　160a
研究成果　87b
阳江市　221a
药品标准　65b
“一带一路”知识产权工作　156b
营造良好社会氛围　9b
粤澳知识产权案件协助处理机制　162a
粤澳知识产权工作小组　39b
粤澳知识产权合作机制　162a
粤澳知识产权交流互访　162b
粤澳知识产权宣传培训　162b
粤澳知识产权研究　163a
粤港澳台区域知识产权合作　158a
粤港澳知识产权交流研讨　160b
粤港澳知识产权信息资源共享　163a
粤港保护知识产权合作专责小组　38b
粤港合作　55b
粤港知识产权合作　38b
粤港知识产权宣传教育　161b
粤港知识产权引导服务　161a
粤台知识产权服务机构交流　163b
粤台知识产权交流合作　163b
云浮市　233b
运用能力培训　176b

Z

展会保护　105a
展会与专业市场执法监管　105b
战略性新兴产业重点项目　42b
战略性新兴产业专利信息资源开发利用计划　85、85a
湛江市　222b
肇庆市　226b

证后监管　79b
政府立法　64b
知识产权保护　2b、63a、102a、183a、186a、189a、195a、199a、200a、203a、206b、210a、212b、217b、220a、221a、223a、224b、227a、228b、230a、232a、234a
知识产权保护长效机制　107b
知识产权保护宣传　71a
知识产权创新能力　44b
知识产权创造　6a、164b、182a、185a、188b、194a、199a、200a、202b、206a、210a、211b、217a、219a、221a、222b、224b、226b、228a、230a、232a、233b
知识产权对外合作　4a
知识产权对外交流与合作　156a
知识产权犯罪　70a
知识产权分析评议服务示范创建　84a
知识产权服务　186b、196a、215a
知识产权服务业　3b
知识产权改革创新　2a
知识产权管理　4b、182a、186b、190b、195b、199b、203a、208a、211a、213b、218a、220b、222a、223a、225a、229a、231a、232b、234b
知识产权管理和服务　201b、227b
知识产权贯标　151a
知识产权合作机制　159a
知识产权获奖　43b
知识产权交流合作　191b
知识产权交流与合作　211a
知识产权交易　98a
知识产权教育　165b、170b、175a
知识产权课题研究　141a
知识产权贸易和法律服务　159b
知识产权能力　63b
知识产权培训　176a
知识产权强国建设先行地　2a
知识产权人才队伍建设　4b
知识产权人才交流　165a
知识产权人才培训　172a
知识产权上量提质活动　177a
知识产权涉外应对　157a
知识产权涉外应对工作　109b
知识产权试点示范　129
知识产权司法保护　103b
知识产权维权援助　109a
知识产权行政保护　6b
知识产权宣传　176a、196b、229b
知识产权宣传培训　165b、187b、191a、199b、202a、203b、209a、214a、218b、222a、223a、226a、228a、231b
知识产权选修课　177a
知识产权学术交流　141b
知识产权研究　173a
知识产权远程教育顺德分站　177b
知识产权运营　92、92a
知识产权运营体系建设　6b
知识产权运用　3a、6a、182b、185a、189a、194b、199a、202b、206a、212a、217a、219b、221a、226b、230a、234a
知识产权战略实施　45a、53a
知识产权执法　164b
知识产权执法及案件协作处理机制　159a
知识产权质押及投融资　94、94a
执法协作　108
职能部门工作概述　41
植物新品种　80
植物新品种保护　103a
质监知识产权保护　103a
中港新三地国际版权法律研讨会　49b
中国专利法律状态数据加工　88a
中山市　217a
中小学知识产权教育工作　178b
重大经济活动知识产权分析评议　84、84a
重大经济科技活动知识产权评议促进计划　84b
重大平台建设　157a
重大外事及交流活动　157a
重大知识产权获奖成果　81

重点企业、区域知识产权高端运营及创新运用　92b
重点、热点　168a
珠海市　188a
主要成果　85b
主要举措　85a、87a、94a
主要特点　74a
主要职责　36a
著作权保护　102b
专利　74
专利保护　102b
专利保险　97、97a
专利代理服务能力建设　132b
专利代理管理　132、132a
专利代理管理工作发展　133a
专利代理行业发展　133b
专利导航新模式　86a
专利电子申请　136a
专利技术的实施　43b
专利联盟规范化、实体化发展　87b
专利权质押登记特点　95a
专利申请和授权　43a、74a
专利信息服务平台　85b
专利信息化建设及推广　88a
专利信息利用促进工作　90a
专利信息情报服务　90b
专利信息推送服务　88b
专利信息资源　61a
专利信息资源开发利用计划项目　54a
专利行政执法　105a
专利行政执法协作　108a
专利运营机制　62a
专题培训　177a
专题研究报告　242
专项推动　46a
专项行动　105a、105b
专项执法行动　65b
转化　98
自律建设　145b
自主创新政策环境　44a
组织参加2015年中国专利信息年会　91b
组织管理　8a
组织架构　36a、37b
作品著作权　54b